UNIVERSITY LIBRARY
UW-STEVENS POINT

W9-CIM-053

The Supreme Court
and
Individual Rights

UNIVERSITY LIBRARY
UW-STEVENS POINT

The Supreme Court
and
Individual Rights

Second Edition

Elder Witt

Congressional Quarterly

1414 22nd Street, N.W., Washington, D.C. 20037

Congressional Quarterly Inc.

Congressional Quarterly Inc., an editorial research service and publishing company, serves clients in the fields of news, education, business, and government. It combines specific coverage of Congress, government, and politics by Congressional Quarterly with the more general subject range of an affiliated service, Editorial Research Reports.

Congressional Quarterly publishes the *Congressional Quarterly Weekly Report* and a variety of books, including college political science textbooks under the CQ Press imprint and public affairs paperbacks on developing issues and events. CQ also publishes information directories and reference books on the federal government, national elections, and politics, including the *Guide to Congress*, the *Guide to the U.S. Supreme Court*, the *Guide to U.S. Elections*, and *Politics in America*. The *CQ Almanac*, a compendium of legislation for one session of Congress, is published each year. *Congress and the Nation*, a record of government for a presidential term, is published every four years.

CQ publishes *The Congressional Monitor*, a daily report on current and future activities of congressional committees, and several newsletters including *Congressional Insight*, a weekly analysis of congressional action, and *Campaign Practices Reports*, a semimonthly update on campaign laws.

An electronic online information system, Washington Alert, provides immediate access to CQ's databases of legislative action, votes, schedules, profiles, and analyses.

Copyright © 1988 Congressional Quarterly Inc.

All rights reserved. No part of this publication may be reproduced or transmitted in any form or by any means, electronic or mechanical, including photocopy, recording, or any information storage and retrieval system, without permission in writing from the publisher.

Printed in the United States of America

Library of Congress Cataloging-in-Publication Data

Witt, Elder.
    The Supreme Court and individual rights.

    Bibliography: p.
    Includes indexes.
    1. Civil rights--United States--Cases. 2. United States. Supreme Court. I. Title.
KF4748.W53   1988   342.73'085   88-6942
ISBN 0-87187-465-2   347.30285

KF
4748
.W53
1988

Contents

Appendix

Indexes

Introduction

The Supreme Court's role as guardian of the rights and liberties of the individual is a new one, a responsibility assumed in the twentieth century.

For most of its history, the Court had little to say about the Constitution's guarantees of individual freedom. Preoccupied with defining the relationship of nation to state, state to state, and government to business, the Court found little occasion and less reason to deal with individual rights.

Indeed, until the twentieth century there was no broad constitutional basis for the assertion of individual rights against government action.

The Constitution itself contains few provisions touching individual rights; and those few have been infrequently invoked. The Bill of Rights operated solely against federal action until adoption of the Fourteenth Amendment in 1868.

That amendment's guarantees of the privileges and immunities of U.S. citizens, due process of law, and equal protection were designed to extend the protection of the Bill of Rights to individuals threatened by state action.

But not until half a century after its ratification was the purpose of this amendment in any way fulfilled. In the 1920s the Court finally began to read its guarantees as its authors had intended.

In the 1960s the promises of due process and equal protection were construed to apply most of the guarantees of the Bill of Rights to the states. In the 1970s and 1980s questions of individual rights versus government authority consumed more and more of the Court's time and became its most controversial and pressing business.

A NARROW BASE: 1789-1865

The Supreme Court deals with cases that arise under the Constitution and the laws of the United States.

Only half a dozen sentences in the original Constitution deal directly with matters of individual rights. The Constitution does forbid suspension of the privilege of the writ of habeas corpus except in time of public emergency.[1] And it prohibits the passage of bills of attainder or ex post facto laws.[2] For almost all crimes, the Constitution requires jury trials in the state where the crime was committed;[3] it defines the crime of treason, sets the standard of evidence, and limits the penalty for that crime.[4] And it provides for extradition of fugitives[5] and forbids religious tests for federal officeholders.[6]

The Demand for Guarantees

Not surprisingly, many persons active in the formulation of the new government—with all-too-fresh memories of governmental oppression—found the lack of more comprehensive guarantees of individual rights a serious deficiency. Historian Charles Warren described the situation:

> Men on all sides contended that, while the first object of a Constitution was to establish a government, its second object, equally important, must be to protect the people against the government. That was something which all history and all human experience had taught.
>
> The first thing that most of the colonies had done, on separating from Great Britain, had been to assure to the people a Bill of Rights, safeguarding against state legislative despotism those human rights which they regarded as fundamental. Having protected themselves by specific restrictions on the power of their state legislatures, the people of this country were in no mood to set up and accept a new national government, without similar checks and restraints. As soon as the proposed Constitution was published, the demand for a national Bill of Rights was heard on all sides.[7]

Practical concerns motivated this demand. Warren wrote:

> They were thinking of facts, not theories. They had lived through bitter years, when they had seen govern-

1

ments, both royal and state, trample on the human rights which they and their ancestors in the colonies and in England had fought so hard to secure. In the seven years prior to the signing of the federal Constitution, they had seen the legislatures of four states ... deprive their citizens of the right to jury trial in civil cases. They had seen the state legislatures ... pass bills of attainder sentencing men to death or banishment without a criminal trial by jury. They had seen the legislatures of nearly all the states deprive persons of their property without due process, by the passage of laws allowing tender of worthless paper and other property in payment of debts and of judgments. They had seen a Massachusetts legislature impair the freedom of the press by confiscatory taxation. They had seen the royal government quarter troops on the inhabitants in time of peace and deny to the people the right of assembly and of petition. They had seen the King's officials search their houses without lawful warrants. They knew that what government had done in the past, government might attempt in the future, whether its ruling power should be royal, state, or national—king, governor, legislature, or Congress. And they determined that, in America, such ruling power should be definitely curbed at the outset. There should be no uncontrolled power in the government of American citizens. Rightly had Jefferson said, "an elective despotism was not the government we fought for." [8]

Thus, a number of the states that ratified the Constitution did so only with the assurance that a top priority of the First Congress would be the approval of a Bill of Rights to be added to the Constitution.

The Bill of Rights

In June 1789 James Madison of Virginia introduced a dozen proposed constitutional amendments in the First Congress, a Bill of Rights generally modeled after existing state bills of rights. Congress approved the amendments in September 1791, and ten of them took effect in December after ratification by the requisite number of states. [9]

These amendments are called the Bill of Rights. As Chief Justice Earl Warren noted, its provisions do not guarantee novel rights, but do "summarize in a striking and effective manner the personal and public liberties which Americans [of that time] ... regarded as their due and as being properly beyond the reach of any government." [10]

The Bill of Rights was conceived to protect the individual against the government. Chief Justice Warren continued:

> The men of our First Congress ... knew ... that whatever form it may assume, government is potentially as dangerous a thing as it is a necessary one. They knew that power must be lodged somewhere to prevent anarchy within and conquest from without, but that this power could be abused to the detriment of their liberties. [11]

The guarantees perform an affirmative as well as a negative function, Zechariah Chafee, Jr., points out:

> They fix a certain point to halt the government abruptly with a "thus far and no farther"; but long before that point is reached they urge upon every official of the three branches of the state a constant regard for certain declared fundamental policies of American life. [12]

The first of these amendments protects freedom of thought and belief. It forbids Congress to restrict freedom of religion, speech, the press, peaceable assembly, and petition.

The Second Amendment ensures the right of the states to maintain militia and, in connection with that state right, the right of the people to keep and bear arms. The Third Amendment restricts government power to quarter soldiers in people's homes. Neither has been the subject of many cases before the federal courts. [13]

The Fourth Amendment protects the individual's right to be secure in his person, house, papers, and effects against unreasonable searches or seizures. This security is ensured by requiring that searches and arrests be authorized by warrants issued only if there is probable cause for the action and when the person to be arrested or the place to be searched and the objects sought are precisely described.

The Fifth Amendment requires indictment of all persons charged in civilian proceedings with capital or otherwise serious crimes. It forbids trying a person twice for the same offense or compelling a person to incriminate himself. It states that no one should be deprived of life, liberty, or property without due process of law, and protects private property against being taken for public use without just compensation.

The Sixth Amendment sets out certain requirements for criminal trials, guaranteeing a speedy and public jury trial for all persons accused of crime, with an impartial jury selected from the area of the crime. The defendant is further guaranteed the right to be notified of the charge against him, to confront witnesses testifying against him, to compel witnesses to come to testify in his favor, and to have the aid of an attorney in his defense.

The Seventh Amendment provides for a jury trial in all common law suits involving more than $20.

The Eighth Amendment forbids excessive bail, excessive fines, and cruel and unusual punishment.

The Ninth and Tenth Amendments do not guarantee specific rights. The Ninth declares that the mention in the Constitution of certain rights should not be interpreted as denying or disparaging other rights retained by the people. The Tenth reserves to the states, or to the people, all powers not delegated by the Constitution to the national government nor prohibited by the Constitution to the states.

The Judicial Role

Madison, father of these amendments, expected the federal courts to play a major role in implementing their guarantees. "Independent tribunals of justice will consider themselves in a peculiar manner the guardians of those rights; they [the courts] will be an impenetrable bulwark against every assumption of power in the Legislative or Executive; they will naturally be led to resist every encroachment upon rights expressly stipulated for in the Constitution by the declaration of rights," he told his fellow members of Congress. [14]

But the Supreme Court itself had little occasion to apply these promises in its first 130 years.

The stringent Alien and Sedition Acts of 1798—severe infringements of the rights and liberties of the individual, particularly those protected by the First Amendment—were never challenged before the High Court. The acts expired early in 1801. (It is worth noting, however, that most of the early members of the Court, in their roles as circuit judges, presided over trials of persons charged with sedition, and displayed no disinclination to enforce that law.) [15]

Slavery, despite the prolonged national debate it engendered, was never dealt with by the Court as a matter of individual rights. The few pronouncements by the Court on the issue demonstrate clearly that the justices saw it as a matter of property rights, not human rights. *(Box, p. 4)*

In 1833 the Court ruled that the Bill of Rights provided no protection against state action, but only against federal authority.

Barron v. Baltimore arose when the owner of a wharf in Baltimore, Maryland, challenged city action that seriously impaired the value of his property by creating shoals and shallows around it. Barron argued that this was a "taking" of his property without just compensation, in violation of the Fifth Amendment.[16]

When Barron's case came before the Supreme Court, Chief Justice John Marshall found the question it posed to be "of great importance, but not of much difficulty." Marshall described Barron's argument: the Fifth Amendment "being in favor of the liberty of the citizen ought to be so construed as to restrain the legislative power of a State, as well as that of the United States." [17]

That argument could not prevail, however, continued the chief justice. The Bill of Rights was adopted to secure individual rights against the "apprehended encroachments of the general government—not against those of the local governments." [18] The Court could find no indication that Congress intended the Bill of Rights to safeguard the individual against state action, and it would not undertake such an extension of those provisions on its own. Marshall concluded:

> Had Congress engaged in the extraordinary occupation of improving the constitutions of the several States by affording the people additional protection from the exercise of power by their own governments in matters which concerned themselves alone, they would have declared this purpose in plain and intelligible language.[19]

Barron v. Baltimore stands to this day, unreversed in its precise finding—that the first Congress, in approving the Bill of Rights, did not intend these amendments to protect the individual against state action but only against action by federal authorities.

THE CIVIL WAR AMENDMENTS

After the Civil War Congress added three new amendments to the Constitution. The language of these additions seemed to overturn the restrictions *Barron v. Baltimore* placed on the guarantees of the Bill of Rights.

The Thirteenth Amendment, adopted in 1865, abolished slavery and involuntary servitude, except for persons sentenced to such service as punishment for crime. It authorizes Congress to pass laws to enforce this guarantee.

The Fifteenth Amendment, adopted in 1870, forbids state or federal authorities to deny or abridge the right of U.S. citizens to vote because of race, color, or previous condition of servitude. It, too, authorized Congress to pass legislation enforcing its prohibition.

The Fourteenth Amendment, the most complex and most litigated of the three, was adopted in 1868. It declares that all persons born or naturalized in the United States are citizens. This is the Constitution's only definition of citizenship.

In addition, the amendment forbids states to abridge any privilege or immunity of U.S. citizens, to deprive any person of life, liberty, or property without due process of law, or to deny to any person the equal protection of the law.

These guarantees are undergirded by a grant of power to Congress to enforce them through legislation. They have been the foundation of the modern revolution in civil rights and criminal procedure, although for decades after their addition to the Constitution they seemed almost useless as protection for individual rights.

The Intent of Congress

The privileges and immunities, due process, and equal protection clauses were intended by their author, Representative John A. Bingham, R-Ohio (1855-1863, 1865-1873), to extend the guarantees of the Bill of Rights against state action. Bingham thought that the privileges and immunities section of the Fourteenth Amendment would be the chief vehicle for this extension.

In 1871 Bingham explained his view of this portion of the amendment, in response to a query from a fellow member of the House. He stated that "the privileges and immunities of citizens of the United States . . . are chiefly defined in the first eight amendments to the Constitution. . . . These eight articles . . . were never limitations upon the power of the States, until made so by the Fourteenth Amendment." [20]

During Senate consideration of the amendment, the chief Senate spokesman in behalf of the proposal had stated that "the great object of the first section of this amendment is . . . to restrain the power of the States and compel them at all times to respect these great fundamental guarantees." [21]

During the process of ratification, however, the other sections of the amendment—concerning apportionment of representatives among the states, the holding of federal posts by persons who had forsaken such offices to support the rebellious states, and the validity of the public debt—were given far more attention than Section 1.

Frustration of the Promise

Almost a century would pass before the hopes explicit in the adoption of the Thirteenth, Fourteenth, and Fifteenth Amendments were fulfilled. In large part, the frustration of their promises was the work of the Court.

Partly in response to waning public enthusiasm for Reconstruction, partly out of concern for healing the wounds of war, partly because the nation had not developed its sensitivity to issues of individual rights, the Court in the postwar decades severely curtailed the operation of the Civil War amendments to protect individual citizens.

The restrictive interpretation of these amendments came in two lines of rulings. In the first, the Court defined narrowly the privileges and immunities, due process, and equal protection clauses of the Fourteenth Amendment, and the similar substantive phrases of the Thirteenth and Fifteenth Amendments. In the second, the Court confined

The Court and the Issue of Slavery . . .

The issue of slavery came to the Supreme Court in its first decades only as a question of international or commercial law or of states' rights and federal power, not as a human rights issue. Not until after the Civil War did the status of the nation's blacks become a question of individual rights rather than property rights.

As the United States celebrated the bicentennial of the Constitution in 1987, Justice Thurgood Marshall reminded the nation that "when the Founding Fathers used the phrase 'We the People' in 1797, they did not have in mind the majority of America's citizens," because the phrase included neither blacks nor women.

The Framers, said Marshall, "could not have imagined, nor would they have accepted, that the document they were drafting would one day be construed by a Supreme Court to which had been appointed a woman and a descendant of an African slave."

Marshall pointed out that "the record of the Framers' debates on the slave question is especially clear: the Southern states acceded to the demands of the New England states for giving Congress broad power to regulate commerce, in exchange for the right to continue the slave trade." [1]

Slavery had a continuing impact upon pre-Civil War constitutional history. As Carl B. Swisher explained:

Concern for the preservation of slavery furnished the driving power back of theories of state rights and of limitation upon the power of the federal government which for many decades hampered the expansion of federal power. Concern for the protection of slavery entered into the interpretation of the commerce clause . . . of clauses having to do with the rights of citizenship, and of other important constitutional provisions. The clash of interest between slavery and non-slavery groups brought on the crisis of a civil war which threatened the complete destruction of the American constitutional system. [2]

Historian Charles Warren also viewed the slavery issue as underlying the early debate over the scope of the commerce power:

[T]hroughout the long years when the question of the extent of the federal power over commerce

was being tested in numerous cases in the court, that question was, in the minds of Southerners, simply coincident with the question of the extent of the Federal power over slavery. [3]

The Court gave firm support to federal power over the subject of fugitive slaves. At the same time, it left as much as possible to the states the question of the status of slaves who had spent time in both slave and free areas.

The Court's divergence from this position—in the *Dred Scott* case of 1857—added fuel to the conflagration that burst out in civil war.

International Law

In the first case involving slavery decided by the Court, the justices held that the slave trade, though by 1825 illegal in the United States, was not illegal under international law. The case involved slaves who arrived in the United States after being removed from a vessel captured by an American warship.

Chief Justice John Marshall made clear in his opinion that the legality of the situation alone, not its morality, was before the Court. He wrote:

In examining claims of this momentous importance; claims in which the sacred rights of liberty and of property come in conflict with each other . . . this Court must not yield to feelings which might seduce it from the path of duty, but must obey the mandates of the law. . . . Whatever might be the answer of a moralist to this question, a jurist must search for its legal solution in those principles of action which are sanctioned by the usages, the national acts, and the general assent of that portion of the world of which he considers himself as a part. [4]

Commercial Law

Four years later, the Court ruled that a slave who died in an abortive rescue attempt after a steamboat fire was a passenger, not freight, for purposes of his owners' damage suit against the vessels involved. "A slave has volition, and has feelings which cannot be entirely disregarded," wrote Chief Justice Marshall.

"He cannot be stowed away as a common package. . . . The carrier has not, and cannot have, the

rigidly the enforcement power these three amendments granted Congress.

Early in the 1870s the Supreme Court first indicated its limited view of the effect of these amendments. The privileges and immunities of U.S. citizenship were a brief list, the Court ruled in the *Slaughterhouse Cases,* and did not include, for example, the right to vote.[22] The Thirteenth Amendment did no more than abolish the institution of slavery, the Court ruled in *United States v. Reese.* Nor did the Fifteenth Amendment grant to anyone a federal right to vote, only the right to exercise the state-granted franchise free of racial discrimination, the justices

---

...A Question of Legality, Not Morality

same absolute control over him that he has over inanimate matter. In the nature of things, and in his character, he resembles a passenger, and not a package of goods." [5]

In 1841 the Court was faced with a case challenging Mississippi's ban on the importation of slaves. But the justices found a way to decide the case without ruling directly on the importation ban.[6]

Fugitive Slave Laws

As the tension between slave and free states built, and the operations of the underground railway accelerated, an increasing number of cases challenged the federal fugitive slave law, enacted in 1793 to govern the return of fugitive slaves from one state to another.

In 1842 the Court affirmed the exclusive power of Congress to regulate these disputes. The justices struck down a Pennsylvania law providing that before a fugitive was returned to his alleged owner or the owners' representative, a hearing should be held before a magistrate to determine the validity of the claim to the supposed fugitive slave.[7]

Six years later the Court reaffirmed the validity of the federal fugitive slave law and specifically disclaimed any power to resolve the moral dilemma it posed.

[S]ome notice should be taken of the argument, urging on us a disregard of the Constitution and the act of Congress in respect to this subject, on account of the supposed inexpediency and invalidity of all laws recognizing slavery or any right of property in man. But that is a political question, settled by each state for itself; and the federal power over it is limited and regulated by the people of the states in the Constitution itself, as one of its sacred compromises, and which we possess no authority as a judicial body to modify or overrule.[8]

On the eve of the Civil War, the Court resolved the most famous of the fugitive slave cases, *Ableman v. Booth.*

Sherman Booth, an abolitionist editor, was prosecuted under the federal fugitive slave law for helping a fugitive slave to escape. The state courts of Wisconsin, Booth's residence, repeatedly issued writs of habeas corpus, ordering federal authorities to release Booth from custody, basing their order on the view that the federal fugitive slave law was unconstitutional.

The Court in March 1859 resoundingly defended the freedom of federal courts from such state interference—and upheld Booth's conviction.[9]

Slave or Free?

The first case in which the Court was asked to decide what effect residence in a free state or territory had on the status of a slave came to the Court in 1850 and was resolved with restraint and without incident.

The persons involved were slaves in Kentucky who worked for a time in the free state of Ohio, but returned to Kentucky to live. The Court held that their status depended on the state where they were residing. No constitutional provision controlled state action on this matter, it held.[10]

The Court reached a similar conclusion seven years later in the landmark case of *Dred Scott v. Sandford,* but unfortunately it did not stop there.

Dred Scott, the alleged slave, brought the case on his own behalf. By holding that Scott's status was determined by the law of the state in which he resided—the slave state of Missouri—the Court also held that he could not bring the suit, as a slave, and thus it had no jurisdiction over the matter at all. The Court then held that slaves were not citizens and that Congress lacked the power to exclude slavery from the territories.[11]

The issue of slavery then became a matter that was to be resolved only on the battlefield; the Supreme Court did not speak again on the subject.

1. Thurgood Marshall, Speech at the Annual Seminar of the San Francisco Patent and Trademark Law Association, May 6, 1987.
2. Carl B. Swisher, *American Constitutional Development,* 2d ed. (Cambridge, Mass.: Houghton Mifflin Co., 1954), 230.
3. Charles Warren, *The Supreme Court in United States History,* 2 vols. (Boston: Little, Brown, 1922, 1926), I:627.
4. *The Antelope,* 10 Wheat. 66 at 114, 121 (1825).
5. *Boyce v. Anderson,* 2 Pet. 150 at 154-155 (1829).
6. *Groves v. Slaughter,* 15 Pet. 449 (1841).
7. *Prigg v. Pennsylvania,* 16 Pet. 539 (1842).
8. *Jones v. Van Zandt,* 5 How. 215 at 231 (1848).
9. *Ableman v. Booth,* 21 How. 506 (1859).
10. *Strader v. Graham,* 10 How. 52 (1851).
11. *Dred Scott v. Sandford,* 19 How. 393 (1857).

held in *United States v. Cruikshank*.[23]

A decade later the Court held in *Hurtado v. California* that the due process guarantee did not extend the specific protections of the Bill of Rights against state action.[24] And in the well-known 1896 ruling in *Plessy v. Ferguson*, the Court found no denial of equal protection in the requirement of segregated public facilities for blacks and whites.[25]

Furthermore, the Court refused to acknowledge that the enforcement clauses of these amendments significantly enlarged federal power to protect individual rights. The enforcement power granted to Congress to implement these provisions was rigidly confined by state prerogatives.

Congress enacted a number of major statutes to enforce the Thirteenth, Fourteenth, and Fifteenth Amendments. By the end of the century, most of their provisions had either been declared invalid by the Court, repealed directly, or rendered obsolete by subsequent legislation.[26] Charles Warren, writing in the 1920s, described the effect of the Civil War amendments upon the nation's black citizens, as a result of these Supreme Court decisions:

> The first section of the 14th Amendment is a prohibitory measure, and the prohibitions operate against the states only, and not against acts of private persons; the fifth section only gives Congress power, by general legislation, to enforce these prohibitions, and Congress may, within bounds, provide the modes of redress against individuals when a State has violated the prohibitions; and though Congress cannot act directly against the states, Congress may regulate the method of appeal to United States courts by any persons whose right under the Amendment has been affected by action of the states. As to the 15th Amendment, though theoretically it is capable of being enforced to a certain extent by direct congressional action, Congress has, in fact, taken few steps toward such enforcement; and only a few acts of a state or of a state officer have been found by the courts to violate it. Meanwhile, the southern states, by constitutional and statutory provisions, which have been in general upheld by the court, have found methods of limiting the negro right to vote.[27]

Early in the twentieth century, one student of these Court rulings declared that the enforcement acts were struck down because "they were in fact out of joint with the times. They did not square with public consciousness, either North or South. They belonged . . . to a more arbitrary period. They fitted a condition of war, not of peace, and suggested autocracy, rather than a democracy!"[28]

But eventually the Court's narrow view of these amendments gave way to a more expansive one, and these amendments provided the groundwork for the modern revolution in civil and criminal rights.

Congress made possible this shift in federal judicial concern by expanding in the class of persons who could ask a federal court to issue a writ of habeas corpus ordering their release from custody. This new law allowed persons detained by state officials to win their release if they could show that their detention was in violation of their constitutional rights. In 1875 Congress enlarged the jurisdiction of the federal courts and expanded the categories of cases they could hear; it gave them the right to hear all cases arising under the Constitution or federal laws. Several years later Congress further expanded Supreme Court jurisdiction, authorizing the Court to hear appeals in criminal cases.

Property, Not People

In one of the most ironic chapters in Supreme Court history, these new powers and guarantees were for half a century wielded much more effectively to protect property than to protect persons.

Developing the doctrine of substantive due process, the Court found the Fourteenth Amendment a useful tool for striking down a wide range of "progressive" state laws—ranging from those setting minimum wages and maximum hours for working men and women to consumer-oriented measures concerning weights and measures of items produced for sale.

Only a few isolated cases kept alive the hope that the Court would eventually exercise its authority to protect the individual against the government.

In 1886 the Court held that the equal protection clause assured aliens the right to run laundries in San Francisco free of discriminatory application of licensing requirements by city officials.[29]

The same year the Court held that the Fourth and Fifth Amendments provided absolute protection from federal seizure for an individual's private papers.[30] Twenty-eight years later—in 1914—the Court provided for enforcement of this protection through an "exclusionary rule"—declaring that persons from whom federal agents took evidence illegally had the right to demand that the evidence be excluded from use in federal court.[31]

In 1915 the Court invoked the Fourteenth Amendment to strike down state laws restricting the right of aliens to work.[32] The Court also held that the Fifteenth Amendment was violated by Oklahoma's use of a grandfather clause that effectively required all blacks—and only blacks—to take a literacy test before being qualified to vote.[33]

World War I brought the most restrictive set of federal laws concerning speech and the press since 1798. Challenged as violating the First Amendment, these laws were upheld by the Court, but the cases posing these questions to the Court were the first steps in the still-continuing process of shaping the standards by which to judge the government's actions restricting individual freedom.

Broadening Protection

However, the Bill of Rights still operated only against federal, not state, action. Because state authorities exert far more impact upon the everyday lives of individual citizens than their federal counterparts, this left most citizens inadequately protected against arbitrary, coercive, and unfair state government action.

The Court's 1925 ruling in *Gitlow v. New York* marked the waning of this view and the beginning of the expansion of federal protection for individual rights. Benjamin Gitlow, a left-wing socialist, was indicted for violating New York's criminal anarchy law by publishing and distributing subversive documents. The material at issue was a "Left Wing Manifesto" calling for class revolution and the organization of a proletariat state to supress the bourgeoisie. He came to the Supreme Court arguing that the state law was unconstitutional, denying him his rights of free speech and free press, guaranteed by the First Amendment.[34]

The Court upheld the law, but in so doing, the majority stated that it now assumed "that freedom of speech and of the press—which are protected by the First Amendment from abridgment by Congress—are among the fundamental personal rights and 'liberties' protected by the due process clause of the Fourteenth Amendment from impairment by the states." [35]

With that decision the Court began reading into the due process guarantee many of the specific rights and liberties set out in the Bill of Rights.

This process, variously described as the incorporation or absorption of the Bill of Rights into the Fourteenth Amendment, continued for a half a century. By the mid-1970s, the Court had extended the Bill of Rights at last to the point that Representative Bingham had intended a century earlier, when Congress approved Section 1 of the Fourteenth Amendment.

The first rights absorbed into the due process clause and thus protected against state action were those set out in the First Amendment. In 1931 the Court for the first time struck down state laws as infringing on the freedom to speak and the freedom of the press.[36] In 1934 it assumed that freedom of religion was likewise protected against state infringement.[37] And in 1937 the Court held the right of peaceable assembly to be so protected.[38]

The Court also began in the 1930s to enforce the equal protection guarantee against racial discrimination by state officials—and to use the due process clause to require fundamental fairness in state dealings with criminal suspects. The groundwork for revolution was laid.

A Double Standard

As the federal courts, led by the Supreme Court, began to assume the role intended for them by Madison and the drafters of the Fourteenth Amendment, the Court indicated that it would apply a stricter standard to laws challenged as infringing on individual rights than it used for those attacked as abridging economic rights.

In *United States v. Carolene Products Co.*, decided in 1938, the Court upheld a federal law barring interstate shipment of certain types of skimmed milk.[39] This ruling reflected the Court's shift away from disapproval of all such laws as interfering too much with states' rights and the free flow of commerce.

Writing for the majority, Justice Harlan Fiske Stone said that the Court would now uphold economic regulation against a constitutional challenge so long as the regulation had a rational basis.[40]

And in a footnote to that statement, the famous Footnote Four, Stone suggested that "[t]here may be narrower scope for operation of the presumption of constitutionality when legislation appears on its face to be within a specific prohibition of the Constitution, such as those of the first ten Amendments." [41] *(Text of footnote, p. 8)*

This meant, Justice Robert H. Jackson said several years later, that the "presumption of validity which attaches in general to legislative acts is frankly reversed in the case of interferences with free speech and free assembly." [42] He explained the reasoning behind this double standard:

> Ordinarily, legislation whose basis in economic wisdom is uncertain can be redressed by the processes of the ballot box or the pressures of opinion. But when the channels of opinion or of peaceful persuasion are corrupted or clogged, these political correctives can no longer be relied on, and the democratic system is threatened at its most vital point. In that event the Court, by intervening, restores the processes of democratic government; it does not disrupt them.[43]

FREEDOM FOR IDEAS

The First Amendment protects against government suppression the unrestricted exchange of ideas. The guarantees of freedom for speech, press, and religion have been "first" in several ways—the first listed in the Bill of Rights and the first of those amendments to be fully applied against state action.

Furthermore, many argue, this amendment is in fact first in importance among the Constitution's guarantees of individual rights. Such a "preferred position" is linked to the function of these freedoms in maintaining an environment that fosters responsive democratic government.

In 1937 Chief Justice Charles Evans Hughes explained:

> The greater the importance of safeguarding the community from incitement to the overthrow of our institutions by force and violence, the more imperative is the need to preserve inviolate the constitutional rights of free speech, free press and free assembly in order to maintain the opportunity for free political discussion, to the end that government may be responsive to the will of the people and that changes, if desired, may be obtained by peaceful means. Therein lies the security of the Republic, the very foundation of constitutional government.[44]

A Charter for Government

Eight years later, Justice Wiley B. Rutledge brought together the Court's acknowledgment of its new role in respect to the rights of the individual, the view of the First Amendment freedoms as "preferred," and the stricter test for laws challenged as violating that freedom:

> The case confronts us again with the duty our system places on this Court to say where the individual's freedom ends and the State's power begins. Choice on that border, now as always delicate, is perhaps more so where the usual presumption supporting legislation is balanced by the preferred place given in our scheme to the great, the indispensable democratic freedoms secured by the First Amendment. . . . That priority gives these liberties a sanctity and a sanction not permitting dubious intrusions. And it is the character of the right, not of the limitation, which determines what standard governs the choice. . . .
>
> For these reasons any attempt to restrict those liberties must be justified by clear public interest, threatened not doubtfully or remotely, but by clear and present danger. The rational connection between the remedy provided and the evil to be curbed, which in other contexts might support legislation against attack on due process grounds, will not suffice. These rights rest on firmer foundation.[45]

'Footnote Four'

In a footnote to its decision in *United States v. Carolene Products Co.*, the Court in 1938 foreshadowed its shift in concern from economic to individual rights:

4. There may be narrower scope for operation of the presumption of constitutionality when legislation appears on its face to be within a specific prohibition of the Constitution, such as those of the first ten Amendments, which are deemed equally specific when held to be embraced within the Fourteenth. See Stromberg v. California, 283 U.S. 359, 369, 370, 51 S.Ct. 532, 535, 536, 75 L. Ed. 1117, 73 A.L.R. 1484; Lovell v. Griffin, 303 U.S. 444, 58 S.Ct. 666, 82 L. Ed. 949, decided March 28, 1938.

It is unnecessary to consider now whether legislation which restricts those political processes which can ordinarily be expected to bring about repeal of undesirable legislation, is to be subjected to more exacting judicial scrutiny under the general prohibitions of the Fourteenth Amendment than are most other types of legislation. On restrictions upon the right to vote, see Nixon v. Herndon, 273 U.S. 536, 47 S.Ct. 446, 71 L.Ed. 759; Nixon v. Condon, 286 U.S. 73, 52 S.Ct. 484, 76 L.Ed. 984, 88 A.L.R. 458; on restraints upon the dissemination of information, see Near v. Minnesota, 283 U.S. 697, 713-714, 718-720, 722, 51 S.Ct. 625, 630, 632, 633, 75 L.Ed. 1357; Grosjean v. American Press Co., 297 U.S. 233, 56 S.Ct. 444, 80 L.Ed. 660; Lovell v. Griffin, supra; on interferences with political organizations, see Stromberg v. California, supra, 283 U.S. 359, 369, 51 S.Ct. 532, 535, 75 L.Ed. 1117, 73 A.L.R. 1484; Fiske v. Kansas, 274 U.S. 380, 47 S.Ct. 655, 71 L.Ed. 1108; Whitney v. California, 274 U.S. 357, 373-378, 47 S.Ct. 641, 647, 649, 71 L.Ed. 1095; Herndon v. Lowry, 301 U.S. 242, 57 S.Ct. 732, 81 L.Ed. 1066; and see Holmes, J., in Gitlow v. New York, 268 U.S. 652, 673, 45 S.Ct. 625, 69 L.Ed. 1138; as to prohibition of peaceable assembly, see De Jonge v. Oregon, 299 U.S. 353, 365, 57 S.Ct. 255, 260, 81 L.Ed. 278.

Nor need we enquire whether similar considerations enter into the review of statutes directed at particular religious, Pierce v. Society of Sisters, 268 U.S. 510, 45 S.Ct. 571, 69 L.Ed. 1070, 39 A.L.R. 468, or national, Meyer v. Nebraska, 262 U.S. 390, 43 S.Ct. 625, 67 L.Ed. 1042, 29 A.L.R. 1446; Bartels v. Iowa, 262 U.S. 404, 43 S.Ct. 628, 67 L.Ed. 1047; Farrington v. Tokushige, 273 U.S. 284, 47 S.Ct. 406, 71 L.Ed. 646, or racial minorities. Nixon v. Herndon, supra; Nixon v. Condon, supra: whether prejudice against discrete and insular minorities may be a special condition which tends seriously to curtail the operation of those political processes ordinarily to be relied upon to protect minorities, and which may call for a correspondingly more searching judicial inquiry. Compare McCulloch v. Maryland, 4 Wheat. 316, 428, 4 L.Ed. 579; South Carolina State Highway Department v. Barnwell Bros., 303 U.S. 177, 58 S.Ct. 510, 82 L.Ed. 734, decided February 14, 1938, note 2, and cases cited.

"The First Amendment," added Justice Rutledge later in his opinion, "is a charter for government, not for an institution of learning."[46]

Concurring, Justice Jackson wrote:

it cannot be the duty, because it is not the right, of the state to protect the public against false doctrine. The very purpose of the First Amendment is to foreclose public authority from assuming a guardianship of the public mind through regulating the press, speech and religion. In this field every person must be his own watchman for truth, because the forefathers did not trust any government to separate the true from the false for us....

This liberty was not protected because the forefathers expected its use would always be agreeable to those in authority or that its exercise would always be wise, temperate, or useful to society.

As I read their intentions, this liberty was protected because they knew of no other way by which free men could conduct representative democracy.[47]

More recently, Justice William J. Brennan, Jr., has discussed the way in which the First Amendment operates to "foster the values of democratic self-government":

The First Amendment bars the State from imposing upon its citizens an authoritative vision of truth. It forbids the State from interfering with the communicative processes through which its citizens exercise and prepare to exercise their rights of self-government. And the Amendment shields those who would censure the State or expose its abuses.[48]

No Absolute Right

But neither the intrinsic importance of free expression nor its "societal function" enshrine in the First Amendment as an absolute ban on all official restrictions on speech, the press, assembly, or religion.

The collective good—the nation's security or the public's safety—warrants some restriction on the individual's freedom to speak, to publish, to gather in groups, and to exercise his or her religious beliefs. The task of the Court has been to balance the community's interest against the individual's rights, to determine when order and safety demand that limits be set to individual freedom.

Wartime, the cold war, and the civil rights movement created the atmosphere within which the Supreme Court has worked to reconcile these competing concerns. The Court's course has been uneven: it has discarded "tests" for determining permissible government constraints almost as soon as it has developed them.

The often mentioned "clear and present danger" test, although little used by the modern Court, nevertheless stands as a symbol of the basic position still held by the Court on free speech questions: only for very good reason may the government suppress speech—and the Court will evaluate the reasons.

Freedom of the press has come more and more frequently before the Court since 1960. The Court has steadfastly rejected all prior restraints upon publication—most dramatically in the Pentagon Papers case of 1971. And although it has rejected efforts by the news media to expand the protection of the First Amendment into special privileges for the press, it has extended new protection to the news media from libel suits brought by public officials or public figures.

Freedom of religion, a guarantee reflecting the original purpose of many of the nation's earliest settlers, has been at issue in some of the Court's most controversial modern rulings. While it has generally upheld laws enacted to enhance the public welfare against challenges that they incidentally curtail the freedom to exercise one's religious beliefs, the Court has turned strict scrutiny on laws challenged as violating the amendment's ban on the establishment of religion. Such scrutiny has resulted in decisions such as those rejecting state efforts to require or allow devotional exercises in public schools or to use public funds to aid parochial schools.

POLITICAL RIGHTS

For the first 130 years of American history, the privilege of political participation was strictly limited. Until well into the twentieth century, the right to vote was the prerogative of the adult white man, and often only of those adult white men who could pay a poll tax, pass a literacy test, or meet other qualifications.

The Constitution barely mentions the right to vote; and there is no mention at all of the right to have that vote counted equally with others nor of the protected freedom of political association. Yet during the twentieth century these rights have won judicial recognition and protection. By 1975 the right to vote belonged to virtually all citizens eighteen years of age and older, regardless of sex or race.

Since 1962, when the Court abandoned its traditional aloofness from the issue of electoral districting, the right to have one's vote count as equal to those of other city or state residents has become firmly established. As it has implemented that right, the Court has redistributed the balance of political power in every state of the Union.

Unrestricted political association—the freedom to associate with others who share one's political views—has been recognized as an individual and institutional right.

Although the Court during the peak of cold war upheld state and federal programs and statutes curtailing the exercise of this freedom, the modern Court considers this freedom to be the core value the First Amendment was intended to protect.

The Suffrage

Congress, not the Court, has led in expansion of the suffrage. Three constitutional amendments were required to lower the barriers of race, sex, and age.

Indeed, it was the Court's narrow view of the privileges, immunities, and rights protected by the Civil War amendments that necessitated adoption of the Nineteenth Amendment to enfranchise women[49] and that rendered the Fifteenth Amendment a hollow promise for most of a century.[50]

After the Civil War, despite the clear language of the Fourteenth and Fifteenth Amendments, the Supreme Court continued to defer to state power to set voter qualifications, steadily upholding a variety of devices used to exclude blacks from voting. In the twentieth century the Court slowly asserted itself and began to strike down the most blatant of these mechanisms—the grandfather clause in 1915, the white primary in 1927 and again in 1944.[51]

But it was left for Congress to take the lead, as it did in the 1960s, abolishing poll tax requirements through a constitutional amendment, suspending literacy tests, and imposing federal control over the electoral machinery of states with high minority population and low voter registration or participation.

At that time the Court's role—although secondary—was crucial. A century earlier, the Court had undercut similar efforts by Congress to guarantee the right to vote against racial discrimination, by adopting a constricted view of the power of Congress to enforce the constitutional amendments adopted in the wake of the Civil War.

In the 1960s the Court gave full backing to the exercise of unprecedented federal power to guarantee civil rights to the nation's blacks.

The most aggressive and effective of the major civil rights statutes was the Voting Rights Act of 1965, which superimposed federal power and machinery upon the electoral processes of states that had long denied blacks the right to vote. In 1966 the Court upheld the law against every point of a multifaceted constitutional challenge by the affected states.[52] Within five years of enactment, more than one million blacks had been newly registered to vote.

Redistricting Revolution

In stark contrast with the Court's reluctance to enforce the clear ban of the Fifteenth Amendment was its unexpected plunge into the subject of legislative redistricting and malapportionment of legislative power.

After decades of declaring such issues "political" and unsuitable for judicial resolution, the Court in 1962 reconsidered. In *Baker v. Carr* the Court announced its reversal, holding that constitutionally based challenges to the malapportionment of state legislative bodies were "federal questions" that federal courts might properly consider.[53] Although the Court in 1962 went no further than that declaration, *Baker v. Carr* set off a judicial revolution that is still reverberating.

The following year the justices declared that the Fourteenth Amendment's guarantee of equal protection—when applied to voting rights—meant "one person, one vote." [54] Each vote cast in an electoral district in a state or in a city should be of equal weight with every other. The application of this rule to federal and state electoral divisions revolutionized the political base of every legislative body of any significance in the nation.

Beliefs and Association

Out of the unlikely context of the antisubversive and anti-civil rights laws of the 1950s and 1960s, the protected freedom of political association won judicial affirmation.

In addition to its constitutional basis in the First Amendment, the right of association has a clear practical basis: no point of view can win recognition in the increasingly complex American society without organized backing.

War slowed the progress of this right toward acknowledged constitutional status. During World War II and the subsequent cold war, Congress and state legislatures sought to protect the nation against subversion with laws and programs that declared a belief in communism or a similar political system and affiliation with such a system criminal, tantamount to treason.

As it had during the Civil War and World War I, the Court reflected its sensitivity to the national mood with decisions upholding the validity of these antisubversive devices. The Court backed the power of Congress to enact laws that effectively made illegal participation in Communist party activities by anyone aware of the party's aims. The Court seemed to sanction the use of guilt by association as a basis for depriving or denying persons jobs.

Yet within a few years of these rulings, the Court began to circumscribe the methods by which such laws could be enforced. Enforcement became so difficult that, in many instances, it was altogether abandoned.

In one line of rulings beginning in 1957, the Court set out strict standards of proof for government efforts to prosecute persons who were members of the U.S. Communist party. Simple association could not properly serve as the basis for denying a person a job, firing him, depriving him of his U.S. passport, or refusing him admission to the bar, held the Court.[55]

Almost simultaneously, in another series of decisions, the Court began to give full recognition to the right of association. These rulings, most of which dealt with civil rights activists, soon had their impact on the Court's view of legislation penalizing simple membership in "subversive" organizations.[56]

By 1967 the right had gained clear constitutional status. As Justice Byron R. White wrote:

The right of association is not mentioned in the Constitution. It is a judicial construct appended to the First Amendment rights to speak freely, to assemble, and to petition for redress of grievances. While the

right of association has deep roots in history and is supported by the inescapable necessity for group action in a republic as large and complex as ours, it has only recently blossomed as the controlling factor in constitutional litigation; its contours as yet lack delineation.[57]

In the 1970s and 1980s the Court defined those contours as it applied the right of association to curtail the exercise of state power over radical student groups, national political party delegations, independent candidates, and party-switching voters. The Court also held that the practice of patronage firing infringed on this freedom.

EQUALITY BEFORE THE LAW

The Fourteenth Amendment's promise of equal protection of the laws was intended, said one of its key advocates, Senator Jacob M. Howard, R-Mich. (1862-1871), to give "to the humblest, the poorest, the most despised of the race, the same rights and the same protection before the law as it gives to the most powerful, the most wealthy, or the most haughty." [58]

Not until well past the middle of the next century, however, was the protection of this guarantee actually extended to the nation's black citizens, to aliens, to women, the poor, and the illegitimate. And even then, the extension was less than complete.

At first, the Supreme Court seemed in accord with the intent of this portion of the Fourteenth Amendment. The equal protection clause, wrote Justice Samuel F. Miller in 1873, was clearly meant to guarantee equal treatment of blacks. He expressed doubt "whether any action of a State not directed by way of discrimination against the negroes as a class . . . will ever be held to come within the purview of this provision." [59]

Six years later, the Court used the equal protection clause to strike down a state law excluding blacks from jury duty. The equal protection guarantee, declared the Court, meant that "the law in the States shall be the same for the black as for the white; that all persons, whether colored or white, shall stand equal before the laws of the States." [60]

But this declaration soon eroded into superficiality. In 1883—with its rulings in the *Civil Rights Cases*—the Court held that the Fourteenth Amendment applied only to state, not individual, action; that individual discrimination did not violate the Thirteenth Amendment; and that Congress could act only to remedy discrimination by a state, not to prevent it before it occurred.[61]

In 1896 the Court in *Plessy v. Ferguson* held reasonable Louisiana's requirement of "equal but separate" accommodations for black and white passengers on railway trains.[62] This ruling, wrote one commentator, left the Fourteenth Amendment's guarantees "virtually nonexistent except as a bulwark of the rights of corporations." [63]

Plessy was the logical outcome of a conservative view of the power of the law. In the majority opinion, written by Justice Henry B. Brown, the Court declared:

If the two races are to meet upon terms of social

equality, it must be the result of natural affinities, a mutual appreciation of each other's merits and a voluntary consent of individuals.... Legislation is powerless to eradicate racial instincts or to abolish distinctions based upon physical differences, and the attempt to do so can only result in accentuating the difficulties of the present situation. If the civil and political rights of both races be equal one cannot be inferior to the other civilly or politically. If one race be inferior to the other socially, the Constitution of the United States cannot put them upon the same plane.[64]

Business interests, generally more able than individuals to present their views to the Court in the late nineteenth and early twentieth century, did not hesitate to use the equal protection clause as a basis from which to challenge state taxes, police regulations, and labor laws.

They too met with no more than a modicum of success. The Court adopted rationality as the test for such challenges and would uphold all such laws so long as they had a reasonable basis. Nevertheless, businessmen persisted, and economic cases accounted for the vast majority of equal protection questions before the Court until 1960.[65]

The Modern View

On the seventieth anniversary of its adoption—in 1938—the Fourteenth Amendment began to take on new strength in its intended role as protector of individual rights. In the first of a line of rulings that would erode the declaration of *Plessy v. Ferguson* into uselessness, the Supreme Court in 1938 held that a state that maintained no "black" law school violated the equal protection promise when it refused to admit a black resident to its "white" state law school, just because of his race.[66]

Six years later, even as the Court upheld the war power of the federal government to remove Japanese-Americans from their West Coast homes, the justices signaled their waning tolerance for laws using racial classifications. In the Court's opinion in *Korematsu v. United States,* the majority stated that "all legal restrictions which curtail the civil rights of a single racial group are immediately suspect" as violations of the Fourteenth Amendment's guarantee of equal protection. Such laws were subject to "the most rigid scrutiny," declared the Court. "Pressing public necessity may sometimes justify the existence of such restrictions; racial antagonism never can." [67]

Led by the National Association for the Advancement of Colored People and its legal defense fund, civil rights groups quickly accepted this clear judicial invitation to challenge the segregation that pervaded American life. In several subsequent cases decided in the late 1940s, the justices indicated their increasing skepticism as to whether separate facilities could ever be truly equal.

Finally, in its ruling in *Brown v. Board of Education,* the Court in 1954 abandoned the "separate but equal" doctrine, and held state segregation of public schools unconstitutional.[68] Eighty-six years after adoption of the Fourteenth Amendment, the Court at last set the nation on the road to fulfilling the promise of equal protection.

Although the Court mandated a change in the nation's direction, progress was slow. In the 1960s the frustration of the nation's blacks erupted in protests, boycotts, sit ins, and demonstrations. The reaction was often violent.

The compound of protest and reaction sparked congressional action. In 1964 Congress passed the most comprehensive civil rights measure since Reconstruction. The Civil Rights Act of 1964 translated the guarantee of equal protection into a statutory requirement of equal opportunity in employment and equal access to public facilities for blacks and whites.

Historian Irving Brant wrote that the 1964 Act brought to fruition "all that a once-aroused nation had attempted" in adopting the Fourteenth Amendment.[69] The Act was immediately challenged as unconstitutional and just as quickly upheld by a unanimous Supreme Court.[70]

In 1968 Congress approved a federal Fair Housing Act. The Court reinforced its provisions with a broadened interpretation of the Civil Rights Act of 1866, which guaranteed similar rights of equal treatment to blacks and whites seeking to sell, buy, or rent housing.[71]

The Expanding Guarantee

In the 1970s and 1980s the Supreme Court faced a range of "second-generation" questions raised by the national effort to ensure equal treatment for blacks and whites. The justices wrestled with the problem of defining proper remedies for past discrimination. White plaintiffs charged that employers engaged in "reverse discrimination"—penalizing innocent members of the majority group in order to compensate minority group members for past unfairness. Mindful of history, however, the Court generally looked with favor on some "affirmative action" to make up for past discrimination.

The protection of the Fourteenth Amendment's guarantee of equality before the law was broadened during the decades as the Court brought aliens and women within its scope. In 1971 the Court formally declared alienage, like race, to be in all circumstances a suspect classification upon which to base laws. Absent a compelling state justification, such laws would be held invalid.[72]

Women fared less well. The Court has not yet declared sex a suspect classification in all circumstances. But since 1971, when the Court for the first time nullified a state law because it violated the equal protection guarantee by treating men and women differently without a sufficient justification,[73] the Court has struck down a variety of federal regulations and state laws for this same reason. It generally employs the rule that classification by gender must serve important governmental objectives and be substantially related to achieving those objectives, in order to be upheld.

FUNDAMENTAL FAIRNESS

The Constitution twice promises the individual that government will not deprive him of life, liberty, or property without due process of law.

Neither of these guarantees—in the Fifth and Fourteenth Amendments—protects absolutely against loss of life, liberty, or property. They simply assure the individual that this deprivation will occur only after the government has adhered to certain standard approved procedures.

But what is due process for the person faced with a sentence of death, or life in prison, or loss of his property?

The Supreme Court has spent more than a century answering that question. The first time it considered the matter, it noted that the phrase "due process" probably meant no more to those who wrote it into the Bill of Rights than simply "by the law of the land"—that is, by accepted legal procedures.[74]

From that matter-of-fact origin, however, the guarantee of due process has expanded into the basic constitutional assurance to the individual that the government will deal fairly with him, even when it suspects or charges him with serious crimes.

The close relationship between procedure and substance, particularly in the nation's judicial system, was pointed out by Justice Rutledge in 1947. "At times," he wrote, "the way in which courts perform their function becomes as important as what they do in the result. In some respects matters of procedure constitute the very essence of ordered liberty under the Constitution."[75]

Despite the many landmark due process decisions that dot the history of the Supreme Court in the twentieth century, the definition of due process remains incomplete. Justice Felix Frankfurter explained why:

Due process of law . . . conveys neither formal nor fixed nor narrow requirements. It is the compendious expression for all those rights which the courts must enforce because they are basic to our free society. But basic rights do not become petrified as of any one time, even though, as a matter of human experience, some may not too rhetorically be called eternal verities. It is of the very nature of a free society to advance in its standards of what is deemed reasonable and right. Representing as it does a living principle, due process is not confined within a permanent catalogue of what may at a given time be deemed the limits or the essentials of fundamental rights.[76]

Frankfurter wrote that in 1949. In the following two decades the Court expanded the meaning of due process to encompass virtually all the specific guarantees of the Bill of Rights.

The Long Debate

The original due process guarantee is contained in the Fifth Amendment. But *Barron v. Baltimore* made plain that its reach was limited to federal action.

The Fourteenth Amendment, added in 1868, included a similar guarantee, specifically directed against state action. But in one of history's odd turnabouts, this provision was used at first by the Court as a means of dismantling state economic regulation. At the same time, the justices were refusing to read into the due process clause any requirement that states use the indictment process for persons charged with capital crimes, or that they provide twelve-man juries to try persons charged with serious crimes, or that they observe the privilege against compelled self-incrimination.[77]

For a century after 1868, the Court and legal scholars argued over whether or not the Fourteenth Amendment's due process guarantee "incorporated" or "absorbed" the

Bill of Rights—making each particular guarantee applicable against state action. As the debate continued from decision to decision, it tended to obscure the growing consensus among the justices that due process meant more than "by the law of the land"—that it indeed represented a promise of fundamental fairness. Frankfurter described it as "representing a profound attitude of fairness between man and man, and more particularly between the individual and the government."[78] Eventually, this consensus rendered the "incorporation" debate moot.

A fundamentally conservative Court in the 1920s began the enlargement of due process. Inherent in the concept of due process, that Court declared, were the guarantees that one's trial would be free from mob domination, that the judge would be impartial, that the jury would be representative of the community, and that one should have the effective aid of an attorney.[79] These the Court first recognized as essential in particular cases—where the crimes were serious and the defendant young, ignorant, or a member of a minority group.

In the 1930s the Court began to apply constitutional standards to the evidence used by state prosecutors. Confessions extracted by torture could not fairly be used against the persons so forced to incriminate themselves, held the Court—decades before it formally extended the Fifth Amendment privilege against compelled self-incrimination to state defendants.[80]

In the 1940s the Court simply assumed that the ban on cruel and unusual punishment applied to the states as well as the federal government.[81] It held that the Fourth Amendment guarantee of personal security against unreasonable search and seizure applied against state action, but declined to require state judges to exclude evidence seized in violation of that guarantee.[82]

The Due Process Revolution

The decade of the 1960s saw the most rapid expansion of the meaning of due process. Led by Chief Justice Warren, the Supreme Court firmly applied the guarantees of the Fourth, Fifth, Sixth, and Eighth Amendments against state action.

In 1960 the Court forbade federal agents to use evidence seized illegally by state agents. In 1961 it required the exclusion of illegally obtained evidence from state trials.[83]

Since 1938 all federal defendants had been guaranteed the aid of an attorney. In 1963 the Supreme Court finally closed the gap between the right of state and federal defendants in that regard. The Court declared that all persons charged with serious crimes in state court were assured the aid of an attorney, who would be appointed by the court and paid by the state, if necessary.[84]

Rejecting "the notion that the Fourteenth Amendment applies to the states only a 'watered-down subjective version of the Bill of Rights,'" the Court in 1964 held that state suspects, like federal suspects, are protected against being forced to incriminate themselves.[85] In 1965 the Court held that this privilege also barred adverse comment, by judge or prosecutor, on a defendant's failure to testify in his own defense.[86] Also that year, the Court held that due process required states to provide a defendant with the right to confront and cross-examine persons who testified against him.[87]

In 1967 the Court held that states were obliged to provide a speedy trial to criminal defendants.[88] In 1968 it added the requirements of a jury trial for all persons charged by the state with serious crimes.[89] Then, on the last day of Chief Justice Warren's tenure, the Court in 1969 applied the ban on double jeopardy to state criminal proceedings.[90]

The Bill of Rights had effectively—and controversially—at last been nationalized. But the process is a continuing one, as a look at the decisions of any recent term will show. In the words of Justice Frankfurter " 'due process,' unlike some legal rules, is not a technical conception with a fixed content.... Due process is not a mechanical instrument. It is not a yardstick. It is a process. It is a delicate process of adjustment." [91]

Notes

1. Article I, Section 9, Clause 2.
2. Article I, Section 9, Clause 3.
3. Article III, Section 2, Clause 3.
4. Article III, Section 3.
5. Article IV, Section 2, Clause 2.
6. Article VI, Section 3.
7. Charles Warren, *Congress, the Constitution and the Supreme Court* (Boston: Little, Brown, 1925), 79-80.
8. Ibid., 81-82.
9. Irving Brant, *The Bill of Rights* (Indianapolis: Bobbs-Merrill Co., 1965), 42-67; Julius Goebel, Jr., *History of the Supreme Court of the United States*, Vol. I: *Antecedents and Beginnings to 1801* (New York: Macmillan Publishing Co., 1971), 413-456.
10. Henry M. Christman, ed., *The Public Papers of Chief Justice Earl Warren* (New York: Simon & Schuster, 1959), 70.
11. Ibid.
12. Zechariah Chafee, Jr., *Free Speech in the United States* (Cambridge, Mass.: Harvard University Press, 1941; reprint ed., New York: Atheneum, 1969), 6-7.
13. Brant, *Bill of Rights*, 486; see also Goebel, *Antecedents and Beginnings*, 633-651.
14. Brant, *Bill of Rights*, 49-50.
15. Ibid., 314; see also Goebel, *Antecedents and Beginnings*, 633-651.
16. *Barron v. Baltimore*, 7 Pet. 243 (1833).
17. Id. at 247.
18. Id. at 250.
19. Ibid.
20. Brant, *Bill of Rights*, 333; see also Carl B. Swisher, *American Constitutional Development*, 2d ed. (Cambridge, Mass.: Houghton Mifflin Co., 1954), 331.
21. Brant, *Bill of Rights*, 336.
22. *Slaughterhouse Cases*, 16 Wall. 36 (1873); *Minor v. Happersett*, 21 Wall. 162 (1875).
23. *United States v. Reese*, 92 U.S. 214 (1876); *United States v. Cruikshank*, 92 U.S. 542 (1876).
24. *Hurtado v. California*, 110 U.S. 516 (1884).
25. *Plessy v. Ferguson*, 163 U.S. 537 (1896).
26. Charles Warren, *The Supreme Court in United States History*, 2 vols. (Boston: Little, Brown & Co., 1922, 1926), II:618.
27. Ibid., 617.
28. William W. Davis, *The Federal Enforcement Acts*, Studies on Southern History and Politics (1914), cited in Warren, *The Supreme Court in United States History*, II:618.
29. *Yick Wo v. Hopkins*, 118 U.S. 356 (1886).
30. *Boyd v. United States*, 116 U.S. 616 (1886).
31. *Weeks v. United States*, 232 U.S. 383 (1914).
32. *Truax v. Raich*, 239 U.S. 33 (1915).
33. *Guinn v. United States*, 238 U.S. 347 (1915).
34. *Gitlow v. New York*, 268 U.S. 652 (1925).
35. Id. at 666.
36. *Stromberg v. California*, 283 U.S. 259 (1931); *Near v. Minnesota*, 283 U.S. 697 (1931).
37. *Hamilton v. Board of Regents*, 293 U.S. 245 (1934).
38. *DeJonge v. Oregon*, 299 U.S. 353 (1937).
39. *United States v. Carolene Products Co.*, 304 U.S. 144 (1938).
40. Id. at 152.
41. Ibid.
42. Robert H. Jackson, *The Struggle for Judicial Supremacy* (New York: Random House, Vintage Books, 1941), 284-285.
43. Ibid.
44. *DeJonge v. Oregon*, 299 U.S. 353 at 365 (1937).
45. *Thomas v. Collins*, 323 U.S. 516 at 529-530 (1945).
46. Id. at 537.
47. Id. at 545-546.
48. *Herbert v. Lando*, 441 U.S. 153 (1979).
49. *Minor v. Happersett*, 21 Wall. 162 (1875).
50. *United States v. Reese* (1876) 92 U.S. 214 (1876); *United States v. Cruikshank*, 92 U.S. 542 (1876).
51. *Guinn v. United States*, 238 U.S. 347 (1915); *Nixon v. Herndon*, 273 U.S. 536 (1927); *Smith v. Allwright*, 321 U.S. 649 (1944).
52. *South Carolina v. Katzenbach*, 383 U.S. 301 (1966).
53. *Baker v. Carr*, 369 U.S. 186 (1962).
54. *Gray v. Sanders*, 372 U.S. 368 (1963).
55. *Yates v. United States*, 354 U.S. 298; *Scales v. United States*, 367 U.S. 203 (1961); *Noto v. United States*, 367 U.S. 290 (1961); *Elfbrandt v. Russell*, 384 U.S. 11 (1966); *Aptheker v. Secretary of State*, 378 U.S. 500 (1964); *Schware v. Board of Bar Examiners*, 353 U.S. 232 (1957); *Keyishian v. Board of Regents*, 385 U.S. 589 (1967); *United States v. Robel*, 389 U.S. 258 (1967).
56. *National Association for the Advancement of Colored People (NAACP) v. Alabama*, 357 U.S. 449 (1958); *NAACP v. Button*, 371 U.S. 415 (1963).
57. *United States v. Robel*, 389 U.S. 258 at 282-283 (1967).
58. Brant, *Bill of Rights*, 337.
59. *Slaughterhouse Cases*, 16 Wall. 36 at 81 (1873).
60. *Strauder v. West Virginia*, 100 U.S. 303 at 307 (1880).
61. *Civil Rights Cases*, 100 U.S. 3 (1883).
62. *Plessy v. Ferguson*, 163 U.S. 537 (1896).
63. Brant, *Bill of Rights*, 367.
64. *Plessy v. Ferguson*, 163 U.S. 537 at 551-552 (1896).
65. Robert J. Harris, *The Quest for Equality* (Baton Rouge: Louisiana State University Press, 1960), 59; cited by C. Herman Pritchett, *The American Constitution*, 2d ed. (New York: McGraw-Hill Book Co., 1968), 682.
66. *Missouri ex rel. Gaines v. Canada*, 305 U.S. 337 (1938).
67. *Korematsu v. United States*, 323 U.S. 214 at 216 (1944).
68. *Brown v. Board of Education*, 347 U.S. 483 (1954).
69. Brant, *Bill of Rights*, 377.
70. *Heart of Atlanta Motel v. United States*, 379 U.S. 241 (1964).
71. *Jones v. Alfred H. Mayer Co.*, 392 U.S. 409 (1968).
72. *Graham v. Richardson*, 403 U.S. 365 (1971).
73. *Reed v. Reed*, 404 U.S. 71 (1971).
74. *Murray's Lessee v. Hoboken Land & Improvement Co.*, 18 How. 272 (1856).
75. *United States v. United Mine Workers*, 330 U.S. 258 at 342 (1947).
76. *Wolf v. Colorado*, 338 U.S. 25 at 27 (1949).
77. *Hurtado v. California*, 110 U.S. 516 (1884); *Maxwell v. Dow*, 176 U.S. 581 (1900); *Twining v. New Jersey*, 211 U.S. 78 (1908).
78. *Joint Anti-Fascist Refugee Committee v. McGrath*, 341 U.S. 123 at 162 (1951).
79. *Moore v. Dempsey*, 261 U.S. 86 (1923); *Tumey v. Ohio*, 273 U.S. 510 (1927); *Norris v. Alabama*, 294 U.S. 587 (1935); *Powell v. Alabama*, 287 U.S. 45 (1932).
80. *Brown v. Mississippi*, 297 U.S. 278 (1936).
81. *Louisiana ex rel. Francis v. Resweber*, 329 U.S. 459 (1947).
82. *Wolf v. Colorado*, 338 U.S. 25 (1949).
83. *Elkins v. United States*, 364 U.S. 206 (1960); *Mapp v. Ohio*, 367 U.S. 643 (1961).

84. *Gideon v. Wainwright,* 372 U.S. 335 (1963).
85. *Malloy v. Hogan,* 378 U.S. 1 at 10-11 (1964).
86. *Griffin v. California,* 380 U.S. 609 (1965).
87. *Pointer v. Texas,* 380 U.S. 400 (1965).
88. *Klopfer v. North Carolina,* 386 U.S. 213 (1967).

89. *Duncan v. Louisiana,* 391 U.S. 145 (1968).
90. *Benton v. Maryland,* 395 U.S. 784 (1969).
91. *Joint Anti-Fascist Refugee Committee v. McGrath,* 341 U.S. 123 at 163 (1951).

Part I

Freedom for Ideas

Of all the liberties guaranteed by the Bill of Rights, the freedoms of the First Amendment are the most widely cherished. Won through revolution, the freedoms of speech, press, religion, peaceable assembly, and petition are values fundamental to the American ideals of individual freedom and representative self-government.

The guarantee of freedom for the individual's expression of ideas and opinions reflects a belief in the worth of each person. So too does the decision to entrust the government of society to the will of its members.

The "First Amendment protects two kinds of interests on free speech," wrote Professor Zechariah Chafee, Jr. "There is an individual interest, the need of many men to express their opinions on matters vital to them if life is to be worth living, and a social interest in the attainment of truth, so that the country may not only adopt the wisest course of action but carry it out in the wisest way." [1]

The two freedoms are inextricably bound together. Professor Thomas I. Emerson observed that freedom of individual expression is essential to preserve a stable community in the face of ever-changing political, economic, and social circumstances, to maintain "the precarious balance between healthy cleavage and necessary consensus." [2]

Suppression of free expression, on the other hand, endangers both the development and liberty of the individual and the stability of representative government. In the words of constitutional historian Thomas M. Cooley,

> Repression of full and free discussion is dangerous in any government resting upon the will of the people. The people cannot fail to believe that they are deprived of rights, and will be certain to become discontented, when their discussion of public measures is sought to be circumscribed by the judgment of others upon their temperance or fairness. They must be left at liberty to speak with the freedom which the magnitude of the supposed wrongs appears in their minds to demand; and if they exceed all the proper bounds of moderation, the consolation must be, that the evil likely to spring from the violent discussion will probably be less, and its correction by public sentiment more speedy, than if the terrors of the law were brought to bear to prevent the discussion. [3]

Justice Louis D. Brandeis explained this relationship:

> Those who won our independence believed that the final end of the State was to make men free to develop their faculties; and that in its government the deliberative forces should prevail over the arbitrary. They valued liberty both as an end and as a means. They believed liberty to be the secret of happiness and courage to be the secret of liberty. They believed that freedom to think as you will and to speak as you think are means indispensable to the discovery and spread of political truth; that without free speech and assembly discussion would be futile; that with them, discussion affords ordinarily adequate protection against the dissemination of noxious doctrine; that the greatest menace to freedom is an inert people; that public discussion is a political duty; and that this should be a fundamental principle of the American government. They recognized the risks to which all human institutions are subject. But they knew that order cannot be secured merely through fear of punishment for its infraction. . . . Believing in the power of reason as applied through public discussion, they eschewed silence coerced by law—the argument of force in its worst form. Recognizing the occasional tyrannies of governing majorities, they amended the Constitution so that free speech and assembly should be guaranteed. [4]

The First Amendment

The First Amendment states: "Congress shall make no law respecting an establishment of religion, or prohibiting the free exercise thereof; or abridging the freedom of speech, or of the press; or the right of the people peaceably to assemble, and to petition the Government for a redress of grievances."

Given the fundamental character of these rights, it seems somewhat ironic that they were not enumerated in the main body of the Constitution. In that document, the framers sought to prevent federal infringement of certain crucial personal rights by prohibiting Congress specifically from enacting ex post facto laws and bills of attainder, requiring religious oaths from government officers, and by limiting suspension of the writ of habeas corpus.

The Constitution's authors were apparently convinced, however, that the limited powers given the central government and their division among three separate and coequal branches of government were sufficient guarantees against abuse of the freedoms of belief and expression. Many of the framers also thought any enumeration of individual rights was bound to be incomplete and would imply that those freedoms not listed were not protected.

Participants in the state ratifying conventions were unsatisfied with these explanations. Some of the colonies agreed to ratify the Constitution only on the condition that these and other critical rights—such as indictment and trial by jury—be added. The First Congress approved twelve amendments and submitted them to the states in the fall of 1789. Two of these—dealing with apportionment of U.S. representatives and compensation of members of Congress—failed to win ratification. The other ten were made part of the Constitution late in 1791.

No Absolute Rights

For nearly 130 years, the Supreme Court had very little occasion to review or interpret the First Amendment. Seven years after its ratification, however, Congress, fearing war with France, curtailed speech and press by passing the Sedition Act of 1798. The law proved so unpopular that it precipitated the fall of the Federalist party that sponsored it and was allowed to expire before constitutional challenges to it reached the Supreme Court.

In the late 1800s the Court reviewed a pair of federal territorial laws outlawing polygamy, which were challenged as abridging the free exercise of religion. The Court held polygamy a crime that could not be justified as a religious practice. The laws against it therefore did not violate the First Amendment.

Not until World War I, when Congress enacted new sedition and espionage acts, was the Supreme Court forced to consider whether the First Amendment's prohibition against federal interference with speech, press, religion, and assembly was absolute or whether certain emergencies might limit its protection.

In a series of nine cases testing the constitutionality of these two wartime laws, the Supreme Court made clear that the guarantees of free speech and press were not absolute. The justices, however, disagreed on the point at which government might curb exercise of these freedoms.

Rights and the States

At the same time, the Court began to consider whether the First Amendment applied to prohibit state as well as federal abridgment of its guarantees. The First Amendment explicitly prohibits only Congress from abridging its guaranteed freedoms.

In *Barron v. Baltimore* (1833), the Court ruled that the Bill of Rights restricted only the federal government and not the states.[5] In 1868 the Fourteenth Amendment was added to the Constitution, forbidding the states to deprive anyone of "liberty" without due process of the law. By 1890 the Court had defined liberty to include economic and property rights, but personal liberties remained outside the Court's view of the Fourteenth Amendment. But as historians Alpheus T. Mason and William M. Beaney observed, "This illogical position could not long endure."[6]

Application of First Amendment strictures to state action began with the case of *Gilbert v. Minnesota* in 1920. Justice Brandeis, dissenting, said he could not believe "that the liberty guaranteed by the Fourteenth Amendment includes only liberty to acquire and enjoy property."[7]

Nonetheless, as late as 1922 a majority of the Court still declared: "[T]he Constitution of the United States imposes upon the States no obligation to confer upon those within their jurisdiction . . . the right of free speech."[8] In 1923, however, the Court began to include personal freedoms in the definition of liberty protected by the Fourteenth Amendment. Liberty, the majority wrote in *Meyer v. Nebraska,*

> denotes not merely freedom from bodily restraint but also the right of the individual to contract, to engage in any of the common occupations of life, to acquire useful knowledge, to marry, establish a home and bring up children, to worship God according to the dictates of his own conscience, and generally to enjoy those privileges long recognized at common law as essential to the orderly pursuit of happiness by free men.[9]

Two years later the Court with little explanation stated that the First Amendment guarantees of free speech and free press were applicable to the states. In *Gitlow v. New York* (1925), it wrote:

> For present purposes we may and do assume that freedom of speech and of the press—which are protected by the First Amendment from abridgment by Congress—are among the fundamental personal rights and "liberties" protected by the due process clause of the Fourteenth Amendment from impairment by the States.[10]

That same year the Court also moved toward including religious liberty within this protection, as it struck down an Oregon law requiring all children to attend public schools. In *Pierce v. Society of Sisters* (1925) the Court said that the right of parents to rear their children as they saw fit included the right to send those children to private and parochial schools.[11]

But it was fifteen more years before the Court explicitly applied the First Amendment ban on governmental interference with free exercise of religion to the states. In 1940 in *Cantwell v. Connecticut,* the Court declared that the Fourteenth Amendment "has rendered the legislatures of the states as incompetent as Congress to enact" such restrictions. The states were specifically barred from passing any laws respecting establishment of religion by the 1947 ruling in *Everson v. Board of Education.*[12]

In 1931 the Supreme Court, for the first time, struck down a state law as an unconstitutional prior restraint on the press. This action came in *Near v. Minnesota.* Six years later, the Court held that the freedom of assembly was guaranteed against state infringement by the First and Fourteenth Amendments. In the case of *DeJonge v. Oregon,* the Court held the right of peaceful assembly to be equally as fundamental as the rights of free speech and press and therefore equally entitled to protection from restriction by the states.

The right of assembly, the Court wrote, "is one that cannot be denied without violating those fundamental principles of liberty and justice which lie at the base of all civil and political institutions, principles which the Fourteenth Amendment embodies in the general terms of its due process clause."[13]

Government Restraints

Government restraints on exercise of First Amendment rights include suppression of the utterance before it is spoken or published and punishment of the person who made the offending utterance.

Prohibition of prior restraints—censorship, severe taxation, and licensing systems, for example—is particularly vital to ensure freedom of the press. The English legal commentator, Sir William Blackstone, thought that liberty of the press lay entirely in allowing "no previous restraints upon publications and not in freedom from censure for criminal matter when published." [14]

But the First Amendment has been interpreted by the Supreme Court to limit subsequent punishment as well as prior restraint. Cooley wrote,

[t]he mere exemption from previous restraints cannot be all that is secured by the constitutional provisions, inasmuch as of words to be uttered orally there can be no previous censorship, and the liberty of the press might be rendered a mockery and a delusion, and the phrase itself a byword, if, while every man was at liberty to publish what he pleased, the public authorities might nevertheless punish him for harmless publications.... The evils to be prevented were not the censorship of the press merely, but any action of the government by means of which it might prevent such free and general discussion of public matters as seems absolutely essential to prepare the people for an intelligent exercise of their rights as citizens. [15]

Although the First Amendment is stated absolutely— "Congress shall make no law..."—few contend that the amendment is an absolute ban on governmental restriction of the amendment's guarantees.

Most justices and constitutional scholars distinguish between pure expression and expression that is in itself conduct or that incites conduct. The first, with a few exceptions, is absolutely protected against governmental infringement; the second is not. Although the Court was speaking specifically of the freedom of religion, its explanation of this distinction in *Cantwell v. Connecticut* (1940) may be applied to all First Amendment freedoms: "[T]he Amendment embraces two concepts—freedom to believe and freedom to act. The first is absolute but, in the nature of things the second cannot be. Conduct remains subject to regulation for the protection of society." [16]

Unprotected Speech

Some forms of expression that fall outside protection of the First Amendment are fairly obvious. Few would apply First Amendment protection to a person who counsels murder or, as Justice Oliver Wendell Holmes, Jr., said, to a "man falsely shouting fire in a theater and causing a panic." Few would argue that publishers are free to print deliberately false and defamatory material about public or private individuals. The outer bounds of First Amendment protection are not fixed. The Supreme Court initially held commercial speech—that which proposed a financial transaction—to be outside the amendment's reach. In a line of rulings beginning in 1975, the Court has reversed that position.

The Court once ruled that libelous statements were unprotected. It has since held false and defamatory statements about public officials and figures protected unless actual malice is proved. Obscenity is still outside the scope of First Amendment protection, but even there the standards for determining what is obscene and what is not have undergone significant change in recent decades, bringing additional material under protection.

Speech and Conduct

Commercial speech, libel, and obscene material are examples of pure expression. What has proved difficult for the Court to determine with consistency is the precise point at which expression becomes conduct that breaches the bounds of First Amendment protection and becomes subject to government restraint and regulation.

Assume, for example, that a man is making an intemperate speech on a controversial issue on a public street corner. Does the First Amendment protect him against punishment for any consequences that speech might have? If not, must the government wait to stop the speech until his listeners take action either against the speaker or the object of his speech? Or may it stop him at the point that it thinks his words will lead to a breach of the peace? Or is it permissible for the government, knowing from past experience that the speaker is a rabble-rouser, to prevent him from speaking at all?

Finding an answer to these questions is made more difficult by the emotional overlay carried by many forms of expression. The voicing of a popular opinion held by a majority is unlikely to raise any First Amendment challenge. But as Justice Robert H. Jackson once observed, the "freedom to differ is not limited to things that do not matter much." [17]

It is the unpopular opinion and minority position on matters of crucial concern that are most likely to draw hostility and hatred from the majority upon whose good will the rights of the minority depend for their continued meaning. And if the unpopular opinion is perceived as a threat to a way of life or a form of government, it may prompt the majority to petition the government to repress the expression. Such suppression is just what the First Amendment was designed to curb, explained Justice Holmes in a dissenting opinion:

Persecution for the expression of opinions seems to me perfectly logical.... But when men have realized that time has upset many fighting faiths, they may come to believe even more than they believe the very foundations of their own conduct that the ultimate good desired is better reached by free trade in ideas—that the best test of truth is the power of the thought to get itself accepted in the competition of the market, and that truth is the only ground upon which their wishes safely can be carried out. That at any rate is the theory of our Constitution. [18]

The Task of Balancing

The Supreme Court's job has been to balance the scales so that personal rights are restricted only so much as needed to preserve an organized and orderly society. This has not been an easy task, for some justices give more weight to certain factors in the equation than others. If, for instance, a judge believes the preservation of First Amendment rights to be worth more than the tranquillity of the established society, the judge may require the society to show that the expression places it in some grave and immediate jeopardy. If, on the other hand, the judge gives the need for an orderly society the same or greater weight than the need for free expression, even a small degree of disruption may be enough for him to justify governmental restraint of the threatening idea.

The Absolute Position

Very few justices have believed that the First Amendment is absolute, that the government may under no circumstances restrict the exercise of free speech, press, religion, or assembly.

Justice Hugo L. Black was one who held this view. "[T]he Amendment provides in simple words that Congress shall make no law . . . abridging freedom of speech or of the press," he wrote in one case. "I read 'no law abridging' to mean no law abridging." [19]

Black elaborated on this in a 1961 dissent:

I believe that the First Amendment's unequivocal command that there shall be no abridgment of the rights of free speech and assembly shows that the men who drafted our Bill of Rights did all the "balancing" that was to be done in this field. . . . [T]he very object of adopting the First Amendment, as well as the other provisions of the Bill of Rights, was to put the freedoms protected there completely out of the area of any congressional control that may be attempted through the exercise of precisely those powers that are now being used to "balance" the Bill of Rights out of existence. [20]

Black's view of the First Amendment meant that he would extend its protection to obscenities and libel. But even Black placed certain kinds of expression outside the reach of the First Amendment. In 1949 he wrote an opinion holding that a particular instance of picketing was so intertwined with illegal labor practices that it lost any First Amendment protection it might otherwise have. And in two cases in the mid-1960s, Black contended that civil rights demonstrations were not protected if they occurred in inappropriate places. *(Details, p. 43)*

Preferred Position

If First Amendment rights generally have not been viewed as absolute, most justices still accord them a preferred position when weighed against competing rights and interests. This preferred position arises from the judicial belief that preservation of these rights is so essential to the maintenance of democratic values as to warrant special judicial consideration.

Justice Benjamin N. Cardozo first voiced this view from the bench in a 1937 case. He suggested that because the freedom of "thought and speech . . . is the matrix, the indispensable condition, of nearly every other form of freedom," First Amendment rights were on a "different plane of social and moral values" than the other rights and freedoms guaranteed by the Bill of Rights. [21]

Cardozo's statement was followed in 1938 by a broad hint that the Court might apply stricter standards to test the validity of laws restricting First Amendment rights than it did in cases involving property and economic rights. Traditionally the Court deferred to legislative judgment in enacting statutes levying taxes and regulating business. So

long as there was a reasonable basis for the regulation, the Court would presume it constitutional.

But in the famous *Carolene Products* footnote, Justice Harlan Fiske Stone wrote that "[T]here may be a narrower scope for operation of the presumption of constitutionality when legislation appears on its face to be within a specific prohibition of the Constitution, such as those of the first ten amendments." [22] *(Text of footnote, p. 8)*

The following year, all but one member of the Court endorsed the premise implicit in that footnote. "Mere legislative preferences or beliefs respecting matters of public convenience may . . . be insufficient to justify such [regulation] as diminishes the exercise of rights [of freedom of speech and press] so vital to the maintenance of democratic institutions," the majority wrote. Furthermore, it was the duty of the courts "to weigh the circumstances and to appraise the substantiality of the reasons advanced" to support regulation of First Amendment rights rather than to defer to legislative judgment. [23]

This special treatment of the First Amendment came to be known as the "preferred position," a phrase first used by Stone, then chief justice, in a dissent in *Jones v. Opelika* (1942). Ironically, the first use by a majority came in the decision that overturned *Jones*. In *Murdock v. Pennsylvania* (1943) the majority flatly stated that "[f]reedom of press, freedom of speech, freedom of religion are in a preferred position." [24]

The fullest elaboration of this attitude came in the 1945 case of *Thomas v. Collins*. Justice Wiley B. Rutledge wrote that it was the Court's duty

to say where the individual's freedom ends and the State's power begins. Choice on that border, now as always delicate, is perhaps more so where the usual presumption supporting legislation is balanced by the preferred place given in our scheme to the great, the indispensable democratic freedoms secured by the First Amendment. . . . That priority gives these liberties a sanctity and a sanction not permitting dubious intrusions. . . .

. . . [A]ny attempt to restrict those liberties must be justified by clear public interest, threatened not doubtfully or remotely, but by clear and present danger. The rational connection between the remedy provided and the evil to be curbed, which in other contexts might support legislation against attack on due process grounds, will not suffice. These rights rest on firmer foundation. Accordingly, whatever occasion would restrain orderly discussion and persuasion, at appropriate time and place, must have clear support in public danger, actual or impending. Only the gravest abuses, endangering paramount interests, give occasion for permissible limitation. [25]

Use of the phrase "preferred position" faded away, but the concept recurs. The Court considers statutes that limit First Amendment rights highly suspect, requiring close judicial attention and compelling justification for their existence. Chief Justice Warren E. Burger stated that consensus in 1978:

Deference to a legislative finding cannot limit judicial inquiry when First Amendment rights are at stake. . . . A legislature appropriately inquires into and may declare the reasons impelling legislative action but the judicial function commands analysis of whether the specific conduct charged falls within the reach of the statute and if so whether the legislation is consonant with the Constitution. Were it otherwise, the scope of freedom of speech and of the press would be subject to legislative definition and the function of the First Amendment as a check on legislative power would be nullified.[26]

A few justices opposed the preferred position concept. Chief among these was Felix Frankfurter, a vigorous advocate of judicial restraint. In 1949 he characterized the preferred position approach to the First Amendment as "a mischievous phrase, if it carries the thought, which it may subtly imply, that any law touching communication is infected with presumptive invalidity."[27]

When he balanced First Amendment rights against competing interests, Frankfurter placed great weight on legislative judgment. Two years later, he wrote:

Free speech cases are not an exception to the principle that we are not legislators, that direct policy making is not our province. How best to reconcile competing interests is the business of legislatures, and the balance they strike is a judgment not to be displaced by ours, but to be respected unless outside the pale of fair judgment.[28]

The Search for a Standard

The Supreme Court has never held the freedoms of speech, press, religion, and assembly to be absolute or unabridgeable. Although it has written specific rules for determining whether speech is obscene or libelous, the Court has been unable to settle on a general standard for determining at what point a form of expression becomes sufficiently threatening to society to justify its being regulated or otherwise restrained by government.

Clear and Present Danger

The first time the Supreme Court ruled directly on the extent to which government might limit speech, Justice Oliver Wendell Holmes, Jr., proposed the "clear and present danger" test as the standard for such regulation. The case, *Schenck v. United States* (1919), was the first of several challenging convictions under the World War I espionage and sedition acts that made it a federal crime to obstruct the U.S. war effort.

Writing for a unanimous Court, Holmes said:

The question in every case is whether the words are used in such circumstances and are of such a nature as to create a clear and present danger that they will bring about the substantive evils that Congress has a right to prevent. It is a question of proximity and degree.[29]

In the eyes of the justices, the fact that the country was engaged in a war made Schenck's efforts to obstruct recruitment a clear and present danger punishable under federal law. *(Details, p. 24)*

Eight months later, a majority of the Court moved away from the clear and present danger standard toward what became known as the "bad tendency" test. This test held that government may punish any speech that tends to interfere with the successful prosecution of a war effort, no matter how remote in time or unlikely the effect of the

interference might be. The majority applied the bad tendency test in several cases.[30] But in 1937 it renewed reliance on the clear and present danger doctrine.

The case concerned a black Communist who went to Georgia to solicit members for the Communist party and to encourage black Georgians to demand equal rights with whites. He was convicted under a state law because a trial court found that his speeches and documents had a dangerous tendency to incite insurrection.

A majority of the Court overturned the conviction on the ground that the speech and documents did not threaten "a clear and present danger of forcible obstruction of a particular state function."[31] *(Details, p. 33)*

Until 1937 the Court had considered free speech questions primarily in the context of seditious speech—utterances that threatened the viability of the established governing and economic system.

After 1937 the Court began to review more cases weighing the constitutional guarantee of free speech against state limitations designed to preserve public peace. In these cases it frequently employed the clear and present danger test. Thus in 1940 the Court held that a state could not constitutionally punish a person for peacefully picketing an employer with whom he had a labor dispute.[32]

In another 1940 case the Court overturned the conviction for breach of the peace of a Jehovah's Witness whose attack on other religions highly incensed two passersby who had consented to listen to it. In the absence of a definitive statute making such conduct a clear and present danger to a substantial interest of the state, the Court said the situation had threatened no "clear and present menace to public peace and order."[33] *(Details, p. 34)*

It soon became apparent that the justices could seldom reach a consensus on whether a danger was "clear and present." In 1949 a majority of the Court held that the clear and present danger to public order was not threatened by a speaker whose speech in a private hall sparked a near-riot by several hundred protestors gathered outside the hall. But in 1951 the Court upheld the conviction of a speaker whose utterances caused one listener to threaten to stop the speaker from continuing his remarks. Here the Court majority held that a clear and present danger of greater disorder warranted restraint of the speaker.[34]

The widely held fear that the American system of government was in danger of subversion by Communists led to enactment of a federal law outlawing membership in the Communist party and the advocacy of the violent overthrow of the established government. *(Discussion of political associations, p. 131)*

The question whether this act was an unconstitutional infringement on free speech came to the Supreme Court in the 1951 case of *Dennis v. United States*. A majority of the Court upheld the federal law, using a substantially revised version of the clear and present danger test.

The justices read the traditional rule as being applicable only when the probability of success of the intended dangerous effect was imminent. Finding this an inadequate protection from subversive activity that included advocacy of the future overthrow of the government by force, Chief Justice Fred M. Vinson wrote that the clear and present danger test must be reinterpreted as follows: "In each case [courts] must ask whether the gravity of the 'evil' discounted by its improbability, justified such invasion of free speech as is necessary to avoid the danger."[35]

With this restatement, the original meaning of the clear and present danger test appeared to be lost. The doctrine was little used after the 1957 case of *Yates v. United States*.[36]

The Balancing Doctrine

The test was replaced for a time by the so-called balancing doctrine, in which the Court weighed the value of preserving free speech against the value of preserving whatever governmental interest that speech might adversely affect. This standard appeared in a 1950 decision sustaining a federal law that denied the protection of the National Labor Relations Act to any union whose officers failed to swear that they were not Communists and did not believe in the violent overthrow of the government.

The majority found that the law's primary purpose was to prevent a union official from using his power to force a strike to advance the Communist cause. In the Court's view this law limited speech only incidentally. It found application of the clear and present danger test inappropriate and turned instead to the balancing test:

> When particular conduct is regulated in the interest of public order, and the regulation results in an indirect, conditional, partial abridgment of speech, the duty of the courts is to determine which of these two conflicting interests demands the greater protection under the particular circumstances presented.[37]

Throughout the cold war period, the Court employed the balancing test to determine the validity of numerous state and federal laws restricting the speech and actions of individuals associated with the Communist party and other allegedly subversive organizations.[38]

But when the Court was asked to weigh the interest of a state in obtaining the membership lists of a state branch of the National Association for the Advancement of Colored People (NAACP) against the members' right to privacy in association, it balanced the scales in favor of the right of association. The Court did not apply the balancing test to other 1960s civil rights cases involving picketing and demonstrations. In 1967 the Court specifically rejected the use of that test in a national security case.[39]

The Court disposed of some of the cold war cases by using the "incitement test," which distinguished between the advocacy of unlawful conduct as abstract doctrine, and advocacy that actually incited action. The first was protected by the First Amendment, the second was not.[40]

Recognizing the inadequacy of these substantive tests, the Court has come to rely on several tests that focus on the challenged statute rather than on the conduct or speech it regulates. The three standards most frequently employed are statutory vagueness, facial overbreadth, and the least restrictive means test. They are based on the premise that laws imposing restrictions that are too broad might inhibit some persons from exercising their constitutionally protected freedoms.

An overly broad statute restricts forms of expression that are protected as well as those that are not. Under the least restrictive means test, government may only restrain expression as much as necessary to achieve its purpose: "[E]ven though the governmental purpose be legitimate and substantial, that purpose cannot be pursued by means that broadly stifle fundamental personal liberties when the end can more narrowly be achieved."[41]

Statutes deficient in any of these respects may be challenged by persons whose speech may in fact be properly punished by the state under the law.

Notes

1. Zechariah Chafee, Jr., *Free Speech in the United States* (Cambridge, Mass.: Harvard University Press, 1941; reprint ed. New York: Atheneum, 1969), 33.
2. Thomas I. Emerson, *The System of Freedom of Expression* (New York: Random House, Vintage Books, 1970), 7.
3. Thomas M. Cooley, *A Treatise on Constitutional Limitations*, 8th ed., 2 vols. (Boston: Little, Brown, 1927), II:901.
4. *Whitney v. California*, 274 U.S. 357 at 375-376 (1927).
5. *Barron v. Baltimore*, 7 Pet. 243 (1833).
6. Alpheus T. Mason and William M. Beaney, *The Supreme Court in a Free Society* (New York: W. W. Norton, 1968), 289.
7. *Gilbert v. Minnesota*, 254 U.S. 325 at 343 (1920).
8. *Prudential Insurance Co. v. Cheek*, 259 U.S. 530 at 538 (1922).
9. *Meyer v. Nebraska*, 262 U.S. 390 at 399-400 (1923).
10. *Gitlow v. New York*, 268 U.S. 652 at 666 (1925).
11. *Pierce v. Society of Sisters*, 268 U.S. 510 (1925).
12. *Cantwell v. Connecticut*, 310 U.S. 296 at 303 (1940); *Everson v. Board of Education*, 330 U.S. 1 (1947).
13. *Near v. Minnesota*, 283 U.S. 697 (1931); *DeJonge v. Oregon*, 299 U.S. 353 at 364 (1937).
14. William Blackstone, *Commentaries on the Laws of England*, quoted in Chafee, *Free Speech*, 9.
15. Cooley, *Constitutional Limitations*, II:885-86.
16. *Cantwell v. Connecticut*, 310 U.S. 296 at 303-04 (1940).
17. *West Virginia State Board of Education v. Barnette*, 319 U.S. 624 at 642 (1943).
18. *Abrams v. United States*, 250 U.S. 616 at 630 (1919).
19. *Smith v. California*, 361 U.S. 147 at 157 (1959).
20. *Konigsberg v. State Board of California*, 366 U.S. 36 at 61 (1961).
21. *Palko v. Connecticut*, 302 U.S. 319 at 327, 326 (1937).
22. *United States v. Carolene Products*, 304 U.S. 144 at 152, fn. 4 (1938).
23. *Schneider v. Irvington*, 308 U.S. 147 at 161 (1939).
24. *Murdock v. Pennsylvania*, 319 U.S. 105 at 115 (1943) overturning *Jones v. Opelika*, 316 U.S. 584 (1942).
25. *Thomas v. Collins*, 323 U.S. 516 at 529-530 (1945).
26. *Landmark Communications Inc. v. Virginia*, 435 U.S. 829 at 843-844 (1978).
27. *Kovacs v. Cooper*, 336 U.S. 77 at 90 (1949).
28. *Dennis v. United States*, 341 U.S. 494 at 539-540 (1951).
29. *Schenck v. United States*, 249 U.S. 47 at 52 (1919).
30. See, for example, *Abrams v. United States*, 250 U.S. 616 (1919); *Pierce v. United States*, 252 U.S. 239 (1920); *Gitlow v. New York*, 268 U.S. 652 (1925).
31. *Herndon v. Lowry*, 301 U.S. 242 at 261 (1937).
32. *Thornhill v. Alabama*, 310 U.S. 88 (1940).
33. *Cantwell v. Connecticut*, 310 U.S. 296 at 311 (1940).
34. *Terminiello v. Chicago* 337 U.S. 1 (1949); *Feiner v. New York*, 340 U.S. 315 (1951).
35. *Dennis v. United States*, 341 U.S. 494 at 510 (1951).
36. *Yates v. United States*, 354 U.S. 298 (1957).
37. *American Communications Association v. Douds*, 399 U.S. 382 at 399 (1950).
38. See, for example, *Konigsberg v. State Bar of California*, 366 U.S. 36 (1961).
39. *NAACP v. Alabama ex rel. Patterson*, 357 U.S. 449 (1958); *Edwards v. South Carolina*, 372 U.S. 229 (1963); *Cox v. Louisiana*, 379 U.S. 536 (1965); *Brown v. Louisiana*, 383 U.S. 131 (1966); *Adderly v. Florida*, 385 U.S. 39 (1967); *United States v. Robel*, 389 U.S. 258 (1967).
40. *Brandenburg v. Ohio*, 395 U.S. 444 (1969).
41. *Shelton v. Tucker*, 364 U.S. 479 at 488 (1960).

Freedom of Speech

Speech is the basic vehicle for communicating ideas, thoughts, and beliefs. The right to speak freely is necessary to the free flow of ideas considered so crucial to the success of representative government in the United States. This belief spurred the residents of the new nation to add to the Constitution a prohibition on government action abridging the freedom of speech.

Although the First Amendment states its protection absolutely, few contend that the right it protects is without limit. And there are forms of speech that merit no First Amendment protection whatsoever. The Supreme Court's task has been to answer two questions raised by this guarantee: What is protected speech and when may such speech be curbed?

The Court has divided speech into two general categories, pure speech and what some of its members call "speech plus."

Verbal expression of thought and opinion, whether spoken calmly in the privacy of one's home or delivered passionately in a soapbox harangue, is the purest form of speech. Constitutional historian C. Herman Pritchett has observed that the "distinctive qualities of pure speech are that it relies for effect only on the power of the ideas or emotions that are communicated by speech and that usually the audience is a voluntary one which chooses to listen to the speaker's message." [1]

Because it does not interfere with or inconvenience others, pure speech is subject to the least amount of government control. The Court, however, recognizes the right of government to curb pure speech that threatens the national security or public safety. It also acknowledges that government has a right to regulate pure speech that does interfere with others.

The broadest official restrictions on pure speech have come during times of war when the Court has upheld federal and state controls on seditious and subversive speech. It has sustained punishment of nonseditious speech that stimulates a violent and hostile reaction. But because the Court considers the varying circumstances attending each free speech case, it has been unable to develop and apply consistently a standard for determining the point at which the threat warrants a restriction on or punishment of the speech.

Certain forms of pure speech and expression fall outside the protection of the First Amendment because they are not essential to communication of ideas and have little social value.

"Fighting words"—public insults calculated to elicit a violent response—fall into this category, as does obscenity. Here again, however, the Court has had great difficulty settling on a standard by which to define the obscene.

Initially the Court placed speech that advertised products and services outside the protection of the First Amendment. Since 1975, however, the Court has recognized that advertisements convey ideas and information of substantial value to the public and so has brought commercial speech under First Amendment coverage.

Expression that makes a symbolic statement has been considered pure speech by the Court. The justices have upheld the right of students to wear armbands and to fly the flag upside down in symbolic protest of the Vietnam War. Although such symbolism may make itself felt on an involuntary audience, it relies for effect, like pure speech, primarily on evocation of an idea or emotion. The Court has also held, however, that symbolic speech, like pure speech, may be so intertwined with conduct that the state may regulate both.

"Speech plus" combines the rights of speech and assembly with a course of conduct—usually parading, demonstrating, or picketing. According to Pritchett, "speech plus" involves:

> physical movement of the participants, who rely less upon the persuasive influence of speech to achieve their purposes and more upon the public impact of assembling, marching and patrolling. Their purpose is to bring a point of view—by signs, slogans, singing or their mere presence—to the attention of the widest possible public, including those uninterested or even hostile.[2]

The Court has upheld the right of persons to engage in speech plus conduct but at the same time it has accorded government the right to regulate the conduct aspect to ensure public safety and order. Such regulation must be precisely drawn and applied in a nondiscriminatory fashion. The government also must have a legitimate and substantial interest to justify the regulation, and the regulation must restrict the speech aspect as little as possible.

One area of speech plus conduct has been held by the Court to have almost no First Amendment protection. Although the Court at first ruled that the information conveyed to the public by labor picketing merited some degree of First Amendment protection, later decisions have virtually reversed this holding. Peaceful labor picketing is protected under federal labor law, however.

The Court has established that government has limited power to prevent public property from being used for public speech and assembly. It has made an exception, however, of property, such as a jailyard, that is dedicated to specific uses making it an inappropriate public forum.

Because it bars only government action abridging speech, the First Amendment generally does not affect speech that occurs on private property. Here, too, there are exceptions. The First Amendment does apply to privately owned company towns that provide all services to its residents that a municipally owned town would. But the owners of private property dedicated to specific public purposes—a shopping mall, for example—may restrict speech on their property that is not directly related to its public use.

SEDITIOUS SPEECH AND NATIONAL SECURITY

Just seven years after ratification of the First Amendment, Congress passed the Sedition Act of 1798. This act set stiff penalties for false, scandalous, or malicious writings about the president, either chamber of Congress, or the government, if published with intent to defame any of them, excite hatred against them, stir up sedition, or aid foreign countries hostile to the United States.

The Republicans charged that it abridged the freedoms of speech and press, but no challenge got to the Supreme Court before the act expired. Although only twenty-five people were arrested and ten convicted under the act, it was extremely unpopular and is credited with bringing about the demise of the Federalist party. Upon taking office in 1801, Republican Thomas Jefferson pardoned all those convicted under it, and several years later Congress refunded their fines, with interest.

Although martial law imposed in some areas during the Civil War substantially curtailed freedoms of speech and press, the constitutionality of these actions was never presented to the Court, and it was not until the United States entered World War I that Congress again passed legislation restricting free speech and free press.

Espionage and Sedition

The Espionage Act of 1917 made it a crime to make false statements with the intent to interfere with the operation of the armed forces or to cause insubordination, disloyalty, or mutiny in the armed forces or to obstruct recruiting and enlistment efforts.

The Sedition Act of 1918 made it a crime to say or do anything to obstruct the sale of government war bonds; or to utter, print, write, or publish anything intended to cause contempt and scorn for the government of the United States, the Constitution, the flag, or the uniform of the armed forces; or to say or write anything urging interference with defense production. The act also made it a crime to advocate, teach, defend, or suggest engaging in any of that conduct proscribed by the law.

Challenges to these laws reached the Supreme Court in 1919 and 1920—after World War I ended. They presented the Court with its first opportunity to define the protection afforded by the First Amendment. Was the right of free speech absolute, or could its exercise be restrained? If the latter, under what circumstances and to what extent might free speech be limited?

The Court's answer to the first question was that the right was not absolute. Under certain circumstances Congress could forbid and punish speech it considered seditious. In those early cases, the Court never seriously examined the federal acts themselves, as it later would scrutinize state laws curbing free speech. Instead, the Court deferred to the congressional judgment that the speech and conduct prohibited by the laws would be detrimental to the success of the war effort.

The Court did not speak as easily or as firmly to the question of acceptable limits on free speech. Although the first decisions were unanimous, the Court quickly divided on this point, with the substantial majority ruling that speech and publications that had the tendency to bring about evils that Congress wished to prevent could be punished. The proofs required to show that speakers or publishers intended their remarks to have evil effects were not particularly strict. In balancing preservation of First Amendment rights against preservation of existing government policies, this majority found the latter interest to have greater weight.

Justices Oliver Wendell Holmes, Jr., and Louis D. Brandeis were an eloquent minority. They held that, to be restricted, speech or publication must raise an immediate danger that its intended effect would damage the war effort. They would require that intent to achieve this effect be proved more by evidence than inference.

The *Schenck* Case

The first of six major seditious speech cases, *Schenck v. United States* (1919), involved the secretary of the Socialist party and others convicted of conspiring to cause insubordination in the armed forces and to obstruct recruiting and enlistment. Schenck printed and distributed fifteen thousand leaflets opposing the recently passed Selective Service law; many were mailed to draftees.

Justice Holmes, who wrote the unanimous opinion affirming Schenck's conviction, described the message: "In impassioned language it intimated that conscription was despotism in its worst form and a monstrous wrong against humanity in the interest of Wall Street's chosen few." The leaflet urged its readers to oppose the draft.

Again in Holmes' words, the pamphlet

described the arguments on the other side [in favor of the draft] as coming from cunning politicians and a mercenary capitalist press, and even silent consent to the conscription law as helping to support an infamous conspiracy. It denied the power to send our citizens away to foreign shores to shoot up the people of other lands, and added that words could not express the condemnation such cold-blooded ruthlessness deserves . . . winding up, "You must do your share to maintain, support and uphold the rights of the people of this country." [3]

At his trial Schenck did not deny that the intended effect of this circular was to persuade people to resist conscription. But he argued that such expression was protected by the First Amendment.

The Court, however, rejected this contention. "We admit that in many places and in ordinary times the defendants in saying all that was said in the circular would have been within their constitutional rights," Holmes wrote. "But the character of every act depends upon the circumstances in which it is done." [4]

Holmes then framed what became known as the "clear and present danger" doctrine. If words raised a clear and present danger of bringing about the evils that Congress had the constitutional authority to prevent, the First Amendment protections of free speech and press must give way and the words could be punished. *(Development of doctrine, p. 21)*

In Holmes's view, Schenck's words, printed during wartime and with the admitted intent to persuade men to refuse induction, presented such a clear and present danger. "When a nation is at war," he wrote, "many things that might be said in time of peace are such a hindrance to its effort that their utterance will not be endured so long as men fight and that no Court could regard them as protected by any constitutional right." [5]

It made no difference that Schenck and his compatriots had not succeeded in obstructing recruitment. "The statute . . . punishes conspiracies to obstruct as well as actual obstruction," Holmes concluded. "If the act, (speaking or circulating a paper), its tendency and the intent with which it is done are the same, we perceive no ground for saying that success alone warrants making the act a crime." [6]

The *Frohwerk* Case

The next two cases, decided on the same day a week after the *Schenck* decision, also unanimously affirmed convictions under the espionage and sedition laws. But in both cases, the evidence showing intent to create a clear and present danger was less convincing than in *Schenck*.

In *Frohwerk v. United States* (1919), Justice Holmes indicated that had more evidence been presented, the defendant might well have been acquitted. Frohwerk had placed in a German-language newspaper twelve articles that the government considered attempts to cause disloyalty and insubordination among the armed forces.

Writing the opinion, Holmes said there was little in the language of the articles to distinguish them from the language Schenck used in his leaflets. But from the trial record, the Court was unable to determine whether the circumstances surrounding the publishing and distribution of the articles were such that no clear and present danger was raised:

> It may be that all this might be said or written even in time of war in circumstances that would not make it a crime. We do not lose our right to condemn either measures or men because the Country is at war. It does not appear that there was any special effort to reach men who were subject to the draft. . . . But we must

take the case on the record as it is, and on that record it is impossible to say that it might not have been found that the circulation of the paper was in quarters where a little breath would be enough to kindle a flame and that the fact was known and relied upon by those who sent the paper out. [7]

The *Debs* Case

In the second case decided that day in 1919 the Court upheld the conviction of well-known Socialist Eugene V. Debs for violating the espionage act by a speech he gave in Canton, Ohio. The government alleged the speech was intended to interfere with recruiting and to incite insubordination in the armed forces.

Debs's speech was primarily about socialism. He discussed its growing popularity and predicted its eventual success. However, he also spoke in support of several people serving sentences for violations of the espionage and sedition acts, saying of one that if she was guilty, then so was he. And he made the statements that "you need to know that you are fit for something better than slavery and cannon fodder" and "You have your lives to lose; you certainly ought to have the right to declare war if you consider a war necessary." On this evidence, a trial jury convicted Debs.

The Supreme Court affirmed the conviction. Based on these statements, wrote Holmes, a jury could reasonably conclude that Debs was opposed "not only [to] war in general but this war, and that the opposition was so expressed that its natural and intended effect would be to obstruct recruiting." [8]

The Court then considered whether Debs actually intended his speech to have this effect. Here Holmes looked at evidence showing that just before speaking, Debs endorsed the view that U.S. involvement in World War I was unjustifiable and should be opposed by all means. Such evidence "that the defendant accepted this view . . . at the time that he made his speech is evidence that if in that speech he used words tending to obstruct the recruiting service he meant that they should have that effect," Holmes said. [9]

The *Abrams* Case

Eight months later, in November 1919, the Court issued its first divided decision in a seditious speech case. *Abrams v. United States* concerned the convictions of five Russian-born immigrants for writing, publishing, and distributing in New York City two allegedly seditious pamphlets criticizing the U.S. government for sending troops into Russia in 1918.

One of the pamphlets described President Woodrow Wilson as a coward and a hypocrite, implying that the real reason for sending troops to Russia was not to protect supplies for use in the war against Germany but to aid those fighting takeover of Russia by Communist revolutionaries. The pamphlet also described capitalism as the "one enemy of the workers."

The second pamphlet, printed in Yiddish, warned workers in munitions factories that their products would be used to kill Russians as well as Germans. It called for a general strike. The five distributed some of these pamphlets by tossing them from a window; others were circulated secretly around the city. The five were each sentenced to twenty years imprisonment.

A seven-justice majority upheld the convictions. Justice John H. Clarke, writing for the majority, quickly dismissed the direct free speech issue by citing the *Schenck* and *Frohwerk* cases as precedents. The only question the Court need answer, Clarke said, was whether there was sufficient evidence presented to the jury to sustain its guilty verdict.

Clarke quoted sections of the two pamphlets—the evidence in the case—and from these excerpts concluded:

the plain purpose of their propaganda was to excite, at the supreme crisis of war, disaffection, sedition, riots, and, as they hoped, revolution, in this country for the

purpose of embarrassing and if possible defeating the military plans of the [U.S.] Government in Europe. . . . Thus it is clear not only that some evidence but that much persuasive evidence was before the jury tending to prove that the defendants were guilty as charged.[10]

This reasoning strayed too far from the clear and present danger test to win the concurrence of Holmes and Brandeis.

Holmes agreed with the majority that the five defendants had advocated a general strike and curtailment of war materials production, but he questioned whether their intent to hinder the war effort had been proved.

Holmes further contended that the espionage and sedition acts required conviction of a speaker only if it was proved that he intended his speech to have the criminal effect proscribed by the law and that the speech must produce or be intended to produce a "clear and imminent danger that it will bring about forthwith certain substantive evils that the United States constitutionally may seek to prevent."

Continuing, he wrote:

But as against dangers peculiar to war . . . the principle of the right to free speech is always the same. It is only the present danger of immediate evil or an intent to bring it about that warrants Congress in setting a limit to the expression of opinion where private rights are not concerned. Congress certainly cannot forbid all effort to change the mind of the country. Now nobody can suppose that the surreptitious publishing of a silly leaflet by an unknown man, without more, would present any immediate danger that its opinions would hinder the success of the government arms or have any appreciable tendency to do so.[11]

Only the Yiddish pamphlet criticizing the U.S. intervention in Russia could afford "even a foundation" for the government's charge, Holmes said.

The *Schaefer* Case

In the next case the Court majority moved even further away from Holmes's clear and present danger test. *Schaefer v. United States* (1920) arose after five officers of a Philadelphia German-language newspaper were convicted of publishing false news items with the intent to promote Germany's success in the war and hamper recruiting efforts.

The articles, generally unfavorable to the U.S. war effort, were reprinted from other publications, but the paper's officers had either added to or omitted parts of the text. One article was found objectionable solely because one word had been mistranslated so that "bread lines" read "bread riots."

Six of the justices voted to reverse the convictions of two of the men but sustained the convictions of the other three. Speaking through Justice Joseph McKenna, the majority said it had no doubt that the statements were deliberately falsified, "the purpose being to represent that the war was not demanded by the people but was the result of the machinations of executive power."[12]

Nor, said the majority, was it unreasonable for a jury to conclude that the additions and omissions were made with the intent that the reprinted articles would have the effect alleged. To readers, McKenna wrote, the articles' "derisive contempt may have been truly descriptive of

---

Treason

Article III, Sec. 3 of the Constitution specifically defines treason against the United States as consisting "only in levying War against them, or in adhering to their Enemies, giving them Aid and Comfort. No Person shall be convicted of Treason unless on the Testimony of two Witnesses to the same overt Act, or on Confession in open Court."

The Supreme Court has reviewed only three charges of treason, all arising from World War II incidents. Two of these decisions left interpretation of part of the law in some doubt; the third added little to the discussion.

In *Cramer v. United States* (1945), Cramer befriended two of the German saboteurs who were landed in the United States in 1942 to sabotage the American war effort. He met twice with them in public places and held some money in safekeeping for one of them.

Cramer was charged with giving aid and comfort to the enemy, but the Supreme Court held, 5-4, that Cramer's traitorous intent had not been proved and that eating and drinking with the enemy did not establish guilt.[1]

The 1947 case of *Haupt v. United States* grew out of the same incident. Haupt was the father of one of the saboteurs and was convicted of giving aid and comfort to the enemy after he sheltered his son, helped him try to find employment in a bomb sight factory, and bought him an automobile. Sustaining the conviction, 8-1, the Court held that sheltering the enemy was an overt act that gave aid and comfort and there was no further need to prove that Haupt had traitorous intent when he took him in his son.[2]

In the third case, *Kawakita v. United States* (1952), the Court held that charges of treason could be brought against an American citizen who had committed a treasonous act against the United States in a foreign country.[3]

1. *Cramer v. United States,* 325 U.S. 1 (1945).
2. *Haupt v. United States,* 330 U.S. 631 (1947).
3. *Kawakita v. United States,* 343 U.S. 717 (1952).

American feebleness and inability to combat Germany's prowess, and thereby [may have served] to chill and check the ardency of patriotism." [13]

Furthermore, the majority held that there was no need to show that the articles presented an immediate danger but only that they tended to have a bad effect. Were the articles, McKenna asked,

> the mere expression of peevish discontent, aimless, vapid and innocuous? We cannot so conclude. We must take them at their word, as the jury did, and ascribe to them a more active and sinister purpose. They were the publications of a newspaper, deliberately prepared, systematic, always of the same trend, more specific in some instances, it may be, than in others. Their effect or the persons affected could not be shown, nor was it necessary. The tendency of the articles and their efficacy were enough for offense ... and to have required more would have made the law useless. It was passed in precaution. The incidence of its violation might not be immediately seen, evil appearing only in disaster, the result of disloyalty engendered and the spirit of mutiny. [14]

Holmes and Brandeis would have acquitted all five defendants on the ground that the articles did not raise a clear and present danger to the government's war efforts. Of one of the reprints, Brandeis wrote:

> It is not apparent on a reading of this article ... how it could rationally be held to tend even remotely or indirectly to obstruct recruiting. But ... the test to be applied ... is not the remote or possible effect. There must be the clear and present danger. Certainly men judging in calmness and with this test presented to them could not reasonably have said that this coarse and heavy humor immediately threatened the success of recruiting. [15]

Brandeis not only chided the majority for failing to apply the test in its review of the case but criticized the lower courts for failing to offer the test to the jury as the standard to be used. Instead, the jury had been instructed to convict if they found that any of the articles would diminish "our will to win" the war.

Brandeis concluded with a strong warning against restricting free speech too readily:

> To hold that such harmless additions to or omissions from news items and such impotent expressions of editorial opinion, as were shown here, can afford the basis even of a prosecution will doubtless discourage criticism of the policies of the Government. To hold that such publications can be suppressed as false reports, subjects to new perils the constitutional liberty of the press....
>
> Nor will this grave danger end with the passing of the war. The constitutional right of free speech has been declared to be the same in peace and in war. In peace, too, men may differ widely as to what loyalty to our country demands; and an intolerant majority, swayed by passion or by fear, may be prone in the future, as it has often been in the past, to stamp as disloyal opinions with which it disagrees. Convictions such as these, besides abridging freedom of speech, threaten freedom of thought and of belief. [16]

Justice Clarke also dissented, but not on free speech grounds.

The *Pierce* Case

The final major case in this series centered on a pamphlet entitled "The Price We Pay," written by an eminent Episcopal clergyman and published by the Socialist party.

A federal district judge in Baltimore acquitted several persons accused of violating the espionage act by distributing the pamphlet in that city. The judge found that the booklet was an attempt to recruit persons to the Socialist party and its philosophy and not an attempt to persuade them to interfere with the war effort.

However, an Albany, New York, judge and jury found the latter to be true. Consequently, several persons who distributed the pamphlet in Albany were convicted of conspiring to attempt to cause insubordination in the armed forces. They appealed to the Supreme Court on the ground that the government failed to show intent to cause insubordination or to prove that distribution of the pamphlet created a clear and present danger that insubordination would result.

Seven justices upheld the convictions in *Pierce v. United States* (1920). Much of their reasoning hinged on the fact that a jury could conclude that several of the statements were false, and that the distributors knew them to be false or distributed them without any regard for whether the statements were false or not. Among those statements the Court majority thought a jury might consider false were the following:

- "Into your homes the recruiting officers are coming. They will take your sons of military age and impress them into the army.... And still the recruiting officers will come; seizing age after age, mounting up to the elder ones and taking the younger ones as they grow to soldier size."
- "The Attorney General of the United States is so busy sending to prison men who do not stand up when the Star Spangled Banner is played, that he has no time to protect the food supply from gamblers."
- "Our entry into [the war] was determined by the certainty that if the allies do not win, J. P. Morgan's loans to the allies will be repudiated, and those American investors who bit on his promises will be hooked."

A jury would also be warranted in concluding that such statements, when circulated, would have a tendency to cause insubordination and that that was the intent of the distributors. Even if a jury was not agreed on the probable effect of the pamphlet, said Justice Mahlon Pitney,

> at least the jury fairly might believe that, under the circumstances existing, it would have a tendency to cause insubordination, disloyalty and refusal of duty in the military and naval forces.... Evidently it was intended, as the jury found, to interfere with the conscription and recruitment services; to cause men eligible for the service to evade the draft; to bring home to them, and especially to their parents, sisters, wives, and sweethearts, a sense of impending personal loss, calculated to discourage the young men from entering the service. [17]

Holmes and Brandeis dissented in an opinion written by Brandeis. They disagreed that the statements cited by the majority were false. The first, regarding recruiting, was eventually proved true. The second, concerning the attorney general, was false if taken literally but was clearly meant to suggest that the attorney general might better spend his time than prosecuting people for allegedly sedi-

The Right and Freedom of Association . . .

The right of an individual to associate with others who share similar beliefs and aspirations is not explicitly granted by the Constitution or the Bill of Rights. But the Supreme Court has found this right implicit within the First Amendment freedoms of speech and assembly and in the concept of liberty protected by the Fourteenth Amendment.

Judicial recognition of this right is of recent vintage. In 1927 a majority of the justices upheld the conviction of a woman for violating California's criminal syndicalism law by associating with people in an organization that advocated overthrow of the government by unlawful means.[1]

In 1928 the Court upheld conviction of a Ku Klux Klan officer who disobeyed a New York statute which required certain organizations to file membership lists with the state. In an opinion from which only one justice dissented, the Court held the statute a proper exercise of the state's police power.[2]

A distaste for implying guilt by association underlay the Court's decision in *DeJonge v. Oregon* (1937), reversing DeJonge's conviction for conducting a public meeting under the auspices of the Communist party. The Court distinguished between the party's illegal intent to overthrow the U.S. government and the protected right of a party member to speak and assemble for lawful purposes.[3] *(Details, p. 32)*

This right was sorely tested during the cold war years, when Americans saw their national security threatened by Communist subversion. Antisubversive laws were repeatedly challenged with the claim that political associations were constitutionally protected. Although this contention won a few adherents on the Court, none of the Court's decisions on these laws during this period was grounded on a right of association. *(Further discussion, p. 131)*

The NAACP Cases

The civil rights movement late in the 1950s moved the Court to recognize a constitutionally protected right of association. At the heart of this issue was membership in the National Association for the Advancement of Colored People (NAACP). The cases arose when several southern states, incensed by the association's pivotal role in the civil rights movement, tried to prevent the NAACP from continuing its activities within their borders.

The NAACP challenged these measures. Not only did the Supreme Court strike them down, but in so doing it found in the First and Fourteenth Amendments an implicit right of association that stood on an equal plane with the explicitly guaranteed freedoms of speech, press, assembly, and religion.

Disclosure of Membership. The first of these cases arose in Alabama. Like many other states,

Alabama had a statute requiring all out-of-state corporations to register with the state before doing business there. Although local branches of the NAACP had operated in Alabama since 1915, it had never registered under the statute, nor had the state indicated it should do so.

In 1956 the state attorney general, charging the NAACP with failure to register, won a temporary restraining order prohibiting the organization from working in the state. The attorney general also requested, and the state court ordered, that the NAACP turn over certain records, including lists of all its Alabama members. The NAACP eventually produced all the records requested except the membership lists. The state court held the organization in contempt, fining it $100,000.

The Supreme Court unanimously reversed the contempt conviction with its decision in the case of *NAACP v. Alabama ex rel. Patterson* (1958). Justice John Marshall Harlan wrote the Court opinion:

> Effective advocacy of both public and private points of view, particularly controversial ones, is undeniably enhanced by group association, as this Court has more than once recognized by remarking upon the close nexus between the freedoms of speech and assembly. . . . It is beyond debate that freedom to engage in association for the advancement of beliefs and ideas is an inseparable aspect of the "liberty" assured by the Due Process Clause of the Fourteenth Amendment.[4]

Furthermore, said Harlan, the right of association also entails the right to privacy in that association. "It is hardly a novel perception that compelled disclosure of affiliation with groups engaged in advocacy may constitute [an] effective . . . restraint on freedom of association."[5]

Turning to the NAACP case, he observed that the association had offered unrebutted evidence that previous public disclosures of its membership had resulted in economic reprisal, loss of employment, and physical violence to members. The Court held that Alabama had not presented a sufficient reason to justify an infringement of this protected right.

The reversal of the contempt citation was not the end of this particular story, however. The Court sent the case back to the state court for a decision on whether the NAACP had violated Alabama law by failing to register. The state court forbade the NAACP to operate in Alabama.[6] The Supreme Court reversed the decision in 1967.[7]

Teachers' Associations. In 1960 the Court struck down an even more subtle attempt to discourage membership in the NAACP. Arkansas law required teachers in state-supported schools to file affi-

... An Implicit First Amendment Guarantee

davits listing all the organizations they had belonged to or contributed to within the last five years. It was widely understood that this law was aimed at exposing teachers who belonged to the NAACP. The case of *Shelton v. Tucker* (1960) came to the Court after teachers whose contracts were not renewed because they refused to comply with the statute charged that the law violated their rights to personal, academic, and associational liberties.

For the majority Justice Potter Stewart wrote there was no question that a state might, in an appropriate investigation of the fitness and competence of its teachers, consider their associational ties. However, the law's "comprehensive interference with associational freedom goes far beyond what might be justified in the exercise of the State's legitimate inquiry into the fitness and competency of its teachers." [8]

Litigation and Solicitation. Using a different method to curb NAACP activities, Virginia in 1956 amended its regulations governing ethical conduct of attorneys to forbid solicitation of clients by an agent of an organization that litigates a case in which it is not a party and has no pecuniary interest.

Litigation aid, including advising persons that they might have a claim, was one of the primary methods the NAACP used in its work for racial equality. The organization sued to stop enforcement of Virginia's new rule, arguing that it infringed its right to associate to help persons seek redress for violations of their rights.

By a 6-3 vote the Supreme Court held in *NAACP v. Button* (1963) that Virginia's statute impermissibly infringed on the right of association. That opinion, written by Justice William J. Brennan, Jr., extended the concept of expression to a point not previously reached by the Court. [9] Brennan wrote:

> [A]bstract discussion is not the only species of communication which the Constitution protects: the First Amendment also protects vigorous advocacy, certainly of lawful ends, against government intrusion.... In the context of NAACP objectives, litigation is not a technique of resolving private differences; it is a means for achieving the lawful objective of equality of treatment by all government ... for the members of the Negro community in this country. It is thus a form of political expression.... And under the conditions of modern government, litigation may well be the sole practicable avenue open to a minority to petition for redress of grievances.
>
> We need not, in order to find constitutional protection for the kind of cooperative, organizational activity disclosed by this record, whereby Negroes seek through lawful means to achieve legitimate political ends, subsume such activity under a narrow, literal conception of freedom of

speech, petition or assembly. For there is no longer any doubt that the First and Fourteenth Amendments protect certain forms of orderly group activity. [10]

The majority held that Virginia's statute was impermissibly vague, risking the "gravest danger of smothering all discussion looking to the eventual institution of litigation" on behalf of minority group members, and that the state had not shown a sufficiently compelling reason for restricting this right to associate. [11] Fifteen years later the Court by a 7-1 vote reaffirmed *Button*, declaring that "collective activity undertaken to obtain meaningful access to the courts is a fundamental right within the protection of the First Amendment." [12]

The final NAACP case in this series arose after a committee established by the Florida legislature to investigate Communist activity in the state obtained information that some former or present Communist party members might be members of the Florida NAACP. The committee called as a witness the president of the Miami branch of the NAACP and asked him to verify this information. He refused and was convicted of contempt, which the Court overturned by a 5-4 vote in *Gibson v. Florida Legislative Investigating Committee* (1963). [13]

Recent Rulings

In the 1980s the U.S. Jaycees and the Rotary Club International tried unsuccessfully to invoke the right of association to shield their all-male clubs from pressure to admit women. Twice the Supreme Court rejected this claim. [14] Both times the justices found—without dissent—that any associational right involved in these cases was far outweighed by society's interest in equal treatment of women and men.

1. *Whitney v. California*, 274 U.S. 357 (1927).
2. *Bryant v. Zimmerman*, 278 U.S. 63 (1928).
3. *DeJonge v. Oregon*, 299 U.S. 353 (1937).
4. *NAACP v. Alabama ex rel. Patterson*, 357 U.S. 44 at 460-461 (1958).
5. Id. at 461.
6. *NAACP v. Alabama ex rel. Patterson*, 360 U.S. 240 (1959); *NAACP v. Gallion*, 368 U.S. 16 (1961).
7. *NAACP v. Alabama ex rel. Flowers*, 377 U.S. 288 (1964); see also *Louisiana ex rel. Gremillion v. NAACP*, 366 U.S. 293 (1961); *Bates v. City of Little Rock*, 361 U.S. 516 (1960).
8. *Shelton v. Tucker*, 364 U.S. 379 at 490 (1960).
9. Thomas I. Emerson, *The System of Freedom of Expression* (New York: Random House, Vintage Books, 1970), 429.
10. *NAACP v. Button*, 371 U.S. 415 at 429-430 (1963).
11. Id. at 434.
12. *In re Primus*, 436 U.S. 412 at 426 (1978), quoting *United Transportation Union v. Michigan Bar*, 401 U.S. 576 at 585 (1971).
13. *Gibson v. Florida Legislative Investigating Committee*, 372 U.S. 539 (1963).
14. *Roberts v. U.S. Jaycees*, 468 U.S. 609 (1984); *Board of Directors of Rotary International v. Rotary Club of Duarte*, __ U.S. __ (1987).

tious statements. The third, regarding the reason for U.S. entry into the war, was an expression of opinion rather than fact. To buttress this last statement, Brandeis noted that some members of Congress found the loans instrumental in the government's decision to enter the war. Brandeis then said:

> To hold that a jury may make punishable statements of conclusions or of opinion, like those here involved, by declaring them to be statements of facts and to be false would practically deny members of small political parties freedom of criticism and of discussion in times when feelings run high and the questions involved are deemed fundamental.[18]

Furthermore, Brandeis continued, even if the statements were false, the government offered no proof showing that the men who distributed the pamphlet knew they were false. Nor was there any proof that the pamphlet intended to dampen military morale. The defendants did not even distribute the pamphlet to military men, Brandeis observed. And finally, he said, there was no indication that distribution of "The Price We Pay" raised a clear and present danger of causing insubordination.

Brandeis again concluded with a warning that the Court majority had placed the guarantee of free speech in a precarious position:

> The fundamental right of free men to strive for better conditions through new legislation and new institutions will not be preserved, if efforts to secure it by argument to fellow citizens may be construed as criminal incitement to disobey the existing law—merely, because the argument presented seems to those exercising judicial power to be unfair in its portrayal of existing evils, mistaken in its assumptions, unsound in reasoning or intemperate in language.[19]

The *Hartzel* Case

Distance in time from actual combat brought calmer voices to the debate on seditious speech. The 1918 sedition law was repealed in 1921, and many of those convicted of violating it, including Debs, were ultimately pardoned or had their sentences reduced.

The Espionage Act was still in force when the United States entered World War II. The Supreme Court reviewed only one conviction made under it during this period. The case concerned a man who printed and sent out several articles urging in hostile and intemperate language that the white race stop fighting each other and band together to war against the yellow races.

The question in *Hartzel v. United States* (1944) was not whether what Hartzel said fell within the reach of the federal law, but whether there was enough evidence to sustain his conviction, the same question prominent in the last three World War I cases. A five-justice majority concluded that the government had not proved beyond a reasonable doubt that Hartzel had intended his statements to incite insubordination in the armed forces.[20]

State Sedition Laws

From time to time, states perceived their internal security to be threatened by radical political forces and, like the federal government, they sought to minimize those threats by restricting the exercise of free speech, free press, and free assembly.

The first round of such state laws was enacted after President William McKinley was assassinated in 1901 by a professed anarchist. The model for these criminal anarchy laws—and for the federal Smith Act of 1940—was New York's 1902 law that defined criminal anarchy as "the doctrine that organized government should be overthrown by force or violence, or by assassination of the executive head or any of the executive officials of government, or by any unlawful means." The law made it a felony for anyone to advocate criminal anarchy by speech or by printing and distributing any material advocating or teaching it.

Following World War I and the Communist revolution of 1917, thirty-three states enacted peacetime sedition or criminal syndicalism statutes. Similar to but broader than the criminal anarchy laws, these statutes made it unlawful to advocate, teach, or aid the commission of a crime, sabotage, or other unlawful act of violence in order to bring about political change or a change in industrial ownership. These laws also made it unlawful to organize or knowingly become a member of an organization that advocated criminal syndicalism.

The Supreme Court initially sustained the constitutionality and application of these laws, but by the late 1930s the Court began to reverse convictions in lower courts, holding either that the law was too vague or broad or that it had been applied to persons whose advocacy of overthrow of the government presented no immediate threat.

During the cold war years, states focused exclusively on preventing Communist infiltration of government. Many required public employees to swear that they did not advocate forceful overthrow of the government. Persons refusing to take such oaths were liable to dismissal; those who lied were subject to prosecution for perjury.

At first the Court sustained convictions under these laws, but as the threat of infiltration receded, the Court began to find several of the loyalty oath statutes unconstitutionally vague. In some instances, the Court found their application violative of due process requirements. *(Loyalty oath cases, pp. 142-150)*

By the late 1960s the fear that Communists would destroy the established order was replaced by concern that the public peace was in jeopardy from civil rights activists, antiwar protestors, and members of the so-called New Left. Once again, several states turned to their criminal anarchy and syndicalism laws to restrain the disturbing speech that came from dissident elements of the society. In its first review of this latest application of a criminal syndicalism law, however, the Court cast doubt on the validity of all such laws. The First Amendment protected the advocacy of forceful overthrow of the government, the Court said, unless that advocacy actually incited someone to undertake such action.

The *Gitlow* Case

The first of these state sedition laws to be tested in the Supreme Court was New York's criminal anarchy law.

Benjamin Gitlow, a member of the left wing of the Socialist party, was convicted under the law for printing and distributing some sixteen thousand copies of the "Left Wing Manifesto." This tract repudiated the moderate stance of the main body of the Socialist party and called for the overthrow of the democratic state by "*class action of* the proletariat *in any form* having as its objective the conquest of the power of the state." It also urged the proletariat to "organize its own state *for the coercion and suppression of the bourgeoisie*."

Gitlow appealed his conviction to the Supreme Court on the ground that the statute unconstitutionally restricted his rights of free speech and free press by condemning certain classes of speech without considering whether they presented a clear and present danger of bringing about the evil that the state had the right to prevent.

Gitlow won one of his arguments. The First Amendment explicitly prohibited only Congress, and not the states, from restricting free speech. Gitlow argued, however, that the First Amendment rights of free speech and free press were implicit in the concept of liberty guaranteed by the Fourteenth Amendment. The Court agreed, almost casually, with this contention. *(Details, p. 18)*

But a majority of the Court nonetheless sustained the conviction in *Gitlow v. New York* (1925). The majority, writing through Justice Edward T. Sanford, first held that Gitlow's manifesto fell within the speech proscribed by the law. It was neither abstract doctrine nor the "mere prediction that industrial disturbances and revolutionary mass strikes will result spontaneously in an inevitable process of evolution in the economic system." [21] Instead, the manifesto urged mass strikes for the purpose of fomenting industrial disturbance and revolutionary action to overthrow the organized government.

The Court next held that the state was within its police power when it punished "those who abuse this freedom [of expression] by utterances inimical to the public welfare, tending to corrupt public morals, incite to crime, or disturb the public peace." [22]

The state need not show that such utterances created a clear and present danger of inciting overthrow of the government but only that they tended to have that effect. Sanford explained:

> That utterances inciting to the overthrow of organized government by unlawful means present a sufficient danger of substantive evil to bring their punishment within the range of legislative discretion is clear. Such utterances, by their very nature, involve danger to the public peace and to the security of the State. They threaten breaches of the peace and ultimate revolution. And the immediate danger is none the less real and substantial, because the effect of a given utterance cannot be accurately foreseen. The State cannot reasonably be required to measure the danger from every such utterance in the nice balance of a jeweler's scale. A single revolutionary spark may kindle a fire that, smouldering for a time, may burst into a sweeping and destructive conflagration. It cannot be said that the state is acting arbitrarily or unreasonably when in the exercise of its judgment as to the measures necessary to protect the public peace and safety, it seeks to extinguish the spark without waiting until it has enkindled the flame or blazed into the conflagration. It cannot reasonably be required to defer the adoption of measures for its own peace and safety until the revolutionary utterances lead to actual disturbances of the public peace or imminent and immediate danger of its own destruction; but it may, in the exercise of its judgment, suppress the threatened danger in its incipiency. [23]

Having upheld the authority of the state to determine that a certain class of speech presented a danger, the majority then refused to consider whether the First Amendment protected specific utterances falling within that class. The majority's reasoning was different from the Court's traditional approach to convictions under federal sedition laws, which condemned certain kinds of actions. Under those laws, speech was unprotected only if the government could prove that the circumstances in which it was uttered made it the equivalent of the proscribed action.

Justices Holmes and Brandeis dissented, arguing that the clear and present danger test should be applied to state, as well as to federal, statutes restricting the right of free speech. If that test is applied to Gitlow's case, wrote Holmes,

> it is manifest that there was no present danger of an attempt to overthrow the government by force on the part of the admittedly small minority who shared [Gitlow's] views. It is said that this manifesto was more than a theory, that it was an incitement. Every idea is an incitement. It offers itself for belief and if believed it is acted on unless some other belief outweighs it or some failure of energy stifles the movement at its birth. The only difference between the expression of an opinion and an incitement in the narrower sense is the speaker's enthusiasm for the result. Eloquence may set fire to reason. But whatever may be thought of the redundant discourse before us it had no chance of starting a present conflagration. If in the long run the beliefs expressed in proletarian dictatorship are destined to be accepted by the dominant forces of the community, the only meaning of free speech is that they should be given their chance and have their way. [24]

The *Whitney* Case

California's criminal syndicalism statute was the next state sedition law tested in the Supreme Court. Anita Whitney, a niece of former Supreme Court justice Stephen J. Field, participated in a convention establishing the California branch of the new Communist Labor party.

At the convention, Whitney advocated adoption of a resolution dedicating the party to seek political change through the ballot, but this proposition was rejected in favor of a resolution urging revolutionary class struggle as the means to overthrow capitalism. Despite her defeat, Whitney continued to participate in the convention and the party. Whitney testified that she had no intention of helping to create an unlawful organization, but she was convicted of violating the California law prohibiting organization and participation in groups advocating criminal syndicalism.

The Supreme Court unanimously sustained her conviction. After holding that the state law was not unconstitutionally vague, Justice Sanford said the majority saw little to distinguish Whitney's actions from Gitlow's manifesto. In fact, Whitney's actions in assembling with others to form a group advocating forceful overthrow of the government posed an even greater danger to the state. Sanford wrote:

> The essence of the offense denounced by the Act is the combining with others in an association for the accomplishment of the desired ends through the advocacy and use of criminal and unlawful methods. It partakes

of the nature of a criminal conspiracy.... That such united and joint action involves even greater danger to the public peace and security than the isolated utterances and acts of individuals is clear. We cannot hold that, as here applied, the Act is an unreasonable or arbitrary .exercise of the police power of the State, unwarrantedly infringing any right of free speech, assembly or association, or that those persons are protected from punishment by the due process clause who abuse such rights by joining and furthering an organization thus menacing the peace and welfare of the state.[25]

Justices Holmes and Brandeis concurred with the majority in a separate opinion written by Brandeis that sounded more like a dissent. Under the California statute, Brandeis wrote,

[t]he mere act of assisting in forming a society for teaching syndicalism, of becoming a member of it, or of assembly with others for that purpose is given the dynamic quality of crime. There is guilt although the society may not contemplate immediate promulgation of the doctrine. Thus the accused is to be punished, not for contempt, incitement or conspiracy, but for a step in preparation, which, if it threatens the public order at all, does so only remotely. The novelty in the prohibition introduced is that the statute aims, not at the practice of criminal syndicalism, nor even directly at the preaching of it, but at association with those who propose to preach it.[26]

Brandeis did not deny that the freedom of assembly, like the freedoms of speech and press, could be restricted by the state, but he again insisted that the restriction be permitted only if the assembly presented a clear and present danger of resulting in the intended evil. The danger must be imminent and serious, he wrote; fear of danger is not enough to restrict the First Amendment freedoms:

To justify suppression of free speech there must be reasonable ground to fear that serious evil will result if free speech is practiced. There must be reasonable ground to believe that the danger apprehended is imminent. There must be reasonable ground to believe that the evil to be prevented is a serious one. Every denunciation of existing law tends in some measure to increase the probability that there will be violation of it. Condonation of a breach enhances the probability. Expressions of approval add to the probability. Propagation of the criminal state of mind by teaching syndicalism increases it. Advocacy of law-breaking heightens it still further. But even advocacy of violation, however reprehensible morally, is not a justification for denying free speech where the advocacy falls short of incitement and there is nothing to indicate that the advocacy would be immediately acted on. The wide difference between advocacy and incitement, between preparation and attempt, between assembling and conspiracy, must be borne in mind. In order to support a finding of clear and present danger it must be shown either that immediate serious violence was to be expected or was advocated, or that the past conduct furnished reason to believe that such advocacy was then contemplated....

... The fact that speech is likely to result in some violence or in destruction of property is not enough to justify its suppression. There must be the probability of serious injury to the State. Among free men, the deterrents ordinarily to be applied to prevent crime are education and punishment for violations of the law, not abridgement of the rights of free speech and assembly.[27]

Although they believed that under these standards the California law improperly restricted Whitney's rights of free speech and assembly, Brandeis and Holmes felt compelled to concur in Whitney's conviction for technical reasons. A few months later, the California governor pardoned Whitney, with reasons that echoed Brandeis's opinion.

The *Fiske* Case

The same day that it decided *Whitney,* the Supreme Court for the first time reversed a conviction for violating a state criminal syndicalism act.

In *Fiske v. Kansas* (1927) the Court for the first time held that the First Amendment guarantee of free speech had been violated by the conviction of Fiske, an organizer for International Workers of the World (IWW). The only evidence introduced at trial to show the unlawful nature of the organization was the IWW preamble, which read in part: "Between these two classes a struggle must go on until the workers of the world organize as a class, take possession of the earth and the machinery of production, and abolish the wage system."

The trial jury apparently assumed that this class struggle would involve the violent overthrow of the government, which would make the IWW and participation in it unlawful under the Kansas statute. But the Supreme Court reversed, seeing no evidence showing that the IWW actually advocated violence or 'other criminal acts to bring about political and industrial change.[28]

The Fiske decision was a turning point. The Court heard three more major cases testing the constitutionality of state criminal syndicalism laws as applied in particular circumstances. In all three, the Court reversed convictions for violating these laws.

The *DeJonge* Case

Two of these cases came to the Court in 1937, ten years after *Fiske. DeJonge v. Oregon* arose after DeJonge was convicted for conducting a public meeting under Communist party auspices. DeJonge maintained he was innocent because he had not advocated or taught any criminal doctrine at the meeting, but merely discussed issues of public concern. The state courts, however, interpreted the statute to make criminal any participation in any meeting sponsored by an organization that advocated at any time the forceful overthrow of the established government.

The Court unanimously reversed DeJonge's conviction, holding that the state's interpretation of the statute was unnecessarily restrictive of the rights of free speech and assembly. In one of the Court's first expositions on the right of assembly, Chief Justice Charles Evans Hughes wrote:

peaceable assembly for lawful discussion cannot be made a crime. The holding of meetings for peaceable political action cannot be proscribed. Those who assist in the conduct of such meetings cannot be branded as criminals on that score. The question, if the rights of free speech and peaceable assembly are to be preserved, is not as to the auspices under which the meeting is held but as to its purpose; not as to the relations of the speakers, but whether their utterances transcend the bounds of the freedom of speech which the Constitution protects. If the persons assembling have committed crimes elsewhere, if they have formed or are engaged in a conspiracy against the public peace and order, they may be prosecuted for their conspiracy or other violation of valid laws. But it is a different matter when the State, instead of prosecuting them for such offense, seizes upon mere participation in a peaceable assembly and a lawful public discussion as the basis for a criminal charge.[29]

The *Herndon* Case

In a second case decided in 1937, a majority of the Court abandoned the "bad tendency" test adopted in *Gitlow* in favor of something more like the clear and present danger standard.

Herndon v. Lowry (1937) concerned a black organizer sent to Atlanta to recruit members for the Communist party. He held three meetings and signed up a few members. He had with him membership blanks, literature on the Communist party, and a booklet entitled "The Communist Position on the Negro Question." This booklet called for self-determination for blacks living in the southern "black belt." The booklet envisioned a black-dominated government separate from the rest of the United States. To achieve this goal, the tract advocated strikes, boycotts, and a revolutionary power struggle against the white ruling class.

Herndon was arrested and convicted of violating a Georgia law that made it unlawful for anyone to attempt to persuade anyone else to participate in an insurrection against the organized government. Herndon appealed his conviction on the grounds that he had said or done nothing to create any immediate danger of an insurrection.

A five-justice majority agreed, holding the state statute too vague and too broad. The state needed to show more than that Herndon's words and actions might tend to incite others to insurrection at some future time. Justice Owen J. Roberts wrote:

> The power of a state to abridge freedom of speech and of assembly is the exception rather than the rule and penalizing even of utterances of a defined character must find its justification in a reasonable apprehension of danger to organized government. The judgment of the legislature is not unfettered. The limitation upon individual liberty must have appropriate relation to the safety of the state.[30]

The majority did not accept the state court's view that Herndon was guilty if he intended an insurrection to occur "at any time within which he might reasonably expect his influence to continue to be directly operative in causing such action by those whom he sought to induce." This view left a jury without any precise standard for measuring guilt, Roberts said, and could conceivably allow a jury to convict a person simply because it disagreed with his opinion:

> The statute, as construed and applied, amounts merely to a dragnet which may enmesh anyone who agitates for a change of government if a jury can be persuaded that he ought to have foreseen his words would have some effect in the future conduct of others. No reasonably ascertainable standard of guilt is prescribed. So

vague and indeterminate are the boundaries thus set to the freedom of speech and assembly that the law necessarily violates the guarantee of liberty embodied in the Fourteenth Amendment.[31]

The four dissenters would have used the bad tendency test to uphold the conviction. They said Herndon's possession of the booklets on black self-determination showed that he intended to distribute them, and noted that he had not denied that intention. They also said it was apparent that by endorsing the self-determination plan, Herndon was advocating insurrection. "Proposing these measures was nothing short of advising a resort to force and violence, for all know that such measures could not be effected otherwise," they wrote.[32]

The *Brandenburg* Case

State criminal syndicalism laws reemerged in the late 1960s as states sought ways to restrain civil rights and antiwar activists. The Court, however, in a 1969 per curiam opinion called into question the continuing validity of most criminal syndicalism laws.

In the case of *Brandenburg v. Ohio*, the Court extended the *Herndon* decision by setting out what has been called the "incitement" test. This standard distinguishes between advocacy of the use of force as an abstract doctrine, which is protected by the First Amendment, and actual incitement to use force, which is not protected.

Brandenburg, the leader of a Ku Klux Klan group, invited a newsman and photographer to film a Klan rally. Parts of the film were subsequently broadcast both locally and nationally. They showed Brandenburg declaring that "if our President, our Congress, our Supreme Court, continues to suppress the white Caucasian race, it's possible that there might have to be some revengance [sic] taken." As a result of the speech shown on the film, Brandenburg was convicted of violating Ohio's criminal syndicalism act.

The Supreme Court reversed the conviction in an unsigned opinion. It observed that the *Brandenburg* case was similar to *Whitney*. Both had assembled with others in a group that advocated unlawful means to change the political order. Although the Court sustained Whitney's conviction in 1927,

> later decisions have fashioned the principle that the constitutional guarantees of free speech and free press do not permit a State to forbid or proscribe advocacy of the use of force or of law violation except where such advocacy is directed to inciting or producing imminent lawless action and is likely to incite or produce such action. . . . Measured by this test, Ohio's Criminal Syndicalism Act cannot be sustained.[33]

The Court also overturned *Whitney*.

PUBLIC SPEECH AND PUBLIC SAFETY

Speech that threatens community peace and order is far more prevalent than speech that jeopardizes the national security. The Supreme Court's role in community peace cases has been much the same as its role in national security cases—to find the balance among the right of an individual to make a public speech, the right of listeners to assemble to hear that speech, and the obligation of the state to maintain public order, safety, and tranquillity.

If the incident involves only verbal or symbolic expression, the balance tips in favor of the right to speak. Government may place no restraint on or punish such speech unless it threatens or actually harms public safety, the Court has held.

However, because the Court examines the individual circumstances of each case, the point at which speech becomes an incitement or a threat to the welfare of the community varies considerably. In neither type of case has the Court been able to devise a general standard for measuring the point at which First Amendment protection must give way to government restriction.

Government may not place any prior restraints on speech, but the Court has ruled that it may regulate the time, place, and manner of speech that is likely to interfere with other rightful uses of public property. This is especially true of speech that is combined with potentially disruptive conduct such as parading or demonstrating.

But the Court has insisted that such regulations be precisely drawn to restrict speech only as much as is necessary and that they be applied and enforced in a nondiscriminatory manner.

Permits and Prior Restraint

Until the Supreme Court applied the First Amendment to the states, it conceded to municipalities absolute authority to regulate and even to prohibit speech on public property. In 1897 the Court sustained the validity of a Boston ordinance prohibiting public speeches on Boston Common without a permit from the mayor. The Supreme Court endorsed the holding of the Massachusetts Supreme Court, which, in an opinion written by Oliver Wendell Holmes, Jr., declared that a legislature

> as representative of the public . . . may and does exercise control over the use which the public may make of such places. . . . For the legislature absolutely or constitutionally to forbid public speaking in a highway or public park is no more an infringement of the rights of a member of the public than for the owner of a private house to forbid it in his house.[34]

Some forty years passed before the Court was obliged to rule again on this question. By that time, it had decided that the First Amendment acted as a bar against state infringement of free speech. In line with that view, cases claiming that government was abridging free speech were getting special scrutiny.

The case of *Hague v. C.I.O.* (1939) arose out of Jersey City, New Jersey, mayor Frank Hague's opposition to attempts to organize workers in the city into closed-shop unions. To discourage these organizing efforts, Hague harassed members of the Committee for Industrial Organization (C.I.O.), searching them when they entered the city, arresting them for distributing union literature, and forcibly throwing some of them out of the city. He also refused to grant any member of the union the permit required by city ordinance before a public speech could be made on public property. The C.I.O. brought suit to stop Hague from enforcing this statute.

The Supreme Court granted the injunction against continued enforcement of the ordinance. Writing for two members of the majority, Justice Roberts said that the right to speak and assemble in public was a privilege and immunity of national citizenship that states and cities could not abridge:

> Wherever the title of streets and parks may rest, they have immemorially been held in trust for the use of the public and, time out of mind, have been used for purposes of assembly, communicating thoughts between citizens, and discussing public questions. Such use of the streets and public places has, from ancient times, been a part of the privileges, immunities, rights and liberties of citizens. The privilege of a citizen of the United States to use the streets and parks for communication of views on national questions may be regulated in the interest of all; it is not absolute, but relative, and must be exercised in subordination to the general comfort and convenience, and in consonance with peace and good order; but it must not, in the guise of regulation, be abridged or denied.[35]

In a concurring opinion, Justices Harlan Fiske Stone and Stanley F. Reed viewed the rights of free speech and assembly as included not in the privileges and immunities clause of the Fourteenth Amendment but in that amendment's prohibition against state deprivation of personal liberty without due process of law. Under the due process guarantee these rights were secured to all persons in the United States and not just to citizens. This broader view was eventually accepted by a majority of the Court.

In the *Hague* case, Roberts indicated that states and cities might regulate certain aspects of public speaking. In 1941 the Court elaborated on this, holding that the time, manner, and place of public speeches or other forms of expression could be regulated so long as the regulation was precisely and narrowly drawn and applied neutrally to all speakers and demonstrators.[36] *(Details, Cox v. New Hampshire, p. 41)*

Disturbing the Peace

Having established in *Hague* the right of individuals to communicate ideas in public places, the Court was quickly faced with the question whether the First Amendment protected speech that sparked a breach of the peace.

Speech to Passersby. The first case raising this issue concerned a Jehovah's Witness named Jesse Cantwell. Seeking converts to his faith in New Haven, Connecticut, in 1938, Cantwell stopped two men on a sidewalk and asked if he could play a phonograph record for them. They agreed, and he played "Enemies," which attacked organized religion in general and Catholicism in particular. The two men, both Catholics, were offended and told Cantwell to go away. There was no violence or other disturbance. Nonetheless, Cantwell was convicted of inciting others to a breach of the peace.

The Supreme Court reversed the conviction in *Cantwell v. Connecticut* (1940), finding the breach-of-the-peace ordinance too vague as applied to Cantwell:

> The offense known as breach of the peace embraces a great variety of conduct destroying or menacing public order and tranquility. It includes not only violent acts

but acts and words likely to produce violence in others. No one would have the hardihood to suggest that the principle of freedom of speech sanctions incitement to riot or that religious liberty connotes the privilege to exhort others to physical attack upon those belonging to another sect. When clear and present danger of riot, disorder, interference with traffic upon the public streets, or other immediate threat to public safety, peace or order, appears, the power of the State to prevent or punish is obvious. Equally obvious is it that a State may not unduly suppress free communication of views, religious or other, under the guise of conserving desirable conditions. Here we have a situation analogous to a conviction under a statute sweeping in a great variety of conduct under a general and indefinite characterization, and leaving to the executive and judicial branches too wide a discretion in its application.[37]

Looking at the facts of the situation, the Court said it found "no assault or threatening of bodily harm, no truculent bearing, no intentional discourtesy, no personal abuse." Absent a statute narrowly drawn to define and

Fighting Words: Insult to Injury

"Fighting words," words so insulting that they provoke violence from the person they are addressed to, are generally unprotected by the First Amendment guarantee of free speech.

The Supreme Court first made this point in the 1942 case of *Chaplinsky v. New Hampshire*. Chaplinsky, a Jehovah's Witness, provoked a public disturbance when he publicly assailed another religion as "a racket," and called a police officer "a God damned racketeer" and "a damned Fascist." He was convicted of violating a state statute making it a crime to call another person "offensive and derisive names" in public.

The Supreme Court sustained the conviction, upholding the statute against a challenge that it violated the guarantee of free speech. "[R]esort to epithets or to personal abuse is not in any proper sense communication of information or opinion safeguarded by the Constitution," the unanimous Court declared:

> Allowing the broadest scope to the language and purpose of the . . . Amendment, it is well understood that the right of free speech is not absolute at all times and under all circumstances. There are certain well-defined and narrowly limited classes of speech, the prevention and punishment of which has never been thought to raise any Constitutional problem. These include the lewd and obscene, the profane, the libelous, and the insulting or "fighting" words—those which by their very utterance inflict injury or tend to incite an immediate breach of the peace. It has been well observed that such utterances are no essential part of any exposition of ideas, and are of such slight social value as a step to truth that any benefit that may be derived from them is clearly outweighed by the social interest in order and morality.[1]

But the Court in *Chaplinsky* was willing to uphold the statute only because the state court had narrowly construed its language to apply to fighting words and no other speech.

The Supreme Court has continued to insist that

statutes penalizing fighting words be narrowly drawn and strictly interpreted. In 1972 the Court affirmed reversal of a Georgia man's conviction for calling a police officer a "son of a bitch" and threatening the officer with physical abuse. The Supreme Court concluded that the state court's interpretation of the statute was too broad, making it applicable to protected speech as well as to fighting words.[2]

In 1971 the Court ruled that a state may not punish as a crime the public display of an offensive word, used as an expression of legitimate protest and not resulting in a breach of the peace. In protest of the Vietnam War, Paul Cohen wore into a Los Angeles courthouse a jacket inscribed with the slogan "Fuck the Draft." He was arrested and convicted under a state breach of the peace law making "offensive conduct" a crime.

Writing for the majority in *Cohen v. California* (1971), Justice John Marshall Harlan described the offending slogan not as conduct but as speech expressing a political viewpoint. Such expression is entitled to First Amendment protection, Harlan said, unless it provoked or intended to provoke a breach of the peace.

The state cannot properly prohibit public display of the offending expletive, Harlan continued. For if a state had the power to outlaw public use of one word, he wrote, it could outlaw the use of other words and such action would run "a substantial risk of suppressing ideas in the process. Indeed, governments might soon seize upon the censorship of particular words as a convenient guise for banning the expression of unpopular views."[3]

The Court later held that the Federal Communications Commission could regulate the times at which radio and television may broadcast offensive words.[4] *(Details, p. 74)*

1. *Chaplinsky v. New Hampshire* 315 U.S. 568 at 571, 572 (1942).
2. *Gooding v. Wilson*, 405 U.S. 518 (1972); see also *Lewis v. City of New Orleans*, 415 U.S. 130 (1974).
3. *Cohen v. California*, 403 U.S. 15 at 26 (1971).
4. *Federal Communications Commission v. Pacifica Foundation*, 438 U.S. 726 (1978).

punish the conduct Cantwell engaged in, his conduct, the Court said, "raised no such clear and present menace to public peace and order as to render him liable" under the general breach of the peace statute.[38]

Near Riot. The next breach-of-the-peace case required the Court to decide to what extent the First Amendment protected speech which provoked a near riot.

Terminiello was a defrocked Catholic priest who in 1946 spoke at a private meeting in Chicago sponsored by the Christian Veterans of America. In his speech Terminiello virulently attacked Jews, blacks, and the Roosevelt administration but did not urge his five hundred listeners to take any specific action.

While he spoke, some one thousand protestors gathered outside the hall, shouting, throwing rocks through windows, and trying to break into the meeting. The police restrained the mob with difficulty. As a result of the disturbance Terminiello was arrested for and convicted of disorderly conduct under an ordinance which made it illegal for anyone to aid in a "breach of the peace or a diversion tending to a breach of the peace."

By a 5-4 vote the Supreme Court reversed Terminiello's conviction without reaching the constitutional issues involved. Instead, the majority held that the trial judge had improperly instructed the jury when he defined a breach of the peace as speech that "stirs the public to anger, invites dispute, brings about a condition of unrest, or creates a disturbance." Some parts of this instruction, the majority felt, would punish speech protected by the First Amendment, and since it was not apparent under which part the jury had convicted Terminiello, the conviction must fall.

Justice William O. Douglas explained the majority position in *Terminiello v. Chicago* (1949):

> [A] function of free speech under our system of government is to invite dispute. It may indeed best serve its high purpose when it induces a condition of unrest, creates dissatisfaction with conditions as they are, or even stirs people to anger. Speech is often provocative and challenging. It may strike at prejudices and preconceptions and have profound unsettling effects as it presses for acceptance of an idea. That is why freedom of speech, though not absolute, . . . is nevertheless protected against censorship or punishment, unless shown likely to produce a clear and present danger of a serious substantive evil that rises far above public inconvenience, annoyance or unrest. . . . There is no room under our Constitution for a more restrictive view. For the alternative would lead to standardization of ideas either by legislatures, courts, or dominant political or community groups.[39]

Chief Justice Fred M. Vinson dissented, contending that Terminiello's speech consisted of "fighting words" that are outside the protection of the First Amendment. *(Fighting words, box, p. 35)*

In a separate dissent joined by Justices Felix Frankfurter and Harold H. Burton, Justice Robert H. Jackson maintained that Terminiello's speech created a "clear and present danger" that a riot would ensue and that the authorities were entitled to act to preserve the public peace "at least so long as danger to public order is not invoked in bad faith, as a cover for censorship or suppression." In conclusion, Jackson wrote:

> The choice [for the courts] is not between order and

liberty. It is between liberty with order and anarchy without either. There is danger that, if the court does not temper its doctrinaire logic with a little practical wisdom, it will convert the constitutional Bill of Rights into a suicide pact.[40]

Street Meeting. Two years later the Supreme Court drew closer to Jackson's position when it affirmed the breach-of-the-peace conviction of a student whose streetcorner speech seemed much less threatening to public order than Terminiello's. The different conclusions in these two cases illustrate the difficulty the Court has had in settling on a general standard by which to determine when speech oversteps the bounds of First Amendment protection. *(Discussion of general standards, pp. 21-22)*

Irving Feiner spoke at an open-air meeting in Syracuse, New York, inviting listeners to attend a meeting that evening of the Progressive party. In the course of his speech, Feiner made insulting remarks about President Harry S. Truman, the American Legion, and the mayor of Syracuse. He also urged blacks to fight for equal rights. Someone complained to the police, who sent two officers to investigate. The crowd was restless and some passersby were jostled and forced into the street. Finally one listener told the officers that if they did not stop Feiner, he would. The police then asked Feiner to stop speaking. When he refused they arrested him for breach of the peace.

The six justices voting to sustain the conviction in *Feiner v. New York* (1951) found that the police had acted not to suppress speech but to preserve public order. Chief Justice Vinson wrote:

> We are well aware that the ordinary murmurings and objections of a hostile audience cannot be allowed to silence a speaker, and are also mindful of the possible danger of giving overzealous police officials complete discretion to break up otherwise lawful public meetings. . . . But we are not faced here with such a situation. It is one thing to say that the police cannot be used as an instrument for the oppression of unpopular views, and another to say that, when as here the speaker passes the bounds of argument or persuasion and undertakes incitement to riot, they are powerless to prevent a breach of the peace.[41]

In dissent, Justice Hugo L. Black said that the majority's decision in effect made the police censors of public speech. Instead, the duty of the police should be to protect the speaker in the exercise of his First Amendment rights, even if that necessitates the arrest of those who would interfere, he said. Justices Douglas and Sherman Minton also dissented.

Prior Restraint

In contrast with its difficulty in defining the point at which speech loses its First Amendment protection, the Court has steadfastly rejected state efforts to place prior restraints on speech. In 1931 the Court held that an injunction against continued publication of a newspaper was an unconstitutional prior restraint of the press.[42] In 1940 it held that a statute which permitted city officials to determine what was a religious cause and what was not amounted to an unconstitutional restraint on the free exercise of religion.[43] But not until 1945 did the Court overturn a state statute as an improper prior restraint on speech.

Union Organizer. The case of *Thomas v. Collins*

arose after Thomas, a union organizer, refused to apply for the organizer's permit required by Texas law. The state issued an injunction to stop Thomas from soliciting for union members. He made a speech advocating union membership anyway and was convicted of contempt. He appealed to the Supreme Court, which voted 5-4 to overturn his contempt conviction.

Elaborating on the reasoning behind the Court's ear-lier permit decisions, Justice Wiley B. Rutledge said it was clear that the injunction against soliciting restrained Thomas's right to speak and the rights of the workers to assemble to hear him. The statute prohibiting solicitation without a permit was so imprecise that it in essence forbade "any language which conveys, or reasonably could be found to convey, the meaning of invitation," Rutledge said. "How one might 'laud unionism,' as the State and the State

Loud Sounds and Free Speech

Does a city impermissibly interfere with freedom of speech by regulating the use of loudspeakers and other amplification devices? Twice this question has come to the Supreme Court, and its decisions have left the matter in some confusion.

In *Saia v. New York* (1948) the Court considered a Lockport, New York, ordinance that prohibited the use of sound equipment without permission from the chief of police. Samuel Saia, a Jehovah's Witness, obtained a permit to amplify religious lectures he gave in a public park. Because some people complained about the noise, Saia's permit was not renewed. He spoke with the loudspeaker anyway and was arrested and convicted of violating the ordinance. He countered that the ordinance violated his right to free speech.

Noise and Sound

The Court, 5-4, struck down the ordinance because it set no standards for granting or denying permits. Justice William O. Douglas explained:

> The present ordinance would be a dangerous weapon if it were allowed to get a hold on our public life. Noise can be regulated by regulating decibels [rather than by barring loudspeakers]. The hours and place of public discussion can be controlled.... Any abuses which loud-speakers create can be controlled by narrowly drawn statutes. When a city allows an official to ban them in his uncontrolled discretion, it sanctions a device for suppression of free communication of ideas.[1]

In dissent Justice Felix Frankfurter insisted that a city has a right to regulate the use of sound amplification to protect the privacy of other users of the park. "Surely there is not a constitutional right to force unwilling people to listen," he said.[2] In a separate dissent Justice Robert H. Jackson drew a distinction between speech and amplification of speech. Regulating amplification, even prohibiting it altogether, in no way interfered with the freedom of speech itself, he said.

The following year, the four dissenters in *Saia* and Chief Justice Fred M. Vinson joined together to sustain a Trenton, New Jersey, ordinance prohibiting the use on all public streets of any sound equipment that emitted "loud and raucous noise."

This language might have been interpreted as barring all use of sound equipment in city streets, but a three-justice plurality in *Kovacs v. Cooper* (1949), for whom Justice Stanley F. Reed spoke, distinguished between "loud and raucous noise" and other sounds which might come from amplifying systems.

Reed agreed that "[a]bsolute prohibition within municipal limits of all sound amplification, even though reasonably regulated in place, time and volume is undesirable and probably unconstitutional as an unreasonable interference with normal activities." But regulation of noise was permissible. The ordinance, Reed said, in no way restricts "communication of ideas or discussion of issues by the human voice, by newspapers, by pamphlets."[3]

Frankfurter and Jackson wrote separate concurring opinions. Justice Hugo L. Black in dissent disagreed with Reed's interpretation of the ordinance, contending that it prohibited all sound amplification. This repudiation of *Saia*, he wrote, was "a dangerous and unjustifiable breach in the constitutional barriers designed to insure freedom of expression."[4]

Sound and Streetcars

In a third case the Court majority held that individuals do not have an absolute right to privacy in public places. A private transit company in the District of Columbia piped music, occasionally interspersed with commercials into its streetcars. Despite a challenge from passengers that the practice violated their right to privacy, the programming was approved by the local public utilities commission.

The Court held that courts had no authority to interfere with such a decision by the commission so long as it was arrived at through proper procedures. Justice Douglas dissented, calling the programming "a form of coercion to make people listen."[5]

1. *Saia v. New York*, 334 U.S. 558 at 562 (1948).
2. Id. at 563.
3. *Kovacs v. Cooper*, 336 U.S. 77 at 81-82, 89 (1949).
4. Id. at 101-102.
5. *Public Utilities Commission of the District of Columbia v. Pollak*, 343 U.S. 451 at 468 (1952).

Supreme Court concede Thomas was free to do, yet in these circumstances not imply an invitation, is hard to conceive," he said.[44]

Consequently the law operated to require Thomas to register in order to make a public speech. This was incompatible with the First Amendment, Rutledge said.

> If the exercise of the rights of free speech and assembly cannot be made a crime, we do not think this can be accomplished by the device of requiring previous registration as a condition for exercising them and making such a condition the foundation for restraining in advance their exercise.[45]

The dissenters would have affirmed Thomas's conviction. Justice Roberts contended that the contempt conviction was based not on Thomas's speech but on his explicit solicitation of workers to join the union in violation of the order not to solicit without a permit. The dissenters thought the registration requirement was well within the powers of the state to regulate business transactions.

Street Speaker. A solid majority of the Court struck down as an unconstitutional prior restraint a permit system applied in *Kunz v. New York*, decided the same day in 1951 as *Feiner*.

New York City had an ordinance that barred worship services on public streets without a permit. Kunz, an ordained Baptist minister, had been granted a permit for one year but his application for renewal was rejected because his vituperative denunciations of Catholics and Jews had created public disturbances. When Kunz spoke without the permit, he was convicted and fined ten dollars. He appealed his conviction to the Supreme Court, which overturned it by an 8-1 vote.

Writing for the majority, Chief Justice Vinson rejected as too arbitrary the New York court's rationale that the permit had been revoked "for good reasons." He said:

> We have here . . . an ordinance which gives an administrative official discretionary power to control in advance the right of citizens to speak on religious matters on the streets of New York. As such, the ordinance is clearly invalid as a prior restraint on the exercise of First Amendment rights.[46]

In lone dissent, Justice Jackson contended that Kunz's speeches were filled with "fighting words," the kind of verbal abuses and insults that were likely to incite violent response and that city officials were entitled to restrain. "The question . . . is not whether New York could, if it tried, silence Kunz, but whether it must place its streets at his service to hurl insults at the passer-by," Jackson said.[47]

Symbolic Speech

Symbolic speech, the expression of ideas and beliefs through symbols rather than words, has generally been held protected by the First Amendment. The Supreme Court first dealt with the issue of symbolic speech in 1931 when it found California's "red flag" law unconstitutional. The statute made it a crime to raise a red flag as a symbol of opposition to organized government, or as "an invitation . . . to anarchistic action, or as an aid to propaganda that is of a seditious character." A state jury convicted Yetta Stromberg of raising a reproduction of the Soviet flag every morning at a children's summer camp, but it did not say which part of the law she violated.

The Supreme Court held that the first clause of the statute was an unconstitutional restriction of free speech because the flying of any banner symbolizing advocacy of a change in government through peaceful means could be penalized. Such punishment would violate the right of free speech. Because it was possible that the jury had believed Stromberg guilty of violating only this clause of the law, its unconstitutionality rendered her conviction a denial of due process. Chief Justice Charles Evans Hughes wrote:

> The maintenance of the opportunity for free political discussion to the end that government may be responsive to the will of the people and that changes may be obtained by lawful means, an opportunity essential to the security of the Republic, is a fundamental principle of our constitutional system. A statute which upon its face, and as authoritatively construed, is so vague and indefinite as to permit the punishment of the fair use of this opportunity is repugnant to the guaranty of liberty contained in the Fourteenth Amendment.[48]

Saluting the Flag

The fullest exposition of symbolism as a form of communication protected by the First Amendment came in the Court's decision in the second wartime "flag salute" case. There the Court ruled that states could not compel school children to pledge allegiance to the American flag. *(Details, pp. 86-88)*

Writing for the majority in *West Virginia State Board of Education v. Barnette* (1943), Justice Jackson said:

> There is no doubt that, in connection with the pledges, the flag salute is a form of utterance. Symbolism is a primitive but effective way of communicating ideas. The use of an emblem or flag to symbolize some system, idea, institution, or personality, is a short cut from mind to mind. Causes and nations, political parties, lodges and ecclesiastical groups seek to knit the loyalty of their followings to a flag or banner, a color or design. The State announces rank, function, and authority through crowns and maces, uniforms and black robes, the church speaks through the Cross, the Crucifix, the altar and shrine, and clerical raiment. Symbols of State often convey political ideas just as religious symbols come to convey theological ones. Associated with many of these symbols are appropriate gestures of acceptance or respect: a salute, a bowed or bared head, a bended knee. A person gets from a symbol the meaning he puts into it, and what is one man's comfort and inspiration is another's jest and scorn.[49]

The First Amendment, Jackson said, no more permitted a state to compel allegiance to a symbol of the organized government than it permitted the state to punish someone who used a symbol to express peaceful opposition to organized government.

Sit-In Demonstrations

Another form of symbolic speech reviewed by the Supreme Court was the student sit in of the early 1960s. To protest racial discrimination in public accommodations, blacks requested service at "whites only" lunch counters and remained there quietly until ejected or arrested.

At least one justice believed that these sit ins were a form of expression guaranteed constitutional protection under some circumstances. In a concurring opinion in *Garner v. Louisiana* (1961), Justice John Marshall Harlan wrote that a sit in was:

> as much a part of the "free trade in ideas" . . . as is verbal expression, more commonly thought of as "speech." It, like speech, appeals to good sense and to "the power of reason as applied through public discussion" . . . just as much, if not more than, a public oration delivered from a soapbox at a street corner. This Court has never limited the right to speak . . . to mere verbal expression.[50]

The Court avoided answering the question whether the First and Fourteenth Amendments protected the protestors from conviction for trespassing on private property.[51]

But two decades later, the Court held that a court could not assess damages for economic losses against the civil rights demonstrators who carried out a sustained nonviolent boycott of the shops of white merchants. The Court held in *NAACP v. Claiborne Hardware Co.* that such a boycott was protected by the First Amendment. Violence, however, was not protected and those who practiced it could be held liable for the damages inflicted.[52]

Antiwar Protests

The unpopularity of the Vietnam War generated several symbolic speech cases. In *United States v. O'Brien* (1968), the Supreme Court refused to view draft card burning, an expression of protest to the war and the draft, as symbolic speech protected by the First Amendment. "We cannot accept the view that an apparently limitless variety of conduct can be labeled 'speech' whenever the person engaging in the conduct intends thereby to express an idea," the majority said. Even if that view were adopted, the majority continued, the First Amendment would not protect draft card burning:

> This Court has held that when "speech" and "nonspeech" elements are combined in the same course of conduct, a sufficiently important governmental interest in regulating the nonspeech element can justify incidental limitations on First Amendment freedoms.[53]

Here, the majority said, Congress had a substantial interest in maintaining the draft registration system as part of its duty to raise and maintain armies.

In 1969, however, the Supreme Court ruled that school officials improperly suspended students for wearing black armbands in symbolic protest of the war in Indochina. The officials said they based the suspensions on their fear that the armbands might create a disturbance among the students. However, the majority wrote in *Tinker v. Des Moines School District,*

> undifferentiated fear or apprehension of disturbance is not enough to overcome the right to freedom of expression. . . . In order for the State in the person of school officials to justify prohibition of a particular expression of opinion, it must be able to show that its action was caused by something more than a mere desire to avoid the discomfort and unpleasantness that always accompany an unpopular viewpoint.[54]

In yet another form of protest against the Vietnam

Right to Remain Silent

The First Amendment guarantees individuals the right to speak freely. The Supreme Court also has held that this guarantee includes a right to remain silent. In other words, the state may not coerce or compel a person to state a position or belief he or she does not voluntarily endorse.

Among the most dramatic examples of this right are the two 1940 cases arising from the refusal of children of Jehovah's Witnesses to salute the American flag in school. In their view, pledging allegiance to the flag violated their religious belief that they should not worship graven images.

The first time the Court considered this matter it held that the flag salute requirement did not violate religious freedom; three years later the Court reversed itself to rule that compulsory flag salutes did abridge the freedom guaranteed by the First Amendment for speech and religious belief.[1] *(Details of cases, p. 86-88)*

More recently, the Court held that the individual's First Amendment freedom included the right to refuse to carry a state-required ideological message on his car license plates.

George Maynard was convicted of a misdemeanor for obscuring the motto on his New Hampshire license plate, which read "Live Free or Die." Affirming a lower court's reversal of Maynard's conviction, the Supreme Court said, "[T]he right of freedom of thought protected by the First Amendment against state action includes both the right to speak freely and the right to refrain from speaking at all."[2]

1. *Minersville School District v. Gobitis,* 310 U.S. 586 (1940), overruled by *West Virginia State Board of Education v. Barnette,* 319 U.S. 624 (1943).
2. *Wooley v. Maynard,* 430 U.S. 705 at 714 (1977).

War, an actor wore an army uniform while he and others performed a protest play on a sidewalk outside an army induction center in Houston. The play depicted U.S. soldiers killing Vietnamese women and children. The actor was arrested and convicted of violating a federal law that made it a crime to wear an official military uniform in a theatrical production unfavorable to the armed forces.

The Supreme Court unanimously overturned that conviction in *Schacht v. United States* (1970), concluding that the wearing of the uniform was part of the actor's speech. "An actor, like everyone else in our country enjoys a constitutional right to freedom of speech, including the right openly to criticize the Government during a dramatic performance," the Court said.[55]

Protest and the Flag

The Supreme Court in three modern cases reversed convictions of persons who used the American flag to symbolize opposition to government policy and the course of public events. In two of these, the Court avoided the question whether such symbolism constituted expression protected by the First Amendment.

Street v. New York (1968) concerned a man who protested the shooting of civil rights activist James Meredith by publicly burning a flag while declaring: "If they did that to Meredith, we don't need an American flag."

He was convicted under a New York law which made it illegal to mutilate a flag or to cast contempt upon it either by words or conduct. Overturning the conviction, the Supreme Court said the statute as applied to Street was too broad because it permitted the punishment of his words, which were protected by the First and Fourteenth Amendments.[56]

In the second case, the Court overturned the conviction of a man who wore a small flag on the seat of his pants. In *Smith v. Goguen* (1974), the Court said the Massachusetts statute, which made contemptuous treatment of the flag a crime, was unconstitutionally vague because it "fails to draw reasonably clear lines between the kinds of non-ceremonial treatment [of the flag] that are criminal and those that are not." [57]

In the third case, the Supreme Court reached the constitutional issue. *Spence v. Washington* (1974) arose when a student flew a flag, on which he had superimposed a peace symbol, upside down from his apartment window. The student was protesting the U.S. invasion of Cambodia and the shooting of four Kent State University student protestors. He was arrested and convicted for violating a Washington statute prohibiting defacement of the flag.

In a per curiam opinion, the Court majority overturned the conviction, holding that the student's conduct was a form of symbolic speech protected under the First Amendment. The majority wrote:

> [T]here can be little doubt that appellant communicated through the use of symbols. . . . [This communication] was a pointed expression of anguish by appellant about the then-current domestic and foreign affairs of his government. An intent to convey a particularized message was present, and in the surrounding circumstances the likelihood was great that the message would be understood by those who viewed it.[58]

Because the communication was protected by the First Amendment, the majority continued, the state could punish the communication only if it clashed with some substantial state interest. But there was no evidence that the flag caused a breach of the peace, and the possibility that some passersby might be offended by the message was not sufficient to warrant restraint of speech.

THE FREEDOM
OF ASSEMBLY

At first the Supreme Court considered the right to peaceable assembly to be a privilege and immunity of national citizenship guaranteed by the Fourteenth Amendment. In the 1876 case of *United States v. Cruikshank,* the Court said:

The right of the people peaceably to assemble for the purpose of petitioning Congress for a redress of grievances, or for any thing else connected with the powers or the duties of the national government, is an attribute of national citizenship, and, as such, under the protection of, and guaranteed by, the United States. The very idea of a government, republican in form, implies a right on the part of its citizens to meet

The Right of Petition

The First Amendment right "to petition the Government for a redress of grievances" had its origins in the Magna Carta and the development of the English parliamentary system.

One of the earliest exercises of the right in the United States occurred in the 1830s when Congress received scores of petitions seeking abolition of slavery in the District of Columbia. The right of petition was later invoked by the unemployed petitioners of Coxey's army of 1894, the bonus marchers in 1932, and participants in the Poor People's Campaign of 1968.

Petitioners are not restricted to seeking redress of grievances only from Congress. They may petition administrative agencies and the courts. Application of the First Amendment to the states through the due process clause of the Fourteenth Amendment has also ensured citizens the right to make their views known to state governments.

Nor is petition of government limited solely to seeking a redress of grievances. Individuals, citizen groups, and corporations all lobby government to persuade it to adopt policies that will benefit their particular interests. A few significant Supreme Court decisions on the right of petition have come in the lobbying area, and they are of limited scope.

In the major decision on this right, the Court upheld the authority of Congress to require certain lobbyists to register. (*United States v. Harriss,* 347 U.S. 612, 1954)

The Court ruled in 1980 that this right was not infringed by military regulations that require the approval of the base commander before military personnel may send a petition to members of Congress. (*Brown v. Glines,* 444 U.S. 348, 1980). In 1985 it held that this right did not protect those who exercise it from being sued for libel for what they include in their petition. (*McDonald v. Smith,* 472 U.S. 479, 1985). Also that year the Court held that the ten dollar limit on what a veteran can pay an attorney for representing him in pursuing claims with the Veterans Administration did not abridge the veterans' right effectively to petition the government for redress. (*Walters v. National Association of Radiation Survivors,* 473 U.S. 305, 1985)

peaceably for consultation in respect to public affairs and to petition for a redress of grievances.[59]

It was more than sixty years before the Court addressed the issue of the right of assembly again. In the 1937 case of *DeJonge v. Oregon,* a majority of the Court recognized, first, that the right of assembly was on an equal status with the rights of free speech and free press, and, second, that it was applicable to the states through the due process clause of the Fourteenth Amendment.

The meaning of this First Amendment protection was simple, the Court said, "peaceable assembly for lawful discussion cannot be made a crime." [60] *(Details, DeJonge case, p. 32)*

Two years later in the case of *Hague v. C.I.O.* a plurality of three justices again held that the right of peaceable assembly was protected by the privileges and immunities clause of the Fourteenth Amendment. Two other justices found this right included in the "liberty" guaranteed by the Fourteenth Amendment due process clause. It is this latter view that has prevailed.[61] *(Details, Hague case, p. 34)*

Parades and Demonstrations

The right peacefully to parade or demonstrate to make known one's views or to support or oppose an issue of public policy is based on the twin guarantees of the rights of free speech and free assembly.

But because parading and demonstrating involves conduct that might interfere with the ability of other members of the public to use the same public places, they have always been considered subject to greater regulation than exercises of pure speech and assembly.

To preserve the freedoms of speech and assembly, the Supreme Court has insisted that parade and demonstration regulations be precisely worded and applied in nondiscriminatory fashion. To preserve the public welfare, the Court has held that not all public places are appropriate sites for public protests.

Time, Place, and Manner

The primary precedent on parades and demonstrations was the 1941 case of *Cox v. New Hampshire.* Cox was one of sixty-eight Jehovah's Witnesses convicted of parading without a permit. He challenged the statute as an improper infringement on his rights of free speech and assembly, but the Supreme Court rejected his argument in a unanimous decision. As construed and applied, the Court said, the ordinance did not allow denial of permits because the views of the paraders might be unpopular; the ordinance was intended only to ensure that paraders would not unduly interfere with others using the streets. Chief Justice Hughes explained:

> If a municipality has authority to control the use of its public streets for parades and processions, as it undoubtedly has, it cannot be denied authority to give consideration, without unfair discrimination, to time, place and manner in relation to the other proper uses of the streets.[62]

Civil Rights Protests

Cases arising out of the civil rights movement of the late 1950s and 1960s gave the Court the opportunity to explore more fully the extent of First Amendment protection for peaceable demonstrations and protests.

In a series of cases arising out of nonviolent demonstrations in southern states, the Supreme Court ruled that peaceful protests conducted according to valid regulations on public property designated for general use were protected by the First Amendment. But peaceful protests on public property reserved for specific purposes might not be protected.

Breach of Peace. The first case in this series arose in Columbia, South Carolina, where in early 1961 some 180 black high school and college students marched to the state capitol grounds to protest discrimination. Between two hundred and three hundred people gathered to watch the peaceful demonstration.

Although there was no threat of violence or other disturbance, the police grew concerned that trouble might flare up and so ordered the demonstrators to disperse within fifteen minutes. The students refused, were arrested, and subsequently convicted of breach of the peace.

The Supreme Court overturned the convictions in *Edwards v. South Carolina* (1963).[63] The Court accepted the state courts' finding that the students' conduct constituted a breach of the peace under state law. But the justices held that the state law was unconstitutionally broad because it penalized the exercise of free speech, assembly, and petition for redress of grievances "in their most pristine and classic form."

Justice Potter Stewart wrote for the Court:

> These petitioners were convicted of an offense so generalized as to be, in the words of the South Carolina Supreme Court, "not susceptible of exact definition." And they were convicted upon evidence which showed no more than that the opinions which they were peaceably expressing were sufficiently opposed to the views of the majority of the community to attract a crowd and necessitate police protection.[64]

Recalling that the majority in *Terminiello v. Chicago* (1949) had held provocative and unsettling speech to be constitutionally protected, Stewart declared that "the Fourteenth Amendment does not permit a State to make criminal the peaceful expression of unpopular views." [65]

In lone dissent, Justice Tom C. Clark would have upheld the convictions because the police were trying to preserve the peace and did not intend to suppress speech.

Similar circumstances attended the arrest and conviction of the Reverend B. Elton Cox for breach of the peace in Baton Rouge, Louisiana. In 1961 Cox led some two thousand black college students in a two-and-one-half block march from the state capitol to a courthouse where twenty-three other students were in jail for their attempts to integrate white lunch counters.

Prior to the march, police officials asked Cox to abandon the demonstration, but he refused. The march was orderly. Once at the courthouse, Cox and the students complied with police instructions to stay on the sidewalk. Between one hundred and three hundred white onlookers watched the students wave picket signs and sing patriotic and religious songs. Cox then spoke to explain the reasons for the demonstration. At its conclusion, he urged the marchers to seek service at the lunch counters.

At this point the sheriff ordered the demonstrators to disperse. Soon afterwards the police fired a tear gas cannis-

The Court and Civil Disobedience

Is a person ever justified in ignoring a law restricting First Amendment freedoms and proceeding to speak or meet in defiance of the law? The Supreme Court has answered both yes and no—depending on the circumstances.

Disobedience Permitted

A person may disobey the law if it is obviously unconstitutional as written. In a long line of cases that includes *Cantwell v. Connecticut* (1940), *Kunz v. New York* (1951), and *Niemotko v. Maryland* (1951), the Court has reversed convictions of persons who spoke or met without a permit, finding that the statute requiring the permit was unconstitutional. *(Details, pp. 48, 38, 84)*

The Supreme Court fully stated this rule in *Shuttlesworth v. City of Birmingham* (1969). The Reverend Fred L. Shuttlesworth was convicted for violating an ordinance that made it an offense to participate in a public demonstration without a permit. Because the ordinance gave city officials complete discretion to determine to whom they would grant permits, the unanimous Court held it unconstitutional. Justice Potter Stewart explained

that a law subjecting the exercise of First Amendment freedoms to the prior restraint of a license, without narrow, objective, and definite standards to guide the licensing authority, is unconstitutional. . . . And our decisions have made clear that a person faced with such . . . [a] law may ignore it, and engage with impunity in the exercise of the right of free expression for which the law purports to require a license.[1]

Defiance Disapproved

But the Court has held that a person may not violate with impunity a valid law restricting First Amendment rights if that law is valid even if it was applied improperly to him. In *Poulos v. New Hampshire* (1953) the defendant was arbitrarily denied a permit to conduct a religious meeting. He went ahead with the meeting and, when arrested, claimed it would have taken too long to appeal the improper denial through legal channels.

The Court sustained the conviction, stating

judicial correction of arbitrary refusal by administrators to perform official duties under valid laws is exulcerating and costly. But to allow applicants to proceed without the required permits to run businesses, erect structures, purchase firearms, . . . hold public meetings without prior safety arrangements . . . is apt to cause breaches of the peace or cause public dangers. The valid

requirements of license are for the good of the applicants and the public. It would be unreal to say that such official failures to act in accordance with state law, redressable by state judicial procedures, are state acts violative of the Federal Constitution. Delay is unfortunate, but the expense and annoyance of litigation is a price citizens must pay for life in an orderly society where the rights of the First Amendment have a real and abiding meaning.[2]

Injunction Defied

Nor may a person defy with impunity an injunction issued forbidding a meeting or demonstration, even if the injunction may be invalid. This situation arose in the controversial case of *Walker v. City of Birmingham* (1967).

In 1963 the Southern Christian Leadership Conference under the guidance of Dr. Martin Luther King, Jr., sponsored a number of demonstrations in Birmingham protesting racial discrimination. City officials refused to issue the required parade permits.

The demonstrators paraded anyhow, and on April 10 a state court issued an injunction ordering them to stop parading without a permit. With no time to fight the injunction in court, the black civil rights activists went ahead with planned demonstrations on April 12 and April 14. King and seven others were later arrested and convicted of contempt of court.

The Supreme Court upheld the convictions, 5-4. The majority acknowledged that the parade permit ordinance might be unconstitutional on its face. But it held that the demonstrators should have obeyed the injunction and challenged its validity in court.

Justice Stewart explained, quoting a 1922 opinion: "An injunction duly issuing out of a court of general jurisdiction with equity powers, upon pleadings properly invoking its action, and served upon persons . . . within the jurisdiction, must be obeyed by them, however erroneous the action of the court may be."[3]

The four dissenters argued that the ordinance and the injunction enforcing it were clearly invalid and that the protestors had the right to continue unpenalized in the exercise of their First Amendment freedoms.

1. *Shuttlesworth v. City of Birmingham*, 394 U.S. 147 at 150-151 (1969).
2. *Poulos v. New Hampshire*, 345 U.S. 395 at 409 (1953).
3. *Walker v. City of Birmingham*, 388 U.S. 307 at 314 (1967) quoting *Howat v. State of Kansas*, 258 U.S. 181 at 189-190 (1922); see also *Carroll v. President and Commissioners of Princess Anne*, 393 U.S. 175 (1968).

ter into the crowd and the demonstrators left the area.

Cox was arrested and convicted of disturbing the peace. The Supreme Court, 7-2, set aside his conviction in *Cox v. Louisiana* (1965). As in *Edwards*, the majority found Louisiana's breach of the peace statute unconstitutionally broad in scope because it penalized persons who were lawfully exercising their rights of free speech, assembly, and petition.[66]

Courthouse Picketing. In a second case arising from those same circumstances, the Court, 5-4, overturned Cox's conviction for violating a Louisiana statute prohibiting picketing or parading "in or near" a courthouse.[67] The Court sustained the validity of the statute, as justified by the state interest protecting the administration of justice from outside influence, the majority said. The statute was precisely drawn so that it did not restrict the rights of free speech and assembly but instead regulated conduct which, though entwined with speech and assembly, was not constitutionally protected.

But the Court also held that the term "near" was so vague that it was not unreasonable for Cox to rely on the interpretation of the police as to how close they might come to the courthouse. By specifically confining the demonstration to a particular segment of the sidewalk, the police had in effect given permission for the demonstration to take place at that particular place. Thus the statute had been applied improperly to convict Cox.

Library Protest. The following year the Court overturned the breach-of-the-peace convictions of five black men who staged a peaceful and orderly protest against racial segregation by refusing to leave a library reserved for white use.

The Court held this demonstration to be constitutionally protected in the case of *Brown v. Louisiana* (1966). The First Amendment freedoms

> embrace appropriate types of action which certainly include the right in a peaceable and orderly manner to protest by silent and reproachful presence, in a place where the protestant has every right to be, the unconstitutional segregation of public facilities.[68]

In dissent Justice Black maintained that the First Amendment did not "guarantee to any person the right to use someone else's property, even that owned by the government and dedicated to other purposes, as a stage to express dissident ideas."[69]

Jailhouse Demonstration. Black's views won the adherence of a majority in a case decided later in 1966. *Adderly v. Florida* arose after blacks demonstrated at a county jail to protest the arrests of several students who had tried to integrate a segregated theater. The demonstrators were convicted of criminal trespass.

Writing the opinion for the five-justice majority, Black acknowledged that the jail, like the capitol grounds in *Edwards*, was public property but there the similarities ended. "Traditionally, state capitol grounds are open to the public. Jails, built for security purposes, are not," he said. Black continued:

> The State, no less than a private owner of property, has power to preserve the property under its control for the use to which it is lawfully dedicated. For this reason there is no merit to the [demonstrators'] argument that they had a constitutional right to stay on

the property over the jail custodian's objections, because this "area chosen for the peaceful civil rights demonstration was not only 'reasonable' but also particularly appropriate. . . ." Such an argument has as its major unarticulated premise the assumption that people who want to propagandize protests or views have a constitutional right to do so whenever and however and wherever they please. That concept of constitutional law was vigorously and forthrightly rejected in [previous cases]. . . . We reject it again.[70]

For the four dissenters, Justice Douglas said the Court was effectively negating *Edwards* and *Cox*. Douglas wrote:

> The jailhouse, like an executive mansion, a legislative chamber, a courthouse, or the statehouse itself . . . is one of the seats of government, whether it be the Tower of London, the Bastille, or a small county jail. And when it houses political prisoners or those who many think are unjustly held, it is an obvious center for protest. . . . Conventional methods of petitioning may be, and often have been, shut off to large groups of our citizens. . . . Those who do not control television and radio, those who cannot afford to advertise in newspapers or circulate elaborate pamphlets may have only a more limited type of access to public officials. Their methods should not be condemned as tactics of obstruction and harassment as long as the assembly and petition are peaceable, as these were.[71]

Residential Area. In 1969 the Court upheld the right of peaceful demonstrators to parade in a residential neighborhood, on the public sidewalks near Chicago mayor Richard Daley's home to urge desegregation of Chicago public schools. White residents grew threatening and, to ward off potential violence, police asked the marchers to disperse. They refused and were arrested. Five were convicted of disorderly conduct.

In a unanimous decision in *Gregory v. City of Chicago*, the Supreme Court overturned the convictions. Because there was no evidence that the marchers' conduct had been disorderly, the Court said the convictions violated due process. The Court also said that the "march, if peaceful and orderly, falls well within the sphere of conduct protected by the First Amendment."[72]

Boycotts and Sleep Ins. Thirteen years later, in 1982, the Court reaffirmed this protection for nonviolent demonstrations. In *NAACP v. Claiborne Hardware Co.*, the Court unanimously ruled that a nonviolent boycott in 1966 by civil rights demonstrators, intended to curtail business at the shops of white merchants in Port Gibson, Mississippi, was speech and conduct protected by the First Amendment. Damages for economic losses suffered as a result of the boycott could not be assessed against those who merely participated in the boycott.

Violence, however, the Court explained, was not protected activity, and a state court could assess damages against those responsible for such violence, but that liability must reflect the individual's participation in violence and could not be lodged against anyone simply because he or she was part of the boycott group.[73]

The following year the Court struck down as unconstitutional a federal law barring all demonstrations on the sidewalks adjacent to its own building.[74]

Then in 1984 came the case of *Clark v. Community for Creative Non-Violence*, in which a group protesting the Reagan administration's treatment of the nation's poor and

Public Speech on Private Property ...

The First Amendment prohibits only government action abridging the freedom of speech. Most First Amendment cases thus involve situations in which speech occurs or is abridged in a public forum or on public property.

Some private property is dedicated to public use, however, and there the question arises whether the property owner becomes subject to the First Amendment prohibition. If that is so, then a private owner may no more restrict exercise of First Amendment freedoms on his property than may a government.

The Company Town

The Court first confronted this issue in the 1946 case of *Marsh v. Alabama.* Chickasaw, Alabama, a suburb of Mobile, was wholly owned by a private corporation. A Jehovah's Witness, Grace Marsh, passed out handbills on a Chickasaw street in violation of a regulation forbidding such distribution. She challenged her subsequent arrest and conviction, claiming that her First Amendment rights had been infringed.

A majority of the Supreme Court agreed. Save for its private ownership, wrote Justice Hugo L. Black, Chickasaw had all the characteristics of any other American town. And its residents had the same interest as residents of municipally owned towns in keeping channels of communication open. "There is no more reason for depriving these people of the liberties guaranteed by the First and Fourteenth Amendments than there is for curtailing these freedoms with respect to any other citizens," Black said.[1]

Picketing and Private Malls - I

In 1968 the Court relied on *Marsh v. Alabama* when it forbade the owner of a private shopping mall to prohibit union picketing of a store in the mall. A nonunion supermarket in a privately owned mall near Altoona, Pennsylvania, was picketed by members of a food employees union who wished to point out that the supermarket did not employ union workers or abide by union pay and working condition requirements. The owners of the store and the shopping center won an injunction forbidding picketing in the mall and its private parking lots.

By a 6-3 vote, the Supreme Court declared the injunction invalid in *Amalgamated Food Employees Union Local 590 v. Logan Valley Plaza* (1968). Noting the similarities between the shopping center and the business district in the company town involved in *Marsh,* Justice Thurgood Marshall observed that the general public had unrestricted access to the mall and that it served as the functional equivalent of a town business district. These circumstances, the majority said, rendered the mall public for purposes of the First Amendment, and consequently its owners could not invoke state trespass laws to prohibit picketing that advanced the communication of ideas. Marshall noted the narrowness of the ruling:

> All we decide here is that because the shopping center serves as the community business block "and is freely accessible and open to the people in the area and those passing through" ... the State may not delegate the power, through the use of its trespass laws, wholly to exclude those members of the public wishing to exercise their First Amendment rights on the premises in a manner and for a purpose generally consonant with the use to which the property is actually put.[2]

Justice Black dissented, contending that the majority erred in its reliance on *Marsh* as a precedent. *Marsh* held that the First Amendment applied when the private property had taken on *all* of the aspects of a town, he said, adding:

> I can find nothing in *Marsh* which indicates that if one of these features is present, e.g., a business district, this is sufficient for the Court to confiscate a part of an owner's private property and give its use to people who want to picket on it.[3]

Handbill Protests in Shopping Centers

Within four years a majority of the Court qualified the ruling in *Logan Valley Plaza,* holding that owners of a private shopping mall could prohibit the distribution of leaflets unrelated to business conducted in the mall.

homeless challenged the administration's ban on camping in certain national parks. When applied to Lafayette Park across from the White House, site of a variety of periodic and ongoing demonstrations, the challengers argued, this ban violated the First Amendment freedom of expression.

The Court, 7-2, upheld the ban—which defined camping as sleeping overnight—as a reasonable restriction on the time, place, and manner in which First Amendment rights could be exercised.[75]

Labor Picketing

The question of how much protection the First Amendment affords labor picketing has deeply troubled the Supreme Court. Picketing clearly conveys a message to the public about the issues in labor disputes and is therefore a form of expression. But unlike most other sorts of parades and demonstrations, picketing also uses economic pressure and coercion to bring about better working condi-

...The First Amendment Restricted

The circumstances in *Lloyd Corporation, Ltd. v. Tanner* (1972) were similar to those in *Marsh* with one major difference. The Lloyd Center was not a company town but a privately owned and operated shopping mall that prohibited the circulation of handbills. Inside the mall, several people attempted to distribute handbills inviting the general public to attend a meeting to protest the Vietnam War. When asked to desist, they did, but then brought suit charging they had been denied their right to free speech.

By a 5-4 vote the Supreme Court rejected the charge. Writing for the majority, Justice Lewis F. Powell, Jr., held that although the shopping mall served the public it still maintained its private character:

> The invitation is to come to the Center to do business with the tenants.... There is no open-ended invitation to the public to use the Center for any and all purposes, however incompatible with the interests of both the stores and the shoppers whom they serve.... This Court has never held that a trespasser or an uninvited guest may exercise general rights of free speech on property privately owned and used nondiscriminatorily for private purposes only.[4]

Writing for the dissenters, Justice Marshall saw nothing to distinguish this case from the Court's holdings in *Marsh* and *Logan Valley Plaza*.

Picketing and Private Malls - II

Four years later the Court moved a step closer to divesting speech on private property used for specific public purposes of any First Amendment protection. But a majority of the Court still refused to overturn the *Logan Valley Plaza* decision, leaving the issue in some confusion.

Hudgens v. National Labor Relations Board (1976) arose after striking employees of a shoe company warehouse decided also to picket the company's retail stores. One of these was situated in a shopping mall whose owners threatened to have the pickets arrested for trespassing if they did not desist. The pickets withdrew but challenged the owners' threat as an unfair labor practice under the National Labor Relations Act.

Before answering that question, the Supreme Court majority felt it necessary to determine whether the picketing was entitled to any First Amendment protection. A majority concluded it was not. Three of the members of the majority held that the *Lloyd* decision had in effect overruled the *Logan Valley Plaza* decision and that, consequently, uninvited speech on private property was not protected. The three other justices comprising the majority did not believe that the *Logan Valley Plaza* decision had been overruled. But they distinguished between the pickets in that case who conveyed information about the operation of a store actually located in the mall and the pickets in *Hudgens* who tried to convey information about a warehouse located away from the mall.

Justices Marshall and William J. Brennan, Jr., dissented. Marshall insisted that when an owner of a private shopping mall invited the public onto his property to conduct business he gave up a degree of privacy to the interests of the public. One of those public interests was "communicating with one another on subjects relating to businesses that occupy" the shopping center. "As far as these groups are concerned," said Marshall, "the shopping center owner has assumed the traditional role of the state in its control of historical First Amendment forums."[5]

Just four years later, however, the Court seemed to move again on this question, holding unanimously that a state could require the owner of a shopping mall to permit students to collect signatures on a petition to Congress within his mall.[6]

1. *Marsh v. Alabama*, 326 U.S. 501 at 508-509 (1946); see also *Tucker v. Texas*, 326 U.S. 517 (1946).
2. *Amalgamated Food Employees Union Local 590 v. Logan Valley Plaza*, 391 U.S. 308 at 319-320 (1968).
3. *Id.* at 332.
4. *Lloyd Corporation, Ltd. v. Tanner*, 407 U.S. 551 at 564-565, 568 (1972).
5. *Hudgens v. National Labor Relations Board*, 424 U.S. 507 at 543 (1976).
6. *PruneYard Shopping Center v. Robins*, 447 U.S. 74 (1980).

tions and, as conduct, can be regulated by government.

Permissible Pickets

Initially courts considered all labor picketing illegal. As labor unions grew in power and acceptability, however, that view began to change. In a 1921 decision the Supreme Court permitted a union to post one picket at each entrance and exit of a factory for the purpose of explaining a union grievance against the employer. Although the First Amendment issue of free speech was not directly raised in this case, the Court acknowledged that "[w]e are a social people and the accosting by one of another in an inoffensive way and an offer by one to communicate and discuss information with a view to influence the other's action are not regarded as aggression or a violation of the other's rights."[76]

In a 1937 decision the Court moved closer to the First

Amendment question. In *Senn v. Tile Layers Union*, it upheld a Wisconsin statute permitting peaceful picketing against a challenge that such picketing constituted a "taking" of the employer's property without due process of law guaranteed by the Fourteenth Amendment. "Clearly, the means which the state authorizes—picketing and publicity—are not prohibited by the Fourteenth Amendment. Members of a union might ... make known the facts of a labor dispute, for freedom of speech is guaranteed by the Federal Constitution," Justice Brandeis wrote for a slim majority.[77]

Full Protection

Three years later in 1940 a substantial majority of the Court drew industrial picketing under the protective wing of the First Amendment. In *Thornhill v. Alabama* (1940) Byron Thornhill appealed his conviction under an Alabama law that forbade picketing. He argued that the statute violated his rights of free speech, assembly, and petition for redress of grievances.

Speaking through Justice Frank Murphy, eight justices held the antipicketing statute invalid. "In the circumstances of our times the dissemination of information concerning the facts of a labor dispute must be regarded as within that area of free discussion that is guaranteed by the Constitution," Murphy wrote.[78]

The picketing did not lose its First Amendment protection just because it might result in some degree of economic coercion, Murphy explained.

> It may be that effective exercise of the means of advancing public knowledge may persuade some of those reached to refrain from entering into advantageous relations with the business establishment which is the scene of the dispute. Every expression of opinion on matters that are important has the potentiality of inducing action in the interests of one rather than another group in society. But the group in power at any moment may not impose penal sanctions on peaceful and truthful discussion of matters of public interest merely on a showing that others may thereby be persuaded to take action inconsistent with its interests.[79]

The following year the Court in *AFL v. Swing* (1941) relied on *Thornhill* to hold that the First Amendment guarantee of free speech was infringed by a state policy limiting picketing to cases where union members had a dispute with their employer, forbidding organizational picketing by unions hoping to persuade nonunion workers to join.[80]

Prior Restraint of Violence

But in another case decided the same day as *AFL v. Swing*, a majority of the Court indicated that the First Amendment did not foreclose prior restraint of picketing in the interest of public safety. By a 6-3 vote, the majority upheld an injunction forbidding a union of milk wagon drivers to engage in picketing because their past picketing had resulted in violence. Justice Frankfurter wrote the opinion for the majority in *Milk Wagon Drivers Union v. Meadowmoor Dairies Inc.* (1941).

"Peaceful picketing is the workingman's means of communication," said Frankfurter, but the First Amendment does not protect "utterance in a context of violence" that becomes "part of an instrument of force." Under the

circumstances of the case, he continued, "it could justifiably be concluded that the momentum of fear generated by past violence would survive even though future picketing might be wholly peaceful."[81]

Third-Party Picketing

In 1942 the Court delivered conflicting decisions on the permissibility of picketing of persons not directly involved in a labor dispute. The conclusion of the two holdings seemed to be that a third party to a labor dispute could be picketed only if the union had no other means to make its views on the dispute effectively known.

In the case of *Bakery and Pastry Drivers v. Wohl* the Court lifted an injunction against a union of bakery truck drivers who had picketed bakeries and groceries using nonunion drivers in order to induce the nonunion drivers to give some of their work to union drivers. The Court majority observed that the mobility and "middle-man" status of the nonunion drivers separated them from the public. Therefore picketing those who did business with them was "the only way to make views, admittedly accurate and peaceful, known."[82]

But in a second case decided the same day, *Carpenters and Joiners Union v. Ritter's Cafe*, the Court sustained an injunction against a carpenters union, forbidding it to picket a cafe owned by a man whose nearby house was being built by a nonunion contractor. The five-justice majority noted that the union's real complaint was with the contractor and that the injunction permitted picketing against his other business enterprises. The Court concluded:

> As a means of communication of the facts of a labor dispute, peaceful picketing may be a phase of the constitutional right of free utterance. But recognition of peaceful picketing as an exercise of free speech does not imply that the state must be without power to confine the sphere of communication to that directly related to the dispute.[83]

In both these cases the majority recognized that industrial picketing, in Justice William O. Douglas's words,

> is more than free speech, since it involves patrol of a particular locality and since the very presence of a picket line may induce action of one kind or another, quite irrespective of the nature of the ideas which are being disseminated. Hence those aspects of picketing make it the subject of restrictive regulation.[84]

Illegal Conduct

The Court moved another step away from *Thornhill* in 1949. Picketing as "conduct" may in some circumstances be so intertwined with illegal labor practices that states may prohibit it, held a unanimous Court in *Giboney v. Empire Storage and Ice Co.*

A Missouri court issued an injunction against a union of ice drivers who had picketed an ice company in order to persuade the company to refuse to sell ice to nonunion drivers. Other unions had observed the picket line, and the company's sales fell by 85 percent. If the company had entered into the proposed union agreement, however, it would have thus violated Missouri's restraint of trade law.

The union contended that because its picketing publicized the facts about the labor dispute it was therefore

Financing Political Speech

When legislators limit the amount anyone can contribute to a candidate or a political campaign or the amount a candidates may spend, they restrict free speech.

After avoiding the issue for years,[1] the Supreme Court in 1976 struck down limits that Congress had imposed on campaign spending. Similar limits upon campaign contributions, however, were upheld.[2] Both provisions were part of the Federal Election Campaign Act of 1974.

"A restriction on the amount of money a person or group can spend on political communication during a campaign necessarily reduces the quantity of expression," declared the Court, "by restricting the number of issues discussed, the depth of their exploration and the size of the audience reached.... [V]irtually every means of communicating ideas in today's mass society requires the expenditure of money."[3]

Acknowledging that the contribution limits also curtailed free speech, the Court found them justified by the government's interest in preventing corruption.

In 1981 a divided Court again upheld contribution limits, in particular a limit of $5,000 per year that an individual or unincorporated association could contribute to a political action committee. But four years later, the Court struck down the federal law limiting to $1,000 the amount that a political action committee could spend independently to promote or prevent the election of publicly funded presidential candidates.

Justice William H. Rehnquist said that in the context of a national campaign, this limit curtailed freedom of speech in the same way as "allowing a speaker in a public hall to express his views while denying him the use of an amplifying system."[4]

In 1978 the Court made clear that corporations also have a right to free speech. Striking down a state law that forbade corporations to spend money to influence voters' decisions on referendum issues, Justice Lewis F. Powell, Jr., wrote:

If the speakers here were not corporations, no one would suggest that the State could silence their proposed speech. It is the type of speech indispensable to decisionmaking in a democracy, and this is no less true because the speech comes from a corporation rather than an individual. The inherent worth of the speech in terms of its capacity for informing the public does not depend upon the identity of the source, whether corporation, association, union or individual.[5]

Powell distinguished this limit from state laws forbidding corporations to contribute to candidates. "The risk of corruption perceived in cases involving candidate elections ... simply is not present in a vote on a public issue," Powell said.[6]

In 1981 the Court struck down a city ordinance limiting to $250 the amount a citizen could contribute to a group taking a position on a ballot issue, reaffirming a citizen's right to contribute as much as he or she wishes to such a debate.[7]

1. *United States v. CIO,* 335 U.S. 106 (1948); *United States v. United Auto Workers,* 352 U.S. 567 (1957); *Pipefitters v. United States,* 407 U.S. 385 (1972).
2. *Buckley v. Valeo,* 424 U.S. 1 (1976).
3. Id. at 19.
4. *California Medical Association v. Federal Election Commission,* 453 U.S. 182 (1981); *Federal Election Commission v. National Conservative Political Action Committee,* 470 U.S. 480 (1985); see also *Federal Election Commission v. Massachusetts Citizens for Life,* ___ U.S. ___ (1986).
5. *First National Bank of Boston v. Bellotti,* 435 U.S. 765 at 777 (1978).
6. Id. at 790.
7. *Citizens Against Rent Control/Coalition for Fair Housing v. City of Berkeley,* 454 U.S. 290 (1981).

entitled to First Amendment protection. The Supreme Court rejected this thesis. In an opinion written by Justice Black, the Court found that the picketing was an integral part of conduct that violated a valid state law and was therefore not protected by the First Amendment. Black wrote: "It has never been deemed an abridgement of freedom of speech or press to make a course of conduct illegal merely because the conduct was in part initiated, evidenced or carried out by means of language."[85]

State Regulation

In a series of cases beginning with *Giboney* and continuing with three decisions in 1950, the Court effectively reversed *Thornhill,* making clear that the expressive aspects of picketing did not protect it from state regulation and prohibition. If the purpose of the picketing could be construed as contrary to state statute or policy, the Court would hold a state-imposed injunction valid.

The first of the 1950 cases blended the aspects of industrial picketing and civil rights demonstrations. In *Hughes v. Superior Court of California,* the Court upheld an injunction forbidding picketing by blacks trying to force a grocer to hire a certain percentage of black employees. Although no state law prohibited racial hiring quotas, the California judge who issued the injunction held the picketing inimical to the state's policy of supporting nondiscrimination. Upholding this judgment, the Court through Justice Frankfurter stated:

It has been amply recognized that picketing, not being the equivalent of speech as a matter of fact, is not its inevitable legal equivalent. Picketing is not beyond the control of a State if the manner in which picketing is conducted or the purpose which it seeks to effectuate gives ground for its disallowance.[86]

In two other cases decided the same day, the Court upheld injunctions against picketing aimed at forcing an employer to pressure his employees to choose the picketing union as their bargaining representative, and against picketing to compel a family business with no employees to operate by union standards.[87]

In the 1953 case of *Local Plumbers Union #10 v. Graham* the Court again held that the speech aspects of picketing did not protect it from regulation. The union claimed that the picketing simply announced to the public that the picketed employer hired nonunion workers, but the Supreme Court found that the major purpose of the picketing was to force the employer to replace his nonunion employees with union workers, action that would violate the state's "right-to-work" law.[88]

In 1957 the Court upheld an injunction against unions engaged in organizational picketing of a nonunion gravel pit. Such picketing violated a state law making it an unfair labor practice for anyone to force an employer "to interfere with any of his employees in the enjoyment of their legal rights."

Writing for the majority in *International Brotherhood of Teamsters, Local 695 v. Vogt*, Justice Frankfurter reviewed the line of cases decided by the Court since the *Thornhill* finding that picketing was protected by the First Amendment. *Thornhill* was still valid, Frankfurter said, because "[s]tate courts, no more than state legislatures, can enact blanket prohibitions against picketing." But, he added, the cases decided since then had

established a broad field in which a state, in enforcing some public policy, whether of its criminal or its civil law, and whether announced by its legislature or its courts, could constitutionally enjoin peaceful picketing aimed at preventing effectuation of that policy.[89]

For the three dissenters, Justice Douglas said that the majority had completely abandoned *Thornhill*. Douglas urged the Court to return to the proposition that the First Amendment protects from state restriction all picketing that is not violent or a part of illegal conduct:

[W]here, as here, there is no rioting, no mass picketing, no violence, no disorder, no fisticuffs, no coercion— indeed nothing but speech, the principles announced in *Thornhill* . . . should give the advocacy of one side of a dispute First Amendment protection.[90]

In 1968 the Court held that the First Amendment forbade a state to delegate to the owner of a shopping mall the power to restrict labor picketing of a store in the mall. But the continuing validity of this decision has since been called into question, and the decision in the *Vogt* case stands as the Court's position on labor picketing's relation to the First Amendment.[91] *(See box, pp. 44-45)*

Soliciting and Canvassing

Door-to-door noncommercial solicitation of a neighborhood by persons seeking financial and moral support for their particular religious, political, or civic cause squarely sets the freedoms of speech, press, and religion against the right of privacy in one's home. Must the right to disseminate ideas give way to privacy or does privacy yield to the uninvited dissemination of ideas?

Professor Zechariah Chafee argued that privacy may be the value more worthy of preservation:

Of all the methods of spreading unpopular ideas . . . [solicitation] seems the least entitled to extensive [First Amendment] protection. The possibilities of persuasion are slight compared with the certainties of annoyance. Great as is the value of exposing citizens to novel views, home is one place where a man ought to be able to shut himself up in his own ideas if he desires.[92]

But the Supreme Court has generally held in solicitation cases that freedom of ideas takes precedence over privacy. To protect their citizens from annoyance, governments may regulate the time and manner of solicitation, and to protect the public from fraud or crime, governments may require solicitors to identify themselves. But such regulations must be narrowly drawn and precisely defined to avoid infringing First Amendment rights.

One of the first solicitation ordinances to fall under Supreme Court scrutiny was a Connecticut statute that prohibited solicitation of money or services without the approval of the secretary of the local public welfare office. The secretary had the discretion to determine if the solicitation was in behalf of a *bona fide* religion or charitable cause. The Supreme Court struck down the statute, in *Cantwell v. Connecticut* (1940):

Without doubt a State may protect its citizens from fraudulent solicitation by requiring a stranger in the community, before permitting him publicly to solicit funds for any purpose, to establish his identity and his authority to act for the cause which he purports to represent. The State is likewise free to regulate the time and manner of solicitation generally, in the interest of public safety, peace, comfort or convenience. But to condition the solicitation of aid for the perpetuation of religious views or systems upon a license, the grant of which rests in the exercise of a determination by state authority as to what is a religious cause, is to lay a forbidden burden upon the exercise of liberty protected by the Constitution.[93]

Although continuing to uphold the authority of a town to require solicitors to meet identification requirements, the Court in 1976 ruled a New Jersey town ordinance too vague to meet First Amendment standards and in 1980 held invalid an Illinois village's ordinance denying the right to solicit funds door-to-door to any group that spent more than a certain percentage on administrative costs. That the Court said was an undue infringement upon free speech.[94]

Membership Solicitation

The 1945 case of *Thomas v. Collins* brought to the Court a First Amendment challenge to a Texas law that required all labor union organizers to register with the state before soliciting union members there.

To test the statute, union organizer R. J. Thomas announced that he would solicit members without registering. A Texas court issued an order restraining Thomas from addressing an organizing rally without the proper credentials, but he defied the order and was subsequently convicted of contempt. Thomas challenged the registration requirement as violating his right of free speech.

The Supreme Court agreed, holding that the First Amendment clearly protected a speech made to solicit persons for membership in a lawful organization:

> That there was restriction upon Thomas' right to speak and the right of the workers to hear what he had to say, there can be no doubt. The threat of the restraining order, backed by the power of contempt, and of arrest for crime, hung over every word. . . . We think a requirement that one must register before he undertakes to make a public speech to enlist support for a lawful movement is quite incompatible with the requirements of the First Amendment.[95]

Doorbells

In 1943 the Court in the case of *Martin v. Struthers* struck down a Struthers, Ohio, ordinance that prohibited all distributors of handbills or other advertisements from knocking on doors or ringing bells to ensure that residents would receive the flyer.

Ignoring this ordinance, a Jehovah's Witness distributed a flyer, which advertised a religious meeting, in a neighborhood where many of the residents were night workers and consequently slept in the daytime. He was arrested and defended himself with the claim that the ordinance was unconstitutional.

The Court agreed, by a 5-4 vote. "While door to door distributors of literature may be either a nuisance or a blind for criminal activities, they may also be useful members of society engaged in dissemination of ideas," wrote Justice Black. He enumerated causes that depended on door-to-door solicitation for their success, observing that this form of dissemination of ideas "is essential to the poorly financed causes of little people."[96] The First Amendment prohibited the community from substituting its judgment for that of an individual in determining whether the individual may receive information.

In dissent, Justice Reed maintained that the ordinance did not violate any First Amendment right but simply respected a homeowner's privacy:

> No ideas are being suppressed. No censorship is involved. The freedom to teach or preach by word or book is unabridged, save only the right to call a householder to the door of his house to receive the summoner's message.[97]

Commercial Speech

Initially, the Supreme Court held that commercial speech—advertising—was unprotected by the First Amendment and therefore subject to regulation and even prohibition by the states.

But in a series of decisions in the 1970s, the Court changed its mind. Finding that commercial speech provides information to which the consuming public has a right, the Court struck down state and local prohibitions of certain advertisements. The Court continued to emphasize, however, that commercial advertising is subject to regulation to prevent false, deceptive, and misleading information and to specify the time, place, and manner of publication and distribution.

Unprotected Speech

Commercial speech was first discussed by the Court in *Schneider v. Irvington* (1939), in which it ruled that the First Amendment prohibited a city from requiring a person soliciting for religious causes to first obtain permission from city officials. However, the Court cautioned, "[w]e are not to be taken as holding that commercial solicitation and canvassing may not be subjected to such regulation as the ordinance [concerned in this case] requires."[98]

Schneider was followed by the Court's unanimous opinion in *Valentine v. Chrestensen* (1942), the case that became the early precedent on commercial speech. Here

Public Employees

Public employees have the same First Amendment right to speak freely as other Americans, but in three recent Supreme Court rulings, the Court considered questions about their ability to exercise that right.

The First Amendment does not protect public employees from dismissal as a result of their complaints about their working conditions or supervisors, the Court held, 5-4, in 1983. In the case of *Connick v. Myers* (461 U.S. 138, 1983), the Court held that nothing in the First Amendment requires a public employer to tolerate action that he feels will undermine his authority or the operation of his office. That same year, the Court held that a federal employee demoted for criticizing his agency had rights under the law to claim remedies for such unconstitutional action and therefore did not have the right to bring a damage suit against his employer to protest the demotion. (*Bush v. Lucas,* 462 U.S. 367, 1983).

The court in 1987 held in *Rankin v. McPherson* (__ U.S. __) that a Texas constable violated the First Amendment rights of a deputy when he fired her for commenting, upon learning of the unsuccessful attempt in 1981 to assassinate President Ronald Reagan, that "if they go for him again, I hope they get him."

Justice Harry A. Blackmun explained that as long as an employee was not in a confidential, policy-making or public-contact role, the danger to the agency's successful function from that employee's private speech is minimal. At some point, he wrote "such concerns are so removed from the effective function of the public employer that they cannot prevail over the free speech rights of the public employee. This is such a case."

The vote was close on this one: 5-4. The dissenters—Chief Justice William H. Rehnquist and Justices Byron R. White, Sandra Day O'Connor, and Antonin Scalia—maintained that "no law enforcement agency is required by the First Amendment to permit one of its employees to 'ride with the cops and cheer for the robbers.'"

the Court held that the First Amendment did not protect commercial handbills even if one side of a handbill contained a statement protesting an ordinance prohibiting the circulation of commercial handbills:

> This Court has unequivocally held that the streets are proper places for the exercise of the freedom of communicating information and disseminating opinion and that, though the states and municipalities may appropriately regulate the privilege in the public interest, they may not unduly burden or proscribe its employment in these public thoroughfares. We are equally clear that the Constitution imposes no such restraint on government as respects purely commercial advertising. Whether, and to what extent, one may promote or pursue a gainful occupation in the streets, to what extent such activity shall be adjudged a derogation of the public right of the user, are matters for legislative judgment.[99]

In a 1951 case salesmen of nationally known magazines claimed that freedom of the press was infringed by ordinances prohibiting door-to-door solicitation for subscriptions without prior consent of the homeowners. The Court rejected the claim. "We agree that the fact that periodicals are sold does not put them beyond the protection of the First Amendment. The selling, however, brings into the transaction a commercial feature," the Court wrote.[100]

Communication of Information

This commercial feature was enough to allow states to bar door-to-door solicitation, but it was not enough to deprive a paid political advertisement of all First Amendment protection. In the landmark libel case of *New York Times v. Sullivan* (1964), the Court held that an advertisement seeking support for the civil rights movement

> was not a commercial advertisement in the sense in which the word was used in *Chrestensen*. It communicated information, expressed opinion, recited grievances, protested claimed abuses, and sought financial support on behalf of a movement whose existence and objectives are matters of the highest public interest.... That the Times was paid for publishing this advertisement is as immaterial in this connection as is the fact that newspapers and books are sold.... Any other conclusion would discourage newspapers from carrying "editorial advertisements" of this type.[101]

This reasoning in the *Times* case was implemented in 1975 when the Court held that Virginia violated the First Amendment when it punished a local newspaper editor for printing an advertisement concerning the availability of legal abortions in New York. The advertisement did more than propose a commercial transaction, the Court said in *Bigelow v. Virginia*. It also conveyed information not only to women who might be interested in seeking an abortion but to people interested in the general issue of whether abortions should be legalized.[102]

The Consumer's Right

The following year, in *Virginia State Board of Pharmacy v. Virginia Citizens Consumer Council, Inc.,* the Court majority abandoned its distinction between advertising which publicly conveyed important information and thereby merited some First Amendment protection and

that which did not.

Agreeing with a lower Court that Virginia could not constitutionally forbid pharmacists to advertise the prices of prescription drugs, the Court wrote:

> Advertising, however tasteless and excessive it sometimes may seem, is nonetheless dissemination of information as to who is producing and selling what product, for what reason, and at what price. So long as we preserve a predominantly free enterprise economy, the allocation of our resources in large measure will be made through numerous private economic decisions. It is a matter of public interest that those decisions, in the aggregate, be intelligent and well informed. To this end, the free flow of commercial information is indispensable.... And if it is indispensable to the proper allocation of resources in a free enterprise system, it is also indispensable to the formation of intelligent opinions as to how that system ought to be regulated or altered. Therefore, even if the First Amendment were thought to be primarily an instrument to enlighten public decisionmaking in a democracy, we could not say that the free flow of information does not serve that goal.[103]

In subsequent cases the Court used this reasoning to rule that a state could not prohibit advertisement of contraceptives, advertisement of prices for routine legal services, or the posting of "For Sale" and "Sold" signs in private yards.[104] Using traditional First Amendment tests, the Court found that the right of the public to the commercial information outweighed any interest the government had in suppressing that information.

In a fourth case, however, the Court held that the First Amendment was not violated by a state bar's disciplinary action against an attorney who solicited clients in person, for pecuniary gain, under circumstances that posed dangers of fraud, undue influence, and intimidation—all of which was conduct the Court thought the state had a right to prevent.[105] Subsequently, however, the Court ruled that states may regulate attorney advertising only to ensure that it is not deceptive or misleading.[106]

More recently, the Court recognized a corporate right of free speech, first acknowledged in the political arena, and often entwined with commercial speech. *(Box, p. 47)*

The Court held that a state cannot forbid a utility to send out statements of its views on controversial matters of public policy as inserts in customer bills—nor can it force a utility to send out inserts carrying messages with which the company does not agree.[107]

It held that a state cannot ban all promotional advertising by a utility—even in light of the state's legitimate interest in energy conservation—but it permitted Puerto Rico to ban advertising of gambling within its borders, even though gambling is legal there.[108]

Notes

1. C. Herman Pritchett, *The American Constitution,* 3d ed. (New York: McGraw-Hill Book Co., 1977), 314.
2. Ibid., 317.
3. *Schenck v. United States* 249 U.S. 47 at 51 (1919).
4. Id. at 52.
5. Ibid.
6. Ibid.
7. *Frohwerk v. United States,* 249 U.S. 204 at 208-209 (1919).
8. *Debs v. United States,* 249 U.S. 211 at 215 (1919).
9. Id. at 216.

10. *Abrams v. United States* 250 U.S. 616 at 623 (1919).
11. Id. at 627, 628.
12. *Schaefer v. United States* 251 U.S. 466 at 481 (1920).
13. Id. at 478.
14. Id. at 479.
15. Id. at 486.
16. Id. at 493-495.
17. *Pierce v. United States*, 252 U.S. 239 at 249 (1929).
18. Id. at 269.
19. Id. at 273; the three minor decisions in this series were *Sugarman v. United States* 249 U.S. 182 (1919); *Stilson v. United States*, 250 U.S. 583 (1919); *O'Connell v. United States*, 253 U.S. 142 (1920).
20. *Hartzel v. United States*, 322 U.S. 680 (1944).
21. *Gitlow v. New York*, 268 U.S. 652 at 665 (1925).
22. Id. at 667.
23. Id. at 669.
24. Id. at 673.
25. *Whitney v. California*, 274 U.S. 357 at 371-372 (1927).
26. Id. at 373.
27. Id. at 376, 378.
28. *Fiske v. Kansas*, 274 U.S. 380 (1927).
29. *DeJonge v. Oregon*, 299 U.S. 353 at 365 (1937).
30. *Herndon v. Lowry*, 301 U.S. 242 at 258 (1937).
31. Id. at 263-64.
32. Id. at 276.
33. *Brandenburg v. Ohio*, 395 U.S. 444 at 447-448 (1969).
34. *Davis v. Massachusetts*, 167 U.S. 43 at 47 (1897).
35. *Hague v. C.I.O.*, 307 U.S. 496 at 515-516 (1939).
36. *Cox v. New Hampshire*, 312 U.S. 569 (1941).
37. *Cantwell v. Connecticut*, 310 U.S. 296 at 308 (1940).
38. Id. at 310, 311.
39. *Terminiello v. Chicago*, 337 U.S. 1 at 4-5 (1949).
40. Id. at 37.
41. *Feiner v. New York*, 340 U.S. 315 at 320-321 (1951).
42. *Near v. Minnesota*, 283 U.S. 697 (1931).
43. *Cantwell v. Connecticut*, 310 U.S. 296 (1940).
44. *Thomas v. Collins*, 323 U.S. 516 at 534-535 (1945).
45. Id. at 540.
46. *Kunz v. New York*, 340 U.S. 290 at 293 (1951).
47. Id. at 298.
48. *Stromberg v. California*, 283 U.S. 359 at 369 (1931).
49. *West Virginia State Board of Education v. Barnette*, 319 U.S. 624 at 632-633 (1943).
50. *Garner v. Louisiana*, 368 U.S. 157 (1961).
51. See, for example, *Peterson v. City of Greenville*, 373 U.S 244 (1963); *Shuttlesworth v. City of Birmingham*, 373 U.S. 26 (1963); *Lombard v. Louisiana*, 373 U.S. 267 (1963); *Gober v. City of Birmingham*, 373 U.S. 374 (1963); *Avent v. North Carolina*, 373 U.S. 375 (1963).
52. *NAACP v. Claiborne Hardware Co.*, 458 U.S. 886 (1982).
53. *United States v. O'Brien*, 391 U.S. 367 at 376 (1968).
54. *Tinker v. Des Moines School District*, 393 U.S. 503 at 508-509 (1969).
55. *Schacht v. United States*, 398 U.S. 58 at 63 (1970).
56. *Street v. New York*, 394 U.S. 576 (1969).
57. *Smith v. Goguen*, 415 U.S. 566 at 574 (1974).
58. *Spence v. Washington*, 418 U.S. 405 at 410-411 (1974).
59. *United States v. Cruikshank*, 92 U.S. 542 at 552 (1876).
60. *DeJonge v. Oregon*, 299 U.S. 353 at 365 (1937).
61. *Hague v. C.I.O.*, 307 U.S. 496 (1939).
62. *Cox v. New Hampshire*, 312 U.S. 569 at 576 (1941).
63. *Edwards v. South Carolina* 372 U.S. 229 (1963). See also *Fields v. South Carolina* 375 U.S. 44 (1963); *Cameron v. Johnson*, 390 U.S. 611 (1968).
64. *Edwards v. South Carolina*, 372 U.S. 229 at 235, 237 (1963).
65. Id. at 237; *Terminiello v. Chicago*, 337 U.S. 1 (1949).
66. *Cox v. Louisiana*, 379 U.S. 536 (1965).
67. *Cox v. Louisiana*, 379 U.S. 559 (1965).
68. *Brown v. Louisiana*, 383 U.S. 131 at 142 (1966).
69. Id. at 166.
70. *Adderly v. Florida*, 385 U.S. 39 at 41, 47-48 (1966).
71. Id. at 49-51.
72. *Gregory v. City of Chicago*, 394 U.S. 111 at 112 (1969).
73. *NAACP v. Claiborne Hardware Co.*, 458 U.S. 886 (1982).
74. *United States v. Grace*, 461 U.S. 171 (1983).
75. *Clark v. Community for Creative Non-Violence*, 468 U.S. 288 (1984).
76. *American Steel Foundries v. Tri-City Central Trades Council*, 257 U.S. 184 at 204 (1921).
77. *Senn v. Tile Layers Union*, 301 U.S. 468 at 478 (1937).
78. *Thornhill v. Alabama*, 310 U.S. 88 at 102 (1940).
79. Id. at 104; see also *Carlson v. California*, 310 U.S. 106 (1940).
80. *AFL v. Swing*, 312 U.S. 321 (1941).
81. *Milk Wagon Drivers Union v. Meadowmoor Dairies, Inc.*, 312 U.S. 287 at 293, 294 (1941).
82. *Bakery and Pastry Drivers v. Wohl*, 315 U.S. 769 at 775 (1942).
83. *Carpenters and Joiners Union v. Ritter's Cafe*, 315 U.S. 722 at 727 (1942).
84. *Bakery and Pastry Drivers v. Wohl*, 315 U.S. 769 at 776-77 (1942).
85. *Giboney v. Empire Storage & Ice Co.*, 336 U.S. 490 at 502 (1949).
86. *Hughes v. Superior Court of California*, 339 U.S. 460 at 465-466 (1950).
87. *Building Service Employees Union v. Gazzam*, 339 U.S. 532 (1950); *International Brotherhood of Teamsters v. Hanke*, 339 U.S. 470 (1950).
88. *Local Plumbers Union #10 v. Graham*, 345 U.S. 192 (1953).
89. *International Brotherhood of Teamsters, Local 695 v. Vogt*, 354 U.S. 284 at 294-295, 293 (1957).
90. Id. at 296.
91. *Amalgamated Food Employees Union v. Logan Valley Plaza*, 391 U.S. 308 (1968), qualified by *Lloyd Corp. Ltd. v. Tanner*, 407 U.S. 551 (1972) and *Hudgens v. National Labor Relations Board*, 424 U.S. 507 (1976).
92. Zechariah Chafee, Jr., *Free Speech in the United States* (Cambridge, Mass.: Harvard University Press, 1941; reprint ed., New York: Atheneum, 1969), 405-6.
93. *Cantwell v. Connecticut*, 310 U.S. 296 at 306-7 (1940); see also *Schneider v. Irvington*, 308 U.S. 147 (1939); *Largent v. Texas*, 318 U.S. 418 (1943).
94. *Hynes v. Oradell*, 425 U.S. 610 (1976); *Village of Schaumburg v. Citizens for a Better Environment*, 444 U.S. 620 (1980).
95. *Thomas v. Collins*, 323 U.S. 516 at 534, 540 (1945). See also *Staub v. City of Baxley*, 355 U.S. 313 (1958).
96. *Martin v. City of Struthers*, 319 U.S. 141 at 145, 146 (1943).
97. Id. at 154-155.
98. *Schneider v. Irvington*, 308 U.S. 147 at 165 (1939).
99. *Valentine v. Chrestensen*, 316 U.S. 52 at 54 (1942).
100. *Breard v. City of Alexandria*, 341 U.S. 622 at 642 (1951).
101. *New York Times Co. v. Sullivan*, 376 U.S. 254 at 266 (1964).
102. *Bigelow v. Virginia*, 421 U.S. 809 (1975).
103. *Virginia State Board of Pharmacy v. Virginia Citizens Consumer Council, Inc.*, 425 U.S. 748 at 765 (1976).
104. *Carey v. Population Services International*, 431 U.S. 678 (1977); *Bates v. Arizona State Bar*, 433 U.S. 350 (1977); *Linmark Associates Inc. v. Township of Willingboro*, 431 U.S. 85 (1977); *Bolger v. Youngs Drug Products Corp.*, 463 U.S. 60 (1983).
105. *Ohralik v. Ohio State Bar Association*, 436 U.S. 447 (1978). See also *Friedman v. Rogers*, 440 U.S. 1 (1979); *Zauderer v. Office of Disciplinary Counsel of the Supreme Court of Ohio*, 471 U.S. 626 (1985).
106. *In re R.M.J.*, 455 U.S. 191 (1982).
107. *Consolidated Edison of New York v. Public Service Commission of New York*, 447 U.S. 530 (1980); *Pacific Gas & Electric Co. v. Public Utilities Commission*, 475 U.S. 1 (1986).
108. *Central Hudson Gas & Electric Co. v. Public Service Commission of New York*, 447 U.S. 557 (1980); *Posadas de Puerto Rico Associates v. Tourism Council of Puerto Rico*, 478 U.S. 328 (1986).

2

Freedom of the Press

Much of the significance of free speech would be lost if speech could not be freely printed and circulated. Not only is it virtually impossible for individuals to disseminate their views on public matters without help from the press—including, in modern times, the broadcast media—but it is also impossible for individuals otherwise to procure for themselves the information they need to make informed judgments on the conduct of government and other matters of public concern.

Thomas Jefferson spelled out the importance of this informing function in 1787, criticizing omission of a free press guarantee from the Constitution. Writing from France, where he had been during the Constitutional Convention, Jefferson said:

> The people are the only censors of their governors; and even their errors will tend to keep these to the true principles of their institution. To punish these errors too severely would be to suppress the only safeguard of the public liberty. The way to prevent these irregular interpositions of the people is to give them full information of their affairs thru the channel of the public papers, & to contrive that those papers should penetrate the whole mass of the people. The basis of our government being the opinion of the people, the very first object should be to keep that right; and were it left to me to decide whether we should have a government without newspapers or newspapers without a government, I should not hesitate for a moment to prefer the latter.[1]

Nearly two hundred years later, Justice Lewis F. Powell, Jr., stated the same case for a free press in the context of modern communications:

> An informed public depends on accurate and effective reporting by the news media. No individual can obtain for himself the information needed for the intelligent discharge of his political responsibilities. For most citizens the prospect of personal familiarity with newsworthy events is hopelessly unrealistic. In seeking out the news the press therefore acts as an agent of the public at large. It is the means by which the people receive that free flow of information and ideas essential to intelligent self-government. By enabling the public to assert meaningful control over the political process, the press performs a crucial function in effecting the societal purpose of the First Amendment.[2]

The First Amendment is premised on the view that its societal purpose can be achieved only if publishers are free to determine for themselves what they will print. Although the First Amendment is usually thought of in terms of individual freedom, it is the societal value that the Supreme Court has stressed in its decisions upholding the guarantee of a free press.

At the least, the guarantee of freedom of the press means freedom from prior restraint or censorship. At the most, the guarantee also means that governments may not punish the press for what it publishes. As is true of many other constitutional guarantees, however, only a few justices have taken this absolute view of free press. Most justices have viewed freedom of the press as subject to certain restrictions.

The Supreme Court has struck down a number of laws as prior restraints on the press. This list includes statutes that forbade continued publication of malicious criticisms of government officials, prohibited circulation of noncommercial handbills, or placed a discriminatory tax on some newspapers.

In 1971 the Supreme Court rejected a request by the Nixon administration to stop publication of the Pentagon Papers. The Court said the government had failed to show sufficient justification for restraining continued publication of the documents. But in that case and others the Court has strongly implied that prior restraints might be permissible under certain extreme circumstances. The Court also has upheld the right of government to regulate certain aspects of publishing, including labor and business practices and the manner and place of distribution of circulars and handbills. These regulations may from time to time operate as prior restraints on the press.

The Court has not guarded the press quite so rigorously against subsequent punishment as against prior restraint. During World War I it upheld the convictions of several persons for publication of articles the Court found in violation of the espionage and sedition acts.

Libel, the printed defamation of an individual, was

long thought by the Court to be outside the protection of the First Amendment. But in the 1960s the Court began to reverse this posture, extending publishers considerable protection against libel suits brought by public officials and public figures. The Court has held that the First Amendment affords less protection from libel suits brought by private individuals, and little if any when the case does not involve a matter of public concern.

A corollary question faced by the Court is whether the First Amendment protects the press against claims that published articles or broadcast reports have impermissibly interfered with individual privacy. In the few cases it has decided involving this issue, the Court has ruled against the privacy claims unless the claimants could prove that the publisher acted with actual malice or displayed reckless disregard for the truth of the report.

The Court still considers obscene publications to be outside the protection of the First Amendment and subject both to prior restraint and subsequent punishment. The justices, however, have great difficulty in defining what is obscene, and the standard, which has been changed many times, continues to evolve as societal mores change.

In the mid-twentieth century freedom of the press has upon occasion collided with the right to impartial and fair administration of justice. Comprehensive reporting of the workings of the justice system is crucial to its fair administration. But news reports—especially of sensational crimes—may injure a defendant's rights by prejudicing the community against him.

Gag rules are one response of trial judges to this situation. With these rules a trial court restricts the information the press may report about a trial. In 1976 the Court reviewed such a gag order and found it an unconstitutional prior restraint. But the Court has also upheld several contempt citations against reporters who defied court-ordered gag rules.

To protect a defendant's right to a fair trial some judges have excluded the press and/or the public from pretrial hearings. In 1979 the Supreme Court upheld such an exclusion order, but in 1980 the Court read the First Amendment to guarantee press and public the right to attend trials.

In recent years the Supreme Court has ruled against the arguments of the press that the First Amendment gives them special privileges. Does the role of the press in a representative government entitle reporters to special access to sources? Gag rules are just one aspect of this access question. Another aspect—access to prisons to view conditions and interview inmates—has been answered negatively by a majority of the Court.

Confidentiality is a more troubling area. Can reporters be required to divulge their news sources to court officials and other law enforcement officers investigating alleged criminal activities? Reporters contend that their relationship with news sources should be privileged just as are the relationships between doctor and patient, lawyer and client, and husband and wife. But the Court has so far rejected this argument, holding that a reporter has no more constitutional right to withhold information that might help resolve a crime than does an ordinary citizen.

In another ruling disappointing to the press, the Court held that the First Amendment does not require police to use subpoenas instead of search warrants when it seeks evidence of a crime from newspaper offices and files. Congress responded to that ruling by passing a law imposing the subpoena requirement.

PRIOR RESTRAINT: CENSORSHIP

Of the effect of censorship on the press, Professor Thomas I. Emerson wrote

A system of prior restraint is in many ways more inhibiting than a system of subsequent punishment: It is likely to bring under government scrutiny a far wider range of expression; it shuts off communication before it takes place; suppression by a stroke of the pen is more likely to be applied than suppression through a criminal process; the procedures do not require attention to the safeguards of the criminal process; the system allows less opportunity for public appraisal and criticism; the dynamics of the system drive toward excesses, as the history of all censorship shows.[3]

It was a history of excesses that impelled the addition of the free press guarantee to the First Amendment. Prior restraint of the press had been widely practiced—and sharply attacked—in England where both church and state authorities had imposed a licensing system on the press from the development of the printing press in the fifteenth century until 1695, when the licensing laws were finally repealed. Indirect censorship through heavy taxation also was common.

Several of the colonies also attempted to censor the press, but these efforts were unpopular and shortlived.

Consequently, when the guarantee of freedom of the press was written it was widely assumed to mean freedom from prior restraint. And, in fact, few prior restraints have been imposed on the press throughout U.S. history.

Public Nuisance

Not until 1931 did the Supreme Court review a case of prior restraint of the press. The case—*Near v. Minnesota*—concerned a state law that prohibited as a public nuisance publication of malicious, scandalous, and defamatory newspapers, magazines, and other publications. The truth of the defamatory allegations was a defense only if the allegations were made with good motive and for justifiable ends.

In 1927 the county attorney for Hennepin County sought an injunction under this statute to halt continued publication of a weekly periodical that had charged that county officials were derelict in their duties regarding a Jewish gangster who ran gambling, bootlegging, and racketeering operations in Minneapolis. The articles charged that the police chief was in collusion with the gangster, that a member of the grand jury investigating the rackets was sympathetic to the gangsters, and that the county attorney seeking the injunction had failed to take adequate measures to stop the vice operations. The publication was clearly a scandal sheet, and its managers seemed prejudiced against Jews.

A state court issued a temporary injunction forbidding continued publication of the newspaper. At the ensuing trial it was concluded that the paper had violated the state statute, and a permanent injunction forbidding further publication of the paper was issued. At every opportunity, Near, the manager of the paper, raised the argument that the law as applied to his paper violated his rights under the Fourteenth Amendment. When the state supreme court affirmed the order for the permanent injunction, Near appealed to the Supreme Court.

By a 5-4 vote the Supreme Court lifted the injunction, holding that the Minnesota statute was an unconstitutional prior restraint on the press in violation of the First and Fourteenth Amendments.

Admittedly, the statute did not operate exactly like the old English licensing laws that required editors to submit all articles to government censors for approval prior to publication, wrote Chief Justice Charles Evans Hughes for the majority. Nonetheless, he continued:

> [i]f we cut through mere details of procedure, the operation and effect of the statute in substance is that public authorities may bring the owner or publisher of a newspaper or periodical before a judge upon a charge of conducting a business of publishing scandalous and defamatory matter—in particular that the matter consists of charges against public officers of official dereliction—and unless the owner or publisher is able and disposed to bring competent evidence to satisfy the judge that the charges are true and are published with good motives and for justifiable ends, his newspaper or periodical is suppressed and further publication is made punishable as a contempt. This is of the essence of censorship.[4]

Acknowledging that freedom of the press from prior restraint was not absolute, Hughes suggested four exceptional situations in which government censorship might be permissible: publication of crucial war information such as the number and location of troops, obscene publications, publications inciting "acts of violence" against the community or violent overthrow of the government, and publications that invade "private rights."

The nature of these exceptions, none of which applied in the pending case, placed "in a strong light the general conception that liberty of the press, historically considered and taken up by the Federal Constitution, has meant, principally although not exclusively, immunity from prior restraints or censorship," Hughes wrote.[5]

Nor had the passage of time lessened the necessity for that immunity, he continued.

> While reckless assaults upon public men, and efforts to bring obloquy upon those who are endeavoring faithfully to discharge official duties, exert a baleful influence and deserve the severest condemnation in public opinion, it cannot be said that this abuse is greater, and it is believed to be less, than that which characterized the period in which our institutions took shape. Meanwhile, the administration of government has become more complex, the opportunities for malfeasance and corruption have multiplied, crime has grown to most serious proportions, and the danger of its protection by unfaithful officials and of the impairment of the fundamental security of life and property by criminal alliances and neglect, emphasizes the primary need of a vigilant and courageous press, especially in great cities. The fact that the liberty of the press may be abused by miscreant purveyors of scandal does not make any the less necessary the immunity of the press

from previous restraint in dealing with official misconduct. Subsequent punishment for such abuses as may exist is the appropriate remedy, consistent with constitutional privilege.[6]

Hughes said the Minnesota statute could not be justified on the grounds that a publisher might avoid its penalties by showing that the defamatory material was true and

---

The Press as Business

When the Court in 1936 struck down certain state taxes on the press as an unconstitutional prior restraint, Justice George Sutherland made clear that the First Amendment does not immunize newspapers from payment of ordinary business taxes.[1] The First Amendment also does not exempt the press from compliance with general laws regulating business and labor relations.

"The publisher of a newspaper has no special immunity from the application of general laws," the Court said in 1937, ruling that the National Labor Relations Act applied to the press.[2] It also held that the press must abide by federal minimum wage and maximum hour standards.[3]

The Court also has held that the press is subject to antitrust laws. In *Associated Press v. United States* (1945), Justice Hugo L. Black said that antitrust laws were vital to preservation of a free press:

> The First Amendment, far from providing an argument against application of the Sherman Act, here provides powerful reasons to the contrary. That Amendment rests on the assumption that the widest possible dissemination of information from diverse and antagonistic sources is essential to the welfare of the public, that a free press is a condition of a free society. Surely a command that the government itself shall not impede the free flow of ideas does not afford nongovernment combinations a refuge if they impose restraints upon that constitutionally guaranteed freedom. Freedom to publish means freedom for all and not for some. Freedom to publish is guaranteed ... but freedom to combine to keep others from publishing is not.[4]

1. *Grosjean v. American Press Company*, 297 U.S. 233 (1936).
2. *Associated Press v. National Labor Relations Board*, 301 U.S. 103 at 132 (1937).
3. *Oklahoma Press Publishing Co. v. Walling*, 327 U.S. 186 (1946).
4. *Associated Press v. United States*, 326 U.S. 1 at 20 (1945); see also: *Lorain Journal Co. v. United States*, 342 U.S. 143 (1951); *United States v. Radio Corporation of America*, 358 U.S. 334 (1959); *Citizen Publishing Company v. United States*, 394 U.S. 131 (1969); *United States v. Greater Buffalo Press, Inc.*, 402 U.S. 549 (1971).

printed with good motives and for justifiable ends. This would place the legislature in the position of deciding what were good motives and justifiable ends and thus "be but a step to a complete system of censorship." [7]

Nor was the statute justified because it was intended to prevent scandals that might disturb the public peace and even provoke assaults and the commission of other crimes. "Charges of reprehensible conduct, and in particular of official malfeasance, unquestionably create a public scandal," Hughes wrote, "but the theory of the constitutional guaranty is that even a more serious public evil would be caused by authority to prevent publication." [8]

The four dissenters, in an opinion written by Justice Pierce Butler, contended that the Minnesota law did not "operate as a *previous* restraint ... within the proper meaning of that phrase." The restraint occurred only after publication of articles adjudged to constitute a public nuisance and served only to prohibit further illegal publications of the same kind. "There is nothing in the statute purporting to prohibit publications that have not been adjudged to constitute a nuisance," Butler said. [9]

Furthermore, the dissenters thought the threat of subsequent punishment inadequate to protect against this sort of evil. Libel laws are ineffective against false and malicious assaults printed by "insolvent publishers who may have purpose and sufficient capacity to contrive to put into effect a scheme ... for oppression, blackmail or extortion." [10]

Restrictive Taxation

The Supreme Court prohibited the use of a more traditional kind of prior restraint in the 1936 case *Grosjean v. American Press Co.*

The Louisiana legislature under the direction of Governor Huey Long placed a state tax of 2 percent on the gross receipts of newspapers that sold advertisements and had circulation in excess of twenty thousand per week. The tax was promoted as a tax on the privilege of doing business, but it had been calculated to affect only nine big city newspapers opposed to the Long regime. The papers immediately sought an injunction in federal district court to stop enforcement of the law on the grounds that the tax violated freedom of the press and, because smaller newspapers were exempt, denied them equal protection.

The federal district court issued the injunction, and a unanimous Supreme Court affirmed that decision solely on First Amendment grounds. The tax "operates as a restraint in a double sense," wrote Justice George Sutherland. "First, its effect is to curtail the amount of revenue realized from advertising, and, second, its direct tendency is to restrict circulation." [11]

Sutherland then reviewed the history of restrictive taxation of the press. The British Parliament had frequently imposed so-called "taxes on knowledge" to suppress criticism of the government. Despite strong opposition, these stamp taxes persisted until 1855.

Massachusetts in 1785 and 1786 imposed both a stamp tax and an advertising tax on newspapers and magazines, but hostility to the taxes was so strong that they were quickly repealed.

Given this background, Sutherland said, the framers of the First Amendment must have meant to prohibit the imposition of such taxes. He continued:

The predominant purpose of the grant of immunity here invoked was to preserve an untrammeled press as a vital source of public information. The newspapers, magazines and other journals of the country, it is safe to say, have shed and continue to shed, more light on the public and business affairs of the nation than any other instrumentality of publicity; and since informed public opinion is the most potent of all restraints upon misgovernment, the suppression or abridgement of the publicity afforded by a free press cannot be regarded otherwise than with grave concern. The tax here involved is bad not because it takes money from the pockets of the ... [newspapers]. If that were all, a wholly different question would be presented. It is bad because, in the light of its history and of its present setting, it is seen to be a deliberate and calculated device in the guise of a tax to limit the circulation of information to which the public is entitled in virtue of the constitutional guaranties: A free press stands as one of the great interpreters between the government and the people. To allow it to be fettered is to fetter ourselves. [12]

Handbills

The Supreme Court has always considered handbills, leaflets, circulars, and other types of flyers containing an individual or group opinion on public issues to be a part of the press entitled to First Amendment protection.

Chief Justice Hughes voiced this principle in 1938:

The liberty of the press is not confined to newspapers and periodicals. It necessarily embraces pamphlets and leaflets. These indeed have been historic weapons in the defense of liberty, as the pamphlets of Thomas Paine and others in our own history abundantly attest. The press in its historic connotation comprehends every sort of publication which affords a vehicle of information and opinion. [13]

Consequently, the Court has been unsympathetic to efforts of municipalities to restrict distribution of such handbills on public property. The arguments that some restriction is necessary to protect the public from fraud or to keep the streets clean have not been considered sufficient to justify the resulting infringement on the freedoms of speech and press. The Court has only limited distribution of noncommercial handbills when distribution has occurred on private property dedicated to specific public purposes. *(Box, p. 44)*

The *Lovell* Case

The first test of a city ordinance controlling distribution of handbills came in the 1938 case of *Lovell v. Griffin.* Alma Lovell, a Jehovah's Witness, distributed religious tracts in Griffin, Georgia, in violation of an ordinance that prohibited circulation of literature of any kind without written permission from the city manager. The Supreme Court struck down the ordinance as an unconstitutional prior restraint on the press. Chief Justice Hughes wrote for a unanimous Court:

The ordinance prohibits the distribution of literature of any kind at any time, at any place, and in any

manner without a permit from the City Manager....
Whatever the motive which induced its adoption, its
character is such that it strikes at the very foundation
of the freedom of the press by subjecting it to license
and censorship.[14]

The Handbill Cases

In a series of cases considered together in 1939, the
Supreme Court struck down four ordinances seeking to

regulate handbill circulation.

The first of these cases, *Schneider v. Irvington,* again
involved a Jehovah's Witness who was convicted of canvassing and distributing religious tracts without the required permit. The Court held that this ordinance, like the
one in *Lovell,* left too much to official discretion.[15]

In the other three cases the Court held unconstitutional ordinances that prohibited all distribution of handbills on public streets.[16]

Justice Owen J. Roberts attempted to explain how a

The Command to Publish

Freedom of the press means that government
may not stop the press from printing nor command it
to print. The Supreme Court has only found one
exception to the rule that government may not dictate the form or content of what the press prints.

The 'Help-Wanted' Case

In 1973 the Court upheld a government order to
a newspaper forbidding it to place help-wanted advertisements under columns labeled "Jobs—Male Interest" and "Jobs—Female Interest" in violation of
an ordinance that prohibited discrimination by sex in
employment. The Court reached that decision by a 5-
4 vote. The majority explained that the help-wanted
ads were commercial speech unprotected by the First
Amendment and that the column heads added by the
newspaper were indistinguishable from that speech.
(Commercial speech, p. 49)

Furthermore, the majority said in *Pittsburgh
Press Co. v. Pittsburgh Commission on Human Relations* (1973), even if commercial speech merited First
Amendment protection, illegal commercial speech
did not:

> The advertisements, as embroidered by their
> placement, signaled that the advertisers were
> likely to show an illegal sex preference in their
> hiring decisions. Any First Amendment interest
> which might be served by advertising an ordi-
> nary commercial proposal and which might argu-
> ably outweigh the governmental interest sup-
> porting the regulation is altogether absent when
> the commercial activity itself is illegal and the
> restriction on advertising is incidental to a valid
> limitation on economic activity.[1]

The Right of Reply

In a decision handed down the following year,
the Court emphasized the narrowness of the *Pittsburgh Press* holding when it struck down a Florida
statute that required newspapers to grant political
candidates equal space to reply to the paper's criti-

cism of their public records.

Writing for a unanimous Court in *Miami Herald
Publishing Co. v. Tornillo* (1974), Chief Justice Warren E. Burger carefully reviewed the arguments in
favor of the law, acknowledging that the diminishing
number of newspapers and the concentration of media ownership meant that frequently only one view of
an issue was published. "Chains of newspapers, national newspapers, national wire and news services,
and one-newspaper towns are the dominant features
of a press that has become noncompetitive and enor-
mously powerful and influential in its capacity to
manipulate popular opinion and change the course of
events," he wrote.[2]

But a governmental command to print specific
information collides with the freedom of the press
guaranteed by the First Amendment, he said, and
under the decisions of the Court

> any such compulsion to publish that which
> " 'reason' tells them should not be published" is
> unconstitutional. A responsible press is an un-
> doubtedly desirable goal, but press responsibility
> is not mandated by the Constitution and like
> many other virtues it cannot be legislated.[3]

In conclusion, Burger wrote:

> A newspaper is more than a passive receptacle or
> conduit for news, comment and advertising. The
> choice of material to go into a newspaper, and
> the decisions made as to limitations on the size
> and content of the paper, and treatment of pub-
> lic issues and public officials—whether fair or
> unfair—constitute the exercise of editorial con-
> trol and judgment. It has yet to be demonstrated
> how governmental regulation of this crucial pro-
> cess can be exercised consistent with First
> Amendment guarantees of a free press as they
> have evolved to this time.[4]

1. *Pittsburgh Press Co. v. Pittsburgh Commission on Human Relations,* 413 U.S. 376 at 389 (1973).
2. *Miami Herald Publishing Co. v. Tornillo,* 418 U.S. 241 at 249
   (1974).
3. Id. at 256.
4. Id. at 258.

Obscenity: An Elusive Definition...

The Supreme Court has never considered obscenity protected by the First Amendment. Obscenity is one of the categories of expression that is unprotected because it is "no essential part of any exposition of ideas, and [is] of . . . slight social value as a step to truth." [1]

But to place obscenity outside the protection of the First Amendment does not end the matter. It only shifts the focus of judicial effort to the problem of defining what is obscene. The problem has proved frustrating; the only criterion the Court has consistently agreed upon is that to be obscene, material must deal with sex.

Blasphemous or sacrilegious expression is not considered obscene, nor, generally, are scatological profanities. Violence has been found obscene only when linked with sex.

As Justice John Marshall Harlan explained when the Court ruled that the phrase "Fuck the Draft" on a jacket in a courthouse was not obscene: "Whatever else may be necessary to give rise to the States' broader power to prohibit obscene expression, such expression must be, in some significant way, erotic." [2]

Most state laws restricting the dissemination of obscene materials date back to the Victorian era. The early standard for obscenity was stated by a British court in the case of *Regina v. Hicklin* (1868): "whether the tendency of the matter charged as obscenity is to deprave and corrupt those whose minds are open to such immoral influences." [3]

As Professor Thomas I. Emerson observed, the *Hicklin* test "brought within the ban of the obscenity statutes any publication containing isolated passages that the courts felt would tend to exert an immoral influence on susceptible persons." [4]

By the 1930s that standard was being rejected as too rigid. In 1934 Appeals Court judge Augustus Hand proposed a new standard:

While any construction of the statute that will fit all cases is difficult, we believe that the proper test of whether a given book is obscene is in its dominant effect. In applying this test, relevancy of the objectionable parts to the theme, the established reputation of the work in the estimation of approved critics, if the book is modern, and the verdict of the past, if it is ancient, are persuasive pieces of evidence. [5]

The *Roth* Standard

Not until 1957 did the Supreme Court begin to define obscenity.

Roth v. United States concerned a federal statute making it a crime to mail materials that were "obscene, lewd, lascivious or filthy," while *Alberts v. California* concerned a state law making it illegal to publish, sell, distribute or advertise any "obscene or indecent" material. Relying heavily on Hand's test, the Court developed what became known as the *"Roth* standard."

Obscene matter, declared the Court, has no First Amendment protection. Justice William J. Brennan, Jr., wrote:

All ideas having even the slightest redeeming social importance—unorthodox ideas, controversial ideas, even ideas hateful to the prevailing climate of opinion—have the full protection of the guaranties, unless excludable because they encroach upon the limited area of more important interests. But implicit in the history of the First Amendment is the rejection of obscenity as utterly without redeeming social importance. [6]

Brennan then proposed a definition of obscenity:

[S]ex and obscenity are not synonymous. Obscene material is material which deals with sex in a manner appealing to prurient interest. The portrayal of sex . . . is not itself sufficient reason to deny material the constitutional protection of freedom of speech and press. [7]

The standard for this determination, Brennan said, was "whether to the average person, applying contemporary standards, the dominant theme of the material taken as a whole appeals to the prurient interest." [8]

Finding that the trial courts in both *Roth* and *Albert* had applied this standard to hold the material in question obscene, the majority upheld convictions under both the federal and state laws.

After *Roth* the Court grew increasingly fragmented on this issue. Seldom did a majority agree on applying a single standard to the material in question. Nonetheless, several important refinements of the *Roth* standard gained a measure of acceptance.

In the 1962 case of *Manual Enterprises v. Day,* Justice Harlan wrote that obscene material must not only appeal to prurient interest but also be patently offensive, "so offensive on their face as to affront current community standards of decency." [9]

Two years later in *Jacobellis v. Ohio* (1964), Justice Brennan added the requirement that the materials in question must be found "utterly without redeeming social importance." [10]

The height of confusion over a definition of obscenity was reached on one day in 1967 when the Court, in deciding three obscenity cases, issued fourteen separate opinions.

In one case the Court ruled that the book *Fanny Hill* was not obscene. The test applied, the prevailing opinion held, was that the dominant theme of the

... And a Changing Standard

book must appeal to prurient interest, that the book must be found patently offensive when judged by contemporary community standards and that it must be found utterly without redeeming social value.

Since the trial court had found that the book might have "some minimal literary value," it was not obscene.[11]

In a second case, the Court came up with a fourth test. This test held that material that might not be obscene on its own might become so if it was placed "against a background of commercial exploitation of erotica solely for the sake of their prurient appeal." [12]

After this point the Court retreated, indicating in a 1967 *per curiam* opinion in *Redrup v. New York* that it would sustain obscenity convictions only to protect juveniles or unwilling adults from exposure to obscene materials or in cases of pandering.[13]

The *Miller* Standard

Then in 1973 a slim majority of the Court endorsed a standard for determining what was obscene. This new standard gave government much more latitude to ban obscene materials than did the *Roth* test.

Writing for the five-justice majority in *Miller v. California* (1973), Chief Justice Warren E. Burger held that states could regulate:

> works which depict or describe sexual conduct. That conduct must be specifically defined by the applicable state law.... A state offense must also be limited to works which, taken as a whole, appeal to the prurient interest in sex, which portray sexual conduct in a patently offensive way, and which, taken as a whole, do not have serious literary, artistic, political or scientific value.[14]

With this standard, Burger said, the Court excluded only hard-core materials from First Amendment protection. As a guideline, he suggested that such materials were those that included "patently offensive representations or descriptions of ultimate sexual acts, normal or perverted, actual or simulated" and "patently offensive representations or descriptions of masturbation, excretory functions, and lewd exhibition of the genitals." [15]

The majority specifically rejected the *Jacobellis* test that to be obscene, materials must be "utterly without redeeming social value." It also rejected the idea that the community standard must be national in scope. "It is neither realistic nor constitutionally sound to read the First Amendment as requiring that the people of Maine or Mississippi accept public depiction of conduct found tolerable in Las Vegas or New York City," Burger wrote.[16]

The following year, the Court made clear that local juries did not have "unbridled discretion" to determine what was obscene, overturning a Georgia jury's finding that the movie "Carnal Knowledge" was obscene.[17]

Subsequently, the Court upheld state laws prohibiting the promotion of sexual performances by children, but struck down a state law banning material just because it incited lust. That covered material that did no more than "arouse 'good, old-fashioned, healthy' interest in sex," said the Court.[18]

In 1982 the Court held that the First Amendment limited the power of public school officials to take books off the library shelves because some parents found the contents objectionable.[19]

But four years later, the Court held that the First Amendment was not offended when school officials suspended a student for a lewd speech at a school assembly. "It is a highly appropriate function of public school education to prohibit the use of vulgar and offensive terms in public discourse," the Court declared.[20]

In a ruling expected to make it more difficult for local communities to hold material obscene, the Court in 1987 declared that local community standards—used in determining whether a book or film appealed to the prurient interest and was patently offensive—should not be used in deciding whether an allegedly obscene book or film had any scientific, literary, or artistic value. Instead a more objective, national standard should be used, ruled the Court in *Pope v. Illinois.*[21]

1. *Chaplinsky v. New Hampshire,* 315 U.S. 568 at 572 (1942).
2. *Cohen v. California,* 403 U.S. 15 at 20 (1971).
3. *Regina v. Hicklin,* L.H. 3 Q.B. 360 at 371 (1868), quoted in Thomas I. Emerson, *The System of Freedom of Expression* (New York: Random House, Vintage Books, 1970), 469.
4. Emerson, *System,* 469.
5. *United States v. One Book Entitled "Ulysses,"* 72 F. 2d 705 at 708 (2d Cir. 1934).
6. *Roth v. United States, Alberts v. California,* 354 U.S. 476 at 484 (1957).
7. Id. at 487-488.
8. Id. at 489.
9. *Manual Enterprises v. Day,* 370 U.S. 478 at 482 (1962).
10. *Jacobellis v. Ohio,* 378 U.S. 184 at 191 (1964).
11. *A Book Named "John Cleland's Memoirs of a Woman of Pleasure" v. Attorney General of Massachusetts,* 383 U.S. 413 at 419 (1966).
12. *Ginzburg v. United States,* 383 U.S. 463 at 466 (1966).
13. *Redrup v. New York,* 386 U.S. 767 (1967).
14. *Miller v. California,* 413 U.S. 15 at 24 (1973).
15. Id. at 25.
16. Id. at 32.
17. *Jenkins v. Georgia,* 418 U.S. 153 (1974).
18. *New York v. Ferber,* 458 U.S. 747 (1982); *Brockett v. Spokane Arcades, Eikenberry v. J-R Distributors,* 472 U.S. 491 (1985).
19. *Board of Education, Island Trees Union Free School District #26 v. Pico,* 457 U.S. 853 (1982).
20. *Bethel School District No. 403 v. Fraser,* 478 U.S. 675 (1986).
21. *Pope v. Illinois,* ___ U.S. ___ (1987).

city might properly regulate circulation of handbills:

> Municipal authorities, as trustees for the public, have the duty to keep their communities' streets open and available for movement of people and property, the primary purpose to which the streets are dedicated. So long as legislation to this end does not abridge the constitutional liberty of one rightfully upon the street to impart information through speech or the distribution of literature, it may lawfully regulate the conduct of those using the streets. For example, a person could not exercise this liberty by taking his stand in the middle of a crowded street, contrary to traffic regulations, and maintain his position to the stoppage of all traffic; a group of distributors could not insist upon a constitutional right to form a cordon across the street and to allow no pedestrian to pass who did not accept a tendered leaflet; nor does the guarantee of freedom of speech or of the press deprive a municipality of power to enact regulations against throwing literature broadcast in the streets. Prohibition of such conduct would not abridge the constitutional liberty since such activity bears no necessary relationship to the freedom to speak, write, print or distribute information or opinion.[17]

The desire to prevent litter was not a sufficient reason to limit circulation of handbills, the Court held. Cities could prevent litter by other methods.

Responding to the argument that cities should be permitted to prohibit the dissemination of handbills in public streets so long as other public places were available for distribution, Roberts wrote that "one is not to have the exercise of his liberty of expression in appropriate places abridged on the plea that it may be exercised in some other place."[18]

Anonymous Handbills

In 1960 the Supreme Court struck down a Los Angeles ordinance that required all handbills to include the name and address of the person preparing, sponsoring, or distributing them.

"There can be no doubt that such an identification requirement would tend to restrict freedom to distribute information and thereby freedom of expression," wrote Justice Hugo L. Black in *Talley v. California*.[19] Throughout history, he observed, persecuted groups and sects have had to resort to anonymous criticism of oppressive practices to avoid further persecutions.

Three justices dissented, maintaining that the Court should weigh the state's interest in preventing fraud against the individual's claimed rights.

Injunctions

In a 1971 case the Supreme Court ruled that a temporary injunction against the publication of certain handbills was an unconstitutional abridgment of the freedoms of speech and press.

The case of *Organization for a Better Austin v. Keefe* arose when an organization that sought to maintain the racial make-up of its neighborhood grew upset with the tactics Keefe used to induce whites to sell their homes to blacks. After Keefe denied the allegations and refused to cooperate with the association, it began to circulate handbills in Keefe's neighborhood describing what it considered

to be his unsavory real estate activities. Keefe then sought and was granted the injunction.

The Supreme Court held that "the injunction, so far as it imposes prior restraint on speech and publication, constitutes an impermissible restraint on First Amendment rights." The fact that the association's aim in circulating the handbills was to coerce Keefe into cooperation with it was "not fundamentally different from the function of a newspaper," the majority said. Nor could the injunction be justified as protecting Keefe's privacy. Keefe was "not attempting to stop the flow of information into his own household, but to the public."[20]

Election-Day Editorials

The basic need to protect free discussion of government lay at the heart of the Court's 1966 decision to strike down an Alabama statute that made it a crime to solicit votes on election day.

A newspaper editor who printed an editorial on election day urging his readers to vote a certain way on a ballot proposition was convicted under this law. A statute setting criminal penalties "for publishing editorials such as the one here silences the press at a time when it can be most effective," wrote Justice Black for the majority in *Mills v. Alabama*. "It is difficult to conceive of a more obvious and flagrant abridgment of the constitutionally guaranteed freedom of the press."[21]

The Pentagon Papers

Publication in June 1971 of articles based upon a classified history of U.S. involvement in Vietnam precipitated an unprecedented confrontation between the U.S. government and the press.

The forty-seven-volume, seven thousand-page history, which soon became known as the "Pentagon Papers," covered the Truman, Eisenhower, Kennedy, and Johnson administrations. It indicated that the U.S. government was more involved in the Vietnamese civil war at almost every stage than U.S. officials had ever publicly admitted.

Copies of the Pentagon Papers were made available to the press by Daniel Ellsberg, an analyst who had helped prepare the report and then become an antiwar activist.

The *New York Times* was the first newspaper to publish articles based on the papers; the first installment appeared in its June 13, 1971, edition. The following day, after the second installment appeared, the Justice Department asked the *Times* to return the documents and to halt publication of the series. The articles, they said, would cause "irreparable injury to the defense interests of the U.S." The *Times* refused to comply.

On June 15 U.S. District Court judge Murray I. Gurfein granted the temporary restraining order requested by the Justice Department against the *Times*, to be in effect until he could hold hearings on the government's request for a permanent injunction.

After the hearings, Gurfein ruled June 19 that the government was not entitled to a permanent injunction against the *Times's* publication of further articles. But Judge Irving R. Kaufman of the U.S. Court of Appeals immediately granted a restraining order against the *Times*, at the Justice Department's request, to permit the government to appeal Judge Gurfein's decision. The appeals court June 23 returned the case to the lower court for further secret hearings and extended until June 25 a restraining order against the *Times*. The *Times* on June 24 petitioned the Supreme Court to review the Court of Appeals order.

The government also sought to restrain the *Washington Post,* which had published its first Pentagon Papers article June 18, from further publications. The *Post* case arrived at the Supreme Court through an involved succession of hearings and temporary restraining orders similar to those in the *Times* case. However, both the district court and the court of appeals in Washington refused the Justice Department's request for a permanent injunction against the *Post*. The government appealed on June 24.

The Court heard arguments on June 26 and announced its decision four days later. By a 6-3 vote, the Court June 30 ruled that the government had failed to meet "the heavy burden of showing justification" for restraining further publications of the Pentagon Papers.[22]

Each of the nine justices wrote a separate opinion. Taken together, these opinions covered the wide range of sentiment that exists when a First Amendment right must be weighed against national security claims.

The Majority

In separate concurring opinions Justices Black and William O. Douglas maintained that freedom of the press was absolute and could not be abridged by the government under any circumstances.

"[E]very moment's continuance of the injunctions against these newspapers amounts to a flagrant, indefensible, and continuing violation of the First Amendment," Black asserted in the last opinion he wrote. "Both the history and language of the First Amendment support the view that the press must be left free to publish news, whatever the source, without censorship, injunctions or prior restraints."[23]

Douglas wrote: "The First Amendment provides that 'Congress shall make no law ... abridging the freedom of speech or of the press.' That leaves, in my view, no room for governmental restraint on the press."[24]

Justice William J. Brennan, Jr., thought the government might properly restrain the press in certain clear emergencies. But the circumstances of this case did not present such an emergency, Brennan said, and there should have been no injunctive restraint. The government sought the injunction on the grounds that the publication "could," "might," or "may" damage national security, Brennan said. "But the First Amendment tolerates absolutely no prior judicial restraints of the press predicated upon surmise or conjecture that untoward consequences may result."[25]

Justices Potter Stewart and Byron R. White both thought that prior restraints might be permissible under certain conditions and that disclosure of some of the information in the Pentagon Papers might be harmful to national interests. "But I cannot say that disclosure of any of them [the papers] will surely result in direct, immediate, and irreparable damage to our Nation or its people," concluded Stewart. "That being so, there can under the First Amendment be but one judicial resolution of the issues before us."[26]

White said he concurred with the majority "only because of the concededly extraordinary protection against prior restraints enjoyed by the press under our constitu-

Prior Restraint

In *Near v. Minnesota* the Supreme Court indicated that obscenity was one form of expression that might be subject to prior restraint.

Twenty-six years later, a majority of five justices upheld, against a challenge of unconstitutional prior restraint, a New York statute that allowed public officials to seek injunctions against the sale of obscene publications.

Contrary to the discussion in *Near,* the majority indicated that the First Amendment might protect even obscene publications from licensing or censorship before publication. But this challenged statute was not such a prior restraint. Instead, the majority said, it "studiously withholds restraint upon matters not already published and not yet found to be offensive." As such it was a valid means "for the seizure and destruction of the instruments of ascertained wrongdoing."[1]

In another 5-4 decision, the Court upheld in 1961 a Chicago ordinance that prohibited public showings of movies found to be obscene. In *Times Film Corp. v. City of Chicago,* the majority held that the doctrine of prior restraint was not absolute and that the censorship procedure was a valid means for controlling the dissemination of obscene movies. In dissent Chief Justice Earl Warren said the majority decision "gives formal sanction to censorship in its purest and most far-reaching form."[2]

In 1965 the Court limited the impact of this decision by prescribing strict rules authorities must follow when censoring films. The burden of proving the film obscene falls on the censor who must license it quickly or seek a restraining order in court. Furthermore, the process must "assure a prompt final judicial decision." The Court has been consistent in enforcing these procedural safeguards.[3]

1. *Kingsley Books v. Brown,* 354 U.S. 436 at 445, 444 (1957).
2. *Times Film Corp. v. City of Chicago,* 365 U.S. 43 at 55 (1961).
3. *Freedman v. Maryland,* 380 U.S. 51 at 59 (1965); see also *Southeastern Promotions, Ltd. v. Conrad,* 420 U.S. 546 (1975), *Roaden v. Kentucky,* 413 U.S. 496 (1973).

tional system." The government's position, White said, is that the necessity to preserve national security is so great that the president is entitled

to an injunction against publication of a newspaper story whenever he can convince a court that the information to be revealed threatens "grave and irreparable" injury to the public interest; and the injunction should issue whether or not ... publication would be lawful ... and regardless of the circumstances by which the newspaper came into possession of the information.

Freedom to Circulate

"Liberty of circulating is as essential to that freedom [of the press] as liberty of publishing; indeed, without the circulation, the publication would be of little value," the Supreme Court said as early as 1878.[1]

But in that case and others, the Court nonetheless upheld the right of Congress to prohibit the use of the mails to circulate materials considered injurious to public morals.

Circulation through the mails of publications espousing unpopular political opinions and doctrines also has been restricted. During the two world wars the government permitted the postmaster general to withdraw second-class mailing privileges from publications that violated the espionage laws. In 1921 the Court upheld this delegation of authority when it sustained the postmaster general's withdrawal of second-class mail rates from the Socialist newspaper, *Milwaukee Leader*, without directly addressing the First Amendment questions implied in the case.[2]

The Court appeared more willing to protect publications that clearly posed no threat to national security. In 1946 it ruled that the postmaster general had exceeded his authority when he withdrew second-class mail privileges from *Esquire* magazine because he determined the magazine's contents fell outside the matter eligible for the special mailing rates. The Court said that Congress had authorized the postmaster general to decide only whether publications contained "information of a public character, literature or art" and not "whether the contents meet some standard of the public good or welfare."[3]

The Court also extended some protection to dissident publications in 1965 when it struck down a 1962 federal statute permitting the postmaster general to deliver "Communist political propaganda" only at the recipient's specific request.[4]

Because obscenity has no First Amendment protection, the Court has consistently sustained federal statutes restricting its dissemination. In 1957 the Court upheld a law prohibiting the mailing of obscene materials and in 1970 it sustained a federal statute allowing individuals to request the post office not to deliver them obscene materials.[5]

In other cases the Court has upheld the right of Congress to bar importation of obscene matter and to prohibit transport of such matter by common carrier through interstate commerce.[6] But in 1983 the Court unanimously struck down a federal law barring the mailing of unsolicited ads for contraceptives.[7]

1. *Ex parte Jackson*, 96 U.S. 727 at 733 (1878); see also *In re Rapier*, 143 U.S. 110 (1892).
2. *United States ex rel. Milwaukee Social Democratic Publishing Co. v. Burleson*, 255 U.S. 407 (1921).
3. *Hannegan v. Esquire*, 327 U.S. 146 at 158-159 (1946).
4. *Lamont v. Postmaster General*, 381 U.S. 301 (1965).
5. *Roth v. United States*, 354 U.S. 476 (1957); *Rowan v. Post Office Department*, 397 U.S. 728 (1970).
6. *United States v. Thirty-seven Photographs*, 402 U.S. 363 (1971); *United States v. 12 200-Ft. Reels of Super 8mm. Film*, 413 U.S. 123 (1973); *United States v. Orito*, 413 U.S. 139 (1973).
7. *Bolger v. Youngs Drug Products Corp.*, 463 U.S. 60 (1983).

At least in the absence of legislation by Congress . . . I am quite unable to agree that the inherent powers of the Executive and the courts reach so far as to authorize remedies having such a sweeping potential for inhibiting publications by the press.[27]

The critical factor for Justice Thurgood Marshall was that Congress had twice refused to give the president authority to prohibit publications disclosing matters of national security or to make such disclosures criminal. It would be a violation of the doctrine of separation of powers, Marshall said,

for this Court to use its power of contempt to prevent behavior that Congress has specifically declined to prohibit. . . . The Constitution provides that Congress shall make laws, the President execute laws, and courts interpret law. . . . It did not provide for government by injunction in which the courts and the Executive can "make law" without regard to the action of Congress.[28]

The Dissenters

Chief Justice Warren E. Burger and Justices John

Marshall Harlan and Harry A. Blackmun dissented. All three lamented the haste with which the cases had been decided. Holding that the press did not enjoy absolute protection from prior restraint, Burger said that the exception which might permit restraint "may be lurking in these cases and would have been flushed had they been properly considered in the trial courts, free from unwarranted deadlines and frenetic pressures."[29]

Burger also thought the papers had been derelict in their duty to report the discovery of stolen property or secret government documents. That duty "rests on taxi drivers, Justices and the *New York Times*," he said.[30]

Justice Harlan listed a number of questions which he said should and would have been considered if the cases had been deliberated more fully. On the merits of the cases, Harlan said the judiciary should not "redetermine for itself the probable impact of disclosure on the national security."[31]

Therefore, Harlan would have sent the cases back to the lower courts for further proceedings, during which time he would have permitted the temporary restraining orders to remain in effect. Harlan said he could "not believe that the doctrine prohibiting prior restraints reaches to the point of preventing courts from maintaining the *status quo* long enough to act responsibly in matters of such national importance." [32]

In his dissent, Justice Blackmun wrote:

The First Amendment, after all, is only one part of the entire Constitution. Article II ... vests in the Executive Branch primary power over the conduct of foreign affairs.... Each provision of the Constitution is important and I cannot subscribe to a doctrine of unlimited absolutism for the First Amendment at the cost of downgrading other provisions.... What is needed here is a weighing, upon properly developed standards, of the broad right of the press to print and of the very narrow right of the government to prevent. [33]

The three dissenters and Stewart and White from the majority indicated that they believed the newspapers might be subject to criminal penalties for publishing classified government documents. But the question never arose. The government's prosecution of Ellsberg for espionage, theft, and conspiracy for leaking the papers was dismissed because of government misconduct. The government brought no further prosecutions.

SUBSEQUENT PUNISHMENT: LIBEL

Libel occurs when something printed or broadcast defames the character or reputation of an individual. The effort to punish publishers for printing defamatory statements can be traced back to England, where state and church authorities suppressed criticism of their policies, calling it sedition.

It is not certain whether the First Amendment guarantee of a free press was intended to prohibit Congress from enacting similar seditious libel laws. Whatever the case, the Federalist-dominated Congress enacted a libel law in 1798, but it proved extremely unpopular and was allowed to expire. Although the validity of the law was never tested, later justices assumed it was unconstitutional. [34]

In any event, Congress has never again enacted a law making general criticism of government officials and their conduct unlawful. It is now well accepted that criticism of government policies and officials is protected by the First Amendment, although specific types of criticism may be punishable. The Sedition Act of 1918, for example, set penalties for interfering with the war effort, and the Smith Act of 1940 punished those who conspired to advocate overthrow of the government. Both types of conduct are considered outside the protection of the First Amendment.

Civil Libel

When anyone is libeled, the question arises as to the proper balance between the need for open discussion of public issues and personalities and the need of individuals for protection against false, irresponsible, and malicious publications.

Certain public figures—judges, legislators, and executive officials—enjoy absolute immunity from libel suits. Certain professionals, such as doctors and lawyers, enjoy a more limited or qualified immunity, but publishers historically have been liable to damage suits.

Libelous publications include those that charge that an individual is guilty of a criminal offense, carries a dread disease such as leprosy or AIDS (acquired immune deficiency syndrome), is incompetent in his or her profession or, if a public official, is guilty of misconduct.

In the United States, truth is a defense to libel. But truth can be expensive to prove. And when the truth involves a matter of judgment, as in a political opinion, it may be impossible to prove. Placing this burden of proof on publishers can lead to self-censorship, a hesitancy to print information about public officials and others influential in public life. Such self-censorship impairs the societal function of the press in a democratic system.

Cognizant of this restrictive impact, several states early in the twentieth century began to enact laws protecting publishers from libel suits in all cases except those where the publisher printed the charges in actual malice. The seminal decision came from the Kansas Supreme Court in the 1908 case of *Coleman v. MacLennan,* in which a political candidate sued a newspaper publisher for libel:

[W]here an article is published and circulated among voters for the ... purpose of giving what the defendant believes to be truthful information concerning a candidate for public office, and for the purpose of enabling such voters to cast their ballots more intelligently, and the whole thing is done in good faith, and without malice, the article is privileged, although the principal matters contained in the article may be untrue in fact and derogatory to the character of the plaintiff, and in such a case the burden is on the plaintiff to show actual malice in the publication of the article. [35]

To protect the communication of information relevant to public affairs, the U.S. Supreme Court—fifty years later—adopted this "actual malice" rule for libel suits brought against publishers by public officials and other personalities in the public eye.

Now libel cases involving anyone of public note immediately pull the First Amendment into play. But the Court in 1985 reminded the country that the First Amendment provides no shield against damage awards in a libel case that involves only private parties and no "matter of public concern."

"We have long recognized that not all speech is of equal First Amendment importance," wrote Justice Powell for the Court in *Dun & Bradstreet Inc. v. Greenmoss Builders.* "It is speech on 'matters of public concern' that is 'at the heart of the First Amendment's protection.'" [36]

New York Times v. Sullivan

The Supreme Court revised the rules for libel in the case of *New York Times Co. v. Sullivan* (1964).

L. B. Sullivan was an elected commissioner of the city of Montgomery, Alabama, responsible for the police department. He sued the *New York Times* and four black clergymen for libel as a result of an advertisement the clergymen had placed in the newspaper on March 29, 1960.

The ad, entitled "Heed Their Rising Voices," called

Group Libel

From time to time states have sought to quell racial and religious intolerance and unrest by enacting group libel laws—laws that make it illegal for anyone to defame groups of people.

Such laws clearly restrain the freedom of the press to discuss public issues concerning particular groups. But in the only case it has heard on the validity of group libel laws, the Supreme Court sustained it, holding that the First Amendment offered no protection for such statements.

The case of *Beauharnais v. Illinois* (1952) concerned a man who headed an organization called the White Circle League. He distributed on Chicago streets leaflets making clearly racist statements about blacks and calling on the mayor and city council to protect white residents and neighborhoods against harassment by blacks.

Beauharnais was convicted of violating an Illinois group libel statute that made it illegal to publish anything defamatory or derogatory about "a class of citizens of any race, color, creed or religion." He appealed his conviction, but the Supreme Court sustained it by a 5-4 vote.

Writing for the majority, Justice Felix Frankfurter observed that it would be libelous to accuse an individual falsely of being a rapist or robber. And, said Frankfurter, "if an utterance directed at an individual may be the object of criminal sanctions, we cannot deny to a State power to punish the same utterance directed at a defined group" unless the state had acted arbitrarily when it passed its group libel law.[1]

Frankfurter mentioned the First Amendment only at the end of his opinion, holding it irrelevant to this case on the basis of the Court's earlier dicta that it afforded no protection for libel.

In a separate dissenting opinion, Justice William O. Douglas wrote:

Intemperate speech is a distinctive characteristic of man. Hot-heads blow off and release destructive energy in the process. . . . So it has been from the beginning; and so it will be throughout time. The Framers . . . knew human nature as well as we do.[2]

The viability of the *Beauharnais* decision as a precedent has been called into question by the Court's later decisions that both civil and criminal libels are within the scope of the First Amendment protections, but the Court has not reconsidered the 1952 decision.[3]

1. *Beauharnais v. Illinois,* 343 U.S. 250 at 258 (1952).
2. Id. at 286-287.
3. See *The New York Times Co. v. Sullivan,* 376 U.S. 254 (1964); *Garrison v. Louisiana,* 379 U.S. 64 (1964); *Ashton v. Kentucky,* 384 U.S. 195 (1966).

attention to the fledgling struggle for civil rights in the South and appealed for funds to support the black student movement, the "struggle for the right-to-vote," and the legal defense of civil rights leader Dr. Martin Luther King, Jr., who had been indicted for perjury in Montgomery.

The advertisement recounted the violence with which the civil rights movement had been met. Sullivan's libel suit was based on two paragraphs that read:

In Montgomery, Alabama, after students sang "My Country, 'Tis of Thee" on the State Capitol steps, their leaders were expelled from school, and truckloads of police armed with shotguns and tear-gas ringed the Alabama State College Campus. When the entire student body protested to state authorities by refusing to re-register, their dining hall was padlocked in an attempt to starve them into submission. . . .

Again and again the Southern violators have answered Dr. King's peaceful protests with intimidation and violence. They have bombed his home almost killing his wife and child. They have assaulted his person. They have arrested him seven times—for "speeding," "loitering" and similar "offenses." And now they have charged him with "perjury"—a *felony* under which they could imprison him for *ten years*.[37]

The advertisement did not refer to Sullivan personally, but Sullivan contended that the references to police included him. He also contended that because arrests are usually made by police, the "they" in "They have arrested" referred to him, and that the "they" who made the arrests were equated with the "they" who bombed King's home and assaulted him.

The two paragraphs contained errors. The students sang the national anthem, not "My Country, 'Tis of Thee." Several students were expelled from the school for demanding service at an all-white lunch counter, but not for leading the demonstration at the capitol. Police were deployed near the campus, but they did not "ring" it. Students protested the expulsions by boycotting classes for a day, not by refusing to re-register. The campus dining room was never padlocked; the only students denied access to it were those who did not have meal tickets. King had been arrested four times, not seven times.

The suit was tried under Alabama libel law, and Sullivan was awarded damages of $500,000. Other plaintiffs in Alabama brought suits against the *Times* seeking damages totaling $5.6 million.

The Supreme Court Decision

The *Times* appealed the decision to the Supreme Court, which unanimously reversed it. Writing for six justices, Justice Brennan dismissed the Court's earlier *dicta* viewing all libel as outside the protection of the First Amendment. "None of . . . [those] cases sustained the use of libel laws to impose sanctions upon expression critical of the official conduct of public officials," he said.

"[L]ibel can claim no talismanic immunity from constitutional limitations. It must be measured by standards that satisfy the First Amendment." [38]

At the outset Brennan distinguished the civil rights advertisement from the kind of commercial speech the Court still held unprotected. The ad primarily communicated information about a public issue of great concern, he said. (Commercial speech, p. 49)

Reviewing the role of a free press in a democratic

society, Brennan said:

> we consider this case against the background of a profound national commitment to the principle that debate on public issues should be uninhibited, robust, and wide-open, and that it may well include vehement, caustic, and sometimes unpleasantly sharp attacks on government and public officials.... The present advertisement, as an expression of grievance and protest on one of the major public issues of our time, would seem clearly to qualify for the constitutional protection. The question is whether it forfeits that protection by the falsity of some of its factual statements and by its alleged defamation of ... [Sullivan].[39]

The courts, said Brennan, have recognized that "erroneous statement is inevitable in free debate, and that it must be protected if the freedoms of expression are to have the 'breathing space' that they 'need ... to survive.' "[40]

This was true of speech about public officials as well as public issues, Brennan said:

> A rule compelling the critic of official conduct to guarantee the truth of all his factual assertions—and to do so on pain of libel judgments virtually unlimited in amount—leads to a comparable "self-censorship."... Under such a rule, would-be critics of official conduct may be deterred from voicing their criticism, even though it is believed to be true and even though it is in fact true, because of doubt whether it can be proved in court or fear of the expense of having to do so.... The rule thus dampens the vigor and limits the variety of public debate. It is inconsistent with the First and Fourteenth Amendments.[41]

Drawing heavily on *Coleman v. MacLennan*, Brennan then set out the standard for determining whether defamatory statements about public officials were protected by the First Amendment:

> The constitutional guarantees require, we think, a federal rule that prohibits a public official from recovering damages for a defamatory falsehood relating to his official conduct unless he proves that the statement was made with 'actual malice'—that is, with knowledge that it was false or with reckless disregard of whether it was false or not.[42]

Applying that rule to the circumstances of the *Sullivan* case, the Court found that there was no evidence that the individual clergymen knew their statements to be false or were reckless in that regard. Although the *Times* had information in its news files that would have corrected some of the errors contained in the advertisement, the Court did not find that the *Times* personnel had acted with any actual malice. The evidence against the *Times*, said Brennan, "supports at most a finding of negligence in failing to discover the misstatements, and is constitutionally insufficient to show the recklessness that is required for a finding of actual malice."[43]

Concurring, Justice Black, joined by Justice Douglas, contended that the First and Fourteenth Amendments prevented a state from ever awarding libel damages to a public official for false statements made about his public conduct. The newspaper and the individual clergymen "had an absolute, unconditional constitutional right to publish in the *Times* advertisement their criticisms of the Montgomery agencies and officials," he wrote.[44]

In another concurring opinion, Justice Arthur J. Gold-

The Right to Publicity

In August 1972 an Ohio television station filmed, without the performer's consent, the entire fifteen-second act of Hugo Zacchini, a "human cannonball" whose "act" consisted of being shot from a cannon into a net two hundred feet away.

After the station showed the film clip on its nightly news program as an item of interest, Zacchini sued, charging that the television station had appropriated his right to control publicity concerning his performance.

The Ohio Supreme Court ruled in favor of the television station. Unless Zacchini showed that the station intentionally meant to harm him or to use the film for some private purpose, its airing of Zacchini's act was protected by the First and Fourteenth Amendments, the court held.

By a 5-4 vote, the Supreme Court overturned that ruling with its decision in *Zacchini v. Scripps-Howard Broadcasting Co.* (1977).

"Wherever the line in particular situations is to be drawn between media reports that are protected and those that are not, we are quite sure that the First and Fourteenth Amendments do not immunize the media when they broadcast a performer's entire act without his consent," wrote Justice Byron R. White for the majority. "The Constitution no more prevents a State from requiring ... [the station] to compensate petitioner for broadcasting his act on television than it would privilege ... [the station] to film and broadcast a copyrighted dramatic work without liability to the copyright owner."

Three of the dissenters held that the broadcast was privileged under the First and Fourteenth Amendments. The film was a simple report on a newsworthy event and shown as part of an ordinary daily news report. The broadcast was therefore no more than a "routine example of the press fulfilling the informing function so vital to our system." (433 U.S. 562 at 574-575, 580, 1977)

berg, again joined by Douglas, also held that the First Amendment provided an absolute right to criticize the public conduct of public officials. He also questioned how much protection the "actual malice" rule would afford publishers. Can "freedom of speech which all agree is constitutionally protected ... be effectively safeguarded by a rule allowing the imposition of liability upon a jury's evaluation of the speaker's state of mind?" he asked.[45]

In a series of subsequent decisions, the Court elaborated on its *New York Times* rule. In *Garrison v. Louisiana* (1964), the Court ruled that the actual malice rule limited state power to impose criminal as well as civil sanctions against persons criticizing the official conduct of public officials. In 1968 the Court ruled that to prove reckless disregard for the truth or falsity of the allegedly libelous statement there must be "sufficient evidence to permit the conclusion that the defendant in fact entertained serious doubts as to the truth of his publications."[46]

In the 1979 case of *Herbert v. Lando,* the Court by a 6-3 vote held that the *New York Times* actual malice standard required inquiry into the editorial process—the pre-publication thoughts, conclusions, and conversations of editors and reporters—by persons who charge they have been libeled by the product of that process.

The Court said that nothing in the First Amendment restricted a person alleging libel from obtaining the evidence necessary to prove actual malice under the *New York Times* rule. To the contrary,

> *New York Times* and its progeny made it essential to proving liability that plaintiffs [alleging libel] focus on the conduct and state of mind of the defendant [publishers]. To be liable, the alleged defamer of public officials or of public figures must know or have reason to suspect that his publication is false. In other cases [brought by private individuals] proof of some kind of fault, negligence perhaps, is essential to recovery. Inevitably, unless liability is to be completely foreclosed, the thoughts and editorial processes of the alleged defamer would be open to examination.[47]

The Court has been seriously divided in determining against what category of person the *New York Times* rule operates. All the justices agreed that public officials and public figures must show actual malice to win damages.

After a brief period when the Court seemed to apply the actual malice standard to suits brought by private individuals involving matters of public concern, it now allows states to set less stringent standards of proof for private citizens alleging libel.

Public Officials

Two years after *New York Times Co. v. Sullivan,* the Court further defined the category of public officials. In the case of *Rosenblatt v. Baer,* a former supervisor of a county ski resort sued a newspaper columnist for an allegedly libelous statement about his management of the recreation area. Without being instructed to use the *New York Times* rule, the jury found in favor of the supervisor. The Supreme Court reversed, but disagreed on their reasons.

Justice Brennan, who wrote the formal Court opinion in which only two other justices concurred, defined "public official":

> There is, first, a strong interest in debate on public issues, and second, a strong interest in debate about those persons who are in a position significantly to influence the resolution of those issues. Criticism of government is at the very center of the constitutionally protected area of free discussion. Criticism of those responsible for government operations must be free, lest criticism of government itself be penalized. It is clear, therefore, that the "public official" designation applies at the very least to those among the hierarchy of government employees who have, or appear to the public to have, substantial responsibility for or control over the conduct of governmental affairs. . . . Where a position in government has such apparent importance that the public has an independent interest in the

qualifications and performance of the person who holds it, beyond the general public interest in the qualifications and performance of all government employees, both elements we identified in *New York Times* are present and the *New York Times* malice standards apply.[48]

Although this has come to be the accepted definition of "public official," a majority of the Court did not initially endorse it. Justice Tom C. Clark concurred in the judgment without an opinion. Justice Douglas concurred, but thought the question should turn on whether the alleged libel involved a public issue rather than a public official. Justice Stewart also agreed with the judgment but cautioned that the actual malice rule should be applied only "where a State's law of defamation has been unconstitutionally converted into a law of seditious libel."[49]

Justice Harlan concurred with the judgment but disagreed with part of Brennan's opinion. Justice Black concurred, maintaining that the First and Fourteenth Amendments forbade all libel judgments against newspaper comment on public issues. Justice Abe Fortas dissented for technical reasons.

The Court was considerably more unified in 1971 when it ruled that candidates for public office were public officials and that the *New York Times* rule protected publishers from libel charges resulting from their decision to print information on the criminal records of these persons.[50]

Public Figures

The wide diversity of views on the applicability of the actual malice rule was again evident in two 1967 decisions in which the Court applied the *New York Times* rule to persons who were not public officials but were nonetheless in the public eye.

The first of these cases, *Curtis Publishing Co. v. Butts,* concerned a libel action brought by former University of Georgia athletic director Wallace Butts against the *Saturday Evening Post,* which was owned by the Curtis Publishing Company.

The *Post* had printed a story in which it alleged that Butts had "fixed" a football game by revealing his team's offensive and defensive plays to the opposing coach, Paul Bryant of the University of Alabama.

At his trial, completed before the Supreme Court issued its malice rule, Butts admitted talking to Bryant but said he had revealed nothing of value to him. Butts was supported by expert witnesses, and there was substantial evidence that the *Post* investigation of the allegation had been gravely inadequate. The jury found in Butts's favor and the final award was $480,000. After the *New York Times* rule was issued, the publishing company asked for another trial, which the state courts denied.

The second case, *Associated Press v. Walker,* concerned an allegedly libelous eyewitness news report that former general Edwin A. Walker had led rioters against federal marshals who were trying to maintain order at the University of Mississippi during turmoil over the enrollment of a black student, James Meredith.

Walker, who had commanded federal troops guarding black students who tried to enter a Little Rock, Arkansas, high school in 1958, was awarded $500,000 in compensatory damages.

The Press and Personal Privacy

Freedom of the press might be justifiably curtailed, wrote Chief Justice Charles Evan Hughes in *Near v. Minnesota* (1931), to prevent the invasion of "private rights." *(Near ruling, p. 54)*

The Court has not yet addressed the specific question whether government may prevent publication of articles that invade a person's privacy, but it has considered whether publications may be punished for such invasions of personal privacy.

Time Inc. v. Hill (1967) brought to the Court a claim of privacy by a family held hostage in their Pennsylvania home in 1952 by three escaped convicts. The convicts treated the family politely and released them unharmed.

A 1953 book entitled *The Desperate Hours* recounted a story similar to the Hill family's experience, but, unlike the actual event, the convicts in the story treated their captives violently. The novel was made into a play and later a film. In an article on the play, *Life* magazine sent actors to the former Hill house where they were photographed acting scenes from the play. The article characterized the play as a reenactment of the Hill incident.

Hill sued the magazine under a New York right of privacy statute that made it a misdemeanor for anyone to use without consent another's name for commercial purposes. The jury found in favor of Hill and the state appeals courts affirmed.

The Supreme Court reversed, 6-3.[1] The Hill family was newsworthy, albeit involuntarily, wrote Justice William J. Brennan, Jr., for the majority. The New York law permitted newsworthy persons to recover if they could show that the article was fictionalized. But, said Brennan, the actual malice standard set out in *New York Times Co. v. Sullivan* (1964) must be applied to this case even though private individuals were involved.[2] Brennan wrote:

> The guarantees for speech and press are not the preserve of political expression or comment upon public affairs, essential as those are to healthy government. One need only pick up any newspaper or magazine to comprehend the vast range of published matter which exposes persons to public view, both private citizens and public officials. Exposure of the self to others in varying degrees is a concomitant of life in a civilized community. The risk of this exposure is an essential incident of a society which places a primary value on freedom of speech and of press.... We have no doubt that the subject of the *Life* article ... is a matter of public interest.... Erroneous statement is no less inevitable in such a case than in the case of comment upon public affairs, and in both, if innocent or merely negligent, "... it must be protected if the freedoms of expression are to have the 'breathing space' that they 'need ... to survive'...."

> ... We create a grave risk of serious impairment of the indispensable service of a free press in a free society if we saddle the press with the impossible burden of verifying to a certainty the facts associated in news articles with a person's name, picture or portrait, particularly as related to nondefamatory matter.[3]

Because the jury had not been instructed that it could award damages to the Hills only if it found the article had been published with actual malice, the majority sent the case back to the lower courts.

In the next case, however, the Court found that a jury had been justified in finding that false statements had been printed with reckless disregard for the truth.

Cantrell v. Forest City Publishing Co. (1974) concerned a published report on the family of a man who had been killed in a bridge collapse. Among the admitted misrepresentations in the article were "quotes" from the man's widow, who had not been interviewed. This was a "calculated falsehood," the majority said, portraying the Cantrell family "in a false light through knowing or reckless untruth."[4]

In *Cox Broadcasting Corporation v. Cohn* (1975) the Court struck down a Georgia law making it illegal to broadcast the name of rape victims. The father of a girl who had died as a result of an assault and rape brought suit against a television station for reporting his daughter's name in two of their news reports. The reporter testified that he had obtained the name of the victim at an open court hearing at which five of six men indicted for the crime pleaded guilty.

The Court said that the First Amendment does not allow states to "impose sanctions for the publication of truthful information contained in official court records open to public inspection." On privacy, the majority wrote:

> If there are privacy interests to be protected in judicial proceedings, the States must respond by means which avoid public documentation or other exposure of private information. Their political institutions must weigh the interests in privacy with the interests of the public to know and of the press to publish.[5]

In 1979 a unanimous Court struck down a state law that forbade newspapers, but not other forms of the press, from reporting the names of juveniles involved in criminal proceedings.[6]

1. *Time Inc., v. Hill*, 385 U.S. 374 (1967).
2. *The New York Times Co. v. Sullivan*, 376 U.S. 254 (1964).
3. *Time Inc. v. Hill*, 385 U.S. 374 at 388, 389 passim (1967).
4. *Cantrell v. Forest City Publishing Co.*, 419 U.S. 245 at 253 (1974).
5. *Cox Broadcasting Corp. v. Cohn*, 420 U.S. 469 at 495, 496 (1975).
6. *Smith v. Daily Mail Publishing Co.*, 443 U.S. 97 (1979).

The Supreme Court unanimously reversed the award in Walker's case but by a 5-4 vote upheld the award of damages to Butts.[51]

All of the justices agreed that both Butts and Walker were public figures, but four of the justices would not have applied the actual malice rule to their cases. Three of the remaining five justices would have applied the actual malice rule, and the other two maintained that freedom of the press absolutely protects publishers from libel suits.

Court's Opinion

Justice Harlan, joined by Justices Clark, Stewart, and Fortas, concluded that Butts and Walker were "public figures." (Chief Justice Earl Warren, the fifth member of the majority, agreed with Harlan's result but not with his reasoning.)

"Butts may have attained that status by position alone and Walker by his purposeful activity amounting to a thrusting of his personality into the 'vortex' of an important public controversy," Harlan said. Both men "commanded sufficient public interest and had sufficient access to the means of counter-argument to be able to 'expose through discussion the falsehood and fallacies' of the defamatory statements." [52]

But those four justices would apply a rule less strict than actual malice in libel cases brought by such public figures. Harlan wrote,

a "public figure" who is not a public official may also recover damages for a defamatory falsehood whose substance makes substantial danger to reputation apparent, on a showing of highly unreasonable conduct constituting an extreme departure from the standards of investigation and reporting ordinarily adhered to by reasonable publishers.[53]

Using this standard, Harlan found that the *Post* had failed to exercise elementary journalistic precautions to determine if the allegation against Butts was true. The libel award to Butts must be sustained. But the award to Walker must be overturned, Harlan said, because nothing in the evidence suggests a "departure from accepted publishing standards." [54]

The remaining five justices agreed with Chief Justice Warren that public figures must prove actual malice under the *New York Times* rule to win libel damages. Applying that rule, it was evident that Walker had not proved actual malice, Warren said. But in Butts's case, the conduct of the *Saturday Evening Post* showed the "degree of reckless disregard for the truth" that constituted actual malice under the rule.

Narrowing the Definition

In 1979 the Supreme Court sharply narrowed the public figure category. In its decisions in the cases of *Wolston v. Reader's Digest Association Inc.* and *Hutchinson v. Proxmire,* the justices held that two men who had been involuntarily thrust into the public eye were not public figures and could recover libel damages without proving actual malice in the publications charged.

Ilya Wolston was convicted of contempt in 1958 for refusing to appear and testify before a grand jury investigating Soviet espionage attempts. Ronald Hutchinson, a scientist, found himself in the public eye after his research—paid for in part with federal funds—was the target

of a "Golden Fleece" award from Senator William Proxmire, D-Wis., who described the research as a waste of tax monies. Neither man, held the Court, was a public figure as a result of this publicity.

The vote in the *Wolston* case was 8-1. Only Justice Brennan dissented. Justice William H. Rehnquist explained that the majority felt that "[a] private individual is not automatically transformed into a public figure just by becoming involved in or associated with a matter that attracts public attention."

"A libel defendant must show more than mere newsworthiness [on the part of the person charging libel] to justify application of the demanding burden of *New York Times,*" wrote Rehnquist.[55]

Moving away from definition and toward procedural safeguards, the Court in 1984 ruled that federal appeal courts reviewing libel awards won by public figures must take a new look at the evidence to see if it proved actual malice. Two years later, the Court held that judges should summarily dismiss libel charges brought by a public figure unless they find clear and convincing evidence of actual malice in the challenged article. And in 1988 the Court denied damages for emotional distress to a public figure who did not prove actual malice.[56]

Private Individuals

The first time the Court considered whether private individuals must prove actual malice to win damages for libel, it splintered into four different groups.

George Rosenbloom, a distributor of nudist magazines, was arrested in a police crackdown on pornography. A local radio station reported that Rosenbloom had been arrested for possession of obscene literature. After he was acquitted of criminal obscenity charges, Rosenbloom sued the radio station for libel. A jury awarded him $750,000, but an appeals court reversed on the grounds that the jury should have been required to apply the *New York Times* actual malice standard to the case.

The Supreme Court affirmed the appeals court, 5-3, in *Rosenbloom v. Metromedia Inc.* (1971). Chief Justice Burger and Justices Brennan and Blackmun agreed that the actual malice rule should be applied to all discussion of public issues, even that including defamatory statements about private individuals.

The First Amendment protects discussion of public issues, Brennan said, and an issue does not become less public

merely because a private individual is involved.... The public's primary interest is in the event; the public focus is on the conduct of the participant and the content, effect, and significance of the conduct, not the participant's prior anonymity or notoriety.[57]

Justice Black concurred, maintaining that the guarantee of a free press protected publishers against all libel suits. Justice White also concurred, holding that the *New York Times* rule protected newspapers who praised public officials—in this case the police who undertook the pornography investigation—and criticized their adversaries.

In dissent, Justices Marshall, Stewart, and Harlan said they would not apply the actual malice rule to libel cases involving private individuals. Justice Douglas did not participate.

The *Gertz* Decision

Three years later the Court shifted, adopting the *Rosenbloom* dissenters' position that the actual malice rule did not apply in libel cases brought by private individuals. Five justices endorsed this view in *Gertz v. Robert Welch, Inc.* (1974).

Elmer Gertz was an attorney who sued a Chicago policeman in behalf of the family of a youth killed by the officer. *American Opinion,* the journal of the John Birch Society, printed an article characterizing Gertz as a "Leninist" with a criminal record who was part of a Communist conspiracy to discredit local police. Charging that the allegations were false, Gertz sued the journal for damages.

The jury awarded him $50,000, but the trial court overruled the jury. Citing *Rosenbloom,* the court said that the First Amendment protected publishers from libel suits in connection with discussions of public interest even if they defamed private individuals unless the individual could prove actual malice on the part of the publisher. The Supreme Court reversed, 5-4.

The majority included the two newest members of the Court, Powell and Rehnquist, who had succeeded Justices Black and Harlan late in 1971. Voting with them were *Rosenbloom* dissenters Marshall and Stewart and, with reservations, Justice Blackmun.

The *New York Times* rule is not appropriate in libel cases involving private individuals, wrote Justice Powell for the majority. Private citizens lack the access of public officials and public figures to "channels of effective communication" to combat allegations about their conduct, he observed. Furthermore, private individuals, unlike public officials and figures, have not voluntarily subjected themselves to public scrutiny. A private person, Powell wrote,

> has relinquished no part of his interest in the protection of his own good name, and consequently he has a more compelling call on the courts for redress of injury inflicted by defamatory falsehood. Thus, private individuals are not only more vulnerable to injury than public officials and public figures; they are also more deserving of recovery.[58]

Therefore, Powell continued, "[S]o long as they do not impose liability without fault, the States may define for themselves the appropriate standard of liability for a publisher or broadcaster of defamatory falsehood injurious to a private individual."[59]

To avoid self-censorship, Powell cautioned, the liability of publications to private-person libel suits must be limited. Therefore, private individuals who proved, for example, only that a publisher had been negligent when he printed false defamatory statements could recover damages only for the actual injury to his reputation. Punitive or presumed damages could be awarded only on a showing that actual malice, as defined by the *New York Times* rule, was intended, Powell held.

Turning to the case at hand, Powell held that Gertz was a private individual despite his active participation in community and professional affairs:

> Absent clear evidence of general fame or notoriety in the community, and pervasive involvement in the affairs of society, an individual should not be deemed a public personality for all aspects of his life. It is preferable to reduce the public-figure question to a more meaningful context by looking to the nature and extent of an individual's participation in the particular

---

Confidentiality

A state may not fine a newspaper for printing a true report of confidential proceedings of a state commission considering disciplinary action against a sitting state judge. This was the Supreme Court's unanimous holding in the case of *Landmark Communications Inc. v. Virginia* (435 U.S. 829, 1978).

After the Norfolk *Virginian-Pilot* printed an accurate report of an inquiry by the state judicial review commission into the conduct of a sitting judge named in the article, the newspaper was indicted, tried, convicted, and fined $500 for violating state law by breaching the confidentiality of the commission's proceedings.

The state justified the law as necessary to protect public confidence in the judicial process, to protect the reputation of judges, and to protect persons who might bring complaints to the commission. The Court held that those interests justified the law protecting the confidentiality of proceedings before the commission, but they did not justify imposing criminal penalties on news media, uninvolved in the commission's proceedings, who breached that confidentiality.

---

controversy giving rise to the defamation.[60]

The majority sent the case back for a new trial, holding, on the one hand, that the jury should not have been allowed to award damages without a finding of fault on the part of *American Opinion,* and, on the other hand, that the trial court had erred in holding that the actual malice standard should be applied.

The dissenting justices, Chief Justice Burger and Justice Brennan, joined by Justice Douglas, maintained that discussions of public interest, including those touching private persons, should be protected by the actual malice rule. Justice White also dissented, claiming that the majority opinion made it almost impossible for a private individual to defend his reputation successfully.

The Court reaffirmed the principles of *Gertz* in *Time v. Firestone.* In its December 22, 1967, issue, *Time* magazine carried an item in its "Milestones" section announcing the divorce of Russell A. Firestone, Jr., heir to the tire fortune, from his third wife, Mary Alice Sullivan. In that item the magazine wrote: "The 17-month intermittent trial produced enough testimony of extramarital adventures on both sides, said the judge, 'to make Dr. Freud's hair curl.' "

This report, as *Time* was soon to discover, was less than accurate. Although Firestone's suit for divorce had charged his wife with adultery and extreme cruelty, the judge in granting him the divorce did not specify that those charges were the grounds upon which the divorce was granted.

When *Time* refused to retract the item, the former Mrs. Firestone sued the magazine for libel. She won a

$100,000 damage judgment. *Time* appealed, claiming that Mrs. Firestone was a public figure and therefore must prove actual malice to win the suit. The magazine also argued that reports of court proceedings are of sufficient public interest that they cannot be the basis for libel judgments—even if erroneous or false and defamatory—unless it is proved that they were published maliciously.

The Supreme Court rejected both of *Time's* arguments and sent the case back to Florida courts to determine whether *Time* had been negligent or was otherwise at fault.

Writing for the majority, Justice Rehnquist stated that Mrs. Firestone was not a public figure despite her involvement in the sensational divorce case. She "did not assume any role of especial prominence in the affairs of society . . . and she did not thrust herself to the forefront of any particular public controversy in order to influence the resolution of the issues involved in it." [61]

Rehnquist noted that in *Gertz* the justices had rejected use of the actual malice rule for all reports of court proceedings. The public interest in such reports, he added, was sufficiently protected under a 1975 decision forbidding the states to allow the media to be sued for reporting true information available to the public in official court records. *(1975 case, p. 67)*

Justice White dissented, saying that the libel award should be upheld. Justice Brennan also dissented, arguing that the First Amendment protected reporting of public judicial proceedings unless actual malice was proved. The third dissenter, Justice Marshall, thought Mrs. Firestone was a public figure and that the *New York Times* actual malice rule should therefore apply.

In 1979 the Court again upheld *Gertz,* ruling that private individuals who were placed in the public eye involuntarily were not "public figures" and therefore did not have to prove actual malice under the *New York Times* rule in order to bring a successful libel suit. But seven years later, the Court seemed to rebalance this particular equation somewhat, holding that private persons who sue for libel must prove both the falsity of the challenged report as well as fault on the part of the media before they can recover damages. [62]

FREE PRESS VERSUS FAIR TRIAL

At times the First Amendment guarantee of freedom of the press collides with the Sixth Amendment's guarantee of trial by an impartial jury.

As Justice Clark wrote in 1966:

A responsible press has always been regarded as the handmaiden of effective judicial administration, especially in the criminal field. . . . The press does not simply publish information about trials, but guards against the miscarriage of justice by subjecting the police, prosecutors, and judicial processes to extensive public scrutiny and criticism. [63]

In this way the public may assure itself that justice is attained, to the benefit both of society and of the individual defendant.

The conflict between the freedom and the right arises from the Constitution's promise that a defendant shall be judged by an impartial jury solely on evidence produced in court, and that both judge and jury shall be free from outside influence. But in cases concerning prominent people or sensational crimes, pretrial publicity can so saturate a community that the pool of unbiased potential jurors is significantly diminished. News accounts and editorials may influence jurors and judges while a case is pending. The question then is what, if any, restrictions on the free press are constitutionally permissible to ensure a fair trial.

Contempt of Court

The Supreme Court has had little tolerance for efforts by judges to restrict criticism of their official conduct. From time to time judges have held in contempt publishers, editors, and writers who have criticized them—while a case was still pending—for the way they have handled it.

The argument in support of such punishment is that public criticism of a judge might influence or coerce him to rule in a way that will maintain the good will of the publisher and the community at large at the expense of the parties in the case.

Federal Courts

The potential for judicial abuse of the contempt power prompted Congress in 1831 to enact a law forbidding the use of contempt citations to punish misbehavior other than that which occurred in court "or so near thereto as to obstruct the administration of justice." In 1918 the Supreme Court allowed the use of the contempt power to curtail a newspaper's criticisms of a judge's conduct in a pending case. [64]

In 1941, however, the Court overruled that decision, holding that the phrase "so near thereto" meant only physical proximity. Thus, federal law as presently construed gives published criticisms of federal judicial conduct absolute protection from summary contempt proceedings. [65]

State Courts

In 1907, several years before the Supreme Court held that the First Amendment freedoms were protected against state action by the Fourteenth Amendment, the Court sustained a contempt citation against a newspaper publisher for publishing articles and a cartoon critical of a state court's actions on pending cases.

If the court determines that a critical publication tends to interfere with the fair administration of justice, wrote Justice Oliver Wendell Holmes, Jr., then the publisher may be punished. "When a case is finished, the courts are subject to the same criticism as other people, but the propriety and necessity of preventing interference with the court of justice by premature statement, argument or intimidation hardly can be denied," he said. [66]

Since 1925, and the application of the First Amendment to the states, the Court has not sustained any contempt citation issued by a judge against a newspaper critical of his actions on a pending case. The leading decision in this area is *Bridges v. California* (1941), in which the Court overturned, 5-4, contempt rulings against a labor leader and an anti-union Los Angeles newspaper.

While a motion for a new trial was pending in a dispute between two competing longshoremen's unions, Bridges, the president of one of the unions, sent a telegram to the U.S. secretary of labor describing as outrageous the judge's initial decision favoring the competing union. Bridges threatened to strike the entire Pacific coast if the original decision were allowed to stand. The telegram was reprinted in several California newspapers.

A companion case to *Bridges, Times-Mirror Co. v. Superior Court of California,* involved a *Los Angeles Times* editorial that urged a trial judge to give severe sentences to two union members found guilty of beating up nonunion truck drivers.

Writing for the five-justice majority overturning the contempt citation against the newspaper, Justice Black said that punishment for contempt improperly restricted freedom of the press. If the contempt citations were allowed to stand, Black said,

> anyone who might wish to give public expression to his views on a pending case involving no matter what problem of public interest, just at the time his audience would be most receptive, would be as effectively discouraged as if a deliberate statutory scheme of censorship had been adopted.[67]

Such a restriction would be permissible only if the criticism raised a clear and present danger that a substantive evil would result, Black continued. The only dangers cited by the court in this case were that the articles might result in disrespect for the court and unfair administration of justice. Black quickly dismissed the first of these rationales:

> The assumption that respect for the judiciary can be won by shielding judges from published criticism wrongly appraises the character of American public opinion. For it is a prized American privilege to speak one's mind, although not always with perfect good taste, on all public institutions. And an enforced silence, however limited, solely in the name of preserving the dignity of the bench, would probably engender resentment, suspicion, and contempt much more than it would enhance respect.[68]

Nor did the Court find any evidence that the articles in question created a clear and present danger of interfering with the fair administration of justice. The judge in the *Los Angeles Times* case was likely to know that a lenient sentence for the two union members would result in criticism from the paper. "To regard it [the editorial], therefore, as in itself of substantial influence upon the course of justice would be to impute to judges a lack of firmness, wisdom, or honor, which we cannot accept as a major premise," Black wrote.[69]

Likewise, the judge in the *Bridges* case was likely to realize that his decision might result in a labor strike. "If he was not intimidated by the facts themselves," Black said, "we do not believe that the most explicit statement of them could have sidetracked the course of justice."[70]

Speaking for the dissenters, Justice Felix Frankfurter said the judges were within their rights to punish comments that had a "reasonable tendency" to interfere with the impartial dispensation of justice. Frankfurter wrote:

> Freedom of expression can hardly carry implications that nullify the guarantees of impartial trials. And since courts are the ultimate resorts for vindicating the

Bill of Rights, a state may surely authorize appropriate historic means [the contempt power] to assure that the process for such vindication be not wrenched from its rational tracks into the more primitive melee of passion and pressure. The need is great that courts be criticized, but just as great that they be allowed to do their duty.[71]

In *Pennekamp v. Florida* (1946), the Court reaffirmed its opinion that editorial comment on the court's handling of a pending case did not present a clear and present danger of interfering with the fair administration of justice and was therefore not punishable. "In the borderline instances where it is difficult to say upon which side the alleged offense falls, we think the specific freedom of public comment should weigh heavily against a possible tendency to influence pending cases," the Court said.[72]

The following year, the Court in *Craig v. Harney* (1947) overturned a contempt citation for articles that gave an unfair and inaccurate account of a trial. The majority found that neither the articles nor a critical editorial constituted "an imminent and serious threat to the ability of the court to give fair consideration" to the pending case.[73]

Although the Court almost totally abandoned use of the clear and present danger test in other contexts during the 1950s, it reaffirmed the use of that test in contempt cases in 1962. *(Discussion of standard, p. 21)*

In *Wood v. Georgia* the Court reversed the contempt citation of a county sheriff who denounced a county judge's order to a grand jury to investigate rumors of purchased votes and other corrupting practices as a "political attempt to intimidate" black voters. The lower court held that the sheriff's criticism, publicized in several news accounts, created a clear and present danger of influencing the grand jury. The Supreme Court disagreed, observing that the lower courts had made no attempt to show how the criticism created "a substantive evil actually designed to impede the course of justice."[74]

Pretrial Publicity

The press contempt cases concerned criticism of judges and their conduct. A more frequent threat to the fair administration of justice is posed by publications that cast defendants in such a bad light that their rights to fair treatment are jeopardized. In those instances the Court has held that trial courts should take regulatory actions to protect the right to a fair trial with the least possible restriction on a free press.

Defense attorneys frequently claim that news reports are so inflammatory and pervasive as to deny their clients due process. The Supreme Court rejected such a claim in the 1951 case of *Stroble v. California,* noting that the publicity had receded six weeks before the trial, that the defendant had not requested a change of venue, and that his publicized confession was voluntary and placed in evidence in open trial.[75]

In 1959 the Court overturned a federal conviction because jurors had been exposed through news accounts to information that was not admitted in evidence at the trial.[76]

Two years later the Supreme Court for the first time reversed a state conviction on grounds that pretrial publicity had denied the defendant due process.

In *Irvin v. Dowd* (1961), Irvin had been arrested and indicted for one of six murders committed in and around Evansville, Indiana. Shortly after Irvin's arrest, the police sent out press releases saying that he had confessed to all six crimes. The news media covered the crimes and the confession extensively; it also reported on previous crimes in which Irvin had been implicated.

Irvin's attorney won a change of venue to a neighboring rural county, but that area was just as saturated by the same news reports. A request for a second change of venue was denied.

The pervasiveness of the news reports was evident during jury selection. Of the 420 potential jurors asked, 370 said that they had some opinion about Irvin's guilt. Eight of the 12 jurors selected said they thought he was guilty even before the trial began.

Given these circumstances, a unanimous Supreme Court found that the jury did not meet the constitutional standard of impartiality. Justice Clark, who wrote the opinion, cautioned, however, that it was not necessary for jurors to

be totally ignorant of the facts and issues involved. In these days of swift, widespread and diverse methods of communication, an important case can be expected to arouse the interest of the public in the vicinity, and scarcely any of those best qualified to serve as jurors will not have formed some impression or opinion as to the merits of the case. This is particularly true in criminal cases. To hold that the mere existence of any preconceived notion as to the guilt or innocence of an accused, without more, is sufficient to rebut the presumption of a prospective juror's impartiality would be to establish impossible standards.[77]

The following year, a narrow majority of the Court held that pretrial publicity had denied Teamsters Union president David D. Beck a fair trial on charges of grand larceny. The adverse publicity, stemming largely from a U.S. Senate investigation, had been diluted by time and by the presence of other labor leaders also under investigation, and both the grand jury and petit jury had been carefully questioned to avoid selection of those unduly influenced by media reports, the majority said.[78]

But in *Rideau v. Louisiana* (1963), the Court held that a murder defendant whose filmed confession was broadcast and seen by three jurors had been denied due process when his effort to win a change of venue was rejected. Clark dissented, arguing that there was no evidence showing that the telecast confession had indelibly marked the minds of the jurors.[79]

Conduct of Trial

The very presence of working news reporters in and near a courtroom during the course of a trial may also jeopardize its fairness. In 1964 the Court had little trouble holding in *Estes v. Texas* that the presence of television cameras, radio microphones, and newspaper photographers at the pretrial hearing and trial of financier Billie Sol Estes denied Estes his right to a fair trial.

"[V]ideotapes of these hearings clearly illustrate that the picture presented was not one of that judicial serenity and calm to which petitioner was entitled," the Court said.[80]

Two years later, in 1966, the Supreme Court in the case of *Sheppard v. Maxwell* laid out some ground rules to ensure fair trials with minimal restriction on the operation of a free press.

The *Sheppard* Case

The 1954 bludgeon murder of a pregnant woman in her suburban Cleveland home and the subsequent arrest, trial, and conviction of her husband, Dr. Sam Sheppard, for that murder excited some of the most intense and sensational press coverage the country had witnessed.

Pretrial publicity as much as proclaimed Sheppard's guilt. Reporters had access to witnesses during the trial itself and frequently published information damaging to Sheppard that could have come only from the prosecuting attorneys. Some of this information was never introduced as evidence. Reporters in the courtroom were seated only a few feet from the jury and from Sheppard and his counsel who were constantly besieged by reporters and photographers as they entered and left the courtroom.

"The fact is that bedlam reigned at the courthouse during the trial and newsmen took over practically the entire courtroom," said the Supreme Court, overturning Sheppard's conviction by an 8-1 vote. "The carnival atmosphere at trial could easily have been avoided since the courtroom and courthouse premises are subject to control of the court," the majority wrote. "[T]he presence of the press at judicial proceedings must be limited when it is apparent that the accused might otherwise be prejudiced or disadvantaged." [81]

Change of venue and postponement of the trial until publicity dies down would be proper if pretrial publicity threatens the fair administration of justice, the Court said. Once the trial has begun, the judge may limit the number of reporters permitted in the courtroom and place strict controls on their conduct while there. Witnesses and jurors should be isolated from the press, and the jury may be sequestered to prevent it from being influenced by trial coverage.

The majority also indicated that the judge should have acted to prevent officials from releasing certain information to the press:

[T]he trial court might well have proscribed extrajudicial statements by any lawyer, party, witness or court official which divulged prejudicial matters, such as the refusal of Sheppard to submit to an interrogation or take any lie detector tests; any statement made by Sheppard to officials; the identity of prospective witnesses or their probable testimony; any belief in guilt or innocence; or like statements concerning the merits of the case. . . .

Being advised of the great public interest in the case, the mass coverage of the press, and the potential prejudicial impact of publicity, the court could also have requested the appropriate city and county officials to promulgate a regulation with respect to dissemination of information about the case by their employees. In addition, reporters who wrote or broadcast prejudicial stories could have been warned as to the impropriety of publishing material not introduced in the proceedings. . . . In this manner, Sheppard's right to a trial free from outside interference would have been given added protection without corresponding curtailment of the news media.[82]

Inmates and Free Speech

Prison rules limiting inmate communications with persons outside the walls must be measured against the First Amendment, held a unanimous Supreme Court in *Procunier v. Martinez* (1974). The justices thus invalidated California regulations allowing prison mailroom officials wide discretion to censor letters to or from inmates.

The traditional "hands-off" policy of the federal courts toward prison regulations is rooted in a realistic appreciation of the fact that "the problems of prisons . . . are complex and intractable, and . . . not readily susceptible of resolution by decree," Justice Lewis F. Powell, Jr., explained.[1]

However, he continued, "[w]hen a prison regulation or practice offends a fundamental constitutional guarantee, federal courts will discharge their duty to protect constitutional rights.... This is such a case."[2]

The Court recognized that censorship of inmate mail jeopardized the First Amendment rights of those free persons who wished to communicate with prisoners. But it also acknowledged that the government had a legitimate interest in maintaining order in penal institutions, an interest that might justify the imposition of certain restraints on inmate correspondence.

To determine whether a censorship regulation constituted an impermissible restraint on First Amendment liberties, the Court set out a two-part test: the regulation must further a substantial governmental interest—not simply the suppression of criticism or other expression—and the restraint on speech "must be no greater than is necessary or essential to the protection of the particular governmental interest involved."[3]

The Court also held that the inmate and author must be informed of the censorship of a particular letter.

Later in the year, the Court held that states were under no First Amendment obligation to permit prisoners to have face-to-face interviews with news reporters. An inmate's First Amendment rights might legitimately be constrained by security, rehabilitative, and discipline considerations, the Court said in *Procunier v. Hillery* (1974).

Referring to *Martinez*, the Court pointed to the mail as one alternative means inmates had of communicating with persons outside the prison.[4]

In 1987 the Court in *Turner v. Safley* announced a standard against which such prison regulations could be measured. If the regulation was reasonably related to legitimate penological interests, said the Court, it would be upheld. The justices then used that standard to strike down a state prison rule forbidding most inmate marriages—but upheld, 5-4, a regulation that bars most correspondence between inmates.[5]

1. *Procunier v. Martinez,* 416 U.S. 396 at 404-405 (1974).
2. Id. at 405-406.
3. Id. at 413.
4. *Procunier v. Hillery,* 417 U.S. 817 (1974).
5. *Turner v. Safley,* ___ U.S. ___ (1987).

Gag Rules

After *Sheppard,* trial judges began to use so-called "gag rules," under which the press is barred by judicial order from publishing articles containing certain types of information about pending court cases. Refusal to comply with the order may result in being held in contempt of court.

Such orders are clearly a prior restraint on publication, and their constitutionality has been challenged repeatedly by the press.

In the Court's first full-scale review of a gag rule, all nine justices held the challenged order an unconstitutional prior restraint on the press. Only three justices, however, said that all gag rules were unconstitutional. Four felt they might be permissible under some circumstances. The remaining two justices indicated their inclination to agree that all gag rules were unconstitutional.

The murder of six members of a family in the small town of Sutherland, Nebraska, in October 1975 was followed by the arrest of Erwin Charles Simants, who was charged with the crimes. Because of the nature of the crimes and the location—a rural area with a relatively small number of potential jurors—the judge issued a gag order on the day of the preliminary hearing. Although that hearing took place in open court, the press was forbidden to report any of the testimony given or the evidence presented. The order remained in effect until the jury was chosen.

Writing the Court's opinion in *Nebraska Press Association v. Stuart* (1976), Chief Justice Burger said that the judge could have used less drastic means than the gag order to ensure that excessive publicity did not make it impossible to assemble an unbiased jury and conduct a fair trial.

"[P]rior restraints on speech and publication are the most serious and the least tolerable infringement on First Amendment rights," Burger wrote. "A prior restraint . . . has an immediate and irreversible sanction. If it can be said that a threat of criminal or civil sanctions after publication 'chills' speech, prior restraint 'freezes' it at least for the time."[83] *(Prior restraint, p. 54)*

Furthermore, said Burger, the right to report evidence given in an open courtroom is a settled principle. "[O]nce a public hearing had been held, what transpired there could not be subject to prior restraint."[84]

But the chief justice refused to rule out the possibility that the circumstances of some particular case might justify imposition of a gag rule. "This Court has frequently denied that First Amendment rights are absolute and has

Radio and Television Broadcasting ...

The modern expansion of the "press" to include radio and television broadcasters generated a new set of First Amendment issues. Because there are only a limited number of broadcast frequencies, the government allocates access to them through a licensing system, a structure that would normally be considered prior restraint of free speech and free press. But as the Supreme Court noted in 1969, "[w]ithout government control the ... [media] would be of little use because of the cacophony of competing voices, none of which could be clearly and predictably heard." [1]

The Court has sustained the right of the Federal Communications Commission (FCC) to determine who receives broadcast licenses, emphasizing that these determinations must be made on neutral principles that do not favor one broadcaster over another because of the particular views espoused. "Congress did not authorize the Commission to choose among applicants upon the basis of their political, economic or social views or upon any other capricious basis," the Court wrote in 1943. [2]

Right of Reply

For almost forty years the FCC required broadcasters to give individuals whose views or records were attacked on the air an opportunity to respond. The commission, to protect what it viewed as the public's right to hear a fair presentation of both sides of a dispute, also required broadcasters who editorialized to offer persons with opposing views the right of reply.

The "fairness doctrine" was challenged in court as a violation of the broadcasters' First Amendment rights to determine the content of broadcasts free from governmental interference. The Court unanimously rejected this argument in 1969. "Where there are substantially more individuals who want to broadcast than there are frequencies to allocate, it is idle to posit an unabridgeable First Amendment right to broadcast comparable to the right of every individual to speak, write, or publish," wrote Justice Byron R. White. [3]

The First Amendment right of viewers and listeners to diverse viewpoints on matters of political, economic, and social concern are paramount to the rights of broadcasters. White said:

A license permits broadcasting, but the licensee has no constitutional right to be the one who holds the license or to monopolize a radio frequency to the exclusion of his fellow citizens. There is nothing in the First Amendment which prevents the Government from requiring a licensee to share his frequency with others and to conduct himself as a proxy or fiduciary with obligations to present those views and voices which are representative of his community and which would otherwise, by necessity, be barred from the airwaves. [4]

Right to Broadcast

The Supreme Court ruled in 1973 that radio and television stations are not required to sell time to all individuals and groups who wish to expound their views on public issues across the airwaves. The Court announced this decision in *Columbia Broadcasting System v. Democratic National Committee.*

Six of the justices, led by Chief Justice Warren E. Burger, held that while the fairness doctrine did require broadcasters to provide a right of reply to opposing views, Congress had firmly rejected the idea that all persons wishing to air their views should have access to broadcast facilities. The fairness doctrine makes the broadcaster responsible for adequate coverage of public issues in a manner that fairly reflects different viewpoints, the six agreed, but since every viewpoint cannot be aired, Congress and the FCC have appropriately left it to the broadcaster to exercise journalistic discretion in selecting those that present a fair picture of the issue.

Five of the six justices saw the basic question as "not whether there is to be discussion of controversial issues of public importance in the broadcast media, but rather who shall determine what issues are to be discussed by whom, and when." [5] Providing a right of access to the airwaves would benefit persons who could afford to buy the time, and these persons could not be held accountable for fairness, they said.

Justice William O. Douglas agreed with the outcome of the majority's reasoning but contended that the First Amendment actually prohibited the government from requiring broadcasters to accept such paid editorial advertisements. Broadcasters, Douglas wrote, are entitled to the same protection under the guarantee of a free press that newspapers receive.

Justices William J. Brennan, Jr., and Thurgood Marshall dissented. By approving the broadcasters' policy of refusing to sell such air time the government was abridging the right of its citizens to free speech, they wrote.

The public nature of the airwaves, the preferred status given to broadcasters to whom the government granted the right to use a certain frequency, the extensive government regulation of broadcast programming, and FCC approval of the challenged policy all combined to make that refusal government action clearly violating the First Amendment ban, Brennan said. The public's First Amendment interest "in the reception of a full spectrum of views presented in a vigorous and uninhibited manner on controversial issues of public importance" was

...Permissible Prior Restraint

thwarted by a policy of refusing paid editorials. Such a policy gave broadcasters nearly exclusive control over the "selection of issues and viewpoints to be covered, the manner of presentation, and, perhaps most important, who shall speak." The fairness doctrine was insufficient to ensure this necessary wide-open exchange of views, said Brennan.[6]

Another side of this issue came to the Court in 1984, and the justices in *FCC v. League of Women Voters of California* struck down a federal law barring editorials on public radio and television programs that received federal grants. This curtailed precisely the sort of speech the Framers meant to protect, wrote Brennan, "speech that is 'indispensable to the discovery and spread of political truth.' "[7]

President Ronald Reagan opposed the fairness doctrine as a First Amendment infringement, and he appointed members of the FCC who agreed with him. After the Supreme Court in June 1987 declined to review a lower court ruling that the FCC could, in its discretion, abandon this doctrine without congressional approval, the FCC voted 4-0 in August to discard it.[8]

Content and Context

The Supreme Court in 1978 upheld against a First Amendment challenge the FCC's power to limit the hours during which radio stations may broadcast material which, although offensive to many listeners, is not obscene.

About two o'clock one afternoon, a New York radio station owned by the Pacifica Foundation aired a recorded monologue by humorist George Carlin. Entitled "Filthy Words," the monologue satirized society's attitude toward certain words, in particular seven which are generally barred from use on the air.

In the monologue, Carlin lists the seven "dirty words" (shit, piss, fuck, cunt, cocksucker, motherfucker, and tits) and then uses them in various forms throughout the recording.

After receiving a parent's complaint that his young son had heard the monologue, the FCC issued an order to the station restricting the hours during which such an "offensive" program could be broadcast. Pacifica challenged the order, arguing that the FCC was regulating the content of a program in violation of the guarantee of free speech.

"No such absolute rule [forbidding government regulation of content] is mandated by the Constitution," said Justice John Paul Stevens for the majority of five. "[B]oth the content and the context of speech are critical elements of First Amendment analysis."[9]

While "some uses of even the most offensive words are unquestionably protected" by the First Amendment, "the constitutional protection accorded to ... such patently offensive ... language [as used in the monologue] need not be the same in every context.... Words that are commonplace in one setting are shocking in another," he said.[10]

The context of the broadcast justified the FCC's regulation, the majority concluded. Because the broadcast media has established a "uniquely pervasive presence," offensive material that is broadcast reaches people in the privacy of their homes "where the individual's right to be let alone plainly outweighs the First Amendment rights of an intruder." Furthermore, the broadcast was "uniquely accessible to children," and the Court has held that speech otherwise protected might be regulated to protect the welfare of children.[11]

The four dissenters held that the majority could and should have avoided dealing with the constitutional issue simply by holding that the Communications Act of 1934 allowed the FCC to ban or restrict the broadcast only of obscene materials.

Media Cross-Ownership

The Supreme Court upheld in 1978 the authority of the FCC to decree an end to common ownership of a community's single newspaper and its only radio or television station. This authority had been challenged with the argument that the ban on cross-media ownership violated freedom of the press.

The commission has broad power "to regulate broadcasting in the 'public interest,' " wrote Justice Marshall for the unanimous Court. The FCC issued its order to encourage diversity of ownership that could possibly result in diversity of viewpoints aired within a community. This was a valid public interest and a rational means of reaching that goal, Marshall said.[12]

1. *Red Lion Broadcasting Co. v. Federal Communications Commission,* 395 U.S. 367 at 376 (1969).
2. *National Broadcasting Company v. United States,* 31 U.S. 190 at 226 (1943); see also *Federal Communications Commission v. SNCN Listeners Guild,* 450 U.S. 582 (1981).
3. *Red Lion Broadcasting Co. v. Federal Communications Commission,* 395 U.S. 367 at 388 (1969).
4. Id. at 389.
5. *Columbia Broadcasting System, Inc. v. Democratic National Committee,* 412 U.S. 94 at 130 (1973).
6. Id. at 184, 187.
7. *Federal Communications Commission v. League of Women Voters of California,* 468 U.S. 364 (1984).
8. *Telecommunications Research and Action Center v. Federal Communications Commission,* 801 F 2d 501, review denied, June 8, 1987.
9. *Federal Communications Commission v. Pacifica Foundation,* 438 U.S. 726 at 744 (1978).
10. Id. at 746-747.
11. Id. at 748, 749.
12. *Federal Communications Commission v. National Citizens Committee for Broadcasting,* 436 U.S. 775 (1978).

consistently rejected the proposition that a prior restraint can never be employed." [85]

"The right to a fair trial by a jury of one's peers is unquestionably one of the most precious and sacred safeguards enshrined in the Bill of Rights," wrote Justice Brennan in a concurring opinion joined by Justices Marshall and Stewart.

But, Brennan added, "I would hold . . . that resort to prior restraints on the freedom of the press is a constitutionally impermissible method for enforcing that right." Judges have less drastic means of ensuring fair trials than by prohibiting press "discussion of public affairs." [86] Eight years later in 1984, however, the Court had no difficulty in upholding a state court order restraining the publication of information about a religious organization obtained through pretrial discovery that took place under court order. [87]

ACCESS AND CONFIDENTIALITY

In a very practical sense, the public delegates to the press the job of gathering, sifting, and reporting the news that shapes its political, economic, and social views of the world. As surrogate for the public, the press attends and reports on events that the vast majority of the public does not or cannot attend.

The news gathering process has been the subject of several Supreme Court cases as the justices have considered whether the First Amendment guarantees the press special access to or special protection for its news sources. The Court generally has refused to adopt such an expansive view of the First Amendment freedom, although the one exception to that view came when the press linked arms with the public in general to argue for access to criminal trials.

In 1979 the Court in *Gannett Co. v. DePasquale* rejected the newspaper chain's claim that it had a constitutional right, under the First and the Sixth Amendments, to attend a pretrial hearing on suppression of evidence in a murder case.

By a vote of 5-4, the Court held that the judge in the case had properly granted the request of the defendants to exclude the press and public from the hearing. Upholding the judge's action were Chief Justice Burger, Justices Stewart, Powell, Rehnquist, and John Paul Stevens. Dissenting were Justices Blackmun, Brennan, White, and Marshall.

The majority based its decision wholly on the Sixth Amendment, reading it literally and finding that it guaranteed the right to a *public* trial only to the person *charged* with crime, not to the public or the press. In this case, the defendants had requested that the pretrial hearing be closed; the judge had granted that request.

Justice Stewart pointed out that closing such a hearing was "often one of the most effective methods that a trial judge can employ to attempt to insure that the fairness of a trial will not be jeopardized by the dissemination of such [prejudicial] information throughout the community before the trial itself has even begun." [88]

Within a year the Court had effectively reversed itself.

By 7-1, the Court in *Richmond Newspapers Inc. v. Commonwealth of Virginia* recognized that both press and public had a First Amendment right of access to trials and pretrial hearings. Justice Rehnquist dissented; Powell did not participate.

In some situations, wrote Chief Justice Burger for the Court, it might be necessary—to ensure a fair trial—to limit access to that trial. But if a judge found such limitations necessary, they must be clearly set out to support his finding that closure of the trial was necessary to preserve some overriding interest. [89]

This trend continued to a surprising climax the following year when the Court ruled in *Chandler v. Florida* that it found nothing in the Constitution—neither in the due process clause nor the guarantee of a fair trial—that precluded a state from permitting television cameras in a courtroom to broadcast trial proceedings. [90]

When the press asks for special access to institutions and persons not generally available to the public, it almost always gets a judicial cold shoulder. Twice the Supreme Court has confronted such a request. On both occasions, the Court held that the press had no greater access to such institutions than that enjoyed by the general public.

In 1974 the Court weighed the right of reporters to gather news within the prison system against society's interest in secure prisons. The Court sustained, 5-4, prison regulations that bar interviews by reporters with inmates they request by name to see. [91]

The regulations prohibiting face-to-face interviews were apparently written to curtail the so-called "big wheel" phenomenon, in which the influence of certain inmates is so enhanced by publicity that disruption and disciplinary problems result.

The majority, with Justice Stewart writing, held that prison officials were justified in adopting the ban on interviews to minimize disruptive behavior.

The ban did not mean that reporters had no access to the prisons, the majority stressed in *Pell v. Procunier, Saxbe v. Washington Post* (1974). Reporters could communicate with specific inmates through the mail. Furthermore, both the California and federal prison systems permitted reporters to visit prisons and to talk with inmates they met in the course of their supervised tour, or with inmates selected by prison officials.

But nothing in the First or Fourteenth Amendments requires "government to afford the press special access to information not shared by members of the public generally," wrote Stewart. [92]

In a dissenting opinion joined by two other justices, Justice Powell saw the ban on interviews as "impermissibly restrain[ing] the ability of the press to perform its constitutionally established function of informing the people on the conduct of their government." [93]

Elaborating on this point, Powell said the government had no legitimate interest in withholding the information reporters might gather in personal interviews:

Quite to the contrary, federal prisons are public institutions. The administration of these institutions, the effectiveness of their rehabilitative programs, the conditions of confinement they maintain, and the experiences of the individuals incarcerated therein are all matters of legitimate societal interest and concern. Respondents [the reporters] do not assert a right to force disclosure of confidential information or to invade in any way the decisionmaking process of governmental officials. Neither do they seek to question any inmate who does not wish to be interviewed. They only seek to be free of an exceptionless prohibition against a method of newsgathering that is essential to effective reporting in the prison context.[94]

County Jails

In 1978 the Court, 4-3, reaffirmed its holding that reporters have no right to greater access than the general public.

In 1972 a federal judge had found conditions in an Alameda County, California, jail to be so shocking as to constitute cruel and unusual punishment. As a result, television station KQED sought access to the prison to interview inmates and film conditions there.

The county sheriff agreed to begin monthly scheduled tours of the prison open to the press and general public but prohibited the use of cameras or sound equipment as well as interviews with inmates. KQED then won an order from a federal judge directing the sheriff to grant the press wider access, to allow the interviews and the use of sound and camera equipment. The sheriff appealed in the case of *Houchins v. KQED, Inc.*

Neither the First nor Fourteenth Amendment mandates "a right of access to government information or sources of information within the government's control," wrote Chief Justice Burger, announcing the decision in an opinion only two other justices joined. The First Amendment does not guarantee access to information, but only the freedom to communicate information once acquired. "[U]ntil the political branches decree otherwise, as they are free to do, the media has no special right of access to the Alameda County Jail different from or greater than that accorded the public generally," Burger wrote.[95]

The fourth member of the majority, Justice Stewart, agreed only that the order was too broad. The three dissenters—Justices Brennan, Stevens, and Powell—argued that "information-gathering is entitled to some measure of constitutional protection . . . not for the private benefit of those who might qualify as representatives of the 'press' but to insure that the citizens are fully informed regarding matters of public interest."[96]

Protecting Confidentiality

Does the First Amendment allow reporters to withhold information from the government to protect a news source? Members of the press contend that the threat of potential exposure will discourage those news sources who, for a variety of reasons, agree to provide information to reporters only if they are assured confidentiality. Not only will the individual reporter's effectiveness be damaged by forced disclosure, they contend, but the public will also suffer, losing information that it is entitled to have. For these reasons they argue that the First Amendment protects the confidentiality of news sources, even if the sources reveal to the reporter information about crimes.

Several states have laws shielding reporters from demands of grand juries, courts, and other investigating bodies for confidential or unpublished information they have collected. But the Supreme Court has refused to recognize a constitutional privilege of journalists to refuse to answer legitimate inquiries from law enforcement officers.

Grand Jury Investigations

In 1972 the Court decided three cases in which reporters challenged grand jury subpoenas for confidential information. These cases concerned:

● Paul M. Branzburg, an investigative reporter for the Louisville *Courier-Journal* who wrote several articles based on personal observations of drug users whom he had promised not to identify. He was then subpoenaed by a grand jury to testify on what he had observed.

● Paul Pappas, a television newsman who was allowed to visit a Black Panthers headquarters during a period of civil unrest on the condition that he not report what he saw. He later was subpoenaed to testify about that visit.

● Earl Caldwell, a black reporter for *The New York Times* who gained the confidence of Black Panthers in the San Francisco area and wrote several articles about them. He was then called to testify before a grand jury about alleged criminal activity among the Panthers.

State courts in *Branzburg* and *Pappas* ruled that the reporters must provide the information sought to the grand juries. The two reporters appealed.

In *Caldwell*, a federal court of appeals reversed a lower court, holding that freedom of the press protected Caldwell not only from testifying but even from appearing before the grand jury. The Justice Department appealed this ruling to the Supreme Court.

By 5-4 the Supreme Court sustained the state courts in *Branzburg v. Hayes* and *In re Pappas*, and reversed the appeals court in *United States v. Caldwell*. "Until now the only testimonial privilege for unofficial witnesses that is rooted in the Federal Constitution is the Fifth Amendment privilege against self-incrimination," wrote Justice White for the majority. "We are asked to create another by interpreting the First Amendment to grant newsmen a testimonial privilege that other citizens do not enjoy. This we decline to do."[97]

The majority denied that any infringement of First Amendment rights was involved in these cases:

We do not question the significance of free speech, press or assembly to the country's welfare. Nor is it suggested that news gathering does not qualify for First Amendment protection; without some protection for seeking out the news, freedom of the press could be eviscerated. But this case involves no intrusions upon speech or assembly, no prior restraint or restriction on what the press may publish and no express or implied command that the press publish what it prefers to withhold. No exaction or tax for the privilege of publishing, and no penalty, civil or criminal, related to the content of published material is at issue here. The use of confidential sources by the press is not forbidden or restricted; reporters remain free to seek news from any source by means within the law. No attempt is made to require the press to publish its sources of information or indiscriminately to disclose them on request.[98]

White observed that the First Amendment did not protect the press from obeying other valid laws such as labor and antitrust regulations. The authority of grand juries to subpoena witnesses was vital to their task:

Fair and effective law enforcement aimed at providing security for the person and property of the individual is a fundamental function of government, and the grand jury plays an important constitutionally mandated role in this process. On the records now before us, we perceive no basis for holding that the public interest in law enforcement and in ensuring effective grand jury proceedings is insufficient to override the consequential, but uncertain, burden on newsgathering which is said to result from insisting that reporters, like other citizens, respond to relevant questions put to them in the course of a valid grand jury investigation or criminal trial.[99]

The majority thought that potential exposure would affect few of a reporter's confidential news sources. "Only where news sources themselves are implicated in crime or possess information relevant to the grand jury's task need they or the reporter be concerned about grand jury subpoenas," White wrote. Nor can we "seriously entertain the notion that the First Amendment protects a newsman's agreement to conceal the criminal conduct of his source ... on the theory that it is better to write about crime than to do something about it," he said.[100]

The majority's "crabbed view of the First Amendment reflects a disturbing insensitivity to the critical role of an independent press in our society," wrote Justice Stewart in a dissent which Justices Marshall and Brennan joined. The majority decision "invites state and federal authorities to undermine the historic independence of the press by attempting to annex the journalistic profession as an investigative arm of government."[101]

Stewart contended that a reporter had a constitutional right to maintain a confidential relationship with news sources. The right to publish must include the right to gather news, he said, and that right in turn must include a right to confidentiality. A reporter's immunity to grand jury probes is not a personal right but the right of the public to maintain an access to information of public concern, Stewart said.[102]

Stewart did not believe the immunity was absolute. Weighed against other constitutional rights, First Amendment rights must be given a preferred position, he said, and government must show a compelling reason for restricting them. He suggested that a reporter be required to appear before a grand jury under certain conditions. The government must:

(1) show that there is probable cause to believe that the newsman has information which is clearly relevant to a specific probable violation of law; (2) demonstrate that the information sought cannot be obtained by alternative means less destructive of First Amendment rights; and (3) demonstrate a compelling and overriding interest in the information.[103]

Justice Douglas also dissented, holding that the First Amendment immunized reporters from grand jury investigations unless they were implicated in a crime. Since this decision, the Court has declined to review several lower court orders finding reporters in contempt for refusing to reveal confidential sources to officials.[104]

Newsroom Searches

The Supreme Court sanctioned a different threat to confidentiality when it ruled in *Zurcher v. The Stanford Daily* (1978) that the First Amendment does not protect newspaper offices from warranted police searches for information or evidence.

The lineup of the justices was almost identical to that in the 1972 "newsman's privilege" cases. Justice Brennan did not participate; Justice Stevens dissented as had Justice Douglas (whom Stevens succeeded) in the earlier case. By 5-3, the Court rejected the argument of the nation's press that police should use subpoenas, not search warrants, to obtain information or evidence from news files, at least so long as the reporter or newspaper was not suspected of any involvement in criminal activity.

A subpoena is a less intrusive means for obtaining evidence than is a search by police armed with a warrant. The subpoena requires a person to search his own home, office, or files for certain specified items. The search warrant authorizes police, unannounced, to enter a home or office by force if necessary to search for the particular material the warrant describes.

Furthermore, a person faced with a search warrant has no opportunity to contest the search before it takes place. But a person subpoenaed to produce information may move to quash the subpoena.

The case arose from a 1971 police search of the offices of the *Stanford Daily,* the campus newspaper of Stanford University. The search occurred after conflict between police and demonstrators at Stanford University Hospital resulted in injury to nine policemen. Police obtained a warrant to search the files, wastebaskets, desks, and photo laboratories at the *Daily's* offices; the object of the fruitless search was evidence of the identity of the demonstrators responsible for the police injuries.

The Supreme Court majority declared that the men who wrote the Fourth Amendment were well aware of the conflict between the government and the press, and if they had felt that special procedures were needed when the government wanted information in the possession of the press, they would have said so.

The First Amendment guarantee of a free press that can gather, analyze, and publish news without governmental interference is sufficiently protected by the Fourth Amendment requirement that searches be reasonable and that warrants be issued by neutral magistrates, wrote Justice White for the majority. He continued:

Properly administered, the preconditions for a warrant—probable cause, specificity with respect to the place to be searched and the things to be seized, and overall reasonableness—should afford sufficient protection against the harms that are assertedly threatened by warrants for searching newspaper offices.[105]

Magistrates could ensure that the search not interfere with publication—and that the warrant be specific enough to prevent officers from rummaging in newspaper files or intruding into editorial decisions. White also said the majority was no more persuaded than it had been in 1972 "that confidential sources will disappear and that the press will suppress news because of fears of warranted searches."[106]

Justice Stewart, joined by Justice Marshall, found it

self-evident that police searches of newspaper offices burden the freedom of the press.... [I]t cannot be denied that confidential information may be exposed to the eyes of police officers who execute a search warrant by rummaging through the files, cabinets, desks and wastebaskets of a newsroom. Since the indisputable effect of such searches will thus be to prevent a newsman from being able to promise confidentiality to his potential sources, it seems obvious to me that a journalist's access to information, and thus the public's will thereby be impaired. . . . The end result, wholly inimical to the First Amendment, will be a diminishing flow of potentially important information to the public.[107]

Justice Stevens disagreed with the majority, arguing that documentary evidence in the possession of an innocent third party should be sought by subpoena rather than search warrant. *(See p. 180.)*

Notes

1. Quoted in Willard Grosvenor Bleyer, *Main Currents in the History of American Journalism* (Boston: Houghton Mifflin Co., 1927), 103.
2. Dissenting opinion in *Saxbe v. Washington Post,* 417 U.S. 843 at 863 (1974).
3. Thomas I. Emerson, *The System of Freedom of Expression* (New York: Random House, Vintage Books, 1970), 506.
4. *Near v. Minnesota,* 283 U.S. 697 at 713 (1931).
5. Id. at 716.
6. Id. at 720.
7. Id. at 721.
8. Id. at 722.
9. Id. at 735, 736.
10. Id. at 738.
11. *Grosjean v. American Press Co.,* 297 U.S. 233 at 244-245 (1936).
12. Id. at 250. See also *Minneapolis Star & Tribune Co. v. Minnesota Commissioner of Revenue,* 460 U.S. 575 (1983) and *Arkansas Writers' Project v. Ragland,* __ U.S. __ (1987).
13. *Lovell v. Griffin,* 303 U.S. 444 at 452 (1938).
14. Id. at 451.
15. *Schneider v. Irvington,* 308 U.S. 147 (1939). See also *Jamison v. Texas,* 318 U.S. 413 (1943).
16. Specific names of these three cases are: *Kim Young v. California, Snyder v. Milwaukee, Nichols v. Massachusetts,* 308 U.S. 147 (1939).
17. *Schneider v. Irvington,* 308 U.S. 147 at 160-161 (1939).
18. Id. at 163.
19. *Talley v. California,* 362 U.S. 60 at 64 (1960).
20. *Organization for a Better Austin v. Keefe,* 402 U.S. 415 at 418, 419, 420 (1971).
21. *Mills v. Alabama,* 384 U.S. 214 at 219 (1966).
22. *New York Times Co. v. United States,* 403 U.S. 713 at 714 (1971).
23. Id. at 715, 717.
24. Id. at 720.
25. Id. at 725-726.
26. Id. at 730.
27. Id. at 730-731, 732.
28. Id. at 742.
29. Id. at 749.
30. Id. at 751.
31. Id. at 757.
32. Id. at 759.
33. Id. at 761.
34. See Holmes's dissent in *Abrams v. United States,* 250 U.S. 616 at 630 (1919); Black's and Douglas's opinion in *Beauharnais v. Illinois,* 343 U.S. 250 at 272 (1952); majority opinion in *The New York Times Co. v. Sullivan,* 376 U.S. 254 (1964).
35. *Coleman v. MacLennan,* 98 P 281 at 281-282 (1908).
36. *Dun & Bradstreet Inc. v. Greenmoss Builders Inc.,* 422 U.S. 749 (1985).
37. *The New York Times Co. v. Sullivan,* 376 U.S. 254 at 257-258 (1964).
38. Id. at 268, 269.
39. Id. at 270-271.
40. Id. at 271-272.

41. Id. at 279.
42. Id. at 279-280.
43. Id. at 288.
44. Id. at 293.
45. Id. at 300.
46. *Garrison v. Louisiana,* 379 U.S. 64 (1964); *Ashton v. Kentucky,* 384 U.S. 195 (1966); *St. Amant v. Thompson,* 390 U.S. 727 at 731 (1968); *Greenbelt Cooperative Publishing Assn. v. Bresler,* 398 U.S. 6 (1970); *Time Inc. v. Pape,* 401 U.S. 279 (1971).
47. *Herbert v. Lando,* 441 U.S. 153 (1979).
48. *Rosenblatt v. Baer,* 383 U.S. 75 at 85-86 (1966).
49. Id. at 93.
50. *Monitor Patriot Co. v. Roy,* 401 U.S. 265 (1971); see also *Ocala Star-Banner Co. v. Damron,* 401 U.S. 295 (1971).
51. *Curtis Publishing Co. v. Butts, Associated Press v. Walker,* 388 U.S. 130 (1967).
52. Id. at 155.
53. Ibid.
54. Id. at 159.
55. *Wolston v. Reader's Digest Association Inc.,* 443 U.S. 157; *Hutchinson v. Proxmire,* 443 U.S. 111 (1979).
56. *Bose Corp. v. Consumers Union of the United States,* 466 U.S. 485 (1984); *Anderson v. Liberty Lobby,* 477 U.S. 242 (1986); *Hustler Magazine v. Falwell,* __ U.S. __.
57. *Rosenbloom v. Metromedia Inc.,* 403 U.S. 29 at 43 (1971).
58. *Gertz v. Robert Welch, Inc.,* 418 U.S. 323 at 345 (1974).
59. Id. at 347.
60. Id. at 352.
61. *Time Inc. v. Firestone,* 424 U.S. 448 at 453 (1976).
62. *Wolston v. Readers' Digest Assn. Inc.,* 443 U.S. 157 (1979); *Hutchinson v. Proxmire,* 443 U.S. 111 (1979); *Philadelphia Newspapers Inc. v. Hepps,* 475 U.S. 767 (1986).
63. *Sheppard v. Maxwell,* 384 U.S. 333 at 350 (1966).
64. *Toledo Newspaper Co. v. United States,* 247 U.S. 402 (1918).
65. *Nye v. United States,* 313 U.S. 33 (1941).
66. *Patterson v. Colorado,* 205 U.S. 454 at 463 (1907).
67. *Bridges v. California, Times-Mirror Co. v. Superior Court of California,* 314 U.S. 252 at 269 (1941).
68. Id. at 270-271.
69. Id. at 273.
70. Id. at 278.
71. Id. at 284.
72. *Pennekamp v. Florida,* 328 U.S. 331 at 347 (1946).
73. *Craig v. Harney,* 331 U.S. 367 at 378 (1947).
74. *Wood v. Georgia,* 370 U.S. 375 at 389 (1962).
75. *Stroble v. California,* 343 U.S. 181 (1951).
76. *Marshall v. United States,* 360 U.S. 310 (1959).
77. *Irvin v. Dowd,* 366 U.S. 717 at 722-723 (1961).
78. *Beck v. Washington,* 369 U.S. 541 (1962).
79. *Rideau v. Louisiana,* 373 U.S. 723 (1963).
80. *Estes v. Texas,* 381 U.S. 532 at 536 (1965).
81. *Sheppard v. Maxwell,* 384 U.S. 333 at 355, 358 (1966).
82. Id. at 361-362.
83. *Nebraska Press Association v. Stuart,* 427 U.S. 539 at 559 (1976).
84. Id. at 568. See also *Cox Broadcasting Corp. v. Cohn,* 420 U.S. 469 (1975).
85. *Nebraska Press Association v. Stuart,* 427 U.S. 539 at 570 (1976).
86. Id. at 572.
87. *Seattle Times Co. v. Rhinehart,* 467 U.S. 1 (1984).
88. *Gannett Co. Inc. v. DePasquale,* 443 U.S. 368 (1979).
89. *Richmond Newspapers v. Commonwealth of Virginia,* 448 U.S. 555 (1980). See also *Globe Newspaper Co. v. Superior Court,* 457 U.S. 596 (1982); *Press-Enterprise Co. v. Superior Court of California, Riverside County,* 464 U.S. 501 (1984); *Press-Enterprise Co. v. Superior Court of California* (1986).
90. *Chandler v. Florida,* 449 U.S. 560 (1981).
91. *Saxbe v. Washington Post Co.,* 417 U.S. 843 (1974); *Pell v. Procunier,* 417 U.S. 817 (1974).
92. *Pell v. Procunier,* 417 U.S. 817 at 834 (1974).
93. Id. at 835.

94. *Saxbe v. Washington Post Co.,* 417 U.S. 843 at 861 (1974).
95. *Houchins v. KQED, Inc.,* 438 U.S. 1 at 15-16 (1978).
96. Id. at 32.
97. *Branzburg v. Hayes; In re Pappas; United States v. Caldwell,* 408 U.S. 665 at 689-90 (1972).
98. Id. at 681-682.
99. Id. at 690-691.
100. Id. at 691, 692.
101. Id. at 725.
102. Id. at 732-733.
103. Id. at 743.
104. See, for example, *Hubbard Broadcasting Co. v. Ammerman,* 436 U.S. 906 (1978); *Tribune Publishing Co. v. Caldero,* 434 U.S. 930 (1977).
105. *Zurcher v. The Stanford Daily,* 436 U.S. 547 at 565 (1978).
106. Id. at 566.
107. Id. at 571-573.

3

Freedom of Religion

It is unthinkable to most Americans that Congress or the president could or would dictate what religious beliefs individuals must hold and what church, if any, they must attend. The freedom to believe as one chooses, or not to believe at all, is as basic to the concept of American democracy as the rights of free speech and press.

The First Amendment's guarantees of free exercise of religion and separation of church and state were the direct products of colonial experience. Many of the colonies were established by settlers fleeing from religious persecution.

Some of the colonialists were themselves intolerant, persecuting those whose religious beliefs and practices were different from their own. Several colonies forbade Catholics and/or non-Christians to hold certain offices and jobs. For a time, there was a state religion in some of the colonies. Others, however, notably Rhode Island, Pennsylvania, and Delaware, tolerated religious diversity.[1]

By the time of the Revolution, belief in religious toleration was well established, and, when the First Amendment was written in 1789, it was religious freedom that led the list of rights Congress was forbidden to abridge. As Justice Joseph Story wrote in his commentaries on the Constitution:

> It was under a solemn consciousness of the dangers from ecclesiastical ambition, the bigotry of spiritual pride, and the intolerance of sects, thus exemplified in our domestic as well as in foreign annals, that it was deemed advisable to exclude from the national government all power to act upon the subject.[2]

The Supreme Court has never viewed either of the religion clauses—"Congress shall make no law respecting an establishment of religion, or prohibiting the free exercise thereof"—as absolute. Freedom to *believe* is absolute, but freedom to *practice* that belief may be circumscribed by government under certain conditions. Government may not directly aid religion, but secular programs that indirectly benefit religious institutions may be permissible.

The Court's task has been to ensure that government remains neutral toward religion. As Chief Justice Warren E. Burger explained in 1970:

> The course of constitutional neutrality in this area cannot be an absolutely straight line; rigidity could well defeat the basic purpose of these provisions, which is to insure that no religion be sponsored or favored, none commanded and none inhibited. The general principle deducible from the First Amendment and all that has been said by the Court is this: that we will not tolerate either governmentally established religion or governmental interference with religion. . . .

> Each value judgment under the Religion Clauses must therefore turn on whether particular acts in question are intended to establish or interfere with religious beliefs and practices or have the effect of doing so. Adherence to the policy of neutrality that derives from an accommodation of the Establishment and Free Exercise Clauses has prevented the kind of involvement that would tip the balance toward government control of churches or governmental restraint on religious practice.[3]

To maintain this neutrality, the Court has developed tests that it applies to the circumstances of each case challenging a supposed violation of the religion clauses.

If a law allegedly interferes with the free exercise of religion, the Court will first examine the statute to see if it carefully describes the conduct that may be restricted. The statute may not be vague or too broad, nor may it leave too much to the discretion of the officials administering it. It may not discriminate on the basis of religion. If the statute is carefully drawn and its purpose and effect are to achieve a secular goal, the restriction likely will be permitted, even if it occasionally restricts a religious exercise.

In recent decisions the Court has been more protective of religious freedom, requiring the government to show that it has a compelling reason for taking any action that indirectly restricts religious liberty, and that no means less restrictive of religious freedom could have accomplished the same secular goal.

If government action is alleged to constitute establishment of religion, the government can successfully defend it only by showing that both the purpose and effect of the action are secular and not intended to aid religion and that the government involvement with religion required by the challenged action is not excessive and does not require continued governmental surveillance of the religious institutions affected.

These, however, are only the general rules. A reading of the cases shows they are not uniformly applied.

THE FREE EXERCISE OF RELIGION

Freedom of religion is inextricably bound up with the other freedoms guaranteed by the First Amendment. Without the freedoms of speech and press, the expression and circulation of religious beliefs and doctrines would be impossible. Without the freedoms of assembly and association, the right to participate with others in public and private religious worship would be curtailed.

So interwoven are these freedoms that both before and after the Court held in 1940 that the Fourteenth Amendment protected the free exercise of religion from restriction by the states, it resolved many cases challenging state infringements on religious liberty by relying on the freedoms of speech and press.

The Court held in *Lovell v. Griffin* (1938) that a municipal prohibition against distribution of handbills without a permit as enforced against a Jehovah's Witness passing out religious circulars was an unconstitutional prior restraint on freedom of the press. And in *Kunz v. New York* (1951), the Court held that arbitrary denial of a public speech permit to a Baptist minister was a violation of the rights of free speech and assembly as well as of religious liberty.[4] *(Details, Lovell case, p. 56; Kunz case, pp. 38, 84)*

As a result of this close relationship, the Supreme Court uses many of the same tests developed in the context of restrictions on free speech and press to determine if government has impermissibly restricted free exercise of religion.

In general the Supreme Court has ruled that states and the federal government may restrict the free exercise of religion if the exercise involves fraud or other criminal activity and there is no other means of protecting the public. Government also may restrict religious practices that threaten public peace and order, but only if the restriction is nondiscriminatory, narrowly drawn, and precisely applied.

The Court also has upheld the right of government, in some circumstances, to compel an individual to take action contrary to his or her religious belief. As the rule was stated late in the 1970s, such a compulsory law will stand against a First Amendment challenge if its primary purpose and effect is to advance a valid secular goal and if the means chosen are calculated to have the least possible restrictive effect on free exercise of religion.

Religion and Criminal Law

In its first direct pronouncement on the First Amendment's protection for the free exercise of religion, the Supreme Court held in 1879 that polygamy was a crime, not a religious practice. *Reynolds v. United States* brought before the Court a Mormon's challenge to the constitutionality of the federal law that barred plural marriages in Utah territory.

Observing that bigamy and polygamy were considered punishable offenses in every state, the Court found "it . . . impossible to believe that the constitutional guaranty of religious freedom was intended to prohibit legislation in respect to this most important feature of social life."[5]

Eleven years later the Court elaborated on this reasoning when it upheld an Idaho territorial statute denying the vote to bigamists, polygamists, and those who advocated plural marriages. In *Davis v. Beason* (1890), the Court for the first time distinguished between protected belief and unprotected conduct:

> It was never intended or supposed that the [First] Amendment could be evoked as a protection against legislation for the punishment of acts inimical to the peace, good order and morals of society. With man's relations to his Maker and the obligations he may think they impose, and the manner in which an expression shall be made by him of his belief on those subjects, no interference can be permitted provided always the laws of society designed to secure its peace and prosperity, and the morals of its people, are not interfered with. However free the exercise of religion may be, it must be subordinate to the criminal laws of the country, passed with reference to actions regarded by general consent as properly the subjects of punitive legislation.[6]

Justice Stephen J. Field, who wrote the Court's opinion, concluded succinctly: "Crime is not the less odious because sanctioned by what any particular sect may designate as religion."[7]

Fraud

The exercise of religious freedom to solicit funds to maintain the religion has occasionally been restricted by states and municipalities wishing to protect their citizens from fraud.

In *Cantwell v. Connecticut* (1940), the Court laid out the type of restriction that might be permitted:

> Nothing we have said is intended even remotely to imply that, under the cloak of religion, persons may, with impunity, commit fraud upon the public. . . . Even the exercise of religion may be at some slight inconvenience in order that a State may protect its citizens from injury. Without doubt a State may protect its citizens from fraudulent solicitation by requiring a stranger in the community . . . to establish his identity and his authority to act for the cause which he purports to represent. The State is likewise free to regulate the time and manner of solicitation generally, in the interest of public safety, peace, comfort or convenience.[8]

In *Martin v. City of Struthers* (1943), the Court held that the possibility that some persons might use house-to-house solicitations as opportunities to commit crimes did not warrant an ordinance prohibiting all solicitors from ringing doorbells to summon the occupants of the house. The Court said that the municipality must find a way of preventing crime that was less restrictive of those persons soliciting for sincere causes.[9] *(Details, p. 49)*

Religion: An Evolving Definition

As the nation's tolerance for religious diversity has broadened, so has the Supreme Court's definition of beliefs it considers religious and therefore entitled to First Amendment protection.

Originally the Court considered religion only in the traditional Judeo-Christian sense, which demanded belief in a divine being. "The term 'religion' has reference to one's views of his relations to his Creator, and the obligations they impose of reverence for his being and character, and of obedience to his will," the Court said in the 1890 case of *Davis v. Beason*.[1]

This view prevailed in 1931, when Chief Justice Charles Evans Hughes wrote that "[t]he essence of religion is belief in a relation to God involving duties superior to those arising from any human relation."[2] This definition became the foundation for the definition adopted by Congress in 1948 of the belief one must hold to qualify for exemption from military service as a conscientious objector. *(Box, p. 87)*

In the 1940s the Court began to move toward a more expansive interpretation of "religion," accepting beliefs that were neither orthodox nor theistically based. In 1943 Justice Felix Frankfurter quoted with approval the words of federal judge Augustus Hand:

It is unnecessary to attempt a definition of religion; the content of the term is found in the history of the human race and is incapable of compression into a few words. Religious belief arises from a sense of the inadequacy of reason as a means of relating the individual to his fellow men and to his universe.... [I]t may justly be regarded as a response of the individual to an inward mentor, call it conscience or God, that is for many persons at the present time the equivalent of what has always been thought a religious impulse.[3]

The following year Justice William O. Douglas, speaking for the Court majority, said that the free exercise of religion "embraces the right to maintain theories of life and of death and of the hereafter which are rank heresy to followers of the orthodox faiths."[4] In 1953 Douglas wrote that "it is no business of courts to say that which is religious practice or activity for one group is not religion under the protection of the First Amendment."[5]

As one commentator noted, these decisions made clear that "the classification of a belief as religion does not depend upon the tenets of its creed."[6]

The breadth of the Court's modern definition of religion was perhaps most clearly stated in its 1961 decision in *Torcaso v. Watkins*:

neither a State nor the federal government can constitutionally force a person "to profess a belief or disbelief in any religion." Neither can constitutionally pass laws nor impose requirements which aid all religions as against non-believers, and neither can aid those religions based on a belief in the existence of God as against those religions founded on different beliefs.[7]

In 1965 the Court reaffirmed its *Torcaso* judgment, viewing as religious any sincere and meaningful belief that occupies a place in the possessor's life parallel to the place God holds in the faith of an orthodox believer. The Court expanded this definition in 1970 to include moral and ethical beliefs held with the strength of traditional religious convictions.[8]

1. *Davis v. Beason*, 133 U.S. 333 at 342 (1890).
2. *United States v. Macintosh*, 283 U.S. 605 at 633-634 (1931).
3. *United States v. Kauten*, 133 P. 2d 703 at 708 (1943), quoted by Justice Felix Frankfurter, dissenting, in *West Virginia State Board of Education v. Barnette*, 319 U.S. 624 at 658-659 (1943).
4. *United States v. Ballard*, 322 U.S. 78 at 86 (1944).
5. *Fowler v. Rhode Island*, 345 U.S. 67 at 70 (1953).
6. "Toward a Constitutional Definition of Religion," *Harvard Law Review* 91 (March 1978) 5:1056.
7. *Torcaso v. Watkins*, 367 U.S. 488 at 495 (1961).
8. *United States v. Seeger*, 380 U.S. 163 at 166 (1965); *Welsh v. United States*, 398 U.S. 333 (1970).

The 'I Am' Movement

Only once has the Supreme Court dealt with the question whether a movement designated as religious by its founders was actually fraudulent. Guy Ballard, the leader of the "I Am" movement, at one point had some three million followers. He and two relatives claimed that their teachings had been dictated by God, that Jesus had personally appeared to them and that they could cure both curable and incurable diseases. They were indicted by the federal government for mail fraud.

The sole question before the Supreme Court in *United States v. Ballard* (1944) was whether the trial jury had been properly instructed that it need not determine whether the Ballards' beliefs were true but only whether the Ballards believed them to be true.

A majority of the Court found the instruction proper. Religious freedom, wrote Justice William O. Douglas,

embraces the right to maintain theories of life and of death and of the hereafter which are rank heresy to followers of the orthodox faiths. Heresy trials are foreign to our Constitution. Men may believe what they cannot prove. They may not be put to the proof of their religious doctrines or beliefs.... The religious views espoused by respondents might seem incredible, if not preposterous, to most people. But if those doctrines are subject to trial before a jury charged with finding their truth or falsity, then the same can be done with the religious beliefs of any sect.[10]

Chief Justice Harlan Fiske Stone dissented, saying that a jury could properly be instructed to determine whether the representations were true or false. Stone said he saw no reason why the government could not submit evidence, for instance, showing that Ballard had never cured anyone of a disease. Justice Robert H. Jackson also dissented, on the ground that the case should have been dismissed altogether. *(Court definitions of religion, p. 83)*

Laws that make employment of children under a certain age a crime have been upheld against claims that they impinge on religious liberty. In 1944 the Court sustained a Massachusetts statute that prohibited girls younger than eighteen from selling newspapers on the streets.

The law had been applied to forbid a nine-year-old Jehovah's Witness from distributing religious literature. The state's interest in protecting children from the harmful effects of child labor "is not nullified merely because the parent grounds his claim to control the child's course of conduct on religion or conscience," the Court wrote in *Prince v. Massachusetts.*[11]

Religion and Social Order

On balance, society's need for order and tranquillity may at times be strong enough to warrant restriction of religious liberty. But the Supreme Court has made it clear that such restrictions must be narrowly drawn and uniformly applied.

The conflict between public order and religious liberty was first raised in *Cantwell v. Connecticut* (1940). Jesse Cantwell, a Jehovah's Witness, played a recording that attacked the Catholic church for two passersby who were Catholic. When they indicated their displeasure with the message, he stopped the record and moved on. The next day he was arrested for breach of the peace.

The Supreme Court overturned the conviction, finding the statute defining breach of the peace too broad, "sweeping in a great variety of conduct under a general and indefinite characterization."[12] This vagueness left too much discretion to officials charged with applying it.

Cantwell, the majority said, had not started a riot or caused anyone else to take action that amounted to a breach of the peace. He therefore raised no "clear and present menace to public peace and order as to render him liable to conviction of the common law offense in question," the Court concluded.[13] *(Details, p. 34)*

Permits

The Court also ruled that permit systems requiring speakers, demonstrators, and paraders to seek a license before undertaking their activity were valid only if narrowly drawn and precisely applied. In *Cantwell* the Court struck down a statute that forbade solicitation for religious causes without a permit because the law allowed a state official discretion to withhold permits if he did not think the cause was a religious one. "[T]o condition the solicitation of aid for the perpetuation of religious views or systems upon a license, the grant of which rests in the exercise of a determination by state authority as to what is a reli-

gious cause, is to lay a forbidden burden upon the exercise of [religious] liberty," the Court wrote.[14]

In *Cox v. New Hampshire* (1941) the Court upheld conviction of a group of Jehovah's Witnesses who paraded without obtaining the required permit. The Court said the statute was not enacted or applied with intent to restrict religious freedom. Rather, it was intended simply to determine the time, manner, and place of parades so as to minimize public disruption and disorder. Such a precisely drawn and applied statute did not unconstitutionally impinge on religious liberty.[15] *(Details, p. 41)*

In *Kunz v. New York* (1951) the Court reversed the conviction of a Baptist minister who continued to give highly inflammatory public street sermons even though his permit to speak on the streets had not been renewed because earlier speeches had caused disorder. The Court said that "an ordinance which gives an administrative official discretionary power to control in advance the right of citizens to speak on religious matters on the streets ... is clearly invalid as a prior restraint on the exercise of First Amendment rights."[16] *(Details, p. 38)*

In another 1951 case the Supreme Court ruled that a city could not deny a permit for a public meeting to a group whose religious views it disapproved. Jehovah's Witnesses had applied for a permit to hold a religious meeting in Havre de Grace, Maryland. The permit was denied after officials questioned the Witnesses about their religious beliefs. The Witnesses held their meeting despite the permit denial and were arrested for disorderly conduct.

The Supreme Court reversed their convictions in *Niemotko v. Maryland* (1951). Denial of a permit to one religious group when permits had been granted to other religious meetings amounted to a denial of equal protection, the Court said.[17]

Two years later the Court reversed the conviction of a Jehovah's Witness who spoke at an open-air meeting in violation of a Pawtucket, Rhode Island, ordinance prohibiting religious addresses in public parks.

During the trial, the state admitted that it had allowed ministers of other churches to deliver sermons at church services held in public parks. The Court ruled that such unequal treatment constituted an improper establishment of religion. "To call the words which one minister speaks to his congregation a sermon, immune from regulation, and the words of another minister an address, subject to regulation, is merely an indirect way of preferring one religion over another," the Court said in *Fowler v. Rhode Island* (1953).[18]

License Fees

The validity of license fees imposed on peddlers was challenged by Jehovah's Witnesses who contested the application of the fees to Witnesses who sold religious literature from door to door.

At first review the Court sustained the license fees. In *Jones v. Opelika* (1942), a five-justice majority ruled that the solicitations were more commercial than religious:

When proponents of religious or social theories use the ordinary commercial methods of sales of articles to raise propaganda funds, it is a natural and proper exercise of the power of the state to charge reasonable fees for the privilege of canvassing. Careful as we may and should be to protect the freedoms safeguarded by the Bill of Rights, it is difficult to see in such enact-

Jehovah's Witnesses: Definers of Freedom

It is a measure of the power of the First Amendment guarantee of the free exercise of religion that its broad interpretation has evolved almost solely in connection with one of the most reviled religious sects in American history. "Probably no sect since the early days of the Mormon Church has been as much a thorn in the communal side and as much a victim of communal hate and persecution as Jehovah's Witnesses," writes one commentator.[1]

Jehovah's Witnesses were originally followers of Charles T. Russell, a Presbyterian who grew disillusioned with all existing religious organizations and began to fashion a new religion in the late 1860s and early 1870s. His followers were first known as Russellites, adopting the name Jehovah's Witnesses after Joseph F. Rutherford succeeded Russell in 1931. In 1884 the sect established the Watchtower Bible and Tract Society to print and disseminate religious literature distributed by the Witnesses.

In 1931 the Witnesses described their mission:

As Jehovah's Witnesses our sole and only purpose is to be entirely obedient to his commandments; to make known that he is the only true and almighty God; that his Word is true and that his name is entitled to all honor and glory; that Christ is God's King ... of authority; that his kingdom is now come, and in obedience to the Lord's commandments we must now declare this good news as a testimony or witness to the nations and to inform the rulers and the people of and concerning Satan's cruel and oppressive organization, and particularly with reference to Christendom, which is the most wicked part of that visible organization ... that God's kingdom is the hope of the world and there is no other.[2]

To carry this message, the Witnesses organized Watchtower Campaigns in the 1930s and 1940s. Each house in a town would be visited by a Witness. If the occupants were willing, the Witness would give them literature, usually for a monetary contribution, and play a phonograph record. The gist of the message is that organized religions, the Roman Catholic church in particular, are rackets. A typical publication, entitled *Enemies*, claimed that:

the greatest racket ever invented and practiced is that of religion. The most cruel and seductive public enemy is that which employs religion to carry on the racket, and by which means the people are deceived and the name of Almighty God is reproached. There are numerous systems of religion, but the most subtle, fraudulent and injurious to humankind is that

which is generally labeled the "Christian religion," because it has the appearance of a worshipful devotion to the Supreme Being, and thereby easily misleads many honest and sincere persons.[3]

Under a chapter entitled "Song of the Harlot," the booklet says: "Referring now to the foregoing scriptural definition of harlot: what religious system exactly fits the prophecies recorded in God's Word? There is but one answer, and that is, the Roman Catholic Church."[4]

Understandably, the Witnesses were not popular in many communities. On more than one occasion members of the sect met with violence from those affronted by their views. Several communities enacted laws to curb the activities of the Witnesses, and it was these laws that the Witnesses challenged in court. According to constitutional historian Robert F. Cushman, members of the sect brought some thirty major cases testing the principles of religious freedom to the Supreme Court beginning in 1938. In most of those cases, the Court ruled in their favor.[5]

The first case brought by the Witnesses was *Lovell v. Griffin* (1938), in which the Court held that religious handbills were entitled to protection of freedom of the press. In another important case, *Cantwell v. Connecticut* (1940), the Court held, first, that the Fourteenth Amendment prohibited abridgment by the states of the free exercise of religion; second, that public officials did not have the authority to determine that some causes were religious and others were not; and third, that a breach of the peace law as applied to a Jehovah's Witness whose message angered two passersby was overbroad and vague and therefore unconstitutional.[6]

Other significant decisions upheld the right of Witnesses to solicit from door to door and to ring homeowners' doorbells, to refuse to salute the flag, and to be exempt from peddler's fees on sales of their literature.[7]

1. Leo Pfeffer, *Church, State and Freedom*, rev. ed. (Boston: Beacon Press, 1967), 650; Pfeffer and Justice Robert H. Jackson's dissenting opinion in *Douglas v. City of Jeannette*, 319 U.S. 157 (1943) served as the main sources for this information.
2. Quoted by Pfeffer, *Church, State and Freedom*, 651.
3. Quoted by Justice Jackson, *Douglas v. City of Jeannette*, 319 U.S. 157 at 171 (1943).
4. Ibid.
5. Robert F. Cushman, *Cases in Civil Liberties*, 2d ed. (Englewood Cliffs, N.J.: Prentice-Hall, 1976), 305.
6. *Lovell v. Griffin*, 303 U.S. 444 (1938); *Cantwell v. Connecticut*, 310 U.S. 296 (1940).
7. *Martin v. City of Struthers*, 319 U.S. 141 (1943); *West Virginia State Board of Education v. Barnette*, 319 U.S. 624 (1943), overruling *Minersville School District v. Gobitis*, 310 U.S. 586 (1940); *Murdock v. Pennsylvania*, 319 U.S. 105 (1943), overruling *Jones v. Opelika*, 316 U.S. 584 (1942).

ments a shadow of prohibition of the exercise of religion or of abridgement of the freedom of speech or the press. It is prohibition and unjustifiable abridgement which is interdicted, not taxation.[19]

The following year, Justice James F. Byrnes, who had voted with the majority, resigned and was replaced by Wiley B. Rutledge, a liberal. The Court decided to consider the license fee issue a second time and this time struck it down, again 5-4.

The case generating the reversal concerned a Jeannette, Pennsylvania, ordinance that placed a tax of $1.50 a day on the privilege of door-to-door solicitation. It also required all persons taking orders for or delivering goods door-to-door to obtain a license from the city.

Without obtaining such a license, Jehovah's Witnesses went from house to house in the town soliciting new members. They requested "contributions" of specific amounts from persons showing an interest in their books and pamphlets but on occasion gave the literature free of charge to residents who were unable to pay. Arrested and convicted of violating the ordinance, the Witnesses claimed it unconstitutionally restricted their religious liberty.

"A state may not impose a charge for the enjoyment of a right granted by the federal constitution," the majority said in *Murdock v. Pennsylvania* (1943), overruling its decision in *Jones v. Opelika*.[20]

The majority held that because Jehovah's Witnesses believe that each Witness is a minister ordained by God to preach the gospel, the license fee constituted a tax on the free exercise of religion. Soliciting new adherents by personal visitation and the sale of religious tracts was an evangelical activity that "occupies the same high estate under the First Amendment as do worship in the churches and preaching from the pulpits," the five justices wrote.[21]

Unlike the majority in *Opelika*, this majority did not hold that the commercial aspects of religious solicitation deprived it of its First Amendment protection:

[T]he mere fact that the religious literature is "sold" by itinerant preachers rather than "donated" does not transform evangelism into a commercial enterprise. If it did, then the passing of the collection plate in church would make the church service a commercial project. The constitutional rights of those spreading their religious beliefs through the spoken and printed word are not to be gauged by standards governing retailers or wholesalers of books.... It is plain that a religious organization needs funds to remain a going concern. But an itinerant evangelist, however misguided or intolerant he may be, does not become a mere book agent by selling the Bible or religious tracts to help defray his expenses or to sustain him. Freedom of speech, freedom of the press, freedom of religion are available to all, not merely to those who can pay their own way.[22]

Almost forty years later, the Court in 1981 addressed a First Amendment challenge by the Hare Krishna sect to a Minnesota state fair rule that required all persons seeking to sell literature or solicit funds at the fair to do so from a fixed booth. In *Heffron v. International Society for Krishna Consciousness* the Court held that this rule was reasonable in light of the state's interest in maintaining order in a public place and that it was not an abridgement of the sect's freedom to exercise their religion. A few months later in 1981, similar considerations of evenhand-

edness were evident as the Court held in *Widmar v. Vincent* that a state university must grant the same access to university buildings to a recognized student group that wishes to hold religious meetings as it does to any recognized group that wishes to meet for any reason.[23]

Religion and Political Duty

Under what circumstances may government compel a person to set aside or subordinate his or her religious beliefs in order to fulfill some officially imposed duty? The Supreme Court generally has upheld statutes aimed clearly at maintaining or improving the public health and welfare even if those laws indirectly infringe on religious liberty.

In 1905 a state law requiring compulsory vaccination against smallpox was sustained against such a challenge, brought by Seventh Day Adventists opposed to it on religious grounds. The Court ruled in *Jacobson v. Massachusetts* that the legislature had acted reasonably to require vaccination in order to suppress a disease that threatened the entire population.[24]

The Supreme Court, however, has remained silent on the question whether the state can force a person to accept medical treatment, including blood transfusions, if such treatment would violate religious beliefs. Although a number of well-publicized cases have arisen in lower courts, the Supreme Court so far has chosen not to adjudicate the issue.

In several instances the Court has determined that the government's interest in imposing a duty upon individual citizens is not great enough to warrant the intrusion on free exercise of religion. Two of the Court's early decisions on this issue illustrate the shifting weights accorded government interests and religious liberty in different situations.

In the 1925 case of *Pierce v. Society of Sisters*, the Court ruled that Oregon could not constitutionally compel all school children to attend public schools. Such compulsion violated the liberty of parents to direct the upbringing of their children, a liberty which includes the right to send children to parochial schools. But in 1934 the Court held that a college student's conscientious objection to war did not excuse him from attending mandatory classes in military science and tactics at the University of California.[25]

Flag Salute Cases - I

By far the most dramatic cases to pose the question of government compulsion versus religious liberty involved school children and the American flag. Could government demand that children be forced to salute the American flag against their religious beliefs? These cases arose as Europe and then the United States entered World War II.

Lillian and William Gobitis, aged twelve and ten, were expelled from a Minersville, Pennsylvania, school in 1936 for refusing to participate in daily flag salute ceremonies. The children were Jehovah's Witnesses who had been taught not to worship any graven image.

Their parents appealed to the local school board to make an exception for their children to the flag salute requirement. When the school board refused, the parents placed the children in a private school and then sued to recover the additional school costs and to stop the school board from requiring the flag salute as a condition for attendance in the public schools.

A federal district Court in Philadelphia and then the Court of appeals upheld the parents' position. The school board appealed to the Supreme Court.

On three earlier occasions the Supreme Court in brief, unsigned opinions had dismissed challenges to flag salute requirements, saying that they posed no substantial federal question. But in each of those cases the result of the dismissal was to sustain the requirement.[26] A dismissal of the Gobitis case would have left the lower court decisions in place, striking down the requirement.

The Court granted review, and the case of *Minersville School District v. Gobitis* was argued in the spring of 1940. The Gobitis children were represented by attorneys for the American Civil Liberties Union; a "friend of the court" brief was filed by the American Bar Association in their behalf.

The Supreme Court voted 8-1, however, to reverse the lower courts and sustain the flag salute requirement. Religious liberty must give way to political authority, wrote Justice Felix Frankfurter for the majority, at least so long as that authority was not used directly to promote or restrict religion.

"Certainly the affirmative pursuit of one's convictions about the ultimate mystery of the universe and man's relation to it is placed beyond the reach of the law," he wrote. On the other hand, he said, the "mere possession of religious convictions which contradict the relevant concerns of a political society does not relieve the citizen from the discharge of political responsibilities."[27]

Was the flag salute a relevant political concern? Frankfurter sidestepped the question, writing that national unity was the basis for national security and that the Court should defer to the local determination that a compulsory flag salute was an effective means of creating that unity:

The influences which help toward a common feeling for the common country are manifold. Some may seem harsh and others no doubt are foolish. Surely, however, the end is legitimate. And the effective means for its attainment are still so uncertain and so unauthenticated by science as to preclude us from putting the widely prevalent belief in flag-saluting beyond the pale of legislative power. It mocks reason and denies our whole history to find in the allowance of a requirement to salute our flag on fitting occasions the seeds of sanction for obeisance to a leader.

The wisdom of training children in patriotic impulses by those compulsions which necessarily pervade so much of the educational process is not for our independent judgment.[28]

Though the members of the Court might find "that the deepest patriotism is best engendered by giving unfettered scope to the most crotchety beliefs," it was not for the Court but for the school board to determine that granting the Gobitis children an exemption from the salute "might cast doubts in the minds of other children which would themselves weaken the effect of the exercise," Frankfurter wrote.[29]

Only Justice Stone dissented, choosing religious liberty over political authority. The compulsory salute, Stone said,

does more than suppress freedom of speech and more than prohibit the free exercise of religion, which concededly are forbidden by the First Amendment.... For by this law the state seeks to coerce these children to express a sentiment which, as they interpret it, they

Religion and War

Since it instituted compulsory conscription in 1917, Congress has exempted from military service those persons who object to war for religious reasons. In 1917 the exemption was relatively narrow, extending only to adherents of a "well-recognized religious sect or organization ... whose existing creed or principles [forbid] its members to participate in war in any form."

Congress expanded the exemption in 1940 to any persons who "by reason of their religious training and belief are conscientiously opposed to participation in war in any form." In 1948 Congress defined "religious training and belief" to mean "an individual's belief in a relation to a Supreme Being involving duties superior to those arising from any human relation but [not including] essentially political, sociological, or philosophical views or a merely personal moral code."

In 1965 this definition was challenged as discriminating against those persons holding strong "religious" convictions but not believing in a Supreme Being in the orthodox sense. The Supreme Court sidestepped the issue by interpreting Congress's definition very broadly. The "test of belief 'in a relation to a Supreme Being' is whether a given belief that is sincere and meaningful occupies a place in the life of its possessor parallel to that filled by the orthodox belief in God of one who clearly qualifies for exemption," the Court said in *United States v. Seeger*.[1]

In 1970 the Court construed the exemption to include persons who objected to all war on moral and ethical grounds. To come within the meaning of the law, wrote Justice Hugo L. Black for the Court in *Welsh v. United States*, opposition to the war must "stem from the registrant's moral, ethical, or religious beliefs about what is right and wrong and ... these beliefs [must] be held with the strength of traditional religious convictions."[2]

But the Supreme Court rejected a contention that conscription unconstitutionally infringed on the religious liberty of those opposed to a particular war as unjust. The Court acknowledged that this ruling impinged on those religions that counseled their members to refuse participation in unjust wars but to fight in those that were just. But the Court said that Congress had acted reasonably and neutrally when it decided that the danger of infringing religious liberty did not outweigh the government interest in maintaining a fairly administered draft service; fairness would be threatened by the difficulty of separating sincere conscientious objectors from fraudulent claimants.[3]

1. *United States v. Seeger*, 380 U.S. 163 at 165-166 (1965).
2. *Welsh v. United States*, 398 U.S. 333 at 340 (1970).
3. *Gillette v. United States*, 401 U.S. 437 (1971).

do not entertain, and which violates their deepest religious convictions.[30]

Moreover, Stone said the school board could have found ways to instill patriotism in its students without compelling an affirmation some students were unwilling to give:

The very essence of the liberty which they [the First and Fourteenth Amendments] guaranty is the freedom of the individual from compulsion as to what he shall think and what he shall say, at least where the compulsion is to bear false witness to his religion. If these guaranties are to have any meaning they must, I think, be deemed to withhold from the state any authority to compel belief or the expression of it where that expression violates religious convictions, whatever may be the legislative view of the desirability of such compulsion.[31]

The majority's reluctance to review legislative judgment was in this case "no more than the surrender of the constitutional protection of the liberty of small minorities to the popular will," Stone said.[32]

The press and the legal profession responded unfavorably to the decision. One commentator noted that more than 170 leading newspapers condemned the decision while only a few supported it.[33] Law review articles almost universally opposed it.

Two years after the *Gobitis* decision, Justices Douglas, Hugo L. Black, and Frank Murphy announced in a dissent from the majority's holding in an unrelated case that they had changed their minds about compulsory flag salutes.

In *Jones v. Opelika* (1942), the majority upheld a statute imposing peddler's fees on Jehovah's Witnesses selling religious publications door to door. Dissenting from this decision as an unconstitutional suppression of the free exercise of religion, Black, Douglas, and Murphy described the majority position as a logical extension of the principles in the *Gobitis* ruling. They wrote:

Since we joined in the opinion in the *Gobitis* case, we think this is an appropriate occasion to state that we now believe that it was ... wrongly decided. Certainly our democratic form of government functioning under the historic Bill of Rights has a high responsibility to accommodate itself to the religious views of minorities however unpopular and unorthodox those views may be. The First Amendment does not put the right freely to exercise religion in a subordinate position. We fear, however, that the opinion in these and in the *Gobitis* case do exactly that.[34]

Flag Salute Cases - II

This reversal of position and the appointment in 1943 of Justice Rutledge, a libertarian with well-established views favoring freedom of religion, indicated that at least four justices might join now-Chief Justice Stone in overruling *Gobitis* if the flag salute issue were reconsidered. That opportunity arose in 1943.

The case in which the Court overturned *Gobitis* was *West Virginia State Board of Education v. Barnette.* After the *Gobitis* decision, the West Virginia Board of Education required all schools to make flag salutes part of their daily routine in which all teachers and pupils must participate. Not only would children be expelled if they refused to salute the flag, they would be declared "unlawfully absent"

from school and subject to delinquent proceedings. Parents of such children were subject to fine and imprisonment. Several families of Jehovah's Witnesses affected by this decree sued for an injunction to stop its enforcement. The federal district court agreed to issue the injunction and the state school board appealed that decision directly to the Supreme Court.

By a 6-3 vote the Supreme Court upheld the lower federal court and reversed *Gobitis*. Writing the opinion, which was announced on Flag Day 1943, Justice Jackson rejected the *Gobitis* view that the courts should defer to the legislative judgment in this matter. "The very purpose of a Bill of Rights was to withdraw certain subjects from the vicissitudes of political controversy, to place them beyond the reach of majorities and officials and to establish them as legal principles to be applied by the courts," he said.[35]

Jackson then turned to the heart of the issue. "National unity as an end which officials may foster by persuasion and example is not in question," he wrote. "The problem is whether under our Constitution compulsion as here employed is a permissible means for its achievement." Jackson's answer was negative. "Compulsory unification of opinion achieves only the unanimity of the graveyard."[36]

For Jackson the issues raised by the compulsory flag salute reached beyond questions of religious liberty to broader concerns for the individual's personal liberty. In one of the most elegant and eloquent passages in Supreme Court history, he wrote:

The case is made difficult not because the principles of its decision are obscure but because the flag involved is our own. Nevertheless, we apply the limitations of the Constitution with no fear that freedom to be intellectually and spiritually diverse or even contrary will disintegrate the social organization. To believe that patriotism will not flourish if patriotic ceremonies are voluntary and spontaneous instead of a compulsory routine is to make an unflattering estimate of the appeal of our institutions to free minds. We can have intellectual individualism and the rich cultural diversities that we owe to exceptional minds only at the price of occasional eccentricity and abnormal attitudes. When they are so harmless to others or to the State as those we deal with here, the price is not too great. But freedom to differ is not limited to things that do not matter much. That would be a mere shadow of freedom. The test of its substance is the right to differ as to things that touch the heart of the existing order.

If there is any fixed star in our constitutional constellation, it is that no official, high or petty, can prescribe what shall be orthodox in politics, nationalism, religion or other matters of opinion or force citizens to confess by word or act their faith therein. If there are any circumstances which permit an exception, they do not now occur to us.[37]

In dissent, Justices Owen J. Roberts and Stanley F. Reed simply stated that they agreed with the majority opinion in *Gobitis*.

But Justice Frankfurter's dissent rivaled Jackson's majority opinion in eloquence. Insisting that the majority had failed to exercise proper judicial restraint, Frankfurter maintained that it was within the constitutional authority of the state school board to demand that public school children salute the American flag. Reading the majority a lecture on their duties as interpreters of the Constitution, Frankfurter began with an unusual personal reference to his own heritage:

> One who belongs to the most vilified and persecuted minority in history is not likely to be insensible to the freedoms guaranteed by our Constitution. Were my purely personal attitude relevant I should wholeheartedly associate myself with the general libertarian views in the Court's opinion, representing as they do the thought and action of a lifetime. But as judges we are neither Jew nor Gentile, neither Catholic nor agnostic. . . . As a member of this Court I am not justified in writing my private notions of policy into the Constitution, no matter how deeply I may cherish them or how mischievous I may deem their disregard. The duty of a judge who must decide which of two claims before the Court shall prevail, that of a State to enact and enforce laws within its general competence or that of an individual to refuse obedience because of the demands of his conscience, is not that of an ordinary person. It can never be emphasized too much that one's own opinion about the wisdom or evil of a law should be excluded altogether when one is doing one's duty on the bench. The only opinion of our own even looking in that direction that is material is our opinion whether legislators could in reason have enacted such a law. In the light of all the circumstances, including the history of this question in this Court, it would require more daring than I possess to deny that reasonable legislators could have taken the action which is before us for review. . . . I cannot bring my mind to believe that the "liberty" secured by the Due Process Clause gives this Court the authority to deny to the State of West Virginia the attainment of that which we all recognize as a legitimate legislative end, namely, the promotion of good citizenship, by employment of the means here chosen.[38]

Saturdays and Sundays

In 1961 the Court set out the modern rule for determining when a state may properly compel obedience to a secular law that conflicts with religious beliefs.

The rule was stated as the Court upheld the validity of Sunday closing laws, challenged as restricting the free exercise of religion. That claim was raised by an Orthodox Jew who observed the Jewish Sabbath, closing his clothing and furniture store on Saturday. To make up the lost revenue, he opened the store on Sunday. When Pennsylvania enacted a Sunday closing law in 1959, he challenged its constitutionality.

The Supreme Court found that the law did not violate the First Amendment. Sunday closing of commercial enterprises was an effective means for achieving the valid state purpose of providing citizens with a uniform day of rest. Although it operated indirectly to make observance of certain religious practices more expensive, the Sunday closing law did not make any religious practice illegal, the majority observed in *Braunfeld v. Brown* (1961).

The Court then announced the rule for judging whether a state law unconstitutionally restricts the exercise of religious liberty:

> If the purpose or effect of a law is to impede the observance of one or all religions or is to discriminate invidiously between religions, that law is constitution-

ally invalid even though the burden may be characterized as being only indirect. But if the State regulates conduct by enacting a general law within its power, the purpose and effect of which is to advance the State's secular goals, the statute is valid despite its indirect burden on religious observance unless the State may accomplish its purpose by means which do not impose such a burden.[39]

Unemployment Compensation

Two years later the Court significantly modified *Braunfeld* by declaring that only a compelling state interest could justify limitations on religious liberty.

Sherbert v. Verner (1963) arose after Adell Sherbert was fired from her South Carolina textile mill job because, as a Seventh-Day Adventist, she refused to work on Saturdays. Because she refused available work, the state denied her unemployment compensation benefits.

Overturning the state ruling by a 7-2 vote, the Court, speaking through Justice William J. Brennan, Jr., explained that the state's action forced Sherbert either to abandon her religious principles in order to work, or to maintain her religious precepts and forfeit unemployment compensation benefits. "Governmental imposition of such a choice puts the same kind of burden upon the free exercise of religion as would a fine imposed against appellant for her Saturday worship," Brennan wrote.[40]

Brennan contended that the state could limit the exercise of an individual's religion only for a compelling state interest. "Only the gravest abuses, endangering paramount interests, give occasion for permissible limitation," he said. Prevention of fraudulent claims was the only reason the state advanced for denying benefits to Sherbert, Brennan noted. To justify that denial, he wrote, the state must show that it cannot prevent such fraud by means that are less restrictive of religious liberty.[41]

In dissent, Justices John Marshall Harlan and Byron R. White held that the Court should have abided by its *Braunfeld* rule. Unemployment compensation was intended to help people when there was no work available, not to aid those who, for whatever reason, refused available work. Maintenance of such a distinction was a valid goal of the state, which affected religion only indirectly, they said.

Twice in the mid-1980s the Court reaffirmed *Sherbert*, holding that a state could not deny employment benefits to a man who quit his job because his religion forbade his participation in weapons production, or to a woman—like Sherbert—fired because she would not work on her Sabbath. On the other hand, the Court has also set limits to state action protecting the right of workers to have their Sabbath off from work. In 1985 the Court in *Thornton v. Caldor Inc.*, ruled unconstitutional a state law giving all employees the right to refuse with impunity to work on their Sabbath. By giving those workers that right, the state gave religious concerns priority over all others in setting work schedules and thereby advanced religion, the Court held.[42]

Compulsory School Attendance

The *Sherbert* ruling was reinforced earlier by the Court's 1972 decision in *Wisconsin v. Yoder*. Old Order Amish parents refused to send their children to school beyond grade eight; this violated Wisconsin's law compelling all children to attend school until they reached age 16. The parents asserted that high school education engendered values contrary to Amish beliefs, which hold that salvation may be obtained only by living in religious, agrarian communities separate from the world and worldly influences.

Expert witnesses testified that compulsory high school education might result not only in psychological harm to Amish children confused by trying to fit into two different worlds, but also in destruction of the Amish community. Despite this testimony, the Wisconsin trial and appeals courts upheld compulsory attendance as a reasonable and constitutional means of promoting a valid state interest.

The state supreme court reversed, ruling that the state had not shown that its interest in compelling attendance was sufficient to justify the infringement on the free exercise of religion. The Supreme Court affirmed that holding.

Chief Justice Burger wrote the Court's opinion. He acknowledged that the provision of public schools was one of the primary functions of the state. But, he added:

> a state's interest in universal education, however highly we rank it, is not totally free from a balancing process when it impinges on fundamental rights and interests, such as those specifically protected by the Free Exercise Clause of the First Amendment, and the traditional interest of parents with respect to the religious upbringing of their children so long as they ... "prepare [them] for additional obligations." [43]

The Court accepted the evidence showing that the traditional Amish community life was based on convictions that would be weakened by forcing teenage children into public schools. The Court also noted that the Amish provided their children with alternative modes of vocational education that accommodated all the interests the state advanced in support of its compulsory attendance law.

Religion and Oath-Taking

Article VI of the Constitution states that "no religious Test shall ever be required as a Qualification to any Office or public Trust under the United States." The Supreme Court in 1961 ruled that under the First Amendment, states are prohibited from requiring religious test oaths.

Ray Torcaso, appointed a notary public in Maryland, was denied his commission when he refused to declare his belief in God, a part of the oath notaries public were required by Maryland law to take. Torcaso sued, challenging the oath as abridging his religious liberty.

A unanimous Supreme Court struck down the oath requirement in *Torcaso v. Watkins* (1961). Justice Black wrote:

> We repeat and again affirm that neither a State nor the Federal Government can constitutionally force a person "to profess a belief or disbelief in any religion." Neither can constitutionally pass laws or impose requirements which aid all religions as against non-believers, and neither can aid those religions based on a belief in the existence of God as against those religions founded on different beliefs. [44]

The Supreme Court in *Torcaso* stated unequivocally that a state may not require a person to swear to a belief he or she does not hold. But may government require a person

to swear a nonreligious oath contrary to religious beliefs? In a series of cases concerning pacifist applicants for U.S. citizenship, the Supreme Court first said yes but then changed its mind.

The naturalization oath requires applicants for citizenship to swear "to support and defend the Constitution and the law of the United States of America against all enemies, foreign and domestic." The naturalization service interpreted this to require that would-be citizens be willing to bear arms in defense of the country. It therefore denied citizenship to two women pacifists and to a fifty-four-year-old Yale Divinity School professor who said he would fight only in wars he believed to be morally justified.

Although the three were qualified in every other way to be citizens and were extremely unlikely ever to be called into active service, the Court upheld the naturalization service's position as reasonable in 1929 in *United States v. Schwimmer* and again in 1931. [45]

Following World War II, the Court reconsidered and reversed these holdings. Again the majority did not reach the constitutional issue but dealt only with the statutory interpretation of the oath.

Girouard v. United States (1946) concerned a Canadian Seventh-Day Adventist who agreed to serve as a noncombatant in the armed forces but refused to bear arms because killing conflicted with his religious beliefs. The majority noted that the oath did not expressly require naturalized citizens to swear to bear arms and ruled that this interpretation need not be read into the oath. Congress, the majority said, could not have intended to deny citizenship in a country noted for its protection of religious beliefs to persons whose religious beliefs prevented them from bearing arms. [46]

The year before it overruled its early decisions in the pacifist naturalization cases, the Supreme Court upheld the Illinois bar's decision to deny admission to an attorney because its required oath conflicted with his beliefs. [47]

That decision has never been overruled, but its effect has been weakened by subsequent decisions. Among the more recent of these was the Court's 1978 ruling in *McDaniel v. Paty* in which the Court struck down as unconstitutional a Tennessee law that forbade clergymen to hold state offices. [48]

Writing the Court's opinion, Chief Justice Burger relied on *Sherbert* as precedent, saying that the state law unconstitutionally restricted the right of free exercise of religion by making it conditional on a willingness to give up the right to seek public office. [49]

Justices Potter Stewart, Thurgood Marshall, and Brennan used *Torcaso* as precedent, and Marshall and Brennan held that the law also violated the establishment clause. [50] Justice White held that the law denied clergymen equal protection of the laws.

ESTABLISHMENT
OF RELIGION

The establishment clause of the First Amendment prohibits Congress from making any law "respecting an establishment of religion." This has been interpreted to mean not only that Congress cannot designate a national church but also that it cannot act to give any direct support to religion.

There is considerable disagreement over how absolutely the two men most responsible for the establishment clause viewed it. Many agree with constitutional expert C. Herman Pritchett, who has written that Thomas Jefferson and James Madison thought that the prohibition of establishment meant that a presidential proclamation of Thanksgiving Day was just as improper as a tax exemption for churches. Others, however, most notably political science professor Robert L. Cord take issue with this view. Cord points out that Madison as president issued at least four Thanksgiving Day proclamations, and Jefferson as president signed an 1802 Act of Congress providing a tax exemption for churches in Alexandria County.[51]

The Supreme Court, which specifically declared the establishment clause applicable to the states in 1947, has never adopted the absolutist position. In its first decision on the clause, the Court sustained a federal construction grant to a Roman Catholic hospital. The Court held that the hospital's purpose was secular and that it did not discriminate among its patients on the basis of religion. The aid therefore only indirectly benefited the church.[52]

Since that decision in 1899, most of the Court's establishment cases have arisen in the areas of taxation and education. The Court has sustained the practice of exempting churches from taxes on the grounds that to tax them would be to entangle government excessively with religion. For much the same reason, the Court has also declined to review legal questions involving controversies within churches.

The Court has barred religious exercises in tax-supported public schools as unconstitutional government advancement of religion. Prayer recitations, Bible readings, and religious instruction, when denominational, favor one religion over others; when nondenominational, they favor all religion over nonreligious beliefs, the Court has said.

The Court, however, has adopted what it describes as a "benevolent neutrality" toward government financial aid to parochial schools. If the aid is secular in its purpose and effect and does not entangle the government excessively in its administration, it is permissible, even if it indirectly benefits the church schools.

Not all justices agree, however, on what aid is secular and what is not. For example, a majority of the Court continues to hold that state textbook loan programs to parochial schools are proper. But a minority insists that because textbooks are essential to the business of teaching, their loan to church-affiliated schools is an unconstitutional establishment of religion.

Tax Exemptions

Historically, the federal government, every state, and the District of Columbia have exempted churches from paying property and income taxes. In 1970 the Supreme Court sustained these exemptions by an 8-1 vote. The case, *Walz v. Tax Commission,* arose when a property owner in New York challenged the state's property tax exemption for religious institutions as an establishment of religion. He contended that the exemption meant that nonexempt property owners made an involuntary contribution to churches.

Internal Church Disputes

The Supreme Court has been reluctant to involve itself in the internal disputes that occasionally arise within churches. Where judicial intervention is unavoidable, the Court has insisted that courts decline to resolve doctrinal questions.

This rule was first developed in *Watson v. Jones* (1872), a dispute over church property between a national church organization and local churches that had withdrawn from the national hierarchy. The case was decided on common law grounds, but had First Amendment overtones:

All who unite themselves to [the central church] do so with an implied consent to [its] government, and are bound to submit to it. But it would be a vain consent, and would lead to the total subversion of such religious bodies, if anyone aggrieved by one of their decisions could appeal to the secular courts and have [it] reversed.[1]

In 1952 the Supreme Court said that the First Amendment gave religious organizations an "independence from secular control or manipulations—in short, power to decide for themselves, free from state interference, matters of church government as well as those of faith and doctrine."[2]

In 1969 the Court again held that both religion clauses forbid interference with doctrine:

First Amendment values are plainly jeopardized when church property litigation is made to turn on the resolution by civil courts of controversies over religious doctrine and practice. If civil courts undertake to resolve such controversies ... the hazards are ever present of inhibiting the free development of religious doctrine and of implicating secular interests in matters of purely ecclesiastical concern.... The Amendment therefore commands civil courts to decide church property disputes without resolving underlying controversies over religious doctrines.[3]

The judicial role is therefore limited to examining the church rules and determining that they have been applied appropriately. Justice Louis D. Brandeis wrote, "In the absence of fraud, collusion, or arbitrariness, the decisions of the proper church tribunals on matters purely ecclesiastical, although affecting civil rights, are accepted in litigation before the secular courts as conclusive."[4]

1. *Watson v. Jones,* 13 Wall. 679 at 728-29 (1872).
2. *Kedroff v. St. Nicholas Cathedral,* 344 U.S. 94 at 116 (1952); see also *Kreshik v. St. Nicholas Cathedral,* 363 U.S. 190 (1960).
3. *Presbyterian Church in the United States v. Mary Elizabeth Blue Hull Memorial Presbyterian Church,* 393 U.S. 440 at 449 (1969).
4. *Gonzalez v. Archbishop,* 280 U.S. 1 at 16 (1929).

Writing for the majority, Chief Justice Burger observed that churches were only one of several institutions—including hospitals, libraries, and historical and patriotic organizations—exempted from paying property taxes. Such exemptions reflected the state's decision that these groups provided beneficial and stabilizing influences in the community and that their activities might be hampered or destroyed by the need to pay property taxes. "We cannot read New York's statute as attempting to establish religion," Burger wrote; "it is simply sparing the exercise of religion from the burden of property taxation levied on private profit institutions." [53]

Thus the exemption met the existing test for determining whether government policy constituted improper establishment of religion. Both the purpose and effect of the exemption were primarily secular, having only an indirect benefit to religion.

But to this test, the Court in *Walz* added a new one: whether the exemption resulted in excessive government involvement with religion. To answer this question, Burger said the Court must consider whether taxing the property would result in more or less entanglement than continuing the exemption.

Observing that taxation would require government valuation of church property, and possibly tax liens and foreclosures, Burger concluded that the "hazards of churches supporting government are hardly less in their potential than the hazards of government supporting churches." Tax exemption, on the other hand, created "only a minimal and remote involvement between church and state.... It restricts the fiscal relationship between church and state, and tends to complement and reinforce the desired separation insulating each from the other." [54]

As churches have moved into quasi-business areas in recent years, the tax question has returned to the Court in several new ways. In 1981 the Court ruled unanimously that church-run elementary and secondary schools were exempt from paying federal or state unemployment taxes. Four years later, however, the Court made clear that this exemption did not extend so far as to protect commercial enterprises of churches from minimum wage, overtime, and recordkeeping requirements of federal labor law. [55]

Religion and Public Schools

"We are a religious people whose institutions presuppose a Supreme Being," wrote Justice Douglas in 1952. [56]

The nation's governmental institutions reflect this belief daily. Each session of the House and Senate opens with a prayer. The Supreme Court begins its sessions with an invocation asking that "God save the United States and this honorable Court." Our currency proclaims, "In God We Trust," and we acknowledge that we are "one nation, under God," each time we recite the pledge of allegiance. These official and public affirmations of religious belief have not escaped legal challenge, but the Supreme Court has dismissed most of them summarily. In 1983 the Court for the first time gave full consideration to a challenge to a state legislature's practice of opening sessions with a prayer. The Court upheld it, finding that it dated back to the First Congress of the United States, the one that also adopted the First Amendment and had "become part of the fabric of our society." [57]

Earlier, the Court refused to review a lower court decision that held that despite inclusion of the phrase "under God" in the pledge of allegiance, the First Amendment did not bar the New York Education Commission from recommending that the pledge be recited in schools. In 1971 the Court declined to stop astronauts from praying on television for God's blessing for a successful trip to the moon. In the same ruling, the lower court had rejected a challenge to the phrase "So help me God" contained in the oath witnesses are required to take in many courts. And in 1979 the Court refused to review a challenge to the words "In God We Trust" on currency. [58]

Although the Court has not proscribed government-sponsored public expression of religious belief on the part of adults, it has flatly prohibited states from requiring or permitting religious exercises by children in public elementary and secondary schools.

Released Time

The first two Supreme Court rulings concerning religious exercises in public schools involved "released time" programs. Employed by school districts across the country, these programs released students from regular classwork, usually once a week, to receive religious instruction. In some cases the students received the instruction in their regular classrooms; sometimes they met in another schoolroom; at other times they met in churches or synagogues. Students participated in the programs voluntarily. Students who did not participate had a study period during the time religious instruction was given.

The first of the released time cases was *Illinois ex rel. McCollum v. Board of Education* (1948). The Champaign, Illinois, school board operated a released time program in which religion teachers came into the public schools once a week to give one half-hour of religious instruction to voluntary participants. The program was challenged as a violation of the First Amendment's establishment clause by the atheist mother of a fifth grader, the only pupil in his class who did not participate in the program.

By an 8-1 vote, the Supreme Court declared the program unconstitutional. "Pupils compelled by law to go to school for secular education are released in part from their legal duty upon the condition that they attend religious classes," wrote Justice Black for the majority. "This is beyond all question a utilization of the tax-established and tax-supported public school system to aid religious groups to spread their faith." [59]

Four justices concurred separately. Not only did the program violate the establishment clause by tending to advance certain religions over others, they said, it also threatened to impede the free exercise of religion. Justice Frankfurter explained:

Religious education so conducted on school time and property is patently woven into the working scheme of the school. The Champaign arrangement thus presents powerful elements of inherent pressure by the school system in the interest of religious sects.... That a child is offered an alternative may reduce the constraint; it does not eliminate the operation of influence by the school in matters sacred to conscience and outside the school's domain. The law of imitation operates, and nonconformity is not an outstanding characteristic of children. The result is an obvious pressure upon children to attend. Again, while the Champaign school population represents only a fraction of the more than two hundred and fifty sects of the nation, not even all the practicing sects in Champaign are willing or able to provide religious instruction.... As a result, the public school system of Champaign actively furthers inculcation in the religious tenets of some faiths, and in the process sharpens the consciousness of religious differences at least among some of the children committed to its care.[60]

Four years later the Court upheld New York City's released time program, in which religious instruction was given during the school day but not in the public schools. In *Zorach v. Clausen* (1952), the Court held, by a 6-3 vote, that this program did not violate the establishment clause. "The First Amendment ... does not say that in every and all respects there shall be a separation of Church and State," wrote Justice Douglas, noting that governments provided churches with general services such as police and fire protection and that public officials frequently said prayers before undertaking their official chores.[61]

The New York program did not significantly aid religion; it simply required that the public schools "accommodate" a program of outside religious instruction. Government, continued Douglas,

> may not coerce anyone to attend church, to observe a religious holiday, or to take religious instruction. But it can close its doors or suspend its operations as to those who want to repair to their religious sanctuary for worship or instruction. No more than that is undertaken here.[62]

Justices Black, Frankfurter, and Jackson held that the program was coercive and a direct aid to religion.

School Prayer

A decade after *Zorach,* the Supreme Court set off an intense new round of controversy over church and state matters with its decisions banning school prayer and Bible reading as regular devotional exercises in public schools. Such exercises, often coupled with recitation of the pledge of allegiance, were common occurrences in classrooms across the country.

As early as 1930 the Supreme Court dismissed for lack of a federal question a state court's refusal to direct the state school superintendent to require Bible reading in public schools. The question of Bible readings in public schools came to the Court again in 1952, but it again dismissed the suit, this time because the parents of the child involved no longer had standing to sue.[63]

Another ten years passed before the Court directly confronted the issue of the constitutionality of devotional practices in public schools. The case of *Engel v. Vitale* arose after New York's State Board of Regents recommended to school districts that they adopt a specified nondenominational prayer to be repeated voluntarily by students at the beginning of each school day. The brief prayer read: "Almighty God, we acknowledge our dependence upon Thee, and we beg Thy blessings upon us, our parents, our teachers, and our country."

The prayer was not universally adopted throughout the state. New York City, for example, chose instead to have its students recite the verse of the hymn "America" that asks God's protection for the country.

The school board of New Hyde Park, New York, adopted the recommended prayer. Parents of ten pupils in the school district, with the support of the New York Civil Liberties Union, brought suit, claiming that the prayer was contrary to their religious beliefs and practices and that its adoption and use violated the establishment clause. The state courts upheld the prayer on the condition that no student be compelled to participate.

Evolution or Creation?

One of the most celebrated trials in American history took place in 1925. John Scopes was convicted and fined $100 for teaching the Darwinian theory of evolution in violation of a Tennessee law that made it illegal to teach anything other than a literal Biblical theory of human creation. Scopes's conviction was reversed by the state supreme court, but the statute was left standing and was never challenged before the U.S. Supreme Court.[1]

Decades later the Supreme Court ruled twice on this issue. In *Epperson v. Arkansas* a public school biology teacher challenged a state law that forbade teachers in state-supported schools from teaching or using textbooks that teach "the theory or doctrine that mankind ascended or descended from a lower order of animals."

The Supreme Court unanimously held this law in violation of the First Amendment. "Arkansas law selects from the body of knowledge a particular segment which it proscribes for the sole reason that it is deemed to conflict with a particular religious doctrine; that is, with a particular interpretation of the Book of Genesis by a particular religious group," held the Court.[2]

In 1987 the Court, 7-2, held that Louisiana violated the First Amendment when it required that any public school teacher who taught evolution must also give equal time to teaching "creation-science." Writing for the majority in *Edwards v. Aguillard,* Justice William J. Brennan, Jr., explained that it was clear that the purpose of the law was "to advance the religious viewpoint that a supernatural being created humankind." [3]

Dissenting were Chief Justice William H. Rehnquist and Justice Antonin Scalia, who criticized the Court for presuming the law unconstitutional because "it was supported strongly by organized religions or by adherents of particular faiths.... Political activism by the religiously motivated is part of our heritage," Scalia wrote. "Today's religious activism may give us [this law] ... but yesterday's resulted in the abolition of slavery, and tomorrow's may bring relief for famine victims." [4]

1. *Scopes v. State,* 154 Tenn. 105, 289 S.W. 363 (1927).
2. *Epperson v. Arkansas,* 393 U.S. 97 at 103 (1968).
3. *Edwards v. Aguillard,* __ U.S. __ (1987).
4. Ibid.

The Supreme Court, 6-1, reversed the state courts, holding that this use of the prayer was "wholly inconsistent with the Establishment Clause." In an opinion written by Justice Black, the majority explained its view:

[T]he constitutional prohibition against laws respecting an establishment of religion must at least mean that in this country it is no part of the business of government to compose official prayers for any group of the American people to recite as a part of a religious program carried on by government.[64]

The fact that the prayer was nondenominational and that students who did not wish to participate could remain silent or leave the room did not free the prayer "from the limitations of the Establishment Clause." Black wrote:

The Establishment Clause, unlike the Free Exercise Clause, does not depend upon any showing of direct governmental compulsion and is violated by the enactment of laws which establish an official religion whether those laws operate directly to coerce nonobserving individuals or not. This is not to say, of course, that laws officially prescribing a particular form of religious worship do not involve coercion of such individuals. When the power, prestige and financial support of government is placed behind a particular religious belief, the indirect coercive pressure upon religious minorities to conform to the prevailing officially approved religion is plain.[65]

In response to the argument that the prayer, if an establishment of religion at all, was a relatively insignificant and harmless encroachment, Black quoted Madison, the chief author of the First Amendment:

[I]t is proper to take alarm at the first experiment on our liberties.... Who does not see that the same authority which can establish Christianity, in exclusion of all other Religions, may establish with the same ease any particular sect of Christians, in exclusion of all other Sects?[66]

Asserting that "the Court has misapplied a great constitutional principle," Justice Stewart dissented. "I cannot see how an 'official religion' is established by letting those who want to say a prayer say it," he said.[67] Stewart compared the regents' prayer to other state-sanctioned religious exercises, such as the reference to God in the pledge to the flag, in the president's oath of office, and in the formal opening of each day's session of the Court itself:

I do not believe that this Court, or the Congress, or the President has by the actions and practices I have mentioned established an "official religion" in violation of the Constitution. And I do not believe the State of New York has done so in this case. What each has done has been to recognize and to follow the deeply entrenched and highly cherished spiritual traditions of our Nation—traditions which come down to us from those who almost two hundred years ago avowed their "firm Reliance on the Protection of divine Providence" when they proclaimed the freedom and independence of this brave new world.[68]

Bible Readings

A year later, the Court affirmed its school prayer decision, declaring unconstitutional the practice of daily Bible readings in public school classrooms.

Two cases, *School District of Abington Township v. Schempp* and *Murray v. Curlett,* were considered together. The *Schempp* case concerned a Pennsylvania statute that required the reading of at least ten verses from the Bible each day, followed by recitation of the Lord's Prayer and the pledge to the flag. Pupils were excused from participating at the request of their parents. The Schempps asserted that certain literal Bible readings were contrary to their Unitarian religious beliefs and brought suit to stop the readings. In the *Murray* case, the challenged reading was required not by state law but by a 1905 city rule. Madalyn Murray and her student son, William, were atheists. They contended that the daily religious exercises placed "a premium on belief as against non-belief and subject[ed] their freedom of conscience to the rule of the majority." They asked that the readings be stopped.

By 8-1 the Court held that the Bible readings in both cases were unconstitutional. The readings were clearly religious exercises prescribed as part of the school curriculum for students compelled by law to attend school. They were held in state buildings and supervised by teachers paid by the state. By these actions the state abandoned the neutrality toward religion demanded by the establishment clause. Justice Tom C. Clark wrote for the majority:

The place of religion in our society is an exalted one, achieved through a long tradition of reliance on the home, the church and the inviolable citadel of the individual heart and mind. We have come to recognize through bitter experience that it is not within the power of government to invade that citadel, whether its purpose or effect be to aid or oppose, to advance or retard. In the relationship between man and religion, the State is firmly committed to a position of neutrality.[69]

It was no defense that the Bible reading exercises might be "relatively minor" encroachments on the First Amendment. "The breach of neutrality that is today a trickling stream may all too soon become a raging torrent," Clark wrote.[70] Nor did the ruling set up a "religion of secularism" in the schools. Schools could permit the study of the Bible for its literary and historical merits; they were only prohibited from using the Bible as part of a devotional exercise.

Finally, Clark said that the ruling did not deny the majority its right to the free exercise of religion. "While the Free Exercise Clause clearly prohibits the use of state action to deny the rights of free exercise to *anyone,* it has never meant that a majority could use the machinery of the State to practice its beliefs." [71]

Opposition from the public to the two school prayer decisions ran high, encouraging both chambers of Congress to consider constitutional amendments that would overrule the decisions. Neither the House nor the Senate was able to produce the two-thirds votes needed to send a proposed amendment to the states for ratification.

For well over twenty years, the Court stayed away from school prayer cases. Then in 1985 it took a long, hard look at the new version of school prayer, a "moment-of-silence" law from Alabama. Twenty-three states had passed such laws. They varied in their particulars, but in general, they permitted teachers to set aside a moment in each public school classroom each day for students to engage in quiet meditative activity.

When Alabama's law was challenged, a federal judge—

School Prayer and Congressional Backlash

"The Supreme Court has made God unconstitutional," declared Senator Sam Ervin, D-N.C. (1954-1974), after the Court's school prayer decision in *Engel v. Vitale*.[1]

Members of Congress, governors, even a former president all spoke out in opposition to the decision. And although the ruling was greeted favorably by the Jewish community and many Christian leaders, several clergymen expressed shock. "I am shocked and frightened that the Supreme Court has declared unconstitutional a simple and voluntary declaration of belief in God by public school children," said Francis Cardinal Spellman. "The decision strikes at the very heart of the Godly tradition in which America's children have for so long been raised."[2]

Reaction to the Court's Bible reading decision was equally adverse and outspoken. "Why should the majority be so severely penalized by the protests of a handful?" asked evangelist Billy Graham.[3]

And despite the opposition of most major religious organizations to any constitutional amendment to overturn the rulings, mail advocating such an amendment flooded into congressional offices.

Becker Amendment

Representative Frank J. Becker, R-N.Y. (1953-1965), introduced a proposed constitutional amendment in 1962. It provided that nothing in the Constitution should be interpreted to bar "the offering, reading from, or listening to prayer or biblical scriptures, if participation therein is on a voluntary basis, in any government or public school institution or place."

The House Judiciary Committee took no action on the proposal. Judiciary Committee chairman Emanuel Celler, D-N.Y. (1923-1973), opposed it.

Dirksen Amendment

Despite the lack of congressional action, the school prayer issue did not disappear.

Senate Minority Leader Everett McKinley Dirksen, R-Ill. (1951-1969), proposed in 1966 an amendment stating that the Constitution should not be interpreted to bar any public school authority from providing for or permitting the voluntary participation of students in prayer. His amendment specifically stated that it did not authorize any government official to prescribe the form or content of a prayer.

But the Senate failed, by nine votes, to give the Dirksen amendment the two-thirds vote needed for passage of a constitutional amendment.

Wylie Amendment

For a few years, congressional interest in a school prayer amendment waned. Then, at the urging of a grassroots organization called the Prayer Campaign Committee, Representative Chalmers P. Wylie, R-Ohio, began to circulate another petition among House members to discharge from a still-opposed House Judiciary Committee a proposed amendment similar to the Dirksen amendment. By September 1971 a majority of the House had signed Wylie's petition and the amendment came to the House floor for debate. On November 8, 1971, the amendment failed by 28 votes to win the approval of the necessary two-thirds majority. The vote was 240-162.

1. Quoted in Leo Pfeffer, *Church, State and Freedom*, rev. ed. (Boston: Beacon Press, 1967), 466.
2. Ibid., 467.
3. Quoted in Congressional Quarterly, "Restore Prayers in Schools: The Move that Failed," *Education for a Nation* (Washington, D.C.: Congressional Quarterly, 1972), 38.

in blithe disregard of a half-century of Supreme Court decisions—declared that the First Amendment did not preclude Alabama from establishing a state religion. Although an appeals court reversed that ruling, the state—backed by the Reagan administration—asked the Supreme Court to reinstate the law. The Court refused, 6-3, agreeing with the appeals court that the law violated the establishment clause. Some moment-of-silence laws might pass muster, said Justices Lewis F. Powell, Jr., and Sandra Day O'Connor, but not one that was so clearly just a subterfuge for returning prescribed prayer to the public schools. For the majority in *Wallace v. Jaffree*, Justice John Paul Stevens declared that it was "established principle that the government must pursue a course of complete neutrality toward religion." Chief Justice Burger dissented, joined by Justices White and William H. Rehnquist, who said it was time for the Court to reassess its precedents on this issue.[72]

Two years later in 1987 the Court took up the question of New Jersey's moment-of-silence law, which might have fallen into the category of those laws that passed constitutional examination. But the Court did not address the issue head-on, resolving it on a different issue altogether.[73]

State Aid to Parochial Schools

The first suit challenging state aid to church-related schools reached the Supreme Court in the 1930 case of *Cochran v. Louisiana Board of Education*.[74]

Louisiana furnished all school children in the state, including those attending parochial schools, secular textbooks paid for with public funds. Cochran, a taxpayer, challenged the statute. Because the Court in 1930 had not yet specifically stated that the Fourteenth Amendment incorporated the religious guarantees of the First Amendment, Cochran's contention was that this use of public funds violated the Fourteenth Amendment's prohibition against state action depriving persons of their property without due process of law.

Rejecting this assertion, the Supreme Court adopted the "child benefit" theory, holding that the provision of free textbooks was designed to further the education of all children in the state and not to benefit church-related schools.

The 1947 case of *Everson v. Board of Education,* in which the Court specifically applied the establishment clause to the states, was also the first case in which the Court was required to consider whether the clause barred public aid to church-operated schools. Elaborating on its reasoning in *Cochran,* the Court ruled 5-4 that, while the establishment clause forbade states from aiding religion, it did not prohibit the states from granting aid to all children in the state without regard to their religious beliefs.

Everson concerned a New Jersey statute that permitted local boards of education to reimburse parents for the costs of sending their children to school on public transportation. Arch Everson, a local taxpayer, challenged as an impermissible establishment of religion the reimbursement of parents of parochial school students.

Writing for the majority, Justice Black offered what would become an often quoted description of the meaning of the establishment clause:

> The "establishment of religion" clause of the First Amendment means at least this: Neither a state nor the Federal Government can set up a church. Neither can pass laws which aid one religion, aid all religions or prefer óne religion over another. Neither can force nor influence a person to go to or to remain away from church against his will or force him to profess a belief or disbelief in any religion. No person can be punished for entertaining or professing any religious beliefs or disbeliefs, for church attendance or non-attendance. No tax in any amount, large or small, can be levied to support any religious activities or institutions, whatever they may be called, or whatever form they may adopt to teach or practice religion. Neither a state nor the Federal Government can, openly or secretly, participate in the affairs of any religious organizations or groups and *vice versa.* In the words of Jefferson, the clause against establishment of religion by law was intended to erect "a wall of separation between Church and State." [75]

Having said that, however, the majority proceeded to uphold the New Jersey statute on the ground that it did not aid religion but was instead public welfare legislation benefiting children rather than schools:

> It is undoubtedly true that children are helped to get to church schools. There is even a possibility that some of the children might not be sent to the church schools if the parents were compelled to pay their children's bus fares out of their own pockets when transportation to a public school would have been paid for by the State.... Similarly, parents might be reluctant to permit their children to attend [church] schools which the state had cut off from such general government services as ordinary police and fire protection, connections for sewage disposal, public highways and sidewalks. Of course, cutting off church schools from these services, so separate and so indisputably marked off from the religious function, would make it far more difficult for the schools to operate. But such is obviously not the purpose of the First Amendment. That Amendment requires the state to be a neutral in its relations with groups of religious believers and nonbelievers; it does not require the state to be their adversary. State power is no more to be used so as to handicap religions, than it is to favor them. [76]

For the four dissenters, Justice Rutledge agreed with the majority that the establishment clause "forbids state support, financial or other, of religion in any guise, form or degree. It outlaws all use of public funds for religious purposes." But to cast this particular case in terms of public welfare, as the majority does, is to ignore "the religious factor and its essential connection with the transportation, thereby leaving out the only vital element in the case," said Rutledge. [77]

Publicly supported transportation of parochial school children benefits not only their secular education but also their religious education, Rutledge asserted. In conclusion he wrote:

> Two great drives are constantly in motion to abridge, in the name of education, the complete division of religion and civil authority which our forefathers made. One is to introduce religious education and observances into the public schools. The other, to obtain public funds for the aid and support of various private religious schools.... In my opinion, both avenues were closed by the Constitution. Neither should be opened by this Court. [78]

Textbooks

It was evident from *Everson* that despite Justice Black's extremely broad interpretation of the establishment clause, the line of separation between church and state was, as a later justice would put it, "a blurred, indistinct and variable barrier depending on all the circumstances of a particular relationship." [79]

The Court now needed to devise some criteria for assessing whether state aid to church schools breached that barrier.

In the twenty years between *Everson* and the next state aid case, the Supreme Court decided the school prayer cases, ruling that the establishment clause did not permit public schools to use prayers and Bible reading as part of their daily exercises and that such exercises violated the clause because they were sectarian in purpose and their primary effect was to advance religion.

The Court first applied these guidelines to a question of state aid to church-related schools in the 1968 case of *Board of Education of Central School District No. 1 v. Allen.* The circumstances were similar to those of the *Cochran* case. New York required local school boards to lend text books purchased with public funds to seventh through twelfth grade students, including those attending parochial schools. The New York requirement was challenged as a violation of the establishment clause. The New York Court of Appeals upheld the requirement and, by a 6-3 vote, the Supreme Court agreed.

Writing for the majority, Justice White explained that the purpose of the requirement was secular, to further the educational opportunities of students at both public or private schools. Because the subject matter of the books was secular, the loan program neither advanced nor inhibited religion, White said.

To the claim that books were critical to the teaching process and that the primary goal of parochial schools was to teach religion, White observed that the Court "has long recognized that religious schools pursue two goals, religious instruction and secular education." Without more evidence, White said the majority could not state that "all teaching in a sectarian school is religious or that the processes of secular and religious training are so intertwined that secular textbooks furnished to students by the public are in fact instrumental in the teaching of religion." [80]

The majority also held that the loan program conformed to the *Everson* "child-benefit" precedent. "[N]o funds or books are furnished to parochial schools, and the financial benefit is to parents and children, not to schools," White wrote.[81]

In separate dissents, Justices William Douglas and Abe Fortas contended that although local public school boards would approve the books for use, in actual practice sectarian authorities would choose the books to be used in the church schools.

Justice Black also dissented, distinguishing between nonideological aid such as transportation or school lunch—which was permissible—and books, which were related to substantive religious views and beliefs, and thus, in his view, were impermissible.

'Parochiaid'

The *Allen* case was decided at a time when rising educational costs compelled more and more parochial school officials to seek direct financial aid from the states. Faced with their own fiscal problems, many states with large numbers of parochial school students were willing to comply on the premise that it would be less expensive to give the church schools aid than to absorb their students into the public system if they were forced to close.

Several states—notably New York, Pennsylvania, and Ohio—passed statutes authorizing direct aid such as teacher salary subsidies, tuition reimbursements, and tuition tax credits. The favorable decision in the *Allen* case and support for such programs from President Richard Nixon and many members of Congress encouraged church and state officials to hope that these so-called "parochiaid" programs might pass constitutional scrutiny. They were to be disappointed.

The first challenges to these direct aid laws reached the Court in 1971. *Lemon v. Kurtzman* and its companion cases concerned a Rhode Island statute that authorized a salary supplement to certain nonpublic school teachers and a Pennsylvania law that established a program to reimburse nonpublic schools for teachers' salaries, textbooks, and instructional materials. In practice the Rhode Island law benefited only Roman Catholic schools while the Pennsylvania law affected more than 20 percent of the students in the state. Both laws stipulated that recipient teachers must teach only secular subjects. The Pennsylvania law stipulated that the textbooks and instructional materials also be secular in nature.

The Court struck down both state laws by unanimous votes. In doing so it added a new requirement to the test for permissible state aid. Writing the Court's opinion, Chief Justice Burger said such aid not only must have a secular legislative purpose and a primary effect that neither advanced nor inhibited religion, but it also must not foster "an excessive government entanglement with religion." [82] The latter requirement was drawn from a 1970 ruling upholding property tax exemptions for church property. (*Walz v. Tax Commission, p. 91*)

To determine whether state entanglement with religion is excessive, Burger said, the Court "must examine the character and purposes of the institutions that are benefited, the nature of the aid that the State provides, and the resulting relationship between the government and the religious authority." [83]

Applying this new test to the Rhode Island statute, the majority found that teacher salary supplements did result in excessive state entanglement with religion. Without continual monitoring, the state could not know with certainty whether a parochial school teacher was presenting subject matter to pupils in the required neutral manner, Burger said. Simple assurances were not sufficient, he said:

> We need not and do not assume that teachers in parochial schools will be guilty of bad faith or any conscious design to evade the limitations imposed by the statute and the First Amendment. We simply recognize that a dedicated religious person, teaching in a school affiliated with his or her faith and operated to inculcate its tenets, will inevitably experience great difficulty in remaining religiously neutral.[84]

The only way to ensure that teachers remained neutral, Burger said, is through "comprehensive, discriminating and continuing state surveillance." Such contact between state and church amounted to excessive entanglement.[85]

By the same reasoning, the salary reimbursement portion of the Pennsylvania statute was invalid, Burger said. Furthermore, the portion of the Pennsylvania law reimbursing church schools for textbooks and instructional materials constituted direct aid to the school rather than to the pupils and their parents.

School Maintenance

Using the same three-part test, the Court in 1973 struck down New York statutes that authorized maintenance and repair grants to certain private and parochial schools, reimbursed low-income parents of nonpublic school students for a portion of the school tuition, and allowed tax credits to parents of nonpublic school students who did not qualify for the tuition reimbursements.

Writing for the majority in *Committee for Public Education and Religious Liberty v. Nyquist*, Justice Powell said that nothing in the statute stipulated that maintenance grants should be used only for secular purposes. Because the state grant could easily be used to "maintain the school chapel, or [cover] the cost of renovating classrooms in which religion is taught, or the cost of heating and lighting those same facilities," the majority could not deny that the primary effect of the grant was to subsidize directly "the religious activities of sectarian elementary and secondary schools" in violation of the establishment clause.[86]

Tuition Grants, Tax Credits

The tuition reimbursement law also unconstitutionally advanced religion, the majority held. Even though it appeared to aid parents, its obvious and primary effect was to aid church schools. Powell wrote:

[I]t is precisely the function of New York's law to provide assistance to private schools, the great majority of which are sectarian. By reimbursing parents for a portion of their tuition bill, the State seeks to relieve their financial burdens sufficiently to assure that they continue to have the option to send their children to religion-oriented schools. And while the other purposes for that aid—to perpetuate a pluralistic educational environment and to protect the fiscal integrity of overburdened public schools—are certainly unexceptionable, the effect of the aid is unmistakably to provide desired financial support for nonpublic, sectarian institutions.[87]

It made no difference to the majority that parents might spend the reimbursement money on something other than tuition:

[I]f the grants are offered as an incentive to parents to send their children to sectarian schools by making unrestricted cash payments to them, the Establishment Clause is violated whether or not the actual dollars given eventually find their way into the sectarian institutions. Whether the grant is labeled a reimbursement, a reward or a subsidy, its substantive impact is still the same.[88]

The majority concluded that the tax credit provisions served to advance religion for the same reasons tuition grants did. Under either the tuition reimbursement or the tax credit, the parent "receives the same form of encouragement and reward for sending his children to nonpublic schools," Powell wrote.[89]

Dissenting from the majority on tuition reimbursement and tax credits, Chief Justice Burger and Justice Rehnquist contended that the programs aided parents and not schools. Justice White would have upheld all three programs. He said that the primary effect of the statutes was not to advance religion but to "preserve the secular functions" of parochial schools.

Ten years later the Court, 5-4, upheld a Minnesota state income tax deduction available to parents of public and private school children. In *Mueller v. Allen,* the Court found permissible a deduction for parental costs of tuition, textbooks, and transportation for elementary and secondary school children up to $700 per older child and $500 per younger child. Critical to the ruling was the fact that this deduction was available both to public and private school patrons, although it was not disputed that the major share of the benefit ran to the latter, since public schools charge no tuition.[90]

Testing Services

On the same day as the *Nyquist* decision, June 25, 1973, the Court also held invalid a New York law that provided per-pupil payments to nonpublic schools to cover the costs of testing and maintaining state-mandated pupil records. Most of the funds were spent on testing—both state-mandated standardized tests and those prepared by teachers to measure the progress of students in regular course work.

The Court found that the statute was invalid as it related to this latter sort of testing because "despite the obviously integral role of testing in the total teaching process," it made no attempt to ensure that teacher-prepared tests were "free of religious instruction." Thus the grants used for testing had the primary effect of advancing religion. And because the Court could not determine which part of the grants was spent on potentially religious activities and which on permissible secular activities, it invalidated the entire statute.[91]

Several years later, the Court found a permissible testing reimbursement arrangement that covered the costs of administering, grading, and reporting the results of standardized tests prepared by the state—as well as the costs of reporting pupil attendance and other basic data required by the state.[92]

Other State Services

In two other cases, *Meek v. Pittinger* (1975) and *Wolman v. Walter* (1977), the Court again used its three-level test to measure the constitutionality of a variety of state services. Under these rulings, the Court allowed states to provide church-affiliated schools with loaned textbooks, standardized testing and scoring services, and speech and hearing diagnostic services. Therapeutic, guidance, and remedial education services could be provided by public school board employees to parochial school students at sites away from the schools, although similar services provided at the schools were impermissible.

The Court in *Wolman* ruled unconstitutional an Ohio law that permitted the state to pay the costs of transportation for parochial school field trips. The majority held that because the schools determined the timing and destination of field trips, they and not parents were the true beneficiaries of the statute, and thus could not be reimbursed. "The field trips are an integral part of the educational experience," the majority said, "and where the teacher works within and for a sectarian institution, an unacceptable risk of fostering of religion is an inevitable byproduct."[93]

The Court also held impermissible as a violation of the establishment clause the loan of instructional materials and equipment either to sectarian schools themselves or to their pupils.

Ruling out direct loans to schools in *Meek,* the Court held that even though the materials were secular in nature the loan "has the unconstitutional primary effect of advancing religion because of the predominantly religious character of the schools benefiting from the Act."[94] In the later *Wolman* case, the majority said it saw no significant difference between lending materials to schools and lending them to pupils; "the state aid inevitably flows in part in support of the religious role of the schools," it said.[95]

The perennial nature of the parochiaid issue—and the Court's firm stance—were illustrated afresh in 1985. On July 1 the Court held that Grand Rapids, Michigan, school officials had "established" religion by providing remedial and enrichment classes to students at forty-one nonpublic schools, forty of which were religiously affiliated. Writing for the majority, Justice Brennan said these classes—conducted during the school day by public school teachers, or after school by parochial school teachers who were paid for this work from public funds—were impermissible. The "symbolic union of church and state inherent in the provision of secular state-provided instruction in the religious school buildings threatens to convey a message of state support for religion," Brennan wrote in *Grand Rapids School District v. Ball.* The vote was 7-2 on the school-day classes, with Justices Rehnquist and White dissenting; it was 5-4 on the after-school classes, with Chief Justice Burger and Justice O'Connor finding them permissible.[96]

That same day the Court, 5-4, also held New York's system for providing remedial and counseling services to disadvantaged children in nonpublic schools unconstitutional. In *Aguilar v. Felton,* the Court found it unacceptable that the city used federal funds to send teachers into private and parochial schools to provide these services during the regular school day. This too advanced religion in symbolic and practical fashion, held the Court, by providing services the private schools would otherwise lack—and by monitoring the program, the city became entangled in church-school affairs. Burger, White, Rehnquist, and O'Connor dissented.[97]

Federal Aid to Parochial Schools

Federal taxpayers, the Court ruled in 1923, do not suffer direct injury from federal decisions on spending, and therefore cannot challenge such decisions in Court.[98]

But in the 1968 case of *Flast v. Cohen,* the Court modified this rule to permit taxpayer suits under certain circumstances—if they challenge a spending or tax program, rather than a regulatory policy, and if the taxpayer can show that the alleged misspending violated a constitutional restriction on congressional spending and taxing powers.

Mrs. Flast challenged as an unconstitutional establishment of religion a program of federal aid to both public and parochial school children. Congress in 1965 had based this education aid program on the "child benefit" theory. Title I of the Elementary and Secondary Education Act of 1965, the major federal aid program, gave grants to educationally disadvantaged children regardless of whether they attended public or private schools.

The Supreme Court in 1968 ruled that Mrs. Flast could bring her suit challenging this program because the establishment clause "operates as a specific constitutional limitation upon the exercise by Congress of the taxing and spending power." [99]

Flast's challenge never returned to the Supreme Court for a decision on the merits of her argument. Another case did, but the justices sidestepped the constitutional issue. *Wheeler v. Barrera* (1974) was brought by parents of nonpublic school students in Missouri who complained that their children were not receiving the same Title I benefits as eligible children attending public schools.

The Court held that to continue receiving Title I funds, the state must comply with the federal requirement to provide parochial school students with remedial services comparable to those given public school students. But, the Court said, these services did not have to be identical.

And because such a program had not yet been instituted, the Court declined to rule whether the provision of publicly employed teachers to teach parochial school students in their own schools would violate the establishment clause.[100] When that question came up eleven years later, the answer was clear: that arrangement did violate the establishment clause.

Aid to Church Colleges

Unlike its lengthy deliberations over government aid to elementary and secondary schools, the Supreme Court

---

The Creche Case

One of the most talked-about church-state cases of the 1980s was the "creche" case from Pawtucket, Rhode Island—*Lynch v. Donnelly* (465 U.S. 668, 1984). In this case, the First Amendment establishment clause was invoked as a basis for challenging the decision of city officials to include a creche, or nativity scene, in their city's annual holiday display that included almost all traditional Christmas symbols.

As it was urged to do by the Reagan administration, the Court, 5-4, upheld as permissible the inclusion of the creche. Writing for the Court, Chief Justice Warren E. Burger declared that "the concept of a 'wall' of separation is a useful figure of speech . . . but . . . not a wholly accurate description of the practical aspects of the relationship that in fact exists between church and state."

"No significant segment of our society and no institution within it can exist in a vacuum or in total or absolute isolation from all the other parts, much less from government," Burger continued. "Nor does the Constitution require complete separation of church and state; it affirmatively mandates accommodation, not merely tolerance, of all religions, and forbids hostility toward any."

Justices William J. Brennan, Jr., Thurgood Marshall, Harry A. Blackmun, and John Paul Stevens dissented. In their view the "primary effect of including a nativity scene in the city's display is . . . to place the government's imprimatur of approval on the particular religious beliefs exemplified by the creche." That clearly violated the First Amendment, they argued.

---

had little difficulty in upholding direct government aid to church-affiliated colleges and universities. In three cases decided in the 1970s, the Court approved state and federal programs aiding sectarian institutions of higher education.

In *Tilton v. Richardson* (1971) the Court upheld federal construction grants to church-affiliated colleges under the Higher Education Facilities Act of 1963. This federal statute permitted church-related schools to receive grants with the understanding that no federally financed building would be used for sectarian purposes.

Writing the opinion for the majority of five, Chief Justice Burger said that because the grants were available to both secular and sectarian schools the law met the test that government aid be secular in purpose. The majority did not find the involvement between the federal government and church-related schools likely to be excessive. The buildings themselves were religiously neutral in character, and since religious indoctrination was not the primary purpose of the colleges, the necessity for government surveillance to maintain the separation between religious and secular education was minimal.

Nor did the federal law advance religion. There was no evidence, said Burger, that "religion seeps into the use of any of these facilities."[101]

The majority, however, did declare unconstitutional a section of the law that permitted the schools to use the buildings for sectarian purposes after twenty years.

Underlying the majority's decision was its presumption that there is a significant difference between the religious aspects of church-related colleges and church-related primary and secondary schools, and between impressionable youngsters and more skeptical young adults. As Burger explained it:

[C]ollege students are less impressionable and less susceptible to religious indoctrination.... The skepticism of the college student is not an inconsiderable barrier to any attempt or tendency to subvert the congressional objectives and limitations. Furthermore, by their very nature, college and postgraduate courses tend to limit the opportunities for sectarian influence by virtue of their own internal disciplines. Many church-related colleges and universities are characterized by a high degree of academic freedom and seek to evoke free and critical responses from their students.[102]

Justice Douglas, speaking for three of the dissenters, objected to the federal law on the grounds that no federal tax revenues should be used to support religious activities of any sort. Justice Brennan also dissented. Using the *Tilton* decision as a precedent, the Court subsequently upheld a South Carolina statute that allowed the state to issue revenue bonds to finance construction of secular facilities at secular and sectarian colleges and universities, and a Maryland program of general annual grants to private colleges, including church-related schools.[103]

Notes

1. Sources on the history of religious freedom in the United States include: Loren P. Beth, *The American Theory of Church and State* (Gainesville: University of Florida Press, 1958); and Leo Pfeffer, *Church, State and Freedom*, rev. ed. (Boston: Beacon Press, 1967).
2. Joseph Story, *Commentaries on the Constitution of the United States*, Sec. 1879; cited in Charles Evans Hughes, *The Supreme Court of the United States: Its Foundations, Methods and Achievements, An Interpretation* (New York: Columbia University Press, 1928), 161.
3. *Walz v. Tax Commission*, 397 U.S. 664 at 669-670 (1970).
4. *Lovell v. Griffin*, 303 U.S. 444 (1938); *Kunz v. New York*, 340 U.S. 290 (1951).
5. *Reynolds v. United States*, 98 U.S. 145 at 165 (1879).
6. *Davis v. Beason*, 133 U.S. 333 at 342-343 (1890).
7. Id. at 345; see also *Cleveland v. United States*, 329 U.S. 14 (1946).
8. *Cantwell v. Connecticut*, 310 U.S. 296 at 306-307 (1940).
9. *Martin v. City of Struthers*, 319 U.S. 141 (1943).
10. *United States v. Ballard*, 322 U.S. 78 at 86, 87 (1944).
11. *Prince v. Massachusetts*, 321 U.S. 158 at 166 (1944).
12. *Cantwell v. Connecticut*, 310 U.S. 296 at 308 (1940).
13. Id. at 311.
14. Id. at 307; See also *Schneider v. Irvington*, 308 U.S. 147 (1939); *Martin v. City of Struthers*, 319 U.S. 141 (1943).
15. *Cox v. New Hampshire*, 312 U.S. 569 (1941).
16. *Kunz v. New York*, 340 U.S. 290 at 293 (1951).
17. *Niemotko v. Maryland*, 340 U.S. 268 (1951).
18. *Fowler v. Rhode Island*, 345 U.S. 67 at 70 (1953).
19. *Jones v. Opelika*, 316 U.S. 584 at 597 (1942).
20. *Murdock v. Pennsylvania*, 319 U.S. 105 at 113 (1943).
21. Id. at 109.
22. Id. at 111; see also *Follett v. City of McCormick*, 321 U.S. 573 (1944).
23. *Heffron v. International Society for Krishna Consciousness*, 452 U.S. 640 (1981); *Widmar v. Vincent*, 454 U.S. 263 (1981).
24. *Jacobson v. Massachusetts*, 197 U.S. 11 (1905).
25. *Pierce v. Society of Sisters*, 268 U.S. 510 (1925); *Hamilton v. California Board of Regents*, 293 U.S. 245 (1934).
26. *Leoles v. Landers*, 302 U.S. 656 (1937); *Hering v. State Board of Education*, 303 U.S. 624 (1938); *Gabrielli v. Knickerbocker, Johnson v. Town of Deerfield*, 306 U.S. 621 (1939).
27. *Minersville School District v. Gobitis*, 310 U.S. 586 at 593, 594-595 (1940).
28. Id. at 598.
29. Id. at 598, 600.
30. Id. at 601.
31. Id. at 604.
32. Id. at 606.
33. Irving Dilliard, "The Flag-Salute Cases," in *Quarrels That Have Shaped the Constitution*, ed. John A. Garraty (New York: Harper & Row, 1964), 234.
34. *Jones v. Opelika*, 316 U.S. 584 at 623-624 (1942).
35. *West Virginia State Board of Education v. Barnette*, 319 U.S. 624 at 638 (1943).
36. Id. at 640, 641.
37. Id. at 641-642.
38. Id. at 646-647.
39. *Braunfeld v. Brown*, 366 U.S. 599 at 607 (1961); see also *Gallagher v. Crown Kosher Super Market*, 366 U.S. 617 (1961).
40. *Sherbert v. Verner*, 374 U.S. 398 at 404 (1963).
41. Id. at 406 quoting *Thomas v. Collins*, 323 U.S. 516 at 530 (1945).
42. *Thomas v. Review Board of the Indiana Employment Security Division*, 450 U.S. 707 (1981); *Hobbie v. Unemployment Appeals Commission of Florida*, __ U.S. __ (1987); *Estate of Thornton v. Caldor, Inc.*, 472 U.S. 703 (1985).
43. *Wisconsin v. Yoder*, 406 U.S. 205 at 214 (1972).
44. *Torcaso v. Watkins*, 367 U.S. 488 at 495 (1961).
45. *United States v. Schwimmer*, 279 U.S. 644 (1929); *United States v. Macintosh*, 283 U.S. 605 (1931); *United States v. Bland*, 283 U.S. 636 (1931).
46. *Girouard v. United States*, 328 U.S. 61 (1946), overturning *United States v. Schwimmer*, 279 U.S. 644 (1929); *United States v. Macintosh*, 283 U.S. 605 (1931); *United States v. Bland*, 283 U.S. 636 (1931).
47. *In re Summers*, 325 U.S. 561 (1945).
48. *McDaniel v. Paty*, 435 U.S. 618 (1978).
49. *Sherbert v. Verner*, 374 U.S. 398 (1963).
50. *Torcaso v. Watkins*, 367 U.S. 488 (1961).
51. C. Herman Pritchett, *The American Constitution*, 3d ed. (New York: McGraw-Hill Book Co., 1977), 402; Robert L. Cord, *Separation of Church and State* (New York: Lambeth Press, 1982), 226.
52. *Bradfield v. Roberts*, 175 U.S. 291 (1899); see also *Quick Bear v. Leupp*, 210 U.S. 50 (1908).
53. *Walz v. Tax Commission*, 397 U.S. 664 at 673 (1970).
54. Id. at 675, 676.
55. *St. Martin Evangelical Lutheran Church and Northwestern Lutheran Academy v. State of South Dakota*, 452 U.S. 640 (1981); *Tony and Susan Alamo Foundation v. Secretary of Labor*, 471 U.S. 290 (1985); see also *Corporation of the Presiding Bishop of the Church of Jesus Christ of the Latter Day Saints v. Amos*, __ U.S. __ (1987).
56. *Zorach v. Clausen*, 343 U.S. 306 at 313 (1952).
57. *Marsh v. Chambers*, 463 U.S. 783 (1983).
58. *Lewis v. Allen*, 379 U.S. 923 (1964); *O'Hair v. Paine*, 432 F 2d 66 (CA 5, 1971); *O'Hair v. Blumenthal* (1979).
59. *Illinois ex rel. McCollum v. Board of Education*, 333 U.S. 203 at 210 (1948).

60. Id. at 227-28.
61. *Zorach v. Clausen,* 343 U.S. 306 at 312 (1952).
62. Id. at 315, 314.
63. *Clithero v. Schowalter,* 284 U.S. 573 (1930); *Doremus v. Board of Education,* 342 U.S. 429 (1952).
64. *Engel v. Vitale,* 370 U.S. 421 at 425 (1962).
65. Id. at 430-431.
66. Id. at 436, quoting James Madison, "Memorial and Remonstrance Against Religious Assessments."
67. Id. at 445.
68. Id. at 450.
69. *School District of Abington Township v. Schempp, Murray v. Curlett,* 374 U.S. 203 at 226 (1963).
70. Id. at 225.
71. Id. at 226.
72. *Wallace v. Jaffree,* 472 U.S. 38 (1985).
73. *Karcher v. May,* ___ U.S. ___ (1987).
74. *Cochran v. Louisiana Board of Education,* 281 U.S. 370 (1930).
75. *Everson v. Board of Education,* 330 U.S. 1 at 15-16 (1947).
76. Id. at 17-18.
77. Id. at 33, 50.
78. Id. at 63.
79. *Lemon v. Kurtzman,* 403 U.S. 602 at 614 (1971).
80. *Board of Education of Central School District No. 1 v. Allen,* 392 U.S. 236 at 245, 248 (1968).
81. Id. at 243-244
82. *Lemon v. Kurtzman,* 403 U.S. 602 at 613 (1971), quoting

Walz v. Tax Commission, 397 U.S. 664 at 674 (1970).
83. Id. at 615.
84. Id. at 618.
85. Id. at 619.
86. *Committee for Public Education and Religious Liberty v. Nyquist,* 413 U.S. 756 at 774 (1973); *Sloan v. Lemon* 413 U.S. 825 (1973).
87. Id. at 783.
88. Id. at 786.
89. Id. at 791.
90. *Mueller v. Allen,* 463 U.S. 388 (1983); see also *Witters v. Washington Department of Services for the Blind* (1986).
91. *Levitt v. Committee for Public Education and Religious Liberty,* 413 U.S. 472 at 480 (1973).
92. *Committee for Public Education and Religious Liberty v. Regan,* 444 U.S. 646 (1980).
93. *Wolman v. Walter,* 433 U.S. 229 at 254 (1977).
94. *Meek v. Pittinger,* 421 U.S. 349 at 363 (1975).
95. *Wolman v. Walter,* 433 U.S. 229 at 250 (1977).
96. *Grand Rapids School District v. Ball,* 473 U.S. 373 (1985).
97. *Aguilar v. Felton,* 473 U.S. 402 (1985).
98. *Frothingham v. Mellon,* 262 U.S. 447 (1923).
99. *Flast v. Cohen,* 392 U.S. 83 at 104 (1968).
100. *Wheeler v. Barrera,* 417 U.S. 402 (1974).
101. *Tilton v. Richardson,* 403 U.S. 672 at 681 (1971).
102. Id. at 686.
103. *Hunt v. McNair,* 413 U.S. 734 (1973); *Roemer v. Maryland Board of Public Works,* 426 U.S. 736 (1976).

Part II

Political Participation

Part of the political history of the United States is the story of the effort to translate the ideals of equality and freedom into political reality. The elusiveness of these goals is reflected in a long line of Supreme Court decisions that deal with the right to vote, the right to have the vote counted equally with all others, and the freedom to associate with persons of similar political views.

The right to vote is the cornerstone of the democratic political system. Yet the Constitution makes little mention of that right, and, for well over a century, the Supreme Court maintained that its source was state, not federal, citizenship.

Five times the Constitution has been amended to extend and protect this basic political right.

In the nation's earliest years, the right to vote was the exclusive prerogative of free white adult property-owning males. Property qualifications were the first restriction abandoned, although vestiges of that requirement remained for more than a century in the form of poll taxes.

The Civil War—and the amendments that marked its close—seemed to promise a new age of broadened political participation. The privileges and immunities clause of the Fourteenth Amendment appeared to many to guarantee all citizens—female as well as male, black as well as white—the right to vote.

But within a decade of its adoption, the Supreme Court made clear that the amendment had no such practical effect. The Constitution of the United States, declared the Court, still granted no one the right to vote. That was a state prerogative. The ruling, in a case brought on behalf of a woman seeking to vote, sparked a drive that lasted forty-five years for another constitutional amendment, granting women the right to vote.

The Fifteenth Amendment spoke plainly: suffrage was not to be restricted because of the race, color, or previous slavery of the potential voter. Yet, insulated from federal action by Court decisions that perpetuated the view that voter qualifications and election regulations were exclusively state responsibilities, state officials successfully employed a variety of devices—literacy tests, grandfather clauses, poll taxes, white primaries—to circumvent the amendment's intent for most of another century.

Although the Supreme Court began as early as 1915 to edge toward a new view of the amendments and the protection they provided for the right to vote, it was Congress, spurred by the civil rights movement of the 1960s, that led in the eventual fulfillment of the promise of the Fifteenth Amendment. The Voting Rights Act of 1965 at last secured to the nation's black citizens the right to vote. To do so, the act asserted federal authority over electoral matters traditionally left in the hands of state officials.

Once Congress acted, the Supreme Court steadily backed its power to ensure the right to vote. The Court heard out the challenges of the states to the new law—and then rejected them resoundingly. In a series of rulings that were a mirror image of those postwar decisions of the 1870s and 1880s, the Court gave the broadest possible reading to the Fifteenth Amendment, the power of Congress to enforce it, and to the 1965 act, making it the most effective civil rights law ever enacted.

At the same time that the Court's modern voting rights decisions were underwriting the expansion of the right to vote, its plunge into the political morass of redistricting cases revolutionized the balance of political power both within Congress and in every state legislature in the nation.

Electoral districts within state boundaries had been a fact of life since early in the nineteenth century when Congress first directed all states with more than one member in the House of Representatives to elect those House members from separate, compact, and contiguous districts. Later in the century, the national legislature required that its electoral districts within each state also be as nearly equal in population as was practicable.

But in 1929 Congress omitted those requirements from its revision of the law. A few years later the Supreme Court found the omission purposeful. Lifting these requirements for congressional districts came just as the nation's population was shifting from primarily rural areas to become an urban majority. For forty years this shift was not reflected in the nation's legislatures.

Farm and rural interests continued to dominate in Congress and in state legislatures. Efforts by urban residents to have district lines redrawn to reflect their new strength—and to win equal weight for their votes—failed.

In large part these attempts were blocked by the insistence of federal courts, led by the Supreme Court, that such challenges were political matters outside judicial power, best dealt with by the malapportioned legislatures that were the heart of the problem. As late as 1946, the Court explicitly reaffirmed this view, describing redistricting challenges as a "political thicket" it would not enter.

But within sixteen years the Court reversed itself. In 1962 it took the first step, ruling that redistricting cases might, after all, present questions susceptible to judicial resolution. This ruling opened the doors of the federal courts to a multitude of suits challenging state and congressional districting and apportionment structures.

As it dealt with these subsequent cases, the Court translated the Fourteenth Amendment's guarantee of equal protection into the rule of "one person, one vote" as the proper measure for redistricting plans. Within a decade it appeared that the standard was in some ways a dual one, applied to require that a state's congressional districts be almost precisely equal in population, while allowing its own legislative electoral districts to vary further from the ideal of precise equality.

In subsequent rulings, the Court also extended the application of this "one person, one vote" rule to a variety of local electoral districts.

The freedom of political association receives no mention in the Constitution at all. Yet in its modern rulings, the Supreme Court has made clear in decisions concerning Communists and civil rights activists, radicals and Republicans, that it considers the freedom to associate with persons of like political views—without penalty from the government—an essential corollary of the First Amendment freedoms of speech, peaceable assembly, and the right to petition the government for redress of grievances.

Like other First Amendment rights—but unlike the right to vote—the freedom of political association may legitimately be restricted by government in order to further other major interests. Thus political association cases present the Court with the task of reconciling individual freedom and the government's need to preserve public peace and national security.

Such reconciliation takes place through a process of weighing and balancing, which inevitably reflects the social and political context in which the justices live and work. Thus it should be no surprise that during periods of severe external threat, the Court has upheld substantial restrictions upon the exercise of this right.

Nowhere is this more obvious than in the decisions of the 1950s and 1960s concerning the efforts of Congress, the executive branch, and state legislatures to curtail the spread of domestic communism and to protect government against infiltration by disloyal persons.

In its early 1950s rulings on these laws and programs, the Court found their restrictive impact on individual freedom justified. As the threat eased, however, the Court found challenges to these laws more and more persuasive. In response, it tightened the standards of proof to ensure that persons were not penalized simply for "guilt by association" or abstract advocacy of revolution, but only for actions that clearly threatened the nation's security. Eventually, this line of rulings vitiated the internal security laws into complete ineffectiveness.

The right of political association—finally recognized even in internal security cases—found its clearest definition in cases involving homegrown forms of activism and more traditional political activities. In the 1960s the Court forbade states to interfere with the right of civil rights activists to associate and work for the advancement of blacks and other minorities. Such associations could not be penalized by the state, held the Court. Later rulings recognized the right of national political parties to this freedom—interpreted to shield those parties from the interference of state courts—and the right of persons holding different views from those of an elected officeholder to keep their jobs nonetheless.

4

The Right to Vote

The gradually broadening suffrage is one of the most significant characteristics of the continuing American experiment in popular government. In 1792 only propertied white males were granted the privilege of voting. By 1972 that right was possessed by all Americans eighteen or older—blacks and whites, women and men.

The Constitution barely mentions the right to vote. It provides for the direct election of members of the House of Representatives, permits states to set voter qualifications, and gives the states the authority to set the times, places, and manner of elections for senators and representatives. Article I, section 4, however, does reserve to Congress the power to override, by law, such state-made election rules.

Early in the history of the republic, popular pressure forced states to drop the restrictive property qualification for voting. The Constitution subsequently has been amended five times to extend the vote to formerly disenfranchised groups.

The Fifteenth Amendment, added in 1870, prohibited denial of the right to vote for reasons of race, color, or previous condition of servitude.

Women, who had sought to win the right to vote through judicial interpretation of the "privileges and immunities" clause of the Fourteenth Amendment, were rebuffed in that effort by the Supreme Court. Uniting into an organized women's suffrage movement, they worked and fought for half a century for the right to vote. Finally, in 1920, the addition of the Nineteenth Amendment forbade restriction of the suffrage on account of sex.

In 1961 the Twenty-third Amendment granted residents of the nation's capital, the District of Columbia, the right to vote in presidential elections. In 1964 the Twenty-fourth Amendment ended all efforts to restrict the right to vote because of lack of wealth or property, outlawing use of a poll tax as a means of abridging the right to vote in federal elections.

Then the age for political participation was formally lowered by the Twenty-sixth Amendment, ratified in 1971, granting all citizens eighteen and older the right to vote in federal elections. With this amendment—and new civil rights legislation finally implementing the Fifteenth Amendment—virtually every adult citizen possessed the right to vote in the nation's elections by 1972.

THE RIGHT AND THE POWER

No other constitutional promise has gone so long unfulfilled as that of the Fifteenth Amendment. Despite the clear language forbidding abridgment of the right to vote because of race or color, state officials succeeded for almost a full century in denying black citizens the right to vote.

The Supreme Court, by its acquiescence, played a critical role in creating this anomalous situation.

The right to vote was viewed by many as doubly guaranteed by the Civil War amendments—protected by the provision of the Fourteenth Amendment safeguarding the privileges and immunities of citizens against state infringement and by the clear language of the Fifteenth Amendment forbidding abridgment of the right to vote because of race, color, or previous condition of servitude.

In addition, voting rights for blacks had been made a condition for readmission to the union for the rebellious states of the Confederacy. And yet, after the presidential election of 1876, the issue of Negro voting rights was again left to state control. As the southern states returned to white rule, they passed laws that effectively defeated the purposes of the amendments.

The Supreme Court created the environment for such systematic state obstruction with a set of rulings in which it adopted the narrowest possible view of the impact of the amendments upon the individual's right to vote. The Court held that the right to vote was chiefly governed by state laws; that its source was the state, not the U.S. Constitution; and that Congress had only limited power to interfere in state regulation of electoral matters.

No Privilege or Immunity

The first of these restrictive rulings came in 1875 with the case of *Minor v. Happersett* in which the Court declared that the U.S. Constitution did not give anyone the right to vote.

Minor v. Happersett was brought by Francis Minor, a St. Louis attorney, on behalf of his wife, president of the Missouri Woman Suffrage Association. The Minors argued that the right to vote was a privilege of U.S. citizenship, protected by the first section of the Fourteenth Amendment. Therefore, the Minors concluded, states could not deny women the right to vote.

Missouri law, however, limited suffrage to males. Happersett, an election registrar, refused to register Mrs. Minor, and the couple filed suit.

Just two years earlier, in the *Slaughterhouse Cases,* the Court had described the privileges and immunities of U.S. citizenship as a brief list not including the right to vote. In line with that decision, the Court rejected the Minors' argument. Chief Justice Morrison R. Waite wrote for the Court that the right to vote was not a privilege or immunity of federal citizenship. The suffrage, Waite stated, had never been coextensive with citizenship:

> The United States has no voters in the States of its creation. . . .
>
> [T]he Constitution of the United States does not confer the right of suffrage upon anyone.

It was still up to the states, Waite said, to define voter qualifications—even for federal elections:

> The [Fourteenth] Amendment did not add to the privileges and immunities of a citizen. It simply furnished an additional guaranty for the protection of such as he already had.
>
> It is clear, therefore, we think, that the Constitution has not added the right of suffrage to the privileges and immunities of citizenship as they existed at the time it was adopted.[1]

No Federal Voting Right

The following year, the Court adopted a similar narrow view of the Fifteenth Amendment.

In *United States v. Reese* and *United States v. Cruikshank,* the Court overturned federal convictions of persons charged with violating the 1870 act enforcing the Fifteenth Amendment's guarantee against denial of voting rights because of race.

In the *Reese* case, state election officials were convicted for violating the law by refusing to receive or count a black man's vote. The Court overturned the convictions, finding the section of the law under which they were charged technically defective.

The Court, again through Chief Justice Waite, stated that "[t]he Fifteenth Amendment does not confer the right of suffrage upon anyone . . . [but] has invested the citizens of the United States with a new constitutional right . . . exemption from discrimination in the exercise of the elective franchise on account of race, color or previous condition of servitude." [2]

United States v. Cruikshank, decided that same day in 1876, dealt with one of the ninety-six indictments resulting from a massacre of sixty blacks in Colfax, Louisiana, in 1873. Disputes over local elections allegedly led William J. Cruikshank and others to shoot down a posse of blacks who had seized the Colfax Courthouse.

Cruikshank and his confederates were indicted under the enforcement act for conspiring to intimidate blacks to prevent their exercise of constitutional rights, including the right to vote. The Supreme Court declared the indictment defective because "it is nowhere alleged in these counts that the wrong contemplated against the rights of these citizens was on account of their race or color." [3]

Chief Justice Waite delivered the opinion of the Court. He declared again that the amendment added nothing to the rights a citizen possessed:

> It simply furnishes an additional guaranty as against any encroachment by the States upon the fundamental rights which belong to every citizen as a member of society. . . . The power of the National Government is limited to the enforcement of this guaranty. . . .
>
> The right to vote in the States comes from the States; but the right of exemption from the prohibited discrimination comes from the United States. The first has not been granted or secured by the Constitution of the United States; but the last has been.
>
> Inasmuch, therefore, as it does not appear in these counts that the intent of the defendants was to prevent these parties from exercising their right to vote on account of their race . . . it does not appear that it was their intent to interfere with any right granted or secured by the Constitution or laws of the United States. We may suspect that race was the cause of the hostility; but it is not so averred.[4]

Exceptions to the View

Despite this limiting interpretation of the new constitutional language concerning the right to vote, the Court upheld federal power to regulate elections generally under the provisions of Article I.

In 1880 in *Ex parte Siebold,* which did not involve charges of racial discrimination, the Court upheld federal power to ensure that elections of federal officials be fairly conducted. Siebold, a state election official, was convicted of violating federal law by stuffing a ballot box in an election of state and federal officers.

The Court upheld his conviction, citing Article I, section 4, to justify federal regulation of the actions of state election officials. Article I, section 4, gave Congress broad concurrent powers to regulate elections along with and independent of state power in that area.[5]

Over the next three decades the Court reaffirmed this position in similar cases.[6]

The Court's narrow view of the Fifteenth Amendment also underwent some modification in 1884 in *Ex parte Yarbrough,* the only early case in which the Court backed the use of federal power to punish the action of private individuals for obstructing the right to vote in a federal election.

In *Yarbrough* the Court held that once an individual acquired the right to vote for federal officers—by meeting state-set voter qualifications—that right was accorded federal protection.

Jasper Yarbrough, a member of the Ku Klux Klan, and some fellow Klansmen attacked a Negro named Berry Saunders and beat him up to prevent his voting in a congressional election. Yarbrough was convicted and sentenced to prison for violating the 1870 Enforcement Act by conspiring to prevent a citizen from voting.

He challenged his conviction, arguing that the 1870 law was unconstitutional, because Congress lacked the authority to act to protect the right to vote in federal elections. The Court, however, upheld his conviction, the federal law, and congressional power to protect the right to vote.

Justice Samuel Miller, writing for the majority, made clear that the right to vote for members of Congress was derived from the federal Constitution—not state laws—and was subject to federal protection:

That a government whose essential character is republican ... has no power to secure this election from the influence of violence, of corruption, and of fraud, is a proposition so startling as to arrest attention. ...

If this government is anything more than a mere aggregation of delegated agents of other States and governments, each of which is superior to the General Government, it must have the power to protect the elections on which its existence depends from violence and corruption.

If it has not this power, it is left helpless before the two great natural and historical enemies of all republics, open violence and insidious corruption. ...

The States in prescribing the qualifications for the most numerous branch of their own Legislatures, do not do this with reference to the election for members of Congress. ... They define who are to vote for the popular branch of their own legislature, and the Constitution of the United States says the same persons shall vote for members of Congress in that State. It adopts the qualification thus furnished as the qualification of its own electors for members of Congress.

It is not true, therefore, that electors for members of Congress owe their right to vote to the state law in any sense which makes the exercise of the right to depend exclusively on the law of the State.[7]

The Fifteenth Amendment, said the Court, did operate in some circumstances as the source of a right to vote. And Congress did have the authority "to protect the citizen in the exercise of rights conferred by the Constitution of the United States essential to the healthy organization of the government itself."[8]

And so, the opinion concluded:

If the Government of the United States has within its constitutional domain no authority to provide against these evils [violence and corruption of elections], if the very sources of power may be poisoned by corruption or controlled by violence and outrage, without legal restraint, then, indeed, is the country in danger and its best powers, its highest purposes, the hopes which it inspires ... are at the mercy of the combinations of those who respect no right but brute force, on the one hand, and unprincipled corruptionists on the other.[9]

But despite Justice Miller's strong words, the Court in general maintained for decades that, in the absence of state action, the acts of private individuals to deny the rights of others to vote were outside the reach of federal power.

In 1903 the Court stated that the provisions of the 1870 Enforcement Act, which might be interpreted "to punish purely individual action [to interfere with voting rights,] cannot be sustained as an appropriate exercise of the power conferred by the Fifteenth Amendment upon Congress."[10]

THE PATTERN OF EXCLUSION

Encouraged by the Court's limiting view of the federal right to vote and of federal power to enforce that right many southern states during the period from 1890 to 1910 rewrote their constitutions or added new requirements for voters to exclude blacks from participation in the political process.[11] The Court by and large left major elements of the program of disenfranchisement untouched for decades.

The strategy of exclusion employed many methods, among them literacy tests, grandfather clauses, all-white primaries, poll taxes, and the racial gerrymander.

Grandfather clauses were held unconstitutional in 1915, and white primaries were finally ruled invalid in 1944. But not until Congress acted did the Court strike down the use of poll taxes and literacy tests.

Ancestry and Literacy

For seventy years, from 1898 until 1969, the Supreme Court upheld the validity of literacy tests for voters.

In 1898 the Court first upheld the validity of literacy tests as voter qualification devices. In *Williams v. Mississippi,* a Negro man was indicted for murder by an all-white grand jury. The jurors were selected from the list of registered voters who had, among other qualifications, passed such a literacy test. Williams challenged the use of the test as unconstitutional.

Williams's attorneys argued that his conviction was invalid because the laws under which the grand jury was selected allowed discrimination in voter registration, thereby violating the equal protection guarantee of the Fourteenth Amendment.

Justice Joseph McKenna, writing for the Court, refused to find the Mississippi statutes in violation of the equal protection clause. The "evil" was not the laws themselves, he wrote, for they did not on their face discriminate against blacks; the only evil resulted from the effect of their discriminatory administration.[12]

Grandfather Clauses

Seventeen years later, however, the Supreme Court held impermissible Oklahoma's combined use of a literacy test and a "grandfather" clause.

The state required all voters to pass a literacy test *or* to show that their ancestors were entitled to vote in 1866. This requirement was challenged as a violation of the Fifteenth Amendment, because in operation it exempted most white males from the literacy test requirement and permitted voter registrars to test primarily blacks, whose ancestors in most cases had not been eligible to vote in 1866.

The state defended its system by arguing that the clause did not deny blacks the right to vote outright; it simply required them all to take the literacy tests. The Fifteenth Amendment, the state continued, did not confer the right to vote on all Negroes; it merely prevented states from denying them the right to vote on purely racial grounds.

With its 1915 decision in *Guinn v. United States,* the Court began moving toward its modern view of the amendment. Unanimously, the Court struck down Oklahoma's system as an unconstitutional evasion of the Fifteenth Amendment. Chief Justice Edward D. White wrote the Court's opinion.

In that opinion, however, the Court continued to affirm state power to require voters to demonstrate some measure of literacy, stating that the establishment of a literacy test requirement was "but the exercise by the state of a lawful power ... not subject to our supervision." [13]

Guinn had limited impact on black voting rights in the South because it dealt only with the grandfather clause. The case, however, was the first in which the Court in a voting rights case looked beyond nondiscriminatory form to discover discriminatory substance.

(In a second Oklahoma case decided that same day, the Court upheld the federal indictments—under the Reconstruction Civil Rights Acts—of county election officials who refused to count certain persons' votes. The Court, in *United States v. Mosely,* declared that: "[T]he right to have one's vote counted is as open to protection by Congress as the right to put a ballot in a box.") [14]

Oklahoma subsequently adopted a requirement that all voters register within a twelve-day period, exempting from the requirement those who had voted in the 1914 elections, prior to *Guinn.* In 1939 the Court held this too was an unconstitutional attempt to disenfranchise blacks in violation of the Fifteenth Amendment.

Justice Felix Frankfurter, writing for the majority, said that the Fifteenth Amendment "nullifies sophisticated as well as simple-minded modes of discrimination. It hits onerous procedural requirements which effectively handicap exercise of the franchise by the colored race although the abstract right to vote may remain unrestricted as to race." [15]

Tests of Understanding

In addition to strict literacy tests, some states also required voters to "understand and explain" an article of the Constitution. The vagueness of one such provision was nullified by a federal court as an arbitrary grant of power to election officials who could and did administer the literacy test in a racially discriminatory fashion and thus violated the Fifteenth Amendment. The fact that the provision itself made no mention of race did not save it from being unconstitutional. The Supreme Court affirmed this ruling in 1949. [16]

But the Court continued to uphold state power to require that its voters demonstrate some measure of literacy. In 1959 the Supreme Court upheld North Carolina's requirement that all voters be able to read and write a section of the state constitution in English. Such a test was not, on its face, a violation of the Fourteenth, Fifteenth or Seventeenth Amendments, the Court held in the case of *Lassiter v. Northampton County Board of Elections.*

Justice William O. Douglas's opinion for the majority stressed that the state had an interest in securing an independent and intelligent electorate. How the state achieved that objective, Douglas said, was a policy question outside the Court's purview:

Literacy and intelligence are obviously not synonymous. Illiterate people may be intelligent voters. Yet in our society ... a state might conclude that only

those who are literate should exercise the franchise.... We do not sit in judgment on the wisdom of that policy. We cannot say, however, that it is not an allowable one measured by constitutional standards.

Of course a literacy test, fair on its face, may be employed to perpetuate that discrimination which the Fifteenth Amendment was designed to uproot. No such influence is charged here.... The present requirement, applicable to members of all races ... seems to us one fair way of determining whether a person is literate.... Certainly we cannot condemn it on its face as a device unrelated to the desire of North Carolina to raise the standards for people of all races who cast the ballot." [17]

But six years later, the Court held Louisiana's test requiring voters to display a reasonable knowledge and understanding of any section of the state or federal constitution to be a violation of the Fifteenth Amendment.

The Court's unanimous opinion, written by Justice Hugo L. Black, viewed the requirement in light of the history of voter discrimination in the state:

The applicant facing a registrar in Louisiana thus has been compelled to leave his voting fate to that official's uncontrolled power to determine whether the applicant's understanding of the Federal or State Constitution is satisfactory. As the evidence showed, colored people, even some with the most advanced education and scholarship, were declared by voting registrars with less education to have an unsatisfactory understanding of the Constitution of Louisiana or of the United States. This is not a test but a trap, sufficient to stop even the most brilliant man on his way to the voting booth. The cherished right of people in a country like ours to vote cannot be obliterated by the use of laws like this, which leave the voting fate of a citizen to the passing whim or impulse of an individual registrar. [18]

Suspension of Literacy Tests

In 1965 Congress, as part of the Voting Rights Act, suspended all literacy tests and similar devices in all areas where less than half the population of voting age had been registered or had voted in the 1964 presidential election.

The act was immediately challenged as infringing upon state power to oversee elections. In *South Carolina v. Katzenbach,* decided in 1966, the Supreme Court upheld Congress's power to pass the law and backed all its major provisions, including that suspending literacy tests. [19]

Chief Justice Earl Warren, who delivered the opinion of the Court, wrote that the provision of the act suspending literacy tests:

was clearly a legitimate response to the problem.... Underlying the response was the feeling that States and political subdivisions which had been allowing white illiterates to vote for years could not sincerely complain about "dilution" of their electorates through the registration of Negro illiterates. Congress knew that continuance of the tests and devices in use at the present time, no matter how fairly administered in the future, would freeze the effect of past discrimination in favor of unqualified white registrants. Congress permissibly rejected the alternative of requiring a complete reregistration of all voters, believing that this would be too harsh on many whites who had enjoyed the franchise for their entire adult lives.[20]

The opinion in *South Carolina v. Katzenbach,* on March 7, 1966, was followed three months later by two decisions that prevented states from disqualifying potential voters simply because they were unable to read or write English.[21]

Reinstatement Denied

Three years later in 1969 the Court rejected the effort of a North Carolina county to have the literacy test reinstated. The Court declared that counties and states that had denied blacks their equal educational opportunity, by operating separate and unequal schools for blacks and whites, had denied blacks the opportunity to acquire the skills necessary to pass a literacy test. And so, the Court held in the case of *Gaston County v. United States,* re-

---

State Requirements: Age, Residence, Property

States historically have imposed various nonracial qualifications upon voters. Supreme Court rulings, however, have limited state power to impose voter requirements related to age, property ownership, or residence for any extended period of time.

Nevertheless, in 1974 the Court affirmed the power of states to exclude convicted felons from the exercise of the franchise. In 1968, in the case of *Green v. New York City Board of Elections,* the Court upheld a New York law that barred convicted, unpardoned felons from voting.[1]

In 1974 the Court reaffirmed that position, ruling that denial of the right to vote to convicted felons did not violate the Fourteenth Amendment.[2]

In 1970 the Court upheld the power of Congress to lower age and residence requirements for participation in federal elections, although not for state or local elections.[3]

Only eleven years earlier, the Court had declared that states had broad powers to set age and residence rules for voters:

> The states have long been held to have broad powers to determine the conditions under which the right of suffrage may be exercised.... Residence requirements, and age ... are obvious examples indicating factors which a State may take into consideration in determining the qualification of voters.[4]

Following that ruling, the Court in 1972 seemed to limit all state-imposed residency requirements for voters to thirty days. In a case involving Tennessee's residency requirement of one year prior to registration as a voter, the Court held that requirement invalid, saying that the state had shown no compelling state interest to justify such a lengthy residency requirement.[5] This decision in *Dunn v. Blumstein* sidestepped, but did not overrule, a 1904 decision upholding a similar Maryland requirement that a voter file a declaration of intent to register one year before his enrollment on the voter lists.[6]

But the Court later left standing Arizona's rule cutting off voter registration fifty days before a primary. The Court indicated that the state had shown the fifty-day period necessary to permit preparation of accurate voter lists.[7]

In an earlier ruling the Court had held that a state could not prevent military personnel stationed within its borders from establishing residence for purposes of voting.[8] And, the Court held in 1970, a state could not deny the right to vote to persons living in a federal enclave in the state, if those persons were otherwise treated as state residents.[9]

By the mid-1970s property requirements for voting in general elections had disappeared from the American electoral process.

In a set of modern rulings the Court made clear that the equal protection guarantee of the Fourteenth Amendment was offended by state efforts to restrict the right to vote.

In 1969 the Court struck down Louisiana's law that limited to property tax payers the right to vote in elections to approve issuance of utility revenue bonds.[10]

The same day the Court held that the equal protection guarantee assured all residents—not merely those who owned or leased property or who had children in the public schools—the right to vote in school district elections.[11]

In 1970 the Court applied the same principle to strike down state efforts to exclude those who did not own property from voting in elections held to approve the issue of general obligation bonds.[12] The Court later struck down laws that limited the right to vote in city bond elections to persons who owned taxable property.[13]

1. *Green v. New York City Board of Elections,* 389 U.S. 1048 (1968).
2. *Richardson v. Ramirez,* 418 U.S. 24 (1974).
3. *Oregon v. Mitchell, Texas v. Mitchell, United States v. Idaho, United States v. Arizona,* 400 U.S. 112 (1970).
4. *Lassiter v. Northampton County Board of Elections,* 360 U.S. 45 at 51 (1959).
5. *Dunn v. Blumstein,* 405 U.S. 330 (1972).
6. *Pope v. Williams,* 193 U.S. 621 (1904).
7. *Marston v. Lewis,* 410 U.S. 679 (1973); *Burns v. Fortson,* 410 U.S. 686 (1973).
8. *Carrington v. Rash,* 380 U.S. 89 (1965).
9. *Evans v. Cornman,* 398 U.S. 419 (1970).
10. *Cipriano v. City of Houma,* 395 U.S. 701 (1969).
11. *Kramer v. Union Free School District No. 15,* 395 U.S. 818 (1969).
12. *Phoenix v. Kolodzieski,* 399 U.S. 204 (1970).
13. *Hill v. Stone,* 421 U.S. 289 (1975).

instatement of a literacy test would simply perpetuate the effects of the dual, unequal educational system that had so long operated to disenfranchise blacks.[22]

Justice John Marshall Harlan wrote for the Court.

Affording today's Negro youth equal educational opportunity will doubtless prepare them to meet, on equal terms, whatever standards of literacy are required when they reach voting age. It does nothing for their parents, however. From this record, we cannot escape the sad truth that throughout the years, Gaston County systematically deprived its black citizens of the educational opportunities it granted to its white citizens. "Impartial" administration of the literacy test today would serve only to perpetuate those inequities in a different form.[23]

The 1965 act, extended for five years in 1970, was amended at that time to suspend literacy tests nationwide and to bring more areas under coverage of its provisions. The Supreme Court upheld the nationwide ban on literacy tests in the 1970 case of *Oregon v. Mitchell.*[24]

In that case, Justice Black explained that such a ban, in light of the long history of discriminatory literacy tests, was well within the power of Congress to enforce the Fifteenth Amendment. In 1975 the law was amended to abolish all literacy tests permanently.

White Primaries

Southern politics was completely dominated by the Democratic party during the first half of the twentieth century. In many areas the Democratic primary was the only significant part of the election process. Winning the primary was tantamount to election. Being excluded from voting in the primary was equivalent to being excluded from voting altogether.

Not until 1941 was it clear, as the result of a Supreme Court ruling, that Congress had the power to regulate primary, as well as general, elections. In fact, in a 1921 decision involving campaign spending—*Newberry v. United States*—the Court seemed to say that Congress lacked this power.[25]

This Court-created doubt encouraged the eleven states that had comprised the Confederacy to begin systematic exclusion of blacks from participation in the primary. The Democratic party was often organized on a statewide or county basis as a private club or association that could freely exclude blacks.

The effort of Texas to use the white primary to shut blacks out of participation in the political process came before the Supreme Court five times.

Nixon v. Herndon: 1927

In 1923 the Texas legislature passed a law forbidding blacks to vote in the state Democratic primary. Dr. L. A. Nixon, a black resident of El Paso, challenged the law, arguing that it clearly violated the Fourteenth and Fifteenth Amendments.

In *Nixon v. Herndon,* decided in 1927, the Supreme Court agreed with Nixon's Fourteenth Amendment claim. "A more direct and obvious infringement," of the equal protection guarantee would be hard to imagine, wrote Justice Oliver Wendell Holmes, Jr., for a unanimous Court.[26]

Nixon v. Condon: 1932

After *Herndon* the legislature authorized state political parties' executive committees to establish their own qualifications for voting in the primary. Nixon again sued, challenging the law as racially discriminatory.

Attorneys for the state argued that the Fourteenth Amendment's equal protection clause did not apply because the party, not state officials, set up the allegedly discriminatory standards.

With Justice Benjamin N. Cardozo writing for the majority of five, the Court held that the executive committee of the Democratic party acted as a delegate of the state in setting voter qualifications, that its action was equivalent to state action and thus within the scope of the equal protection guarantee it violated.[27]

Grovey v. Townsend: 1935

The Texas Democratic party forthwith, without state direction or authorization, voted to limit party membership to whites.

In 1935, with its decision in *Grovey v. Townsend,* the Supreme Court unanimously held that the political party was not acting as a creature of the state and that its action was thus unreachable under either the Fourteenth or Fifteenth Amendments. The Court in this case viewed the political party as a private club, a voluntary association of private individuals, whose actions—even in controlling access to the vote—were not restricted by the Constitution.[28]

United States v. Classic: 1941

Only six years later, however, the Court began to cut away the foundation on which *Grovey v. Townsend* was based. In 1941—in *United States v. Classic*—the Court discarded the *Newberry* restriction on federal power to regulate primary elections.

Classic was not a racial discrimination case at all. Classic, an overzealous opponent of Louisiana governor Huey Long, was convicted of falsifying election returns. His conviction was based on the federal law that made it a crime "to injure, oppress, threaten or intimidate any citizen in the free exercise or enjoyment of any right or privilege secured to him by the Constitution." He challenged his conviction, arguing that the right to vote in a primary election was not a right secured by the Constitution.

The prosecution in *Classic* was initiated by the newly formed civil rights section of the Justice Department set up by Attorney General Frank Murphy and later directed by Attorney General Robert Jackson, both of whom became members of the Supreme Court. The case was argued before the Court by Herbert Wechsler, a former law clerk to Justice Harlan Fiske Stone and by Jackson.

The Court upheld Classic's conviction and declared that the primary was an integral part of the election process. The authority of Congress under Article I, section 4, to regulate elections included the authority to regulate primary elections, wrote Justice Stone, "when, as in this case, they are a step in the exercise by the people of their choice of representatives in Congress." [29]

Smith v. Allwright: 1944

Three years later, in 1944, the Court overturned *Grovey* and held the all-white primary unconstitutional.

Smith v. Allwright arose out of the refusal of S. S. Allwright, a county election official, to permit Lonnie E. Smith, a black man, to vote in the 1940 Texas Democratic primary. Smith sued Allwright for damages. Lower federal courts denied Smith the right to bring suit, citing *Grovey v. Townsend* as placing this sort of discrimination beyond federal control.

Smith was represented before the Supreme Court by two attorneys for the National Association for the Advancement of Colored People, William H. Hastie and Thurgood Marshall, both later distinguished judges, with Marshall becoming the first black member of theCourt.

The Court heard arguments twice in the case. On April 3, 1944, the Court held the white primary unconstitutional as a violation of the Fifteenth Amendment.

The seven justices appointed by Roosevelt since the *Grovey* decision, along with Stone, who had voted with the majority in *Grovey*, found state action evident in the number of state laws regulating primary elections.

Writing for the majority, Justice Stanley Reed linked *Classic* and *Smith v. Allwright:*

> The fusing by the *Classic* case of the primary and general elections into a single instrumentality for choice of officers has a definite bearing on the permissibility under the Constitution of excluding Negroes from primaries.... *Classic* bears upon *Grovey v. Townsend* not because exclusion of Negroes from primaries is any more or less state action by reason of the unitary character of the electoral process but because the recognition of the place of the primary in the electoral scheme makes clear that state delegation to a party of the power to fix the qualifications of primary elections is delegation of a state function that may make the party's action the action of the state.[30]

Thus, held the Court, Allwright's action was state action abridging Smith's right to vote just because of his race, a clear violation of the Fifteenth Amendment.

Only Justice Owen J. Roberts sounded a dissenting voice as the Court overturned *Grovey v. Townsend*, a decision not yet a decade old. Author of the Court's opinion in *Grovey*, Roberts warned that by overruling such a recent decision, the Court "tends to bring adjudications of this tribunal into the same class as a restricted railroad ticket, good for this day and train only." [31]

Terry v. Adams: 1953

In 1953, with still another Supreme Court decision, the relentless effort of Texas Democrats—and politicians in other southern states—to maintain the white primary at last came to an end.

Since 1889 the Jaybird party, an all-white Democratic organization in one Texas county, had declared itself a private club and had submitted political candidates' names in an unofficial county white primary. The successful candidate in the Jaybird primary invariably entered and won the following Democratic primary and general election.

The Court struck down this strategem as a violation of the Fifteenth Amendment, finding the use of racially exclusive private clubs as a· political caucus a violation of the Fifteenth Amendment. Justice Black wrote in the majority opinion in *Terry v. Adams:*

> [T]he Jaybird primary has become an integral part, indeed the only effective part, of the elective process that determines who shall rule and govern in the county. The effect of the whole procedure, Jaybird primary plus Democratic primary plus general election, is to do precisely that which the Fifteenth Amendment forbids—strip Negroes of every vestige of influence in selecting the officials who control the local county matters that intimately touch the daily lives of citizens.[32]

Poll Taxes

In the early days of the republic, poll taxes replaced landholding, property, and other more burdensome requirements for voters, but most poll taxes were eliminated by the time of the Civil War.

This sort of tax was revived in the early 1890s, as one of the devices used to restrict the suffrage to white voters in the South. The ostensible reason for reintroduction of the poll tax was to "cleanse" the state of such election abuses as repeat voting.

A Legitimate Tax

In 1937 the Supreme Court upheld the constitutionality of the poll tax against the challenge that it violated the equal protection guarantee of the Fourteenth Amendment. In *Breedlove v. Suttles,* the Court held that the tax assessed upon voters by Georgia was a legitimate means of raising revenue. It was not a denial of equal protection, held the Court, because, on its face, it applied to Negro and white voters alike.

The Court, for whom Justice Pierce Butler wrote the opinion, rejected the notion that the Georgia tax was an impermissible levy on a federally guaranteed right.[33]

After the Populist era many states had voluntarily dropped use of the poll tax. Proposals to abolish it were introduced in every Congress from 1939 to 1962. By 1960 only four states still required its payment by voters. In August 1962 the House approved a constitutional amendment—already accepted by the Senate—that outlawed poll taxes in federal elections.

Constitutional Amendment

The poll tax ban was ratified as the Twenty-fourth Amendment January 23, 1964. The first Supreme Court decision interpreting the amendment came in 1965. The Court in *Harman v. Forssenius* struck down Virginia's effort to anticipate the poll tax ban by giving voters in federal elections the option of paying the levy or filing a certificate of residence before each election.

The Court held that the reregistration/residence requirement for persons who chose to exercise their right to vote without paying a poll tax subverted the effect of the Twenty-fourth Amendment.[34]

In 1966 the Court held the poll tax an unconstitutional requirement for voting in state and local elections as well. "Wealth, like race, creed, or color is not germane to one's ability to participate intelligently in the electoral process," wrote Justice Douglas for the Court in *Harper v. State Board of Elections*. Thus the Court struck down Virginia's $1.50 poll tax as a violation of the equal protection clause, overruling *Breedlove v. Suttles*.[35]

Douglas explained the Court's reasoning.

> We conclude that a State violates the Equal Protection

Clause of the Fourteenth Amendment whenever it makes the affluence of the voter or payment of any fee an electoral standard. Voter qualifications have no relation to wealth nor to paying or not paying this or any other tax....

To introduce wealth or payment of a fee as a measure of a voter's qualifications is to introduce a capricious or irrelevant factor.... In this context—that is, as a condition of obtaining a ballot—the requirement of fee paying causes an "invidious" discrimination ... that runs afoul of the Equal Protection Clause.[36]

Justices Black and Harlan wrote dissents. Black argued that the majority was merely incorporating its notion of good government policy into the Constitution. Harlan, with whom Justice Potter Stewart concurred, described the majority opinion as "wholly inadequate" to explain why a poll tax was "irrational or invidious." [37]

The Racial Gerrymander

Even as the white primary, literacy tests, and poll taxes were disappearing from the electoral framework of the South, the Supreme Court struck down still another device used to disenfranchise black voters.

Northern and southern states both made some use of the racial gerrymander—the practice of drawing election district boundary lines to dilute or eliminate any concentration of black voting strength in a single district.

In 1960 the case of *Gomillion v. Lightfoot* brought this practice before the Supreme Court, which found it a clear violation of the Fifteenth Amendment. The Court's ruling was notable for two other reasons: it predated by two years the Court's abandonment of its traditional hands-off policy toward redistricting and reapportionment questions, and the majority opinion was written by Justice Frankfurter, who had been the Court's most articulate spokesman for this hands-off policy. *(Details, p. 120)*

Alabama had redefined the boundaries of the city of Tuskegee to exclude virtually all black voters. The excluded blacks sought a court order halting enforcement of the law, which had changed the shape of the city limits from a square to a twenty-eight-sided figure, removing all but four or five qualified black voters from within the city while not removing a single white voter.

Professor C. G. Gomillion of Tuskegee Institute and the other affected black citizens argued both that the gerrymander denied them due process and equal protection under the Fourteenth Amendment and infringed their right to vote in violation of the Fifteenth Amendment.

The Supreme Court unanimously declared the gerrymander unconstitutional. The right of the states to control the boundaries of their political subdivisions is subject to constitutional limitation, it held.

Justice Frankfurter wrote the Court's opinion. Frankfurter had been the author of the Court's opinion in the 1946 case of *Colegrove v. Green*, which declared that the Court ought not to enter the "political thicket" of redistricting questions because they were political questions beyond the competence of the Courts to resolve.[38]

Frankfurter distinguished between *Gomillion* and *Colegrove*, pointing out that *Colegrove* involved involuntary nonracial disparities in districts created by population

shifts, not state action, while *Gomillion,* on the other hand, involved intentional racial discrimination by the state.

When a legislature thus singles out a readily isolated segment of a racial minority for special discriminatory treatment, it violates the Fifteenth Amendment. In no case involving unequal weight in voting distribution that has come before the Court did the decision sanction a differentiation on racial lines whereby approval was given to unequivocal withdrawal of the vote solely from colored citizens. Apart from all else, these considerations lift this controversy out of the so-called "political" arena and into the conventional sphere of constitutional litigation....

While in form this is merely an act redefining metes and bounds, if the allegations are established, the inescapable human effect of this essay in geometry and geography is to despoil colored citizens, and only colored citizens, of their theretofore enjoyed voting rights.[39]

Justice Charles E. Whittaker's concurring opinion pointed out that this application of the Fifteenth Amendment extended the meaning of that amendment, guaranteeing not only the right to vote but also the right to vote in a particular district. The equal protection clause of the Fourteenth Amendment would have been a preferable basis for the ruling, Whittaker wrote:

[I]nasmuch as no one has the right to vote in a political division, or in a local election concerning only an area in which he does not reside, it would seem to follow that one's right to vote in Division A is not abridged by a redistricting that places his residence in Division B *if* he there enjoys the same voting privileges as all others in that Division.

But it does seem clear to me that accomplishment of a State's purpose ... of "fencing Negro citizens out of" Division A and into Division B is an unlawful segregation of races of citizens in violation of the Equal Protection Clause of the Fourteenth Amendment.[40]

In 1962 Manhattan voters brought suit charging that a New York congressional districting law was irrational, discriminatory, and unequal and segregated voters by race and national origin, concentrating white voters in the Seventeenth—"Silk Stocking"—District, and nonwhite and Puerto Rican voters in the Eighteenth, Nineteenth, and Twentieth Congressional Districts.

The Supreme Court found no constitutional violation. Its opinion noted that since Manhattan was a mosaic of ethnic and racial groups, almost any combination of arbitrarily drawn congressional district lines would result in some pattern of racial imbalance subject to challenge as unconstitutional.[41] *(Later ruling, p. 126)*

RIGHT AND POWER: A BROAD VIEW

Although the Court had struck down the use of grandfather clauses and white primaries before 1950, it was

The Right to Run for Public Office

In the late 1960s and 1970s the Supreme Court struck down a number of state-imposed restrictions on the right to run for public office, ruling that they violated the Fourteenth Amendment's guarantee of equal protection.

In 1969 the Court held that a state law requiring valid nominating petitions for independent presidential electors to include the signatures of at least two hundred persons from each of fifty counties—among the total of twenty-five hundred signatures required—violated the "one person, one vote" rule. By setting this arbitrary quota for each of that many counties, held the Court, the law discriminated against voters residing in the more heavily populated counties of the state.[1] With this ruling in *Moore v. Ogilvie*, the Court reversed a 1948 decision upholding the same requirement.[2]

Three years later, in 1972, the Court struck down a state's practice of basing the size of filing fees for candidates on the estimated total cost of an election. This practice, held the Court, discriminated against candidates who could not afford to pay large fees.[3] In 1974 the Court held it unconstitutional for a state to set mandatory high filing fees in order to prevent poor people from running for office.[4]

In a broad-ranging decision relying heavily on First Amendment principles, the Supreme Court in the 1976 case of *Buckley v. Valeo* struck down congressional limits on the amount candidates for president might spend. In that same ruling, however, the justices upheld the limits placed on individual contributions to campaigns and on the contributions of corporate political action committees.[5] *(Details, p. 47)*

Two other rulings reduced the burden that states may impose upon new political parties seeking to win a place on the state ballot. In a 1968 ruling in a case initiated by the American Independent party, the Court struck down Ohio's substantially more burdensome requirements for small or newly organized parties wishing to obtain a place on the ballot. The Court declared that laws that placed heavier burdens on parties other than the Republican and Democratic parties violated the guarantee of equal protection.[6]

Six years later, however, the Court held that a state might properly require new and minority parties seeking a ballot spot to secure a certain number of voter signatures endorsing its effort—and to require that those signatures belong to persons who had not voted in a party primary or otherwise participated in another party's nominating process during that year. This restriction, held the Court, was simply a reasonable means for the state to use in protecting the integrity of its nominating process.[7]

1. *Moore v. Ogilvie*, 394 U.S. 814 (1969).
2. *MacDougall v. Green*, 335 U.S. 281 (1948).
3. *Bullock v. Carter*, 405 U.S. 134 (1972).
4. *Lubin v. Panish*, 415 U.S. 709 (1974).
5. *Buckley v. Valeo*, 424 U.S. 1 (1976).
6. *Williams v. Rhodes*, 393 U.S. 23 (1968).
7. *American Party of Texas v. White, Hainsworth v. White*, 415 U.S. 767 (1974); see also *Munro v. Socialist Workers Party*, __ U.S. __ (1986).

Congress that at last asserted federal power to ensure the right of black citizens to vote.

A constitutional amendment ratified in 1964 outlawed the use of poll taxes in federal elections; the Voting Rights Act of 1965 suspended use of literacy tests and set up federal machinery to protect the opportunity of blacks to register and vote.

Congress began reasserting its authority to enforce the Fifteenth Amendment in 1957. The amendment authorizes Congress to pass appropriate legislation to enforce it. But in the years immediately after adoption of the amendment, efforts to pass enforcing legislation were proscribed by the Court's restrictive view of this power.

The Civil Rights Act of 1957 set up the Civil Rights Commission, which was charged, among other tasks, with studying the problem of voter discrimination. The act also authorized the attorney general to bring lawsuits to halt public and private interference with the right of blacks to vote, and expanded federal jurisdiction over such suits. The Court upheld the investigatory procedures of the commission and the authorization of federal voting rights suits.[42]

Responding to reports that progress in securing voting rights for blacks was still slow even under the provisions of the 1957 act, Congress in 1960 passed a measure that permitted the U.S. attorney general to sue a state for deprivation of voting rights if the individuals named initially as defendants—usually voting registrars—should leave office. This provision remedied a situation that had arisen in a suit brought by the United States against Alabama voting officials.[43]

In addition, Title VI of the 1960 law authorized the appointment of special federal "voting referees" to oversee voter registration in selected counties where a federal court found a pattern of voter discrimination.

The Civil Rights Act of 1964, in its first title, mandated state adoption of standard procedures and requirements for all persons seeking to register to vote. The law also required local officials to justify rejecting a potential voter who had completed the sixth grade or had equivalent evidence of intellectual competence. Other provisions of the 1964 law expedited the movement of voting rights cases to the Supreme Court.[44]

In two cases brought under the 1964 act, the Supreme Court sanctioned the government's efforts to break the pattern of case-by-case litigation of voting rights violations.

The Court upheld federal power to challenge a state's entire constitutional legal framework for voter registration and conduct of elections.[45]

The Voting Rights Act

But progress was still slow. In Dallas County, Alabama, three new federal laws and four years of litigation produced the registration of only 383 black voters out of a potential pool of 15,000 blacks of voting age.

On March 8, 1965, the Reverend Martin Luther King, Jr., led a "Walk for Freedom" to dramatize the need for additional efforts in behalf of registering black voters in Selma, Alabama, and elsewhere in the South. The violence of the reaction of local white law enforcement officers and white bystanders to King's peaceful demonstration drew nationwide attention to the problem.

A week later, President Lyndon B. Johnson addressed a joint session of Congress to ask passage of a new voting rights measure to close the legal loopholes that had so long allowed local officials to stall black voter registration. Johnson explained that "no law that we now have on the books . . . can ensure the right to vote when local officials are determined to deny it."[46]

Later that month, testifying before a Senate committee on the need for such legislation, NAACP official Roy Wilkins—appearing on behalf of the Leadership Conference on Civil Rights—urged Congress to "transform this retail litigation method of registration into a wholesale administration procedure registering all who seek to exercise their democratic birthright."[47]

Within five months, Congress had approved the sweeping Voting Rights Act of 1965. The law suspended literacy tests and provided for the appointment of federal supervisors of voter registration in all states and counties where literacy tests (or similar qualifying devices) were in effect as of November 1, 1964, and where fewer than 50 percent of the voting age residents were registered to vote or did vote in the 1964 presidential election.

The law established criminal penalties for persons found guilty of interfering with the voting rights of others. State or county governments brought under the coverage of the law were required to obtain federal approval of any new voting laws, standards, practices, or procedures before implementing them. A covered state or county could "escape" from the law's provisions if it could convince a three-judge federal court in the District of Columbia that no racial discrimination in registration or voting had occurred in the previous five years.

The act placed federal registration machinery in six southern states (Alabama, Georgia, Mississippi, South Carolina, Louisiana, and Virginia), Alaska, twenty-eight counties in North Carolina, three counties in Arizona, and one in Idaho.

It was the most effective civil rights legislation ever enacted. Within four years, almost one million blacks had registered to vote under its provisions.[48]

Judicial Support

Not surprisingly, this unprecedented assertion of federal power over electoral and voting matters was immedi-

ately challenged as exceeding congressional authority and encroaching on states' rights. But times and the Court had changed since the post-Civil War era, and in 1966 the Supreme Court firmly backed the power of Congress to pass such a law.

In *South Carolina v. Katzenbach,* the state asked the Court to halt implementation of the law, charging that Congress had overstepped itself in suspending state voting standards, authorizing the use of federal election examiners, and adopting a "triggering" formula that resulted in its affecting some states, but not others.

At the Court's invitation, Alabama, Georgia, Louisiana, Mississippi, and Virginia filed briefs in support of South Carolina's challenge. Twenty other states filed briefs in support of the law.

South Carolina charged that by suspending voter qualification "tests and devices" in some states, Congress violated the principle that all states were equal. It also alleged that the law denied the affected states due process of law by presuming that high minority population coupled with low voter participation demonstrated the existence of racially discriminatory voting practices. Due process was also denied, argued South Carolina, by the law's failure to allow judicial review of the findings putting the law into effect in a state. Furthermore, the state maintained, the act was an unconstitutional bill of attainder, punishing certain states, and that it violated the separation of powers by using legislative means to find certain states guilty of discrimination.

Taking a far broader view both of the right to vote and congressional power to enforce and protect that right than had the Court of the 1870s and 1880s, the Supreme Court in 1966 rejected all challenges to the act.

"Congress," wrote Chief Justice Warren for eight members of the Court, "has full remedial powers to effectuate the constitutional prohibition against racial discrimination in voting."[49] He continued:

The Voting Rights Act was designed by Congress to banish the blight of racial discrimination in voting, which has infected the electoral process in parts of our country for nearly a century. . . . Congress assumed the power to prescribe these remedies from Section 2 of the Fifteenth Amendment, which authorizes the National Legislature to effectuate by "appropriate" measures the constitutional prohibition against racial discrimination in voting. We hold that the sections of the Act which are properly before us are an appropriate means for carrying out Congress' constitutional responsibilities and are consonant with all other provisions of the Constitution. We therefore deny South Carolina's request that enforcement of these sections of the act be enjoined.[50]

Warren responded to the challenges to each particular provision. With respect to the coverage formula, Warren said that it was "rational in both practice and theory." The suspension of tests and devices "was a legitimate response to the problem for which there is ample precedent in Fifteenth Amendment cases." The federal approval requirement for new voting rules in the states covered by the act, Warren observed, "may have been an uncommon exercise of congressional power, as South Carolina contends, but the Court has recognized that exceptional conditions can justify legislative measures not otherwise appropriate." The appointment of federal election examiners was "clearly an appropriate response to the problem, closely related to remedies authorized in prior cases." [51]

Justice Black concurred in part and dissented in part. He agreed that Congress had the power under the Fifteenth Amendment to suspend literacy tests and to authorize federal examiners to register qualified voters. But Black objected to the provisions that suspended any changes in state voting laws until the state obtained approval of the change from the attorney general or the federal district court in the District of Columbia. This provision, Black argued, "so distorts our constitutional structure of government as to render any distinction drawn in the Constitution between state and federal power almost meaningless." [52]

Also in 1966, in *Katzenbach v. Morgan* the Court upheld the portion of the Voting Rights Act that permitted persons educated in accredited "American-flag" schools to vote even if they were unable to read and write English. The provision was aimed at enfranchising Puerto Ricans educated in such schools, living in the United States, but unable to demonstrate literacy in English. [53]

Although the basic constitutionality of the Voting Rights Act was now settled, a steady stream of voting rights cases came to the Court well into the mid-1980s, testing the scope and application of the law. The Court steadfastly backed the act and the broadest possible interpretation and application of its provisions.

In the 1969 case of *Gaston County v. United States*, the Court refused to allow a North Carolina county to reinstate a literacy test. Writing the Court's opinion, Justice Harlan linked the county's earlier maintenance of segregated schools and the literacy level of its blacks and declared that to reinstitute the literacy qualification for voters would simply perpetuate the inequality of the denial of equal educational opportunity. [54] *(Details, p. 111)*

In a number of other cases the Court upheld the preclearance requirement for a wide variety of laws and practices affecting the right to vote. [55]

In 1978 the Court even extended the requirement to apply to a county school board's rule that any employee running for state office must take leave from his post without pay during the period of active candidacy. The Court held both that the rule was a voting standard, practice, or procedure subject to the requirement and that the county school board was a political subdivision subject to the provisions of the Voting Rights Act. Four justices dissented on the first point, three on the second. [56]

Earlier, the Court held that annexation of contiguous areas by communities covered by the act was prohibited without prior federal approval. [57]

In 1975, however, the Court held in the case of *Richmond v. United States* that a federally approved annexation plan did not violate the Voting Rights Act—even if it reduced the percentage of black voters in the city's population—so long as there were legitimate objective reasons for the annexation. [58]

In two cases decided in 1977—*Briscoe v. Bell* and *Morris v. Gressette*—the Court also sustained the act's limits on judicial review of the formula that put the law into effect in certain areas, and on judicial review of the attorney general's decision to approve changes in voting laws or practices. [59]

Despite its willingness to affirm the sweeping provisions of the 1965 law as originally enacted and as amended, the Court has refused to interpret it as forbidding all use of racial criteria in redistricting or as requiring that blacks be given proportional representation on elected bodies.

In its 1976 decision in *Beer v. United States,* the Court upheld a city's reapportionment of the districts from which city council members were chosen. The change resulted in an increase in the number of black council members, but not in a proportional representation of black voters among the council members. The Court held that the Voting Rights Act was satisfied so long as such changes did not reduce the voting strength of racial minorities. [60]

And—although the Court in *Gomillion v. Lightfoot* had held as unconstitutional any redistricting that was clearly intended to deny or dilute the right of blacks to vote—it held in 1977 that states could still use some racial criteria in drawing electoral districts for members of the state legislature.

In *United Jewish Organizations of Williamsburgh v. Carey,* the Court upheld New York's 1974 redistricting law that purposely redrew certain districts with nonwhite majorities of at least 65 percent. The county affected was one of three in the state brought under the coverage of the Voting Rights Act by the 1970 amendments to that law.

The Hasidic Jewish community of the Williamsburgh section of Brooklyn objected to the redrawn lines because the new boundaries divided their voting strength between two districts. The Jewish community argued that such use of racial criteria in the redistricting plan deprived them of equal protection guaranteed by the Fourteenth Amendment and diluted their voting strength in violation of the Fifteenth Amendment.

The Constitution does not prevent all use of racial criteria in districting and apportionment, wrote Justice Byron R. White for seven members of the majority. Nor, he continued, does it "prevent a State subject to the Voting Rights Act from deliberately creating or preserving black majorities in particular districts in order to ensure that its reapportionment plan complies with [the act]."

"There is no doubt," White continued, that the state in drawing new district lines, "deliberately used race in a purposeful manner. But its plan represented no racial slur or stigma with respect to whites or any other race, and we discern no discrimination violative of the Fourteenth Amendment nor any abridgment of the right to vote on account of race within the meaning of the Fifteenth Amendment." [61]

In 1980 the Court for the first time narrowed the reach of the Voting Rights Act, ruling 6-3 in *Mobile v. Bolden* that it did not reach a voting system that was found discriminatory in effect, unless there was evidence that the system was also discriminatory in its intent.

Justice Stewart wrote the opinion, declaring that "the Fifteenth Amendment does not entail the right to have Negro candidates elected," but only guaranteed that blacks be able to "register and vote without hindrance." The fact that no black had ever been elected city commissioner under Mobile's challenged system of at-large elections was not enough to prove the system in violation of the Voting Rights Act or the Constitution. [62]

The dissenters were Justices Marshall, White, and William J. Brennan, Jr. Marshall protested the Court's acquiescence in the "vote dilution" that occurred in this situation for black residents of Mobile. He was not arguing for proportional representation of blacks, he said, but simply that it was not permissible for "the right to vote [to be] . . . granted in form, but denied in substance." [63]

The Mobile decision set off an immediate reaction on Capitol Hill. In 1982 Congress extended the Voting Rights Act, writing into the law specific language to overturn

Mobile by declaring that a voting practice or law that had the effect of discriminating against blacks or other minorities violated the law, whatever its intent.[64]

In 1986 the Court applied that new test in *Thornburg v. Gingles,* ruling that six of North Carolina's multimember legislative districts impermissibly diluted the strength of black votes in the state. The fact that very few blacks had been elected from those districts was enough to prove that the system was in violation of the law, the Court held.[65]

Notes

1. *Minor v. Happersett,* 88 U.S. 627 at 629 (1874).
2. *United States v. Reese,* 92 U.S. 563 at 564 (1876).
3. *United States v. Cruikshank,* 92 U.S. 542 at 555 (1876).
4. Id. at 554-556.
5. *Ex parte Siebold,* 100 U.S. 371 (1880).
6. *Ex parte Clarke,* 100 U.S. 399 (1880); *United States v. Gale,* 109 U.S. 65 (1883). *In re Coy,* 127 U.S. 731 (1888); *United States v. Mosely,* 238 U.S. 383 (1915).
7. *Ex parte Yarbrough,* 110 U.S. 651 at 657-658, 663-664 (1884).
8. Id. at 666.
9. Id. at 667.
10. *James v. Bowman,* 190 U.S. 127 at 139 (1903).
11. C. Vann Woodward, *The Strange Career of Jim Crow,* 2d rev. ed. (New York: Oxford University Press, 1966), 82-93.
12. *Williams v. Mississippi,* 170 U.S. 213 at 225 (1898).
13. *Guinn v. United States,* 238 U.S. 347 at 366 (1915).
14. *United States v. Mosley,* 238 U.S. 383 at 386 (1915).
15. *Lane v. Wilson,* 307 U.S. 268 at 275 (1939).
16. *Davis v. Schnell,* 336 U.S. 933 (1949).
17. *Lassiter v. Northampton County Board of Elections,* 360 U.S. 45 at 51-54 (1959).
18. *Louisiana v. United States,* 380 U.S. 145 at 152-153 (1965).
19. *South Carolina v. Katzenbach,* 383 U.S. 301 (1966).
20. Id. at 328, 334.
21. *Katzenbach v. Morgan,* 384 U.S. 641 (1966); *Cardona v. Power,* 384 U.S. 672 (1966).
22. *Gaston County v. United States,* 395 U.S. 285 (1969).
23. Id. at 296-297.
24. *Oregon v. Mitchell,* 400 U.S. 112 (1970).
25. *Newberry v. United States,* 256 U.S. 232 (1921).
26. *Nixon v. Herndon,* 273 U.S. 536 at 541 (1927).
27. *Nixon v. Condon,* 286 U.S. 73 (1932).
28. *Grovey v. Townsend,* 295 U.S. 45 (1935).
29. *United States v. Classic,* 313 U.S. 299 at 317 (1941).
30. *Smith v. Allwright,* 321 U.S. 649 at 660 (1944).
31. Id. at 669.
32. *Terry v. Adams,* 345 U.S. 461 at 469-470 (1953).
33. *Breedlove v. Suttles,* 302 U.S. 277 (1937).
34. *Harman v. Forssenius,* 380 U.S. 528 (1965).
35. *Harper v. Virginia State Board of Elections,* 383 U.S. 663 at 668 (1966).
36. Id. at 666, 668.
37. Id. at 683, 686.
38. *Colegrove v. Green,* 328 U.S. 549 (1946).
39. *Gomillion v. Lightfoot,* 364 U.S. 339 at 346-347 (1960).
40. Id. at 349.
41. *Wright v. Rockefeller,* 376 U.S. 52 (1964).
42. *United States v. Raines,* 362 U.S. 17 (1960); *Hannah v. Larch,* 363 U.S. 420 (1960).
43. Congressional Quarterly, *Congress and the Nation,* vol. 1 (Washington, D.C.: Congressional Quarterly, 1965), 1628; *United States v. Alabama,* 362 U.S. 602 (1960).
44. Congressional Quarterly, *Congress and the Nation,* vol. 1, 1638.
45. *United States v. Louisiana,* 380 U.S. 145 (1965); *United States v. Mississippi,* 380 U.S. 128 (1965).
46. Lyndon B. Johnson, *Public Papers of the Presidents of the United States, Lyndon B. Johnson, 1965,* Book I (Washington, D.C.: U.S. Government Printing Office, 1966), March 15, 1965, 282.
47. U.S. Congress. Senate. Judiciary Committee. Voting Rights (Part II), Statement of Roy Wilkins, 89th Cong. 1st Sess. 1965, 1005.
48. Congressional Quarterly, *Congress and the Nation,* vol. II (Washington, D.C.: Congressional Quarterly, 1969), 354, 356-365.
49. *South Carolina v. Katzenbach,* 383 U.S. 301 at 326 (1966).
50. Id. at 308.
51. Id. at 330, 334, 336.
52. Id. at 358.
53. *Katzenbach v. Morgan,* 384 U.S. 641 (1966).
54. *Gaston County v. United States,* 395 U.S. 285 (1969).
55. *Allen v. Virginia Board of Elections,* 393 U.S. 544 (1969); *Hadnott v. Amos,* 394 U.S. 358 (1969); see also *McDaniel v. Sanchez,* 452 U.S. 130 (1981); *Hathorn v. Lovorn,* 457 U.S. 255 (1982); *City of Port Arthur, Texas v. United States,* 459 U.S. 159 (1982); *NAACP v. Hampton County Election Commission,* 470 U.S. 166 (1985).
56. *Dougherty County Board of Education v. White,* 435 U.S. 921 (1978).
57. *Perkins v. Mathews,* 400 U.S. 379 (1971); see also *City of Pleasant Grove v. United States,* __ U.S. __ (1987).
58. *Richmond v. United States,* 422 U.S. 358 (1975).
59. *Briscoe v. Bell,* 432 U.S. 404 (1977); *Morris v. Gressette,* 432 U.S. 491 (1977).
60. *Beer v. United States,* 425 U.S. 130 (1976).
61. *United Jewish Organizations of Williamsburgh v. Carey,* 430 U.S. 144 at 161, 165 (1977).
62. *City of Mobile v. Bolden,* 446 U.S. 55 at 65 (1980).
63. Id. at 141.
64. Congressional Quarterly, *Congress and the Nation,* vol. VI, 680.
65. *Thornburg v. Gingles,* 478 U.S. 30 (1986).

5

The Right to an Equal Vote

In the early 1960s, as Congress was moving to fulfill at last the promise of the Fifteenth Amendment, the Supreme Court sparked a second revolution in the nation's electoral system, based on the equal protection guarantee of the Fourteenth Amendment. In 1962 the Court abandoned its long-standing policy of noninterference in the malapportionment of population among a state's electoral districts. By the end of the decade, the Court's rulings had required that almost all the nation's legislative and congressional district lines be redrawn.

The equal protection guarantee meant that one person's vote should be counted equally with another's. Thus the standard by which these redistricting efforts were measured was that of "one person, one vote."

CONGRESS, DISTRICTS, AND PEOPLE

Article I, section 4 of the Constitution gives Congress the power to override state-set rules governing the election of senators and representatives. The section reads:

The Times, Places and Manner of holding Elections for Senators and Representatives shall be prescribed in each State by the Legislature thereof; but the Congress may at any time by Law make or alter such Regulations, except as to the Places of chusing Senators.

Congress exercised this power in 1842 to require that members of the House be elected from separate districts within each state. In 1872 Congress added the requirement that these districts be of approximately equal population. Subsequent reapportionment statutes, including those enacted in 1901 and 1911, contained the specification that congressional districts be "contiguous and compact territory and containing as nearly as practicable an equal number of inhabitants." [1]

But the next such law, passed in 1929, omitted these requirements, and the Supreme Court in 1932 held the omission intentional and the standards thus no longer in effect. In the case of *Wood v. Broom* the Court upheld a Mississippi redistricting law that failed to provide compact, contiguous, and population-equal districts. [2]

This decision came at a critical time in the nation's demographic history. The 1920 census showed that, for the first time, more Americans lived in cities than in rural settings. The implication was clear: the voice of the farmer in the legislature and in Congress would grow fainter, while that of the city dweller would increase in strength.

But for forty years, while the Supreme Court maintained a hands-off policy, rural interests delayed the political impact of this shift in population.

The Court steadfastly held that challenges to malapportionment were political questions, outside its purview. In 1946 the Court refused to intervene in Illinois, reaffirming its intention to stay out of the "political thicket" of redistricting and reapportionment.

But within two decades the Court reversed that stance of restraint. With the decision announced in *Baker v. Carr*, the Court abandoned its view that malapportionment was a strictly political question. In subsequent rulings the Court moved into the thicket, requiring the redrawing of state legislative and congressional district lines to ensure each voter's ballot equal weight in the state electoral process.

'The Political Thicket'

The case of *Colegrove v. Green* was brought to the Supreme Court in 1946 by Kenneth W. Colegrove, a Northwestern University professor of political science. He challenged Illinois congressional districts as so unequal in population that they in fact denied voters in the more populous districts the equal protection of the law guaranteed by the Fourteenth Amendment. The numerical disparity between these districts, he pointed out, was as large as 800,000 persons.

The Supreme Court, 4-3, threw out his case without addressing the equal protection issue. Justice Robert H.

Jackson did not take part in the decision; the seat of the chief justice was vacant—Chief Justice Harlan Fiske Stone died two months before the decision was announced.[3]

Justice Felix Frankfurter wrote the Court's opinion, joined by Justices Stanley F. Reed and Harold H. Burton. Frankfurter noted that the case could be resolved simply on the same basis as *Wood v. Broom*. Because Congress had omitted the equal population standard from the reapportionment law now in effect, there was no such requirement for states to follow in drawing district lines.

But practical considerations as well dictated the Court's decision not to intervene. Frankfurter continued:

> due regard for the effective working of our Government revealed this issue to be of a peculiarly political nature and therefore not meet for judicial determination. . . .
>
> Nothing is clearer than that this controversy concerns matters that bring courts into immediate and active relations with party contests. From the determination of such issues this Court has traditionally held aloof. It is hostile to a democratic system to involve the judiciary in the politics of the people. . . .
>
> . . . due regard for the Constitution as a viable system precludes judicial correction [of the evils protested here]. Authority for dealing with such problems resides elsewhere. . . . The short of it is that the Constitution [Article I, section 4] has conferred upon Congress exclusive authority to secure fair representation by the States in the popular House and left to that House determination whether States have fulfilled their responsibility. If Congress failed in exercising its powers, whereby standards of fairness are offended, the remedy ultimately lies with the people. Whether Congress faithfully discharges its duty or not, the subject has been committed to the exclusive control of Congress. . . .
>
> To sustain this action would cut very deep into the very being of Congress. Courts ought not to enter this political thicket. The remedy for unfairness in districting is to secure State legislatures that will apportion properly, or to invoke the ample powers of Congress.[4]

The critical fourth vote was cast by Justice Wiley B. Rutledge, who wrote a separate opinion explaining that he did not endorse the position set out by Frankfurter that issues of districting were not proper matters for judicial determination, but that in this case he thought the Court properly dismissed the matter in order to avoid collision with the political departments of the government.[5]

Justices Hugo L. Black, William O. Douglas, and Frank Murphy dissented, finding the matter well within the power of the federal courts to redress constitutional grievances caused by state action.

Black wrote: "What is involved here is the right to vote guaranteed by the Federal Constitution. It has always been the rule that where a federally protected right has been invaded the federal courts will provide the remedy to rectify the wrong done."[6]

Population disparities such as those in this case clearly violated the Fourteenth Amendment, the dissenters concluded, and the Court should grant relief.

Colegrove stood for sixteen years as a firmly planted obstacle to judicial inquiry into the apportionment of state legislatures, as well as into the distribution of population among congressional districts.

Race and Redistricting

But in 1960—with Justice Frankfurter speaking for the Court—the Supreme Court made an exception to its refusal to intervene in such matters. Civil rights and redistricting converged in the case of *Gomillion v. Lightfoot*, and the Supreme Court was persuaded by a claim of racial discrimination to strike down an Alabama law redrawing Tuskegee's voting boundary lines to eliminate nearly every black voter from the city's limits.[7] *(Details, p. 114)*

Justice Frankfurter drew a clear line between redistricting challenges based on the Fourteenth Amendment, like *Colegrove*, and those based on the Fifteenth Amendment, like *Gomillion*.

> The decisive facts in this case . . . are wholly different from the considerations found controlling in *Colegrove*.
>
> That case involved a complaint of discriminatory apportionment of congressional districts. The appellants in *Colegrove* complained only of a dilution of the strength of their votes as a result of legislative inaction over a course of many years. The petitioners here complain that affirmative legislative action deprives them of their vote and the consequent advantages that the ballot affords. . . .
>
> When a state exercises power wholly within the domain of state interest, it is insulated from federal judicial review. But such insulation is not carried over when state power is used as an instrument of circumventing a federally protected right.[8]

Baker v. Carr

By 1962 only three members of the *Colegrove* Court remained on the bench: Frankfurter, Black, and Douglas—the latter two, dissenters from the 1946 ruling.

By that year, as well, studies made clear that the once slight advantage in representation of rural voters in state legislatures had become extremely distorted representation. Rural districts held nearly twice as many seats as they would have been entitled to by apportionment on a population basis alone. A similar degree of population imbalance also existed with respect to congressional districts.

In the 1962 Tennessee redistricting case of *Baker v. Carr*, the Supreme Court took its first step into the political thicket of legislative reapportionment.[9]

The Tennessee legislature had failed to reapportion itself for sixty years, despite the fact that the state constitution required decennial reapportionment after each census. By 1960 population shifts from rural to urban regions of the state had created dramatic disparities in the pattern of representation for state house and senate seats. Justice Tom C. Clark in his concurring opinion in *Baker v. Carr* pointed out that two-thirds of the members of the state senate were elected by slightly more than one-third of the state's population, while two-thirds of the members of the house were elected by 40 percent of the state's voters.[10]

Appeals to the legislature to reapportion itself were futile. A suit brought in state court was rejected on the grounds that state courts—like federal courts—should stay out of such legislative matters. The city dwellers who brought the state suit then appealed to the federal courts, charging that the "unconstitutional and obsolete" appor-

Political Questions and Judicial Answers

The "political question" doctrine that the Supreme Court invoked in 1946 to avoid addressing the issue of legislative malapportionment is one of the oldest of the Court's rationales for *not* deciding a case.

In his classic discussion of judicial power in *Marbury v. Madison,* Chief Justice John Marshall declared:

The province of the court is, solely, to decide on the rights of individuals, not to inquire how the executive, or executive officers, perform duties in which they have a discretion. Questions in their nature political, or which are, by the Constitution and laws, submitted to the executive, can never be made in this court.[1]

In the ensuing years the Court used this doctrine as a convenient device for avoiding collisions with Congress, the president, or the states on matters ranging from foreign relations to malapportioned congressional districts.

The attributes of the doctrine are quite variable. One modern justice has observed that they "in various settings, diverge, combine, appear, and disappear in seeming disorderliness."[2]

The Constitution provides that the United States shall guarantee to every state a republican form of government. When the question of enforcing that guarantee came for the first time to the Supreme Court in 1849, however, the Court made clear that this was a "political question" beyond its reach.

The case of *Luther v. Borden* involved two competing groups, each asserting that they were the lawful government of Rhode Island. In the Court's opinion, Chief Justice Roger B. Taney stated firmly that it was up to Congress to decide which government was the legitimate one. He explained:

when the senators and representatives of a State are admitted into the councils of the Union, the authority of the government under which they are appointed, as well as its republican character, is recognized by the proper constitutional authority.

And its decision is binding on every other department of the government, and could not be questioned in a judicial tribunal.[3]

The Court has remained quite consistent in applying the political question doctrine to avoid addressing "guaranty clause" challenges to state action.[4]

In another early nineteenth century ruling, the Court placed questions of foreign policy and foreign affairs firmly in the "political question" category. In 1829 the Court refused to settle an international border question, stating that it was not the role of the courts to assert national interests against foreign powers.[5] That point has been reaffirmed throughout the Court's history, based firmly on the view that in foreign affairs the nation should speak with a single voice.[6]

In similar fashion, the Court has generally invoked the political question doctrine to refuse to intervene in questions of legislative process or procedure, leaving their resolution to Congress or the states.

The exception to that general practice has come in cases raising questions of basic constitutional standards—such as the power of Congress to legislate on certain matters, or the propriety of one chamber's action excluding a member who meets constitutional qualifications[7]—or in matters where Congress and the president are deadlocked over an issue.[8]

For most of the nation's history, the Court also viewed challenges to state decisions allocating population among electoral districts as a political question. It was in this vein that Justice Felix Frankfurter wrote in *Colegrove v. Green* (1946) that for Courts to involve themselves in malapportionment controversies was "hostile to a democratic system."[9]

But sixteen years later, the Court in *Baker v. Carr* found the *Colegrove* ruling based on too broad a definition of "political questions." For the new majority, Justice William J. Brennan, Jr., explained:

it is the relationship between the judiciary and the coordinate branches of the Federal Government, and not the federal judiciary's relationship to the States, which gives rise to the "political questions.". . . The nonjusticiability of a political question is primarily a function of the separation of powers.[10]

The basic question of fairness involved in *Baker v. Carr,* wrote Brennan, was constitutional, not political, and was therefore well within the jurisdiction of the Court. Simply "the presence of a matter affecting state government does not [in and of itself] render the case nonjusticiable."[11]

1. *Marbury v. Madison,* 1 Cr. 137 at 170 (1803).
2. *Baker v. Carr,* 369 U.S. 186 at 210 (1962).
3. *Luther v. Borden,* 7 How. 1 at 42 (1849).
4. *Pacific States Telephone and Telegraph Co. v. Oregon,* 223 U.S. 118 (1912).
5. *Foster v. Neilson,* 2 Pet. 253 at 307 (1829).
6. *Oetjen v. Central Leather Co.,* 246 U.S. 297 at 302 (1918); *United States v. Curtiss-Wright Export Corporation,* 299 U.S. 304 (1936).
7. *Hawke v. Smith,* 253 U.S. 221 (1920); *Coleman v. Miller,* 307 U.S. 433 (1939); *Powell v. McCormack,* 395 U.S. 486 (1969).
8. *Pocket Veto Case,* 279 U.S. 655 (1929).
9. *Colegrove v. Green,* 328 U.S. 549 at 554 (1946).
10. *Baker v. Carr,* 369 U.S. 186 at 210 (1962).
11. Id. at 232.

tionment system denied them the equal protection of the laws promised by the Fourteenth Amendment.

In *Baker v. Carr*, the Court ruled 6-2 that constitutional challenges to legislative malapportionment could properly be considered by federal courts. Such claims were "justiciable," held the Court in the decision announced on March 26, 1962, abandoning the view that they were political questions outside the competence of the courts.

The Court stopped there. It did not go on to address the merits of the challenge to malapportionment.

The Opinion

Justice William J. Brennan, Jr., wrote the Court's opinion in *Baker v. Carr*. With surprising ease, the majority resolved the question of federal jurisdiction over the case. The complaint clearly arose under one of the provisions of the U.S. Constitution, Brennan wrote, so it fell within the federal judicial power as defined in Article III. "An unbroken line of our precedents sustains the federal courts' jurisdiction of the subject matter of federal constitutional claims of this nature." [11]

Then, turning to the question of the voters' standing to bring the case, Brennan explained that they did have such standing because they had been deprived of an interest they sought to defend.

These appellants seek relief in order to protect or vindicate an interest of their own.... Their constitutional claim is, in substance, that the 1901 statute [setting up the existing districting and apportionment structure] constitutes arbitrary and capricious state action, offensive to the Fourteenth Amendment in its irrational disregard of the standard of apportionment prescribed by the State's Constitution or of any standard, effecting a gross disproportion of representation to voting population. [12]

This holding did not require the Court to decide the merits of the voters' allegations, Brennan wrote. But he did consider the critical question of the justiciability of the issue—its suitability to judicial solution.

Did this suit present a "political question" outside the proper scope of the Supreme Court's consideration? Brennan's answer was no.

He explained:

the mere fact that the suit seeks protection of a political right does not mean it presents a political question.... It is argued that apportionment cases, whatever the actual wording of the complaint, can involve no federal constitutional right except one resting on the guaranty of a republican form of government, and that complaints based on that clause have been held to present political questions which are nonjusticiable.

We hold that the claim pleaded here neither rests upon nor implicates the Guaranty Clause and that its justiciability is therefore not foreclosed by our decisions of cases involving that clause. The District Court misinterpreted *Colegrove v. Green* and other decisions of this Court on which it relied. [13]

The guaranty clause to which Brennan referred is the provision in Article IV of the Constitution that states that the United States shall guarantee to every state a republican form of government. One of the first major expositions of the "political question" doctrine in the 1849 case of *Luther v. Borden* involved this guarantee. The Court held

its enforcement to be a political question, left to the political branches—Congress and the president—and outside judicial competence. [14]

Justice Charles E. Whittaker, who retired a week later, did not participate in the decision.

Concurring Opinions

Justices Douglas, Clark, and Potter Stewart wrote concurring opinions.

Douglas emphasized the Court's frequent role as protector of voting rights.

Clark would have gone further and considered the merits of the particular complaint and granted relief: "[No] one, not even the State nor the dissenters, has come up with any rational basis for Tennessee's apportionment statute." [15] Nevertheless, Clark recommended that federal courts intrude in reapportionment matters only as a last resort.

Stewart reiterated that the Court had decided only that such Fourteenth Amendment challenges to malapportionment were justiciable matters and that the persons bringing this case had standing to sue.

Dissenting Opinions

Justices Frankfurter and John Marshall Harlan dissented. In what was his last major opinion, Frankfurter criticized the majority for "[s]uch a massive repudiation of the experience of our whole past in asserting destructively novel judicial power." The Court had, he argued, allowed a "hypothetical claim resting on abstract assumptions" to become "the basis for affording illusory relief for a particular evil even though it foreshadows deeper and more pervasive difficulties in consequence." [16]

Frankfurter went on to say that to give judges the task of "accommodating the incommensurable factors of policy" involved in reapportionment plans was "to attribute ... omnicompetence to judges." By this decision, he wrote, the Supreme Court gave the nation's courts the power "to devise what should constitute the proper composition of the legislatures of the fifty States." The Court had overlooked the fact, he added, "that there is not under our Constitution a judicial remedy for every political mischief, for every undesirable exercise of legislative power." [17]

Justice Harlan found the Tennessee plan rational and wrote that he saw "nothing in the Equal Protection Clause or elsewhere in the Federal Constitution which expressly or impliedly supports the view that state legislatures must be so structured as to reflect with approximate equality the voice of every voter.... In short, there is nothing in the Federal Constitution to prevent a State, acting not irrationally, from choosing any electoral legislative structure it thinks best suited to the interests, temper, and customs of its people." [18]

Harlan concluded with a strong criticism of the majority's action, saying that "what the Court is doing reflects more an adventure in judicial experimentation than a solid piece of constitutional adjudication." [19]

'One Person, One Vote'

The decision in *Baker v. Carr* opened the doors of federal courtrooms across the country to litigants challenging state and congressional apportionment systems. But it provided no standards to guide federal judges in measuring the validity of challenged systems.

With its subsequent rulings in 1963 and 1964, the Supreme Court formulated a standard, known far and wide as the "one man, one vote" or "one person, one vote" rule.

Two new justices participated in these decisions. After *Baker v. Carr,* Justices Whittaker and Frankfurter retired. President John F. Kennedy appointed Byron R. White to replace Whittaker and Arthur J. Goldberg to succeed Frankfurter.

The Rule Announced

The "one person, one vote" rule was first set out by the Court almost exactly one year after *Baker v. Carr.* But the case in which the announcement came did not involve legislative districts.

In *Gray v. Sanders* the Court found that Georgia's county-unit primary system for electing state officials—a system which weighted votes to give advantage to rural districts in statewide primary elections—denied voters the equal protection of the laws.

Justice Douglas's opinion for eight members of the Court rejected the state's effort to defend this weighted vote system by analogy to the electoral college system. The electoral college system was included in the Constitution because of specific historical concerns, Douglas wrote, but that inclusion "implied nothing about the use of an analogous system by a State in a statewide election." [20]

All votes in a statewide election must have equal weight, held the Court:

How then can one person be given twice or 10 times the voting power of another person in a statewide election merely because he lives in a rural area or because he lives in the smallest rural county? Once the geographical unit for which a representative is to be chosen is designated, all who participate in the election are to have an equal vote—whatever their race, whatever their sex, whatever their occupation, whatever their income, and wherever their home may be in that geographical unit. This is required by the Equal Protection Clause of the Fourteenth Amendment. The concept of "we the people" under the Constitution visualizes no preferred class of voters but equality among those who meet the basic qualification. The idea that every voter is equal to every other voter in his State, when he casts his ballot in favor of one of several competing candidates, underlies many of our decisions. . . . The conception of political equality from the Declaration of Independence to Lincoln's Gettysburg Address, to the Fifteenth, Seventeenth, and Nineteenth Amendments can mean only one thing—one person, one vote. [21]

Justice Harlan again dissented:

The Court's holding surely . . . flies in the face of history . . . "one person, one vote" has never been the universally accepted political philosophy in England, the American Colonies, or in the United States. . . . I do not understand how, on the basis of these mere numbers, unilluminated as they are by any of the complex and subtle political factors involved, a court of law can say, except by judicial fiat, that these disparities are in themselves constitutionally invidious. [22]

The Rule Applied

The Court's rulings in *Baker* and *Gray* concerned the equal weighting and counting of votes cast in state elections. In 1964, deciding the case of *Wesberry v. Sanders,* the Court applied the "one person, one vote" principle to congressional districts and set equality, not rationality, as the standard for congressional redistricting.

'One Man, One Vote' At City Hall

In several recent rulings the Supreme Court has extended the application of the "one person, one vote" rule to some local, as well as state and national, electoral districts.

In 1967 the Court ruled that county school board members, each representing a local board, from districts of disparate population, were not subject to this rule because the county board performed administrative, not legislative, functions. [1]

But in *Avery v. Midland County* the Court ruled in 1968 that when a state delegates lawmaking power to local government and provides for election by district of the officials exercising that power, those districts must be of substantially equal population. [2]

Two years later the Court ruled that the "one person, one vote" rule must be applied to any election—state or local—of persons performing governmental functions:

If one person's vote is given less weight through unequal apportionment, his right to equal voting participation is impaired just as much when he votes for a school board member as when he votes for a state legislator. . . . [T]he crucial consideration is the right of each qualified voter to participate on an equal footing in the election process. [3]

In 1973, however, the Court held that the constitutional guarantee of equal protection did not demand that the "one person, one vote" rule be applied to special-purpose electoral districts such as those devised to regulate water supplies in the West. In such districts, the Court held, states may restrict the franchise to landowners and weigh the votes of each person according to the property he owns. [4]

1. *Sailors v. Board of Education,* 387 U.S. 105 (1967); see also *Dusch v. Davis,* 387 U.S. 112 (1967).
2. *Avery v. Midland County,* 390 U.S. 474 (1968).
3. *Hadley v. Junior College District of Metropolitan Kansas City, Mo.,* 397 U.S. 50 at 55 (1970).
4. *Salyer Land Co. v. Tulare Water District; Associated Enterprises Inc. v. Toltec Watershed Improvement District,* 410 U.S. 743 (1973).

Voters in Georgia's Fifth Congressional District—which included Atlanta—complained that the population of their congressional district was more than twice the ideal state average of 394,312 persons per district. By its failure to redistrict, the state denied them equal protection of the laws, they charged. They also challenged Georgia's apportionment scheme as a violation of Article I, Section 2 of the Constitution that declares that members of the House of Representatives are to be elected "by the people."

A federal district Court dismissed the case in 1962, but the Supreme Court 6-3 reversed the lower Court decision in February 1964.

Justice Black, speaking for six members of the Court, explained:

> We hold that, construed in its historical context, the command of Art. I, Sec. 2, that Representatives be chosen "by the People of the several States" means that as nearly as is practicable, one man's vote in a congressional election is to be worth as much as another's. . . .
>
> To say that a vote is worth more in one district than in another would not only run counter to our fundamental ideas of democratic government, it would cast aside the principle of a House of Representatives elected "by the People."
>
> While it may not be possible to draw congressional districts with mathematical precision, that is no excuse for ignoring our Constitution's plain objective of making equal representation for equal numbers the fundamental goal of the House of Representatives.[23]

Black's view was sharply attacked by Justice Harlan, who dissented:

> The upshot of all this is that the language of Art. I, [Sections] 2 and 4, the surrounding text, and the relevant history are all in strong and consistent direct contradiction of the Court's holding. The constitutional scheme vests in the States plenary power to regulate the conduct of elections for Representatives, and, in order to protect the Federal Government, provides for congressional supervision of the States' exercise of their power. Within this scheme, the appellants do not have the right which they assert, in the absence of provision for equal districts by the Georgia Legislature or the Congress. The constitutional right which the Court creates is manufactured out of whole cloth.[24]

Justice Black did not invoke the equal protection clause in the case. Speculation as to why Black based this ruling on historical grounds rather than on the Fourteenth Amendment suggests that his choice was a compromise among members of the Court.[25]

Four months later, however, eight members agreed on the requirements of the Fourteenth Amendment for state reapportionment.

State Legislative Districts

By a vote of 8-1, the Supreme Court on June 15, 1964, ruled that the Fourteenth Amendment required equally populated electoral districts for both houses of bicameral state legislatures.

This decision is known by the title of a case from Alabama, *Reynolds v. Sims.* But because the case was accompanied to the Supreme Court by a number of others concerning other state legislatures, the Court's decision immediately affected reapportionment in New York, Maryland, Virginia, Delaware, and Colorado. Ultimately, every state legislature felt the impact of *Reynolds v. Sims.*

Writing for the Court what he would often describe as the most significant opinion of his judicial career, Chief Justice Earl Warren stated that the "controlling criterion" for any reapportionment plan must be equal population.[26]

The Court rejected the suggestion that a state might, by analogy to the federal system, constitute one house of its legislature on the basis of population and the other on an area basis.[27]

The Equal Protection Clause required substantially equal representation of all citizens. The Court did not provide any precise formula for defining "substantially equal" and left it to lower Courts to work out a useful standard.

Justice Harlan—the lone dissenter—said the Court's rule had no constitutional basis, and that the drafters of the Fourteenth Amendment had not meant to give the federal government authority to intervene in the internal organization of state legislatures.

Majority Opinion. Chief Justice Warren set forth the reasoning behind the "one person, one vote" rule with clarity and firmness:

> The right to vote freely for the candidate of one's choice is of the essence of a democratic society, and any restrictions on that right strike at the heart of representative government. And the right of suffrage can be denied by a debasement of suffrage or dilution of the weight of a citizen's vote just as effectively as by wholly prohibiting the free exercise of the franchise. . . .
>
> Legislators represent people, not trees or acres. Legislators are elected by voters, not farms or cities or economic interests. As long as ours is a representative form of government, and our legislatures are those instruments of government elected directly by and directly representative of the people, the right to elect legislators in a free and unimpaired fashion is a bedrock of our political system. . . .
>
> . . . The fact that an individual lives here or there is not a legitimate reason for overweighting or diluting the efficacy of his vote. The complexions of societies and civilizations change, often with amazing rapidity. A nation once primarily rural in character becomes predominantly urban. Representation schemes once fair and equitable become archaic and outdated. But the basic principle of representative government remains, and must remain, unchanged—the weight of a citizen's vote cannot be made to depend on where he lives. Population is, of necessity, the starting point for consideration and the controlling criterion for judgment in legislative apportionment controversies. A citizen, a qualified voter, is no more nor no less so because he lives in the city or on the farm. This is the clear and strong command of our Constitution's Equal Protection Clause. This is an essential part of the concept of a government of laws and not men. . . .
>
> The Equal Protection Clause demands no less than substantially equal state legislative representation for all citizens, of all places as well as of all races.
>
> We hold that as a basic constitutional standard, the Equal Protection Clause requires that the seats in both houses of a bicameral state legislature must be apportioned on a population basis. Simply stated, an

individual's right to vote for state legislators is unconstitutionally impaired when its weight is in substantial fashion diluted when compared with votes of citizens living in other parts of the State.[28]

The Court recognized the impossibility of attaining mathematical precision in election district populations:

[T]he Equal Protection Clause requires that a State make an honest and good faith effort to construct districts, in both houses of its legislature, as nearly of equal population as is practicable. We realize that it is a practical impossibility to arrange legislative districts so that each one has an identical number of residents, or citizens, or voters. Mathematical exactness or precision is hardly a workable constitutional requirement.[29]

Warren wrote that in applying the equal population principle:

[S]omewhat more flexibility may therefore be constitutionally permissible with respect to state legislative apportionment than in congressional districting. . . . For the present, we deem it expedient not to attempt to spell out any precise constitutional tests. What is marginally permissible in one State may be unsatisfactory in another, depending on the particular circumstances of the case. Developing a body of doctrine on a case-by-case basis appears to us to provide the most satisfactory means of arriving at detailed constitutional requirements in the area of state legislative apportionment.[30]

Dissenting Opinion. Justice Harlan again dissented, arguing that judicial intervention in reapportionment questions was "profoundly ill advised and constitutionally impermissible." This series of decisions, Harlan said, would weaken the vitality of the political system and "cut deeply into the fabric of our federalism." The Court's ruling gave "support to a current mistaken view of the Constitution and the constitutional function of this Court. This view, in a nutshell, is that every major social ill in this country can find its cure in some constitutional 'principle,' and that this Court should 'take the lead' in promoting reform when other branches of government fail to act. The Constitution is not a panacea for every blot upon the public welfare, nor should this Court, ordained as a judicial body, be thought of as a haven for reform movements." [31]

HOUSE DISTRICTS: STRICT EQUALITY

Five years elapsed between the Court's admonition in *Wesberry v. Sanders,* urging states to make a good-faith effort to construct congressional districts as nearly of equal population as is practicable, and the Court's next application of constitutional standards to redistricting.

In 1967 the Court hinted at the strict stance it would adopt two years later. With two unsigned opinions, the Court sent back to Indiana and Missouri for revision redistricting plans for congressional districts that allowed variations of as much as 20 percent from the average district population.[32]

Political Gerrymanders

The Supreme Court opened the door on a whole new category of political cases on June 30, 1986, ruling that political gerrymanders are subject to constitutional review by federal courts—even if the disputed districts meet the "one person, one vote" test.

"The issue is one of representation," wrote Justice Byron R. White in *Davis v. Bandemer* (478 U.S. 109), "and we decline to hold that such claims are never justiciable."

Davis v. Bandemer came to the Court as a challenge by Indiana Democrats to a 1981 reapportionment of seats for the state legislature. The Democrats argued that the Republican-drawn map so heavily favored the Republican party that it effectively denied Democrats in the state appropriate representation. In the 1982 election, based on the remap, the GOP won a disproportionate share of the seats in the state legislature.

The Republicans responded by arguing that this was a "political question" outside the jurisdiction of federal courts.

The Court, 6-3, rejected that argument, holding that such challenges were justiciable. Dissenting on that point were Chief Justice Warren E. Burger and Justices Sandra Day O'Connor and William H. Rehnquist. They warned, in O'Connor's words, that "the losing party . . . in every reapportionment will now be invited to fight the battle anew in federal court."

But the Court then went on, 7-2, to reject the Democratic challenge to that alleged gerrymander. "Relying on a single election to prove unconstitutional discrimination," wrote White, was "unsatisfactory."

"Unconstitutional discrimination occurs," he continued, "only when the electoral system is arranged in a manner that will consistently degrade a voter's or a group of voters' influence on the political process as a whole."

To prove unconstitutional discrimination through a political gerrymander, both discriminatory intent and effect must be shown, said White. The question to be asked in evaluating such a challenge is "whether a particular group has been unconstitutionally denied its chance to effectively influence the political process. . . . Such a finding of unconstitutionality must be supported by evidence of continued frustration of the will of a majority of the voters or effective denial to a minority of voters of a fair chance to influence the political process."

Justices Lewis F. Powell, Jr., and John Paul Stevens dissented on that point, arguing that "no one factor should be dispositive." They would have invalidated the Indiana remap.

Two years later Missouri's revised plan returned to the Court for full review. With its decision in the case of *Kirkpatrick v. Preisler,* the Court 6-3 rejected the plan. It was unacceptable, held the majority, because it allowed a variation of as much as 3.1 percent from perfectly equal population districts.[33]

The Court thus made clear its strict application of "one person, one vote" to congressional redistricting. Minor deviations from the strict principle of equal population were permissible only when the state provided substantial evidence that the variation was unavoidable.

Writing for the majority, Justice Brennan declared that there was no "fixed numerical or percentage population variance small enough to be considered *de minimis* and to satisfy without question the 'as nearly as practicable' standard." [34]

Brennan continued:

The whole thrust of the "as nearly as practicable" approach is inconsistent with adoption of fixed numerical standards which excuse population variances without regard to the circumstances of each particular case....

The extent to which equality may practicably be achieved may differ from State to State and from district to district.... Unless population variances among congressional districts are shown to have resulted despite such effort, the State must justify each variance, no matter how small....

... to consider a certain range of variances *de minimis* would encourage legislators to strive for that range rather than for equality "as nearly as practicable." ... to accept population variances, large or small, in order to create districts with specific interest orientations is antithetical to the basic premise of the constitutional command to provide equal representation for equal numbers of people.[35]

Justice Abe Fortas concurred with the majority but felt that the Court had set a standard of "near-perfection" difficult to achieve:

Whatever might be the merits of insistence on absolute equality if it could be obtained, the majority's pursuit of precision is a search for a will-o'-the wisp. The fact is that any solution to the apportionment and districting problem is at best an approximation because it is based upon figures which are always to some degree obsolete. No purpose is served by an insistence on precision which is unattainable because of the inherent imprecisions in the population data on which districting must be based.[36]

Justices Harlan, Stewart, and White dissented. White called the majority's ruling "an unduly rigid and unwarranted application of the Equal Protection Clause which will unnecessarily involve the courts in the abrasive task of drawing district lines." [37] Harlan wrote that the decision transformed "a political slogan into a constitutional absolute. Strait indeed is the path of the righteous legislator. Slide rule in hand, he must avoid all thought of county lines, local traditions, politics, history, and economics, so as to achieve the magic formula: one man, one vote." [38]

In another congressional redistricting case decided the same day, the Court in *Wells v. Rockefeller* rejected New York's redistricting plan as out of line with equal protection standards.

The New York plan resulted in districts of nearly equal size within regions of the state, but not of equal population throughout the state. That was unacceptable, held the Court, in light of the fact that the state could not and did not claim that its legislators had made a good-faith effort to achieve precise mathematical equality among its congressional districts.

Brennan wrote again for the Court:

To accept a scheme such as New York's would permit groups of districts with defined interest orientations to be overrepresented at the expense of districts with different interest orientations. Equality of population among districts in a substate is not a justification for inequality among all the districts in the State.[39]

The effect of this line of rulings from *Baker* through *Kirkpatrick* was felt in every state. By the end of the 1960s, thirty-nine of the forty-five states that elect more than one member of the House had redrawn their district lines. But because the new districts were based on 1960 census figures, population shifts during the decade left the new districts far from equal in population.

The redistricting following the 1970 census, however, resulted in substantial progress toward population equality among each state's congressional districts. Three hundred eighty-five of the 435 members of the House of Representatives elected in 1972 were chosen from districts that varied less than 1 percent from their state's average congressional district population.[40]

In 1973 the Court unanimously reaffirmed the strict standard for congressional districts set out in *Kirkpatrick.* The Court invalidated Texas's 1971 redistricting plan that allowed a difference of almost 5 percent between the most populous and the least populous congressional district.[41]

Justice White, writing the opinion in the case of *White v. Weiser,* said that these differences were avoidable. Chief Justice Warren E. Burger and Justices William H. Rehnquist and Lewis F. Powell, Jr., concurred, but added that had they been members of the Court in 1969, they would have dissented from the rule of strict equality set out in *Kirkpatrick v. Preisler.*

Ten years later, on June 22, 1983, the Court again emphasized the strict standard of "one person, one vote," but this time the Court was not at all unanimous. Divided 5-4 in *Karcher v. Daggett,* the Court struck down New Jersey's congressional redistricting plan that was based on the 1980 census. Although the variation between the most populous district and the least populous district was less than 1 percent, the Court held that the difference must be justified as necessary to achieve some important state goal. New Jersey had not provided that justification, held the Court. Justice Brennan wrote the opinion; Justices White, Powell, Rehnquist, and Burger dissented.[42]

STATE DISTRICTS: MORE LEEWAY

Baker v. Carr began the revolution in state legislatures of the nation, allowing federal courts to address the problem of malapportionment. *Reynolds v. Sims* marked the second phase in the process, establishing the "one person, one vote" standard for legislative districting.

The third and longest phase was characterized by the Supreme Court's effort to resolve the tension between the goal of equal population, demanded by the Fourteenth Amendment, and state definitions of democratic representation that often took factors other than population into account.

In this effort, which extended over the fifteen years following *Reynolds v. Sims,* the Court indicated a preference for single-member, not multimember, electoral districts. It continues to insist that reapportionment is primarily a legislative responsibility. And since 1973, it has been willing to tolerate more deviation from absolutely equal population for state than for congressional districts.

Multimember Districts

In 1965, in *Fortson v. Dorsey,* the Supreme Court rejected a constitutional challenge to Georgia's use of single-member and multimember districts for electing members of the state senate. This system was challenged as intended to minimize the voting strength of certain minority groups.

Although the Court held that those allegations had not been proved, Justice Brennan in the opinion made clear that the Court was not giving blanket approval to multimember districts:

It might well be that, designedly or otherwise, a multi-member constituency apportionment scheme, under the circumstances of a particular scheme, would operate to minimize or cancel out the voting strength of racial or political elements of the voting population. When this is demonstrated it will be time enough to consider whether the system still passes constitutional muster.[43]

The following year, the Court refused to disturb a similar electoral system for Hawaii's senate, emphasizing that the task of setting up such systems should be left to legislators, not judges.[44]

Again in 1971, in a case from Indiana, the Court refused to hold multimember districts per se unconstitutional, requiring proof that the particular districts challenged in fact operated to dilute the votes of certain groups or certain persons.[45]

Two years later, however, the Court did require the disestablishment of two multimember districts for electing members of the Texas house, holding them impermissible in light of the history of political discrimination against blacks and Mexican-Americans residing in those areas.[46]

Population Equality

Beginning in 1967, with *Swann v. Adams,* the Court defined the outer limits of population variance for state legislative districts. In that case, the Court held unconstitutional Florida's plan that permitted deviations of as much as 30 percent and 40 percent from population equality.

Minor variations from equality would be tolerated if there were special justifications for it, held the Court, but it would be left to the state to prove the justification sufficient. Justice White wrote the opinion:

Reynolds v. Sims ... recognized that mathematical exactness is not required in state apportionment plans. *De minimis* variations are unavoidable, but variations of 30 percent among senate districts and 40 percent among house districts can hardly be deemed *de minimis* and none of our cases suggests that differences of this magnitude will be approved without a satisfactory explanation grounded on acceptable state policy.[47]

White said that the Court in *Reynolds* had limited the permissible deviations to "minor variations" brought about by "legitimate considerations incident to the effectuation of a rational state policy ... such ... as the integrity of political subdivisions, the maintenance of compactness and contiguity in legislative districts or the recognition of natural or historical boundary lines."[48]

Justice Harlan, joined by Justice Stewart, dissented, saying that Florida's plan was a rational state policy. Harlan noted that in striking down the plan "because neither the State nor the District Court justified the relatively minor variations in population among some of the districts," the Court "seems to me to stand on its head the usual rule governing this Court's approach to legislative enactments, state as well as federal, which is ... that they come to us with a wrong presumption of regularity and constitutionality."[49]

After the Court's insistence in the 1969 decision in *Kirkpatrick v. Preisler* that congressional districts be precisely equal in population, doubts arose about the flexibility left to states in drawing state legislative electoral districts not absolutely equal in the number of inhabitants.

But in 1973 the Court in *Mahan v. Howell* reiterated the more relaxed application of the "one person, one vote" standard to state legislative districts. The Court declared that "in the implementation of the basic constitutional principle—equality of population among the districts—more flexibility was constitutionally permissible with respect to state legislative reapportionment than in congressional redistricting."[50] Virginia's legislative reapportionment statute, enacted after the 1970 census, allowed as much as a 16.4 percent deviation from equal population in the districts from which members of the state house were elected. When this was challenged in federal court as too wide a disparity, the lower court agreed, citing *Kirkpatrick v. Preisler* and *Wells v. Rockefeller,* both of which concerned congressional districts.

By a 5-3 vote the Supreme Court reversed the lower court, with Justice Rehnquist speaking for the majority. Justice Powell did not participate in the decision; Justices Brennan, Douglas, and Thurgood Marshall dissented.

The Court upheld the state districting plan, finding the population variance not excessive.

Justice Rehnquist cited *Reynolds v. Sims* in support of the majority's view that some deviation from equal population was permissible for state legislative districts so long as it was justified by rational state policy. He explained the reason behind the Court's application of different standards to state and congressional redistricting plans:

almost invariably, there is a significantly larger number of seats in state legislative bodies to be distributed within a State than congressional seats and ... therefore it may be feasible for a State to use political subdivision lines to a greater extent in establishing state legislative districts while still affording adequate statewide representation....

By contrast, the court in *Wesberry v. Sanders* ...

recognized no excuse for the failure to meet the objective of equal representation for equal numbers of people in congressional districting other than the practical impossibility of drawing equal districts with mathematical precision. Thus, whereas population alone has been the sole criterion of constitutionality in congressional redistricting under Art. I ... broader latitude has been afforded the State under the Equal Protection Clause in state legislative redistricting because of the considerations enumerated in *Reynolds v. Sims*. ... The dichotomy between the two lines of cases has consistently been maintained....

Application of the "absolute equality" test of *Kirkpatrick* and *Wells* to state legislative redistricting may impair the normal functioning of state and local governments. ...

We hold that the legislature's plan for apportionment of the House of Delegates may reasonably be said to advance the rational state policy of respecting the boundaries of political subdivisions. The remaining inquiry is whether the population disparities among the districts which have resulted from the pursuit of this plan exceed constitutional limits. We conclude that they do not.[51]

Rehnquist noted, however, that the 16 percent deviation from equality "may well approach tolerable limits."

In dissent, Justice Brennan, joined by Justices Douglas and Marshall, argued for a stricter application of the "one person, one vote" principle, saying:

The principal question presented for our decision is whether on the facts of this case an asserted state interest in preserving the integrity of county lines can justify the resulting substantial deviations from population equality....

... The Constitution does not permit a State to relegate considerations of equality to secondary status and reserve as the primary goal of apportionment the service of some other state interest.[52]

Several months later in 1973, the Court, in the case of *Gaffney v. Cummings*, upheld Connecticut's reapportionment of its legislature, despite a maximum deviation of 7.8 percent from mathematical equality in the population of the districts.[53]

Justice White wrote for the majority that state legislative reapportionment plans need not place an "unrealistic emphasis on raw population figures" when to do so might "submerge ... other considerations and itself furnish a ready tool for ignoring factors that in day-to-day operation are important to an acceptable representation and apportionment arrangement."[54]

White also warned that strict adherence to arithmetic could frustrate achievement of the goal of fair and effective representation "by making the standards of reapportionment so difficult to satisfy that the reapportionment task is recurringly removed from legislative hands and performed by federal courts."[55]

He continued:

We doubt that the Fourteenth Amendment requires repeated displacement of otherwise appropriate state decision making in the name of essentially minor deviations from perfect census population equality that no one, with confidence, can say will deprive any person of fair and effective representation in his state legislature.

That the Court was not deterred by the hazards of the political thicket when it undertook to adjudicate the reapportionment cases does not mean that it should become bogged down in a vast, intractable apportionment slough, particularly when there is little if anything to be accomplished by doing so.[56]

The same day it announced its decision upholding Connecticut's reapportionment in *Gaffney*, the Court in the case of *White v. Regester* upheld a similar plan for the Texas legislature, despite a 9.9 percent variation in the populations of the largest and smallest districts. In the same case, however, the Court required revision of the plan to eliminate two multimember districts in areas with histories of discrimination against racial and ethnic minority-group voters.[57]

Ten years later the Court again affirmed its willingness to give states more leeway in drawing their legislative districts than in drawing their congressional district lines. The same day that it struck down, 5-4, New Jersey's congressional redistricting plan with less than 1 percent variation between districts, it upheld, 5-4, Wyoming's law that gave each county one representative in the state's lower house—even though the population variance among the counties was enormous. The Court said that this arrangement was permissible in light of the state interest in giving each county its own representative.[58]

Court Plans: A Closer Look

Since 1975 the Court has distinguished between the standards it applied to state redistricting plans drawn by legislators and to those drawn by judges. Stricter standards applied to the latter. In the North Dakota case of *Chapman v. Meier*, the Court disapproved a court-ordered plan for the state legislature that allowed up to 20 percent population variance among districts.[59]

Court-ordered redistricting plans should not include multimember districts or allow more than a minimal variation from the goal of equal population, held the Court, unless unique state features or significant state policy justified those characteristics.

Justice Harry A. Blackmun spoke for the unanimous Court, stating that "absent particularly pressing features calling for multimember districts, a United States district court should refrain from imposing them upon a State."[60]

A 20 percent population variance, he continued, was not permissible "simply because there is no particular racial or political group whose voting power is minimized or cancelled." Moreover, Blackmun stated, neither sparse population nor the geographic division of the state by the Missouri River, "warrant[ed] departure from population equality."[61]

Reaffirming this position in the 1977 case of *Connor v. Finch*, the Court, by a 7-1 vote, overturned a court-ordered reapportionment plan for the Mississippi state legislature because it allowed population variations of up to 16.5 percent in senate districts and of up to 19.3 percent among house districts. The population variance was defended as necessary to preserve the integrity of county lines within legislative districts.[62]

The Court found this insufficient in light of the stricter standards set out in *Chapman v. Meier* for court-ordered plans.

Notes

1. For general background see Congressional Quarterly, *Guide to U.S. Elections* (Washington, D.C.: Congressional Quarterly, 1975), 523-539.
2. *Wood v. Broom,* 287 U.S. 1 (1932).
3. *Colegrove v. Green,* 328 U.S. 549 (1946).
4. Id. at 552, 553-554, 556.
5. Id. at 564.
6. Id. at 574.
7. *Gomillion v. Lightfoot,* 364 U.S. 339 (1960).
8. Id. at 346, 347.
9. *Baker v. Carr,* 369 U.S. 186 (1962).
10. Id. at 253.
11. Id. at 201.
12. Id. at 207.
13. Id. at 209.
14. *Luther v. Borden,* 7 How. 1 (1849).
15. *Baker v. Carr,* 369 U.S. 186 at 258 (1962).
16. Id. at 267.
17. Id. at 268-270.
18. Id. at 332, 334.
19. Id. at 339.
20. *Gray v. Sanders,* 372 U.S. 368 at 378 (1963).
21. Id. at 379-381.
22. Id. at 384, 388.
23. *Wesberry v. Sanders,* 376 U.S. 1 at 7-8 (1964).
24. Id. at 42.
25. Richard O. Claude, *The Supreme Court and the Electoral Process* (Baltimore: John Hopkins Press, 1970), 213n.-214n.
26. *Reynolds v. Sims,* 377 U.S. 533 at 567 (1964).
27. Id. at 573-574.
28. Id. at 555, 562, 567-568.
29. Id. at 577.
30. Id. at 578.
31. Id. at 624-625.
32. *Duddleston v. Grills,* 385 U.S. 155; *Kirkpatrick v. Preisler,* 385 U.S. 450 (1967).
33. *Kirkpatrick v. Preisler* 394 U.S. 526 (1969).
34. Id. at 530.
35. Id. at 530-531, 533.
36. Id. at 538-539.
37. Id. at 553.
38. Id. at 549-550.
39. *Wells v. Rockefeller,* 394 U.S. 542 at 546 (1969).
40. Congressional Quarterly, *Guide to U.S. Elections,* 538.
41. *Karcher v. Daggett,* 462 U.S. 725 (1983).
42. *White v. Weiser,* 412 U.S. 783 (1973).
43. *Forton v. Dorsey* 379 U.S. 433 at 439 (1965).
44. *Burns v. Richardson,* 384 U.S. 73 (1966).
45. *Whitcomb v. Chavis,* 403 U.S. 124 (1971).
46. *White v. Regester,* 412 U.S. 755 (1973).
47. *Swann v. Adams,* 385 U.S. 440 at 444 (1967).
48. Ibid.
49. Id. at 447.
50. *Mahan v. Howell,* 410 U.S. 315 at 321 (1973).
51. Id. at 321-323, 328.
52. Id. at 339-340.
53. *Gaffney v. Cummings,* 412 U.S. 736 (1973).
54. Id. at 749.
55. Ibid.
56. Id. at 749-750.
57. *White v. Regester,* 412 U.S. 755 (1973).
58. *Brown v. Thomson,* 462 U.S. 835 (1983).
59. *Chapman v. Meier,* 420 U.S. 1 (1975).
60. Id. at 19.
61. Id. at 24-25.
62. *Connor v. Finch,* 431 U.S. 407 (1977).

Freedom of Political Association

The freedom to espouse any political belief and to associate with others sharing that belief is, in the words of the modern Supreme Court, "the core of those activities protected by the First Amendment." [1]

Judicial recognition of this freedom is new, exclusively a development of the midtwentieth century. A corollary of the First Amendment freedoms of speech and belief, the judicially enunciated right of political association has its origin in the post-World War I rulings in which the Court first attempted to reconcile the government's need to protect itself against internal subversion with the First Amendment protection for free speech.

This freedom is not absolute. The Court has condoned its curtailment, especially during times of national peril when the line between freedom of political association and treasonable conspiracy blurs.

In its longest series of rulings on this freedom—those involving the antisubversive programs of the cold war era—the Court labored to strike the proper balance. Traced decision by decision, the constitutional freedom is ill defined. But by the end of that effort—which consumed almost two decades—the Court was firm on one point: guilt by association is impermissible. Individuals must not be found guilty simply because they belong to a particular group.

The nation's first internal security laws were enacted within the same decade as the Bill of Rights. The Alien and Sedition Acts of 1798 set severe penalties for persons found guilty of criticizing the government or government officials. The laws expired before they were ever challenged before the Supreme Court itself.

During the Civil War, military officials imposed many restrictions upon individual rights and expression. But, again, the constitutionality of those actions was never questioned before the Court.

The Supreme Court first found itself face to face with the question of permissible government restrictions upon political belief and expression in 1919. During World War I, Congress passed the Espionage Act of 1917 and the Sedition Act of 1918 to penalize persons who spoke or published statements with the intent of interfering with the nation's military success, or with the effect of bringing the flag, the Constitution, the government, or the military

uniform into disrepute, or of promoting the cause of the enemy. Hundreds of persons were convicted.

In a series of cases decided after the end of the war, the Court upheld these laws but began to formulate tests to gauge when such restriction of speech and expression was permissible and when it was not. [2]

Increasing concern about the threat of communism, which intensified after the end of World War II, sparked the passage of federal laws intended to protect the nation against Communist subversion. These laws restricted the exercise—by persons holding certain views—of the freedom of political belief, expression, and association. In cases arising under these laws the modern Court attempted to reconcile the demands of political freedom with the requirements of internal security.

The famous if often-disregarded "clear and present danger" test for determining when official restriction or punishment may be imposed upon the exercise of the right to speak was set out by the Court in 1919 in the case of *Schenck v. United States.* Schenck was convicted under the Espionage Act for mailing out circulars to men eligible for the military draft urging them to resist the draft, which he described as unconstitutional despotism.

Although the Court upheld his conviction, finding that his actions constituted a clear and present threat that illegal action would result, it did set out the new standard.

Writing for the unanimous Court, Justice Oliver Wendell Holmes, Jr., declared:

> The most stringent protection of free speech would not protect a man in falsely shouting fire in a theatre and causing a panic. It does not even protect a man from an injunction against uttering words that may have all the effect of force.... The question in every case is whether the words used are used in such circumstances and are of such a nature as to create a clear and present danger that they will bring about the substantive evils that Congress has a right to prevent. [3]

Later in 1919—and again in 1920—Holmes dissented with Justice Louis D. Brandeis when the Court upheld three more convictions under the World War I Espionage and Sedition Acts.

In these cases, to the dismay of Holmes and Brandeis,

the Court relaxed its standard for government curtailment of free expression of political ideas. The majority espoused the view that the "bad tendency" of an individual's speech or action, rather than the actual threat of danger, was sufficient to justify punishment. The new test, stated the majority, did not require that an utterance's "effect or the persons affected ... be shown.... The tendency of the articles and their efficacy were enough for offense." [4]

In dissent Justice Brandeis opposed this "bad tendency" test both because it eliminated consideration of the speaker's intent and because it ignored the relevance of the likelihood that danger would result. He restated the clear and present danger test in the case of *Schaefer v. United States,* saying:

> This is a rule of reason. Correctly applied, it will preserve the right of free speech both from suppression by tyrannous majorities and from abuse by irresponsible, fanatical minorities. [5]

The 1920s were a period of intolerance in the United States. Many states, following the example of Congress, passed laws penalizing persons for expressing or acting upon views of political truth that were perceived as subversive. In 1925 and again in 1927 the Court upheld convictions of persons holding such views. In both instances, Holmes and Brandeis disagreed with the majority's view that the clear and present danger test had no application at all to laws that punished advocacy of the forcible overthrow of government.

In *Gitlow v. New York* the Court in 1925 upheld the conviction of Benjamin Gitlow, a leader of the left wing of the Socialist party, for violating provisions of the New York criminal anarchy statute by publishing thousands of copies of a manifesto setting out his beliefs.

The decision is particularly important because in it the Court for the first time assumed that the First Amendment freedoms of speech and the press protected from abridgment by Congress were among the fundamental personal liberties protected by the Fourteenth Amendment against impairment by the states.

But the Court made clear that the First Amendment "does not confer an absolute right to speak or publish, without responsibility, whatever one may chose." [6]

And, it emphasized, challenges to state laws alleged to restrict the freedom of speech or the press must overcome a strong presumption in favor of the constitutionality of state legislation. If the state thought the statute necessary, and the Court agreed, then the only other question was whether the language used or the action punished was prohibited by the state law.

In 1927 the Court upheld the conviction of Anita Whitney—who happened to be the niece of former Supreme Court justice Stephen J. Field—for violating the California Syndicalism Act of 1919 by her part in organizing the California Communist Labor party. Whitney had participated in the convention setting up the state party and was an alternate member of its state executive committee. With the decision in *Whitney v. California,* the majority of the Court appeared to allow persons to be punished simply for associating with groups which espoused potentially illegal acts.

Justices Holmes and Brandeis agreed in upholding the conviction, because the clear and present danger test had not been used as part of Whitney's defense at trial. But in a concurring opinion that often read like a dissent, Brandeis challenged laws that exalted order over liberty:

Those who won our independence by revolution were not cowards. They did not fear political change. They did not exalt order at the cost of liberty. To courageous, self-reliant men, with confidence in the power of free and fearless reasoning applied through the processes of popular government, no danger flowing from speech can be deemed clear and present, unless the incidence of the evil apprehended is so imminent that it may befall before there is opportunity for full discussion. If there be time to expose through discussion the falsehood and fallacies, to avert the evil by the processes of education, the remedy to be applied is more speech, not enforced silence. Only an emergency can justify repression. Such must be the rule if authority is to be reconciled with freedom. [7]

During the 1930s the Supreme Court, now under the leadership of Chief Justice Charles Evans Hughes, extended *Gitlow's* protection of First Amendment freedoms against state action, while it repudiated the guilt-by-association rule it seemed to adopt in *Whitney.*

In 1931 the Court reversed the conviction of Yetta Stromberg, a supervisor in a youth camp operated by the Young Communist League in California, for violating the state law prohibiting display of a red flag as an "emblem of opposition to organized government." Such a flag was raised by Stromberg each morning at the camp for a flag-salute ceremony. In holding the state law invalid under the due process guarantee of the Fourteenth Amendment, the Court ignored Stromberg's Communist party affiliation. [8]

Six years later, in 1937, the Court overturned the conviction of a man named DeJonge for violating Oregon's criminal syndicalism law when he presided over a public meeting called by the Communist party to protest police brutality in a longshoremen's strike. That same year, the Court reversed the conviction of a Communist organizer in Georgia for attempting to recruit members and distributing literature about the party. [9]

In each case the Court focused upon the actions of the individual, emphasizing personal guilt rather than guilt by association. In the Court's opinion in DeJonge's case, Chief Justice Hughes wrote that the state could not punish a person making a lawful speech simply because the speech was sponsored by an allegedly "subversive" organization.

Hughes's opinion made no reference to the clear and present danger test. He assumed that incitement to violence would not be protected by the First Amendment. The essence of his opinion for the unanimous Court was an affirmation of the political value of the rights of free speech and association:

> The greater the importance of safeguarding the community from incitements to the overthrow of our institutions by force and violence, the more imperative is the need to preserve inviolate the constitutional rights of free speech, free press and free assembly in order to maintain the opportunity for free political discussion, to the end that government may be responsive to the will of the people and that changes, if desired, may be obtained by peaceful means. Therein lies the security of the Republic, the very foundation of constitutional government.... The question, if the rights of free speech and peaceable assembly are to be preserved, is not as to the auspices under which the meeting is held but as to its purpose; not as to the relations of the speakers, but whether their utterances transcend the bounds of the freedom of speech. [10]

Aliens and Communism

Congress, by virtue of its control over immigration and naturalization, has virtually unlimited power to regulate the activities of aliens in the United States and to deport those it finds undesirable. But in several decisions the modern Supreme Court has curtailed this power when it was used to penalize aliens for membership in the Communist party.

Party membership alone—without evidence of the member's advocacy of forcible or violent overthrow of the government—was insufficient reason to revoke an individual's naturalization, the Court ruled in 1943. By a 6-3 vote in the case of *Schneiderman v. United States,* the Court reversed the government's decision to revoke naturalization papers granted to William Schneiderman in 1927 when he was a member of the Communist party.[1]

The Alien Registration Act of 1940 provided for deportation of aliens who were members of the party. In 1952 the Court upheld the application of this provision even to aliens whose membership had terminated before the 1940 law took effect.[2] Congress included similar provisions in the Internal Security Act of 1950 and the Immigration and Nationality Act of 1952.

In 1954 the Court upheld deportation of a resident alien because of his Communist party membership, even though it was not clear that he was aware of the party's advocacy of the violent overthrow of the government. Congress, said the Court, had virtually unrestricted power to deport aliens.[3]

But in 1957 and 1963, the Court applied stricter standards to similar deportation decisions. In the cases of *Rowoldt v. Perfetto* and *Gastelum-Quinones v. Kennedy,* the Court required the government to prove not only that the alien was a member of the party but also that he understood the political implications of that membership before it might permissibly order him to leave the country.[4]

Writing for the Court in *Gastelum-Quinones,* Justice Arthur J. Goldberg explained:

> there is a great practical and legal difference between those who firmly attach themselves to the Communist Party being aware of all of the aims and purposes attributed to it, and those who temporarily join the Party, knowing nothing of its international relationships and believing it to be a group solely trying to remedy unsatisfactory social or economic conditions, carry out trade-union objectives, eliminate racial discrimination, combat unemployment, or alleviate distress and poverty.[5]

1. *Schneiderman v. United States,* 320 U.S. 118 (1943).
2. *Harisiades v. Shaughnessy,* 342 U.S. 580 (1952).
3. *Galvan v. Press,* 347 U.S. 522 (1954).
4. *Rowoldt v. Perfetto,* 355 U.S. 115 (1957); *Gastelum-Quinones v. Kennedy,* 374 U.S. 469 (1963).
5. *Gastelum-Quinones v. Kennedy,* 374 U.S. 469 at 473 (1963).

COMMUNISM AND COLD WAR

World communism posed a double-edged threat to the survival of the American system. Militarily, the spread of Communist-dominated regimes across the globe posed the most serious external challenge the West had ever faced. And ideologically, the appeal of Communist theory to some in the United States resulted in enactment of laws intended to curtail the advocacy of those ideas and penalize those who espoused them. Some observers of this reaction wondered if legislators at home would in fact strangle the very freedoms that military and diplomatic personnel abroad were working to preserve.

Justice William O. Douglas expressed this concern in 1951:

> In days of great tension when feelings run high, it is a temptation to take shortcuts by borrowing from the totalitarian techniques of our opponents. But when we do, we set in motion a subversive influence of our own design that destroys us from within.[11]

The three major federal laws enacted to discourage the growth of communist-affiliated organizations in the United States were the Smith Act of 1940, the McCarran Act of 1950, and the Communist Control Act of 1954.

The Smith Act made it a crime to advocate the violent overthrow of the government or to organize or to belong to any group advocating such revolutionary action. The McCarran Act required all Communist-action or Communist-front groups to register with the Justice Department and disclose their membership lists; that law further penalized members of such groups by prohibiting their holding of government or defense-related jobs or using U.S. passports.

The Communist Control Act of 1954 declared that the Communist party was an instrument of treasonable conspiracy against the U.S. government and thus deprived of all the rights and privileges of political parties and legal entities in the United States.

Debate over the constitutionality of these laws—and the loyalty-security programs and oath requirements that accompanied them—resounded frequently in the nation's courtrooms, including that of the Supreme Court. One's conclusion turned upon one's view of communism—was it a valid political movement, espousal of which and association with which was protected by the First Amendment? Or was it a treasonable conspiracy, which the Constitution itself viewed as punishable?[12]

In the first decade of the cold war, the Supreme Court—reflecting the mood of the nation—generally upheld the provisions and application of these laws. In so doing, the majority avoided ruling directly on the challenge that they impermissibly abridged the First Amendment guarantee of freedom of political association.

Then, beginning in 1957, as the cold war thawed, the Court began to restrict their application, finding them often used in too sweeping a fashion. The Constitution specifies that no one shall be found guilty of treason without evidence of overt treasonous acts. The Supreme Court began to insist that these internal security laws be used only to penalize persons who knowingly and actively sought to promote Communist revolution in the United States, not simply to punish persons who had at some time found other social and economic or philosophical tenets of the movement attractive.

In the decade from 1957 through 1967, the coalescence of a libertarian majority on the Court under Chief Justice Earl Warren resulted in decisions that forced the government to cease prosecuting persons under the Smith Act, to abandon its effort to force registration of the Communist party and other Communist-affiliated groups, and to cease denying passports and defense industry jobs to members of such groups.

In addition, the Court—which had earlier condoned the use of loyalty oaths by state and local governments attempting to ensure the loyalty of their employees—struck down many such oaths as improper restrictions upon the freedom to believe and to speak freely and to associate with others of like belief.

Article VI of the Constitution requires state and federal officeholders to swear to uphold the Constitution of the United States. Congress and state legislatures during the cold war era in particular imposed other oaths deemed appropriate as a condition of public office.

The Smith Act

The Alien Registration Act of 1940 required all aliens living in the United States to register with the government; any found to have past ties to "subversive organizations" could be deported. *(Box, p. 133)*

But Title I of that act—the Smith Act—affected citizens as well as aliens. Intended to thwart Communist activity in the United States, the measure was the nation's first peacetime sedition law since the infamous Sedition Act of 1795. Yet it attracted little attention at the time of its passage in 1940. Thomas I. Emerson observed that: "Enactment of the bill reflected not so much a deliberate national determination that the measure was necessary to protect internal security as an unwillingness of members of Congress to vote against legislation directed at the Communist Party." [13]

The Smith Act made it a crime "to knowingly or willfully advocate, abet, advise, or teach the duty, necessity, desirability, or propriety of overthrowing or destroying any government in the United States by force or violence." It forbade the publication or display of printed matter teaching or advocating forcible overthrow of the government. And in language directly curtailing the freedom of association, the law made it a crime to organize any group teaching, advocating, or encouraging the overthrow or destruction of government by force or to become a "knowing" member of any organization or group dedicated to the violent overthrow of any government in the United States.

In 1948 the government indicted eleven leaders of the Communist party in the United States, charging them with violating the Smith Act by conspiring to form groups teaching the overthrow of the government by force or violence. The eleven were convicted after a long and sensational trial.

In upholding the convictions, Judge Learned Hand spoke for the federal court of appeals and used a "sliding scale" rule for applying the clear and present danger test in sedition cases: "In each case [courts] must ask whether the gravity of the 'evil,' discounted by its improbability, justifies such invasion of free speech as is necessary to avoid the danger," Hand said.[14]

The Act Upheld: *Dennis*

In 1951 the Supreme Court by a vote of 6-2 upheld the convictions—and the constitutionality of the Smith Act. Justice Tom C. Clark did not take part in the Court's decision in *Dennis v. United States.* The eight voting members of the Court disagreed widely over the proper way to measure the validity of sedition laws against the restraints they placed on First Amendment freedoms of expression and association.

Chief Justice Fred M. Vinson, speaking for Justices Stanley F. Reed, Harold H. Burton, and Sherman Minton, gave lip service to the clear and present danger test but seemed in fact to apply the "sliding scale" rule. The Smith Act, wrote Vinson, did not allow persons to be punished simply for peaceful study and discussion of revolutionary concepts: "Congress did not intend to eradicate the free discussion of political theories, to destroy the traditional rights of Americans to discuss and evaluate ideas without fear of governmental sanction." [15] But, he wrote:

Overthrow of the Government by force and violence is certainly a substantial enough interest for the Government to limit speech. Indeed, this is the ultimate value of any society, for if a society cannot protect its very structure from armed internal attack, it must follow that no subordinate value can be protected. If, then, this interest may be protected, the literal problem which is presented is what has been meant by the use of the phrase "clear and present danger" of the utterances bringing about the evil within the power of Congress to punish.

Obviously, the words cannot mean that before the Government may act, it must wait until the *putsch* is about to be executed, the plans have been laid and the signal is awaited. If Government is aware that a group aiming at its overthrow is attempting to indoctrinate its members and to commit them to a course whereby they will strike when the leaders feel the circumstances permit, action by the Government is required. . . . Certainly an attempt to overthrow the Government by force, even though doomed from the outset because of inadequate numbers or power of the revolutionists is a sufficient evil for Congress to prevent. . . .

The damage which such attempts create both physically and politically to a nation makes it impossible to measure the validity in terms of the probability of success. . . .

Politics and the Right to a Passport

Cold war legislation forbade any member of the Communist party to apply for a U.S. passport, but that was not the first time this privilege had been denied to persons who seemed ideologically out of line with prevailing U.S. thought. The Passport Act of 1926, the basis for modern passport administration, authorized the State Department to deny travel documents to applicants with criminal records and to noncitizens.

From 1917 until 1931, passports generally were refused to members of the American Communist party. During the cold war, the State Department resumed that practice. Then, in the 1950 McCarran Act, Congress forbade members of any registered Communist political action or front organization to apply for or to use a passport.

Although the registration provisions were successfully resisted, the State Department nevertheless did deny passports to a number of individuals thought to be Communists, acting under its own rules and the discretion granted it by the Immigration and Nationality Act of 1952.

Freedom to Travel

In *Kent v. Dulles*, decided in 1958, the Supreme Court held that Congress had not authorized the Secretary of State to deny passports to persons because of their beliefs or associations. Furthermore, held the Court, the right to travel is an aspect of liberty of which the citizen cannot be deprived without due process of law.

The Court, 5-4, reversed the State Department's denial of a passport to artist Rockwell Kent, who refused to submit an affidavit disclaiming any affiliation with Communist groups.

Justice William O. Douglas wrote:

we are dealing here with citizens who have neither been accused of crimes or found guilty. They are being denied their freedom of movement solely because of their refusal to be subjected to inquiry into their beliefs and associations. They do not seek to escape the law nor to violate it. They may or may not be Communists. But assuming they are, the only law which Congress has passed expressly curtailing the movement of Communists across our borders has not yet become effective. It would therefore be strange to infer that pending the effectiveness of that law, the Secretary has been silently granted by Congress the larger, the more pervasive power to curtail in his discretion the free movement of citizens in order to satisfy himself about their beliefs or associations.[1]

The dissenting justices—Harold H. Burton, John Marshall Harlan, Charles E. Whittaker, and Tom C. Clark—found the denial proper.

In the wake of *Kent*, the Eisenhower administration asked Congress to authorize the State Department to deny passports to persons with Communist affiliations. Congress did not do so.[2]

The Court's decision in 1961 in *Communist Party v. Subversive Activities Control Board* upheld the order to the party to register under the McCarran Act and made operative the provisions of the act that denied passports to Communist party members. *(Details of decision, p. 140)*

The State Department revoked the passports of several leading Communist party officials including Herbert Aptheker, one of the party's leading intellectuals. In its 1964 decision in *Aptheker v. Secretary of State*, the Court, 6-3, declared the passport denial provisions of the McCarran Act unconstitutional as infringements of the freedom to travel.

Writing for the majority, Justice Arthur J. Goldberg explained that the law violated the guarantee of due process by failing to distinguish between knowing and unknowing party membership and by arbitrarily excluding any consideration of the purpose of the proposed travel.[3] Justices Harlan, Clark, and Byron R. White dissented.

The following year, the Court in *Zemel v. Rusk* upheld the power of the State Department to impose geographic area limitations on the use of U.S. passports.[4] But several subsequent decisions made clear that such limitations, although valid, are practically unenforceable.[5]

Freedom to Travel Denied

In 1981 the Court in *Haig v. Agee* upheld the power of the secretary of state to revoke a citizen's passport. Philip Agee was not a Communist, but a former Central Intelligence Agency official. He had worked as an undercover CIA agent and undertook, upon leaving the agency, to expose CIA agents abroad in order to drive them out of the countries where they were working.

The secretary of state revoked Agee's passport stating that his activities caused serious damage to the national security. Agee challenged the revocation as a violation of his First Amendment right to criticize the government, but the Court decided against him, 7-2.[6]

1. *Kent v. Dulles*, 357 U.S. 117 at 130 (1958).
2. *Congress and the Nation*, vol. I (Washington, D.C.: Congressional Quarterly, 1965), 1650.
3. *Aptheker v. Secretary of State*, 378 U.S. 500 (1964).
4. *Zemel v. Rusk*, 381 U.S. 1 (1965).
5. *United States v. Laub*, 385 U.S. 475 (1967); *Travis v. United States*, 385 U.S. 491 (1967).
6. *Haig v. Agee*, 453 U.S. 280 (1981).

The formation ... of such a highly organized conspiracy, with rigidly disciplined members subject to call when the leaders ... felt that the time had come for action, coupled with the inflammable nature of world conditions ... convince us that their convictions were justified.... And this analysis disposes of the contention that a conspiracy to advocate, as distinguished from the advocacy itself, cannot be constitutionally restrained, because it comprises only the preparation. It is the existence of the conspiracy which creates the danger.... If the ingredients of the reaction are present we cannot bind the Government to wait until the catalyst is added....

... Petitioners intended to overthrow the Government of the United States as speedily as the circumstances would permit. Their conspiracy to organize the Communist Party and to teach and advocate the overthrow of the Government of the United States by force and violence created a "clear and present danger" of an attempt to overthrow the Government by force and violence. They were properly and constitutionally convicted for violation of the Smith Act.[16]

Concurring, Justice Felix Frankfurter observed:

Suppressing advocates of overthrow inevitably will also silence critics who do not advocate overthrow but fear that their criticism may be so construed. No matter how clear we may be that the defendants now before us are preparing to overthrow our Government at the propitious moment, it is self-delusion to think that we can punish them for their advocacy without adding to the risks run by loyal citizens who honestly believe in some of the reforms these defendants advance. It is a sobering fact that in sustaining the convictions before us we can hardly escape restriction on the interchange of ideas.[17]

First Amendment guarantees must be balanced against the nation's need to protect itself, Frankfurter stated:

The appellants maintain that they have a right to advocate a political theory, so long, at least, as their advocacy does not create an immediate danger of obvious magnitude to the very existence of our present scheme of society. On the other hand, the Government asserts the right to safeguard the security of the Nation by such a measure as the Smith Act. Our judgment is thus solicited on a conflict of interests of the utmost concern to the well-being of the country.[18]

The responsibility for reconciling this conflict of values lay primarily with Congress, not the Court, wrote Frankfurter. The Court should only set aside the laws reflecting the judgment of Congress in such matters if it found no reasonable basis for the judgment, or if it found the law too indefinite to meet the demands of due process or breaching the separation of powers. The Court was responsible for ensuring fair procedures in the enforcement of the law and for requiring substantial proof to justify conviction, but "[b]eyond these powers we must not go; we must scrupulously observe the narrow limits of judicial authority even though self-restraint is alone set over us."[19]

Justice Robert H. Jackson, in his concurring opinion, declared that the clear and present danger test was inadequate when applied to laws intended to curtail the spread of the Communist conspiracy:

The authors of the clear and present danger test never applied it to a case like this, nor would I. If applied as it is proposed here, it means that the Communist plotting is protected during its period of incubation; its preliminary stages of organization and preparation are immune from the law; the Government can move only after imminent action is manifest, when it would, of course, be too late.[20]

The law of conspiracy was "an awkward and inept remedy" when applied to the threat of subversion presented by the Communist party, which Jackson described as "a state within a state, an authoritarian dictatorship within a republic." But despite the awkwardness of the instrument, Jackson wrote, he found no constitutional reason for denying the government its use: "There is no constitutional right to gang up on the Government."[21]

Justices Hugo L. Black and Douglas dissented. Black argued that the conspiracy section of the Smith Act should be held void as a prior restraint on the exercise of First Amendment freedoms of speech and the press.

Black noted that the eleven Communist leaders had not been charged with an actual attempt to overthrow the government but only with agreeing "to assemble and to talk and publish certain ideas at a later date. The indictment is that they conspired to organize the Communist Party and to use speech or newspapers ... to teach and advocate the forcible overthrow of the Government. No matter how it is worded, this is a virulent form of prior censorship of speech and press, which I believe the First Amendment forbids."[22]

Douglas also reminded his colleagues that the defendants were not on trial for conspiring to overthrow the government, but only for organizing groups advocating its overthrow. He warned of the "vice of treating speech as the equivalent of overt acts of a treasonable or seditious character," noting that the Constitution allowed punishment for treason only upon evidence of overt treasonable acts:

[N]ever until today has anyone seriously thought that the ancient law of conspiracy could constitutionally be used to turn speech into seditious conduct. Yet that is precisely what is suggested.... We deal here with speech alone, not with speech *plus* acts of sabotage or unlawful conduct. Not a single seditious act is charged in the indictment....

Free speech has occupied an exalted position because of the high service it has given our society. Its protection is essential to the very existence of a democracy.... We have founded our political system on it. It has been the safeguard of every religious, political, philosophical, economic, and racial group amongst us. We have counted on it to keep us from embracing what is cheap and false; we have trusted the common sense of our people to choose the doctrine true to our genius and to reject the rest.... We have above all else feared the political censor....

There comes a time when even speech loses its constitutional immunity. Speech innocuous one year may at another time fan such destructive flames that it must be halted in the interests of the safety of the Republic. That is the meaning of the clear and present danger test. When conditions are so critical that there will be no time to avoid the evil that the speech threatens, it is time to call a halt. Otherwise, free speech which is the strength of the Nation will be the cause of its destruction.

Yet free speech is the rule, not the exception. The restraint to be constitutional must be based on more than fear, on more than passionate opposition . . . on more than a revolted dislike for its contents. . . .

Free speech—the glory of our system of government—should not be sacrificed on anything less than plain and objective proof of danger that the evil advocated is imminent. On this record no one can say that petitioners and their converts are in such a strategic position as to have even the slightest chance of achieving their aims.[23]

In the wake of the *Dennis* decision, new Smith Act conspiracy prosecutions were brought involving 121 defendants—all second-rank U.S. Communist party officials. Other prosecutions were also brought against individuals for their party membership. Convictions were secured in every case brought to trial between 1951 and 1956. The courts of appeal affirmed the convictions and the Supreme Court denied petitions for review.

Strict Standards of Proof: *Yates*

Late in 1955, however, the Court agreed to review the convictions of fourteen persons charged with Smith Act violations.

The decision of the Court in these cases, generally known by the name of one, *Yates v. United States,* was announced in June 1957. By imposing strict standards of proof upon the government in such prosecutions, the Court effectively curtailed further use of the Smith Act to prosecute members of the American Communist party.

The decision marked a major shift in the Court's attitude toward the Smith Act, although it left untouched its earlier declaration in *Dennis* that the act was constitutional.

The defendants who brought before the Court the cases of *Yates v. United States, Schneiderman v. United States,* and *Richmond v. United States* were charged with organizing and participating in a conspiracy, namely the Communist party of the United States, to advocate the overthrow of the government by force.

By a 6-1 vote the Supreme Court in *Yates* found that the government had waited too long to indict these persons for their involvement in the organization of the party in the United States, that the trial judge had erred in his instructions to the jury concerning what they must find to convict the defendants on the advocacy charges, and that the evidence in several cases was insufficient to prove the charges. The Court reversed all the convictions, acquitting those of the defendants against whom the evidence was insufficient and ordering new trials for the others.

Not participating in the ruling were Justice William J. Brennan, Jr., and Justice Charles E. Whittaker.[24]

The majority took a narrow view of the scope of the Smith Act provision making it unlawful to organize a group advocating violent overthrow of the government. The majority, explained Justice John Marshall Harlan in the Court's opinion, defined "organize" in respect to the formation of the U.S. Communist party as an activity that took place in 1945 with the party's founding in this country, rejecting the government's definition of "organize" as an ongoing process. Because the defendants were not indicted on this charge until 1951, the three-year statute of limitations on such charges rendered that part of the indictment invalid, held the Court.

Harlan wrote:

Stated most simply, the problem is to choose between two possible answers to the question: when was the Communist Party "organized"? Petitioners contend that the only natural answer to the question is the formation date—in this case, 1945. The Government would have us answer the question by saying that the Party today is still not completely "organized"; that "organizing" is a continuing process that does not end until the entity is dissolved. . . .

We conclude . . . that since the Communist Party came into being in 1945, and the indictment was not returned until 1951, the three-year statute of limitations had run on the "organizing" charge, and required the withdrawal of that part of the indictment from the jury's consideration.[25]

Furthermore, held the Court, the trial judge had misinterpreted the Court's meaning in the *Dennis* decision when he instructed the jury. He failed to distinguish properly between advocacy of an abstract doctrine, a protected activity, and advocacy intended to promote unlawful action, a punishable activity under the Smith Act. In restating Vinson's ruling in *Dennis,* Justice Harlan discarded the clear and present danger test altogether. In *Dennis,* he wrote, the punishable advocacy did not create any danger of immediate revolution but "was aimed at building up a seditious group and maintaining it in readiness for action at a propitious time." [26]

Harlan continued:

In failing to distinguish between advocacy of forcible overthrow as an abstract doctrine and advocacy of action to that end, the District Court appears to have been led astray by the holding in *Dennis* that advocacy of violent action to be taken at some future time was enough. . . . The District Court apparently thought that *Dennis* obliterated the traditional dividing line between advocacy of abstract doctrine and advocacy of action. . . .

The essence of the *Dennis* holding was that indoctrination of a group in preparation for future violent action, as well as exhortation to immediate action, by advocacy found to be directed to "action for the accomplishment" of forcible overthrow, to violence as "a rule or principle of action," and employing "language of incitement," . . . is not constitutionally protected when the group is of sufficient size and cohesiveness, is sufficiently oriented towards action, and other circumstances are such as reasonable to justify apprehension that action will occur.

This is quite a different thing from the view of the District Court here that mere doctrinal justification of forcible overthrow, if engaged in with the intent to accomplish overthrow, is punishable *per se* under the Smith Act. That sort of advocacy, even though uttered with the hope that it may ultimately lead to violent revolution, is too remote from concrete action to be regarded as the kind of indoctrination preparatory to action which was condemned in *Dennis.* . . .

The essential distinction is that those to whom the advocacy is addressed must be urged to do something, now or in the future, rather than merely to *believe* in something. . . .

We recognize that distinctions between advocacy and teaching of abstract doctrines, with evil intent, and that which is directed to stirring people to action, are often subtle and difficult to grasp, for in a broad

No Bills of Attainder or Ex Post Facto Laws

One of the few provisions of the original Constitution affecting individual rights is the terse sentence in Article I, Section 9: "No Bill of Attainder or ex post facto Law shall be passed."

This prohibition has been the subject of only a few Supreme Court cases. Three acts of Congress have been held to be bills of attainder—and one of those is also the only instance in which the Court has found that Congress passed an ex post facto law.

A bill of attainder, stated the Court in 1867, is "a legislative act which inflicts punishment without a judicial trial." [1] In that year, with its ruling in *Ex parte Garland*, the Court struck down a law enacted in 1865 that barred attorneys from practicing before federal courts unless they swore an oath that they had remained loyal to the Union throughout the Civil War. Persons who swore falsely could be charged with and convicted of perjury.

A. H. Garland of Arkansas had been admitted to practice law before the federal courts during the 1860 Supreme Court term. When Arkansas seceded from the Union, Garland went with his state, becoming first a representative and later a senator in the Confederate Congress. He received a full pardon in 1865 from President Andrew Johnson for his service to the Confederacy. In *Ex parte Garland* he argued that he should be allowed to resume his federal practice without taking the required oath.[2]

The Supreme Court agreed with him, 5-4, finding the test oath requirement invalid as a bill of attainder. Justice Stephen J. Field explained that lawyers who had served the Confederacy could not take the oath without perjuring themselves. Therefore,

> the act, as against them, operates as a legislative decree of perpetual exclusion. And exclusion from any of the professions or any of the ordinary avocations of life for past conduct can be regarded in no other light than as punishment for such conduct.[3]

In addition, the Court held the test oath invalid as an ex post facto law, prohibiting an attorney from practicing before a federal court if he did not take the oath—and thus punishing him for past acts not defined as illegal at the time they were committed.

Almost eighty years passed before the Court again applied the bill of attainder clause to hold a law invalid. The 1946 case of *United States v. Lovett* arose after Representative Martin Dies, D-Texas (1931-1945, 1953-1959), chairman of the House Committee on Un-American Activities, listed thirty-nine federal employees as "irresponsible, unrepresentative, crackpot, radical bureaucrats" who were affiliated with "communist front organizations." Dies urged that Congress refuse to appropriate the funds necessary to pay these employees' salaries.

After a special subcommittee of the House Appropriations Committee heard testimony in secret session, it pronounced three of the thirty-nine—individuals named Lovett, Watson, and Dodd—guilty of subversive activities and unfit to hold their government jobs. Congress then passed a provision barring appropriations to pay the salaries of the three. President Franklin D. Roosevelt signed the bill, but made clear that he viewed that particular provision as an unconstitutional bill of attainder.

In 1946 a majority of the Court agreed with Roosevelt. Justice Hugo L. Black wrote that "legislative acts, no matter what their form, that apply either to named individuals or to easily ascertainable members of a group in such a way as to inflict punishment on them without a judicial trial are bills of attainder prohibited by the Constitution." [4]

The most recent of the Court's rulings striking down an act of Congress as a bill of attainder is the 1965 case of *United States v. Brown*, which concerned a provision of the Labor Management and Reporting Act of 1959. The provision made it a crime for anyone to serve as an officer or employee of a labor union if he were a member of the Communist party or had been a member at any time in the previous five years.[5]

Designed to prevent politically motivated strikes, the provision replaced a section of the Taft-Hartley Act of 1947 that had required unions seeking access to the National Labor Relations Board to file affidavits swearing that none of the union's officers were members of or affiliated with the Communist party. In 1950 the Court had upheld that requirement.[6] *(Details, p. 144)*

The Court, however, found the successor provision unconstitutional as a bill of attainder. "The statute," wrote Chief Justice Earl Warren, "designates in no uncertain terms the persons who possess the feared characteristics and therefore cannot hold union office without incurring criminal liability— members of the Communist Party." [7]

Brown differed from *Douds*, Warren explained, because the Taft-Hartley provision could be escaped by persons who resigned from the Communist party. The newer provision, however, applied to persons who had been members of the party before its enactment.[8]

1. *Cummings v. Missouri*, 4 Wall. 277 (1867).
2. *Ex parte Garland*, 4 Wall. 333 (1867).
3. Id. at 377.
4. *United States v. Lovett*, 328 U.S. 303 at 315 (1946).
5. *United States v. Brown*, 381 U.S. 437 (1965).
6. *American Communications Association v. Douds*, 339 U.S. 382 (1950).
7. *United States v. Brown*, 381 U.S. 437 at 450 (1965).
8. Id. at 457-458.

sense, as Mr. Justice Holmes said . . . "Every idea is an incitement." But the very subtlety of these distinctions required the most clear and explicit instructions with reference to them.[27]

The Court, wrote Harlan, also found the evidence of advocacy geared to action deficient in a number of the cases: "however much one may abhor even the abstract preaching of forcible overthrow or believe that forcible overthrow is the ultimate purpose to which the Communist Party is dedicated, it is upon the evidence in the record that the petitioners must be judged in this case."[28]

Justices Black and Douglas concurred in part and dissented in part. Both felt that all the prosecutions of these defendants should be dropped because the Smith Act provisions upon which the charges were based "abridge freedom of speech, press and assembly in violation of the First Amendment."[29]

"I believe that the First Amendment forbids Congress to punish people for talking about public affairs, whether or not such discussion incites to action, legal or illegal," Black wrote.[30]

In a separate dissenting opinion Justice Clark said that all of the convictions should be upheld, in line with *Dennis*. Clark noted that although the Communists in *Yates* were lower in the hierarchy than those defendants in *Dennis*, they served "in the same army and were engaged in the same mission."[31]

The *Yates* requirement that the government show a connection between advocacy and action, between participation in the Communist party and forcible overthrow of the government, ended most Smith Act prosecutions. The government decided to drop charges against those of the *Yates* defendants who, in light of the Court's ruling, could have been retried.

Membership Prosecutions

Despite the Court's narrow view of the Smith Act's "organizing" and "advocating" provisions, prosecutions remained possible under the clause that forbade "knowing" membership in any group advocating forcible overthrow of the government. When coupled with the registration provisions of the 1950 McCarran Act, this provision seemed to constitute compulsory self-incrimination in violation of the Fifth Amendment guarantee against such coercion. *(McCarran Act, this page)*

In 1961 the Supreme Court for the first time reviewed convictions of persons under the membership clause. In those rulings, the Court upheld the constitutionality of the provision, but measured the government's proof in such cases against the strict *Yates* standard of evidence.

In the case of *Scales v. United States*, the Court affirmed the conviction of Junius Scales, director of a Communist training school, and upheld the constitutionality of the membership clause. The vote was 5-4. Chief Justice Warren and Justices Black, Douglas, and Brennan dissented.

Justice Harlan, again the spokesman for the majority, distinguished between active, "knowing" membership and passive, merely nominal membership in a subversive organization. The membership clause, properly applied, did not violate the First Amendment guarantees of free political expression and association, he explained. In *Dennis* the Court had established two points in that regard:

the advocacy with which we are here concerned is not constitutionally protected speech, and . . . that a combination to promote such advocacy, albeit under the aegis of what purports to be a political party, is not such association as is protected by the First Amendment.

We can discern no reason why membership, when it constitutes a purposeful form of complicity in a group engaging in this same forbidden advocacy, should receive any greater degree of protection from the guarantees of that amendment.[32]

Harlan continued:

The clause does not make criminal all association with an organization which has been shown to engage in illegal advocacy. There must be clear proof that a defendant "specifically intend[s] to accomplish [the aims of the organization] by resort to violence.". . . Thus the member for whom the organization is a vehicle for the advancement of legitimate aims and policies does not fall within the ban of the statute: he lacks the requisite specific intent "to bring about the overthrow of the government as speedily as circumstances would permit." Such a person may be foolish, deluded, or perhaps merely optimistic, but he is not by this statute made a criminal.[33]

Justices Douglas and Brennan and Chief Justice Warren based their dissent primarily on the view that the 1950 Internal Security Act specifically immunized persons from prosecution under the Smith Act membership clause.

In a separate opinion Justice Douglas charged that the Court was legalizing guilt by association, an action with which he strongly disagreed. In his separate opinion Justice Black reiterated his view that the First Amendment "absolutely forbids Congress to outlaw membership in a political party or similar association merely because one of the philosophical tenets of that group is that the existing government should be overthrown by force at some distant time in the future when circumstances may permit."[34]

In a companion case, *Noto v. United States*, the Court reversed the membership clause conviction of John Francis Noto, holding the evidence insufficient under the *Yates* rule to justify the conviction. There was no dissent from the decision to reverse the conviction. Justice Harlan wrote for the Court:

the mere abstract teaching of Communist theory, including the teaching of the moral propriety or even moral necessity for a resort to force and violence, is not the same as preparing a group for violent action and steeling it to such action. There must be some substantial direct or circumstantial evidence of a call to violence now or in the future which is both sufficiently strong and sufficiently pervasive to lend color to the otherwise ambiguous theoretical material regarding Communist Party teaching, and to justify the inference that such a call to violence may fairly be imputed to the Party as a whole, and not merely to some narrow segment of it.[35]

The McCarran Act

Deeming the Smith Act insufficient protection against the domestic Communist movement, Congress in 1950 approved the Internal Security—or McCarran—Act, over the veto of President Harry S. Truman. The purpose of the act was to expose party leaders and members of Communist-front groups by requiring that all Communist-front and Communist-action organizations register with the attorney general. Public exposure, it was thought, would curtail the activities of such groups.

Title I of the McCarran Act established a five-member Subversive Activities Control Board (SACB), appointed by the president, to determine, subject to judicial review, whether a particular organization was a Communist-action or Communist-front group and whether certain individuals were among the members.

Once the SACB decided that an organization was such a Communist group, the organization was required to register with the Justice Department and provide to the government lists of its officers and members. Members of registered groups were barred from federal jobs, jobs in defense-related industries, and from applying for or using U.S. passports.[36]

The penalties for failure to register were heavy fines and long prison terms. Compliance with the law, however, made the subject a likely candidate for investigation by a legislative committee or prosecution under the Smith Act. The act did, however, state that holding offices in, or being a member of a Communist organization should not in itself be a crime and that registration should not be used as evidence against a person being prosecuted for violating any criminal law.

In November 1950 the attorney general filed a petition with the SACB to compel the Communist party of the United States to register as a Communist-action organization. That action began an unsuccessful fifteen-year battle to force registration of the party. The judicial record involved three decisions by the court of appeals and two reviews by the Supreme Court. The case record included 15,000 pages of testimony and 507 documentary exhibits. The SACB twice ordered the party to register. The party appealed both orders to the courts.[37]

Registration Order Upheld

In 1961 the Supreme Court upheld the second registration order in an apparent victory for the government. The case of *Communist Party v. Subversive Activities Control Board* was decided by a 5-4 vote. The majority rejected the party's arguments that the registration provisions were unconstitutional as a bill of attainder and as violations of the First Amendment's guarantees of freedom.[38] *(Bill of attainder rulings, p. 138)*

Justice Frankfurter, writing for Justices Clark, Harlan, Whittaker, and Potter Stewart, found—in one of the longest opinions in the Court's history—that the evidence confirmed the SACB ruling that the party was a Communist-action group within the scope of the McCarran Act registration provisions. The provisions of that law did not constitute a bill of attainder, Frankfurter declared:

It attaches not to specified organizations but to described activities in which an organization may or may not engage. The singling out of an individual for legislatively prescribed punishment constitutes an attainder whether the individual is called by name or described in terms of conduct which, because it is past conduct, operates only as a designation of particular persons.... The Subversive Activities Control Act is not of that kind. It requires the registration only of

organizations which, after the date of the Act, are found to be under the direction, domination, or control of certain foreign powers and to operate primarily to advance certain objectives.[39]

Nor, held the majority, did the law violate First Amendment guarantees. Other federal statutes demanded registration and disclosure, Frankfurter noted. In requiring registration Congress balanced private rights of free speech and association against the public interest in disclosure:

Where the mask of anonymity which an organization's members wear serves the double purpose of protecting them from popular prejudice and of enabling them to cover over a foreign-directed conspiracy, infiltrate into other groups, and enlist the support of persons who would not, if the truth were revealed, lend their support ... it would be a distortion of the First Amendment to hold that it prohibits Congress from removing the mask.[40]

Frankfurter emphasized the foreign-dominated character of the Communist party in the United States:

There is no attempt here to impose stifling obligations upon the proponents of a particular political creed as such, or even to check the importation of particular political ideas from abroad for propagation here. The Act compels the registration of organized groups which have been made the instruments of a long-continued, systematic, disciplined activity directed by a foreign power and purposing to overthrow existing government in this country.[41]

The majority found it premature to consider the challenge that the registration provisions violated the Fifth Amendment privilege against compelled self-incrimination, pointing out that this privilege must be claimed by an individual and that it was not now evident that the party officers would make such a claim. In similar fashion, the majority refused to rule on the constitutionality of any other sanctions that might be imposed upon members of the party, once it was registered.

Chief Justice Warren and Justices Brennan, Black, and Douglas dissented in separate opinions, citing a wide variety of reasons for their disagreement with the majority.

Warren would have remanded the case to the SACB for reconsideration of credibility of the testimony of two key government witnesses.

Justice Black protested that the Subversive Activities Control Act of 1950 effectively outlawed the Communist party, a direct violation of the First Amendment:

The first banning of an association because it advocates hated ideas—whether that association be called a political party or not—marks a fateful moment in the history of a free country. That moment seems to have arrived for this country.... This whole Act, with its pains and penalties, embarks this country, for the first time, on the dangerous adventure of outlawing groups that preach doctrines nearly all Americans detest. When the practice of outlawing parties and various public groups begins, no one can say where it will end. In most countries such a practice once begun ends with a one-party government.[42]

Justices Douglas and Brennan found the registration provisions in violation of the Fifth Amendment. Justice Douglas wrote:

The Court and State Sedition Laws

Loyalty oath requirements and loyalty dismissal programs were not the only state response to concern about Communist subversion. Many states during the 1940s and 1950s passed their own sedition laws to punish persons for plotting to overthrow the U.S. government.

In 1956, however, the Supreme Court held that Congress had preempted such state laws, occupying the field of federal sedition prosecutions with passage of the Smith Act, the McCarran Act, and the Communist Control Act. This decision in *Pennsylvania v. Nelson* limited state sedition statutes to punishing sedition against state or local—not federal—government.

Steve Nelson, an avowed Communist, had been convicted for violating Pennsylvania's sedition law by his words and actions concerning the federal government. He was sentenced to serve twenty years in prison, and to pay a $10,000 fine and prosecution costs of $13,000. The state supreme court held that the state law had been superseded by the Smith Act—a ruling the Supreme Court upheld and extended.

Chief Justice Earl Warren surveyed the relevant provisions of the Smith, McCarran, and Communist Control Acts and declared:

the conclusion is inescapable that Congress has intended to occupy the field of sedition. Taken as a whole they evince a congressional plan which makes it reasonable to determine that no room has been left for the States to supplement it.

Therefore, a state sedition statute is superseded regardless of whether it purports to supplement the federal law.[1]

"Since 1939," he noted, "in order to avoid a hampering of uniform enforcement of its program by sporadic local prosecutions, the Federal Government has urged local authorities not to intervene in such matters, but to turn over to the federal authorities immediately and unevaluated all information concerning subversive activities."[2]

Justices Stanley F. Reed, Harold H. Burton, and Sherman Minton dissented.

Following the decision, all pending proceedings under state sedition laws were dismissed or abandoned. Congress considered a measure reversing the Court's decision but did not complete action on such a bill.

In 1965 the Court further curtailed state subversion laws, holding Louisiana's Subversive Activities Criminal Control Act unconstitutionally vague.[3] And in 1969 the Court in the case of *Brandenburg v. Ohio* struck down Ohio's Criminal Syndicalism Act, declaring illegal the use of advocacy of violence, crime, sabotage, and terrorism to accomplish industrial or political reform. This ruling overturned the Court's 1927 decision in *Whitney v. California*, upholding an almost identical California law.[4] *(Details, p. 132)*

1. *Pennsylvania v. Nelson*, 350 U.S. 497 at 504 (1956).
2. Id. at 505-506.
3. *Dombrowski v. Pfister*, 380 U.S. 479 (1965).
4. *Brandenburg v. Ohio*, 395 U.S. 444 (1969), overturning *Whitney v. California*, 274 U.S. 357 (1927).

Signing as an officer or director of the Communist Party—an ingredient of an offense that results in punishment—must be done under the mandate of law. That is compulsory incrimination of those individuals and, in my view, a plain violation of the Fifth Amendment.[43]

Enforcing Provisions Nullified

But as subsequent rulings made clear, the Court had upheld only the power of Congress to require registration of Communist-front and Communist-action groups; it would not give similar sanction to the implementing provisions of the McCarran Act.

In 1964 the Court held invalid the passport restrictions imposed by the act on members of registered organizations. *(Box, p. 135)* In 1965, in the case of *Albertson v. Subversive Activities Control Board*, the Court held that the registration requirements, when applied to individuals, violated the Fifth Amendment privilege against compelled self-incrimination.

And in 1967 the Court declared unconstitutional the provision that barred members of registered organizations from jobs in defense-related facilities.

Congress responded, first by rewriting the registration provisions, and eventually by allowing the SACB to die.[44]

Registration and Incrimination

The most severe of these Court-inflicted blows to the McCarran Act was its 1965 ruling in *Albertson v. Subversive Activities Control Board*, a sequel to the 1961 decision upholding the SACB registration order to the Communist party.

Party officers refused to comply with a final notice from the Justice Department that set November 19, 1961, as the deadline for registration of the party. The government subsequently obtained criminal indictments against the party for its failure to register, and an SACB order directed party officers to register personally.

The officers refused and appealed to the federal courts, citing their Fifth Amendment privilege against self-incrimination as justification for their refusal.

With the Court's decision in the case of *Albertson v. Subversive Activities Control Board,* the officers of the Communist party won a clear-cut victory. The Court held unanimously that the information sought in the registration forms included material that was self-incriminating. Thus, compulsion to register did violate the officers' Fifth Amendment privilege. Brennan wrote the Court's opinion.

The Court rejected the government's argument that the information sought through the registration forms was no more incriminating than that on a tax return. While questions on tax returns were "neutral on their face and directed at the public at large," wrote Brennan, the registration questions were aimed at "a highly selective group inherently suspect of criminal activities." Continuing, he explained that in this case the Fifth Amendment privilege was asserted "not . . . in an essentially non-criminal and regulatory area of inquiry, but against an inquiry in an area permeated with criminal statutes where response to any of the form's questions in context might involve the petitioners in the admission of a crucial element of a crime." [45]

This ruling effectively ended the long effort by the government to force registration of the party. [46]

Association and Jobs

Two years later, in *United States v. Robel,* the Court declared that the McCarran Act also abridged the right of political association insofar as it denied all members of Communist-action or Communist-front organizations the right to hold jobs in defense-related industries. The ban, held the Court 6-2, was too broad, taking in all types of members, not simply active and knowing advocates of violent revolution.

Robel, a member of the Communist party, worked as a machinist in a Seattle shipyard determined by the secretary of defense to be a defense facility. Robel stayed on the job after the final registration deadline for the party and so was charged with violation of the act.

Chief Justice Warren's opinion for the majority viewed this portion of the law as establishing guilt purely by association:

When Congress' exercise of one of its enumerated powers clashes with those individual liberties protected by the Bill of Rights, it is our "delicate and difficult" task to determine whether the resulting restriction on freedom can be tolerated. . . . The Government emphasizes that the purpose of . . . [the contested ban] is to reduce the threat of sabotage and espionage in the nation's defense plants. The Government's interest in such a prophylactic measure is not insubstantial. But it cannot be doubted that the means chosen to implement that governmental purpose in this instance cut deeply into the right of association. [It] . . . put appellee to the choice of surrendering his organizational affiliation, regardless of whether his membership threatened the security of a defense facility or giving up his job. . . . The statute quite literally establishes guilt by association alone, without any need to establish that an individual's association poses the threat feared by the Government in proscribing it. The inhibiting effect on the exercise of First Amendment rights is clear.

Warren added, however, that "nothing we hold today should be read to deny Congress the power under narrowly drawn legislation to keep from sensitive positions in de-

fense facilities those who would use their positions to disrupt the Nation's production facilities. [47]

Justices Byron R. White and Harlan dissented. White wrote that in Robel's case

the interest in anticipating and preventing espionage or sabotage would outweigh the deterrent impact of job disqualification. . . . In the case before us the Court simply disagrees with the Congress and the Defense Department, ruling that Robel does not present a sufficient danger to the national security to require him to choose between membership in the Communist Party and his employment in a defense facility. . . . I much prefer the judgment of Congress and the Executive Branch that the interest of respondent in remaining a member of the Communist Party . . . is less substantial than the public interest in excluding him from employment in critical defense industries. [48]

In the fall of 1967 Congress revised the definition of Communist-front organization in the McCarran Act. Another amendment to the act eliminated the registration requirement and authorized the SACB to place on a public register the names of individuals and organizations it found to be Communist.

In 1968 Attorney General Ramsey Clark asked the board to conduct hearings on seven individuals thought to be members of the Communist party. The SACB issued orders against three of the individuals, declaring them to be members of a Communist-action organization. The Board's order was set aside by the District of Columbia Court of Appeals in 1969, holding that mere membership in the Communist party was protected by the First Amendment. [49]

Federal Loyalty Programs

To ensure that only "loyal" persons held federal jobs, Presidents Truman and Dwight Eisenhower instituted federal loyalty programs that provoked considerable controversy.

Critics of the programs argued that through them the government penalized persons for a state of mind rather than for overt acts of disloyalty, and dismissed persons from jobs purely on the grounds of guilt by association. Defenders of the programs pointed out that there was no constitutional right to hold a government job and that the government had a right to protect itself from internal subversion. Moreover, dismissal from a government job did not imply guilt but only that some question existed as to one's fitness for government employment.

The Truman Program

In 1947 President Truman by executive order established a loyalty program for all civilian employees of the executive branch. Executive Order 9835 established a Loyalty Review Board within the Civil Service Commission to coordinate agency loyalty policies and to serve as the final board of appeal in loyalty dismissal cases. Loyalty investigations were required for all present government employees and for all applicants for government jobs. Dismissal of individuals from government posts or denial of a job was permitted when "on all the evidence, reasonable grounds exist for belief that the person involved is disloyal to the

Government of the United States." (In 1951 this standard was modified to allow dismissal when "there is a reasonable doubt as to the loyalty of the person involved.")

In the 1940s Congress authorized summary dismissal of employees of the Departments of State, Defense, Army, Navy, and Air Force and the Atomic Energy Commission when dismissal was considered necessary or advisable in the interest of national security. In 1950 Congress extended this authority to the Departments of the Treasury, Commerce, and Justice.

The Eisenhower Program

In 1953 President Eisenhower extended this summary dismissal power to all executive branch agencies and replaced the Truman loyalty program with a more stringent loyalty-security program established by Executive Order 10450.

Under the Eisenhower program a suspected employee bore the burden of proving his employment "clearly consistent" with national security. The order also sanctioned dismissal for reasons other than disloyalty: for example, personal behavior, sexual misconduct, excessive use of drugs or alcohol, and physical or mental disorders.[50]

Loyalty Programs Sustained

The Supreme Court never squarely addressed the substantial constitutional questions raised by the federal loyalty and security programs, although it did rule in a number of cases during the 1950s concerning individual dismissals. Three constitutional provisions were implicated in government loyalty programs: the First Amendment guarantees of freedom of expression and political association; the Fifth Amendment guarantee that government would not deprive one of liberty or property without due process of law; and the Article I ban on the passage of bills of attainder.

Only the due process question received any extended consideration by the Court in these cases.

The first rulings came in 1951. In *Joint Anti-Fascist Refugee Committee v. McGrath* the Court upheld the authority of the attorney general, under the Truman loyalty program, to maintain and furnish to the Loyalty Review Board a list of allegedly subversive organizations. The Court held, however, that the attorney general had exceeded that authority and acted arbitrarily in placing the names of three particular organizations—including the Anti-Fascist Refugee Committee—on that list.

The vote was 5-3. Justice Clark, attorney general when the case was filed, did not participate in the decision. Justice Burton—joined only by Justice Douglas—wrote the opinion announcing the judgment of the Court. That opinion carefully avoided the First Amendment issues of political association raised by use of this list.

In concurring opinions, Justices Black, Douglas, Frankfurter, and Jackson questioned the constitutionality of the list in light of the guarantee of due process and the prohibition on a bill of attainder. Justice Frankfurter wrote that although the designation as "Communist" actually imposed no legal sanction on the listed organizations,

in the conditions of our time such designation drastically restricts the organizations, if it does not proscribe them. . . . Yet, designation has been made without notice, without disclosure of any reasons justifying it,

without opportunity to meet the undisclosed evidence or suspicion on which designation may have been based, and without opportunity to establish affirmatively that the aims and acts of the organization are innocent.

Frankfurter concluded that such action

to maim or decapitate, on the mere say-so of the Attorney General, an organization to all outward-seeming engaged in lawful objectives is so devoid of fundamental fairness as to offend the Due Process Clause of the Fifth Amendment.[51]

Justices Reed and Minton and Chief Justice Vinson dissented, finding the due process guarantee inapplicable and rejecting any First Amendment challenge to use of the list.

So long as petitioners are permitted to voice their political ideas . . . it is hard to understand how any advocate of freedom of expression can assert that their right has been unconstitutionally abridged. As nothing in the orders or regulations concerning this list limits the teachings or support of these organizations, we do not believe that any right of theirs under the First Amendment is abridged by publication of the list.[52]

The same day, the Court, evenly divided 4-4, upheld, without opinion, the decision of the loyalty board to dismiss Dorothy Bailey, a training officer in the United States Employment Service. Justice Clark again did not participate in the decision.

The even division within the Court left standing an appeals court ruling finding Bailey's removal valid. Because there was no constitutional right to federal employment, her dismissal did not violate due process, and, the majority of the lower court continued, the First Amendment did not bar removal of persons from office for political reasons. There was no opinion from the Supreme Court, as is the practice in cases in which the justices are evenly divided.[53]

In 1955 the Court ruled that the Loyalty Review Board had exceeded its authority in discharging a public health officer as a security risk, after the officer had twice been cleared of any suspicion of disloyalty by agency loyalty boards.[54] In 1956 the Court held unjustified the summary dismissal of an inspector with the Food and Drug Administration on loyalty grounds. The Court ruled that dismissal from a nonsensitive position could not be justified as necessary in the interest of national security.[55]

In 1959 the Court weakened the federal government's effort to carry out its loyalty program by casting doubt on the propriety of the procedures used in revoking security clearances and dismissing employees on the basis of information from anonymous sources. With its ruling in the case of *Greene v. McElroy,* the Court forced the president to revise those procedures.[56]

William L. Greene lost his job as vice president of an engineering firm engaged in defense contract work after his security clearance was revoked. The review board revoking the clearance relied on confidential reports, never available to Greene, even though he appeared at the hearings of the board to respond to the charges against him.

As a result of loss of his clearance, Greene was unable to find another job in the field of aeronautical engineering. He challenged the revocation of his clearance as depriving him of his livelihood and thus of liberty and property without due process of law guaranteed by the Fifth Amendment.

The Court, 8-1, agreed that the denial of access to the evidence against Greene had been improper, depriving him of the opportunity to respond and rebut the charges. Neither Congress nor the president had authorized the Defense Department thus to classify the employees of a contractor as security risks without giving them the opportunity to confront and examine the evidence against them, held the Court.

Chief Justice Warren, writing for five members of the majority, carefully narrowed the reach of the ruling:

[P]etitioner's work opportunities have been severely limited on the basis of a fact determination rendered after a hearing which failed to comport with our traditional ideas of fair procedure. The type of hearing was the product of administrative decision not explicitly authorized by either Congress or the President. Whether those procedures under the circumstances comport with the Constitution we do not decide. Nor do we decide whether the President has inherent authority to create such a program, whether congressional action is necessary, or what the limits on executive or legislative authority may be.

We decide only that in the absence of explicit authorization from the President or Congress the respondents were not empowered to deprive petitioner of his job in a proceeding in which he was not afforded the safeguards of confrontation and cross-examination.[57]

Justices Frankfurter, Harlan, and Whittaker concurred with the Court's judgment.

Justice Clark dissented, arguing that no one has "a constitutional right to have access to the Government's military secrets. . . . What for anyone else would be considered a privilege at best has for Greene been enshrouded in constitutional protection. This sleight of hand is too much for me."

Clark warned that the majority was casting a cloud over the entire federal loyalty-security program, which could result in "a rout of our internal security."[58]

Early in 1960 President Eisenhower issued an executive order restricting the use of informants whose identities must be protected and granting additional rights to persons accused as security risks to confront and cross-examine their accusers.[59]

In 1961, however, the Court, 5-4, upheld the national security dismissal of a short-order cook in a cafeteria on the premises of the Naval Gun Factory in Washington, D.C. The Court in *Cafeteria and Restaurant Workers Union v. McElroy* held this action well within the authority granted by Congress to the executive to control security on military bases.[60]

Loyalty Oaths and Labor

Along with the institution of the federal loyalty-security program came the proliferation of requirements that persons holding certain posts take loyalty oaths or sign affidavits to demonstrate their loyalty to the U.S. government. In a long line of rulings, the Supreme Court first upheld and then circumscribed both the use and the usefulness of such requirements.

Labor Affidavit Upheld

Concern over Communist infiltration of the labor movement and "political strikes" spurred Congress to include in the Taft-Hartley Act, the Labor Management Relations Act of 1947, a provision requiring officers of all labor organizations wishing to benefit from the protections and guarantees of federal labor law to sign affidavits that they were not members of, or affiliated, with the Communist party, and that they did not believe in or hold membership in any organization teaching or believing in the forcible, illegal, or unconstitutional overthrow of the federal government. Unions whose officers did not sign such affidavits were denied all protection of and services from the National Labor Relations Board.

In 1950 the Supreme Court upheld that requirement as within the power of Congress. In the case of *American Communications Association v. Douds*, Chief Justice Vinson explained:

There can be no doubt that Congress may, under its constitutional power to regulate commerce among the several States, attempt to prevent political strikes and other kinds of direct action designed to burden and interrupt the free flow of commerce.[61]

The affidavit requirement, held the Court, was a reasonable means of attaining that end.

Congress could rationally find that the Communist Party is not like other political parties in its utilization of positions of union leadership as means by which to bring about strikes and other obstructions of commerce for purposes of political advantage.[62]

The Court recognized, Vinson continued, that:

By exerting pressures on unions to deny office to Communists and others identified therein . . . [the affidavit requirement] undoubtedly lessens the threat to interstate commerce, but it has the further necessary effect of discouraging the exercise of political rights protected by the First Amendment. Men who hold union offices often have little choice but to renounce Communism or give up their offices.[63]

In response to the challenge that the affidavit requirement was an unconstitutional curtailment of individual freedom, Vinson wrote that the requirement

does not interfere with speech because Congress fears the consequences of speech; it regulates harmful conduct which Congress has determined is carried on by persons who may be identified by their political affiliations and beliefs. The [National Labor Relations] Board does not contend that political strikes, the substantive evil at which . . . [the requirement] is aimed, are the present or impending products of advocacy of the doctrines of Communism or the expression of belief in overthrow of the Government by force. . . . Speech may be fought with speech. Falsehoods and fallacies must be exposed, not suppressed, unless there is not sufficient time to avert the evil consequences of noxious doctrine by argument and education. That is the command of the First Amendment. But force may and must be met with force. . . . [The affidavit requirement] is designed to protect the public not against what Communists and others identified therein advocate or believe, but against what Congress has concluded they have done and are likely to do again.[64]

Politics and Loyalty at the Bar

Concerned about Communist infiltration of the legal profession, several states began in the 1950s inquiring into the political affiliation and associations of persons seeking admission to the practice of law. This line of inquiry produced a series of Supreme Court decisions that covered almost two decades.

When Illinois bar examiners questioned George Anastaplo about his political beliefs, he refused on principle to respond, asserting that the questions invaded areas protected by the First and Fourteenth Amendments. He was denied admission to the bar. In 1955 the Supreme Court upheld the denial by refusing to review his appeal.[1]

Two years later, however, the Court ruled that questionable political affiliations alone, or the simple refusal to answer questions about one's political associations, did not give a state a basis for concluding that an applicant lacked the proper moral character for admission to the practice of law.

In *Schware v. New Mexico Board of Bar Examiners,* the board had concluded that Rudolph Schware lacked the requisite "good moral character" because he had used aliases during the 1930s to obtain jobs in businesses that discriminated against Jews, because he had been arrested several times, and because he had been a member of the Communist party from 1932-1940.

The Supreme Court unanimously reversed the board's decision. Justice Hugo L. Black wrote the opinion, refuting the board's inference that because Schware had belonged to the Communist party he was of bad moral character.[2]

Raphael Konigsberg was denied admission to the California bar because he, like Anastaplo, refused to answer questions about his political affiliations. The Court overturned the state's action the same day it reversed the lower court decision in *Schware.* Konigsberg's record of public and military service testified sufficiently to his loyalty, held the Court.[3]

Admission Not Guaranteed

But, as both Anastaplo and Konigsberg discovered, Supreme Court reversal of the state's initial refusal to admit them to the practice of law did not guarantee their admission. On the basis of *Schware* and *Konigsberg,* Anastaplo asked Illinois to reconsider his application for admission to the bar. After lengthy proceedings, the state again rejected it.

In 1961 the Supreme Court, 5-4, upheld the state's action. The majority said that the state had a legitimate interest in examining the qualifications of persons seeking to practice law in the state—and that questions about his political background were a proper element in that examination.

By continuing to refuse to answer those questions, Anastaplo, the Court held, obstructed the state's inquiry, and denial of admission was a legitimate response.[4]

A second ruling in Konigsberg's case was announced the same day. Also 5-4, the Court upheld California bar officials' refusal to admit Konigsberg—not because of concern about his character but simply because he too persisted in his refusal to answer questions germane to its inquiry, thereby obstructing the state's examining process.[5]

Evidence of Character

Ten years later, in two decisions announced the same day in 1971, the Supreme Court marked the boundary line for such questioning.

By 5-4, the Court held that the First Amendment forbade a state to exclude an applicant from admission to the bar solely on the basis of his refusal to state whether he had ever belonged to an organization advocating the violent overthrow of the government—without any other evidence of disloyalty or unfitness. Justice Black wrote the opinion; dissenting were Justices John Marshall Harlan, Byron R. White, and Harry A. Blackmun and Chief Justice Warren Burger.[6]

But the same day, with Justice Potter Stewart joining those dissenters, the Court, 5-4, held that states could require applicants for admission to the bar to be of good moral character and loyal to the Constitution. It made no difference that the "loyalty" requirement included taking an oath in support of the state and federal constitutions and responding to two questions concerning membership in any organization advocating overthrow of the government by force or violence, with the specific intent of furthering that goal.[7]

In this case, the majority was careful to point out that there was no indication that any applicant had been denied admission to the bar because of his answers to these questions or his refusal to answer them. "It is well settled," wrote Justice Stewart, "that Bar Examiners may ask about Communist affiliation as a preliminary to further inquiry into the nature of the association and may exclude an applicant for refusal to answer."[8]

1. *In re Anastaplo,* 348 U.S. 946 (1955).
2. *Schware v. New Mexico Board of Bar Examiners,* 353 U.S. 232 (1957).
3. *Konigsberg v. State Bar of California,* 353 U.S. 252 (1957).
4. *In re Anastaplo,* 366 U.S. 82 (1961).
5. *Konigsberg v. State Bar of California,* 366 U.S. 36 (1961).
6. *In re Stolar, Baird v. State Bar of Arizona,* 401 U.S. 23 (1971).
7. *Law Students Civil Rights Research Council v. Wadmond,* 401 U.S. 154 (1971).
8. Id. at 165-166.

Justices Clark, Minton, and Douglas did not take part in this decision.

Justice Frankfurter concurred in upholding the membership portion of the affidavit but dissented from the majority opinion upholding the portion involving belief alone.

Justice Jackson also concurred in part and dissented in part, making a similar distinction between the membership and the belief portions of the affidavit:

all parts of this oath which require disclosure of overt acts of affiliation or membership in the Communist Party are within the competence of Congress to enact ... any parts of it that call for a disclosure of belief unconnected with any overt act are beyond its power.[65]

Earlier in his opinion, Jackson had phrased his view in less abstract terms:

I think that under our system, it is time enough for the law to lay hold of the citizen when he acts illegally, or in some rare circumstances when his thoughts are given illegal utterance. I think we must let his mind alone.[66]

In a vigorous dissenting opinion, Justice Black criticized his colleagues for allowing the government to restrict the right to think:

Freedom to think is inevitably abridged when beliefs are penalized by imposition of civil disabilities.... Like anyone else, individual Communists who commit overt acts in violation of valid laws can and should be punished. But the postulate of the First Amendment is that our free institutions can be maintained without proscribing or penalizing political belief, speech, press, assembly, or party affiliation. This is a far bolder philosophy than despotic rulers can afford to follow. It is the heart of the system on which our freedom depends.[67]

Labor Office Ban Voided

In 1959 Congress replaced the affidavit requirement—which proved ineffective since some Communists were willing to take the oath and risk prosecution for perjury—with a flat prohibition against members of the Communist party holding any union office. The new section of the federal labor law, part of the Management Reporting and Disclosure Act of 1959, also disqualified anyone who had been a member of the party during the last five years.[68]

In 1965 the Supreme Court held this ban unconstitutional as a violation of the provision forbidding Congress to pass bills of attainder.

In *United States v. Brown*, Archie Brown, a member of the Communist party, challenged the operation of the law that forbade him to serve on the executive board of a local of the International Longshoremen's and Warehousemen's Union. He also based his challenge on First and Fifth Amendment grounds, but the Court found it unnecessary to consider those.

By a 5-4 vote the Supreme Court ruled in his favor. Chief Justice Earl Warren wrote:

Congress undoubtedly possesses power under the Commerce Clause to enact legislation designed to keep from positions affecting interstate commerce persons who may use such positions to bring about political strikes. In ... [this prohibition] however, Congress has

exceeded the authority granted it by the Constitution. The statute does not set forth a generally applicable rule decreeing that any person who commits certain acts or possesses certain characteristics (acts and characteristics which, in Congress' view, make them likely to initiate political strikes) shall not hold union office, and leave to courts and juries the job of deciding what persons have committed the specified acts or possess the specified characteristics. Instead, it designates in no uncertain terms the persons who possess the feared characteristics and therefore cannot hold union office without incurring criminal liability—members of the Communist Party....

We do not hold today that Congress cannot weed dangerous persons out of the labor movement.... Rather, we make again the point ... that Congress must accomplish such results by rules of general applicability. It cannot specify the people upon whom the sanction it prescribes is to be levied. Under our Constitution, Congress possesses full legislative authority, but the task of adjudication must be left to other tribunals.[69]

In dissent, Justice White, joined by Justices Clark, Harlan, and Stewart, criticized the majority's distinction between the legislative function of making rules and the judicial function in applying those rules to particular individuals or groups. White wrote that the Court took "too narrow [a] view of the legislative process." [70]

In two other cases related to the non-Communist affidavit requirement, the Court in the 1960s reversed convictions of union members who had sworn falsely that they were not Communists. The Court decided both cases without dealing with the First Amendment claim of freedom of political association or the Fifth Amendment privilege protecting individuals against compelled self-incrimination.[71]

Teachers and Oaths

The most frequent state reaction to the threat of Communist subversion was passage of a law requiring public employees—particularly teachers—to take a loyalty oath affirming that they had not been and were not members of the Communist party.

During the 1950s the Court upheld the constitutionality of such oaths, but by 1967 it had reversed itself, finding that most oaths came too close to guilt by association, demanding little evidence of actual subversive activity. In the 1970s the Court upheld several laws requiring state employees to take affirmative oaths promising to uphold the Constitution and to oppose the violent overthrow of the government.

Gerende and *Garner*

The Court's first loyalty oath rulings came in 1951. In *Gerende v. Board of Supervisors of Elections,* the Court upheld Maryland's law requiring every candidate for public office to file an affidavit disavowing involvement in any attempt to overthrow the government by force or violence.[72]

Two months later, on the same day that it upheld the constitutionality of the Smith Act, the Court in *Garner v. Board of Public Works of the City of Los Angeles* upheld a

Los Angeles ordinance requiring city employees to affirm their loyalty through oath and affidavit.

Public employees had to state whether they ever had been members of the Communist party and to swear that they had not advocated the overthrow of state or federal government in the previous five years, that they had not and would not be affiliated with any group advocating such

overthrow during the period they held a city job.

Seventeen employees refused to comply and were dismissed. They sued for reinstatement, challenging the oath and affidavit requirement as unconstitutional as a bill of attainder, an ex post facto law, and a violation of their freedom of speech, assembly, and right to petition the government for redress of grievances.[73]

Politics and Public Employees

Despite the First Amendment's guarantee of freedom for political association, the Supreme Court has consistently upheld the power of Congress and state legislatures to limit the political activity of public employees. The Court first made this point in 1947: the limited burden such laws place upon the right of political association is justified by the government's interest in having its employees chosen on the basis of merit, not political loyalty.

The end of the spoils system for filling federal posts brought with it laws limiting the political activities of government workers.

In 1876 Congress prohibited government employees from requesting, giving, or receiving money for political purposes from any federal official. The Civil Service Act of 1883 forbade federal officials to use their positions to influence the political action of their subordinates.

The Hatch Act of 1939 prohibited federal employees from taking active part in political campaigns or the management of political party activities. Office of Personnel Management (formerly the Civil Service Commission) regulations subsequently have denied government workers the right to participate in the following political activities: running for office, distributing campaign literature, taking an active role in political campaigns, circulating nominating petitions, attending political conventions as other than a spectator, and publishing or signing a letter soliciting votes for a candidate.

In 1947 the Supreme Court in *United Public Workers v. Mitchell* upheld, 4-3, these restrictions on the political activities of government employees. Justices Frank Murphy and Robert H. Jackson did not take part in the decision. Justices Wiley Rutledge, Hugo L. Black, and William O. Douglas dissented.

Justice Stanley F. Reed, speaking for the Court, declared that there was no constitutional objection to the finding of Congress that an efficient public service was best obtained by prohibiting active participation by public employees in political campaigns. The conclusion was a reasonable one, well within the power of Congress. Reed continued:

> For regulation of employees it is not necessary that the act regulated be anything more than an act reasonably deemed by Congress to

interfere with the efficiency of the public service. . . .

> We have said that Congress may regulate the political conduct of Government employees "within reasonable limits," even though the regulation trenches to some extent upon unfettered political action. The determination of the extent to which political activities of governmental employees shall be regulated lies primarily in Congress. Courts will interfere only when such regulation passes beyond the generally existing conception of governmental power.[1]

Reed added, however, that the concept of government power might change, indicating that some future court might find these restrictions impermissible.

But sixteen years later, in 1973, the Court again rebuffed First Amendment challenges to federal and state prohibitions on partisan political activity by public employees. By 6-3, the Court again upheld the validity of the Hatch Act.

Justice Byron R. White wrote for the majority in the case of *Civil Service Commission v. Letter Carriers:*

> [I]t is in the best interest of the country, indeed essential, that federal service should depend upon meritorious performance rather than political service, and that the political influence of federal employees on others and on the electoral process should be limited.[2]

Justices Douglas, William J. Brennan, Jr., and Thurgood Marshall dissented.

In a companion case, *Broadrick v. Oklahoma State Personnel Board,* the Court 5-4 sustained a state law prohibiting employees from partisan political activity.[3] Justice Potter Stewart, who voted with the majority in the Hatch Act case, joined the dissenters in this case.

1. *United Public Workers v. Mitchell,* 330 U.S. 75 at 101, 102 (1947).
2. *Civil Service Commission v. Letter Carriers,* 413 U.S. 548 at 557 (1973).
3. *Broadrick v. Oklahoma State Personnel Board,* 413 U.S. 601 (1973).

The Court upheld the affidavit requirement 7-2, but the oath only 5-4. Justice Clark, writing for the majority, explained that they did not view the ordinance as a bill of attainder because it did not punish anyone, but simply set standards of qualification and eligibility for city jobs. It was not an ex post facto law, he continued, because it involved activity that for the seven previous years had been proscribed for city employees. The majority did not address the First Amendment issues directly.

Justices Frankfurter and Burton concurred in the decision to uphold the affidavit requirement, but dissented from the majority's ruling upholding the oath. Frankfurter wrote:

> The Constitution does not guarantee public employment. City, State and Nation are not confined to making provisions appropriate for securing competent professional discharge of the functions pertaining to diverse governmental jobs. They may also assure themselves of fidelity to the very presuppositions of our scheme of government on the part of those who seek to serve it.[74]

Frankfurter explained that he would have overturned the oath requirement because it was "not limited to affiliation with organizations known at the time to have advocated overthrow of government.... How can anyone be sure that an organization with which he affiliates will not at some time in the future be found ... to advocate overthrow of government by 'unlawful means'?"[75]

Burton found the retroactive nature of the oath invalid under the Court's decisions concerning bills of attainder and ex post facto laws.

Justices Black and Douglas found all aspects of the requirement objectionable, holding both the oath and the affidavit requirements invalid as bills of attainder.

Loyalty Dismissals

Loyalty oath requirements for state or city employees were often linked with programs for the removal of public employees whose loyalty was suspect.

In 1952 the Supreme Court upheld a New York law setting up a state list of subversive organizations—those advocating the violent overthrow of the government—and providing that membership in any listed organization would constitute prima facie evidence justifying dismissal from a public post.

The law was intended to ensure the doctrinal orthodoxy of teachers and other officials in the New York public school system. Before dismissal, an individual who was a member of such an organization was entitled to a full hearing and judicial review of the decision to dismiss him. With its decision in *Adler v. Board of Education, City of New York,* the Court 6-3 sustained the law.[76]

For the majority, Justice Minton wrote:

> That the school authorities have the right and the duty to screen the officials, teachers and employees as to their fitness to maintain the integrity of the schools as a part of ordered society, cannot be doubted. One's associates, past and present, as well as one's conduct, may properly be considered in determining fitness and loyalty. From time immemorial, one's reputation has been determined in part by the company he keeps.[77]

Disqualification from a job under the law, wrote Minton, did not deny one the right of free speech and assembly.

"His freedom of choice between membership in the organization and employment in the school system might be limited, but not his freedom of speech or assembly."[78]

Justices Frankfurter, Black, and Douglas dissented. Frankfurter argued that the Court should have dismissed the case without ruling on the law. Douglas and Black found the law a violation of the First Amendment. It "proceeds on a principle repugnant to our society—guilt by association," wrote Douglas.[79] He elaborated:

> Youthful indiscretions, mistaken causes, misguided enthusiasms—all long forgotten—become the ghosts of a harrowing present. Any organization committed to a liberal cause, any group organized to revolt against a hysterical trend, any committee launched to sponsor an unpopular program becomes suspect. These are the organizations into which Communists often infiltrate. Their presence infects the whole, even though the project was not conceived in sin. A teacher caught in that mesh is almost certain to stand condemned. Fearing condemnation, she will tend to shrink from any association that stirs controversy. In that manner freedom of expression will be stifled....
>
> What happens under this law is typical of what happens in a police state. Teachers are under constant surveillance; their pasts are combed for signs of disloyalty; their utterances are watched for cues to dangerous thoughts. A pall is cast over the classrooms. There can be no real academic freedom in that environment. Where suspicion fills the air and holds scholars in line for fear of their jobs, there can be no exercise of the free intellect....
>
> Of course the school systems ... need not become cells for Communist activities; and the classrooms need not become forums for propagandizing the Marxist creed. But the guilt of the teacher should turn on overt acts. So long as she is a law-abiding citizen, so long as her performance within the public school system meets professional standards, her private life, her political philosophy, her social creed should not be the cause of reprisals against her.[80]

Initial Limitation

But late in the same year as *Adler,* the Court unanimously struck down an Oklahoma loyalty program that penalized knowing *and* unknowing members of certain proscribed organizations. The law challenged in *Wieman v. Updegraff* required all state officers and employees to take a loyalty oath and excluded from public jobs those persons who had been members of certain organizations, regardless of their knowledge of the organization's purposes. With this ruling the Court began to impose limits upon state loyalty oaths by requiring, at the least, that membership be a conscious endorsement of an organization's aims and doctrines before it was used as a basis for a state-imposed penalty.

Justice Clark, in the Court's opinion, made clear that in *Garner* and *Adler* only "knowing" membership resulted in disqualification for or dismissal from a public job. But under Oklahoma law, "membership alone disqualifies."[81]

This was a critical difference:

> the fact of association alone [under the challenged law] determines disloyalty and disqualification; it matters not whether association existed innocently or knowingly. To thus inhibit individual freedom of movement

is to stifle the flow of democratic expression and controversy at one of its chief sources. . . . Indiscriminate classification of innocent with knowing activity must fall as an assertion of arbitrary power. The oath offends due process.[82]

Justice Jackson, who had not heard the case argued, did not participate in the decision.

Penalizing the Privilege

Four years later, the Court held it unconstitutional for a state or city automatically to dismiss an employee if he invoked his constitutional privilege against self-incrimination to avoid answering questions about his political associations.

At issue in *Slochower v. Board of Higher Education of New York City* was the city's summary dismissal of a Brooklyn College professor because, in testimony before the Senate internal security subcommittee, he had refused to answer questions about his political associations before 1941, invoking the Fifth Amendment.

Slochower was suspended without notice, hearing, or an opportunity to explain or discuss the reasons for the termination of his tenure. This action came under a provision of the city charter that automatically terminated the tenure of any public official who invoked the Fifth Amendment to avoid answering questions related to official conduct. Slochower sued, challenging his dismissal as improper and the city charter provision as unconstitutional because it penalized the exercise of a federally guaranteed constitutional right.

The Court ruled in his favor—but on different grounds. Summary dismissal, the Court held 5-4, violated Slochower's right to due process of law. The city board of education, wrote Justice Clark for the majority, had erred in treating his assertion of his Fifth Amendment privilege as a "conclusive presumption of guilt."

Such interpretation of the assertion of a constitutional right was impermissible, Clark continued: "The privilege against self-incrimination would be reduced to a hollow mockery if its exercise could be taken as equivalent to a confession of guilt." [83] Because no valid inference of guilt could be made, the Court sustained Slochower's claim of privilege before the Senate subcommittee and ruled that there was no basis for his dismissal.

Justice Reed, speaking also for Justices Burton and Minton, dissented, arguing that "the city does have reasonable ground to require its employees either to give evidence regarding facts of official conduct within their knowledge or to give up the positions they hold." [84] Justice Harlan, in a separate dissenting opinion, wrote that the majority had "misconceived" the nature of the city charter provision in question and had "unduly circumscribed the power of the State to ensure the qualifications of its teachers." [85]

The State's Right to Inquire

In two 1958 decisions, however, the Court again upheld the right of states to question employees about their associations, in examining their overall qualifications for state employment.

In *Lerner v. Casey* a subway conductor refused to tell his superiors whether he was a member of the Communist party. He was dismissed as a person of doubtful loyalty and reliability.[86] In *Beilan v. Board of Public Education,*

School District of Philadelphia, a school teacher, who refused to tell his superintendent whether he had earlier held a position in the Communist party, was dismissed as incompetent.[87]

The five-man majority in both cases—Harlan, Burton, Frankfurter, Clark, and Whittaker—stressed that the subway conductor and the school teacher were dismissed because they refused to answer questions put by their employers—action that constituted evidence of incompetency and unreliability.

In a concurring opinion, Justice Frankfurter said the two employees were "terminated because of their refusals to answer questions relevant . . . to an inquiry by their supervisors into their dependability. When these two employees were discharged, they were not labeled "disloyal." They were discharged because governmental authorities, like other employers, sought to satisfy themselves of the dependability of employees in relation to their duties." [88]

In dissent, Chief Justice Warren and Justices Brennan, Black, and Douglas argued that the two employees had been branded disloyal by the inquiry into their political associations and activities. In his dissenting opinion, Brennan wrote, "more is at stake here than the loss of positions of public employment for unreliability or incompetence. Rather, it is the simultaneous public labeling of the employees as disloyal that gives rise to our concern." [89]

The Shift of the Sixties

With a series of decisions begining in 1958—initially involving civil rights, not Communist, groups—the Supreme Court gave formal recognition to a First Amendment freedom of political association. *(Details, pp. 28-29)*

In line with this development came a clear shift in the Court's willingness to back government inquiry into the affiliations of its employees and government-imposed penalties upon persons whose affiliations seemed suspect. The *Aptheker* and *Robel* rulings of 1964 and 1967 reflected the change. *(Details, pp. 135, 142)*

And the Court, in a set of rulings in the mid-1960s, effectively reversed most of its key decisions upholding state government loyalty oath and loyalty program requirements, finding that they were too broad to comport with the freedom guaranteed by the First Amendment. The first of these freedom-of-association rulings was the 1958 decision in *National Association for the Advancement of Colored People v. Alabama.*[90]

Two years later the Court struck down a state law that required public school teachers to file affidavits listing all their organizational memberships. In its opinion in *Shelton v. Tucker,* the Court found this requirement to go "far beyond what might be justified in the exercise of the State's legitimate inquiry into the fitness and competency of its teachers." [91]

The following year, the Court first applied this new view to loyalty oaths, striking down a Florida law that required state employees to swear that they had never lent "aid, support, advice, counsel or influence to the Communist Party." Employees who did not sign such an oath were fired.

In its opinion in this case of *Cramp v. Board of Public Instruction,* the Court held this oath far too vague, "completely lacking in . . . terms susceptible of objective measurement." [92] A law describing prohibited acts " 'in terms so vague that men of common intelligence must necessarily guess at its meaning and differ as to its application violates the first essential of due process of law,'" wrote Justice Stewart for the unanimous Court.[93]

In 1964 Washington State's loyalty oath for teachers was struck down on the basis of similar reasoning.[94] And in 1966 and 1967, this shift culminated in decisions effectively nullifying *Gerende, Garner,* and *Adler.*

Elfbrandt and *Garner*

The first of these rulings came in the case of *Elfbrandt v. Russell.* Barbara Elfbrandt, a Quaker teacher in Arizona, challenged the constitutionality of the state laws that required state employees to take a loyalty oath. The oath itself simply affirmed support for the constitutions and laws of the state and the United States, but the state legislature had by law provided that the oath would be considered violated by knowing membership in the Communist party. The law made clear that any employee who took the oath and at the time or later became a willing, knowing member of the Communist party could be prosecuted for perjury.

By 5-4 the Supreme Court held this combination of oath and interpretative statute too broad to meet constitutional standards. Justice Douglas explained that the major flaw was the failure of the state to acknowledge that many people might join organizations such as the Communist party without actually sharing the organization's unlawful purposes. The challenged law, he continued, was predicated on the doctrine of guilt by association:

> Those who join an organization but do not share its unlawful purposes and who do not participate in its unlawful activities surely pose no threat, either as citizens or as public employees.... This Act threatens the cherished freedom of association protected by the First Amendment, made applicable to the States through the Fourteenth Amendment.... A law which applies to membership without the "specific intent" to further the illegal aims of the organization infringes unnecessarily on protected freedoms. It rests on the doctrine of "guilt by association" which has no place here.[95]

With this ruling, the Court effectively, if implicitly, overturned *Garner,* which had upheld that sort of oath. The four dissenting justices, White, Clark, Harlan, and Stewart said that the oath should be upheld in light of the Court's earlier decisions acknowledging the right of states to condition public employment upon the requirement that employees abstain from knowing membership in subversive organizations.

Keyishian and *Adler*

The following year the Court struck down the New York law it had upheld in *Adler.* The vote in *Keyishian v. Board of Regents of the University of the State of New York* was again 5-4. Justice Brennan wrote the majority opinion.

The law authorized the board of regents to prepare a list of subversive organizations and to deny jobs to teachers belonging to those organizations. The law made membership in the Communist party prima facie evidence for disqualification from employment. Four university faculty members subject to dismissal under the law challenged its constitutionality.

The Court found the law too vague and too sweeping, penalizing "[m]ere knowing membership without a specific intent to further the unlawful aims" of the Communist party.[96] The question of vagueness, noted Brennan, had not been placed before the Court in *Adler.* The majority described New York's complex of criminal anarchy and loyalty laws as "a highly efficient *in terrorem* mechanism" that operated to curtail First Amendment freedom:

> It would be a bold teacher who would not stay as far as possible from utterances or acts which might jeopardize his living by enmeshing him in this intricate machinery....
>
> Our Nation is deeply committed to safeguarding academic freedom, which is of transcendent value to all of us and not merely to the teachers concerned. That freedom is therefore a special concern of the First Amendment, which does not tolerate laws that cast a pall of orthodoxy over the classroom.[97]

Four justices—Clark, Harlan, Stewart, and White—dissented. Writing for the dissenters Justice Clark declared: "[T]he majority has by its broadside swept away one of our most precious rights, namely, the right of self preservation."[98]

A few months later, the Court 6-3 struck down the Maryland loyalty oath law it had upheld in *Gerende.* Justice Douglas explained that the oath was so vague that it violated the due process guarantee of the Fourteenth Amendment. Its capricious application could "deter the flowering of academic freedom as much as successive suits for perjury," he wrote.[99] Justices Harlan, Stewart, and White dissented.

POLITICAL ASSOCIATION: A CONTEMPORARY VIEW

As the threat of domestic subversion faded, and questions of domestic politics came again to the foreground of national attention, the Supreme Court in the 1970s and 1980s continued to define various aspects of this freedom of political association.

Loyalty Oaths

The Court continued to support state requirements that employees take affirmatively worded loyalty oaths, declaring their support for the existing system of constitutional government, in place of those disavowing any affiliation with groups intending to overthrow that system.

In 1971 the Court upheld a state requirement that teachers take such an oath, making clear in its opinion that persons could be properly dismissed for refusing to take such an oath only after they were given a hearing.[100] The following year the Court, 4-3, upheld a state requirement that all employees swear to "oppose the overthrow of the government by force, violence or by any illegal or unconstitutional method."[101]

Also in 1971 and 1972 the Court upheld state requirements that applicants for admission to the state bar take affirmative oaths of loyalty to the state and federal constitutions. But the Court at the same time limited strictly the power of state officials to penalize those who would not take such oaths.[102] *(See box, p. 145)*

In 1974 the Court held unanimously that a state infringed this freedom when it required political parties seeking a place on the ballot to swear that they did not advocate the violent overthrow of local, state, or federal government.

In *Communist Party of Indiana v. Whitcomb,* Justice Brennan reaffirmed the Court's view that " 'the constitutional guarantees of free speech and free press do not permit a State to forbid or proscribe advocacy of the use of force or of law violation except where such advocacy is directed to inciting or producing imminent lawless action and is likely to incite or produce such action.' " [103]

Political Parties

Political parties—and in one case a radical student organization—have won Court rulings making clear their right of association, and the point at which state officials could limit its exercise. In the 1972 case *Healy v. James* the Court held that, without evidence that the group would have adverse effects on campus life, university officials could not constitutionally refuse to recognize a local chapter of the radical organization, Students for a Democratic Society.[104]

Several decisions in the next two years set out the Court's view of the permissible restrictions a state might place on persons wishing to change political parties as voters or candidates. In 1973 the Court upheld a state requirement that voters who wished to vote in a party's primary have enrolled in that party at least thirty days before the last general election.[105]

Later in the year, the Court held that the First Amendment limited the scope of such a state requirement. The Court struck down as abridging the right of political association a state rule forbidding a person to vote in the primary of one party if he had voted in that of another party within the preceding twenty-three months.[106] Early in 1974, however, the Court upheld a state requirement that independent candidates disaffiliate themselves from a party one year before the primary election of the year in which they wish to run as independents.[107]

In 1975 the Court held that national political parties, as well as individuals, have a constitutional right of political association. In *Cousins v. Wigoda* the Court held that this right was infringed by state court efforts to penalize one set of state delegates who were seated at the Democratic National Convention, by convention decision, instead of another set of delegates from the state. The case arose out of the 1972 convention—to which two opposing sets of Democratic delegates went from Illinois, one committed to the presidential candidacy of Senator George S. McGovern, D-S.D. (1963-1981), and the other set chosen and led by Mayor Richard J. Daley of of Chicago.[108]

The party's right of association was further defined in 1981 when the Court, 6-3, upheld Wisconsin's right to hold an open primary in which voters participate without declaring their allegiance to a particular party. But, held the Court, the state could not compel the national party to recognize the primary results if to do so would violate the

party's rules and infringe on its right of association.[109]

A year later the Court struck down Ohio's law requiring candidates for office to disclose the names and addresses of campaign contributors. By 6-3 the Court held that such disclosure, particularly of contributors to minor parties, might subject the persons whose names were disclosed to harassment, violating their freedom of association.[110]

And in 1986 the Court told the states they could not require political parties to hold only "closed primaries" in which only party members could vote. A political party may make that decision, wrote Justice Thurgood Marshall, but the state may not do it for a party.[111]

Patronage Firing

Twice the Court has upheld laws restricting the partisan political activity of federal and state workers, finding the curtailment of First Amendment rights justified by the interest in having government jobs filled on the basis of merit, not political loyalty. *(Box, p. 147)*

In 1976 and again in 1980, the Court dealt with the other side of the patronage hiring issue—patronage firing. And in those decisions the Court held that the freedom of political association was violated by that practice.

The case of *Elrod v. Burns,* like *Cousins,* arose in Illinois. It had been the practice that all employees of the Cook County sheriff's office, who were not covered by civil service regulations and who were not of the same party as the newly elected sheriff, were fired by the incoming sheriff—who would then replace them with persons of political affiliation similar to his.

This, held the Court 5-3, violated the First Amendment. Writing for the Court, Justice Brennan explained:

> though freedom of belief is central, "[t]he First Amendment protects political association as well as political expression." . . . There can no longer be doubt that freedom to associate with others for the common advancement of political beliefs and ideas is a form of "orderly activity" protected by the First and Fourteenth Amendments.[112]

Brennan cited as precedent the decision in *Keyishian* nine years earlier, noting that in that case the Court "squarely held that political association alone could not, consistently with the First Amendment, constitute adequate ground for denying public employment." [113] *(Details, p. 150)*

Then, moving to weigh the state's justification for patronage firing against its curtailment of individual freedom, Brennan cited the cases in which the Court had upheld the Hatch Act limitations on partisan political activity by government employees—*United Public Workers v. Mitchell* and *Civil Service Commission v. Letter Carriers.*[114] Those limitations were upheld, he explained, as a justifiable way of eliminating patronage—the very practice which Illinois now argued to preserve.

By forbidding the firing of persons simply because of their political affiliation, Brennan continued, the Court was not outlawing political parties.

> Parties are free to exist and their concomitant activities are free to continue. We require only that the rights of every citizen to believe as he will and to act

and associate according to his beliefs be free to continue as well.

    In summary, patronage dismissals severely restrict political belief and association. Though there is a vital need for government efficiency and effectiveness, such dismissals are on balance not the least restrictive means for fostering that end. . . . [P]atronage dismissals cannot be justified by their contribution to the proper functioning of our democratic process through their assistance to partisan politics since political parties are nurtured by other, less intrusive and equally effective methods. More fundamentally, however, any contribution of patronage dismissals to the democratic process does not suffice to override their severe encroachment on First Amendment freedoms.[115]

Justices Lewis F. Powell, Jr., and William H. Rehnquist and Chief Justice Warren E. Burger dissented, holding that the patronage system contributed to the democratization of politics and to sustaining grass-roots interest in government—considerations that outweighed the limited intrusion of patronage firing on First Amendment freedoms.

Notes

1. *Elrod v. Burns*, 427 U.S. 347 at 356 (1976).
2. *Schenck v. United States*, 249 U.S. 47 (1919); *Frohwerk v. United States*, 249 U.S. 204 (1919); *Debs v. United States*, 249 U.S. 211 (1919).
3. *Schenck v. United States*, 249 U.S. 47 at 52 (1919).
4. *Schaefer v. United States*, 251 U.S. 466 at 482 (1920).
5. Id. at 479.
6. *Gitlow v. New York*, 268 U.S. 652 at 666 (1925).
7. *Whitney v. California*, 274 U.S. 357 at 377 (1927).
8. *Stromberg v. California*, 283 U.S. 359 (1931).
9. *DeJonge v. Oregon*, 299 U.S. 353 (1937); *Herndon v. Lowry*, 301 U.S. 242 (1937).
10. *DeJonge v. Oregon*, 299 U.S. 353 at 365 (1937).
11. *Joint Anti-Fascist Refugee Committee v. McGrath*, 341 U.S. 123 at 174 (1951).
12. Congressional Quarterly, *Congress and the Nation*, vol. I (Washington, D.C.: Congressional Quarterly, 1965), 1645-1670.
13. Thomas I. Emerson, *The System of Freedom of Expression* (New York: Random House, 1970), 110.
14. *Dennis v. United States*, 341 U.S. 494 at 510 (1951).
15. Id. at 502.
16. Id. at 509, 510-511, 516-517.
17. Id. at 549.
18. Id. at 518-520.
19. Id. at 525-526.
20. Id. at 570.
21. Id. at 577.
22. Id. at 579.
23. Id. at 584-585, 590.
24. *Yates v. United States*, 354 U.S. 298 (1957); see also the Court's review of Yates's conviction for contempt: *Yates v. United States*, 355 U.S. 66 (1957); 356 U.S. 363 (1958).
25. *Yates v. United States*, 354 U.S. 298 at 306-307, 312 (1957).
26. Id. at 321.
27. Id. at 320-322, 324-325, 326-327.
28. Id. at 329-330.
29. Id. at 339.
30. Id. at 340.
31. Id. at 345.
32. *Scales v. United States*, 367 U.S. 203 at 228-229 (1961).
33. Id. at 229-230.
34. Id. at 260.
35. *Noto v. United States*, 367 U.S. 290 at 297-298 (1961).
36. *Congress and the Nation*, vol. I, 1650-1651.
37. Ibid., 1653.
38. *Communist Party v. Subversive Activities Control Board*, 367 U.S. 1 (1961).
39. Id. at 86.
40. Id. at 102-103.
41. Id. at 105.
42. Id. at 137, 145.
43. Id. at 181.
44. *Congress and the Nation*, vol. II, 413-415; vol. III, 489; Vol. IV, 570.
45. *Albertson v. Subversive Activities Control Board*, 382 U.S. 70 at 79 (1965).
46. *Congress and the Nation*, vol. II, 418.
47. *United States v. Robel*, 389 U.S. 258 at 265, 266-267 (1967).
48. Id. at 285.
49. *Boorda v. Subversive Activities Control Board*, 421 F. 2d 1142 (D.C. Cir. 1969).
50. For general background on loyalty programs, see *Congress and the Nation*, vol. I, 1663-1668.
51. *Joint Anti-Fascist Refugee Committee v. McGrath*, 341 U.S. 123 at 161 (1951).
52. Id. at 200.
53. *Bailey v. Richardson*, 341 U.S. 918 (1951).
54. *Peters v. Hobby*, 349 U.S. 331 (1955).
55. *Cole v. Young*, 351 U.S. 536 (1956); see also *Service v. Dulles*, 354 U.S. 363 (1957).
56. *Greene v. McElroy*, 360 U.S. 474 (1959).
57. Id. at 508.
58. Id. at 511, 524.
59. *Congress and the Nation*, vol. I, 1667-1668.
60. *Cafeteria and Restaurant Workers Union v. McElroy*, 367 U.S. 886 (1961).
61. *American Communications Association v. Douds*, 339 U.S. 382 at 390 (1950).
62. Id. at 391.
63. Id. at 393.
64. Id. at 396.
65. Id. at 445.
66. Id. at 444.
67. Id. at 446, 452-453.
68. *Congress and the Nation*, vol. I, 568, 611.
69. *United States v. Brown*, 381 U.S. 437 at 449-450, 461 (1965).
70. Id. at 474.
71. *Killian v. United States*, 368 U.S. 231 (1961); *Raymond Dennis et al. v. United States*, 384 U.S. 855 (1966).
72. *Gerende v. Board of Supervisors of Elections*, 341 U.S. 56 (1951).
73. *Garner v. Board of Public Works of the City of Los Angeles*, 341 U.S. 716 (1951).
74. Id. at 724-725.
75. Id. at 726, 728.
76. *Adler v. Board of Education, City of New York*, 342 U.S. 485 (1952).
77. Id. at 493.
78. Ibid.
79. Id. at 508.
80. Id. at 509, 510, 511.
81. *Wieman v. Updegraff*, 344 U.S. 183 at 190 (1952).
82. Id. at 191.
83. *Slochower v. Board of Higher Education of New York City*, 350 U.S. 551 at 557 (1956).
84. Id. at 561.
85. Id. at 565.
86. *Lerner v. Casey*, 357 U.S. 468 (1958).
87. *Beilan v. Board of Public Education, School District of Philadelphia*, 357 U.S. 399 (1958).
88. Id. at 410.
89. Id. at 418; see also *Speiser v. Randall*, 357 U.S. 513 (1958).
90. *National Association for the Advancement of Colored Peo-*

ple v. Alabama, 357 U.S. 449 (1958).

91. *Shelton v. Tucker*, 364 U.S. 479 at 490 (1960).
92. *Cramp v. Board of Public Instruction, Orange County, Fla.*, 368 U.S. 278 at 286 (1961).
93. Id. at 287.
94. *Baggett v. Bullitt*, 377 U.S. 360 at 367 (1964).
95. *Elfbrandt v. Russell*, 384 U.S. at 17-19 (1966).
96. *Keyishian v. Board of Regents of the University of the State of New York*, 385 U.S. 589 at 606 (1967).
97. Id. at 601, 603.
98. Id. at 628.
99. *Whitehill v. Elkins*, 389 U.S. 54 at 62 (1967).
100. *Connell v. Higginbotham*, 403 U.S. 207 (1971).
101. *Cole v. Richardson*, 405 U.S. 676 (1972).
102. *In re Stolar, Baird v. State Bar of Arizona*, 401 U.S. 23, 1 (1971); *Law Students Civil Rights Research Council v. Wadmond*, 401 U.S. 154 (1971).
103. *Communist Party of Indiana v. Whitcomb*, 414 U.S. 441 at 448 (1974).
104. *Healy v. James*, 408 U.S. 169 (1972).
105. *Rosario v. Rockefeller*, 410 U.S. 752 (1973).
106. *Kusper v. Pontikes*, 414 U.S. 51 (1973).
107. *Storer v. Brown, Frommhagen v. Brown*, 415 U.S. 724 (1974).
108. *Cousins v. Wigoda*, 419 U.S. 477 (1975).
109. *Democratic Party of the United States v. LaFollette*, 450 U.S. 107 (1981).
110. *Brown v. Socialist Workers '74 Campaign Committee*, 459 U.S. 81 (1982).
111. *Tashjian v. Republican Party of Connecticut*, ___ U.S. ___ (1986).
112. *Elrod v. Burns*, 427 U.S. 347 at 357 (1975).
113. Id. at 358.
114. *United Public Workers v. Mitchell*, 330 U.S. 75 (1947); *Civil Service Commission v. Letter Carriers*, 413 U.S. 548 (1973).
115. *Elrod v. Burns*, 427 U.S. 347 at 372-373; see also *Branti v. Finkel*, 445 U.S. 507 (1981).

Part III

Due Process

Due process of law is a flexible concept that eludes precise definition, but essentially it embodies a promise that government will deal fairly with the individual. In the twentieth century the Supreme Court read into that guarantee a wide range of rights, including those granted in other provisions of the Bill of Rights—guarantees until then applicable only against federal, not state, infringement.

Due process is primarily a guarantee of fair procedures, of *how* the government must act, not of *what* they must do. It is difficult to overestimate the importance of procedure, noted Justice William O. Douglas, pointing out that most of the provisions of the Bill of Rights were procedural. "It is procedure," he wrote, "that spells much of the difference between rule by law and rule by whim or caprice. Steadfast adherence to strict procedural safeguards is our main assurance that there will be equal justice under law." [1]

Procedural rights are of great significance for persons charged with crimes. The Bill of Rights assures an individual accused of a crime fair treatment. Every criminal case is a legal contest between the individual and government. A crime is an offense against society. Government is society's agency to prosecute the offender, but it is an uneven match. The power of the individual defendant is no match for the power of government unless the individual has guarantees he will be treated fairly.

Procedural rights are not based on sentimental concern for criminals. The guarantees were not devised to coddle them or to provide technical loopholes through which dangerous persons escape the consequences of their acts. "Due process of law is not, primarily, the right of the accused," David Fellman has written. "It is basically the community's assurance that prosecutors, judges and juries will behave properly, within rules distilled from long centuries of concrete experience." [2]

Although the procedural safeguards of the Bill of Rights are known primarily for their importance to persons suspected or accused of crime, they operate as well to shield all individuals against arbitrary, despotic, or unduly intrusive government action. They assure an individual charged with a crime notice of the charge against him, a speedy and public trial by an impartial jury, the opportunity to confront witnesses accusing him and to compel witnesses in his favor to appear, and the aid of an attorney in preparing and presenting his defense.

Furthermore, these guarantees promise the individual that he will not be subjected to unreasonable search or arrest by government officials, compelled to incriminate himself, deprived of life, liberty, or property without due process of law, tried for a serious offense without being formally charged in an indictment, tried twice for the same action by the same sovereign, subject to excessive bail or excessive fines, or sentenced to suffer cruel and unusual punishment.

Originally, these guarantees applied directly only to persons tried in federal courts, even though most persons charged with crimes in the United States are tried in state and local courts. But since 1868 the Fourteenth Amendment has guaranteed the individual due process and equal protection from state, as well as federal, authorities. Beginning in the 1930s, the Court has read those guarantees as extending most of the specific procedural protections of the Bill of Rights to persons tried in state courts.

The judicial expansion of due process reached its climax in the 1960s, but the revolutionary decisions of that time. In the 1920s and 1930s, the Court under the leadership of successive chief justices, William Howard Taft and Charles Evans Hughes, began to apply the fundamental requirements of fair procedure to state trials, even while individual justices wrangled over whether the Fourteenth Amendment extended the guarantees of the Bill of Rights to defendants in state cases.

At first, the Court rejected any wholesale incorporation theory, preferring a more selective approach. The majority began developing a list of fundamental rights that states must honor. The selective incorporation debate came to a dramatic end in the 1960s. In a series of rulings, the Court resoundingly rejected any idea that only a watered-down Bill of Rights applied to the states. The Court extended to state defendants the protection of the controversial exclusionary rule, the right to appointed counsel, the privilege against compelled self-incrimination, the right to confront prosecution witnesses, the right to a speedy trial, the right to a jury trial, and the protection against double jeopardy.

The Protection of Substantive Due Process...

With the development of the doctrine of substantive due process, the Supreme Court became guardian of property rights against restrictive state laws. It scrutinized state laws, looking at what states chose to regulate rather than on how they regulated. This doctrine transformed a guarantee of procedural fairness for persons into the basis for the Court's role as monitor of economic regulation.

Substantive due process was first hinted at in a dissenting opinion in the *Slaughterhouse Cases* in 1873. Even as the Court rejected a challenge by butchers to a state grant of a slaughterhouse monopoly, which, they argued, denied them the opportunity to practice their trade, in violation of due process, Justice Joseph P. Bradley agreed that "a law which prohibits a large class of citizens from adopting . . . or from following a lawful employment . . . does deprive them of liberty as well as property, without due process of law." [1]

Four years later in *Munn v. Illinois,* the Court edged closer to Bradley's view. Although the justices upheld a state law that regulated grain elevator rates, they did so only after considering the substance of the business regulated. The Court found that grain storage was one of a class of businesses "affected with a public interest" and thus subject to such state regulation. [2]

This decision was the first in a line of rulings stretching over half a century, in which the Court looked to the character of the activity regulated to determine whether it was properly within the state's domain.

In *Mugler v. Kansas,* concerning a state prohibition law, Justice John Marshall Harlan explained the Court's view of its responsibility for scrutinizing the substance of challenged laws:

> The courts are not bound by mere forms, nor are they to be misled by mere pretenses. They are at liberty—indeed, are under a solemn duty—to look at the substance of things, whenever they enter upon the inquiry whether the legislature has transcended the limits of its authority. If, therefore, a statute purporting to have been enacted to protect the public health, the public morals, or the public safety, has no real or substantial relation to those objects, or is a palpable invasion of rights secured by the fundamental law, it is the duty of the courts to so adjudge, and thereby give effect to the Constitution. [3]

Three years later, in 1890, the Court in *Chicago, Milwaukee and St. Paul R.R. Co. v. Minnesota* first used substantive due process to strike down a state law regulating economic matters, ruling that the courts should have the final word on the reasonableness of railroad rates. [4]

Freedom of Contract

Although many state laws were challenged as a denial of due process, [5] it was primarily in the areas of rate setting, price regulation, and wage and hour laws that the Court agreed with the challenge.

Wage and hour legislation was found to infringe upon "freedom of contract"—an aspect of liberty first acknowledged in *Allgeyer v. Louisiana* (1897). The personal liberty the due process guarantee protected included the individual's right "to live and work where he will; to earn his livelihood by any lawful calling; to pursue any livelihood or avocation, and for that purpose to enter into all contracts which may be proper, necessary and essential to his carrying out to a successful conclusion the purposes above mentioned," held the Court. [6]

With these doctrines—that business affected with a public interest could be regulated by the state, and that government should not interfere with the freedom of contract—the Supreme Court plunged into a new role as judge of the substance of state economic regulation.

Under the "public interest" rubric, the Court upheld state regulation of such varied matters as insurance and stockyards. [7] To protect the "freedom of contract," the Court struck down a number of the first wage and hour laws passed by the states. In 1898, in *Holden v. Hardy,* the Court upheld a law setting the ten-hour day as the maximum that miners might work. [8] But seven years later, in *Lochner v. New York,* the Court struck down a law setting the ten-hour day and the sixty-hour week as the maximum for bakers. [9]

The Court saw a critical difference between the working conditions of mines and bakeries. Miners worked in palpably unhealthy conditions, to which their exposure should be limited; bakers were subject to less risk of injury or illness in their working environment. [10]

In its 1923 decision in *Adkins v. Children's Hospital,* the Court struck down the District of Columbia's minimum wage law for women. Justice George Sutherland, for the five-man majority, described the law as "simply and exclusively a price-fixing law" in violation of the freedom of contract. [11]

Demise of Substantive Due Process

The Depression and the New Deal created pressures that inexorably forced the Supreme Court to drop its use of substantive due process to monitor economic regulation.

Beginning in 1934 with *Nebbia v. New York,* the Court abdicated its role as "super-legislature," leaving decisions on the wisdom and appropriateness of

...From Property Rights to Privacy Concerns

economic legislation to legislators. In *Nebbia* the Court upheld a state law regulating milk prices, even though the milk industry was not one "affected with a public interest." [12] The Court thus ceased to distinguish between some lines of business and others for the purpose of finding some subject to state regulation and others exempt.

Nevertheless, the Court continued to use the "freedom of contract" doctrine to nullify a state minimum wage law for women. In *Morehead v. Tipaldo,* a five-man majority in 1936 declared:

> The right to make contracts about one's affairs is a part of the liberty protected by the due process clause. Within this liberty are provisions of contracts between employer and employee fixing the wages to be paid.[13]

But the tide of public opinion had already turned against this sort of judicial second-guessing. In 1936 both major parties repudiated the *Morehead* decision. The following year, after President Franklin D. Roosevelt had brandished his plan to "pack" the Court, the justices reversed themselves. In *West Coast Hotel v. Parrish* the Court upheld a Washington state minimum wage law for women, overruling *Adkins* and *Morehead.*[14]

Four years later, in *United States v. Darby Lumber Co.,* the Court upheld federal power to set minimum wage and maximum hour standards for workers involved in interstate commerce.[15]

In 1941, as the unanimous Court upheld a state law regulating the fees that employment agencies might charge, Justice William O. Douglas wrote: "We are not concerned ... with the wisdom, need, or appropriateness of the legislation. Differences of opinion on that score suggest a choice which 'should be left where ... it was left by the Constitution—to the states and to Congress.' " [16]

Subsequently, the Court has declared that it does not "sit as a superlegislature to weigh the wisdom of legislation nor to decide whether the policy it expresses offends the public welfare." [17]

From Property to Privacy

Yet even as the Court sounded the epitaph for the use of substantive due process to justify its supervision of economic regulation, it was developing a line of rulings under the equal protection guarantee that led it again to consider the substance of state legislation.

In 1942 the Court in *Skinner v. Oklahoma* struck down a state law that allowed habitual criminals to be sterilized. This law was a denial of equal protection, held the Court, because of its substance—because it allowed the state to deprive an individual of "one of the basic civil rights of man." [18]

Matters of personal choice in family life have been the primary beneficiary of the "new substantive due process" approach foreshadowed in *Skinner.*

One landmark in this area was the 1965 declaration in *Griswold v. Connecticut* that privacy was a value protected by the Constitution.[19] In that case the Court struck down a state law forbidding all use of birth control devices. Although Justice Douglas, writing the majority opinion, was careful not to rest the conclusion upon the due process clause, Justice Hugo L. Black—in dissent—found the ruling a direct descendant of *Lochner v. New York.* This too was substantive due process, he warned, and it was "no less dangerous when used to enforce this Court's views about personal rights than those about economic rights." [20]

Eight years later Justice William H. Rehnquist sounded the same complaint, dissenting from the Court's 1973 decision in *Roe v. Wade,* which struck down state laws banning abortion. "As in Lochner and similar cases applying substantive due process standards," Rehnquist wrote, the standard adopted in *Roe v. Wade* "will inevitably require this Court to examine the legislative policies and pass on the wisdom of these policies." [21]

1. *Slaughterhouse Cases,* 16 Wall. 36 at 122 (1873).
2. *Munn v. Illinois,* 94 U.S. 113 (1877).
3. *Mugler v. Kansas,* 123 U.S. 623 at 661 (1887).
4. *Chicago, Milwaukee and St. Paul R.R. Co. v. Minnesota,* 134 U.S. 418 (1890); see also *Smyth v. Ames,* 169 U.S. 466 (1898).
5. *Powell v. Pennsylvania,* 127 U.S. 678 (1888); *Jacobson v. Massachusetts,* 197 U.S. 11 (1905); *Austin v. Tennessee,* 179 U.S. 343 (1900); *Packer Corp. v. Utah,* 285 U.S. 105 (1932); *Euclid v. Ambler Realty Co.,* 272 U.S. 365 (1926).
6. *Allgeyer v. Louisiana,* 165 U.S. 578 at 589 (1897).
7. *German Alliance Insurance Co. v. Lewis,* 233 U.S. 389 (1914); *Cotting v. Godard,* 183 U.S. 79 (1901).
8. *Holden v. Hardy,* 169 U.S. 366 (1898).
9. *Lochner v. New York,* 198 U.S. 45 (1905).
10. *Muller v. Oregon,* 208 U.S. 412 (1908); *Bunting v. Oregon,* 243 U.S. 426 (1917). For examples of substantive due process and labor matters, see *Adair v. United States,* 208 U.S. 161 (1908); *Coppage v. Kansas,* 236 U.S. 1 (1915); *Lincoln Federal Labor Union v. Northwestern Iron & Metal Co.,* 335 U.S. 525 (1949).
11. *Adkins v. Children's Hospital,* 261 U.S. 525 at 554 (1923).
12. *Nebbia v. New York,* 291 U.S. 502 (1934); see also *Petersen Baking Co. v. Burns,* 290 U.S. 570 (1934).
13. *Morehead v. Tipaldo,* 298 U.S. 587 at 610 (1936).
14. *West Coast Hotel v. Parrish,* 300 U.S. 379 (1937).
15. *United States v. Darby Lumber Co.,* 312 U.S. 100 (1941); see also *Olsen v. Nebraska,* 313 U.S. 236 (1941), *Federal Power Commission v. Hope Natural Gas,* 320 U.S. 551 (1944).
16. *Olsen v. Nebraska,* 313 U.S. 236 at 246 (1941).
17. *Day-Brite Lighting, Inc. v. Missouri,* 342 U.S. 421 at 423 (1952); see also *Williamson v. Lee Optical of Oklahoma,* 348 U.S. 483 (1955).
18. *Skinner v. Oklahoma,* 316 U.S. 535 (1942).
19. *Griswold v. Connecticut,* 381 U.S. 479 (1965); see also *Eisenstadt v. Baird,* 405 U.S. 438 (1972); *Roe v. Wade,* 410 U.S. 113 (1973); *Doe v. Bolton,* 410 U.S. 179 (1973).
20. *Griswold v. Connecticut,* 381 U.S. 479 at 522 (1965).
21. *Roe v. Wade,* 410 U.S. 113 at 174 (1973).

Early View

Early in its history, during the tenure of Chief Justice John Marshall, the Supreme Court held that the Bill of Rights limited only the federal government, not the states. In 1833 the Supreme Court set out this conclusion in *Barron v. Baltimore*.[3]

With Marshall writing, the Court rejected the argument of a Baltimore wharf-owner that the Fifth Amendment guaranteeing just compensation to persons whose private property was taken for public use applied against all governments, not just the federal government.

No, wrote Marshall, this was not the intent of those who approved and ratified the Bill of Rights:

The Constitution was ordained and established by the people of the United States for themselves, for their own government, and not for the government of the individual States.... The powers they conferred on this government were to be exercised by itself; and the limitations on power, if expressed in general terms, are naturally, and, we think, necessarily applicable to the government created by the instrument.

... the provision in the fifth amendment to the Constitution, declaring that private property shall not be taken for public use without just compensation, is intended solely as a limitation on the exercise of power by the government of the United States, and is not applicable to the legislation of the States.[4]

Congress and Due Process

Although the justices refused to extend the Fifth Amendment's guarantee of due process against *state* action, the Court in 1856 applied that guarantee to legislative action by Congress, making clear that all branches of the *federal* government were bound by it.

In *Murray's Lessee v. Hoboken Land and Improvement Company* the Court upheld an act of Congress authorizing the Treasury Department to issue warrants against the property of federal revenue collectors who were indebted to the federal government.[5] The law had been challenged as allowing the taking of property without due process.

In the majority opinion by Justice Benjamin R. Curtis, the Court began its effort to define due process as any process that did not conflict with specific constitutional provisions or established judicial practices. Curtis wrote:

That the warrant now in question is legal process, is not denied. It was issued in conformity with an act of Congress. But is it "due process of law?" The Constitution contains no description of those processes which it was intended to allow or forbid. It does not even declare what principles are to be applied to ascertain whether it be due process. It is manifest that it was not left to the legislative power to enact any process which might be devised. The article is a restraint on the legislative as well as on the executive and judicial powers of the government, and cannot be so construed as to leave Congress free to make any process "due process of law," by its mere will. To what principles, then, are we to resort to ascertain whether this process enacted by Congress, is due process? To this the answer must be twofold. We must examine the Constitution itself, to see whether this process be in

conflict with any of its provisions. If not found to be so, we must look to those settled usages and modes of proceeding existing in the common and statute law of England, before the emigration of our ancestors and which are shown not to have been unsuited to their civil and political condition by having been acted on by them after the settlement of this country.[6]

Substantive Due Process

Twelve years after that ruling, the Fourteenth Amendment became part of the Constitution, forbidding the states to deprive any person of life, liberty, or property without due process of law.

Oddly, this due process guarantee was initially used with a great deal more effect to protect property than life or liberty. This was the result of the development of the doctrine of substantive due process—the view that the substance, as well as the procedures, of a law must comply with due process. *(Box, pp. 158-159)*

In the mid-twentieth century, Justice Robert H. Jackson compared the two types of due process:

Procedural due process is more elemental and less flexible than substantive due process. It yields less to the times, varies less with conditions, and defers much less to legislative judgment. Insofar as it is technical law, it must be a specialized responsibility within the competence of the judiciary on which they do not bend before political branches of the Government, as they should on matters of policy which comprise substantive law.[7]

Due Process and the States

For sixty-five years after the Fourteenth Amendment was ratified, its due process clause provided little protection to persons tried in state and local courts.

In 1884 the Court held that due process did not require states to use indictments to charge persons with capital crimes, despite the Fifth Amendment provision requiring indictments in similar federal cases. In 1900 the Court held that the due process guarantee did not require states to use twelve-man juries. In 1908 the Court held that the Fifth Amendment privilege against compelled self-incrimination did not protect state defendants.

Hurtado v. California

In the indictment case, *Hurtado v. California*, the Court upheld the murder conviction and death sentence of Joseph Hurtado, charged without an indictment.[8] He challenged his conviction, arguing that under Justice Curtis's definition of due process in *Hoboken*, he had been denied due process.

The Court's ruling, relaxing the earlier standard for the demands of due process upon state criminal procedures, blurred the *Hoboken* definition. Writing for the Court, Justice Stanley Matthews redefined due process as "any legal proceeding enforced by public authority, whether sanctioned by age and custom, or newly devised in the discretion of the legislative power, in furtherance of the general public good, which regards, and preserves these principles of liberty and justice." [9]

However, Matthews continued:

It is not every Act, legislative in form, that is law. Law is something more than mere will exerted as an act of power. It must be not a special rule for a particular person or a particular case, ... thus excluding, as not due process of law, Acts of attainder, Bills of pains and penalties, Acts of confiscation, Acts reversing judgments, and Acts directly transferring one man's estate to another, legislative judgments and decrees, and other similar, special, partial and arbitrary exertions of power under the forms of legislation. Arbitrary power, enforcing its edicts to the injury of the persons and property of its subjects, is not law, whether manifested as the decree of a personal monarch or of an impersonal multitude.[10]

Adopting reasoning diametrically opposed to that of Curtis in *Hoboken*, the majority ruled that because the Fifth Amendment expressly included *both* the indictment requirement *and* the due process guarantee, the indictment requirement was obviously not included as an element of due process.

In dissent Justice John Marshall Harlan set out the "incorporation" approach. In his view the Fourteenth Amendment guarantee of due process "incorporated" many of the specific guarantees of the Bill of Rights, effectively nullifying *Barron v. Baltimore* by applying them against state action.

Harlan argued that the Court's reasoning in *Hurtado* could open the door for states to deny defendants many other rights.

If the presence in the Fifth Amendment of a specific provision for grand juries in capital cases, alongside the provision for due process of law in proceedings involving life, liberty or property, is held to prove that "due process of law" did not, in the judgment of the framers of the Constitution, necessarily require a grand jury in capital cases, inexorable logic would require it to be, likewise, held that the right not to be put twice in jeopardy of life and limb for the same offense, nor compelled in a criminal case to testify against one's self—rights and immunities also specifically recognized in the Fifth Amendment—were not protected by that due process of law required by the settled usages and proceedings existing under the common and statute law of England at the settlement of this country. More than that, other Amendments of the Constitution proposed at the same time, expressly recognize the right of persons to just compensation for private property taken for public use; their right, when accused of crime, to be informed of the nature and cause of the accusation against them, and to a speedy and public trial, by an impartial jury of the State and district wherein the crime was committed; to be confronted by the witnesses against them; and to have compulsory process for obtaining witnesses in their favor. Will it be claimed that these rights were not secured by the "law of the land" or by "due process of law," as declared and established at the foundation of our government?[11]

Selective Incorporation

Eventually the Court would adopt an approach of "selective incorporation" of the guarantees of the Bill of Rights into the due process clause of the Fourteenth Amendment. Justice Samuel F. Miller wrote:

If ... it were possible to define what it is for a State to deprive a person of life, liberty or property without due process of law, in terms which would cover every exercise of power thus forbidden to the State, and exclude those which are not, no more useful construction could be furnished by this or any other court to any part of the fundamental law.

But, apart from the imminent risk of failure to give any definition which would be at once perspicuous, comprehensive and satisfactory, there is wisdom, we think, in the ascertaining of the intent and application of such an important phrase in the Federal Constitution, by the gradual process of judicial inclusion and exclusion, as the cases presented for decision shall require, with the reasoning on which such decisions may be founded. This court is, after an experience of nearly a century, still engaged in defining the obligation of contracts, the regulation of commerce, and other powers conferred on the Federal Government, or limitations imposed upon the States.[12]

Maxwell v. Dow

In 1900 the Court ruled in *Maxwell v. Dow* that the Fourteenth Amendment did not require state juries to be composed of twelve persons.

Justice Harlan again dissented, protesting the contrast between the Court's vigorous use of substantive due process and its reluctance to enforce procedural due process:

If then the "due process of law" required by the Fourteenth Amendment does not allow a State to take private property without just compensation, but does allow the life or liberty of the citizen to be taken in a mode that is repugnant to the settled usages and the modes of proceeding authorized at the time the Constitution was adopted and which was expressly forbidden in the National Bill of Rights, it would seem that the protection of private property is of more consequence than the protection of the life and liberty of the citizen.[13]

Twining v. New Jersey

Eight years later the Court in *Twining v. New Jersey* refused to hold that due process was denied state defendants by a judge's calling the jury's attention to the defendant's failure to testify in his own defense, implying that such silence was an admission of guilt. The defendants had claimed that the judge's comments violated their Fifth Amendment right to remain silent rather than incriminate themselves. They argued that this right was a fundamental "privilege or immunity" of federal citizenship protected against state action by the Fourteenth Amendment.

The Court rejected the claim and upheld the decision of the state court sustaining conviction. Justice William H. Moody's opinion also denied that the Fourteenth Amendment guarantee of due process extended the protection of the first eight amendments against state action:

The essential elements of due process of law, already established ... are singularly few, though of wide application and deep significance.... Due process requires that the court which assumes to determine the rights of parties shall have jurisdiction ... and that there shall be notice and opportunity for hearing given the parties.[14]

But Justice Moody left open the possibility that additional due process requirements could be imposed upon the states.

It is possible that some of the personal rights safeguarded by the first eight Amendments against national action may also be safeguarded against state action, because a denial of them would be a denial of due process of law.... If this is so, it is not because those rights are enumerated in the first eight Amendments, but because they are of such a nature that they are included in the conception of due process of law.[15]

'Fundamental' Rights

This emphasis on rights became increasingly prevalent in the 1920s and 1930s as the Court began to rule that some rights were so fundamental to fair treatment that the due process guarantee required states to observe them.

In *Palko v. Connecticut,* decided in 1937, the Court explained that some rights were "implicit in the concept of ordered liberty" and thus protected by due process against state infringement. In *Palko,* however, the Court again rejected the "incorporation" theory.

Palko had been tried twice by Connecticut for the same murder. He challenged his conviction, arguing that the second trial violated the Fifth Amendment guarantee against double jeopardy. The Court refused to reverse his conviction, declaring that the protection against double jeopardy was not one of those rights which due process required the states to observe.

For the Court, Justice Benjamin N. Cardozo gave a "status report" on due process and state action:

The right to trial by jury and the immunity from prosecution except as the result of an indictment may have value and importance. Even so, they are not of the very essence of a scheme of ordered liberty. To abolish them is not to violate a "principle of justice so rooted in the traditions and conscience of our people as to be ranked as fundamental." ... What is true of jury trials and indictments is true also, as the cases show, of the immunity from compulsory self-incrimination.... This too might be lost, and justice still be done.... The exclusion of these immunities and privileges from the privileges and immunities protected against the action of the states has not been arbitrary or casual. It has been dictated by a study and appreciation of the meaning, the essential implications, of liberty itself.

We reach a different plane of social and moral values when we pass to the privileges and immunities that have been taken over from the earlier articles of the federal bill of rights and brought within the Fourteenth Amendment by a process of absorption....

[T]he process of absorption has had its source in the belief that neither liberty nor justice would exist if they were sacrificed.... This is true ... of freedom of thought and speech.... Fundamental too in the concept of due process, and so in that of liberty, is the thought that condemnation shall be rendered only after trial.... The hearing, moreover, must be a real one, not a sham or a pretense, *Moore v. Dempsey*.... For that reason, ignorant defendants in a capital case were held to have been condemned unlawfully when in truth, though not in form, they were refused the aid of counsel, *Powell v. Alabama*.[16]

A decade later, with its decision in *Adamson v. California,* the Court reaffirmed its holding in *Twining* that the self-incrimination guarantee did not operate against state action—and its general view that the Fourteenth Amendment did not incorporate the Bill of Rights.[17]

Arguing for the "incorporation" theory and dissenting from *Adamson* were four members of the Court—Justices Hugo L. Black, Frank Murphy, William O. Douglas, and Wiley B. Rutledge. They argued that the Fourteenth Amendment was originally intended "to extend to all the people of the nation the complete protection of the Bill of Rights."[18] Black and Douglas would continue to serve on the Court through the 1960s—and find their views at last espoused by a majority of the Court as it extended virtually all those protections to all persons.

Notes

1. *Joint Anti-Fascist Refugee Committee v. McGrath,* 341 U.S. 123 at 179 (1951).
2. David Fellman, *The Defendant's Rights* (New York: Rinehart & Co., 1958), 3-4.
3. *Barron v. Baltimore,* 7 Pet. 243 (1833).
4. Id. at 247, 250-251.
5. *Murray's Lessee v. Hoboken Land and Improvement Co.,* 18 How. 272 (1856).
6. Id. at 276-277.
7. *Shaughnessy v. United States ex rel. Mezei,* 345 U.S. 206 at 224 (1953).
8. *Hurtado v. California,* 110 U.S. 516 (1884); see also *Pennoyer v. Neff,* 95 U.S. 714 (1878).
9. *Hurtado v. California,* 110 U.S. 516 at 537 (1884).
10. Id. at 535-536.
11. Id. at 547-548.
12. *Davidson v. New Orleans,* 95 U.S. 97 at 104 (1877).
13. *Maxwell v. Dow,* 1976 U.S. 581 at 614 (1900).
14. *Twining v. New Jersey,* 211 U.S. 78 at 110-111 (1908).
15. Id. at 99.
16. *Palko v. Connecticut,* 302 U.S. 319 at 325 (1937).
17. *Adamson v. California,* 332 U.S. 46 at 53 (1947).
18. Id. at 89.

7

A Fair Trial

Anyone accused of a crime is constitutionally guaranteed a hearing on the charges against him, an opportunity to force the government to prove the charges, and a chance to present a rebuttal to that evidence.

In the 1920s the Supreme Court began to use the due process clause to require that states ensure that trials be held free of mob domination, and be conducted before an impartial judge and a fairly chosen jury.

As early as 1915 the Court acknowledged that a trial could be so dominated by outside pressures that its outcome would deny the defendant due process. But the Court refused to intervene in the case of *Frank v. Mangum,* finding that the state in that instance provided the defendant sufficient opportunity through appellate review to win correction of this denial of his rights.[1]

Eight years later, however, the Court approved federal intervention to order release of five black men, sentenced to die after a trial so dominated by racial tensions that it became a travesty of justice. Justice Oliver Wendell Holmes, Jr., wrote in *Moore v. Dempsey:*

> if the case is that the whole proceeding is a mask—that counsel, jury, and judge were swept to the fatal end by an irresistible wave of public passion, and that the state courts failed to correct that wrong—neither perfection in the machinery for correction nor the possibility that the trial court and counsel saw no other way of avoiding an immediate outbreak of the mob can prevent this court from securing to the petitioners their constitutional rights.[2]

Four years after *Moore* the Court in 1927 applied the due process clause to require that state and local trials be held before impartial judges without any personal stake in their outcome. In *Tumey v. Ohio* the Court held unconstitutional a system that permitted the presiding judge to take a portion of every fine he assessed against persons found guilty of violating the state's prohibition law.[3]

Chief Justice William Howard Taft declared:

> All matters of judicial qualification may not involve constitutional validity.... But it certainly violates the 14th Amendment and deprives a defendant in a criminal case of due process of law to subject his liberty or

property to the judgment of a court, the judge of which has a direct, personal, substantial pecuniary interest in reaching a conclusion against him in his case.[4]

The Court emphasized that the judge's interest must be both personal and substantial. In 1928 it limited the effect of *Tumey* when it held that, in a town where the mayor-judge received a fixed salary for his duties, payment of half the fines to the town treasury did not violate due process of law.[5]

In 1972, however, the Court ruled that due process was denied persons charged with traffic offenses and tried by the mayor of another Ohio township. The Court based its decision on the fact that the fines collected from traffic violators provided a substantial portion of village revenues.

Justice William J. Brennan, Jr., reasoned that although the mayor received no personal benefit or income from convictions, the "possible temptation" to convict "may ... exist when the mayor's executive responsibilities for village finances may make him partisan to maintain the high level of contributions from the mayor's court." [6]

In 1976 the Court held that due process does not require that a judge be an attorney. In *North v. Russell* the Court considered a due process challenge to Kentucky's two-tiered state court system under which small towns were permitted to employ nonlawyer judges for police courts.

Lonnie North challenged his conviction by such a court and a nonlawyer judge for drunken driving, claiming that it violated his right to due process. The Supreme Court rejected this argument.

Chief Justice Warren E. Burger wrote:

> Our concern in prior cases with judicial functions being performed by nonjudicial officers has also been directed at the need for independent, neutral and detached judgment, not at legal training....
>
> We conclude that the Kentucky two-tier trial court system with lay judicial officers in the first tier in smaller cities and an appeal of right with a *de novo* trial before a traditionally law-trained judge in the second does not violate either the due process or equal protection guarantees of the Constitution of the United States.[7]

Justices Potter Stewart and Thurgood Marshall dissented. They found the use of nonlawyer judges a violation of the guarantees of due process and of the assistance of legal counsel.

THE RIGHT TO A JURY TRIAL

The system of trial by jury is a distinctive feature of the Anglo-American system of justice, dating back as far as the fourteenth century.

The men who wrote the Constitution included in Article III the flat requirement that "The Trial of all Crimes, except in Cases of Impeachment, shall be by Jury."

Not content with this single provision, those who drafted the Bill of Rights included additional guarantees of that right in the grand jury requirement of the Fifth Amendment, in the "speedy and public trial by an impartial jury" requirement of the Sixth Amendment, and in the Seventh Amendment requirement of jury trials in common-law suits involving more than $20.

This right has been the subject of many Supreme Court rulings concerning the size, selection, and unanimity of juries, as well as a defendant's decision to waive the right to a jury trial, usually as a result of plea bargaining.

In federal cases, the Court has been unwavering in insisting that a jury in a criminal case must consist of twelve people and must reach a unanimous verdict. (In federal civil cases, however, juries may be as small as six members.)[8]

The meaning of a jury trial was set out by the Court in *Patton v. United States.*

> That it means a trial by jury as understood and applied at common law, and includes all the essential elements as they were recognized in this country and England when the Constitution was adopted, is not open to question. Those elements were: 1) That the jury should consist of twelve men, neither more nor less; 2) that the trial should be in the presence and under the superintendence of a judge having power to instruct them as to the law and advise them in respect of the facts; and 3) that the verdict should be unanimous.[9]

State Trials

Not for a full century after adoption of the due process clause, however, did the Court apply the right to trial by jury to the states.

In *Walker v. Sauvinet,* decided in 1876, the Court held that the Seventh Amendment right to trial by jury in civil cases was not a privilege or immunity of federal citizenship protected against state action.[10] Then, in *Maxwell v. Dow* (1900), the Court ruled that neither the privileges and immunities clause of the Fourteenth Amendment nor the due process clause required that state juries consist of twelve persons. "Trial by jury has never been affirmed to

be a necessary requisite of due process of law," declared the Court.[11]

With a line of decisions beginning in the 1930s, however, the Court made clear that *if* a state provided a trial by jury to a defendant, it was required to use fair procedures in selecting a jury that would represent a cross section of the community and would be relatively unbiased. *(Details, p. 167)*

Not until 1968, however, on the centennial of the adoption of the Fourteenth Amendment, did the Court hold that the right to trial by jury for persons charged with serious crimes applied to the states. In *Duncan v. Louisiana* the Court applied the Sixth Amendment right to a jury trial to the states, as a necessary ingredient of due process.[12]

Gary Duncan, charged with battery in Louisiana courts, was denied a jury trial, convicted, and sentenced to a fine and two years in prison. Duncan appealed to the Supreme Court, arguing that this denial of a jury trial violated his right to due process. The Supreme Court agreed. Justice Byron R. White wrote:

> Because we believe that trial by jury is fundamental to the American scheme of justice, we hold that the Fourteenth Amendment guarantees a right of jury trial in all criminal cases which—were they to be tried in a federal court—would come within the Sixth Amendment's guarantee.[13]

By applying the right to jury trial to the states the Court created two new questions. Were states now required to use only twelve-person juries? Must all state jury verdicts be unanimous?

Small Juries

The answer to the first question came quickly—and it was no. In *Williams v. Florida,* decided in 1970, the Court held it proper for states to use juries composed of as few as six persons in noncapital cases.[14]

Williams was tried for robbery by a six-man jury, which Florida law allowed in all noncapital cases. Writing for the Court, Justice White acknowledged:

> We do not pretend to be able to divine precisely what the word "jury" imported to the Framers, the First Congress, or the States in 1789. It may well be that the usual expectation was that the jury would consist of 12, and that hence, the most likely conclusion to be drawn is simply that little thought was actually given to the specific question we face today. But there is absolutely no indication in "the intent of the Framers" of an explicit decision to equate the constitutional and common law characteristics of the jury. Nothing in this history suggests, then, that we do violence to the letter of the Constitution by turning to other than purely historical considerations to determine which features of the jury system, as it existed at common law, were preserved in the Constitution. The relevant inquiry, as we see it, must be the function which the particular feature performs and its relation to the purposes of the jury trial. Measured by this standard, the 12-man requirement cannot be regarded as an indispensable component of the Sixth Amendment....
>
> ... [T]he essential feature of a jury obviously lies in the interposition between the accused and his accuser of the common-sense judgment of a group of

Due Process for Delinquents

Juveniles, the Court has ruled, possess some, but not all, of the due process rights assured to adults through the due process clause and the Sixth Amendment. Juvenile court proceedings are considered civil, not criminal, hearings. They are designed to shelter a young offender from the exposure of a public trial, giving him the opportunity to begin anew without the handicap of publicity or a criminal record.

Until 1967 only general elements of due process and fair treatment were applied to these proceedings. But in 1967 the Court in *In re Gault* held that juveniles charged with violating the law did have the right to confront and cross-examine persons presenting the evidence against them. Furthermore, the Court declared that juveniles had the same rights as adults to notice, aid of counsel, and protection against self-incrimination.[1]

In 1970 the Court held that due process required that juveniles be found delinquent by proof "beyond a reasonable doubt"—rather than by any lesser standard. In *In re Winship*, the justices found that Samuel Winship, a twelve-year-old found guilty "by a preponderance of the evidence" of stealing money from a woman's pocketbook, had been denied his due process rights. The standard of proof of guilt "beyond a reasonable doubt" was an essential element of due process and fair treatment applicable to juvenile as well as adult proceedings, held the Court.[2]

The following year, however, in *McKeiver v. Pennsylvania* and *In re Burrus,* the Court refused to extend the right to trial by jury to juvenile court proceedings.[3]

Justice Harry A. Blackmun explained:

If the jury trial were to be injected into the juvenile court system as a matter of right, it would bring with it into that system the traditional delay, the formality and the clamor of the adversary system and, possibly, the public trial. . . .

If the formalities of the criminal adjudicative process are to be superimposed upon the juvenile court system, there is little need for its separate existence. Perhaps that ultimate disillusionment will come one day, but for the moment we are disinclined to give impetus to it.[4]

Four years later, the Court extended the Fifth Amendment protection against double jeopardy to minors, ruling that a defendant found in juvenile court to have violated the law could not subsequently be tried for the same act as an adult.[5]

1. *In re Gault,* 387 U.S. 1 (1967).
2. *In re Winship,* 397 U.S. 358 (1970).
3. *McKeiver v. Pennsylvania, In re Burrus,* 403 U.S. 528 (1971).
4. Id. at 550-551.
5. *Breed v. Jones,* 421 U.S. 519 at 529 (1975).

laymen, and in the community participation and shared responsibility which results from the group's determination of guilt or innocence. The performance of this role is not a function of the particular number of the body which makes up the jury. To be sure the number should probably be large enough to promote group deliberation, free from outside attempts at intimidation, and to provide a fair possibility for obtaining a representative cross section of the community. But we find little reason to think that these goals are in any meaningful sense less likely to be achieved when the jury numbers six, than when it numbers 12—particularly if the requirement of unanimity is retained. And, certainly the reliability of the jury as a factfinder hardly seems likely to be a function of its size.[15]

In 1978 the Court made plain that juries must consist of at least six persons, rejecting Georgia's use of a five-person jury.[16]

The same day the Court resolved the question of jury size with *Williams,* it answered another question: What crimes were serious enough to require states to provide a jury trial? In *Baldwin v. New York* the Court held that states must provide trial by jury for all persons charged with offenses that could be punished by more than six months in prison.[17]

Unanimous Juries

In 1972 the Court held that state juries need not reach their verdicts unanimously. This ruling came in *Johnson v. Louisiana* and *Apodaca v. Oregon.*[18]

In the Louisiana case the Court upheld a state jury's 9-3 verdict convicting a man of robbery. Writing for the majority, Justice White declared that "want of jury unanimity is not to be equated with the existence of a reasonable doubt" concerning a defendant's guilt.

The Court rejected the defendant's argument "that in order to give substance to the reasonable doubt standard which the State, by virtue of the Due Process Clause of the Fourteenth Amendment, must satisfy in criminal cases . . . that clause must be construed to require a unanimous jury verdict in all criminal cases."[19]

White wrote:

this Court has never held jury unanimity to be a requisite of due process of law. . . . Appellant offers no evidence that majority jurors simply ignore the reasonable doubts of their colleagues or otherwise act irresponsibly in casting their votes in favor of conviction, and before we alter our own longstanding perceptions about jury behavior and overturn a considered legislative judgment that unanimity is not essential to reasoned jury verdicts, we must have some basis for doing so other than unsupported assumptions. . . .

Of course, the State's proof could perhaps be regarded as more certain if it had convinced all 12 jurors instead of only nine. . . . But the fact remains that nine jurors—a substantial majority of the jury—were convinced by the evidence. In our view disagreement of three jurors does not alone establish reasonable doubt. . . . That rational men disagree is not in itself equivalent to a failure of proof by the State, nor does it indicate infidelity to the reasonable-doubt standard.[20]

In the Oregon case Robert Apodaca and two other men had been convicted of burglary, larceny, and assault with a deadly weapon. The men had been convicted by twelve-member juries voting 11-1 and 10-2 for a verdict of guilty. Oregon law required that juries reach their verdicts by no less a majority than 10-2. The Supreme Court affirmed these convictions, using reasoning similar to that in the Louisiana case.

In 1979 the Court in *Burch v. Louisiana* faced a ques-

Due Process: The Right to Notice

Formal notice of charges—or of legal proceedings affecting one's rights—is one of the essential elements of due process.

All parties who are to become involved in legal proceedings must be informed in advance of trial of the specific charges against them to give them time to prepare their defense or, in the case of modern class action cases, to withdraw from the affected class.

The Supreme Court has held that in civil and criminal proceedings alike, notice must be given promptly and with sufficient specificity to permit preparation of an adequate defense. In addition, the Court has extended the due process requirement of notice to protect consumers from a unilateral seizure of property by creditors and to shield individuals from some administrative actions.

The concept of notice is included in both the Fifth and Sixth Amendments. The Fifth Amendment provides that no one "shall be held to answer for a capital, or otherwise infamous crime, unless on a presentment or indictment of a Grand Jury, except in cases arising in the land or naval forces, or in the militia." The Court in its 1884 ruling in *Hurtado v. California* held that this requirement of an indictment applied only to persons charged with federal crimes. That decision has never been reversed.[1]

The Sixth Amendment states that in *all* criminal prosecutions the defendant has the right "to be informed of the nature and cause of the accusation" against him. This more general rule has been accepted as basic to a fair trial.

Both the Sixth Amendment and due process require that laws describing certain actions as criminal be sufficiently specific to place persons on notice as to what acts are proscribed. As the Court wrote in 1926, "a statute which either forbids or requires the doing of an act in terms so vague that men of common intelligence must necessarily guess at its meaning and differ as to its application, violates the first essential of due process of law."[2]

Therefore, the Court has held "void for vagueness" laws that do not define with reasonable specificity the nature of forbidden conduct, and has set aside indictments that are insufficiently precise in stating the charges against an individual.

In testing laws challenged as unconstitutionally vague, the Court balances the right to notice against the imprecise language and political considerations inherent in the process of writing laws. Justice Tom C. Clark in 1952 set out the Court's view of these factors:

A criminal statute must be sufficiently definite to give notice of the required conduct to one who would avoid its penalties, and to guide the judge in its application and the lawyer in defending one charged with its violation. But few words possess the precision of mathematical symbols, most statutes must deal with untold and unforeseen variations in factual situations, and the practical necessities of discharging the business of government inevitably limit the specificity with which legislators can spell out prohibitions. Consequently, no more than a reasonable degree of certainty can be demanded. Nor is it unfair to require that one who deliberately goes perilously close to an area of proscribed conduct shall take the risk that he may cross the line.[3]

In later rulings, the Supreme Court extended the concept of notice, holding that it is required in a variety of situations outside of those occurring in the enforcement of the criminal law.

In 1969 and 1972 the Court held that due process required that consumers be notified before their wages were garnisheed or property repossessed for nonpayment of debts.[4]

The Court in 1970 applied the notice requirement to termination of welfare benefits.[5] Two years later, it held that a teacher fired after ten years of service was entitled to notice and a hearing.[6] And in 1975 the Court held that students were entitled to notice of charges before they were suspended from public schools for misbehavior.[7]

1. *Hurtado v. California*, 110 U.S. 516 (1884).
2. *Connally v. General Construction Co.*, 269 U.S. 385 at 391 (1926).
3. *Boyce Motor Lines, Inc. v. United States*, 342 U.S. 337 at 340 (1952).
4. *Sniadach v. Family Finance Corp. et al.*, 395 U.S. 337 (1969); *Fuentes v. Shevin*, 407 U.S. 67 (1972).
5. *Goldberg v. Kelly*, 397 U.S. 254 (1970).
6. *Perry v. Sinderman*, 408 U.S. 593 (1972).
7. *Goss v. Lopez*, 419 U.S. 565 (1975).

tion posed by the "intersection" of its decisions allowing states to use juries of fewer than twelve persons and those allowing state juries to reach their verdicts by less than unanimous votes.

In that case the Court held that a jury as small as six persons must reach its verdict unanimously. The Court held that a defendant charged with a nonpetty crime was denied his Sixth Amendment right to trial by jury if the state allowed him to be convicted by a less than unanimous vote of a six-man jury.[21]

An Impartial Jury

The fairness of an individual's trial is further safeguarded by the selection of an impartial jury. The defendant is protected against bias due to race, sex, employment, or class by the "cross section" principle that forbids systematic exclusion from juries of identifiable segments of the community.

Long before *Duncan v. Louisiana* required states to provide jury trials, the Court was demanding that state juries, if provided, be fairly selected. "It is part of the established tradition in the use of juries as instruments of public justice," declared the Court in 1940, "that the jury be a body truly representative of the community. For racial discrimination to result in the exclusion from jury service of otherwise qualified groups not only violates our Constitution and the laws enacted under it but is at war with our basic concepts of a democratic society and a representative government."[22]

Three decades later the Court reiterated this point, holding that state laws were unconstitutional if they resulted in the exclusion of women from juries. In these rulings the Court reaffirmed the fair cross section requirement as fundamental to the right to a jury trial.[23]

Congress incorporated this principle into the Federal Jury Selection and Service Act of 1968, which—a century after adoption of the Fourteenth Amendment—forbade discrimination in the selection of jury panels based on race, color, religion, sex, national origin, or economic status.[24]

Racial Bias

Racial discrimination in jury selection has been the subject of Supreme Court rulings for more than one hundred years. Both the due process and the equal protection guarantees of the Fourteenth Amendment furnish a basis for federal courts to review state jury selection practices alleged to be discriminatory. Most often the equal protection clause has served as the more effective of the two provisions in this area.

In 1880 the Court struck down Virginia and West Virginia laws that excluded blacks from jury service.[25] But the Court made clear in another decision the same year that it would not require state officials to ensure that blacks actually did serve on juries.[26] In other words, the mere absence of black jurors from any particular panel would not serve as a constitutional basis for challenging the jury's decision.

For the next half-century this superficial approach prevailed, and blacks continued to be excluded from local juries. Then, in 1935, in the "Second Scottsboro Case"—*Norris v. Alabama*—the Court looked behind the language of the state law to its effect, finding it unconstitutional.[27]

Witnesses for the Defense

The right to present a defense includes the power to use subpoenas and similar legal means to compel witnesses to appear in one's behalf at trial.

In 1967 the Supreme Court ruled that this right applied in state as well as federal trials. In *Washington v. Texas* the Court declared that:

> The right to offer the testimony of witnesses, and to compel their attendance if necessary, is in plain terms the right to present a defense, the right to present the defendant's version of the facts as well as the prosecution's to the jury so it may decide where the truth lies. Just as an accused has a right to confront the prosecution's witnesses for the purpose of challenging their testimony, he has the right to present his own witnesses to establish a defense. This right is a fundamental element of due process of law. (*Washington v. Texas*, 388 U.S. 14 at 19, 1967)

One of the "Scottsboro boys," Clarence Norris, a black convicted of raping a white woman, challenged his conviction as a violation of equal protection, pointing out that blacks were systematically eliminated from the pools of potential state jurors—including those who indicted and tried him. The Supreme Court reversed his conviction.

Chief Justice Charles Evans Hughes described the Court's responsibility as "to inquire not merely whether it [the equal protection guarantee] was denied in express terms but also whether it was denied in substance and effect."[28] Pointing out that no black had served on a jury in that county within the memory of any person living, Hughes found that sufficient basis for reversal.

Twelve years later, in the case of *Patton v. Mississippi*, the Court found similar justification for reversing the murder conviction of a black man indicted and convicted by all-white juries.

The Supreme Court held the long exclusion of blacks from juries a denial of equal protection. Justice Hugo L. Black delivered the opinion of a unanimous Court:

> When a jury selection plan, whatever it is, operates in such way as always to result in the complete and long-continued exclusion of any representative at all from a large group of negroes, or any other racial group, indictments and verdicts returned against them by juries thus selected cannot stand. . . . [O]ur holding does not mean that a guilty defendant must go free. For indictments can be returned and convictions can be obtained by juries selected as the Constitution commands.[29]

In subsequent cases, the Court upheld good-faith efforts by state officials to secure competent juries representative of the community. In 1953 the Court approved the use of taxpayers' rolls as the basis from which names were selected for jury service.[30]

The Court then began to rule against token selection of blacks for jury duty, or systems of jury selection that made it easy to exclude blacks. In *Avery v. Georgia* the Court struck down a system using different colored pieces of paper for black persons eligible for jury duty than for white persons. In *Whitus v. Georgia,* the justices invalidated the selection of jurors from tax records that were racially separated.[31]

In 1954 in *Hernandez v. Texas* the Court held that the Fourteenth Amendment forbade the systematic or arbitrary exclusion of any substantial racial group from jury service. A unanimous Court ruled that in a county where 14 percent of the population was of Mexican or Latin American descent, it violated equal protection to exclude all such persons from juries.[32]

In the mid-1980s the Court reaffirmed the importance of eliminating racial bias from the juryroom. In the 1986 case of *Vasquez v. Hillery* the Court ruled that anyone indicted by a grand jury selected in racially discriminatory fashion had the right to a new trial, regardless of the length of time since the discriminatory indictment. Such discrimination is a "grave constitutional trespass," wrote Justice Marshall. It "undermines the structural integrity of the criminal tribunal itself."[33]

Later the same year the Court, 7-2, held it unconstitutional for prosecutors to use peremptory challenges to exclude blacks from juries. Overruling a 1965 decision in *Swain v. Alabama,* the Court held that it was no longer necessary for there to be evidence of a pattern or practice of such exclusions before that practice could successfully be challenged.[34]

Blue Ribbon Juries

The Supreme Court has upheld the use of specially qualified panels of jurors for difficult cases. In *Fay v. New York,* decided in 1947, the Court considered a New York law that forbade selection of jury panels on the basis of race, creed, color, or occupation, but provided for the use of "blue ribbon" juries. Two union officials convicted of conspiracy and extortion by a blue ribbon jury claimed that these panels excluded laborers, craftsmen, and service employees, discriminating against certain economic classes and thus violating the due process and equal protection guarantees.

The Court upheld the system and the convictions. Justice Robert H. Jackson explained:

> We fail to perceive on its face any constitutional offense in the statutory standards prescribed for the special panel. The Act does not exclude, or authorize the clerk to exclude, any person or class because of race, creed, color or occupation. It imposes no qualification of an economic nature beyond that imposed by the concededly valid general panel statute. Each of the grounds of elimination is reasonably and closely related to the juror's suitability for the kind of service the special panel requires or to his fitness to judge the kind of cases for which it is most frequently utilized. Not all of the grounds of elimination would appear relevant to the issues of the present case. But we know of no right of defendants to have a specially constituted panel which would include all persons who might be fitted to hear their particular and unique case.[35]

In dissent Justices Frank Murphy, Hugo L. Black, Wiley B. Rutledge, and William O. Douglas protested that use of blue ribbon juries conflicted with the fair cross section requirement. Murphy wrote:

> There is no constitutional right to a jury drawn from a group of uneducated and unintelligent persons. Nor is there any right to a jury chosen solely from those at the lower end of the economic and social scale. But there is a constitutional right to a jury drawn from a group which represents a cross-section of the community. And a cross-section of the community includes

---

The Disruptive Defendant

Inherent in the defendant's right to confront and cross-examine those persons who testify against him is the right to attend his trial.[1]

In 1970, however, the Supreme Court held that this right was not absolute and that a defendant who persistently disrupted trial proceedings by noisy and disorderly conduct was not denied his constitutional rights when the judge had him removed from the courtroom.

In *Illinois v. Allen* the defendant had constantly interrupted the trial proceedings with noisy outbursts and insulting language. The judge finally ordered him removed from the courtroom until he agreed to behave.

At the conclusion of the trial, which resulted in his conviction, the defendant filed a petition for habeas corpus relief, claiming that he had been denied his right to a fair trial because of his enforced absence from the courtroom during the presentation of most of the state's case against him.

A unanimous Supreme Court rejected that argument. Justice Hugo L. Black wrote:

> It is essential to the proper administration of criminal justice that dignity, order, and decorum be the hallmarks of all court proceedings in our country. The flagrant disregard in the courtroom of elementary standards of proper conduct should not and cannot be tolerated. We believe trial judges confronted with disruptive, contumacious, stubbornly defiant defendants must be given sufficient discretion to meet the circumstances of each case. No one formula for maintaining the appropriate courtroom atmosphere will be best in all situations. We think there are at least three constitutionally permissible ways for a trial judge to handle an obstreperous defendant like Allen: 1) bind and gag him, thereby keeping him present; 2) cite him for contempt; 3) take him out of the courtroom until he promises to conduct himself properly.[2]

1. *Lewis v. United States,* 146 U.S. 370 (1892).
2. *Illinois v. Allen,* 397 U.S. 337 at 343-344 (1970); see also *Mayberry v. Pennsylvania,* 400 U.S. 455 (1971).

The Right to a Public Trial

The Sixth Amendment guarantees persons charged with crimes a public trial; the First Amendment guarantees the press and public the right to attend criminal trials.

In 1979 the Supreme Court held that the Sixth Amendment guarantee is solely for the benefit of the defendant, not for the public in general or the press. *(Details, p. 76; see also p. 54)*

In *Gannett Co. v. DePasquale,* the Court held that a trial judge could close to the press and the public a pretrial hearing on evidence in a murder case, if closure was needed to protect the defendant's right to a fair trial *(Gannett Co. v. DePasquale, 443 U.S. 368, 1979).*

"To safeguard the due process rights of the accused, a trial judge has an affirmative constitutional duty to minimize the effects of prejudicial pretrial publicity," wrote Justice Potter Stewart, noting that one of the most effective means of minimizing publicity is to close pretrial proceedings to both the public and the press.

"The Sixth Amendment," Stewart continued, "surrounds a criminal trial with guarantees ... that have as their overriding purpose the protection of the accused from prosecutorial and judicial abuses. Among the guarantees that the Amendment provides to a person charged with the commission of a criminal offense, and to him alone, is the 'right to a speedy and public trial, by an impartial jury.' The Constitution nowhere mentions any right of access to a criminal trial on the part of the public; its guarantee, like the others enumerated, is personal to the accused."

(Five years later, in *Waller v. Georgia,* 467 U.S. 39, 1984, the Court held that a defendant's right to a public trial means that a judge may close pretrial hearings to the public over a defendant's objection only if some overriding interest will be prejudiced by an open hearing.)

The year after *Gannett,* however, the Supreme Court found in the First Amendment the very guarantee of access that it had found absent in the Sixth. In *Richmond Newspapers v. Virginia,* the Court agreed with a First Amendment challenge brought by the press and overturned the decision of a trial judge to close a murder trial to press and public.

"We hold that the right to attend criminal trials is implicit in the guarantees of the First Amendment," wrote Chief Justice Warren E. Burger. "[W]ithout the freedom to attend such trials, which people have exercised for centuries, important aspects of freedom of speech and 'of the press could be eviscerated.' "

Burger acknowledged that in some situations the only way to preserve the right to a fair trial is to limit the access of press and public. But, said Burger, if such limitations were necessary they should be outlined clearly and backed by written findings on the part of the judge that closure was essential to preserve an overriding state interest. *(Richmond Newspapers v. Virginia,* 448 U.S. 555, 1980)

persons with varying degrees of training and intelligence and with varying economic and social positions. Under our Constitution, the jury is not to be made the representative of the most intelligent, the most wealthy or the most successful, nor of the least intelligent, the least wealthy or the least successful. It is a democratic institution, representative of all qualified classes of people.[36]

Women on Juries

Although the Court as early as 1946 disapproved of the exclusion of women from federal jury panels, it took thirty more years before that disapproval extended to state juries. As recently as 1961, in the case of *Hoyt v. Florida,* the Court upheld a Florida statute that made jury service by women voluntary. Women interested in being included on jury lists had to record with the county their willingness to serve.[37]

Gwendolyn Hoyt, accused of murdering her husband with a baseball bat, challenged the constitutionality of the voluntary jury service statute. Failure to include women on the jury, she claimed, denied women defendants the equal protection of the law.

The Court rejected this argument, saying that Florida law did not exclude all women from jury service, but simply permitted them to avail themselves of a broad exemption from that duty. At the time, the Court noted, seventeen states granted women this privilege.

For the Court Justice John Marshall Harlan wrote that "woman is still regarded as the center of home and family life." In light of that, he continued, "[w]e cannot say that it is constitutionally impermissible for a State ... to conclude that a woman should be relieved from the civic duty of jury service unless she herself determines that such service is consistent with her own special responsibilities."[38]

Fourteen years later the Court reversed itself and overturned *Hoyt.* In *Taylor v. Louisiana* the Court in 1975 found no rational, let alone compelling reason for exempting women from jury duty. The Court found the law unconstitutional, in conflict with the Sixth Amendment right of a defendant to be tried by an impartial jury drawn from a fair cross section of the community.[39]

In 1979 the Court reaffirmed this position, striking down a Missouri law that exempted women from jury duty upon their request. Leaving room for states to exempt from jury duty persons responsible for the care of children and other dependents, the Court held that the broader, sex-based exemption denied defendants their right to a jury that fairly represented their community.[40]

Jail Before Trial

Twice during the 1980s the Supreme Court approved the practice of preventive detention—of holding certain defendants in jail before their trial. The first case involved the pretrial detention of dangerous juveniles; the second, the pretrial detention of organized crime figures.

In *Schall v. Martin, Abrams v. Martin* (467 U.S. 253, 1984), the Court voted 6-3 to uphold New York's law permitting pretrial detention of juveniles when there is a serious risk that the juvenile may commit a serious crime before trial. This fell well within the bounds of due process, wrote Justice William H. Rehnquist for the Court. Detention in such a case, he continued, protects both the juvenile and society. Justices William J. Brennan, Jr., Thurgood Marshall, and John Paul Stevens dissented.

Three years later the Court reaffirmed and broadened its approval for pretrial detention, upholding the relevant provisions of a 1984 federal law. The case of *United States v. Salerno* (___ U.S. ___, 1987) arose from the pretrial detention of Anthony Salerno and Vincent Cafaro, indicted in New York on racketeering charges. The Court ruled—again 6-3—that neither due process nor the ban on excessive bail were violated when a judge decided that the suspect involved posed a danger to the community if he were freed on bail pending trial.

THE RIGHT TO A SPEEDY TRIAL

As early as 1905 the Supreme Court made clear that the right to a speedy trial is a relative matter, "consistent with delays and depend[ent] upon circumstances."[41]

The Court has adopted a balancing approach in cases alleging that a defendant has been denied this right. The justices weigh the particular facts to determine the reasons for the delay and the effect of the delay on the defendant.

In *United States v. Provoo* the Court in 1955 upheld dismissal of an indictment of a defendant who—although ready for trial since 1951 and protesting governmental requests for delay—had not been tried. The Court explained that the lapse of time, the death or disappearance of witnesses, and the protracted confinement of the defendant had seriously jeopardized his opportunity to defend himself.[42]

Dismissal of the charges, the unanimous Court held firmly in 1973, is the only appropriate remedy for denial of this right. In *Strunk v. United States* the Court found reduction of sentence insufficient remedy for delay of trial to the point that the right was denied.[43]

The Court has held that this right does not apply to delays before a person is accused of a crime, but, rather, only to the interval between arrest and trial.

In 1971 Justice White explained:

[T]he Sixth Amendment speedy trial provision has no application until the putative defendant becomes an "accused". . . .

. . . On its face, the protection of the amendment is activated only when a criminal prosecution has begun and extends only to those persons who have been "accused" in the course of that prosecution. These provisions would seem to afford no protection to those not yet accused, nor would they seem to require the Government to discover, investigate, and accuse any person within any particular period of time.[44]

In 1977 the Court reaffirmed this point, rejecting in *United States v. Lovasco,* the argument that a defendant was denied due process by a good-faith investigative delay between the commission of an offense and the time of his indictment.[45] Justice Marshall wrote:

prosecutors do not deviate from "fundamental conceptions of justice" when they defer seeking indictments until they have probable cause to believe an accused is guilty; indeed it is unprofessional conduct for a prosecutor to recommend an indictment on less than probable cause. . . . From the perspective of potential defendants, requiring prosecutions to commence when probable cause is established is undesirable because it would increase the likelihood of unwarranted charges being filed, and would add to the time during which defendants stand accused but untried. . . .

Penalizing prosecutors who defer action . . . would subordinate the goal of "orderly expedition" to that of "mere speed." This the Due Process Clause does not require. We therefore hold that to prosecute a defendant following investigative delay does not deprive him of due process, even if his defense might have been somewhat prejudiced by the lapse of time.[46]

In *Klopfer v. North Carolina* the Court in 1976 held that the due process clause required protection of the right to speedy trial against abridgment by the states.[47] The Court unanimously struck down a North Carolina law that allowed indefinite postponement of a criminal prosecution without dismissal of the indictment. The defendant would remain at liberty, but the prosecutor could restore the case to the docket any time a judge agreed such action to be appropriate.

Speaking for the Court, Chief Justice Earl Warren explained that this procedure "clearly denies the petitioner the right to a speedy trial which we hold is guaranteed to him by the Sixth Amendment. . . . We hold here that the right to a speedy trial is as fundamental as any of the rights secured by the Sixth Amendment."[48]

Federal and state officials operated until the 1970s on the assumption that an accused's failure to demand a speedy trial meant that he acquiesced in delay of proceedings. In 1972 in *Barker v. Wingo,* the Court rejected the view "that a defendant who fails to demand a speedy trial forever waives his right."[49]

Justice Lewis F. Powell, Jr., reaffirmed the Court's "balancing approach" to speedy trial claims:

The approach we accept is a balancing test, in which

the conduct of both the prosecution and the defendant are weighed.

A balancing test necessarily compels courts to approach speedy-trial cases on an *ad-hoc* basis. We can do little more than identify some of the factors which courts should assess in determining whether a particular defendant has been deprived of his right. Though some might express them in different ways, we identify four such factors: Length of delay, the reason for the delay, the defendant's assertion of his right, and prejudice to the defendant. . . .

We regard none of the four factors identified above as either a necessary or sufficient condition to the finding of a deprivation of the right of speedy trial. Rather they are related factors and must be considered together with such other circumstances as may be relevant. In sum, these factors have no talismanic qualities; courts must still engage in a difficult and sensitive balancing process. But, because we are dealing with a fundamental right of the accused, this process must be carried out with full recognition that the accused's interest in a speedy trial is specifically affirmed in the Constitution.[50]

Barker v. Wingo prompted Congress—against the advice of the Justice Department and federal judges—to pass the Speedy Trial Act of 1974 to reduce delays in federal trials. The act established a deadline of one hundred days between arrest or indictment and trial. Failure to meet the deadline would result in dismissal of the charges.[51]

In 1982 the Court further defined this right in *United States v. MacDonald,* ruling that this guarantee applied to the period between arrest and indictment, not to a period after military charges have been dropped and before a civilian indictment has been obtained. In this ruling, the Court explained its view that the right to a speedy trial was not intended to prevent prejudice to the defense as a result of the passage of time, but was instead intended to limit the impairment of liberty of an accused before trial and to shorten the disruption of life caused by pending criminal charges.[52]

THE RIGHT TO CONFRONT WITNESSES

The Sixth Amendment guarantees federal defendants the right to confront and cross-examine their accusers. In *Mattox v. United States,* decided in 1895, the Supreme Court defined the purpose of this confrontation rule:

The primary object . . . was to prevent depositions or ex parte affidavits . . . being used against the prisoner in lieu of a personal examination and cross-examination of the witness in which the accused has an opportunity, not only of testing the recollection and sifting the conscience of the witness, but of compelling him to stand face to face with the jury in order that they may look at him, and judge by his demeanor upon the stand and manner in which he gives his testimony whether he is worthy of belief.[53]

Subsequently, the Court struck down an act of Congress for violating this right by allowing the record of a case in which persons were convicted of stealing government property to be used as evidence—at the trial of the person charged with receiving that property—that the property was stolen. In the opinion, the Court further explained the purpose of this confrontation clause:

Televising Trials

Although he steadfastly opposed the introduction of cameras into the Supreme Court chamber, Chief Justice Warren E. Burger nonetheless in 1981 wrote the Court's opinion in *Chandler v. Florida* (449 U.S. 560) permitting states to televise trials.

For almost half a century, cameras had been unwelcome in the nation's courtrooms, in reaction to some sensational news coverage during trials of the 1920s and 1930s. The American Bar Association (ABA) had in fact declared, as one of the canons of judicial ethics, that all photographic and broadcast coverage of trials should be prohibited.

But during the 1970s attitudes began to change. In 1978 the ABA began considering relaxation of this ban, and the Conference of State Chief Justices voted to allow each state to develop guidelines for the use of cameras in the courtroom.

Florida began to experiment with televised trials in 1977. One of the trials covered by television was that of Noel Chandler and Robert Granger, former Miami Beach policemen charged with burglary. They challenged their convictions, arguing that the television coverage had denied them a fair trial.

Chandler and Granger argued that the Court in *Estes v. Texas* (381 U.S. 532, 1964) had declared that all photographic or broadcast coverage of a criminal trial was a denial of due process. (*Details, p. 72*)

No indeed, responded Chief Justice Burger for the Court. *Estes* "does not stand as an absolute ban on state experimentation with an evolving technology, which, in terms of modes of mass communication, was in its relative infancy in 1964, and is, even now, in a state of continuing change."

He continued: "Any criminal case that generates a great deal of publicity presents some risks that the publicity may compromise the right of the defendant to a fair trial. The risk of juror prejudice in some cases does not justify an absolute ban on news coverage of trials by the printed media [or of] . . . all broadcast coverage."

"Dangers lurk in this, as in most experiments, but unless we were to conclude that television coverage under all conditions is prohibited by the Constitution, the states must be free to experiment," Burger concluded.

a fact which can be primarily established only by witnesses cannot be proved against an accused ... except by witnesses who confront him at the trial, upon whom he can look while being tried, whom he is entitled to cross-examine, and whose testimony he may impeach.... The presumption of the innocence of an accused attends him throughout the trial, and has relation to every fact that must be established to prove his guilt beyond a reasonable doubt.[54]

This presumption was denied the defendant in this case, held the Court, because "he was put upon the defensive almost from the outset of the trial by reason alone of what appeared to have been *said* in another criminal prosecution with which he was not connected and at which he was not entitled to be represented."[55]

Many of the Court's pronouncements on the confrontation clause have focused on efforts by prosecutors to use hearsay evidence—prior, out-of-court statements of persons unavailable to testify and be cross-examined—at trial.

In general, the Court allows use of such evidence only when there is sufficient reason to consider it credible. In *Pointer v. Texas*, decided in 1965, the Court held this right of confrontation to be "a fundamental right essential to a fair trial in a criminal prosecution" and therefore applicable to defendants in state trials through the due process clause.[56]

Pointer involved a trial in which a state prosecutor attempted to use the transcript of a witness' testimony taken at a preliminary hearing, where he was not subject to cross-examination. The prosecutor had made no effort to secure the personal appearance of the witness at the trial. The Court threw out that evidence.

Although in recent years the Court seems to have relaxed some of its earlier restrictions on the use of hearsay evidence or out-of-court statements, it has reaffirmed the high priority it places upon this right in assuring a fair trial.[57]

In 1973 the Court 8-1 held that a defendant on trial for murder had been denied a fair trial and due process by the state judge's strict application of the hearsay rule to prevent the introduction of testimony by three men to whom a fourth man had confessed the crime with which the defendant was charged.[58]

And in 1974, with Chief Justice Burger writing the opinion, the Court held that a defendant was denied his right of confrontation when the trial judge forbade cross-examination of a key witness, a juvenile, about his delinquency record and probationary status, matters that could have impeached the credibility of his testimony.[59]

Notes

1. *Frank v. Mangum*, 237 U.S. 309 (1915).
2. *Moore v. Dempsey*, 261 U.S. 86 at 91 (1923).
3. *Tumey v. Ohio*, 273 U.S. 510 (1927).
4. Id. at 523.
5. *Dugan v. Ohio*, 277 U.S. 261 (1928).
6. *Ward v. Village of Monroeville*, 409 U.S. 57 at 60 (1972).
7. *North v. Russell*, 427 U.S. 328 at 337, 339 (1976). See also *Fisher v. Pace*, 336 U.S. 155 (1949); *Sacher v. United States*, 343 U.S. 1 (1952).
8. *Colgrove v. Battin*, 413 U.S. 149 (1973).
9. *Patton v. United States*, 281 U.S. 276 at 288 (1930); see also *Singer v. United States*, 380 U.S. 24 (1965).
10. *Walker v. Sauvinet*, 92 U.S. 90 (1876).
11. *Maxwell v. Dow*, 176 U.S. 581 at 603 (1900).
12. *Duncan v. Louisiana*, 391 U.S. 145 (1968).
13. Id. at 149.
14. *Williams v. Florida*, 399 U.S. 78 (1970).
15. Id. at 98-101.
16. *Ballew v. Georgia*, 435 U.S. 223 (1978).
17. *Baldwin v. New York*, 399 U.S. 66 (1970).
18. *Johnson v. Louisiana*, 406 U.S. 356 (1972); *Apodaca v. Oregon*, 406 U.S. 404 (1972).
19. *Johnson v. Louisiana*, 406 U.S. 356 at 359 (1972).
20. Id. at 359, 362.
21. *Burch v. Louisiana*, 441 U.S. 130 (1979); *Brown v. Louisiana*, 447 U.S. 323 (1980).
22. *Smith v. Texas*, 311 U.S. 128 at 130 (1940).
23. *Taylor v. Louisiana*, 419 U.S. 522 (1975); *Duren v. Missouri*, 439 U.S. 357 (1979).
24. Congressional Quarterly, *Congress and the Nation*, vol. II (Washington, D.C.: Congressional Quarterly, 1969), 385.
25. *Ex parte Virginia*, 100 U.S. 339 (1880); *Strauder v. West Virginia*, 100 U.S. 303 (1880); see also *Rose v. Mitchell*, 443 U.S. 545 (1979).
26. *Virginia v. Rives*, 100 U.S. 313 (1880).
27. *Norris v. Alabama*, 294 U.S. 587 (1935).
28. Id. at 590.
29. *Patton v. Mississippi*, 332 U.S. 463 at 469 (1947).
30. *Brown v. Allen*, 344 U.S. 443 (1953).
31. *Cassell v. Texas*, 339 U.S. 282 (1950); *Whitus v. Georgia*, 385 U.S. 545 (1967); *Avery v. Georgia*, 345 U.S. 559 (1952).
32. *Hernandez v. Texas*, 347 U.S. 475 (1954).
33. *Vasquez v. Hillery*, 474 U.S. 254 (1986).
34. *Batson v. Kentucky*, 476 U.S. 79 (1986); see also *Griffith v. Kentucky, Brown v. United States*, ___ U.S. ___ (1987).
35. *Fay v. New York*, 332 U.S. 261 at 270-272 (1947); see also *Moore v. New York*, 333 U.S. 565 (1948).
36. Id. at 299-300.
37. *Ballard v. United States*, 329 U.S. 187 (1946); *Hoyt v. Florida*, 368 U.S. 57 (1961).
38. Id. at 62.
39. *Taylor v. Louisiana*, 419 U.S. 522 (1975).
40. *Duren v. Missouri*, 439 U.S. 357 (1979).
41. *Beavers v. Haubert*, 198 U.S. 77 at 87 (1905).
42. *United States v. Provoo*, 350 U.S. 857 (1955); see also *Pollard v. United States*, 352 U.S. 354 (1957); *United States v. Ewell*, 383 U.S. 116 (1966).
43. *Strunk v. United States*, 412 U.S. 434 (1973).
44. *United States v. Marion*, 404 U.S. 307 at 313 (1971).
45. *United States v. Lovasco*, 431 U.S. 783 (1977).
46. Id. at 790-791, 795-796.
47. *Klopfer v. North Carolina*, 386 U.S. 213 (1967).
48. Id. at 222-223.
49. *Barker v. Wingo*, 407 U.S. 514 (1972).
50. Id. at 530, 533.
51. Congressional Quarterly, *Congress and the Nation*, vol. IV (Washington, D.C.: Congressional Quarterly, 1977), 576.
52. *United States v. MacDonald*, 435 U.S. 850 (1982); see also *United States v. Loud Hawk*, 474 U.S. 302 (1986).
53. *Mattox v. United States*, 156 U.S. 237 at 242-243 (1895).
54. *Kirby v. United States*, 174 U.S. 47 at 55 (1899).
55. Id. at 56.
56. *Pointer v. Texas*, 380 U.S. 400 (1965); see also *Douglas v. Alabama*, 380 U.S. 415 (1965).
57. *California v. Green*, 399 U.S. 149 (1970); *Dutton v. Evans*, 400 U.S. 74 (1970). See also *Nelson v. O'Neil*, 402 U.S. 622 (1971); *Harrington v. California*, 395 U.S. 250 (1969); *Schneble v. Florida*, 405 U.S. 427 (1972); *United States v. Inadi*, 475 U.S. 387 (1986); *Delaware v. Van Arsdall*, 475 U.S. 673 (1986); *Richardson v. Marsh*, ___ U.S. ___ (1987), *Cruz v. New York*, ___ U.S. ___ (1987).
58. *Chambers v. Mississippi*, 410 U.S. 284 (1973).
59. *Davis v. Alaska*, 415 U.S. 308 (1974).

8

Search and Seizure

"The security of one's privacy against arbitrary intrusion by the police," wrote Justice Felix Frankfurter in 1946, "is basic to a free society."

"The knock at the door, whether by day or by night," he continued, "as a prelude to a search, without authority of law but solely on the authority of the police, did not need the commentary of recent history to be condemned as inconsistent with the conception of human rights enshrined in the history and the basic constitutional documents of English-speaking peoples." [1]

The Fourth Amendment's guarantee of the "right of the people to be secure in their persons, houses, papers and effects, against unreasonable searches and seizures" was intended to protect the individual against this sort of arbitrary invasion of his privacy by police or other authorities.

The guarantee of personal security against unreasonable search and seizure is buttressed by the second portion of the amendment, the warrant clause. It underscores the "reasonableness" requirement for searches and seizures by stating that "no Warrants shall issue, but upon probable cause, supported by Oath or affirmation, and particularly describing the place to be searched and the person or things to be seized."

The Supreme Court has held that a valid warrant—one issued by a neutral and detached magistrate upon his finding of probable cause—is an essential element of compliance with the Fourth Amendment prohibition against unreasonable search and seizure.

This is perhaps the single most stable element in Fourth Amendment doctrine. As the Court itself has acknowledged, "translation of the abstract prohibition against 'unreasonable searches and seizures' into workable guidelines for the decision of particular cases is a difficult task which has for many years divided the Court.

"Nevertheless, one governing principle, justified by history and by current experience, has consistently been followed: except in certain carefully defined classes of cases, a search of private property without proper consent is 'unreasonable' unless it has been authorized by a valid search warrant." [2]

The warrant must be sufficiently specific to remove the element of discretion from those persons who are to execute it. The Court has recognized two primary exceptions to the warrant requirement for searches: a search related to a lawful arrest and a search of a moving vehicle may be conducted without warrants.

Although the Court generally has resisted arguments for new exceptions to the warrant requirement, it has held that neither aerial surveillance nor police searches of privately owned open fields need be authorized by warrant. [3]

Since 1914 the Court has used a controversial method of enforcing the Fourth Amendment guarantee. The "exclusionary rule" is the Court's insistence that evidence obtained in violation of the Fourth Amendment rights of a defendant may not be used as evidence against him.

Not until 1949 did the Supreme Court consider applying the Fourth Amendment guarantee and the exclusionary rule to state defendants. In *Wolf v. Colorado* the Court seemed to say that the rights protected by the Fourth Amendment were so basic to "the concept of ordered liberty" that they were protected against state action through the due process clause of the Fourteenth Amendment. Nevertheless, the Court in *Wolf* expressly declined to apply the exclusionary rule against state officials. [4]

In 1961, however, the Court reversed *Wolf* and in *Mapp v. Ohio* extended the full protection of the guarantee to state defendants. [5] Two years later in *Ker v. California* the Court stated that the Fourth Amendment guarantee as applied to state action was in all respects the same as that applied to federal action. [6]

THE NEUTRAL MAGISTRATE

The Constitution requires that search and arrest warrants be issued by a neutral and detached magistrate. Justice Robert H. Jackson in 1948 explained why:

The point of the Fourth Amendment, which often is not grasped by zealous officers, is not that it denies law

Private Search

The Fourth Amendment protects individuals only against searches and seizures by government agents, not by private individuals.

The Supreme Court set out this rule in 1921 in *Burdeau v. McDowell.* After McDowell was dismissed from his corporate job, his former employers blew open the lock on his private office safe, broke the lock on his desk drawer, and delivered the contents of desk and safe to the Justice Department, which was investigating McDowell's role in a mail fraud scheme.

McDowell challenged the seizure of the evidence as a violation of his right to be secure in his "papers and effects" against unreasonable search and seizure. The Supreme Court rebuffed his challenge, holding that the Fourth Amendment reached only government action; acts committed by private individuals, as in McDowell's case, were outside the protection of that guarantee. McDowell could, the Court noted, institute a private suit against those individuals who took his papers and turned them over to the government. *(Burdeau v. McDowell,* 256 U.S. 465, 1921)

enforcement the support of the usual inferences which reasonable men draw from evidence. Its protection consists in requiring that those inferences be drawn by a neutral and detached magistrate instead of being judged by the officer engaged in the often competitive enterprise of ferreting out crime. Any assumption that evidence sufficient to support a magistrate's disinterested determination to issue a search warrant will justify the officers in making a search without a warrant would reduce the Amendment to a nullity and leave the people's homes secure only in the discretion of police officers.... When the right of privacy must reasonably yield to the right of search is, as a rule, to be decided by a judicial officer, not by a policeman or Government enforcement agent.[7]

The Court emphasized the importance of this requirement again in 1971. In *Coolidge v. New Hampshire* the Court forbade the use of evidence obtained in a police search based on a warrant issued by the state official who was the chief investigator and prosecutor in the case. "Since he was not the neutral and detached magistrate required by the Constitution," stated the Court, "the search stands on no firmer ground than if there had been no warrant at all."[8]

The following year, however, the Court ruled that municipal court clerks may issue search warrants in cases involving the breach of municipal laws.

The Court stated that there was no Fourth Amendment "commandment ... that all warrant authority must reside exclusively in a lawyer or judge." Justice Lewis F. Powell, Jr., wrote the Court's opinion:

The substance of the Constitution's warrant requirements does not turn on the labelling of the issuing party. The warrant traditionally has represented an independent assurance that a search and arrest will not proceed without probable cause to believe that a crime has been committed and that the person or place named in the warrant is involved in the crime. Thus an issuing magistrate must meet two tests. He must be neutral and detached, and he must be capable of determining whether probable cause exists for the requested arrest or search.... If ... detachment and capacity do conjoin, the magistrate has satisfied the Fourth Amendment's purpose.[9]

PROBABLE CAUSE

A magistrate must find "probable cause" to issue a warrant. Probable cause has been variously defined, but the Court has made clear, on one hand, that while the term "means less than evidence which would justify condemnation,"[10] on the other hand, it does require "belief that the law was being violated on the premises to be searched; and ... the facts ... are such that a reasonably discreet and prudent man would be led to believe that there was a commission of the offense charged."[11]

A warrant is not valid, the Court has held, if it is based only upon a sworn allegation without adequate support in fact. In the 1933 case of *Nathanson v. United States,* the Court set out this rule:

Under the Fourth Amendment, an officer may not properly issue a warrant to search a private dwelling unless he can find probable cause therefore from facts or circumstances presented to him under oath or affirmation. Mere affirmation of belief or suspicion is not enough.[12]

The Court has held valid, however, warrants based on hearsay and has not required direct personal observation of the facts or circumstances justifying the warrant by the individual who seeks it.[13] But the magistrate must be satisfied that the informant, whose identity need not be disclosed, is credible or his information reliable.[14]

In 1978 the Court granted the right to a hearing to a defendant who claimed that police obtained evidence against him by using lies to convince a magistrate of probable cause. Justice Harry A. Blackmun, writing for the Court in *Franks v. Delaware,* made clear the majority's view that "a warrant ... would be reduced to a nullity if a police officer was able to use deliberately falsified allegations to demonstrate probable cause."[15]

Only if an individual cannot or does not consent to a search are police required to obtain a warrant. Voluntary consent of the individual who owns or occupies the place to be searched validates the search.

But, the Court held in 1973, the individual who is asked to consent to a search need not be informed that he may refuse. In *Schneckloth v. Bustamonte* the Court discussed the elements of voluntary consent. The majority, for whom Justice Potter Stewart wrote, concluded:

'Stop and Frisk' Searches Held Reasonable

The Supreme Court has held that the police practice of stopping suspicious persons and "frisking" them for weapons is a reasonable "search" within the boundaries of the Fourth Amendment. The Court has found such searches permissible even without a search warrant or enough information to constitute probable cause for arrest.

In *Terry v. Ohio* (1968) Chief Justice Earl Warren announced "that there must be a narrowly drawn authority to permit a reasonable search for weapons for the protection of the police officer, where he has reason to believe that he is dealing with an armed and dangerous individual, regardless of whether he has probable cause to arrest the individual for a crime. The officer need not be absolutely certain that the individual is armed; the issue is whether a reasonably prudent man in the circumstances would be warranted in the belief that his safety or that of others was in danger." [1]

The limited nature of this authority was emphasized by the Court in a companion case, *Sibron v. New York*. In *Sibron* the Court held impermissible a police officer's search of a suspect, finding it in violation of the *Terry* standard. Chief Justice Warren explained the difference in the two cases:

The search for weapons approved in *Terry* consisted solely of a limited patting of the outer clothing of the suspect for concealed objects which might be used as instruments of assault. Only when he discovered such objects did the officer in *Terry* place his hands in the pockets of the man he searched. In this case, with no attempt at an initial limited exploration for arms, [the] patrolman ... thrust his hand into Sibron's pocket and took from him envelopes of heroin. ... The search was not reasonably limited in scope to the accomplishment of the only goal which might conceivably have justified its inception—the protection of the officer by disarming a potentially dangerous man. Such a search violates the guarantee of the Fourth Amendment, which protects the sanctity of the person against unreasonable intrusions on the part of all government agents. [2]

Four years later the Court in *Adams v. Williams* upheld as proper an officer's stopping a motorist, based upon an informant's tip, reaching into the car and taking a handgun from the person's waistband. The gun was not visible from outside the car; the policeman would not have known of its existence without the informant's tip. [3] The Court stated that "[s]o long as the officer is entitled to make a forcible stop and has reason to believe that the suspect is armed and dangerous, he may conduct a weapons search limited in scope to this protective purpose." [4]

In 1983 the Court ruled that police officers could conduct the same sort of protective search of the interior of a car they have stopped—just as they could pat down or frisk a suspect on the street. [5]

In 1985 the Court eased its rules about the length of time police could detain a suspect under *Terry*. In *United States v. Sharpe* the Court held that it was not unreasonable or unconstitutional for police to detain for twenty minutes the driver of a car stopped on the highway and suspected of transporting drugs, while other law enforcement agents located a truck that had been traveling with the car and confirmed their suspicions that it carried narcotics. [6]

1. *Terry v. Ohio*, 392 U.S. 1 at 27 (1968).
2. *Sibron v. New York*, 392 U.S. 40 at 65-66 (1968).
3. *Adams v. Williams*, 407 U.S. 143 (1972).
4. Id. at 146.
5. *Michigan v. Long*, 463 U.S. 1032 (1983).
6. *United States v. Sharpe*, 470 U.S. 675 (1985).

We hold only that when the subject of a search is not in custody and the State attempts to justify the search on the basis of his consent, the Fourth and Fourteenth Amendments require that it demonstrate that the consent was in fact voluntarily given, and not the result of duress or coercion, express or implied. Voluntariness is a question of fact to be determined from all the circumstances, and while the subject's knowledge of a right to refuse is a factor to be taken into account, the prosecution is not required to demonstrate such knowledge as a prerequisite to establishing a voluntary consent. [16]

Justices William J. Brennan, Jr., William O. Douglas, and Thurgood Marshall dissented, saying that they failed to see "how our citizens can meaningfully be said to have waived something as precious as a constitutional guarantee without ever being aware of its existence." [17]

The following year, in *United States v. Matlock*, the Court held that when one occupant of a house consents to search of the premises, the search is proper and evidence uncovered in it may be used against another occupant. [18]

PROPERTY, PAPERS, AND EFFECTS

The Supreme Court's first major ruling on the scope of the Fourth Amendment's protection for individual privacy and security came in 1886. The case was *Boyd v. United States.*[19]

In *Boyd* the Court established that the Fourth Amendment protected individuals against subpoenas, as well as searches, for private business papers, and forbade such subpoenas as unreasonable if they forced the person to whom they were directed to produce self-incriminating evidence.

The Boyds had contracted with the federal government to furnish plate glass for a post office and courthouse building in Philadelphia. They agreed to discount the price of the glass in return for permission to import it duty-free. Subsequently, the government charged that the Boyds had taken advantage of the agreement by importing more glass than the contract permitted.

The government sought forfeiture of the contract. At trial the judge ordered the Boyds to produce the invoice showing the amount of imported glass they had received. Under protest, the Boyds complied with the order. They were convicted.

The Supreme Court reversed their conviction and ordered a new trial, declaring that the subpoena had violated both their Fourth Amendment and Fifth Amendment rights. For the majority, Justice Joseph P. Bradley explained:

It is our opinion, therefore, that a compulsory production of a man's private papers to establish a criminal charge against him or to forfeit his property is within the scope of the Fourth Amendment to the Constitution, in all cases in which a search and seizure would be.

Bradley concluded that compulsory production of a man's private papers was an unreasonable search and seizure under the Fourth Amendment, saying:

The principles laid down in this opinion affect the very essence of constitutional liberty and security ... they apply to all invasions, on the part of the Government and its employees, of the sanctity of a man's home and the privacies of life. It is not the breaking of his doors and the rummaging of his drawers that constitutes the essence of the offence: but it is the invasion of his indefeasible right of personal security, personal liberty and private property, where that right has never been forfeited by his conviction of some public offense.... Breaking into a house and opening boxes and drawers are circumstances of aggravation; but any forcible and compulsory extortion of a man's own testimony or of his private papers to be used as evidence to convict him of crime or to forfeit his goods is within the condemnation of that judgment. In this regard the Fourth and Fifth Amendments run almost into each other....

We have already noticed the intimate relation between the two Amendments. They throw great light on each other. For the "unreasonable searches and seizures" condemned in the Fourth Amendment are almost always made for the purpose of compelling a man to give evidence against himself, which in criminal cases is condemned in the Fifth Amendment; and compelling a man "in a criminal case to be a witness against himself," which is condemned in the Fifth Amendment, throws light on the question as to what is an "unreasonable search and seizure" within the meaning of the the Fourth Amendment. And we have

been unable to perceive that the seizure of a man's private books and papers to be used in evidence against him is substantially different from compelling him to be a witness against himself.[20]

The Exclusionary Rule

In order to avoid the cumbersome and expensive remedy of retrial for persons convicted on the basis of evidence seized in violation of their Fourth Amendment rights, the Court in 1914 adopted the exclusionary rule.

Set out first by the Court in *Weeks v. United States,* the rule allows a defendant who feels that evidence obtained in violation of his rights will be used against him to require the trial court to exclude it from use.[21]

Weeks was arrested without a warrant. Federal agents searched his home, also without a warrant, and took from it documents and letters used as evidence against him at trial. After his conviction, he challenged the conviction as obtained in violation of his rights.

The Supreme Court agreed. In the Court's opinion Justice William R. Day explained that exclusion of such evidence was necessary to discourage unlawful practices by law enforcement agents:

The tendency of those who execute the criminal laws of the country to obtain conviction by means of unlawful seizures and enforced confessions ... should find no sanction in the judgments of the courts, which are charged ... with the support of the Constitution.... ... If letters and private documents can thus be seized and held and used in evidence against a citizen accused of an offense, the protection of the 4th Amendment, declaring his right to be secure against such searches and seizures, is of no value, and, so far as those thus placed are concerned, might as well be stricken from the Constitution.[22]

The Court concluded both that the seizure of the letters by a federal agent and the refusal of the judge to honor Weeks's request for their return before they were used as evidence were violations of his constitutional rights.

'Mere Evidence'

The Court's next major Fourth Amendment decision— *Gouled v. United States*—set out the rule that "mere evidence" could not properly be seized by government officials, even with a search warrant. In *Gouled* the Court also held that a search of a place to which access had been gained by stealth rather than force still fell within the searches prohibited by the Fourth Amendment.[23]

In *Gouled* an acquaintance of Felix Gouled called upon him at his office on the pretext of paying a friendly visit. The visit, as it turned out, was at the direction of federal agents. Gouled was suspected of attempting to defraud the government in regard to some defense contracts. While Gouled was out of the room, the acquaintance removed some documents from the premises. Those documents were later introduced as evidence against Gouled, who was convicted of conspiracy to defraud the government. He challenged the use of the documents as evidence, arguing that

Border Searches

Since the earliest days of the nation's history Congress has authorized warrantless searches of persons entering the country at its borders. Until quite recently it was assumed that such searches were outside the scope of the Fourth Amendment guarantee.

But in a series of rulings in the mid-1970s, the Supreme Court held that the Fourth Amendment did apply to those searches that were part of the U.S. Border Patrol's effort to control illegal immigration.

In 1973 the Court in *Almeida-Sanchez v. United States* held that roving patrols violated the Fourth Amendment guarantee when they searched vehicles as far as one hundred miles from the border without a search warrant or probable cause to suspect that the car contained illegal aliens.[1]

Two years later the unanimous Court extended *Almeida-Sanchez* to hold that roving patrols could not even stop a car for questioning of its occupants unless there was more cause than the fact that the occupants appeared to be Mexican.[2] The same day, the Court held that border patrol officers at fixed checkpoints away from the border itself must have probable cause or a warrant before they searched cars at the checkpoint without the driver's consent.[3]

But the following year, the Court held that border patrol officers need not have probable cause or a warrant before they stopped cars for brief questioning at fixed checkpoints. Justice Lewis F. Powell, Jr., made clear the Court's distinction between searches and stops for questioning:

> While the need to make routine checkpoint stops is great, the consequent intrusion on Fourth Amendment interests is quite limited....
>
> Neither the vehicle nor its occupants is searched, and visual inspection of the vehicle is limited to what can be seen without a search. This objective intrusion—the stop itself, the questioning, and the visual inspection—also existed in roving-patrol stops. But we view checkpoint stops in a different light because the subjective intrusion—the generating of concern or even fright on the part of lawful travelers—is appreciably less in the case of a checkpoint stop....
>
> ... the reasonableness of the procedures followed in making these checkpoint stops makes the resulting intrusion on the interests of the motorists minimal. On the other hand, the purpose of the stops is legitimate and in the public interest.... Accordingly, we hold that the stops and questioning at issue may be made in the absence of any individualized suspicion at reasonably located checkpoints.[4]

1. *Almeida-Sanchez v. United States*, 413 U.S. 266 (1973).
2. *United States v. Brignoni-Ponce*, 422 U.S. 873 (1975).
3. *United States v. Ortiz*, 422 U.S. 891 (1975).
4. *United States v. Martinez-Fuerte, Sifuentes v. United States*, 428 U.S. 543 at 557-558, 561-562 (1976).

it violated his Fourth and Fifth Amendment rights.

The Supreme Court upheld his challenge, applying *Weeks* to exclude both the letters taken by the visitor and additional evidence obtained as a result of the first seizure. The Court's ruling was based on the surreptitious and warrantless nature of the search, and on the nature of the letters seized. The letters were mere evidence, and thus were outside the zone of reasonable seizures.

The Court of the late nineteenth and early twentieth centuries was very sensitive to property interests. Both in *Boyd* and *Gouled* the Court indicated that the government had a right to seize from an individual only that property to which the individual himself had no right—or a right inferior to the government's. With this reasoning, the only proper targets of search warrants were the fruits and instruments of crime and contraband.

Justice John H. Clarke set out this mere evidence rule:

> Although search warrants have ... been used in many cases ever since the adoption of the Constitution, and although their use has been extended from time to time to meet new cases within the old rules, nevertheless it is clear that, at common law and as the result of the *Boyd* and *Weeks Cases* ... they may not be used as a means of gaining access to a man's house or office and papers solely for the purpose of making search to secure evidence to be used against him in a criminal or penal proceeding, but that they may be resorted to only when a primary right to such search and seizure may be found in the interest which the public or the complainant may have in the property to be seized, or in the right to the possession of it, or when a valid exercise of the police power renders possession of the property by the accused unlawful, and provides that it may be taken.[24]

Although this rule severely limits the use of search warrants, in practice its impact was less dramatic. Congress never authorized the use of search warrants for mere evidence, and the Federal Rules of Criminal Procedure limited the objects of federal warrants to instrumentalities and fruits of crime.

Lower courts, however, construed those categories broadly, including many things only remotely connected with a crime as instruments of the crime. By the time the Court discarded the rule in 1967, Justice Brennan would remark that so many exceptions to the rule had been created—and such confusion over what was evidence and what was an instrument of crime—that it was questionable what effect the rule still had.

The Exclusionary Rule: Effective Remedy...

In 1914 the Supreme Court announced the controversial "exclusionary rule," which barred from federal courts evidence seized in violation of the ban on unreasonable search and seizure.

The Court set out the rule in *Weeks v. United States.*[1]

It has subsequently been applied to bar use of evidence taken in violation of other constitutional rights as well, in particular the Fifth Amendment privilege against self-incrimination and the Sixth Amendment right to counsel.

Not until 1961, however, did the rule operate in state courts.[2]

The rule has been the subject of continuing legal controversy. By denying prosecutors the use of evidence, the rule can cause the collapse of the government's case and the freeing of a person who may be guilty. As Justice Benjamin Cardozo wrote before he came to the Supreme Court bench, "The criminal is to go free because the constable has blundered."[3]

Some, including Chief Justices Warren E. Burger and William H. Rehnquist, feel that this is too high a price for society to pay for inadvertent violations of constitutional guarantees. Burger suggested that the rule should be abandoned and replaced with some less costly remedy—such as a law authorizing persons whose rights are so violated by law enforcement officers to sue the particular offending individuals for monetary damages.

In *Silverthorne Lumber Co. v. United States* (1920) the Court made clear that the exclusionary rule forbade *all* use of illegally obtained evidence in federal courts.[4]

A generation later, however, the Court held that narcotics illegally seized by federal officials could be used to impeach a defendant's credibility after he had testified that he had never used them, and that only the person whose rights were violated by the search and seizure could invoke the exclusionary rule.[5]

Wolf v. Colorado

In 1949 the Court held in *Wolf v. Colorado* that the Fourth Amendment guarantee protected individuals against state as well as federal action. The Court declined, however, to apply the exclusionary rule to enforce this guarantee against state officials.[6]

In *Wolf* a deputy sheriff had seized a doctor's appointment book without a warrant, interrogated patients whose names he found in the book, and thereby obtained evidence to charge Wolf with performing illegal abortions.

Wolf challenged the use of such evidence, arguing that it had been illegally seized and should be excluded. The Supreme Court, however, sustained his conviction.

Justice Felix Frankfurter wrote for the majority that:

> the immediate question is whether the basic right to protect against arbitrary intrusion by the police demands the exclusion of logically relevant evidence obtained by an unreasonable search and seizure.... When we find that in fact most of the English-speaking world does not regard as vital to such protection the exclusion of evidence thus obtained, we must hesitate to treat this remedy as an essential ingredient of the right....
>
> Granting that in practice the exclusion of evidence may be an effective way of deterring unreasonable searches, it is not for this Court to condemn as falling below the minimal standards assured by the Due Process Clause a State's reliance upon other methods which, if consistently enforced, would be equally effective....
>
> We hold, therefore, that in a prosecution in a State Court for a State crime the Fourteenth Amendment does not forbid the admission of evidence obtained by an unreasonable search and seizure.[7]

But even though the Court in *Wolf* refused to apply the rule to exclude *all* illegally seized evidence from use in state courts, there were some instances of police conduct so shocking to the Court that it reversed convictions thereby obtained.

One such case was *Rochin v. California*, decided in 1952. In *Rochin* state police officers had "seized" evidence from a suspect by pumping his stomach to recover two capsules of drugs which he had swallowed at the time of his arrest. The Court held the resulting conviction invalid. Frankfurter wrote the opinion for the unanimous Court, decrying such methods as "conduct that shocks the conscience, ... methods too close to the rack and the screw to permit of constitutional differentiation."[8]

The 'Silver Platter' Doctrine

The Supreme Court in *Weeks v. United States* announced two rules of evidence for federal courts.

One was the exclusionary rule: federal prosecutors could not use evidence obtained by federal agents in violation of the Fourth Amendment protection against unreasonable search and seizure.

The second rule was the "silver platter" doctrine: federal prosecutors *could* use evidence obtained by *state* agents through unreasonable search and seizure, if that evidence was obtained without federal participation and was turned over to the federal officials, in other words, handed to them on a silver platter.

The incongruity of these two rules was explained

...or Expensive Constitutional Right?

by the Court's view in 1914 that the Fourth Amendment did not apply to state action. But after the Court reversed that view in *Wolf v. Colorado* in 1949, the silver platter doctrine survived for eleven more years. Finally, in *Elkins v. United States,* the Court in 1960 repudiated that practice. Writing for the Court, Justice Potter Stewart declared:

> surely no distinction can logically be drawn between evidence obtained in violation of the Fourth Amendment and that obtained in violation of the Fourteenth [through which the ban against unreasonable search and seizure was applicable to the states]. The Constitution is flouted equally in either case. To the victim it matters not whether his constitutional right has been invaded by a federal agent or by a state officer.[9]

Mapp v. Ohio

The Supreme Court extended the exclusionary rule to the states in *Mapp v. Ohio,* decided in 1961. In *Mapp* the Court finally declared that "the exclusionary rule is an essential part of both the Fourth and Fourteenth Amendments."[10]

Cleveland police, suspecting that a law violator was hiding in a certain house, broke in the door, manhandled the woman resident, a Miss Mapp, and searched the entire premises without a warrant. A trunk containing obscene materials was found in the house. Mapp was tried and convicted for possession of obscene materials.

The Supreme Court overturned Mapp's conviction because the evidence used against her had been unconstitutionally seized. Justice Tom C. Clark wrote to reverse *Wolf* insofar as it dealt with the exclusionary rule:

> Nothing can destroy a government more quickly than its failure to observe its own laws, or worse, its disregard of the charter of its own existence. . . .
>
> The ignoble shortcut to conviction left open to the State [by allowing use of illegally obtained evidence] tends to destroy the entire system of constitutional restraints on which the liberties of the people rest. Having once recognized that the right to privacy embodied in the Fourth Amendment is enforceable against the States, and that the right to be secure against rude invasions of privacy by state officers is, therefore, constitutional in origin, we can no longer permit that right to remain an empty promise.[11]

Justices Frankfurter, John Marshall Harlan, and Charles E. Whittaker dissented.

The Court in the 1970s limited the use of the exclusionary rule to overturn convictions, reflecting the lack of enthusiasm of some members of the Court for the rule. Chief Justice Burger said in *Bivens v. Six Unknown Named Agents,* decided in 1971, that he preferred an alternative remedy—perhaps a damage suit against the offending officials.[12]

The Court subsequently refused to forbid prosecutors to use illegally obtained evidence when questioning witnesses before grand juries, or to direct federal judges to release persons challenging their state convictions as obtained with illegally seized evidence. So long as the state has provided an opportunity for a full, fair hearing of the defendant's challenge to that evidence, held the Court, there was no constitutional obligation for federal courts to use the writ of habeas corpus to enforce the exclusionary rule.[13]

In the 1980s the Court approved a significant exception to the exclusionary rule, an exception that some dissenting justices warned might eventually swallow the rule.

In 1984 the Court approved a "good faith" exception to the rule, permitting the use of illegally obtained evidence at trial if the police who seized it had a search warrant and thought they were acting legally—only to find that because of some "technical" flaw, their search was in fact illegal. In such a case, wrote Justice Byron R. White, the exclusion of valid evidence has no deterrent effect and exacts too high a price from society.[14]

The same year the Court also approved an "inevitable discovery" exception to the exclusionary rule—permitting evidence taken in violation of a defendant's rights to be used at trial if the prosecutor can show that the evidence ultimately would have been discovered by lawful means.[15]

1. *Weeks v. United States,* 232 U.S. 383 (1914).
2. *Mapp v. Ohio,* 367 U.S. 643 (1961).
3. *People v. Defore,* 242 N.Y. 13 at 21, 150 N.B. 585 (1926).
4. *Silverthorne Lumber Co. v. United States,* 251 U.S. 385 (1921).
5. *Walder v. United States,* 347 U.S. 62 (1954); see also *Stefanelli v. Minard,* 342 U.S. 117 (1951); *Goldstein v. United States,* 316 U.S. 114 (1942).
6. *Wolf v. Colorado,* 338 U.S. 25 (1949).
7. Id. at 28-29, 31, 33.
8. *Rochin v. California,* 342 U.S. 165 (1952), but see *Irvine v. California,* 347 U.S. 128 (1954); *Breithaupt v. Abrams,* 352 U.S. 432 (1957).
9. *Elkins v. United States,* 364 U.S. 206 at 215 (1960).
10. *Mapp v. Ohio,* 367 U.S. 643 at 657 (1961).
11. Id. at 659, 660.
12. *Bivens v. Six Unknown Named Agents,* 403 U.S. 388 (1971); see also *Monroe v. Pape,* 365 U.S. 176 (1961).
13. *United States v. Calandra,* 414 U.S. 338 (1974); *Stone v. Powell, Wolff v. Rice,* 428 U.S. 465 (1976); see also *United States v. Janis,* 428 U.S. 433 (1976).
14. *United States v. Leon,* 468 U.S. 897 (1984), *Massachusetts v. Sheppard,* 468 U.S. 981 (1984); see also *Maryland v. Garrison,* __ U.S. __ (1987); *Illinois v. Krull,* __ U.S. __ (1987).
15. *Nix v. Williams,* 467 U.S. 431 (1984).

Searching for Evidence

The Court abandoned the "mere evidence" rule in 1967, announcing this shift in *Warden v. Hayden*.[25] Hayden, a robbery suspect, was arrested in his home. In a warrantless search of the house by police at the time of the arrest, clothing was found that matched that described by witnesses as worn by the robber, and weapons allegedly used in the holdup.

Hayden was convicted of armed robbery on the basis of this evidence. He appealed, claiming that the clothing was seized in violation of *Gouled*. The Court, 8-1, rejected his challenge. Justice Brennan declared:

Nothing in the language of the Fourth Amendment supports the distinction between "mere evidence" and instrumentalities, fruits of crime, or contraband. On its face, the provision assures the "right of the people to be secure in their persons, houses, papers and effects . . . ," without regard to the use to which any of these things are applied. This "right of the people" is certainly unrelated to the "mere evidence" limitation. Privacy is disturbed no more by a search directed to a purely evidentiary object than it is by a search directed to an instrumentality, fruit, or contraband. A magistrate can intervene in both situations, and the requirements of probable cause and specificity can be preserved intact. Moreover, nothing in the nature of property seized as evidence renders it more private than property seized, for example, as an instrumentality; quite the opposite may be true. Indeed, the distinction is wholly irrational, since, depending on the circumstances, the same "papers and effects" may be "mere evidence" in one case and "instrumentality" in another.[26]

Brennan declared discredited the twin premises upon which the Court in *Gouled* based the "mere evidence" rule—"that property interests control the right of the government to search and seize" and "that government may not seize evidence simply for the purpose of proving crime." [27]

Privacy, not property, was the primary interest protected by the Fourth Amendment, reasoned the majority, and "[t]he requirements of the Fourth Amendment can secure the same protection of privacy whether the search is for 'mere evidence' or for fruits, instrumentalities or contraband" [28]

In conclusion, Brennan wrote:

The "mere evidence" limitation has spawned exceptions so numerous and confusion so great, in fact, that it is questionable whether it affords meaningful protection. But if its rejection does enlarge the area of permissible searches, the intrusions are nevertheless made after fulfilling the probable cause and particularity requirements of the Fourth Amendment and after the intervention of "a neutral and detached magistrate." . . . The Fourth Amendment allows intrusions upon privacy under these circumstances, and there is no viable reason to distinguish intrusions to secure "mere evidence" from intrusions to secure fruits, instrumentalities, or contraband.[29]

Justice Abe Fortas, joined by Chief Justice Earl Warren, agreed that Hayden's clothing was properly used as evidence against him, but criticized the majority's repudiation of the mere evidence rule as needless and dangerous.

In dissent, Justice Douglas argued that there were two zones of privacy—one that was completely protected from official intrusion and one that could be invaded by a reasonable, usually warranted, search by government agents. Douglas would place personal effects like Hayden's clothes in the first category. He explained:

The right of privacy protected by the Fourth Amendment relates in part of course to the precincts of the home or the office. But it does not make them sanctuaries where the law can never reach. . . . A policeman in "hot pursuit" or an officer with a search warrant can enter any house, any room, any building, any office. The privacy of those *places* is of course protected against invasion except in limited situations. The full privacy protected by the Fourth Amendment is, however, reached when we come to books, phamphlets [*sic*], papers, letters, documents, and other personal effects. . . . By reason of the Fourth Amendment the police may not rummage around among these personal effects, no matter how formally perfect their authority may appear to be. They may not seize them. If they do, those articles may not be used as evidence. Any invasion whatsoever of those personal effects is "unreasonable" within the meaning of the Fourth Amendment.[30]

To Douglas, "the constitutional philosophy" was clear:

The personal effects and possessions of the individual (all contraband and the like excepted) are sacrosanct from prying eyes, from the long arm of the law, from any rummaging by police. Privacy involves the choice of the individual to disclose or to reveal what he believes, what he thinks, what he possesses. The article may be a nondescript work of art, a manuscript of a book, a personal account book, a diary, invoices, personal clothing, jewelry, or what not.[31]

Douglas concluded:

That there is a zone that no police can enter—whether in "hot pursuit" or armed with a meticulously proper warrant—has been emphasized by *Boyd* and by *Gouled*. They have been consistently and continuously approved. I would adhere to them and leave with the individual the choice of opening his private effects (apart from contraband and the like) to the police or keeping their contents and their integrity inviolate. The existence of that choice is the very essence of the right of privacy. Without it the Fourth Amendment and the Fifth are ready instruments for the police state that the Framers sought to avoid.[32]

Rulings Against Private Papers

The abolition of the mere evidence rule curtailed Fourth Amendment protection for private papers.

Two 1976 decisions made this point. In *United States v. Miller* the Court ruled that bank records of a depositor's transactions were not private papers protected by the amendment.[33] And in *Andresen v. Maryland,* the Court undercut *Boyd* to allow use of an attorney's business records as evidence against him.[34] Because police had a warrant for the search in which they seized those papers, there was no valid Fourth Amendment challenge to their use, the Court held. And the justices rejected the attorney's argument that, as in *Boyd,* the use of these papers against him violated his Fifth Amendment privilege against compelled self-incrimination.

Two years later the Court rejected the argument of a campus newspaper that a search of its offices by police with a warrant violated the First and the Fourth Amendments. The *Stanford Daily* offices were searched by police looking for photographs or notes revealing the identity of individual demonstrators responsible for injuries to police during a protest. Such documents were clearly mere evidence, and there was no allegation that the newspaper or any of its employees had engaged in any wrongdoing. The newspaper contended that police should have subpoenaed the information, rather than searching its offices. The Court ruled that the Fourth Amendment did not restrict permissible searches to those places occupied by persons suspected of crimes. "Under existing law," wrote Justice Byron R. White for the majority in *Zurcher v. The Stanford Daily*, "valid warrants may be issued to search *any* property, whether or not occupied by a third party, at which there is probable cause to believe that the fruits, instrumentalities, or evidence of a crime will be found." [35]

Justice John Paul Stevens, one of the dissenters from the *Zurcher* decision, took this opportunity to express his concern about the implications of *Warden v. Hayden.*

> Countless law abiding citizens ... may have documents in their possession that relate to an ongoing criminal investigation. The consequences of subjecting this large category of persons to unannounced police searches are extremely serious.[36]

Stevens continued:

> Possession of contraband or the proceeds or tools of crime gives rise to two inferences: that the custodian is involved in the criminal activity, and that, if given notice of an intended search, he will conceal or destroy what is being sought. The probability of criminal culpability justifies the invasion of his privacy; the need to accomplish the law enforcement purpose of the search justifies acting without advance notice and by force, if necessary....
>
> Mere possession of documentary evidence, however, is much less likely to demonstrate that the custodian is guilty of any wrongdoing....
>
> The only conceivable justification for an unannounced search of an innocent citizen is the fear that, if notice were given, he would conceal or destroy the object of the search. Probable cause to believe that the custodian is a criminal, or that he holds a criminal's weapons, spoils, or the like, justifies that fear.... But if nothing said under oath in the warrant application demonstrates the need for an unannounced search by force, the probable cause requirement is not satisfied. In the absence of some other showing of reasonableness, the ensuing search violates the Fourth Amendment.[37]

ARRESTS AND SEARCHES

The Supreme Court has never applied the warrant requirement of the Fourth Amendment as strictly to arrests—the seizure of one's person—as to searches. The Court has applied the common law rule to arrests, approving warrantless arrests by law enforcement officers for crimes committed in their presence and for other crimes where there are reasonable grounds for their action.[38]

In 1925 the Court stated that "[t]he usual rule is that a police officer may arrest without warrant one believed by the officer upon reasonable cause to have been guilty of a felony." [39]

Half a century later the Court noted that it had never invalidated an arrest supported by probable cause just because the arresting officer did not have an arrest warrant. To impose a warrant requirement on all arrests, the Court said, would "constitute an intolerable handicap for legitimate law enforcement." [40]

Probable cause, however, is essential to justify a warrantless arrest.[41] The Court has declared unconstitutional the warrantless detention of suspects apprehended in a police dragnet, declaring that such "investigatory arrests" must be authorized by warrants if the evidence they uncover is to be used in court.[42]

In *United States v. Watson* the Court in 1976 upheld the warrantless arrest of a suspect in a public place, based upon probable cause.[43] Justice White elaborated on the Court's view of the warrant requirement for arrests:

> Law enforcement officers may find it wise to seek arrest warrants where practicable to do so, and their judgments about probable cause may be more readily accepted where backed by a warrant issued by a magistrate.... But we decline to transform this judicial preference into a constitutional rule when the judgment of the Nation and Congress has for so long been to authorize warrantless public arrests on probable cause rather than to encumber criminal prosecutions with endless litigation with respect to the existence of exigent circumstances, whether it was practicable to get a warrant, whether the suspect was about to flee, and the like.[44]

Joined by Justice Brennan, Justice Marshall dissented, saying:

> A warrant requirement for arrests would ... minimize the possibility that such an intrusion into the individual's sacred sphere of personal privacy would occur on less than probable cause. Primarily for this reason, a warrant is required for searches. Surely there is no reason to place greater trust in the partisan assessment of a police officer that there is probable cause for an arrest than in his determination that probable cause exists for a search.[45]

Later in the same term the Court upheld the warrantless arrest by police of a suspect in her own home, into which police officers followed her after they saw her standing on her front porch. This ruling came in *United States v. Santana.*[46]

Justice William H. Rehnquist explained that under the Court's interpretation of the Fourth Amendment, the suspect's front porch was a "public" place:

> She was not in an area where she had any expectation of privacy.... She was not merely visible to the public but as exposed to public view, speech, hearing and touch as if she had been standing completely outside her house....
>
> We thus conclude that a suspect may not defeat

The Fourth Amendment ...

The Fourth Amendment requires building, health, and fire inspectors to obtain warrants for administrative searches of private premises, the Court has ruled. But the justices have also held that warrants for such searches do not need to meet the same strict "probable cause" standards mandated for warrants in criminal investigations.

On the other hand, the Court has held that warrants are not required when welfare workers enter the homes of clients for interviews, nor when inspectors visit regulated business establishments such as gun and liquor stores and junkyards.

In 1959 the Court in *Frank v. Maryland* upheld the warrantless inspection of a private dwelling by a city health official seeking the source of a rat infestation. In *Frank* the Court stated that the protection of the Fourth Amendment did not apply:

> No evidence for criminal prosecution is sought.... Appellant is simply directed to do what he could have been ordered to do without any inspection, and what he cannot properly resist, namely, act in a manner consistent with the maintenance of minimum community standards of health.[1]

Only eight years later the Court overturned *Frank.* In *Camara v. Municipal Court* it declared that administrative searches were indeed "significant intrusions upon the interests protected by the Fourth Amendment."

Camara refused to permit a housing inspector of the San Francisco Health Department to make a inspection of his apartment without a search warrant. The Court upheld Camara's position, stating:

We may agree that a routine inspection of the physical condition of private property is a less hostile intrusion than the typical policeman's search for the fruits and instrumentalities of crime. For this reason alone, *Frank* differed from the great bulk of Fourth Amendment cases.... But we cannot agree that the Fourth Amendment interests at stake in these inspection cases are merely "peripheral." It is surely anomalous to say that the individual and his private property are fully protected by the Fourth Amendment only when the individual is suspected of criminal behavior.[2]

In a second ruling announced the same day, the Court declared that government agents must obtain a warrant for administrative entries into the nonpublic portions of commercial establishments. In *See v. City of Seattle* the Court established broad guidelines for such searches.[3]

The Court in the 1978 case of *Marshall v. Barlow's, Inc.,* denied government inspectors from the Occupational Safety and Health Administration the right to make warrantless random safety inspections of nonpublic working areas on business premises over the owner's objection. If consent was not given to the search, a warrant must be obtained, the Court held.

Relying on *Camara,* the Court held that the "Warrant Clause of the Fourth Amendment protects commercial buildings as well as private homes.... That an employee is free to report, and the Government is free to use, any evidence of non-compliance with OSHA that the employee observes furnishes no justification for federal agents to enter a place of business from which the public is restricted and to conduct their own warrantless search."[4]

---

an arrest which has been set in motion in a public place, and is therefore proper under *Watson,* by the expedient of escaping to a private place.[47]

Justices Marshall and Brennan again dissented.

Four years later the Court set a limit on this type of warrantless arrest, ruling 6-3 in *Payton v. New York,* that police may not enter a home to arrest its occupant without a warrant for the arrest or the consent of the occupant. Chief Justice Burger and Justices White and Rehnquist dissented.[48]

Searches Incident to Arrest

When police arrest a suspect, the Court has held it reasonable—even without a search warrant—for them to search both the person arrested and, to some limited extent, his immediate surroundings. The justices have viewed

such searches as necessary to protect the lives of the arresting officers, to prevent the fugitive's escape, and to prohibit the destruction of evidence.

In 1925 the Court in *Agnello v. United States* acknowledged this exception to the warrant requirement:

> The right without a search warrant contemporaneously to search persons lawfully arrested while committing crime, and to search the place where the arrest is made in order to find and seize things connected with the crime as its fruits, or as the means by which it was committed, as well as weapons and other things to effect an escape from custody is not to be doubted.[49]

Twenty-two years later in 1947, in *Harris v. United States,* the Court read this exception broadly.[50] Harris was arrested in his apartment by FBI agents and charged with mail fraud and forgery. Without a search warrant, the agents searched his entire apartment for five hours. They found no evidence of mail fraud or forgery, but they did

... and Administrative Searches

The Court has made exceptions to the warrant requirement for administrative searches of premises occupied by gun dealers and liquor establishments, both of which are regulated by federal law. The Court has ruled that the premises of such business establishments may be inspected during regular business hours by government agents without a warrant. In *Colonnade Catering Corp. v. United States* the Court held that in certain industries subject to particular government oversight there can be no expectation of privacy for the proprietor or the premises.

A federal agent of the alcohol and tobacco tax division of the Internal Revenue Service made a warrantless inspection of a locked storeroom and forcibly seized illegal liquor. Justice William O. Douglas declared that "Congress has broad power to design such powers of inspection under the liquor laws as it deems necessary to meet the evils at hand." [5]

In *United States v. Biswell* the Court upheld the warrantless search of a pawnbroker's storeroom by a federal agent who discovered two illegal weapons there. Relying on *Colonnade Catering,* the Court declared:

where, as here, regulatory inspections further urgent federal interest, and the possibilities of abuse and the threat to privacy are not of impressive dimensions, the inspection may proceed without a warrant where specifically authorized by statute. [6]

In *New York v. Burger* the Court in 1987 brought auto junkyards, which are regulated by the state, within this exception to the warrant requirement. [7]

Twice—in 1978 and again in 1984—the Court has insisted that fire officials inspecting the premises on which a suspicious fire occurred must have a warrant, unless the inspection occurs during or immediately after the fire.

In *Michigan v. Tyler* the Court held:

an entry to fight a fire requires no warrant, and ... once in the building, officials may remain there for a reasonable time to investigate the cause of the fire. Thereafter, additional entries to investigate ... must be made pursuant to the warrant procedures governing administrative searches. [8]

The Court underscored this point in *Michigan v. Clifford,* declaring the warrantless entry and search of a burned residence five hours after the fire was extinguished, without notice to the absent residents, was a violation of the Fourth Amendment. [9]

In contrast, the Court has held since the 1970 case of *Wyman v. James* that home visits by a welfare worker to a prospective client raised no valid Fourth Amendment issues. The visit, agreed the Court, might be both "rehabilitative and investigative," but it nevertheless was not "a search in the traditional criminal law context" to which the warrant requirement applied. [10]

1. *Frank v. Maryland,* 359 U.S. 360 at 366 (1959).
2. *Camara v. Municipal Court,* 387 U.S. 523 at 530 (1967).
3. *See v. City of Seattle,* 387 U.S. 541 (1967).
4. *Marshall v. Barlows, Inc.,* 436 U.S. 307 at 311, 315 (1978).
5. *Colonnade Catering Corp. v. United States,* 397 U.S. 72 at 76 (1970).
6. *United States v. Biswell,* 406 U.S. 311 at 317 (1972).
7. *New York v. Burger,* ___ U.S. ___ (1987).
8. *Michigan v. Tyler,* 436 U.S. 499 at 511 (1978).
9. *Michigan v. Clifford,* 464 U.S. 287 (1984).
10. *Wyman v. James,* 400 U.S. 309 at 317-318 (1971).

discover several stolen Selective Service draft cards. Harris was subsequently convicted for illegal possession of those cards.

He challenged the validity of the search and the seizure of the cards, but the Court upheld the search as valid, incident to his arrest. Harris was in control of the entire four-room apartment, it reasoned, and thus the search could extend beyond the room in which he was arrested.

Chief Justice Fred M. Vinson declared that "[s]earch and seizure incident to lawful arrest is a practice of ancient origin and has long been an integral part of the law-enforcement procedures of the United States." [51]

Justices Frankfurter, Jackson, Frank Murphy, and Wiley B. Rutledge dissented. Murphy wrote:

The Court today has resurrected and approved, in effect, the use of the odious general warrant or writ of assistance, presumably outlawed forever from our society by the Fourth Amendment. A warrant of arrest, without more, is now sufficient to justify an unlimited search of a man's home from cellar to garret for evidence of any crime, provided only that he is arrested in his home. Probable cause for the search need not be shown; an oath or affirmation is unnecessary; no description of the place to be searched or the things to be seized need be given; and the magistrate's judgment that these requirements have been satisfied is now dispensed with. In short, all the restrictions put upon the issuance and execution of search warrants by the Fourth Amendment are now dead letters as to those who are arrested in their homes. [52]

The following year, however, the Court seemed to narrow the definition of a search which was permissible, without a warrant, pursuant to a valid arrest. *Trupiano v. United States* involved the arrest of several persons on a farm in New Jersey for operating an illegal still—and the seizure, without a warrant, of the still, which the arresting agents had observed in operation during the arrest. [53]

The Supreme Court held the warrantless arrest valid, but not the seizure of the still. For the majority, Justice Murphy wrote that no reason was offered why the federal agents could not have obtained a search warrant before moving in to make the arrest "except [their] indifference to the legal process for search and seizure which the Constitution contemplated." [54]

Murphy continued:

A search or seizure without a warrant as an incident to a lawful arrest has always been considered to be a strictly limited right. It grows out of the inherent necessities of the situation at the time of the arrest. But there must be something more in the way of necessity than merely a lawful arrest.... Otherwise the exception swallows the general principle, making a search warrant completely unnecessary wherever there is a lawful arrest, and so there must be some other factor in the situation that would make it unreasonable or impracticable to require the arresting officer to equip himself with a search warrant. [55]

Later in 1948 the Court reiterated this last point in its ruling in *McDonald v. United States:*

Where ... officers are not responding to an emergency, there must be compelling reasons to justify the absence of a search warrant. A search without a warrant demands exceptional circumstances.... We cannot ... excuse the absence of a search warrant without a showing by those who seek exemption from the constitutional mandate that the exigencies of the situation made that course imperative. [56]

Although the "exigent circumstances" requirement of *McDonald* for warrantless searches generally has survived, *Trupiano's* insistence that a warrant be required whenever obtaining one was practicable was short-lived.

In 1950 the Court in *United States v. Rabinowitz* declared that "[t]o the extent that *Trupiano* ... requires a search warrant solely upon the basis of the practicability of procuring it rather than upon the reasonableness of the search after a lawful arrest, that case is overruled." [57]

In *Rabinowitz* the Court separated the question of the reasonableness of a search from the warrant requirement. Justice Sherman Minton explained:

What is a reasonable search is not to be determined by any fixed formula. The Constitution does not define what are "unreasonable" searches and, regrettably, in our discipline we have no ready litmus-paper test. The recurring questions of the reasonableness of searches must find resolution in the facts and circumstances of each case....

The relevant test is not whether it is reasonable to procure a search warrant, but whether the search was reasonable. That criterion in turn depends on the facts and circumstances—the total atmosphere of the case. [58]

The attempted separation of the reasonableness standard from the warrant requirement and the use of the "total atmosphere" test resulted in considerable confusion over what sort of warrantless searches were permissible incident to a valid arrest. [59]

In 1969 the Court overruled *Rabinowitz* and *Harris* and returned to the view that the warrant and reasonableness requirements were indeed linked. This shift was announced in *Chimel v. California.* [60] The Court overturned a burglary conviction because it was based on evidence seized without a warrant incident to arrest, but from too extensive a search to be justified by the arrest alone.

Searches incident to arrest were only reasonable insofar as they involved the person arrested and the area immediately under his control—from which he could obtain a weapon or within which he could destroy evidence, declared the Court.

Justice Stewart wrote for the majority:

No consideration relevant to the Fourth Amendment suggests any point of rational limitation, once the search is allowed to go beyond the area from which the person arrested might obtain weapons or evidentiary items. The only reasoned distinction is one between a search of the person arrested and the area within his reach on the one hand, and more extensive searches on the other....

The search here went far beyond the petitioner's person and the area from within which he might have obtained either a weapon or something that could have been used as evidence against him. There was no constitutional justification, in the absence of a search warrant, for extending the search beyond that area. The scope of the search was, therefore, "unreasonable" under the Fourth and Fourteenth Amendments, and the petitioner's conviction cannot stand. [61]

Justice White, joined by Justice Hugo L. Black, dissented:

where as here the existence of probable cause is independently established and would justify a warrant for a broader search for evidence, I would follow past cases and permit such a search to be carried out without a warrant, since the fact of arrest supplies an exigent circumstance justifying police action before the evidence can be removed, and also alerts the suspect to the fact of the search so that he can immediately seek judicial determination of probable cause in an adversary proceeding and appropriate redress. [62]

The following year in *Vale v. Louisiana* the Court held that a street arrest of a narcotics suspect did not constitute an "exigent circumstance" to justify a warrantless search of his house. [63]

Then, in *Coolidge v. New Hampshire,* decided in 1971, the Court ruled that the arrest of a suspect inside his house did not justify a search of his automobile parked in the driveway. [64]

But the Court has never retreated from its view that a suspect under lawful arrest may properly be subjected to full search of his person without a warrant, that such a search is reasonable under the Fourth Amendment, and that evidence found in such a search is admissible.

The Court reaffirmed these points in 1973 in *United States v. Robinson* and *Gustafson v. Florida,* both involving motorists stopped for violations of auto or traffic laws and found to possess illegal drugs. The subsequent narcotics convictions of both were upheld. [65]

Automobile Searches

In addition to the fact that warrants are not always required for searches incident to arrest, the Court since 1925 has allowed some warrantless searches of moving vehicles, especially automobiles.

The landmark case in this area is *Carroll v. United States,* decided in 1925.[66] George Carroll was convicted of transporting liquor for sale in violation of the federal prohibition law and the Eighteenth Amendment. The contraband liquor used as evidence against him had been taken from his car by federal agents acting without a search warrant.

But the Supreme Court sustained Carroll's conviction against his contention that this seizure violated his Fourth Amendment rights. Writing for the Court, Chief Justice William Howard Taft explained:

> the guaranty of freedom from unreasonable searches and seizures by the Fourth Amendment has been construed, practically since the beginning of the government, as recognizing a necessary difference between a search of a store, dwelling house, or other structure in respect of which a proper official warrant readily may be obtained and a search of a ship, motor boat, wagon, or automobile for contraband goods, where it is not practicable to secure a warrant, because the vehicle can be quickly moved out of the locality or jurisdiction in which the warrant must be sought.[67]

Subsequent rulings involving police searches of automobiles, without warrants, for contraband, have made clear the breadth of this exception to the warrant requirements. In 1931 the Court upheld the search of a parked car as reasonable because police could not know when the suspect might move it.[68] The Court in 1948 appeared to limit this exception to situations in which Congress had authorized warrantless searches of moving vehicles suspected of involvement in violating federal laws.[69] But the following year the justices in *Brinegar v. United States* upheld, as reasonable, warrantless searches of automobiles whenever police had probable cause to believe the cars were involved in illegal activity.[70]

This remains the rule, as the Court has repeatedly emphasized in cases in which it has refused to declare evidence to be admissible when it was discovered in a search for which there was no probable cause.[71]

After the Court in *Mapp v. Ohio* applied the exclusionary rule to state proceedings—and in *Ker v. California* declared the standard the same for state and federal action under the Fourth Amendment—the Court applied the same rules for warrantless auto searches to state police and federal agents.

The Court gives police leeway in such searches. It has upheld the search of a car without a warrant as long as a week after the arrest of its owner, when the government had a proprietary interest in the car because it was subject to forfeiture under state law.[72] It has allowed police to make such searches of autos after they have been towed to the police garage from the site of an arrest.[73]

The justices have refused to exclude evidence obtained in the routine warrantless search of an impounded vehicle as inadmissible,[74] or to require that a warrant be obtained before police take paint samples from the exterior of a car parked in a public parking lot.[75]

In 1978 the Court in *Rakas v. Illinois* held that passengers did not have the right to challenge the warrantless search of the vehicle in which they were riding or the use of evidence seized in that search against them. That decision tied the Fourth Amendment rights of persons in cars more closely to property concepts than in earlier cases.

For the five-man majority, Justice Rehnquist emphasized that Fourth Amendment rights could only be asserted

---

'Seizure' of Traits

The Supreme Court has consistently held that certain physical characteristics that individuals consistently display are not protected by the Fourth Amendment from government "seizure" and use as evidence.

Writing for the Court in 1910, Justice Oliver Wendell Holmes, Jr., held that such revelations were not compelled self-incrimination. The Fifth Amendment, wrote Holmes, did not demand "an exclusion of his body as evidence when it may be material."[1]

This principle was subsequently extended to rebut Fourth Amendment challenges to the use of evidence such as voice samples and handwriting examples obtained from suspects.[2]

The Court also has held that minor intrusions on a suspect's body do not violate the Fourth Amendment. But it has outlawed more drastic intrusions as offending both the Fourth Amendment and the "sense of justice."

Thus although the Court has upheld the extraction of blood samples and the taking of fingernail scrapings from suspects, it has rejected the use of a stomach pump to obtain—from a suspect's digestive system—evidence of narcotics possession.[3]

1. *Holt v. United States,* 218 U.S. 245 at 253 (1910).
2. *United States v. Dionisio,* 410 U.S. 1 (1973); *United States v. Mara,* 410 U.S. 19 (1973); *United States v. Wade,* 388 U.S. 218 (1967); *Gilbert v. California,* 388 U.S. 263 (1967); see also *United States v. Euge,* 444 U.S. 707 (1980).
3. *Rochin v. California,* 342 U.S. 165 (1952); *Breithaupt v. Abram,* 352 U.S. 432 (1957); *Schmerber v. California,* 384 U.S. 757 (1966); *Cupp v. Murphy,* 412 U.S. 291 (1973); *South Dakota v. Neville,* 459 U.S. 553 (1983); *Winston v. Lee,* 470 U.S. 753 (1985), but see *United States v. Montoya de Hernandez,* 473 U.S. 531 (1985).

---

by the person whose privacy was invaded: "A person who is aggrieved by an illegal search and seizure only through the introduction of damaging evidence secured by a search of a third person's premises or property has not had any of his Fourth Amendment rights infringed."[76]

The warrantless search in this case was proper because it was based on probable cause: the car fit the description of a getaway car used in a nearby robbery. And because the passengers did not claim that they owned either the car or the items seized, they could not challenge the search, the seizure, or the use of discovered evidence against them as a violation of the Fourth Amendment guarantee.

The four dissenting justices, for whom Justice White wrote, criticized the majority for implying that the Fourth Amendment protected property interests rather than privacy interests. The Court in this ruling, wrote White, was declaring "open season" for auto searches.[77]

Four months later, however, the Court appeared to allay White's fears with its 8-1 decision in *Delaware v.*

The Ultimate Arrest

The Supreme Court invoked the Fourth Amendment guarantee against unreasonable seizure in 1985 to declare that police may not use deadly force to stop a fleeing felon—unless they have reason to believe that he threatens the life of people nearby.

In *Tennessee v. Garner* the father of an unarmed fifteen-year-old boy, who was shot and killed by police as he fled a burglarized house, won a 6-3 decision declaring that "a police officer may not seize an unarmed non-dangerous suspect by shooting him dead." (471 U.S. 1)

Over the dissenting votes of Chief Justice Warren E. Burger and Justices Sandra Day O'Connor and William Rehnquist, Justice Byron R. White wrote for the Court that "the use of deadly force to prevent the escape of all felony suspects, whatever the circumstances, is constitutionally unreasonable."

Prouse. With White writing the majority opinion, the Court held impermissible the state police practice of randomly stopping motorists—without any probable cause—to check licenses and registrations. The Court decided that such "seizures" of the person and any subsequent searches violated the Fourth Amendment and that evidence of a drug law violation discovered in a car after such a random stop could not be admitted as evidence in state court.[78]

The difficulty of administering this exception was well illustrated with a pair of rulings in 1981 and 1982. On July 1, 1981, the Court in *Robbins v. California* ruled that police needed a search warrant to open a closed piece of luggage or other closed container found in a lawfully searched car. The vote was 6-3, with Justices Rehnquist, Stevens, and Harry A. Blackmun dissenting.[79]

On June 1, 1982, the Court reversed itself. Stevens wrote in *United States v. Ross* that police officers who have probable cause to suspect that drugs or other contraband are in a car they have stopped may search the entire vehicle as thoroughly as if they had a warrant, including all containers and packages in the car that might contain the object of the search. Justices White, Brennan, and Marshall dissented.[80]

ELECTRONIC EAVESDROPPING

Not until 1967 did the Supreme Court bring electronic eavesdropping and surveillance techniques within the scope of the Fourth Amendment guarantee of security against unreasonable search and seizure. From 1928 until 1967 the Court held firmly that the Fourth Amendment applied only when there was physical entry and seizure of tangible items; it did not apply to overheard conversations.

This rule was set out in *Olmstead v. United States,* which involved a bootlegging operation against which evidence was gathered through the use of wiretaps. The defendants challenged this method of obtaining evidence, arguing that it violated their Fourth Amendment rights. The Court, with Chief Justice Taft writing its opinion, rejected that claim:

The well-known historical purpose of the 4th Amendment, directed against general warrants and writs of assistance, was to prevent the use of governmental force to search a man's house, his person, his papers, and his effects, and to prevent their seizure against his will. . . .

The Amendment itself shows that the search is to be of material things—the person, the house, his papers or his effects. The description of the warrant necessary to make the proceeding lawful is that it must specify the place to be searched and the person or *things* to be seized. . . .

The Amendment does not forbid what was done here. There was no searching. There was no seizure. The evidence was secured by the use of the sense of hearing and that only. There was no entry of the houses or offices of the defendants. . . .

The language of the Amendment can not be extended and expanded to include telephone wires reaching to the whole world from the defendant's house or office. . . .

Congress may, of course, protect the secrecy of telephone messages by making them, when intercepted, inadmissible in evidence in Federal criminal trials. . . . But the courts may not adopt such a policy by attributing an enlarged and unusual meaning to the 4th Amendment.[81]

In dissent Justice Oliver Wendell Holmes, Jr., wrote, "[A]part from the Constitution, the government ought not to use evidence obtained, and only obtainable, by a criminal act. . . . I think it a less evil that some criminals should escape than that the government should play an ignoble part."[82]

Justice Louis D. Brandeis also dissented, arguing that wiretapping was clearly a search within the meaning of the Fourth Amendment, which he described as intended to protect "the sanctities of a man's home and the privacies of life." He added that the Fourth Amendment guarantee must, to retain its validity, be read with an awareness of new threats to the security it was intended to protect:

Subtler and more far-reaching means of invading privacy have become available to the government. Discovery and invention have made it possible for the government, by means far more effective than stretching upon the rack, to obtain disclosure in court of what is whispered in the closet.

Furthermore, Brandeis argued, wiretapping was itself a crime under federal law, and government agents should not be allowed to commit crimes to catch criminals:

Decency, security, and liberty alike demand that government officials shall be subjected to the same rules of conduct that are commands to the citizen. In a government of laws, existence of the government will be imperiled if it fails to observe the law scrupulously. Our government is the potent, the omnipresent, teacher. For good or ill, it teaches the whole people by its example. Crime is contagious. If the government becomes a law-breaker, it breeds contempt for law; it invites every man to become a law unto himself; it invites anarchy. To declare that in the administration of the criminal law the end justifies the means—to declare that the government may commit crimes in order to secure the conviction of a private criminal— would bring terrible retribution. Against that pernicious doctrine this court should resolutely set its face.[83]

In 1934 Congress included in the Federal Communications Act the statement that "no person not being authorized by the sender shall intercept any communication and divulge or publish the existence, contents, substance, purport, effect or meaning of such intercepted communication to any person."

Three years later, in *Nardone v. United States*, the Court read this provision as forbidding federal agents, as well as all other persons, to intercept and disclose telephone messages by the use of wiretaps. In that and a similar case in 1939, the Court excluded from use in federal courts any evidence obtained, directly or indirectly, from wiretaps.[84]

Two wartime rulings announced in 1942, however, allowed some use of evidence obtained by electronic surveillance. In *Goldstein v. United States* the Court held that wiretap evidence could be used against persons other than those whose conversations had been overheard. And in *Goldman v. United States* the Court held that the use of a "bug"—an electronic listening device, not a wiretap on telephone lines—was not in violation of the Communications Act provision, which applied only to actual interference with communication wires and telephone lines.[85]

In 1961, however, the Court began to take a tougher view of electronic surveillance as an impermissible intrusion into personal privacy. In *Silverman v. United States* the Court held that the Fourth Amendment was violated by the use of a "spike-mike" driven into a building wall to allow police to overhear conversations within the building. The fact that the device, although tiny, actually penetrated the building wall was sufficient to constitute physical intrusion in violation of the search-and-seizure provision.[86]

Six years later, the Court finally abandoned *Olmstead* and brought electronic surveillance of all types within the proscription of the Fourth Amendment.

Katz v. United States involved evidence obtained by government agents who placed a listening device on the outside of a public telephone booth and through it obtained information from telephone conversations which led to the prosecution of individuals involved in illegal book-making activities.[87]

Justice Stewart explained: "The fact that the electronic device employed ... did not happen to penetrate the wall of the booth can have no constitutional significance."[88] He continued:

the Fourth Amendment protects people, not places. What a person knowingly exposes to the public, even in his own home or office, is not a subject of Fourth Amendment protection.... But what he seeks to preserve as private, even in an area accessible to the public, may be constitutionally protected....

Students and Bureaucrats

In the mid-1980s the Court for the first time explicitly applied the Fourth Amendment's guarantee to public school students and government workers.

In each case, however, the application seemed a hollow victory—at least to the particular students and workers involved in the cases of *New Jersey v. T. L. O.* and *O'Connor v. Ortega*. The Court, having applied the constitutional guarantee, found that in both the environment of a school and a government office, certain searches did not require warrants.

In *New Jersey v. T. L. O.* the Court held that school officials did not need a search warrant or probable cause to conduct a reasonable search of a student. Instead, wrote Justice Byron R. White for the Court, school officials may search a student so long as "there are reasonable grounds for suspecting that the search will turn up evidence that the student has violated or is violating either the law or the rules of the school." (469 U.S. 325, 1985).

Two years later, the Court in *O'Connor v. Ortega* declared that "individuals do not lose Fourth Amendment rights merely because they work for the government instead of a private employer." But Justice Sandra Day O'Connor went on to say that supervisors do not need warrants for searching desk drawers and office files for routine work-related purposes or to investigate work-related misconduct. (__ U.S. __, 1987)

... [W]hat he [Katz] sought to exclude when he entered the booth was not the intruding eye—it was the uninvited ear. He did not shed his right to do so simply because he made his calls from a place where he might be seen.[89]

Two years later, in 1969, the Court made clear its intention of penalizing government agents for engaging in improper electronic surveillance. In *Alderman v. United States, Butenko v. United States,* and *Ivanov v. United States,* the Court held that the government must turn over all material obtained by illegal surveillance to the defendant whose Fourth Amendment rights had been violated by its collection and against whom such evidence might be used. The defendant could then examine the information to ascertain what parts of it the government might plan to use against him and to challenge its use.[90]

The government, dismayed by this ruling, chose to drop a number of prosecutions rather than disclose the method and the content of some particular instances of surveillance.

Following *Katz,* Congress in the 1968 Crime Control and Safe Streets Act provided statutory authorization for federal use of judicially approved electronic surveillance. The law set out procedures to be followed by federal agents in obtaining approval for such surveillance, first from Justice Department officials and then from a federal judge who would issue a warrant for this type of search and seizure.

The law provided that applications for warrants must be approved either by the attorney general himself or by a specially designated assistant attorney general.[91]

Twice in the 1970s the Court signaled its determination to apply the warrant requirement to wiretaps at least as strictly as it applied it to other types of searches. In 1972 the Court unanimously rejected the contention of the Nixon administration that the 1968 law did not require judicial approval of warrants for wiretaps or surveillance in national security cases.[92] Two years later, the Court effectively nullified hundreds of criminal prosecutions based on evidence obtained by surveillance with its finding that Attorney General John N. Mitchell had not himself signed the applications for the warrants authorizing the surveillance and had allowed an aide other than the designated assistant attorney general to approve the applications.[93]

In 1979, however, the Court held that because Congress must have recognized that most electronic bugs can only be installed by agents who secretly enter the premises, warrants authorizing such surveillance need not explicitly authorize covert entry.[94]

Notes

1. *Wolf v. Colorado*, 338 U.S. 25 at 27-28 (1949).
2. *Camara v. Municipal Court*, 387 U.S. 523 at 528-529 (1967).
3. *GM Leasing Corporation v. United States*, 429 U.S. 338 (1977); *Michigan v. Tyler*, 436 U.S. 499 (1978); *Mincey v. Arizona*, 437 U.S. 385 (1978); but see also *Oliver v. United States, Maine v. Thornton*, 466 U.S. 170 (1984); *California v. Ciraolo*, 476 U.S. 207 (1986), *Dow Chemical v. United States*, 476 U.S. 227 (1986).
4. *Wolf v. Colorado*, 338 U.S. 25 (1949).
5. *Mapp v. Ohio*, 367 U.S. 643 (1961).
6. *Ker v. California*, 374 U.S. 23 (1963).
7. *Johnson v. United States*, 333 U.S. 10 at 13-14 (1948).
8. *Coolidge v. New Hampshire*, 403 U.S. 443 at 453 (1971); see also *Lo-Ji Sales v. New York*, 442 U.S. 319 (1979).
9. *Shadwick v. City of Tampa, Fla.*, 407 U.S. 345 at 350 (1972).
10. *Locke v. United States*, 7 Cr. 339 at 348 (1813); see *Arizona v. Hicks*, __ U.S. __ (1987) for Court's continued insistence upon "probable cause."
11. *Dumbra v. United States*, 268 U.S. 435 at 441 (1925); see also *Byars v. United States*, 273 U.S. 28 (1927); *Draper v. United States*, 358 U.S. 307 (1959).
12. *Nathanson v. United States*, 290 U.S. 41 at 47 (1933); see also *Giordanello v. United States*, 357 U.S. 480 (1958); *Aguilar v. Texas*, 378 U.S. 108 (1964); *Spinelli v. United States*, 393 U.S. 410 (1969); *United States v. Ventresca*, 380 U.S. 102 at 108-109 (1965).
13. *Jones v. United States*, 362 U.S. 257 (1960).
14. *Rugendorf v. United States*, 367 U.S. 528 (1964); *McCray v. Illinois*, 386 U.S. 300 (1967); see also *Whitely v. Warden*, 401 U.S. 560 (1971); *United States v. Harris*, 403 U.S. 573 (1971); *Adams v. Williams*, 407 U.S. 143 (1972).
15. *Franks v. Delaware*, 438 U.S. 154 at 168 (1978).
16. *Schneckloth v. Bustamonte*, 412 U.S. 218 at 248-249 (1973).
17. Id. at 277.
18. *United States v. Matlock*, 415 U.S. 164 (1974).
19. *Boyd v. United States*, 116 U.S. 616 (1886).
20. Id. at 630, 633.
21. *Weeks v. United States*, 232 U.S. 383 (1914).
22. Id. at 392-393.
23. *Gouled v. United States*, 255 U.S. 298 (1921).
24. Id. at 309.
25. *Warden v. Hayden*, 387 U.S. 294 (1967).
26. Id. at 301-302.
27. Id. at 304, 306.
28. Id. at 306-307.
29. Id. at 309-310.
30. Id. at 320.
31. Id. at 323.
32. Id. at 325.
33. *United States v. Miller*, 425 U.S. 435 (1976).
34. *Andresen v. Maryland*, 427 U.S. 463 (1976).
35. *Zurcher v. The Stanford Daily*, 436 U.S. 547 at 554 (1978).
36. Id. at 579.
37. Id. at 581-583.
38. *Ex parte Burford*, 3 Cr. 448 (1805); *Kurtz v. Moffitt*, 115 U.S. 487 (1885).
39. *Carroll v. United States*, 267 U.S. 132 at 156 (1925).
40. *Gerstein v. Pugh*, 420 U.S. 103 at 113 (1975).
41. *Ker v. California*, 374 U.S. 23 (1963).
42. *Davis v. Mississippi*, 394 U.S. 721 at 727 (1969); *Dunaway v. New York*, 442 U.S. 200 (1979).
43. *United States v. Watson*, 423 U.S. 411 (1976).
44. Id. at 423-424.
45. Id. at 447.
46. *United States v. Santana*, 427 U.S. 38 (1976); see *Johnson v. United States*, 333 U.S. 10 at 16, note 7 (1948) for use of the term "hot pursuit."
47. *United States v. Santana*, 427 U.S. 38 at 42-43 (1976).
48. *Payton v. New York, Riddick v. New York*, 445 U.S. 573 (1980); see also *Welsh v. Wisconsin*, 466 U.S. 740 (1984).
49. *Agnello v. United States*, 269 U.S. 20 at 30 (1925); *Marron v. United States* 275 U.S. 192 (1927).
50. *Harris v. United States*, 331 U.S. 145 (1947)
51. Id. at 150-151.
52. Id. at 183.
53. *Trupiano v. United States*, 334 U.S. 699 at 706 (1948).
54. Id. at 708.
55. Ibid.
56. *McDonald v. United States*, 335 U.S. 451 at 454, 456 (1948).
57. *United States v. Rabinowitz*, 339 U.S. 56 at 66 (1950).
58. Id. at 63, 66.
59. *Kremen v. United States*, 353 U.S. 346 (1957); *Abel v. United States*, 362 U.S. 217 at 238 (1960); *Chapman v. United States*, 365 U.S. 610 (1961); *Ker v. California*, 374 U.S. 23 (1963).
60. *Chimel v. California*, 395 U.S. 752 (1969).
61. Id. at 766, 768.
62. Id. at 780.
63. *Vale v. Louisiana*, 399 U.S. 30 (1970).
64. *Coolidge v. New Hampshire*, 403 U.S. 443 (1971); see also *United States v. Edwards*, 415 U.S. 800 (1974).
65. *United States v. Robinson*, 414 U.S. 218 (1973); *Gustafson v. Florida*, 414 U.S. 260 (1973).
66. *Carroll v. United States*, 267 U.S. 132 (1925).
67. Id. at 153.
68. *Husty v. United States*, 282 U.S. 694 (1931); see also *Scher v. United States*, 305 U.S. 251 (1938).
69. *United States v. Di Re*, 332 U.S. 581 (1948).
70. *Brinegar v. United States*, 338 U.S. 160 (1949); see also *California v. Carney*, 471 U.S. 386 (1985).
71. *Henry v. United States*, 361 U.S. 98 (1959); *Rios v. United States*, 364 U.S. 253 (1960).
72. *Cooper v. California*, 386 U.S. 58 (1967).
73. *Chambers v. Maroney*, 399 U.S. 42 (1970); *Preston v. United States*, 376 U.S. 364 (1964).
74. *Cady v. Dombrowski*, 413 U.S. 433 (1973); *South Dakota v. Opperman*, 428 U.S. 364 (1976).
75. *Cardwell v. Lewis*, 417 U.S. 583 (1974).
76. *Rakas v. Illinois*, 439 U.S. 128 (1978).
77. Id. at 409.
78. *Delaware v. Prouse*, 440 U.S. 648 (1979).
79. *Robbins v. California*, 453 U.S. 420 (1981).
80. *United States v. Ross*, 456 U.S. 798 (1982).

81. *Olmstead v. United States*, 277 U.S. 438 at 463-466 (1928).

82. Id. at 469-470.

83. Id. at 473, 485.

84. *Nardone v. United States*, 302 U.S. 379 (1937); *Weiss v. United States*, 308 U.S. 321 (1939); *Nardone v. United States*, 308 U.S. 338 (1939); see also *Rathbun v. United States*, 355 U.S. 107 (1957); *Benanti v. United States*, 355 U.S. 96 (1957).

85. *Goldstein v. United States*, 316 U.S. 114 (1942); *Goldman v. United States*, 316 U.S. 129 (1942); see also *On Lee v. United States*, 343 U.S. 747 (1952).

86. *Silverman v. United States*, 365 U.S. 505 (1961); see also *Wong Sun v. United States*, 371 U.S. 471 (1963); *Berger v. New York*, 388 U.S. 41 (1967); *Osborn v. United States*, 385 U.S. 323 (1966).

87. *Katz v. United States*, 389 U.S. 247 (1967).

88. Id. at 353.

89. Id. at 351.

90. *Alderman v. United States, Butenko v. United States, Ivanov v. United States*, 394 U.S. 165 (1969).

91. Congressional Quarterly, *Congress and the Nation*, vol. II (Washington, D.C.: Congressional Quarterly, 1969), 326-327.

92. *United States v. U.S. District Court*, 407 U.S. 297 (1972).

93. *United States v. Giordano*, 416 U.S. 505 (1974).

94. *Dalia v. United States*, 441 U.S. 238 (1979).

9

Self-Incrimination

The fundamental meaning of the Fifth Amendment privilege against self-incrimination is clear: no one "shall be compelled in any criminal case to be a witness against himself."

A person may not be forced to confess, required to testify, or provide evidence that could convict him. When charged with a crime, an individual defendant is free to plead not guilty. And no inference of guilt may be drawn either from his decision not to testify at his own trial or to remain silent when interrogated by police.[1]

The privilege is not an absolute right to silence. The right must be claimed; it is waived unless invoked. And when it is claimed, a judge decides whether its assertion is justified.[2] The accused waives that right when he agrees to testify in his own defense, and thus becomes subject to cross-examination.

A witness called to testify before a grand jury, a congressional committee, or an administrative hearing risks a contempt citation if he refuses to appear. Once on the stand, however, he may refuse to answer particular questions on the grounds that the answers will tend to incriminate him.[3] But he may not assert the privilege just because he fears other adverse consequences of his testimony, such as public ridicule or general disrepute.[4]

And once incriminating facts have been revealed voluntarily, a witness cannot then assert his Fifth Amendment privilege to avoid disclosure of further details.[5]

The privilege is a personal one and may not be invoked to protect anyone else. It is to be asserted only by "natural" persons, not by corporations, labor unions, or other organizations.[6] Individuals in possession of public records or those of an organization cannot claim the Fifth Amendment privilege to protect those records, even if they contain information incriminating to the witness. Only purely personal and private documents and papers in the possession of the owner are protected by the privilege.[7]

The Court has affirmed repeatedly that innocent persons as well as guilty ones may invoke this privilege. In doing so, the Court rejects the assumption that anyone who "takes the Fifth" must be guilty. The Court has declared it unconstitutional for a state to punish employees who refuse to testify about employment-related activities, after being ordered to waive their privilege against self-incrimination.

It has reversed convictions of public employees based on testimony obtained through such coercion, and held that states may not fire persons just because they invoke this privilege.[8] (Details, pp. 148-150)

Congress, in the course of regulating certain forms of business and political activity found highly susceptible to illegal diversion or influence, has passed a number of federal laws requiring detailed records, reports, registration, and/or tax payments related to membership in some groups, to drug and firearms transactions, and to gambling.

Until the 1960s the Court generally upheld such registration and tax provisions,[9] but beginning with its decision in the Communist party registration case of *Albertson v. Subversive Activities Control Board* in 1965, the Court held that compliance with such requirements violated the Fifth Amendment.[10] (Details, pp. 141-142)

In the late 1960s and early 1970s the Court struck down many of these registration provisions on Fifth Amendment grounds. Congress subsequently rewrote some of the offending laws to omit the self-incriminatory provisions.[11]

PRIVILEGE AND IMMUNITY

Immunity statutes, in use throughout American history, represent the government's effort to reconcile its need for information with the Fifth Amendment privilege against compelled self-incrimination.

These laws protect individuals who furnish information to the government from prosecutions based on their own coerced testimony. Most immunity laws contain an exception for perjury: if the immunized witness provides false information, he is subject to prosecution for perjury using his words.

Justice Lewis F. Powell, Jr., noted once that immunity laws "seek a rational accommodation between the imperatives of the privilege and the legitimate demands of government to compel citizens to testify." [12]

The modern Court has condoned as constitutional a narrower form of immunity than that approved during the nineteenth century. Early statutes allowed immunization of witnesses from prosecution for any crime revealed in their testimony, a so-called "immunity bath." Later statutes, however, allowed some indirect use of immunized testimony to obtain other evidence of the witness' wrongdoing.

In 1892, in one of its earliest rulings concerning the Fifth Amendment privilege, the Supreme Court held this more limited immunity insufficient protection for the witness. In *Counselman v. Hitchcock* the Court unanimously ordered the release from custody of Charles Counselman, a railroad official, held in contempt of court after he declined to answer certain questions from a grand jury, asserting his constitutional privilege against compelled self-incrimination. Counselman challenged his detention as a violation of his Fifth Amendment rights and sought release through a writ of *habeas corpus.* The Supreme Court agreed with his challenge.

In its opinion, written by Justice Samuel Blatchford, the Court held that grand jury witnesses, as well as persons already charged with crimes, could assert this privilege.

In addition, the Court found this limited immunity, which left the witness still subject to indirect use of his testimony against him, insufficient because it "does not supply a complete protection from all the perils against which the constitutional prohibition was designed to guard, and is not a full substitute for that prohibition." [13]

"In view of the constitutional provision," concluded Justice Blatchford, "a statutory enactment, to be valid, must afford absolute immunity against future prosecution for the offense to which the question relates." [14]

This decision was interpreted as a requirement that immunity must protect a witness from all prosecution for the criminal "transactions" revealed in immunized testimony, not just against the "use" of the testimony itself as evidence.

Concerned that the Fifth Amendment privilege could be used to block inquiry into alleged violations of the Interstate Commerce Act, Congress in 1892 provided that witnesses appearing in Interstate Commerce Commission investigations could be granted this type of "transactional" immunity.

In 1896, by a 5-4 vote, the Court upheld the new law in *Brown v. Walker.* In so doing, the Court made clear that the privilege was to be claimed only to protect the witness himself, not any third party, and only to protect him from prosecution, not simply from "personal odium and disgrace."

The Court upheld Brown's contempt sentence. A railway company auditor, he refused to answer certain questions from a grand jury, claiming his Fifth Amendment privilege. The Court held that this assertion was not appropriate, since the privilege was being claimed to shield others from prosecution.

Justice Henry B. Brown viewed the privilege as meaning only that the witness was secure from criminal prosecution. This interpretation, he said, established an appropriate equilibrium between the private right and the public welfare.

The clause of the Constitution in question is obviously susceptible of two interpretations. If it be construed literally, as authorizing the witness to refuse to disclose any fact that might tend to incriminate, disgrace, or expose him to unfavorable comments, then, as he must necessarily to a large extent determine upon his own conscience and responsibility whether his answer to the proposed question will have that tendency ... the practical result would be, that no one could be compelled to testify to a material fact in a criminal case.... If, upon the other hand, the object of the provision be to secure the witness against a criminal prosecution, which might be aided directly or indirectly by his disclosure, then, if no such prosecution be possible,—in other words, if his testimony operate as a complete pardon for the offense to which it relates,—a statute absolutely securing to him such immunity from prosecution would satisfy the demands of the clause in question. ...

It can only be said in general that the clause should be construed, as it was doubtless designed, to effect a practical and beneficent purpose—not necessarily to protect witnesses against every possible detriment which might happen to them from their testimony, nor to unduly impede, hinder, or obstruct the administration of criminal justice....

The design of the constitutional privilege is not to aid the witness in vindicating his character but to protect him against being compelled to furnish evidence to convict him of a criminal charge.... While the constitutional provision in question is justly regarded as one of the most valuable prerogatives of the citizen, its object is fully accomplished by the statutory immunity, and we are therefore of opinion that the witness was compellable to answer.[15]

The issue of what constituted true immunity was again raised during the 1950s when the Eisenhower administration proposed, and Congress approved, the Immunity Act of 1954. Its purpose was to prevent witnesses, called to testify in government subversion inquiries, from refusing to answer questions on grounds of self-incrimination. The act granted immunity from prosecution for criminal activity revealed during compelled testimony.

But the law was challenged in congressional testimony by Communist party members who alleged that the 1954 act did not provide true immunity in light of the many disabilities—including loss of employment and public criticism—imposed on party members.

In 1956 the Court upheld the 1954 act in *Ullmann v. United States.* Justice Felix Frankfurter, citing *Brown v. Walker,* described the 1893 immunity statute upheld in *Brown* as now "part of our constitutional fabric." [16] Frankfurter continued:

We are not dealing here with one of the vague, undefinable, admonitory provisions of the Constitution whose scope is inevitably addressed to changing circumstances.... [T]he history of the privilege establishes not only that it is not to be interpreted literally, but also that its sole concern is ... with the danger to a witness forced to give testimony leading to the infliction of "penalties affixed to the criminal acts." ... Immunity displaces the danger. Once the reason for the privilege ceases, the privilege ceases.[17]

Justices William O. Douglas and Hugo L. Black dissented, urging the Court to overrule *Brown v. Walker* and adopt the literal view "that the right of silence created by the Fifth Amendment is beyond the reach of Congress.[18] Douglas wrote:

the Fifth Amendment was written in part to prevent any Congress, any court, and any prosecutor from prying open the lips of an accused to make incriminating statements against his will. The Fifth Amendment protects the conscience and the dignity of the individual, as well as his safety and security, against the compulsion of the government....

The critical point is that the Constitution places the right of silence *beyond the reach of government.* The Fifth Amendment stands between the citizen and his government. When public opinion casts a person into the outer darkness, as happens today when a person is exposed as a Communist, the government brings infamy on the head of the witness when it compels disclosure. That is precisely what the Fifth Amendment prohibits.[19]

In the Organized Crime Control Act of 1970, Congress approved a more limited grant of "use" immunity to witnesses in organized crime cases. Rather than providing immunity from prosecution for any offense in which the witness was implicated through his testimony, the law simply forbade the use of any of his compelled testimony or derivative evidence against him. Under the 1970 Act, however, a witness could be prosecuted for crimes mentioned in his testimony if the evidence used in the prosecution was developed independently of his testimony.[20]

In *Kastigar v. United States* the Court found this narrower "use" immunity constitutional.

The privilege has never been construed to mean that one who invokes it cannot subsequently be prosecuted. Its sole concern is to afford protection against being forced to give testimony leading to the infliction of "penalties affixed to . . . criminal acts." Immunity from the use of compelled testimony, as well as evidence derived directly and indirectly therefrom affords this protection.[21]

The Court found this use immunity sufficient, because the law required the state—in prosecuting an immunized witness—to show that its evidence had not been derived from his immunized testimony.

Justice Powell wrote:

A person accorded this immunity . . . and subsequently prosecuted, is not dependent for the preservation of his rights upon the integrity and good faith of the prosecuting authorities. . . . This burden of proof which we reaffirm as appropriate . . . imposes on the prosecution the affirmative duty to prove that the evidence it proposes to use is derived from a legitimate source wholly independent of the compelled testimony.[22]

Justices Douglas and Thurgood Marshall dissented. Douglas wrote:

When we allow the prosecution to offer only "use" immunity we allow it to grant far less than it has taken away. For while the precise testimony that is compelled may not be used, leads from that testimony may be pursued and used to convict the witness. My view is that the Framers put it beyond the power of Congress to *compel* anyone to confess his crimes. . . . Government acts in an ignoble way when it stoops to the end which we authorize today.[23]

PROTECTIONS EXTENDED

Twice—in 1908 and 1947—the Supreme Court rejected arguments that the due process guarantee of the Fourteenth Amendment extended the privilege against self-incrimination to state defendants. In both cases the Court permitted state officials to draw unfavorable inferences from a defendant's failure to testify in his own behalf.

In *Twining v. New Jersey,* decided in 1908, the Court stated that the privilege was not inherent in due process, but "separate from and independent of" it.[24] In 1947 the Court reaffirmed this stance with its decision in *Adamson v. California,* refusing to find the privilege essential to a system of "ordered liberty." [25]

Furthermore, the Court in several cases held that the Fifth Amendment did not protect an individual from a state's use of testimony compelled by federal authority or from federal use of testimony compelled by state authority.[26]

But in 1964 in *Malloy v. Hogan* the Court reconsidered *Twining* and *Adamson* and declared that the Fifth Amendment guarantee against self-incrimination did extend to state proceedings.

Malloy, convicted of illegal gambling activities, refused to testify before a state investigation of gambling operations in Hartford County, Connecticut. Malloy claimed that to testify would compel him to incriminate himself. He was held in contempt and sentenced to prison.

Malloy appealed, but the Connecticut supreme court held that the Fifth Amendment's privilege against self-incrimination was not available to a witness in a state proceeding.

The Supreme Court, 5-4, reversed the state court and upheld Malloy's claim, holding that the Fourteenth Amendment guaranteed him the protection of the Fifth Amendment's privilege against self-incrimination.

Justice William J. Brennan, Jr., wrote the majority opinion, declaring:

The Fourteenth Amendment secures against state invasion the same privilege that the Fifth Amendment guarantees against federal infringement—the right of a person to remain silent unless he chooses to speak in the unfettered exercise of his own will, and to suffer no penalty . . . for such silence. . . .

It would be incongruous to have different standards determine the validity of a claim of privilege based on the same feared prosecution, depending on whether the claim was asserted in a state or federal court. Therefore, the same standards must determine whether an accused's silence in either a federal or state proceeding is justified. . . . It must be considered irrelevant that the petitioner was a witness in a statutory inquiry and not a defendant in a criminal prosecution, for it has long been settled that the privilege protects witnesses in similar federal inquiries.[27]

Justices Byron R. White, Potter Stewart, John Marshall Harlan, and Tom C. Clark dissented from what they viewed as the step-by-step incorporation of the first eight amendments under the due process clause of the Fourteenth Amendment. Justice Harlan wrote:

> The consequence of such an approach ... is inevitable disregard of all relevant differences which may exist between state and federal criminal law and its enforcement. ...

The Court's approach in the present case is in fact nothing more or less than "incorporation" in snatches. If, however, the Due Process Clause *is* something more than a reference to the Bill of Rights and protects only those rights which derive from fundamental principles ... it is just as contrary to precedent and just as illogical to incorporate the provisions of the Bill of Rights one at a time as it is to incorporate them all at once.[28]

On the same day the Court announced its decision in *Malloy v. Hogan*—June 15, 1964—it decided *Murphy v.*

Justice and the Plea Bargain ...

The plea bargain, in which a defendant exchanges a plea of guilty for a prosecutor's promise of less severe punishment than could be expected after trial—has become a fixture of the American system of criminal justice. It has been described as "a mainstay of the criminal justice system in state and federal courts where 80 percent or more of the serious cases and 90 percent or more of the less serious offenses are resolved through pleas of guilty."[1]

There is no constitutional or statutory basis for plea bargaining. Its origin and survival are based on sheer pragmatism.

As the Supreme Court explained in 1977:

> Properly administered, they [plea bargains] can benefit all concerned. The defendant avoids extended pretrial incarceration and the anxieties and uncertainties of a trial; he gains a speedy disposition of his case, the chance to acknowledge his guilt, and a prompt start in realizing whatever potential there may be for rehabilitation. Judges and prosecutors conserve vital and scarce resources. The public is protected from the risks posed by those charged with criminal offenses who are at large on bail while awaiting completion of criminal proceedings.[2]

Formal Recognition

In 1970 the Court for the first time formally recognized the practice of plea bargaining. In *Brady v. United States* the Court upheld its use, finding that it provided a "mutuality of advantage" for the state and for the defendant.[3]

Brady was charged with kidnapping under provisions of a federal law that provided for imposition of the death sentence for that crime upon the recommendation of a jury after trial. He pleaded guilty, foregoing trial and ensuring that he would not receive the death penalty.

Two years earlier the Court in *United States v. Jackson* had struck down that portion of the federal kidnapping law under which Brady had been charged, arguing that by allowing a death sentence *only* after trial, the law had the "inevitable effect" of penalizing both the exercise of the Fifth Amendment right *not* to plead guilty and the Sixth Amendment

right to trial by jury.[4] Brady cited this ruling in challenging his conviction, claiming that his guilty plea was invalid because it was "coerced" by unconstitutional provisions and by his desire to avoid the death penalty.

With Justice Byron R. White as its spokesman, the Court unanimously sustained the plea bargaining process and Brady's conviction:

> For a defendant who sees slight possibility of acquittal, the advantages of pleading guilty and limiting the probable penalty are obvious—his exposure is reduced, the correctional processes can begin immediately, and the practical burdens of a trial are eliminated. For the State there are also advantages—the more promptly imposed punishment after an admission of guilt may more effectively attain the objective of punishment; and with the avoidance of trial scarce judicial and prosecutorial resources are conserved. ...
>
> [W]e cannot hold that it is unconstitutional for the State to extend a benefit to a defendant who in turn extends a substantial benefit to the State and who demonstrates by his plea that he is ready and willing to admit his crime.[5]

Keeping the Bargain

In later rulings the Court has emphasized that guilty pleas are admissible only if knowingly and voluntarily made—although it has condoned some forms of pressure in plea negotiations—and it has usually required prosecutors to keep their bargains.

In *Santobello v. New York* the Court in 1971 held that the state's failure to keep its commitment to recommend a reduced sentence in exchange for a guilty plea required that the defendant be given the opportunity for a trial.

Chief Justice Warren E. Burger wrote:

> his phase of the process of criminal justice and the adjudicative element in accepting a plea of guilty, must be attended by safeguards to insure the defendant what is reasonably due in the circumstances. Those circumstances will vary, but a constant factor is that when a plea rests in any significant degree on a promise or agreement

The Waterfront Commission of New York Harbor. In that case the Court said the Fifth Amendment protects a state witness against incrimination under federal as well as state law and a federal witness against incrimination under state as well as federal law. Immunity granted under federal law protects against state prosecution and vice versa.

Murphy, subpoenaed to testify about a work stoppage at New Jersey piers, refused to answer questions on the grounds that his answers would tend to incriminate him. Granted immunity under New York and New Jersey laws, Murphy still refuscd to testify because the immunity failed to protect him from federal prosecution. The court held Murphy in contempt.

The Supreme Court vacated the contempt judgment. Justice Arthur J. Goldberg's opinion for a unanimous Court set out the constitutional rule:

... A Guilty Plea, a Lesser Penalty

of the prosecutor, so that it can be said to be part of the inducement or consideration, such promise must be fulfilled.[6]

Two years later the Court in *Tollett v. Henderson* refused to allow a defendant who had pleaded guilty to murder to challenge his conviction by arguing that the grand jury that indicted him was unfairly selected.

Justice William H. Rehnquist explained that a guilty plea represented a break in the chain of events that preceded it: "When a criminal defendant has solemnly admitted in open court that he is in fact guilty of the offense with which he is charged, he may not thereafter raise independent claims relating to the deprivation of constitutional rights that occurred prior to the entry of the plea." [7]

In a similar vein, the Court in 1984 refused in *Mabry v. Johnson* to rule that once a plea bargain was made, a defendant had a constitutional right to have it enforced. If a prosecutor decides to withdraw the bargain before a plea of guilty is entered, that withdrawal cannot serve as the basis for challenging a later guilty plea entered in keeping with another, less favorable, plea bargain. In 1987 the Court held in *Ricketts v. Adamson* that when a defendant breaches a plea bargain and refuses to testify against others a second time, as he had promised, the state does not breach the double jeopardy guarantee when it prosecutes him for murder—even though he has already pleaded guilty to a lesser offense and begun serving time.[8]

Permissible Pressure

To be valid, a guilty plea must be voluntarily made and entered with full knowledge of its implications. The Court set aside a second-degree murder conviction of a man who pleaded guilty without realizing that he was admitting that he *intended* to kill his victim, holding that a defendant's failure to receive adequate notice of the offense to which he pleaded guilty resulted in an involuntary plea.[9]

The Court held in 1978, however, that due process does not deprive the prosecutor of valid bargaining tools. By a 5-4 vote, the justices backed a prosecutor's threat of an additional justified indictment if the defendant did not accept a plea bargain.

The Court announced this decision in *Bordenkircher v. Hayes.* Hayes had two prior felony convictions and had been charged with a third felony. In plea negotiations the prosecutor offered to recommend a reduced sentence in return for a guilty plea—and threatened that if the bargain was not accepted he would reindict Hayes under a "habitual criminal" law that would have made him subject to a mandatory life sentence if convicted.

Hayes rejected the bargain, was reindicted, convicted, and received a life sentence. He challenged the prosecutor's actions as "vindictive"; the Court rejected that challenge.

Justice Potter Stewart explained that

in the "give-and-take" of plea bargaining, there is no ... element of punishment or retaliation so long as the accused is free to accept or reject the prosecutor's offer....

There is no doubt that the breadth of discretion that our country's legal system vests in prosecuting attorneys carries with it the potential for both individual and institutional abuse. And broad though that discretion may be, there are undoubtedly constitutional limits upon its exercise. We hold only that the course of conduct engaged in by the prosecutor in this case, which no more than openly presented the defendant with the unpleasant alternatives of foregoing trial or facing charges on which he was plainly subject to prosecution, did not violate the Due Process Clause of the Fourteenth Amendment.[10]

1. Alpheus T. Mason and William M. Beaney, *American Constitutional Law,* 6th ed. (Englewood Cliffs N.J.: Prentice-Hall 1978), 669.
2. *Blackledge v. Allison,* 431 U.S. 63 at 71 (1977).
3. *Brady v. United States,* 397 U.S. 742 at 752 (1970); see also *Boykin v. Alabama,* 395 U.S. 238 (1969).
4. *United States v. Jackson,* 390 U.S. 570 (1968).
5. *Brady v. United States,* 397 U.S. 742 at 752-753 (1970); see also *North Carolina v. Alford,* 400 U.S. 25 (1970).
6. *Santobello v. New York,* 404 U.S. 257 at 262 (1971).
7. *Tollett v. Henderson,* 411 U.S. 258 at 267 (1973).
8. *Mabry v. Johnson,* 467 U.S. 504 (1984); *Ricketts v. Adamson,* ___ U.S. ___ (1987).
9. *Henderson v. Morgan,* 426 U.S. 637 (1976).
10. *Bordenkircher v. Hayes,* 434 U.S. 357 at 363, 365 (1978); see also *Corbitt v. New Jersey,* 439 U.S. 212 (1978).

a state witness may not be compelled to give testimony which may be incriminating under federal law unless the compelled testimony and its fruits cannot be used in any manner by federal officials in connection with a criminal prosecution against him. We conclude, moreover, that in order to implement this constitutional rule and accommodate the interests of the State and Federal Governments in investigating and prosecuting crime, the Federal Government must be prohibited from making any such use of compelled testimony and its fruits.[29]

The following year, the Court reinforced the *Malloy* ruling with *Griffin v. California*. Effectively reversing *Twining* and *Adamson* in their specific holdings concerning judicial or prosecutorial comment on the silence of defendants, the Court held that the Fifth Amendment "forbids either comment by the prosecution on the accused's silence or instructions by the Court that such silence is evidence of guilt."[30]

Writing for the Court in *Griffin*, Justice Douglas explained:

> comment on the refusal to testify is a remnant of the "inquisitorial system of criminal justice," . . . which the Fifth Amendment outlaws. It is a penalty imposed by courts for exercising a constitutional privilege. It cuts down on the privilege by making its assertion costly.[31]

COERCED CONFESSIONS

Confessions, the Court stated long ago, are "among the most effectual proofs in the law" but they are admissible as evidence only when given voluntarily.[32] This has long been the rule in federal courts, where the Fifth Amendment clearly applies.[33]

Since 1936 the same rule has governed the use of confessions in state courts. The inevitable question with which the Court has thus been faced time and again is how to determine when a confession is voluntary.

The first time the Court ruled on the use of confessions—in 1884—the Court defined as involuntary a confession that "appears to have been made, either in consequence of inducements of a temporal nature . . . or because of a threat or promise . . . which, operating upon the fears or hopes of the accused . . . deprive him of that freedom of will or self-control essential to make his confession voluntary within the meaning of the law."[34]

A dozen years later the Court restated the standard for determining when a confession was admissible: "The true test of admissibility is that the confession is made freely, voluntarily, and without compulsion or inducement of any sort."[35]

This test, as the Court acknowledged in 1897, had to be applied every time the use of a confession was challenged. The judge should consider "the circumstances surrounding, and the facts established to exist, in reference to the confession, in order to determine whether it was shown to have been voluntarily made." In all federal trials, the resolution of this issue was controlled by the Fifth Amend-

ment command that no person be compelled to incriminate himself.[36]

Delay in charging a suspect with a crime was one of the first factors pointed out by the Court as of significant value in making this determination. Several federal laws made clear that when a person was arrested, he should be taken promptly before a magistrate and charged. In 1943 the Supreme Court gave compelling force to this requirement by holding that confessions obtained after "unnecessary delay" in a suspect's arraignment could not be used as evidence in federal court.

In *McNabb v. United States* the Court overturned the convictions of several men for murdering a federal revenue agent. The most important elements in the prosecution's case were incriminating statements made by the defendants after three days of questioning by federal officers in the absence of any defense counsel and before they were formally charged with any crime.

The Court based its decision on the statutory requirements of prompt arraignment, and on the Court's general power to supervise the functioning of the federal judicial system, rather than on the Fifth Amendment.

Justice Frankfurter explained that the Court's supervisory role obligated it to establish and maintain "civilized standards of procedure and evidence" for federal courts.[37] The purpose of the ban on unnecessary delay between arrest and arraignment, he continued, was plain:

> A democratic society, in which respect for the dignity of all men is central, naturally guards against the misuse of the law enforcement process. Zeal in tracking down crime is not in itself an assurance of soberness of judgment. Disinterestedness in law enforcement does not alone prevent disregard of cherished liberties. Experience has therefore counseled that safeguards must be provided against the dangers of the overzealous as well as the despotic. The awful instruments of the criminal law cannot be entrusted to a single functionary. The complicated process of criminal justice is therefore divided into different parts, responsibility for which is separately vested in the various participants upon whom the criminal law relies for its vindication. Legislation . . . requiring that the police must with reasonable promptness show legal cause for detaining arrested persons, constitutes an important safeguard—not only in assuring protection for the innocent but also in securing conviction of the guilty by methods that commend themselves to a progressive and self-confident society. For this procedural requirement checks resort to those reprehensible practices known as the "third degree" which, though universally rejected as indefensible, still find their way into use. It aims to avoid all the evil implications of secret interrogation of persons accused of crime. It reflects not a sentimental but a sturdy view of law enforcement. It outlaws easy but self-defeating ways in which brutality is substituted for brains as an instrument of crime detection.[38]

The Federal Rules of Criminal Procedure subsequently incorporated this rule, and in 1957 the Court in *Mallory v. United States* reaffirmed its importance. In *Mallory* the Court nullified a death sentence imposed upon a rapist who "confessed" to the crime during a delay of more than eighteen hours between his arrest and his arraignment. The Court warned that such "unwarranted detention" could lead "to tempting utilization of intensive interrogation, easily gliding into the evils of 'the third degree' "—precisely what the rule was intended to avoid.[39]

Mallory generated fierce criticism and prompted Congress to revise the statutory rule to allow some use of evidence obtained during such delays. In 1968 Congress included in the Crime Control and Safe Streets Act a provision stating that delay in arraignment was not an absolute bar to federal use of a confession obtained during the period of delay.

Decades before it applied the Fifth Amendment to state action, the Supreme Court unanimously forbade states to use coerced confessions to convict persons of crimes.

The concept of basic fairness implicit in the Fourteenth Amendment guarantee of due process served as the basis for the Court's declaration of this prohibition in its 1936 ruling in *Brown v. Mississippi*. With that decision the Court for the first time overturned a state conviction because it was obtained by using a confession extracted by torture.

Mississippi defended its use of this confession by citing the 1908 decision in *Twining v. New Jersey*—that state defendants did not enjoy the protection of the Fifth Amendment privilege against compelled self-incrimination.

The Court rejected that defense, stating flatly that "the question of the right of the state to withdraw the privilege against self-incrimination is not here involved." [40] Chief Justice Charles Evans Hughes saw a distinction between "compulsion" forbidden by the Fifth Amendment and "compulsion" forbidden by the Fourteenth Amendment's due process clause.

> The compulsion to which the . . . [Fifth Amendment] refer[s] is that of the processes of justice by which the accused may be called as a witness and required to testify. Compulsion by torture to extort a confession is a different matter. . . .
>
> Because a state may dispense with a jury trial, it does not follow that it may substitute trial by ordeal. The rack and torture chamber may not be substituted for the witness stand. . . . It would be difficult to conceive of methods more revolting to the sense of justice than those taken to procure the confessions of these petitioners, and the use of the confessions thus obtained as the basis for conviction and sentence was a clear denial of due process.[41]

Over the next three decades the Court judged each case in which state use of a confession was challenged by looking at the "totality of the circumstances" surrounding the arrest and interrogation. In these cases Chief Justice Hughes's neat distinction between physical coercion and other forms of compulsion soon blurred.

In 1940 the Court affirmed *Brown* in *Chambers v. Florida*. In *Chambers* four black men had been convicted of murder on the basis of confessions obtained after days of being held incommunicado and interrogated by law enforcement officials. The unanimous Court overturned their convictions, acknowledging that psychological coercion, as well as physical torture, could produce involuntary confessions whose use violated due process.

Justice Black wrote the Court's opinion, declaring:

> The determination to preserve an accused's right to procedural due process sprang in large part from knowledge of the historical truth that the rights and liberties of people accused of crime could not be safely

---

The 'Public Safety' Exception

The same year the Court approved its first exceptions to the exclusionary rule—1984—it also for the first time approved an exception to the strict requirement, set out in *Miranda v. Arizona*, that police, before questioning someone in custody, advise him of his right to remain silent and his right to have the aid of an attorney. (*Exclusionary rule exceptions, see p. 176*)

In *New York v. Quarles*, decided by votes of 5-4 and 6-3, the Court recognized a "public safety" exception to *Miranda*. Police arresting a suspect in a grocery store and failing to see the gun they expected him to be carrying acted appropriately, the Court held, in asking first "Where's the gun?" and *then* advising him of his rights as *Miranda* requires. The suspect's answer to that question, and any evidence that answer produces, may be used in court.

Almost as significant to many observers as the decision itself was a dissenting opinion by Sandra Day O'Connor, who was then the newest member of the court and a conservative. Effectively illustrating how firmly *Miranda* was enshrined in precedent and worthy of respect from conservative as well as liberal jurists, O'Connor wrote:

> Were the Court writing from a clean slate, I could agree . . . [with permitting use of the answer to the "public safety" question]. But *Miranda* is now the law . . . and the Court has not provided sufficient justification for blurring its now clear strictures. (*New York v. Quarles*, 467 U.S. 649 at 660, 1984)

---

entrusted to secret inquisitorial processes. . . .

> For five days petitioners were subjected to interrogations culminating in . . . [an] all night examination. Over a period of five days they steadily refused to confess and disclaimed any guilt. The very circumstances surrounding their confinement and their questioning without any formal charges having been brought, were such as to fill petitioners with terror and frightful misgivings. Some were practically strangers in the community. . . . The haunting fear of mob violence was around them in an atmosphere charged with excitement and public indignation. . . . To permit human lives to be forfeited upon confessions thus obtained would make of the constitutional requirement of due process of law a meaningless symbol. . . .
>
> Due process of law, preserved for all by our Constitution, commands that no such practice as that disclosed by this record shall send any accused to his death.[42]

The Court in subsequent decisions acknowledged that some situations were so inherently coercive that evidence produced from them was inadmissible, but not until the mid-1960s did it develop any hard-and-fast rules concerning the admissibility of the products of prolonged interrogation of suspects in police custody.[43]

Voluntariness, not veracity, was the key to whether a confession was admissible. As Justice Frankfurter explained in the Court's 1961 decision in *Rogers v. Richmond*:

Our decisions ... have made clear that convictions following the admission into evidence of confessions which are involuntary ... cannot stand. This is so not because such confessions are unlikely to be true but because the methods used to extract them offend an underlying principle in the enforcement of our criminal law: that ours is an accusatorial and not an inquisitorial system—a system in which the State must establish guilt by evidence independently and freely secured and may not by coercion prove its own charge against an accused out of his own mouth.[44]

CONFESSIONS AND COUNSEL

The Fifth Amendment privilege against compelled self-incrimination was inextricably linked with the Sixth Amendment right to counsel by the Court's mid-1960s rulings in *Escobedo v. Illinois* and *Miranda v. Arizona*.

The Court as late as 1958 had ruled that confessions could be voluntary and admissible even when obtained from a suspect who was denied the opportunity to consult with legal counsel during his interrogation by police.[45]

But in 1964 the Court reversed that view. In *Massiah v. United States* the Court declared that an indicted person could not properly be questioned or otherwise persuaded to make incriminating remarks in the absence of his lawyer.[46] Coupled with the Court's ruling later that term in *Malloy v. Hogan*, extending the Fifth Amendment privilege to state defendants, *Massiah* laid the ground work for *Escobedo*.

A week after *Malloy* the Court announced its decision in the case of Danny Escobedo, convicted of murder in Illinois on the basis of his own words. In *Escobedo v. Illinois* the Court discarded the voluntarism standard for determining the admissibility of confessions, moving away from the "totality of the circumstances" approach to concentrate on the procedures followed by police in obtaining a confession.[47]

Escobedo repeatedly asked for and was denied the opportunity to see his attorney during his interrogation by police. Incriminating statements he made during this time were used as evidence against him. He challenged his conviction as a denial of his right to counsel. The Court agreed, but found the reason for denial of that right in the fact that Escobedo had not been adequately informed of his constitutional right to remain silent rather than to be forced to incriminate himself.

Justice Goldberg wrote the majority opinion. Dissenting were Justices Harlan, White, Clark, and Stewart.

The year before, the Court had declared in *Gideon v. Wainwright* that the Sixth Amendment required that every person accused of a serious crime be provided the aid of an attorney.[48] Justice Goldberg reasoned in *Escobedo* that the right guaranteed in *Gideon* would be a hollow one if it did not apply until after police obtained a confession. Goldberg wrote:

We have ... learned ... that no system of criminal justice can, or should, survive if it comes to depend for its continued effectiveness on the citizens' abdication through unawareness of their constitutional rights. No system worth preserving should have to *fear* that if an accused is permitted to consult with a lawyer, he will become aware of, and exercise, these rights. If the exercise of constitutional rights will thwart the effectiveness of a system of law enforcement, then there is something very wrong with that system.

We hold, therefore, that where, as here, the investigation is no longer a general inquiry into an unsolved crime but has begun to focus on a particular suspect, the suspect has been taken into police custody, the police carry out a process of interrogations that lends itself to eliciting incriminating statements, the suspect has requested and been denied an opportunity to consult with his lawyer, and the police have not effectively warned him of his absolute constitutional right to remain silent, the accused has been denied "the Assistance of Counsel" in violation of the Sixth Amendment ... and that no statement elicited by police during the interrogation may be used against him at a criminal trial.[49]

Justice White's dissenting opinion, joined by Justices Clark and Stewart, criticized the majority's holding that any incriminating statement made by an arrested suspect who was denied the opportunity to see his lawyer was inadmissible:

By abandoning the voluntary-involuntary test ... the Court seems driven by the notion that it is uncivilized law enforcement to use an accused's own admissions against him at his trial. It attempts to find a home for this new and nebulous rule of due process by attaching it to the right of counsel guaranteed in the federal system by the Sixth Amendment and binding upon the States by virtue of the due process guarantee of the Fourteenth Amendment. ... The right to counsel now not only entitles the accused to counsel's advice and aid in preparing for trial but stands as an impenetrable barrier to any interrogation once the accused has become a suspect.[50]

Two years after *Escobedo* the Supreme Court in *Miranda v. Arizona*[51] set out "concrete constitutional guidelines" for the custodial interrogation practices of state and local police.[52]

Ernesto Miranda was convicted of kidnapping and rape in Arizona. The prosecution used as evidence against him statements Miranda had made to police during his interrogation. He was not advised of his rights to remain silent and to consult an attorney. Miranda challenged his conviction as obtained in violation of the Fifth Amendment privilege.

By the same 5-4 vote as in *Escobedo*, the Court upheld his challenge. It ruled that prosecutors were constitutionally forbidden to use incriminating statements obtained from suspects during interrogation unless strict procedural safeguards had been followed to guarantee that the suspect was aware of his constitutional rights to remain silent and to have the aid of an attorney.

"The presence of counsel," stated Chief Justice Earl Warren for the majority, was "the adequate protective device" to "insure that statements made in the government-established atmosphere are not the product of compulsion." [53]

Warren, summarizing the Court's holding, said:

the prosecution may not use statements, whether exculpatory or inculpatory, stemming from custodial interrogation of the defendant unless it demonstrates the use of procedural safeguards effective to secure the privilege against self-incrimination. By custodial interrogation, we mean questioning initiated by law enforcement officers after a person has been taken into custody or otherwise deprived of his freedom of action in any significant way. As for the procedural safeguards to be employed, unless other fully effective means are devised to inform accused persons of their right of silence and to assure a continuous opportunity to exercise it, the following measures are required. Prior to any questioning, the person must be warned that he has a right to remain silent, that any statement he does make may be used as evidence against him, and that he has a right to the presence of an attorney, either retained or appointed. The defendant may waive effectuation of these rights, provided the waiver is made voluntarily, knowingly and intelligently. If, however, he indicates in any manner and at any stage of the process, that he wishes to consult with an attorney before speaking there can be no questioning. Likewise, if the individual is alone and indicates in any manner that he does not wish to be interrogated, the police may not question him. The mere fact that he may have answered some questions or have volunteered some statements on his own does not deprive him of the right to refrain from answering any further inquiries until he has consulted with an attorney and thereafter consents to be questioned. [54]

The Fifth Amendment, continued Warren, required that whenever a suspect indicated, before or during interrogation, that he wished to remain silent, all interrogation must cease. "At this point he has shown that he intends to exercise his Fifth Amendment privilege," wrote the Chief Justice. Therefore "any statement taken after the person invokes his privilege cannot be other than the product of compulsion, subtle or otherwise." [55]

As in *Escobedo* Justices Clark, Harlan, White, and Stewart dissented, arguing that they felt the Court should continue to use the "totality of the circumstances" approach to determining the admissibility of confessions. Justice Harlan criticized the ruling as "poor constitutional law." He continued:

I think it must be frankly recognized at the outset that police questioning allowable under due process precedents may inherently entail some pressure on the suspect and may seek advantage in his ignorance or weaknesses. . . . Until today, the role of the Constitution has been only to sift out *undue* pressure, not to assure spontaneous confessions. The Court's new rules aim to offset these minor pressures and disadvantages intrinsic to any kind of police interrogation. The rules do not

serve due process interests in preventing blatant coercion since . . . they do nothing to contain the policeman who is prepared to lie from the start. [56]

Justice White said that the majority misread the Fifth Amendment prohibition against compelled self-incrimination:

Confessions and incriminating admissions, as such, are not forbidden evidence; only those which are compelled are banned. I doubt that the Court observes these distinctions today. . . .

The obvious underpinning of the Court's decision is a deep-seated distrust of all confessions. . . .

The rule announced today . . . is a deliberate calculus to prevent interrogations, to reduce the incidence of confessions and pleas of guilty and to increase the number of trials. Criminal trials, no matter how efficient the police are, are not sure bets for the prosecution, nor should they be if the evidence is not forthcoming. . . . There is, in my view, every reason to believe that a good many criminal defendants, who otherwise would have been convicted on what this Court has previously thought to be the most satisfactory kind of evidence, will now, under this new version of the Fifth Amendment, either not be tried at all or will be acquitted if the State's evidence, minus the confession, is put to the test of litigation. [57]

A week after *Miranda* the Court held that it would not apply the decision retroactively to invalidate convictions obtained in trials begun before its announcement on June 13, 1966. A similar rule applied in cases to which *Escobedo* might apply, held the Court. [58]

Mallory v. United States, Escobedo v. Illinois, and *Miranda v. Arizona,* together with rulings extending the specific protections of the Bill of Rights to state defendants, brought criticism of the Warren Court to a crescendo in the late 1960s.

One of the major themes of the 1968 presidential campaign was "law and order"—a phrase that Richard Nixon, the successful candidate, used as a basis for his criticism of the Court's rulings.

Also in 1968 Congress—responding to similar complaints that the Court was in fact encouraging crime by impeding law enforcement officers in their duties—included in the 1968 Crime Control and Safe Streets Act provisions intended to blunt or overrule the effect of *Mallory* and *Miranda*. By stating that confessions could be used in federal courts whenever the judge found them voluntary, Congress attempted to abandon the procedural guidelines set out in *Miranda* and return to the old voluntary-involuntary test for prosecutorial use of incriminating statements. The 1968 law, however, affected only federal trials, not state trials. The states remained bound by the *Miranda* requirements.

Despite opposition to *Miranda*, the Supreme Court stood by that decision. Early in 1969 the Court held that *Miranda* required that police, before questioning an individual in his own home, warn him of his constitutional rights as soon as he was effectively in custody. [59]

President-elect Nixon promised during his 1968 campaign to appoint men to the Supreme Court who would be less receptive to the arguments of criminal defendants and more responsive to the reasoning of law enforcement officers. Even before the election, Chief Justice Warren had announced his plans to retire.

In the spring of 1969 Nixon named—and the Senate confirmed—Warren E. Burger, a conservative appeals court judge, as Warren's successor. In 1970 Burger was joined on the bench by another Nixon appointee, Harry A. Blackmun. And in 1971 Nixon filled two more seats on the Court with Justices Powell and William H. Rehnquist.

Despite numerous opportunities, the Court with its new chief justice and new members did not overturn *Miranda*. The Court in the 1970s did, however, decline to extend *Miranda* to persons other than suspects in police custody—and it did allow some indirect use of statements from persons not warned of their rights.

The first of these rulings came in 1971 in *Harris v. New York*. By a 5-4 vote, the Court held that although statements made by a defendant before he was advised of his rights could not be used as evidence against him, they could be used to impeach his credibility if he took the stand in his own defense and contradicted what he had said before trial.

Chief Justice Burger observed:

> Some comments in the *Miranda* opinion can indeed be read as indicating a bar to use of an uncounseled statement for any purpose, but discussion of that issue was not at all necessary to the Court's holding, and cannot be regarded as controlling. *Miranda* barred the prosecution from making its case with statements of an accused while in custody prior to having or effectively waiving counsel. It does not follow from *Miranda* that evidence inadmissible against an accused in the prosecution's case in chief is barred for all purposes, provided of course that the trustworthiness of the evidence satisfies legal standards. . . .
>
> The shield provided by *Miranda* cannot be perverted into a license to use perjury by way of a defense, free from the risk of confrontation with prior inconsistent utterances.[60]

Justices Black, Brennan, Douglas, and Marshall dissented, warning that this ruling "goes far toward undoing much of the progress made in conforming police methods to the Constitution." [61]

Three years later, the Court in *Michigan v. Tucker* upheld the prosecution's use of a statement made by a suspect not fully warned of his rights as a "lead" for locating a prosecution witness. Writing the opinion, Justice Rehnquist emphasized that the procedures *Miranda* required were safeguards for constitutional rights, but were not themselves constitutionally guaranteed.[62]

In 1975 the Court in *Oregon v. Hass* reaffirmed *Harris*.[63] Later that year the Court ruled that, although a suspect's assertion of his right to silence must terminate police interrogation of him about one crime, it does not foreclose subsequent police efforts, after an interval and a second warning of his rights, to question him about another crime.[64]

And in 1976 the Court in *United States v. Mandujano* refused to require that *Miranda* warnings be given to grand jury witnesses before they testify—even though they may be potential defendants.[65]

The Court has also held that a juvenile suspect's request to see his probation officer is not an assertion of his Fifth Amendment privilege, requiring police to cease questioning him, and that a probationer does not need *Miranda* warnings before being asked about crimes by his probation officer.[66]

In 1985 the Court ruled that an initial unwarned admission of guilt—given voluntarily in a noncoercive environment—does not so taint any subsequent confession as to bar its use in court.[67] And the following year the Court held, 7-2, that the fact of mental illness does not necessarily disable someone from voluntarily and intelligently waiving his constitutional rights to silence and the aid of an attorney.[68]

Notes

1. *Bruno v. United States,* 308 U.S. 287 (1939); *Griffin v. California,* 380 U.S. 609 (1965); *United States v. Hale,* 422 U.S. 171 (1975); *Doyle v. Ohio, Wood v. Ohio,* 427 U.S. 610 (1976).
2. *Hoffman v. United States,* 341 U.S. 479 (1951); *Mason v. United States,* 244 U.S. 362 (1917); *Rogers v. United States,* 340 U.S. 367 (1951); *United States v. Monia,* 317 U.S. 424 (1943).
3. *Emspak v. United States,* 349 U.S. 190 (1955).
4. *Heike v. United States,* 227 U.S. 131 (1913); *Brown v. Walker,* 161 U.S. 591 (1896).
5. *Rogers v. United States,* 340 U.S. 367 at 372-374 (1951); see also *Blau v. United States,* 340 U.S. 159 (1950).
6. *Hale v. Henkel,* 201 U.S. 43 (1906); *United States v. White,* 322 U.S. 694 (1944); *Bellis v. United States,* 417 U.S. 85 (1974).
7. *Wilson v. United States,* 221 U.S. 361 (1911); *Shapiro v. United States,* 335 U.S. 1 (1948); see also *Mancusi v. DeForte,* 392 U.S. 364 (1968); *Couch v. United States,* 409 U.S. 322 (1973); *United States v. Kasmir, Fisher v. United States,* 425 U.S. 391 (1976).
8. *Garrity v. New Jersey,* 385 U.S. 493 (1967); *Spevack v. Klein,* 385 U.S. 511 (1967); *Slochower v. Board of Higher Education of New York City,* 350 U.S. 551 (1956); *Garner v. Broderick,* 392 U.S. 273 (1968); *Lefkowitz v. Cunningham,* 431 U.S. 801 (1977).
9. *United States v. Doremus,* 249 U.S. 86 (1919); *United States v. Sanchez,* 340 U.S. 42 (1950); *Sonzinsky v. United States,* 300 U.S. 506 (1937); *United States v. Kahriger,* 345 U.S. 22 (1953).
10. *Albertson v. Subversive Activities Control Board,* 382 U.S. 70 (1965).
11. *Grosso v. United States,* 390 U.S. 62 (1968); *Marchetti v. United States,* 390 U.S. 39 (1968); *Haynes v. United States,* 390 U.S. 85 (1968); *Leary v. United States,* 395 U.S. 6 (1969); see also *Minor v. United States, Buie v. United States,* 396 U.S. 87 (1969), *United States v. Freed,* 41 U.S. 601 (1971).
12. *Kastigar v. United States,* 406 U.S. 441 at 446 (1972).
13. *Counselman v. Hitchcock,* 142 U.S. 547 at 585-586 (1892).
14. Ibid.
15. *Brown v. Walker,* 161 U.S. 591 at 595, 596, 605-606, 610 (1896).
16. *Ullmann v. United States,* 350 U.S. 422 at 438 (1956).
17. Id. at 438-439.
18. Id. at 440.
19. Id. at 449, 454.
20. Congressional Quarterly, *Congress and the Nation,* vol. III (Washington, D.C.: Congressional Quarterly, 1973), 273.
21. *Kastigar v. United States,* 406 U.S. 441 at 453 (1972).
22. Id. at 460.
23. Id. at 466-467.
24. *Twining v. New Jersey,* 211 U.S. 78 at 106 (1908).
25. *Adamson v. California,* 332 U.S. 46 at 54 (1947).
26. *United States v. Murdock,* 284 U.S. 141 (1931); *Feldman v. United States,* 322 U.S. 487 (1944); *Knapp v. Schweitzer,* 357 U.S. 371 (1958).
27. *Malloy v. Hogan,* 378 U.S. 1 at 8, 11 (1964).
28. Id at 16, 27.
29. *Murphy v. The Waterfront Commission of New York Harbor,* 378 U.S. 52 at 79 (1964).

30. *Griffin v. California*, 380 U.S. 609 at 615 (1965).
31. Id. at 614; see also *Lakeside v. Oregon*, 435 U.S. 333 (1978).
32. *Hopt v. Utah*, 110 U.S. 574 at 585 (1884).
33. *Bram v. United States*, 168 U.S. 532 (1897).
34. *Hopt v. Utah*, 110 U.S. 574 at 584-585 (1884).
35. *Wilson v. United States*, 162 U.S. 613 at 623 (1896).
36. *Bram v. United States*, 168 U.S. 532, at 561, 542 (1897).
37. *McNabb v. United States*, 318 U.S. 332 at 340 (1943).
38. Id. at 343-344.
39. *Mallory v. United States*, 354 U.S. 449 at 453 (1957).
40. *Brown v. Mississippi*, 297 U.S. 278 at 285 (1935).
41. Id. at 285-286.
42. *Chambers v. Florida*, 309 U.S. 227 at 237, 239-240, 241 (1940).
43. *Lisenba v. California*, 314 U.S. 219 (1941); *Ashcraft v. Tennessee*, 322 U.S. 143 (1944); *Fikes v. Alabama*, 352 U.S. 191 (1957); *Spano v. New York*, 360 U.S. 315 (1959); *Lynumn v. Illinois*, 372 U.S. 528 (1963); *Townsend v. Sain*, 372 U.S. 293 (1963); *Haynes v. Washington*, 373 U.S. 503 (1963).
44. *Rogers v. Richmond*, 365 U.S. 534 at 540-541 (1961); see also *Stein v. New York*, 346 U.S. 156 (1953); *Jackson v. Denno*, 378 U.S. 368 (1964).
45. *Crooker v. California*, 357 U.S. 433 (1958); *Cicencia v. LaGay*, 357 U.S. 504 (1958), overruled by *Miranda v. Arizona*, 384 U.S. 436 (1966).
46. *Massiah v. United States*, 377 U.S. 201 (1964).
47. *Escobedo v. Illinois*, 378 U.S. 478 (1964).
48. *Gideon v. Wainwright*, 372 U.S. 335 (1963).
49. *Escobedo v. Illinois*, 378 U.S. 478 at 490-491 (1964).
50. Id. at 496.
51. *Miranda v. Arizona*, 384 U.S. 436 (1966), was one of four cases reviewed by the Court and resolved together. The others were: *Vignera v. New York, Westover v. United States, California v. Stewart.*
52. *Miranda v. Arizona*, 384 U.S. 436 at 441-442 (1966).
53. Id. at 466.
54. Id. at 444-445.
55. Id. at 474.
56. Id. at 515-516.
57. Id. at 536, 537, 541-542.
58. *Johnson v. New Jersey*, 384 U.S. 719 (1966).
59. *Orozco v. Texas*, 394 U.S. 324 (1969).
60. *Harris v. New York*, 401 U.S. 222 at 224, 226 (1971).
61. Id. at 232.
62. *Michigan v. Tucker*, 417 U.S. 433 (1974).
63. *Oregon v. Hass*, 420 U.S. 714 (1975).
64. *Michigan v. Mosley*, 423 U.S. 96 (1975).
65. *United States v. Mandujano*, 425 U.S. 564 (1976).
66. *Fare v. Michael C.*, 442 U.S. 707 (1979).
67. *Minnesota v. Murphy*, 465 U.S. 420 (1984).
68. *Oregon v. Elstad*, 470 U.S. 298 (1985).

10

The Aid of Legal Counsel

The Sixth Amendment stipulates that "in all criminal prosecutions, the accused shall enjoy the right ... to have the assistance of counsel for his defense."

Despite this unambiguous language, only persons charged with federal crimes punishable by death have been guaranteed this right throughout American history.[1] The right of all other defendants, federal and state, to the aid of an attorney has traditionally depended upon their ability to hire and pay their own lawyer.

But beginning in the 1930s the Supreme Court vastly enlarged the class of persons who have the right to legal counsel—appointed and paid by the state if necessary—in preparing and presenting a defense. In 1932 the Court declared this right so fundamental that the Fourteenth Amendment's due process clause required states to provide the effective aid of counsel to all defendants charged with capital crimes.[2] Six years later the Court held that the Sixth Amendment required that all federal defendants be provided an attorney.[3]

This expansion of the Sixth Amendment right to counsel continued during the 1960s and 1970s, when the Court ruled that the amendment guaranteed the aid of an attorney to all state defendants charged with crimes that could be considered serious. In the 1980s the Court further expanded the right to include a guarantee that indigents who are defending themselves with a claim of insanity are entitled to the aid of a court-appointed and publicly paid psychiatrist.[4]

A FUNDAMENTAL RIGHT

The Court's first modern ruling on the right to counsel came in the "First Scottsboro Case"—*Powell v. Alabama*—in 1932.

Nine young illiterate black men, aged thirteen to twenty-one, were charged with the rape of two white girls on a freight train passing through Tennessee and Alabama. Their trial was held in Scottsboro, Alabama, where community hostility to the defendants was intense.

The trial judge appointed all the members of the local bar to serve as defense counsel. But when the trial began, no attorney appeared to represent the defendants. The judge, on the morning of the trial, appointed a local lawyer who undertook the task with reluctance. The defendants were convicted.

They challenged their convictions, arguing that they were effectively denied aid of counsel because they did not have the opportunity to consult with their lawyer and prepare a defense. The Supreme Court agreed, 7-2.

Writing for the Court, Justice George Sutherland explained:

> It is hardly necessary to say that the right to counsel being conceded, a defendant should be afforded a fair opportunity to secure counsel of his own choice. Not only was that not done here, but such designation of counsel as was attempted was either so indefinite or so close upon the trial as to amount to a denial of effective and substantial aid.[5]

The action of the judge in appointing all members of the local bar as defense counsel was "little more than an expansive gesture" that resulted in no aid to the defendants in the critical pretrial period, the Court said.[6]

Citing the Court's acknowledgment in *Twining v. New Jersey* two dozen years earlier that some of the rights guaranteed in the Bill of Rights might be so fundamental that a denial of them by a state would be a denial of due process, the Court declared that "the right to the aid of counsel is of this fundamental character."[7] *(Details, p. 161)*

In the Scottsboro case the Court's decision leaned heavily upon the circumstances of the case and the characteristics of the defendants in finding the denial of effective aid of counsel a denial of due process. Sutherland wrote:

> In the light of the facts ... the ignorance and illiteracy of the defendants, their youth, the circumstances of public hostility, the imprisonment and the close surveillance of the defendants by the military forces, the

fact that their friends and families were all in other states and communication with them necessarily difficult, and above all that they stood in deadly peril of their lives—we think the failure of the trial court to give them reasonable time and opportunity to secure counsel was a clear denial of due process.

But . . . assuming their inability, even if opportunity had been given, to employ counsel, as the trial court evidently did assume, we are of opinion that, under the circumstances just stated, the necessity of counsel was so vital and imperative that the failure of the trial court to make an effective appointment of counsel was likewise a denial of due process within the meaning of the Fourteenth Amendment. Whether this would be so in other criminal prosecutions, or under other circumstances, we need not determine. All that it is necessary now to decide, as we do decide, is that in a capital case, where the defendant is unable to employ counsel, and is incapable adequately of making his own defense because of ignorance, feeblemindedness, illiteracy or the like, it is the duty of the court, whether requested or not, to assign counsel for him as a necessary requisite of due process of law; and that duty is not discharged by an assignment at such a time or under such circumstances as to preclude the giving of effective aid in the preparation and trial of the case.[8]

Since 1790 federal law implementing the Sixth Amendment guarantee has required that persons charged with capital crimes in federal courts be provided an attorney.[9] In 1938 the Court held that the Sixth Amendment required this assurance for *all* federal defendants. This was the ruling in *Johnson v. Zerbst.*[10]

John Johnson, a Marine, was charged with passing counterfeit money, He was tried and convicted in civil court without the aid of an attorney to act in his defense. He challenged his conviction as obtained in violation of his constitutional rights.

The Supreme Court found his argument persuasive, and upheld his claim. Justice Hugo L. Black spoke for a majority of the Court:

The Sixth Amendment . . . embodies a realistic recognition of the obvious truth that the average defendant does not have the professional legal skill to protect himself when brought before a tribunal with power to take his life or liberty, wherein the prosecution is presented by experienced and learned counsel. That which is simple, orderly and necessary to the lawyer—to the untrained laymen . . . may appear intricate, complex, and mysterious. . . .

. . . The Sixth Amendment withholds from federal courts, in all criminal proceedings, the power and authority to deprive an accused of his life or liberty unless he has or waives the assistance of counsel. . . .

. . . While an accused may waive the right to counsel, whether there is a proper waiver should be clearly determined by the trial court. . . .

Since the Sixth Amendment constitutionally entitles one charged with crime to the assistance of counsel, compliance with this constitutional mandate is an essential jurisdictional prerequisite to a federal court's authority to deprive an accused of his life or liberty [unless the right has been properly waived]. . . . If the accused, however, is not represented by counsel and has not competently and intelligently waived his constitutional right, the Sixth Amendment stands as a

jurisdictional bar to a valid conviction and sentence depriving him of his life or his liberty.[11]

THE APPOINTMENT OF COUNSEL

Johnson v. Zerbst, with its emphatic declaration of the right of federal defendants to have an attorney, provided no aid to state defendants. And for thirty years after *Powell v. Alabama,* the Court refused to rule that the Sixth Amendment, in addition to the general due process guarantee of the Fourteenth Amendment, extended the right to legal counsel to state defendants.

The primary effect of this judicial posture was to withhold the aid of counsel from indigent state defendants charged with noncapital crimes. The Court first declared, in the 1942 case of *Betts v. Brady,* that "appointment of counsel is not a fundamental right" for such state defendants.[12] The due process guarantee of the Fourteenth Amendment, held the Court, did not require states to appoint counsel in every criminal case where it was requested by the defendant. A state legislature might choose to write such a requirement into state law, the Court added.

The vote was 6-3. Justice Owen J. Roberts declared for the majority:

The Sixth Amendment of the national Constitution applies only to trials in federal courts. The due process clause of the Fourteenth Amendment does not incorporate, as such, the specific guarantees found in the Sixth Amendment although a denial by a state of rights or privileges specifically embodied in that and others of the first eight amendments may, in certain circumstances, or in connection with other elements, operate, in a given case, to deprive a litigant of due process of law in violation of the Fourteenth. Due process of law is secured against invasion by the federal Government by the Fifth Amendment and is safeguarded against state action in identical words by the Fourteenth. The phrase formulates a concept less rigid and more fluid than those envisaged in other specific and particular provisions of the Bill of Rights. Its application is less a matter of rule. Asserted denial is to be tested by an appraisal of the totality of facts in a given case. That which may, in one setting, constitute a denial of fundamental fairness, shocking to the universal sense of justice, may, in other circumstances, and in the light of other considerations, fall short of such denial.[13]

Justice Roberts acknowledged that *Johnson v. Zerbst* raised the question "whether the constraint laid by the [Sixth] amendment upon the national courts expresses a rule so fundamental and essential to a fair trial, and so, to due process of law, that it is made obligatory upon the States by the Fourteenth Amendment."[14]

The Court's answer was no. Justice Roberts wrote that Betts—unlike Powell of the Scottsboro case—was a man forty-three years old, "of ordinary intelligence and ability." He was not so handicapped by lack of counsel that he was denied the fundamental fairness promised by the due process clause. And so, concluded the Court, while "the Fourteenth Amendment prohibits the conviction and incarceration of one whose trial is offensive to the common and fundamental ideas of fairness and right, and while want of counsel in a particular case may result in a conviction lacking in such fundamental fairness, we cannot say that the amendment embodies an inexorable command that no trial for any offense, or in any court, can be fairly conducted and justice accorded a defendant who is not represented by counsel." [15]

Justice Black, joined by Justices Frank Murphy and William O. Douglas in dissent, urged that the same rule apply in state as in federal courts:

> A practice cannot be reconciled with "common and fundamental ideas of fairness and right," which subjects innocent men to increased dangers of conviction merely because of their poverty....
>
> Denial to the poor of the request for counsel in proceedings based on charges of serious crime has long been regarded as shocking to the "universal sense of justice" throughout this country. [16]

Under *Betts*, then, the Court considered the special circumstances of each case to determine if denial of counsel denied the defendant fair treatment. The Court upheld some of the state convictions challenged due to lack of counsel, but in most cases it found circumstances that warranted reversal. Among those were the conduct of the trial judge or the youth, ignorance, or lack of legal sophistication of the defendants. [17]

In 1963 the Supreme Court unanimously discarded this case-by-case approach, overruling *Betts v. Brady* to hold that the right to the assistance of counsel was so fundamental that the Fourteenth Amendment due process clause extended the Sixth Amendment guarantee to state defendants. States were henceforth required to provide counsel for all defendants charged with felonies and unable to pay a lawyer. This was the decision in *Gideon v. Wainwright*. [18]

Clarence Earl Gideon, an indigent, was tried and convicted in a Florida state court of a felony—breaking and entering a poolroom to commit a misdemeanor. He requested and was denied a court-appointed attorney. The judge based his refusal on the fact that Gideon's crime—unlike that in the *Powell* case—was not a capital one. Gideon conducted his own defense.

Convicted and sentenced to spend five years in prison, Gideon prepared his own petitions asking a federal court to declare his conviction invalid because it was obtained in violation of his constitutional right to counsel, and to order his release. The Supreme Court finally agreed to hear Gideon's case, and appointed a well-known Washington attorney, Abe Fortas, to argue on his behalf. The Court specifically requested that both sides in the case argue the additional question: should *Betts v. Brady* be reconsidered?

The Court's opinion in *Gideon*, reconsidering and reversing *Betts v. Brady*, was written by Justice Black, who had dissented from *Betts*. Looking back to *Powell v. Alabama*, in which the Court had described the right to counsel as fundamental to a fair trial, Black wrote:

> The fact is that the Court in *Betts v. Brady* made an abrupt break with its own well-considered precedents. In returning to these old precedents, sounder we believe than the new, we but restore constitutional principles established to achieve a fair system of justice. Not only these precedents but also reason and reflection require us to recognize that in our adversary system of criminal justice, any person haled into court,

'Guiding Hand'

One of the classic descriptions of the importance of the aid of an attorney at trial came in the landmark 1932 decision in *Powell v. Alabama*, the "First Scottsboro Case." Writing for the Court, Justice George Sutherland discussed the basic requirements of due process:

> It has never been doubted by this court, or any other so far as we know, that notice and hearing are preliminary steps essential to the passing of an enforceable judgment, and that they, together with a legally competent tribunal having jurisdiction of the case, constitute basic elements of the constitutional requirement of due process....
>
> What, then, does a hearing include? Historically and in practice, in our own country at least, it has always included the right to the aid of counsel when desired and provided by the party asserting the right. The right to be heard would be, in many cases, of little avail if it did not comprehend the right to be heard by counsel. Even the intelligent and educated layman has small and sometimes no skill in the science of law. If charged with crime, he is incapable, generally, of determining for himself whether the indictment is good or bad. He is unfamiliar with the rules of evidence. Left without the aid of counsel he may be put on trial without a proper charge, and convicted upon incompetent evidence, or evidence irrelevant to the issue or otherwise inadmissible. He lacks both the skill and knowledge adequately to prepare his defense, even though he have a perfect one. He requires the guiding hand of counsel at every step in the proceedings against him. Without it, though he be not guilty, he faces the danger of conviction because he does not know how to establish his innocence. If that be true of men of intelligence, how much more true is it of the ignorant and illiterate, or those of feeble intellect. If in any case, civil or criminal, a state or federal court were arbitrarily to refuse to hear a party by counsel, employed by and appearing for him, it reasonably may not be doubted that such a refusal would be a denial of a hearing, and, therefore, of due process in the constitutional sense. *(Powell v. Alabama,* 287 U.S. 45 at 68-69, 1932)

The Right to Refuse Counsel

In a case that seemed to turn inside-out the series of rulings expanding the right of defendants to have the assistance of an attorney, the Supreme Court in 1975 held that defendants also have the right to *refuse* legal assistance.

In *Faretta v. California* the Court ruled that individuals have the right to conduct their own defense and to reject counsel who have been appointed to represent them.

Justice Potter Stewart acknowledged that recognition of this right seemed "to cut against the grain of this court's decisions holding that the Constitution requires that no accused can be convicted and imprisoned unless he has been accorded the right to the assistance of counsel." However, Stewart continued, "it is one thing to hold that every defendant, rich or poor, has the right to the assistance of counsel, and quite another to say that a state may compel a defendant to accept a lawyer he does not *want*." *(Faretta v. California,* 422 U.S. 806 at 832-833, 1975)

who is too poor to hire a lawyer, cannot be assured a fair trial unless counsel is provided for him. This seems to us to be an obvious truth.... Lawyers to prosecute are everywhere deemed essential to protect the public's interest in an orderly society.... That government hires lawyers to prosecute and defendants who have the money hire lawyers to defend are the strongest indications of the widespread belief that lawyers in criminal courts are necessities, not luxuries.[19]

'Adequate Protective Device'

In 1964 the Supreme Court further tightened the requirement that states observe the right to counsel. With its controversial ruling in *Escobedo v. Illinois,* the Court linked that right to the Fifth Amendment privilege against self-incrimination. In *Escobedo* a divided Court held that a suspect in custody had an absolute right to the aid of an attorney during police interrogation.[20] *(Details, p. 198)*

Two years later, with its decision in *Miranda v. Arizona,* the Court declared the presence of counsel "the adequate protective device necessary to make the process of police interrogation conform to the dictates of the [Fifth Amendment] privilege."[21]

"Accordingly," wrote Chief Justice Earl Warren, "we hold that an individual held for interrogation must be clearly informed that he has the right to consult with a lawyer and to have the lawyer with him during interrogation."[22]

In 1972 the Court held that the right to counsel applied not only to state defendants charged with felonies, but in all trials of persons for offenses serious enough to warrant a jail sentence. Speaking for the unanimous Court in *Argersinger v. Hamlin,* Justice Douglas looked back both to *Powell* and *Gideon:*

> Both *Powell* and *Gideon* involved felonies. But their rationale has relevance to any criminal trial, where an accused is deprived of liberty. *Powell* and *Gideon* suggest that there are certain fundamental rights applicable to all such criminal prosecutions....
>
> The requirement of counsel may well be necessary for a fair trial even in a petty offense prosecution. We are by no means convinced that legal and constitutional questions involved in a case that actually leads to imprisonment even for a brief period are any less complex than when a person can be sent off for six months or more....
>
> Under the rule we announce today, every judge will know when the trial of a misdemeanor starts that no imprisonment may be imposed, even though local law permits it, unless the accused is represented by counsel.[23]

Seven years later, in 1979, the Court limited *Argersinger,* holding that the right to counsel did not apply in trials of lesser offenses where no sentence of imprisonment *was* imposed, even though such a sentence *could* have been imposed.

The Court was divided 5-4. For the majority, Justice William H. Rehnquist reaffirmed the key holding in *Argersinger,* that no one could receive a prison sentence if he had not been afforded the aid of an attorney at trial. But Rehnquist said that *Argersinger* did not require reversal of a man's conviction for shoplifting, a crime for which he was fined fifty dollars, even though he had not been provided an attorney, and even though a year in jail was a possible sentence for his crime.[24]

'Critical Stage'

In *Powell v. Alabama* the Court in 1932 indicated the importance of timing in the provision of legal assistance to a defendant.[25] The Court described the period between arrest and trial as a critical one in the preparation of a defense.

Many subsequent rulings on the right to counsel have worked to define the "critical stage" at which the right applies, the time counsel must be made available if requested by the suspect or defendant.

In *Hamilton v. Alabama,* decided in 1961, the Court held that arraignment was such a critical stage, at least in some states.[26] Later, *Escobedo* and *Miranda* emphatically held that the right applied once a suspect was in custody and subject to interrogation.[27]

In 1967 the Court in *United States v. Wade*—and its state counterpart, *Gilbert v. California*—held that police lineups also were such a critical stage.[28] The Court declared inadmissible any in-court identification of defendants based on pretrial lineups conducted in the absence of the defendant's attorney.

Writing for a unanimous Court in *Wade,* Justice William J. Brennan, Jr., observed:

> the principle of *Powell v. Alabama* and succeeding

The Question of Interrogation

Critical to the meaning of *Miranda v. Arizona,* forbidding police to continue interrogation of a suspect after he invoked his right to remain silent or to have his lawyer present, was the meaning of the term *interrogation.*[1]

Fourteen years after *Miranda,* the Court adopted a broad definition of this key word. Interrogation, the Court declared unanimously in *Rhode Island v. Innis,* means more than just the direct questioning of a suspect by police. It includes other "techniques of persuasion," such as staged lineups, intended to evoke statements from a suspect. Indeed, said the Court, interrogation occurs any time police use words or actions "that they *should have known* were reasonably likely to elicit an incriminating response" from a suspect.

This broad definition did not, the Court held, 6-3, encompass events that transpired in the case actually before them. Thomas Innis, arrested for murder, led police to the murder weapon after he overheard policemen conversing among themselves about the possibility of children finding and being harmed by the weapon they were seeking. Because this evocative conversation occurred in a police car without Innis's attorney present, he challenged his eventually incriminating statements as obtained in violation of *Miranda.* The Court rejected this argument, holding that the conversation he overheard did not qualify as interrogation.[2]

In 1981 the Court reaffirmed its broad view of interrogation, ruling that a defendant should be warned, prior to an interview with a state-appointed psychiatrist, that he had the right to refuse to answer the psychiatrist's questions and to have his attorney present during the interview.[3]

The whole area of police conversation with a suspect raises difficult points of distinction. In 1981 the Court in *Edwards v. Arizona* was unanimous in insisting that once a defendant has said he wants his attorney present, all interrogation must cease and may not resume until the attorney is present—or the defendant initiates a new conversation.[4]

Two years later, the Court emphasized the latter point, ruling 5-4 that a suspect who invokes his right to counsel but later, before counsel arrives, asks police "Well, what is going to happen to me now?" is not denied his rights when police remind him of his request for counsel—and then go on to continue the conversation.[5]

Police use of a well-placed informer can also constitute interrogation, the Court has held. In *United States v. Henry* in 1980, the Court held that a suspect was denied the right to counsel when the government obtained and used incriminating statements by planting an informer in his cell prior to trial.[6]

The Court reaffirmed this ruling in *Maine v. Moulton* in 1985, but a year later, drew the line between solicited and unsolicited incriminating statements, permitting police to use *unsolicited* remarks made by a suspect to a police informer in his cell.[7]

1. *Miranda v. Arizona,* 384 U.S. 436 (1966), reaffirmed in *Michigan v. Jackson, Michigan v. Bladel,* 475 U.S. 625 (1986).
2. *Rhode Island v. Innis,* 446 U.S. 291 (1980).
3. *Estelle v. Smith,* 451 U.S. 454 (1981).
4. *Edwards v. Arizona,* 451 U.S. 477 (1981), applied retroactively to cases pending on appeal, *Shea v. Louisiana,* 470 U.S. 51 (1985).
5. *Oregon v. Bradshaw,* 462 U.S. 1039 (1983).
6. *United States v. Henry,* 447 U.S. 264 (1980).
7. *Maine v. Moulton,* 474 U.S. 159 (1985); *Kuhlmann v. Wilson,* 477 U.S. 436 (1986).

cases requires that we scrutinize *any* pretrial confrontation of the accused to determine whether the presence of his counsel is necessary to preserve the defendant's basic right to a fair trial as affected by his right meaningfully to cross-examine the witnesses against him and to have effective assistance of counsel at the trial itself.[29]

In *Gilbert* the Court applied the same rule to state proceedings.

Wade was undercut by Congress. In the Crime Control and Safe Streets Act of 1968, Congress included a provision allowing use of such lineup identification evidence at trial in federal courts, even if obtained in the absence of counsel.

And in 1972 the Court further limited the effect of *Wade* and *Gilbert.* The defendants in those cases had already been indicted when they were placed in the lineup. In *Kirby v. Illinois* the Court ruled that the right to counsel did not apply to persons in such lineups who had not yet been indicted. The right did not take effect, the Court held,

until "formal prosecutorial proceedings" were under way.[30] Justice Potter Stewart explained:

> The initiation of judicial criminal proceedings is far from a mere formalism. It is the starting point of our whole system of adversary criminal justice. For it is only then that the Government has committed itself to prosecute and only then that the adverse positions of Government and defendant have solidified. It is then that a defendant finds himself faced with the prosecutorial forces of organized society, and immersed in the intricacies of substantive and procedural criminal law. It is this point, therefore, that marks the commencement of the "criminal prosecutions" to which alone the explicit guarantees of the Sixth Amendment are applicable.[31]

The principle of *Wade* and *Gilbert* was further eroded in 1973 when the Court held that it was not necessary for a defendant's attorney to be present at a postindictment photographic identification session with potential witnesses.[32]

At the other end of the criminal justice process—appeal of conviction—the Court in 1974 called a halt to the gradual extension of the right to appointed counsel.

In *Ross v. Moffit* the Court held that the state's constitutional obligation to provide appointed counsel for indigents appealing their convictions did not extend past the point where their right to appeal had been effectively exhausted.[33]

'Effective' Aid

As the Court made clear in *Powell v. Alabama,* the effective aid of counsel means more than the mere physical presence of an attorney at trial.

In *Powell* the Court held that the judge's gesture of appointing the entire local bar as defense counsel—and the failure of any particular individuals to assume that role before trial—deprived the defendants of the *effective* aid of counsel.

Other factors can deprive a defendant of the sort of legal representation to which the Sixth Amendment—or due process generally—entitles him. Conflict of interest is one. In the 1942 case of *Glasser v. United States,* the Court found that a judge had denied defendants the effective aid of counsel by requiring a single attorney to represent them both.[34] In that opinion, the majority declared:

> Upon the trial judge rests the duty of seeing that the trial is conducted with solicitude for the essential rights of the accused.... Of equal importance with the duty of the court to see that an accused has the assistance of counsel is its duty to refrain from embarrassing counsel in the defense of an accused by insisting, or indeed, even suggesting, that counsel undertake to concurrently represent interests which might diverge from those of his first client, when the possibility of that divergence is brought home to the court.[35]

In 1978 the Court elaborated on that point, stating in *Holloway v. Arkansas:*

> Joint representation of conflicting interests is suspect because of what it tends to prevent the attorney from doing.... Generally speaking, a conflict may ... prevent an attorney from challenging the admission of evidence prejudicial to one client but perhaps favorable to another, or from arguing at the sentencing hearing the relative involvement and culpability of his clients in order to minimize the culpability of one by emphasizing that of another.... The mere physical presence of an attorney does not fulfill the Sixth Amendment guarantee when the advocate's conflicting obligations has [sic] effectively sealed his lips on crucial matters.[36]

Competence of counsel, however, is more difficult to challenge. The Court in the 1970s rejected the effort of several persons to challenge their convictions, based on guilty pleas, with the argument that they were the result of advice from incompetent counsel. The Court declared that defendants must assume a certain degree of risk that their attorneys would make some "ordinary error" in assessing the facts of their case and the law that applied, and that such error was not a basis for reversing a conviction.[37]

In 1984, however, the Court for the first time set out a standard for use in reviewing a defendant's claim that he had been denied the effective aid of an attorney.

"The benchmark for judging any claim of ineffectiveness," wrote Justice Sandra Day O'Connor, herself not many years from acting as a trial judge in Arizona, "must be whether counsel's conduct so undermined the proper functioning of the adversarial process that the trial cannot be relied on as having produced a just result." In *Strickland v. Washington* she explained that to win reversal of a conviction or invalidation of a sentence, a defendant must show that his attorney made errors so serious at trial that they resulted in his being denied a fair trial.

The proper standard, O'Connor continued, is "reasonably effective assistance. And the lawyer, she said, deserves the benefit of the doubt. "Judicial scrutiny of counsel's performance must be highly deferential.... Because of the difficulties inherent in making the evaluation, a court must indulge a strong presumption that counsel's conduct falls within the wide range of reasonable professional assistance."[38]

Applying that standard to another case decided the same day, May 14, 1984, the Court in *United States v. Cronic* was unanimous in holding that an appeals court was wrong to infer that a defendant was denied the right to counsel because the appointed counsel lacked criminal law experience, and was given only a brief time to prepare for trial. Such a conclusion, wrote Justice John Paul Stevens, must be supported by evidence of serious errors by the lawyer so prejudicial that the defendant was denied a fair trial.[39]

In 1985 the Court for the first time found a case in which this standard worked to prove the defendant's claim. In *Evitts v. Lucey* the Court held that an attorney's failure to file a statement of appeal by the legal deadline constituted evidence that he was not providing his client the effective aid of counsel.[40]

Notes

1. Stat. 73, 92 (1789); 1 Stat. 112, 118 (1790), now 18 *United States Code* 563.
2. *Powell v. Alabama,* 287 U.S. 45 (1932).
3. *Johnson v. Zerbst,* 304 U.S. 458 (1938).
4. *Gideon v. Wainwright,* 372 U.S. 335 (1963); *Argersinger v. Hamlin,* 407 U.S. 25 (1972); *Ake v. Oklahoma,* 470 U.S. 68 (1985).
5. *Powell v. Alabama,* 287 U.S. 45 at 53 (1932).
6. Id. at 56-57.
7. Id. at 68.
8. Id. at 71.
9. 1 *Stat.* 73, 92 (1789); 1 *Stat.* 112, 118 (1790); now 18 *United States Code* 563.
10. *Johnson v. Zerbst,* 304 U.S. 458 (1938).
11. Id. at 462-463, 465, 467-468.
12. *Betts v. Brady,* 316 U.S. 455 (1942).
13. Id. at 461-462.
14. Id. at 465.
15. Id. at 473.
16. Id. at 476.
17. *Canizio v. New York,* 327 U.S. 82 (1946); *Bute v. Illinois,* 333 U.S. 640 (1948); *Tomkins v. Missouri,* 323 U.S. 485 (1945); *Townsend v. Burk,* 334 U.S. 736 (1948); *White v. Ragen,* 324 U.S. 760 (1945); *DeMeerleer v. Michigan,* 329 U.S. 663 (1947); *Marino v. Ragen,* 332 U.S. 561 (1947); *Rice v. Olsen,* 324 U.S. 786 (1945).

18. *Gideon v. Wainwright,* 372 U.S. 335 (1963).
19. Id. at 343-344.
20. *Escobedo v. Illinois,* 378 U.S. 478 (1964).
21. *Miranda v. Arizona,* 384 U.S. 436 at 466 (1966).
22. Id. at 471.
23. *Argersinger v. Hamlin,* 407 U.S. 25 at 32-33, 40 (1972).
24. *Scott v. Illinois,* 440 U.S. 367 (1979).
25. *Powell v. Alabama,* 287 U.S. 45 (1932).
26. *Hamilton v. Alabama,* 368 U.S. 52 (1961).
27. *Escobedo v. Illinois,* 378 U.S. 478 (1964); *Miranda v. Arizona,* 384 U.S. 436 (1966).
28. *United States v. Wade,* 388 U.S. 218 (1967); *Gilbert v. California,* 388 U.S. 263 (1967).
29. *United States v. Wade,* 388 U.S. 218 at 227 (1967).
30. *Kirby v. Illinois,* 406 U.S. 682 (1972); but see also *Coleman v. Alabama,* 399 U.S. 1 (1970).
31. *Kirby v. Illinois,* 406 U.S. 682 at 689-690 (1972).
32. *United States v. Ash,* 413 U.S. 300 (1973).
33. *Ross v. Moffit,* 417 U.S. 600 (1974).
34. *Glasser v. United States,* 315 U.S. 60 (1942).
35. Id. at 71, 76.
36. *Holloway v. Arkansas,* 435 U.S. 475 at 489-490 (1978).
37. *Mann v. Richardson,* 397 U.S. 759 (1970); *Tollett v. Henderson,* 411 U.S. 258 (1973).
38. *Strickland v. Washington,* 466 U.S. 668, at 689 (1984).
39. *United States v. Cronic,* 466 U.S. 648 (1984).
40. *Evitts v. Lucey,* 469 U.S. 387 (1985).

11

Double Jeopardy

To restrain the government from repeated prosecutions of an individual for one particular offense, the prohibition against double jeopardy was included in the Fifth Amendment. The Supreme Court has held that this guarantee protects an individual both against multiple prosecutions for the same offense and against multiple punishments for the same crime.

Until 1969 the double jeopardy clause applied only to federal prosecutions. In that year the Supreme Court in *Benton v. Maryland* held that the due process guarantee of the Fourteenth Amendment extended this protection to persons tried by states as well.[1]

A defendant is placed in jeopardy at the time his jury is sworn in,[2] although if a mistrial is declared under certain circumstances[3] or if the jury fails to agree on a verdict,[4] the double jeopardy clause does not forbid his retrial.

If he is convicted, he may waive his immunity against double jeopardy and seek a new trial, or he may appeal the verdict to a higher court. If the conviction is set aside for a reason other than insufficient evidence, he may be tried again for the same offense.[5]

If he is acquitted, the double jeopardy clause absolutely bars any further prosecution of him for that crime, even if the acquittal was the result of error.[6]

The double jeopardy guarantee, however, protects only against repeated prosecutions by a single sovereign government. Thus, it is not violated when a person is tried on both state and federal charges arising from a single offense. Many acts are offenses under both federal and state laws.

The Court established this rule in the 1922 case of *United States v. Lanza.* Lanza was convicted for violating Washington State's prohibition law. Then he was indicted on the same grounds for violating the federal prohibition law. The federal district judge dismissed his indictment as a violation of the double jeopardy guarantee. The government appealed the dismissal, and the Supreme Court reversed it, 6-3.

Chief Justice William Howard Taft wrote:

We have here two sovereignties, deriving power from different sources, capable of dealing with the same subject-matter within the same territory. Each may, without interference by the other, enact laws to secure prohibition. . . . Each government, in determining what shall be an offense against its peace and dignity, is exercising its own sovereignty, not that of the other.

It follows that an act denounced as a crime by both national and state sovereignties is an offense against the peace and dignity of both, and may be punished by each. The 5th Amendment, like all the other guaranties in the first eight amendments, applies only to proceedings by the Federal government . . . and the double jeopardy therein forbidden is a second prosecution under authority of the Federal government after a first trial for the same offense under the same authority. Here the same act was an offense against the state of Washington, because a violation of its law, and also an offense against the United States under the National Prohibition Act. The defendants thus committed two different offenses by the same act, and a conviction by a court of Washington of the offense against that state is not a conviction of the different offense against the United States, and so is not double jeopardy.[7]

The *Lanza* rule survives. In 1959 and again in 1985 the Court reaffirmed its opinion that multiple prosecutions by different sovereigns—including two states—for the same offense did not violate the double jeopardy clause.[8] However, because a state and a city are not separate sovereigns, the double jeopardy guarantee does protect an individual against prosecution by both for one offense.[9]

The separate sovereignties doctrine was applied by the Court in the 1978 case of *United States v. Wheeler.* There the Court ruled that the double jeopardy clause did not protect an American Indian defendant convicted in tribal court from being tried by federal authorities for the same offense.[10]

In 1985 the Court ruled against a defendant's challenge to being tried in two different states for two parts of the same crime—the murder of his wife. One state—where the murder was committed—charged him for the murder; the second—where he dumped the body—charged him for that crime. The Supreme Court, with Justice Sandra Day O'Connor writing the opinion in *Heath v. Alabama,* found nothing in this situation to violate the double jeopardy guarantee.[11]

The double jeopardy clause also protects an individual

who successfully appeals his conviction on a lesser charge from being retried on the original charge.

In the 1957 case of *Green v. United States* the Court ruled that Green, tried for first-degree murder but convicted of murder in the second degree—a verdict that he successfully appealed—could not be tried again for first-degree murder after he won a new trial on appeal. The Court said that Green had been once in jeopardy for first-degree murder and that appeal of his conviction for a different crime did not constitute a waiver of his protection against double jeopardy. The Court explained:

> The underlying idea, one that is deeply ingrained in at least the Anglo-American system of jurisprudence, is that the State with all its resources and power should not be allowed to make repeated attempts to convict an individual for an alleged offense, thereby subjecting him to embarrassment, expense and ordeal and compelling him to live in a continuing state of anxiety and insecurity, as well as enhancing the possibility that even though innocent he may be found guilty.[12]

In 1937—in the often-cited decision in *Palko v. Connecticut*—the Court rejected the idea that the Fourteenth Amendment due process clause applied the double jeopardy guarantee to state action.

Palko was convicted of second-degree murder and sentenced to life imprisonment. The state sought and won a new trial claiming that legal errors had occurred at trial. At a second trial Palko was found guilty of first-degree murder and sentenced to die. He challenged his second conviction as a violation of the double jeopardy guarantee and of due process.

The Court rejected this argument, excluding the double jeopardy guarantee from the list of guarantees that had been "absorbed" into due process. That protection, Justice Benjamin N. Cardozo wrote for the majority, was not "of the very essence of a scheme of ordered liberty."[13] He then elaborated:

> Is that kind of double jeopardy to which the statute has subjected him a hardship so acute and shocking that our polity will not endure it? Does it violate those "fundamental principles of liberty and justice which lie at the base of all our civil and political institutions?"... The answer surely must be "no." ... The state is not attempting to wear the accused out by a multitude of cases with accumulated trials. It asks no more than this, that the case against him shall go on until there shall be a trial free from the corrosion of substantial legal error.... This is not cruelty at all, nor even vexation in any immoderate degree. If the trial had been infected with error adverse to the accused, there might have been review at his instance, and as often as necessary to purge the vicious taint. A reciprocal privilege, subject at all times to the discretion of the presiding judge ... has now been granted to the state. There is here no seismic innovation. The edifice of justice stands, its symmetry, to many, greater than before.[14]

Thirty-two years later, in 1969, the Court overruled *Palko*. In its last announced decision under Chief Justice Earl Warren, the Court in *Benton v. Maryland* declared that the double jeopardy clause did apply to the states through the due process guarantee of the Fourteenth Amendment. Justice Thurgood Marshall delivered the majority opinion:

Our recent cases have thoroughly rejected the *Palko* notion that basic constitutional rights can be denied by the States so long as the totality of the circumstances does not disclose a denial of "fundamental fairness." Once it is decided that a particular Bill of Rights guarantee is "fundamental to the American scheme of justice," ... the same constitutional standards apply against both the State and Federal Governments. *Palko's* roots had thus been cut away years ago. We today only recognize the inevitable.[15]

Justices John Marshall Harlan and Potter Stewart dissented from this "march toward 'incorporating' much, if not all, of the Federal Bill of Rights into the Due Process Clause."[16]

A dozen years later, a case similar to *Palko* came to the Court. *Bullington v. Missouri* arose after Robert Bullington was convicted of murder, for which he could have been sentenced to death. Instead, the jury sentenced him to life in prison without eligibility for parole for fifty years.

Bullington won a new trial, and the state declared that it would again seek a death sentence for him. Bullington objected, arguing that the double jeopardy clause precluded his being once again placed in jeopardy of a death sentence—after a jury had already decided that he should not be executed.

The Supreme Court, 5-4, agreed with him. The state should not have a second chance to try to convince a jury to sentence Bullington to die, wrote Justice Harry A. Blackmun. Once a jury had decided that he should not die for his crime, Bullington's right to be secure against double jeopardy forbade the state, even at a new trial, to seek the death penalty. Dissenting were Chief Justice Warren E. Burger and Justices Byron R. White, Lewis F. Powell, Jr., and William H. Rehnquist.[17]

The same day the Court announced its decision in *Benton*—June 23, 1969—it held in *North Carolina v. Pearce* that the double jeopardy guarantee limited the authority of a judge to impose a harsher sentence than the original upon a defendant whose first conviction had been set aside for a new trial.[18]

Unless there were objective reasons related to the conduct of the defendant after the imposition of the first sentence, and unless those reasons were set out in the record of the case, a judge could not impose a harsher sentence after retrial, the Court held. Furthermore, time already served on the first sentence must be credited against the new sentence.

Pearce was convicted of assault with intent to rape and sentenced to twelve to fifteen years in prison. After serving several years, he won reversal of his conviction and a new trial. Convicted in the second trial, Pearce was sentenced to eight years in prison. When this new sentence was added to the time he had already served, it amounted to a longer sentence than the original one.

Justice Stewart wrote the Court's opinion, holding the new sentence a violation of the double jeopardy guarantee unless the time already served was credited against it:

> The Court has held today, in *Benton v. Maryland* ... that the Fifth Amendment guarantee against double jeopardy is enforceable against the States through the Fourteenth Amendment. That guarantee has been said to consist of three separate constitutional protections. It protects against a second prosecution for the same offense after acquittal. It protects against a second

prosecution for the same offense after conviction. And it protects against multiple punishments for the same offense. This last protection is what is necessarily implicated in any consideration of the question whether, in the imposition of sentence for the same offense after retrial, the Constitution requires that credit must be given for punishment already endured. . . .

We hold that the constitutional guarantee against multiple punishments for the same offense absolutely requires that punishment already exacted must be fully "credited" in imposing sentence upon a new conviction for the same offense. If upon a new trial, the defendant is acquitted, there is no way the years he spent in prison can be returned to him. But if he is reconvicted, those years can and must be returned—by subtracting them from whatever new sentence is imposed.[19]

In 1973, however, the Court refused to apply these limitations to resentencing by a *jury* after retrial.[20]

In the mid-1970s the Supreme Court in several rulings began to expand the government's right to appeal a judge's decision to dismiss charges against a defendant after the trial was underway. Such appeals had been thought impermissible under the general rule that the prosecution may not appeal a verdict of acquittal.

In 1975 the Court in *United States v. Wilson* held that the double jeopardy guarantee did not foreclose a government appeal of a trial judge's decision to dismiss charges against a defendant who had already been found guilty.[21]

The Court reasoned that the double jeopardy clause did not foreclose an appeal of such a postverdict dismissal of charges inasmuch as the success of the appeal would only result in reinstatement of the verdict, not in a new trial.

In another case decided that same day, the Court seemed to make the possibility of further proceedings against the defendant a crucial element in determining the permissibility of such appeals. In *United States v. Jenkins* the Court held that the double jeopardy clause did forbid the government to appeal a ruling dismissing an indictment when a successful appeal might result in further proceedings.[22]

Three years later, however, the Court overruled *Jenkins* with its decision *United States v. Scott.*[23] By a 5-4 vote the Court held that the government could appeal a trial judge's decision to grant a defendant's motion to dismiss charges in midtrial. The Court held that the double

jeopardy guarantee did not forbid an appeal of that ruling—or retrial of the defendant—because a defendant, in seeking dismissal of the charges based on grounds unrelated to his guilt or innocence, had made a voluntary choice to risk retrial for the same offense.

The double jeopardy clause, held the majority, protected an individual against government oppression through multiple prosecutions, but not against the consequences of his own voluntary choice.

Notes

1. *Benton v. Maryland,* 395 U.S. 784 (1969).
2. *Downum v. United States,* 372 U.S. 734 (1963); *Crist v. Bretz,* 437 U.S. 28 (1978).
3. *Wade v. Hunter,* 336 U.S. 684 (1949); *United States v. Dinitz,* 424 U.S. 600 (1976); *Lee v. United States,* 432 U.S. 23 (1977); *Oregon v. Kennedy,* 456 U.S. 667 (1982).
4. *United States v. Perez,* 9 Wheat. 579 (1824); *Richardson v. United States,* 468 U.S. 317 (1984).
5. *United States v. Ball,* 163 U.S. 662 (1896); *Hudson v. Louisiana,* 450 U.S. 40 (1981); *Smalis v. Pennsylvania,* 476 U.S. 140 (1986), but see *Tibbs v. Florida,* 457 U.S. 31 (1982).
6. *United States v. Sanges,* 144 U.S. 310 (1892); *United States v. Ball,* 163 U.S. 662 (1896); *Fong Foo v. United States,* 369 U.S. 141 (1962); *Sanabria v. United States,* 437 U.S. 54 (1978).
7. *United States v. Lanza,* 260 U.S. 377 at 382 (1922).
8. *Abbate v. United States,* 359 U.S. 187 (1959); *Bartkus v. Illinois,* 359 U.S. 121 (1959); see also *Petite v. United States,* 361 U.S. 529 (1960); *Heath v. Alabama,* 474 U.S. 82 (1985).
9. *Waller v. Florida,* 397 U.S. 387 (1970).
10. *United States v. Wheeler,* 435 U.S. 313 (1978).
11. *Heath v. Alabama,* 474 U.S. 82 (1985).
12. *Green v. United States,* 355 U.S. 184 at 187-188 (1957); see also *Price v. Georgia,* 398 U.S. 323 (1970).
13. *Palko v. Connecticut,* 302 U.S. 319 at 325 (1937).
14. *Id.* at 328.
15. *Benton v. Maryland,* 395 U.S. 784 at 795 (1969).
16. *Id.* at 808.
17. *Bullington v. Missouri,* 451 U.S. 430 (1981); see also *Arizona v. Rumsey,* 467 U.S. 203 (1984), and *Poland v. Arizona,* 476 U.S. 147 (1986).
18. *North Carolina v. Pearce,* 395 U.S. 711 (1969), but see also *Texas v. McCullough,* 475 U.S. 134 (1986).
19. *North Carolina v. Pearce,* 395 U.S. 711 at 717.
20. *Chaffin v. Stynchcombe,* 412 U.S. 17 (1973).
21. *United States v. Wilson,* 420 U.S. 332 (1975).
22. *United States v. Jenkins,* 420 U.S. 358 (1975).
23. *United States v. Scott,* 437 U.S. 82 (1978).

12

Cruel and Unusual Punishment

The Eighth Amendment prohibits "cruel and unusual" punishment but does not specify what is cruel and unusual. The Supreme Court has interpreted this prohibition flexibly, measuring punishments against "evolving standards of decency." Although it has refused, for example, to outlaw the death penalty as invariably cruel and unusual, it has applied the constitutional standard to prohibit states from imposing prison sentences upon those found "guilty" of drug addiction. The Court has said that it views the amendment as prohibiting punishments it found barbaric or disproportionate to the crime.

Since early in the twentieth century, the Supreme Court has weighed the severity of a challenged sentence against the seriousness of the crime. In 1910 the Court in *Weems v. United States* declared the Eighth Amendment ban violated by a law that allowed a person convicted of falsifying a public record to be assessed a heavy fine, sentenced to fifteen years at hard labor, and subjected to several other sanctions.[1]

Nearly a half century later the Court in *Trop v. Dulles* reversed a military court's decision to strip of U.S. citizenship a man who had been convicted of desertion during wartime. The majority, for whom Chief Justice Earl Warren spoke, found such "denationalization" a cruel and unusual punishment "forbidden by the principle of civilized treatment guaranteed by the Eighth Amendment."[2]

Warren then set out an often quoted description of this constitutional provision:

The exact scope of the constitutional phrase "cruel and unusual" has not been detailed by this Court.... The basic concept underlying the Eighth Amendment is nothing less than the dignity of man. While the State has the power to punish, the Amendment stands to assure that this power be exercised within the limits of civilized standards. Fines, imprisonment and even execution may be imposed depending upon the enormity of the crime, but any technique outside the bounds of these traditional penalties is constitutionally suspect.... The Court [has] recognized ... that the words of the Amendment are not precise, and that their scope is not static. The Amendment must draw its meaning from the evolving standards of decency that mark the progress of a maturing society.[3]

EIGHTH AMENDMENT AND THE STATES

Capital punishment has been discussed by the Supreme Court in virtually every cruel and unusual punishment case it has decided, even if the death penalty was not the punishment challenged.

As early as 1892 the Court refused to apply the Eighth Amendment ban to state action.[4] In the midtwentieth century that position was quietly abandoned, but not until 1962 did the Court hold that a state violated that prohibition by authorizing an unusually cruel punishment.

One of the most bizarre of the Court's death penalty cases was that of *Louisiana ex rel. Francis v. Resweber*, decided in 1947.

Willie Francis was sentenced to die by electrocution. On the appointed day Francis was put in the electric chair, the switch was thrown—and nothing happened. A mechanical failure in the operating mechanism prevented the electricity from reaching Francis.

Francis then appealed to the Supreme Court, asking them to forbid the state a second execution attempt because it would constitute cruel and unusual punishment. The Court denied Francis' appeal, by a vote of 5-4.[5]

Speaking for the majority, Justice Stanley F. Reed assumed that the Eighth Amendment ban applied to state action, but did not find that action in Francis's case to be cruel and unusual.

[T]he fact that petitioner has already been subjected to a current of electricity does not make his subsequent execution any more cruel in the constitutional sense than any other execution. The cruelty against which the Constitution protects a convicted man is cruelty inherent in the method of punishment, not the necessary suffering involved in any method employed to extinguish life humanely. The fact that an unforeseeable accident prevented the prompt consummation of the sentence cannot, it seems to us, add an element of cruelty to a subsequent execution. There is no purpose to inflict unnecessary pain nor any unnecessary pain involved in the proposed execution.... We cannot agree that the hardship imposed upon the petitioner rises to that level of hardship denounced as denial of due process because of cruelty.[6]

Justice Harold H. Burton, joined by Justices William O. Douglas, Frank Murphy, and Wiley B. Rutledge, dissented.

Fifteen years after refusing to halt Willie Francis's execution, the Court in 1962 for the first time used the Eighth Amendment to invalidate a state law.

In *Robinson v. California* the Court held it impermissibly cruel and unusual punishment for a state to impose prison sentences upon persons found to be drug addicts.

Justice Potter Stewart wrote the majority opinion for six members of the Court:

This statute ... is not one which punishes a person for the use of narcotics, for their purchase, sale or possession, or for antisocial or disorderly behavior resulting from their administration. It is not a law which even purports to provide or require medical treatment. Rather, we deal with a statute which makes the "status" of narcotic addiction a criminal offense....

It is unlikely that any State ... would attempt to make it a criminal offense for a person to be mentally ill, or a leper, or to be afflicted with a venereal disease ... in the light of contemporary human knowledge, a law which made a criminal offense of such a disease would doubtless be universally thought to be an infliction of cruel and unusual punishment in violation of the Eighth and Fourteenth Amendments....

... We hold that a state law which imprisons a person thus afflicted as a criminal ... inflicts a cruel and unusual punishment in violation of the Fourteenth Amendment.[7]

Justices Byron R. White and Tom C. Clark dissented.

In 1968 the Court refused to apply *Robinson* to forbid states to punish public drunkenness.

In *Powell v. Texas* the Court upheld a Texas law under which Leroy Powell was convicted of being intoxicated in a public place. He attacked the law as cruel and unusual punishment, because it punished him for being a chronic alcoholic.

By a 5-4 vote the Court rejected that challenge. Justice Thurgood Marshall delivered the majority opinion, distinguishing the law in *Powell* from that in *Robinson.*

[A]ppellant was convicted, not for being a chronic alcoholic, but for being in public while drunk on a particular occasion. The State of Texas thus has not sought to punish a mere status, as California did in *Robinson;* nor has it attempted to regulate appellant's behavior in the privacy of his home. Rather, it has imposed upon appellant a criminal sanction for public behavior which may create substantial health and safety hazards, both for appellant and for members of the general public, and which offends the moral and esthetic sensibilities of a large segment of the community.[8]

Justice Abe Fortas, in a dissent joined by Justices Douglas, Stewart, and William J. Brennan, Jr., said the appellant was powerless to avoid drinking and, once intoxicated, could not prevent himself from appearing in public places.

CAPITAL PUNISHMENT

In the decade from 1968 through 1978 the Supreme Court zigzagged its way through a series of rulings on the question of capital punishment. By 1980 it was clear that the Court was not ready to outlaw the death penalty as out of line with contemporary standards of decency.

The first in this line of rulings was *Witherspoon v. Illinois,* decided in 1968.

In *Witherspoon* the Court held that states could not exclude from juries in capital cases all persons opposed to the death penalty. Such exclusion of a sizable group, held the Court, resulted in a jury which was not fairly representative of the community. *(Jury selection, pp. 163-169)*

Justice Stewart spoke for the majority:

in a nation less than half of whose people believe in the death penalty, a jury composed exclusively of such people [those favoring capital punishment] cannot speak for the community. Culled of all who harbor doubts about the wisdom of capital punishment—of all who would be reluctant to pronounce the extreme penalty—such a jury can speak only for a distinct and dwindling minority.... In its quest for a jury capable of imposing the death penalty, the State produced a jury uncommonly willing to condemn a man to die.[9]

Three years later the Court upheld, against a due process challenge, state laws that left completely to the discretion of the jury the decision whether to impose a sentence of death upon a particular defendant. This was the Court's ruling in the 1971 case of *McGautha v. California,* reached by a 6-3 vote.

Justice John Marshall Harlan, speaking for six members of the Court, declared that:

In light of history, experience, and the present limitations of human knowledge, we find it quite impossible to say that committing to the untrammeled discretion of the jury the power to pronounce life or death in capital cases is offensive to anything in the Constitution.[10]

In dissent, Justices William Brennan, Marshall, and Douglas argued that states should be required to set guidelines for this irrevocable jury decision.

Only a year later, however, the Court effectively reversed *McGautha.*

By a 5-4 vote the Court in *Furman v. Georgia, Jackson v. Georgia,* and *Branch v. Texas* invalidated all existing death penalty statutes.

State laws like those of Georgia and Texas, held the majority, left too much discretion to juries in imposing this ultimate penalty. The result was a "wanton and freakish" pattern of its use which violated the Eighth Amendment ban on cruel and unusual punishments.[11]

The Court that had rejected a Fourteenth Amendment due process challenge in *McGautha* upheld an Eighth Amendment challenge in *Furman.*

The majority was composed of the five justices who had served under Chief Justice Warren: Douglas, Brennan, Stewart, White, and Marshall. Each wrote a separate opinion. Dissenting were the four members named to the Court

Bail: Neither Absolute Nor Excessive

The Eighth Amendment states that "[e]xcessive bail shall not be required." Throughout U.S. history, federal law has provided that persons arrested for noncapital offenses shall be granted the right to post bail and win release to participate in preparing their defense.

Bail is money or property pledged by an accused person to guarantee his appearance at trial. The accused is thus permitted to go free on bond. Failure to appear at trial—"jumping bail"—carries criminal penalties, plus forfeiture of the pledged bond.

The Supreme Court has held that a presumption in favor of granting bail exists in the Bill of Rights. Justice Horace Gray wrote in 1895:

> The statutes of the United States have been framed upon the theory that a person accused of crime shall not, until he has been finally adjudged guilty in the court of last resort, be absolutely compelled to undergo imprisonment or punishment, but may be admitted to bail, not only after arrest and before trial, but after conviction and pending a writ of error.[1]

The Eighth Amendment's bail provisions limit federal courts, not state courts. In 1894 the Court ruled in *McKane v. Durston* that the Eighth Amendment provision on bail did not apply to the states.[2]

The Federal Rules of Criminal Procedure provide that the amount of bail shall be determined by the nature and circumstances of the offense, the weight of the evidence, the defendant's ability to pay, and his general character.[3] Under the 1966 Bail Reform Act, almost all persons charged with noncapital federal offenses are able to obtain release on personal recognizance or unsecured bond.[4]

The leading Supreme Court decision on the question of excessive bail is *Stack v. Boyle,* decided in 1951. Twelve Communist leaders in California were indicted for conspiracy under the Smith Act. Bail was fixed at $50,000 for each defendant. The defendants moved to reduce the amount of bail on the grounds that it was excessive in violation of the Eighth Amendment.

The Supreme Court agreed. Chief Justice Fred M. Vinson delivered the opinion of the Court saying:

> This traditional right to freedom before conviction permits the unhampered preparation of a defense, and serves to prevent the infliction of punishment prior to conviction.... Unless this right to bail before trial is preserved, the presumption of innocence, secured only after centuries of struggle, would lose its meaning.
>
> The right to release before trial is conditioned upon the accused's giving adequate assurance that he will stand trial and submit to sentence if found guilty.... Bail set at a figure higher than an amount reasonably calculated to fulfill this purpose is "excessive" under the Eighth Amendment....
>
> If bail in an amount greater than that usually fixed for serious charges of crimes is required in the case of any of the petitioners, that is a matter to which evidence should be directed in a hearing....
>
> In the absence of such a showing, we are of the opinion that the fixing of bail before trial in these cases cannot be squared with the statutory and constitutional standards for admission to bail.[5]

The following spring, however, the Court held that the Eighth Amendment did not guarantee an absolute right to bail. Certain alien Communists had been detained prior to a final determination on their deportation. Their application for bail was denied by the attorney general acting under provisions of the 1950 Internal Security Act.

The Court divided 5-4 in rejecting their argument that bail should be granted. Justice Stanley F. Reed, writing for the majority in *Carlson v. Landon,* stated that the Eighth Amendment did not guarantee all persons detained by federal authority the right to be released on bail:

> The bail clause was lifted with slight changes from the English Bill of Rights Act. In England that clause has never been thought to accord a right to bail in all cases, but merely to provide that bail shall not be excessive in those cases where it is proper to grant bail. When this clause was carried over into our Bill of Rights, nothing was said that indicated any different concept. The Eighth Amendment has not prevented Congress from defining the classes of cases in which bail shall be allowed in this country. Thus, in criminal cases, bail is not compulsory where the punishment may be death.... We think, clearly, here that the Eighth Amendment does not require that bail be allowed.[6]

Justices Hugo L. Black, Felix Frankfurter, William O. Douglas, and Harold H. Burton dissented. Black wrote, "The plain purpose of our bail Amendment was to make it impossible for any agency of Government, even the Congress, to authorize keeping people imprisoned a moment longer than was necessary."[7]

1. *Hudson v. Parker,* 156 U.S. 277 at 285 (1895).
2. *McKane v. Durston,* 153 U.S. 684 (1894).
3. Federal Rules of Criminal Procedure, Rule 46(c).
4. Congressional Quarterly, *Congress and the Nation,* vol. II (Washington, D.C.: Congressional Quarterly, 1969), 315-316.
5. *Stack v. Boyle,* 342 U.S. 1 at 4-5, 6, 7 (1951).
6. *Carlson v. Landon,* 342 U.S. 524 at 545-546 (1952).
7. Id. at 557-558.

by President Richard M. Nixon—Chief Justice Warren E. Burger and Justices Harry A. Blackmun, Lewis F. Powell, Jr., and William H. Rehnquist. Justice Douglas wrote:

> Under these laws no standards govern the selection of the penalty. People live or die, dependent on the whim of one man or of 12....
>
> ... these discretionary statutes are unconstitutional in their operation. They are pregnant with discrimination and discrimination is an ingredient not compatible with the idea of equal protection of the laws that is implicit in the ban on "cruel and unusual" punishments.[12]

Justice Brennan found the death penalty "uniquely degrading to human dignity" no matter how the decision was reached:[13]

> Death is an unusually severe and degrading punishment; there is a strong probability that it is inflicted arbitrarily; its rejection by contemporary society is virtually total; and there is no reason to believe that it serves any penal purpose more effectively than the less severe punishment of imprisonment. The function of these principles is to enable a court to determine whether a punishment comports with human dignity. Death, quite simply, does not.[14]

Justice Stewart found the method of the use of this penalty under existing law to be the critical point in his decision:

> These death sentences are cruel and unusual in the same way that being struck by lightning is cruel and unusual. For, of all the people convicted of rapes and murders in 1967 and 1968, many just as reprehensible as these, the petitioners are among a capriciously selected random handful upon whom the sentence of death has in fact been imposed ... the Eighth and Fourteenth Amendments cannot tolerate the infliction of a sentence of death under legal systems that permit this unique penalty to be so wantonly and so freakishly imposed.[15]

Justice White took a similar view:

> The imposition and execution of the death penalty are obviously cruel in the dictionary sense. But the penalty has not been considered cruel and unusual punishment in the constitutional sense because it was thought justified by the social ends it was deemed to serve. At the moment that it ceases realistically to further these purposes, however, the emerging question is whether its imposition ... would violate the Eighth Amendment. It is my view that it would, for its imposition would then be the pointless and needless extinction of life with only marginal contributions to any discernible social or public purposes....
>
> It is ... my judgment that this point has been reached with respect to capital punishment as it is presently administered under the statutes involved in these cases.[16]

Justice Marshall found the death penalty both "excessive" and "morally unacceptable." He wrote that "the average citizen would, in my opinion, find it shocking to his conscience and sense of justice. For this reason alone capital punishment cannot stand."[17]

Chief Justice Burger, writing for the dissenting justices, based their position in large part on their view of the

---

Cruel Punishment

The Court in the 1980s addressed a number of cases in which punishment other than the death penalty was challenged as in violation of the Eighth Amendment.

In 1980 the Court, 5-4, refused to hold that it was unconstitutionally cruel and unusual punishment for a state to impose a mandatory life sentence upon a "three-time loser"—even though the three crimes of which this defendant had been convicted were all relatively petty, nonviolent crimes. Justice William H. Rehnquist wrote the opinion in *Rummel v. Estelle;* Justices William J. Brennan, Jr., Thurgood Marshall, Lewis F. Powell, Jr., and John Paul Stevens dissented.[1]

That same year, however, the Court ruled that individuals who felt that federal officials had violated their Eighth Amendment right had the right to sue those officials for damages.[2]

Just three years later, the Court reversed the position it took in *Rummel.* In *Solem v. Helm,* the Court, again 5-4, but this time with Justice Harry A. Blackmun joining the *Rummel* dissenters, the Court held that South Dakota violated the Eighth Amendment when it imposed a life sentence without possibility of parole on a man convicted on seven separate occasions of nonviolent felonies.

This decision marked the first time this provision had been used to judge the relative severity of a prison sentence.[3]

1. *Rummel v. Estelle,* 445 U.S. 263 (1980).
2. *Carlson v. Green,* 446 U.S. 14 (1980).
3. *Solem v. Helm,* 463 U.S. 277 (1983).

---

respective roles of judges and legislators:

> If legislatures come to doubt the efficacy of capital punishment, they can abolish it, either completely or on a selective basis. If new evidence persuades them that they have acted unwisely, they can reverse their field and reinstate the penalty to the extent it is thought warranted. An Eighth Amendment ruling by judges cannot be made with such flexibility or discriminating precision.[18]

Furman effectively struck down all existing death penalty laws. The Court, however, left open two avenues that states could follow in enacting new laws, limiting jury discretion sufficiently to ensure that the death penalty would be imposed in a less capricious manner.

States could remove almost all discretion from the decision by making death the mandatory punishment for certain crimes. Or the states could provide a two-stage procedure in capital cases—a trial at which the issue of guilt or innocence was determined and then, for those persons found guilty, a second proceeding at which evidence might be presented before the decision was reached on whether to impose a sentence of death.

Thirty-five states passed new death penalty statutes. Ten chose the mandatory route; the other twenty-five, the two-stage procedure. By 1976 both types of new laws were back before the Supreme Court, and the Court again was asked to declare whether death in and of itself was a cruel and unusual—hence unconstitutional—punishment for any crime in the United States.

The Court refused to outlaw capital punishment in 1976. In *Gregg v. Georgia* and two companion cases, *Proffitt v. Florida* and *Jurek v. Texas*, the Court refused to declare the death penalty unconstitutional in all circumstances. Justices Brennan and Marshall dissented.

Justice Stewart set out the majority position:

> [W]e are concerned here only with the imposition of capital punishment for the crime of murder, and when a life has been taken deliberately by the offender, we cannot say that the punishment is invariably disproportionate to the crime. It is an extreme sanction, suitable to the most extreme of crimes.[19]

So the Court would not overrule the judgment of state legislatures and declare capital punishment *per se* unconstitutional. Justice Stewart continued:

> Considerations of federalism, as well as respect for the ability of a legislature to evaluate, in terms of its particular State, the moral consensus concerning the death penalty and its social utility as a sanction, require us to conclude, in the absence of more convincing evidence, that the infliction of death as a punishment for murder is not without justification and thus is not unconstitutionally severe. . . .
>
> . . . We hold that the death penalty is not a form of punishment that may never be imposed, regardless of the circumstances of the offense, regardless of the character of the offender, and regardless of the procedure followed in reaching the decision to impose it.[20]

Justices Brennan and Marshall dissented. Brennan argued that death was now an uncivilized and unconstitutional punishment, writing that the Court "inescapably has the duty, as the ultimate arbiter of the meaning of our Constitution, to say whether, when individuals condemned to death stand before our Bar, 'moral concepts' require us to hold that the law has progressed to the point where we should declare that the punishment of death, like punishments on the rack, the screw and the wheel, is no longer morally tolerable in our civilized society."[21]

Justice Marshall found death an excessive, shocking, and unjust punishment in all cases, and would declare it invariably cruel and unusual punishment, forbidden by the Eighth Amendment.

Of equal or greater practical significance, the Court in *Gregg, Jurek,* and *Proffitt* approved as constitutional the new two-stage procedure adopted by Georgia, Florida, Texas, and twenty-two other states for imposing the death sentence. This procedure, wrote Justice Stewart, met the objections that had caused the Court in *Furman* to invalidate the existing state laws:

> The basic concern of *Furman* centered on those defendants who were being condemned to death capriciously and arbitrarily. Under the procedures before the Court in that case, sentencing authorities were not directed to give attention to the nature or circumstances of the crime committed or to the character or record of the

defendant. Left unguided, juries imposed the death sentence in a way that could only be called freakish. The new . . . sentencing procedures, by contrast, focus the jury's attention on the particularized nature of the crime and the particularized characteristics of the individual defendant. While the jury is permitted to consider any aggravating or mitigating circumstances, it must find and identify at least one statutory aggravating factor before it may impose a penalty of death. In this way the jury's discretion is channeled. No longer can a jury wantonly and freakishly impose the death sentence; it is always circumscribed by the legislative guidelines.[22]

The same day—July 2, 1976—the Court struck down state laws that made death the mandatory penalty for first-degree murder. This ruling came in *Woodson v. North Carolina* and *Roberts v. Louisiana.*[23]

The Court divided 5-4; Justices Brennan and Marshall became part of the majority with Justices Stewart, Powell, and John Paul Stevens. Dissenting were Chief Justice Burger and Justices Blackmun, White, and Rehnquist.

The Court held that mandatory death penalty statutes "simply papered over the problem of unguided and unchecked jury discretion" and were constitutionally unsatisfactory because they failed to allow room for consideration of the individual defendant and the particular crime.[24]

The majority refused to approve "[a] process that accords no significance to relevant facets of the character and record of the individual offender or the circumstances of the particular offense," finding that such a process "excludes from consideration in fixing the ultimate punishment of death the possibility of compassionate or mitigating factors stemming from the diverse frailties of humankind."[25]

The majority opinion concluded:

> we believe that in capital cases the fundamental respect for humanity underlying the Eighth Amendment . . . requires consideration of the character and record of the individual offender and the circumstances of the particular offense as a constitutionally indispensable part of the process of inflicting the penalty of death.[26]

Subsequently, the Court used similar reasoning in striking down a state law that made death the mandatory sentence for anyone convicted of the first-degree murder of a police officer, or for a prison inmate serving a life sentence without possibility of parole and yet convicted of murdering a fellow inmate.[27]

A CONTINUING REVIEW

The decade following *Gregg* and *Woodson* brought to the Court a steady stream of capital punishment cases—some arguing that laws approved in *Gregg* had been misapplied in a particular case, others bringing new broad-based challenges to the death penalty itself.

In 1977 in *Coker v. Georgia* the Court held that death was an excessive penalty for the crime of rape, striking down state laws that made rape a capital crime.[28]

And in 1978 the Court invalidated Ohio's death penalty law for murder because it limited too strictly the sort of mitigating factors that could be considered in the decision whether to impose the death penalty. Chief Justice Burger wrote for the Court in *Lockett v. Ohio, Bell v. Ohio.* Only Justice Rehnquist dissented.[29]

The Court has reemphasized in case after case that the Eighth Amendment requires that the sentencing judge or jury consider *all* relevant aspects of an individual offender's character, record, and crime—particularly any mitigating factors—before rendering a sentence.[30]

The question of whether a sentence of death can be imposed upon someone who participated in a crime that included murder but was not himself the killer has come to the Court twice in recent years. In *Enmund v. Florida* in 1982, the Court, 5-4, overturned a death sentence imposed upon the driver of a getaway car who neither killed anyone nor witnessed the killings. It was disproportionate, and therefore cruel and unusual, for him to be sentenced to death, wrote Justice White for the majority. Chief Justice Burger and Justices Rehnquist, Powell, and Sandra Day O'Connor dissented.[31]

Five years later, however, the Court narrowed *Enmund.* Also by a 5-4 vote—with O'Connor writing the opinion—the Court in *Tison v. Arizona* ruled that accomplices could indeed be executed if their participation in the crime was major and if they displayed reckless indifference to the value of human life. Justice White joined the majority in this case.[32]

In 1984 the Court rebuffed the argument that the Constitution required state courts to review a death sentence to ensure that it was proportional to the punishment imposed on others convicted of similar crimes. Such review was permitted, but not required by the Constitution, the Court held, 7-2, in *Pulley v. Harris.*[33]

That same year, the Court, 6-3, held that a judge was free to disregard a jury's recommendation of a life sentence and to impose a sentence of death instead. Nothing in the Constitution gave juries sole power to impose a death sentence, the Court held in *Spaziano v. Florida.*[34]

In 1985, seventeen years after its ruling in *Witherspoon,* which set out a rule to govern exclusion of jurors with scruples about the death penalty, the Court discarded the *Witherspoon* rule and adopted one that made exclusion easier.

With Rehnquist as its spokesman, the Court, 7-2, declared that a juror could be excluded when his views would "prevent or substantially impair the performance of his duties as a juror in accordance with his instructions and oath." This rule, adopted in *Wainwright v. Witt,* was much more permissive of exclusion than the *Witherspoon* rule, which permitted exclusion only if it was unmistakable that a juror's view were so strong as to prevent his making an impartial decision on the defendant's guilt.[35]

The following year, the Court reaffirmed this stance, rejecting the argument that to exclude opponents of the death penalty from juries offended the constitutional requirement that the jury be drawn from a cross section of the community and that it be impartial. But in 1987 the Court declared, 5-4, that anytime a potential juror was wrongly disqualified for expressing doubts about capital punishment, the defendant was entitled to a new trial.[36]

In 1986 the Court held that the Constitution forbade the execution of an insane prisoner.[37]

Then in 1987 the Court disposed of what was said to be the last broad-based challenge to the death penalty. By a 5-4 vote in *McCleskey v. Kemp* the Court held that statistics showing race-related disparities in the imposition of the death penalty were not enough to sustain constitutional challenges to state death penalty laws.

For the majority Justice Powell wrote that "apparent disparities in sentencing are an inevitable part of our criminal justice system." The disparities shown in this case were not so great as to indicate that then entire system was so infected that it must be struck down. Justices Brennan, Marshall, Blackmun, and Stevens dissented.[38]

The continuing close balance on this issue was evident only two months later, when the Court, again 5-4, and again with Powell as its voice, held that the use of "victim impact statements"—concerning the effect of a murder on a victim's family—was unconstitutional, creating a risk that a jury might impose a sentence of death in arbitrary and capricious fashion.[39]

Notes

1. *Weems v. United States,* 217 U.S. 349 (1910).
2. *Trop v. Dulles,* 356 U.S. 86 at 99 (1958).
3. Id. at 99-101.
4. *O'Neil v. Vermont,* 144 U.S. 323 (1892).
5. *Louisiana ex rel. Francis v. Resweber,* 329 U.S. 459 (1947).
6. Id. at 464.
7. *Robinson v. California,* 370 U.S. 660 at 666, 667 (1962).
8. *Powell v. Texas,* 392 U.S. 514 at 532 (1968).
9. *Witherspoon v. Illinois,* 391 U.S. 510 at 520-521 (1968).
10. *McGautha v. California,* 402 U.S. 183 at 207 (1971).
11. *Furman v. Georgia, Jackson v. Georgia, Branch v. Texas,* 408 U.S. 238 (1972).
12. Id. at 253, 256-257.
13. Id. at 291.
14. Id. at 305.
15. Id. at 309-310.
16. Id. at 312-313.
17. Id. at 369.
18. Id. at 404.
19. *Gregg v. Georgia,* 428 U.S. 153 at 187 (1976); *Proffitt v. Florida,* 428 U.S. 325 (1976); *Jurek v. Texas,* 428 U.S. 262 (1976).
20. *Gregg v. Georgia,* 428 U.S. 153 at 186-187 (1976).
21. Id. at 229.
22. Id at 206-207.
23. *Woodson v. North Carolina,* 428 U.S. 280 (1976); *Roberts v. Louisiana,* 428 U.S. 325 (1976).
24. *Woodson v. North Carolina,* 428 U.S. 280 at 302 (1976).
25. Id. at 304.
26. Id.
27. *Roberts v. Louisiana,* 431 U.S. 633 (1977); *Sumner v. Shuman,* ___ U.S. ___ (1987).
28. *Coker v. Georgia,* 433 U.S. 583 (1977).
29. *Lockett v. Ohio,* 438 U.S. 586 (1978); *Bell v. Ohio,* 438 U.S. 637 (1978).
30. *Eddings v. Oklahoma,* 455 U.S. 104 (1982); *Skipper v. South Carolina,* 476 U.S. 1 (1986); *Hitchcock v. Dugger,* ___ U.S. ___ (1987).
31. *Enmund v. Florida,* 458 U.S. 782 (1982).
32. *Tison v. Arizona,* ___ U.S. ___ (1987).
33. *Pulley v. Harris,* 465 U.S. 37 (1984).
34. *Spaziano v. Florida,* 468 U.S. 447 (1984).
35. *Wainwright v. Witt,* 469 U.S. 412 (1985).
36. *Lockhart v. McCree,* 476 U.S. 162 (1986); *Gray v. Mississippi,* ___ U.S. ___ (1987).
37. *Ford v. Wainwright,* 477 U.S. 399 (1986).
38. *McCleskey v. Kemp,* ___ U.S. ___ (1987).
39. *Booth v. Maryland,* ___ U.S. ___ (1987).

Part IV

Equal Rights

The Fourteenth Amendment to the Constitution forbids any state to "deny any person within its jurisdiction the equal protection of the laws." Upholding that right of equal protection, the Supreme Court in 1954 struck down state laws segregating blacks from whites in public schools, touching off a civil rights revolution that has widened over the decades to include discrimination against women, the aged, the handicapped, and aliens and which has not yet reached its conclusion.

The guarantee of equal protection prohibits arbitrary discrimination, such as laws that restrict a person's right to vote, to travel from state to state, or to marry whomever he or she pleases. The equal protection clause is both the weapon securing and the armor safeguarding the civil rights of many distinct groups of people.

In the closing decades of the twentieth century, the equal protection clause has become so well established as a shield against discrimination that it may be forgotten that this interpretation of the clause is a modern development. The Fourteenth Amendment, ratified in 1868, was intended primarily to prevent discrimination against the blacks whose citizenship it confirmed. But the Supreme Court soon interpreted it into uselessness.

Segregation of the races was an unassailable fact of life in the late nineteenth century and for most of the twentieth century. The equal protection clause was invoked primarily, although not often successfully, against allegedly unfair and unequal taxation and regulation of economic and commercial affairs. Not until the late 1930s did the clause begin to protect those persons and groups intended to be its primary beneficiaries.

Whether applied to civil rights or property rights, the equal protection clause has never been interpreted by the Court to require a law to treat all groups it affects just the same. Laws by their very nature distinguish between categories of people, classes of property, and kinds of actions. For the most part, such distinctions are desirable, even necessary in an organized society. But some may be capricious or malicious and thereby deny equal protection to the classified group. Thus the question a court must answer whenever a law is challenged as a violation of equal protection is not whether a classification may be made but whether the classification is permissible.

Traditional Standard

The first standard developed by the Supreme Court for measuring a particular classification against the equal protection guarantee grew largely out of its review of state tax and economic regulation. Here the Court deferred more often than not to the judgment of the states.

Not surprisingly, its standard for review of such alleged violations was minimal. The Court was satisfied that a classification was valid if a state could show that it had a reasonable basis. This traditional standard for testing the validity of classifications—still pertinent to appropriate cases today—was summarized by the Court in 1911:

> The equal protection clause of the Fourteenth Amendment does not take from the State the power to classify in the adoption of police laws, but admits of the exercise of a wide scope of discretion in that regard, and avoids what is done only when it is without any reasonable basis and is therefore purely arbitrary....
>
> A classification having some reasonable basis does not offend against the clause merely because it is not made with mathematical nicety or because in practice it results in some inequality....
>
> When the classification in such a law is called in question, if any state of facts reasonably can be conceived that would sustain it, the existence of that state of facts at the time the law was enacted must be assumed....
>
> One who assails the classification in such a law must carry the burden of showing that it does not rest upon any reasonable basis, but is essentially arbitrary.[1]

Invoking only this permissive standard, the Court upheld few challenges to laws on equal protection grounds. The Court noted in 1927 the clause had become no more than "the usual last resort of constitutional arguments."[2]

Modern Standard

The Court's shift in focus from property rights to individual rights in the late 1930s led it to develop a more

Federal Equal Protection

Nowhere does the Constitution explicitly require the federal government to ensure equal protection of its laws against arbitrary discrimination. The Supreme Court, however, has found this requirement implicit in the Fifth Amendment's guarantee of due process of law. The Court explained this finding in the 1954 case of *Bolling v. Sharpe* in which it struck down the federal government's requirement that black and white pupils in the District of Columbia attend separate schools:

> The Fifth Amendment ... does not contain an equal protection clause as does the Fourteenth Amendment which applies only to the states. But the concepts of equal protection and due process, both stemming from our American ideal of fairness, are not mutually exclusive. The "equal protection of the law" is a more explicit safeguard of prohibited unfairness than "due process of law," and, therefore, we do not imply that the two are always interchangeable phrases. But, as this Court has recognized, discrimination may be so unjustifiable as to be violative of due process. (347 U.S. 483 at 499, 1954)

The Court reaffirmed this finding in several later cases: *Weinberger v. Wiesenfeld*, 420 U.S. 636 at 638, note 2 (1975); *Buckley v. Valeo*, 424 U.S. 1 at 93 (1976); *Hampton v. Mow Sun Wong*, 426 U.S. 88 at 100 (1976); *Davis v. Passman*, 442 U.S. 228 (1979).

probing standard for examining charges of denial of equal protection. Under this so-called active standard, classifications that are "inherently suspect" or that affect what the Court considers to be fundamental rights or interests require a greater degree of justification for their existence than simple rationality. A state must prove not only that it has a compelling governmental interest for making the challenged classification, but also that it can achieve that interest in no other way.

The development of this modern standard came in separate stages. In 1944 the Court declared race to be a suspect category requiring this heightened judicial scrutiny. But the Court then did not expressly apply this standard in its most important decision on racial discrimination, the 1954 ruling striking down state-imposed school segregation as a violation of equal protection. Classifications by alienage came in for heightened review as early as 1948, but not until 1971 did the Court explicitly describe alienage as a suspect category.

As early as 1942 the Court indicated that the equal protection clause protected all individuals from state deprivation of certain fundamental rights. But twenty years passed before the Court began to elaborate on this premise.

Much of the development of this modern equal protection standard began after Congress passed the 1964 Civil Rights Act, which prohibited discrimination on the grounds of race, color, national origin, or religion in most privately owned public accommodations. It also prohibited job discrimination on these grounds and on the basis of sex.

Passage of the 1965 Voting Rights Act authorized federal action to enforce the rights of blacks to vote. In 1968 Congress barred discrimination in the sale and rental of housing.

As a result of these federal laws, minorities and other groups traditionally victimized by discrimination brought more and more suits charging a denial of equal protection. In reviewing these cases, the Court has moved further and further from the traditional "reasonable basis" standard.

Race and alienage are the only two categories to which the Supreme Court has accorded suspect status.

The Court first declared race a suspect category in 1944. The case was *Korematsu v. United States* and involved a U.S. citizen of Japanese descent who defied a World War II military order requiring all persons of Japanese descent living on the West Coast to report to relocation centers. The Court ruled against Korematsu and held that the wartime emergency necessitated the unusual detention. But in so deciding, it announced that it would give classifications by race increased attention:

> It should be noted ... that all legal restrictions which curtail the civil rights of a single racial group are immediately suspect. That is not to say that all such restrictions are unconstitutional. It is to say that courts must subject them to the most rigid scrutiny. Pressing public necessity may sometimes justify the existence of such restrictions; racial antagonism never can.[3]

Ten years later, its 1954 school desegregation decisions made abundantly clear the meaning of "rigid scrutiny."

But it was not until 1967 that the Court expressly acknowledged that all racial classifications were "inherently suspect." This rather anticlimactic declaration came in a case in which the Court struck down a Virginia statute that made it a crime for residents to enter into interracial marriages. *(Racial equality, p. 227)*

As early as 1886 the Court held that the Fourteenth Amendment protected aliens as well as citizens. But during the next sixty years, the Court, applying the traditional standard of review, found most statutes challenged as discriminating against aliens were in fact based on some reasonable—and therefore permissible—objective.

In 1948 the Court began to require more than simple rationality to justify such laws. But not until 1971 did the Court explicitly acknowledge that such classifications were inherently suspect, requiring a compelling interest as justification.

"Aliens as a class are a prime example of a 'discrete and insular' minority ... for whom ... heightened judicial solicitude is appropriate," said the Court.[4]

However, because the Constitution gives Congress exclusive authority over naturalization and, by extension, immigration, the Court has been reluctant to judge federal alienage classification laws as strictly as similar state laws. *(Alienage, p. 269)*

All the modern cases challenging discrimination on the basis of sex have occurred since 1969. The Court has applied the traditional standard of review to the majority of them, and more often than not found that the state had a rational basis to justify treating women differently from men.

In one line of decisions, however, the Court has held that classifications by sex were impermissible. On the grounds of administrative efficiency, the statutes struck down in these cases presumed that all men behaved in one way and all women in another, failing to allow for any variation from the unproved assumption. The Court found such presumptions arbitrary, too broad, and unjustified by mere administrative convenience.

In a case decided in 1976, a slim majority of the Court adopted a test that fell between the "reasonable basis" standard and the "compelling governmental interest" test. This standard requires the state to show that its sex-based classification was necessary to achieve some "important governmental objective." [5]

The Court has upheld both the 1964 Civil Rights Act ban on job discrimination on the grounds of sex and the 1963 Equal Pay Act requiring that men and women be paid the same for the same work.

But the Court has steadily refused to describe differential treatment of pregnant women as sex discrimination. Such a classification is based not on gender but on physical condition, a majority of the Court has held, ruling that classification by physical condition did not violate either the equal protection clause or the 1964 Civil Rights Act. *(Sex discrimination, p. 275)*

The Court has refused to apply the compelling interest standard to test laws that discriminate against illegitimate children and the poor. Nonetheless, it has treated most cases involving classification by legitimacy with more than minimal scrutiny, striking down several laws distinguishing illegitimate children from their legitimate siblings on the grounds that such classifications were arbitrary and archaic. The Court has found discrimination against the poor unconstitutional when it deprives the indigent of a fundamental right or interest. But the Court has not applied the equal protection clause to protect the poverty-stricken from deprivation of rights not considered "fundamental."

Fundamental Interests

The Court first articulated its "fundamental interest" standard in the 1942 case of *Skinner v. Oklahoma*. The justices were unanimous as they struck down an Oklahoma statute that authorized sterilization of criminals who had committed two felonies "involving moral turpitude":

We are dealing here with legislation which involves one of the basic civil rights of man. Marriage and procreation are fundamental to the very existence and survival of the race. The power to sterilize, if exercised, may have subtle, far-reaching and devastating effects. In evil or reckless hands it can cause races or types which are inimical to the dominant group to wither and disappear. There is no redemption for the individual whom the law touches. . . . He is forever deprived of a basic liberty. We mention these matters . . . merely in emphasis of our view that strict scrutiny of the classification which a State makes in a sterilization law is essential, lest unwittingly or otherwise invidious discriminations are made against groups or types of individuals in violation of the constitutional guaranty of just and equal laws. [6]

The fundamental interest doctrine next emerged in 1964, when the Court held that the equal protection guarantee required states to create electoral districts each of which had substantially the same number of voters. In *Reynolds v. Sims* the Court wrote:

Undoubtedly, the right of suffrage is a fundamental matter in a free and democratic society. Especially since the right to exercise the franchise in a free and unimpaired manner is preservative of other basic civil and political rights, any alleged infringement of the right of citizens to vote must be carefully and meticulously scrutinized. [7]

In 1969, the Court elaborated:

[I]f a challenged state statute grants the right to vote to some *bona fide* residents of requisite age and citizenship and denies the franchise to others, the Court must determine whether the exclusions are necessary to promote a compelling state interest.

    . . . [T]he deference usually given to the judgment of legislators does not extend to decisions concerning which resident citizens may participate in the election of legislators and other public officials. . . . [W]hen we are reviewing statutes which deny some residents the right to vote, the general presumption of constitutionality afforded state statutes and the traditional approval given state classifications if the Court can conceive of a "rational basis" for the distinctions made are not applicable. [8]

Applying this stricter standard, the Court has struck down a number of statutes because they restricted the right to vote. States have no compelling reason to deny the right to vote to persons simply because they have not resided in the state for a certain period of time, or because they are too poor to pay a poll tax. Filing fees that prevent poor candidates from seeking office also are unconstitutional, as are statutes that keep off the ballot all candidates except those belonging to the two major political parties. *(Voting participation cases, p. 289)*

Durational residency requirements also violate another fundamental interest guarded by the equal protection clause—the right to travel unrestricted from state to state. The Court has debated for several decades the source of this right, sometimes finding it in the interstate commerce clause of Article I of the Constitution, at other times in the privileges and immunities clause of the Fourteenth Amendment. In 1966 the Court abandoned the debate:

The constitutional right to travel from one State to another . . . occupies a position fundamental to the concept of our Federal Union. It is a right that has been firmly established and repeatedly recognized. . . . Although there have been recurring differences in emphasis within the Court as to the source of the constitutional right of interstate travel, there is no need here to canvass those differences further. All heve agreed that the right exists. [9]

Using this reasoning, the Court in 1969 declared requirements that persons live in a state for a certain period of time before becoming eligible for welfare benefits to be a violation of equal protection and thus unconstitutional. The Court said such requirements unconstitutionally restricted the poor in the exercise of their right to travel interstate.

The Supreme Court has designated one other such

matter a fundamental right. That right—access to justice—has been foreclosed at times to poor people who could not afford the fees required either to file suit or hire an attorney, or pay for a transcript to prepare an appeal. In many of these instances, the Court has held that the fee requirement impermissibly violated the indigent's guarantee of due process as well as equal protection of the laws. *(Access to justice, p. 287)*

The fundamental interest doctrine has been criticized from the bench, first by Justice John Marshall Harlan and then by Justice William H. Rehnquist, who replaced Harlan on the bench. Both contended that the Court exceeds its power when it singles out certain rights and interests for special protection. Harlan wrote in 1969:

> [W]hen a statute affects only matters not mentioned in the Federal Constitution and is not arbitrary or irrational, I must reiterate that I know of nothing which entitles this Court to pick out particular human activities, characterize them as "fundamental," and give them added protection under an unusually stringent equal protection test.[10]

In 1972 Rehnquist added that "[t]his body of doctrine created by the Court can only be described as a judicial superstructure, awkwardly engrafted upon the Constitution itself."[11]

Since 1969 the Court has refused to classify any other right or interest as fundamental. Although it hinted in 1969 that it might place "food, shelter and other necessities of life" in the fundamental right category, the Court in 1972 held that the assurance of adequate housing was not a fundamental interest.[12] And in 1973 a majority of the Court held that the right to an education was neither explicitly nor implicitly guaranteed by the Constitution. The majority added that it was "not the province of this Court to create substantive constitutional rights in the name of guaranteeing equal protection of the laws."[13]

Notes

1. *Lindsley v. Natural Carbonic Gas Co.*, 220 U.S. 61 at 78-79 (1911); see also *McGowan v. Maryland*, 366 U.S. 420 (1961); *Williamson v. Lee Optical Co.*, 348 U.S. (1955); *Kotch v. Board of River Pilot Commissioners*, 330 U.S. 552 (1947); *Royster Guano Co. v. Virginia*, 253 U.S. 412 (1920).
2. *Buck v. Bell*, 274 U.S. 200 at 208 (1927).
3. *Korematsu v. United States*, 323 U.S. 214 at 216 (1944).
4. *Graham v. Richardson*, 403 U.S. 365 at 372 (1971).
5. *Craig v. Boren*, 429 U.S. 190 at 197 (1976).
6. *Skinner v. Oklahoma*, 316 U.S. 535 at 541 (1942).
7. *Reynolds v. Sims*, 377 U.S. 533 at 561-562 (1964).
8. *Kramer v. Union Free School District*, 395 U.S. 621 at 627-628 (1969).
9. *United States v. Guest*, 383 U.S. 745 at 757, 759 (1966).
10. *Shapiro v. Thompson*, 394 U.S. 618 at 662 (1969).
11. *Weber v. Aetna Casualty & Surety Co.*, 406 U.S. 164 at 179 (1972).
12. *Shapiro v. Thompson*, 394 U.S. 618 at 627 (1969); *Lindsey v. Normet*, 405 U.S. 56 (1972).
13. *San Antonio Independent School District v. Rodriguez*, 411 U.S. 1 at 33 (1973).

Racial Equality

The Fourteenth Amendment, said the Supreme Court in 1880,

> was designed to assure to the colored race the enjoyment of all the civil rights that under the law are enjoyed by white persons, and to give to that race the protection of the general government, in that enjoyment, whenever it should be denied by the States. It not only gave citizenship and the privileges of citizenship to persons of color, but it denied to any State the power to withhold from them the equal protection of the laws, and authorized Congress to enforce its provisions.[1]

Another seventy-five years would pass before black people would receive any substantial benefit from the Fourteenth Amendment's protections. Even as the Court spoke in 1880, southern states had begun to separate white from black in what would result in almost complete social, legal, and political segregation of the two races.

The Court itself played a role in creating the climate that allowed segregation to flourish. In its first actions regarding blacks after the Civil War, the Court admitted a black attorney to the Supreme Court bar and ruled that a black woman could sue for damages a railroad company that had forcibly removed her from a train after she refused to sit in the "colored" car.[2]

But in the 1873 *Slaughterhouse Cases*, the Court divided 5-4 in ruling that citizens held two distinct types of citizenship, one federal and one state. The Fourteenth Amendment, the majority held, protected a person only from state infringement on such privileges and immunities of national citizenship as the right to petition the federal government and the right to vote in federal elections. The privileges and immunities conferred by citizenship in a state were outside federal protection. This decision, intact today, divested the privileges and immunities clause of any substantive protection it might have afforded citizens of either race.[3]

In the *Slaughterhouse* opinion, the majority characterized the amendment's equal protection clause as primarily of use to protect blacks from unjust discrimination. In deciding the 1880 case of *Strauder v. West Virginia*, the Court utilized the clause to strike down a state law that barred blacks from jury service.

Three years later, however, the Court significantly narrowed the protection of the clause for blacks. In the 1883 *Civil Rights Cases*, the Court nullified an 1875 federal law that gave all persons, regardless of color, "the full and equal enjoyment" of public transportation, inns, theaters, and "other places of public amusement."[4] The Court held that the Fourteenth Amendment prohibited only state-imposed discrimination, and not that imposed by individuals acting privately. Congress therefore had overstepped its authority when it sought to stop private businessmen from discriminating against blacks. Furthermore, the Court said, the amendment only empowered Congress to remedy acts of state discrimination; Congress could not enact a general law in anticipation of discriminatory state actions.

By 1883 the fervor of Reconstruction had worn thin. As one historian wrote, "Other than Negroes and their faithful friends, the people were tired of giving special protection to the former slaves. It was felt to be time for the return to power of the dominant factions in the several communities."[5]

Against this background, the decision in the *Civil Rights Cases* had particular significance. Political scientist Alan F. Westin attributed two primary effects to it:

> [F]irst, it destroyed the delicate balance of federal guarantee, Negro protest and private enlightenment which was producing a steadily widening area of peacefully integrated public facilities in the North and South during the 1870s and early 1880s. Second, it had an immediate and profound effect on national and state politics as they related to the Negro. By denying Congress power to protect the Negro's rights to equal treatment, the Supreme Court wiped the issue of civil rights from the Republican party's agenda of national responsibility. At the same time, those Southern political leaders who saw anti-Negro politics as the most promising avenue to power could now rally the "poor whites" to the banner of segregation.[6]

Thirteen years later, in 1896, the Supreme Court sanctioned the "separate but equal" doctrine developed to justify state-imposed racial segregation. In its decision in *Plessy v. Ferguson*, a majority of the Court held that so long as the facilities provided blacks were equal to those provided whites, state laws requiring segregation did not violate the equal protection or due process clauses of the Fourteenth Amendment. Nor did the Court view separation of the races as pinning on blacks a badge of slavery in violation of the Thirteenth Amendment.[7]

In the wake of this decision, state-ordered segregation invaded almost every aspect of daily life in the former Confederate states. Blacks throughout the South were required to use separate streetcars, waiting rooms, toilets, and water fountains. They attended different schools and were segregated in parks and theaters, mental hospitals, and prisons. At the same time, blacks were almost completely disenfranchised in those states by devices such as the poll tax, property and literacy tests, and the white primary. *(Details of voting rights cases, p. 107)*

Although there was comparatively little official segregation in northern and western states, whites there generally regarded blacks as inferiors and there was little intermingling of the two races.

When the United States entered its brief but intense period of imperialism at the end of the nineteenth century, bringing some eight million nonwhites under its domination, northern attitudes grew steadily more sympathetic to the racist views of southern whites.

As the U.S. Commission on Civil Rights wrote in understatement: at the end of the nineteenth century, the "very concept of civil rights seemed to have passed out of existence, and the prospects for the future were not encouraging."[8]

SEGREGATION UNDER ATTACK

During the first third of the twentieth century, segregation by law appeared firmly entrenched, but the events that would lead to its demise were taking shape. The National Association for the Advancement of Colored People (NAACP), which would lead the court fight to end racial discrimination, was founded in 1909, and the National Urban League in 1911. World War I contributed markedly to rising black aspirations.

Many of the 360,000 blacks who fought to make the world safe for democracy began to wonder when they might begin to enjoy democracy's benefits. The Great War also spurred a black migration to the north where blacks found defense industry work.

Racial tension escalated. In the first year after the war's end, more than seventy blacks were lynched. The Ku Klux Klan enjoyed revived popularity in the North and South. In 1919 bloody race riots broke out in twenty-five cities across the nation. Historian John Hope Franklin described this time as "the greatest period of interracial strife the nation had ever witnessed."[9]

In three school segregation cases the Supreme Court refused to review the separate but equal doctrine, although in 1914 it did strike down a state law because it did not provide blacks with exactly the same train accommodations it provided whites.

In 1917 the Court struck down a municipal ordinance that prohibited blacks from living on the same streets as whites. This decision did not end residential segregation, however, because private restrictive covenants quickly replaced the illegal ordinances. These covenants, attached to the deed or title to property, forbade the white owner to sell to blacks. The Supreme Court upheld the covenants in 1926, reiterating its view that the Fourteenth Amendment did not reach private discrimination.

Blacks as a group were among the most severely burdened by the Great Depression of the 1930s. Although many blacks had left the Republican party to vote for Woodrow Wilson in 1912, only to be disillusioned when he did little to advance their civil rights, many thousands more swung their support to Franklin Delano Roosevelt in the 1936 and 1940 elections. The Democratic administration did try to improve the economic condition of both races, but segregation continued unabated. Blacks nonetheless had won recognition as a political power, and by the 1940s militant individuals and organized groups demanding an end to segregation were beginning to make themselves heard.

These demands steadily gained adherents as the ironies of World War II became increasingly apparent. The inconsistency of sending black and white soldiers to fight against Germany's vile racial policies while continuing to practice racial segregation at home became too obvious to ignore.

The cold war further intensified this paradox. Communist countries pointed to American racial policies in an effort to undermine the appeal of the democratic system that the United States was attempting to persuade the rest of the world to adopt. No reasonable person could deny the irony, as C. Vann Woodward observed, of the United States competing with the Soviet Union for the friendship of the people of the Orient and Africa while continuing to treat Orientals and blacks in the United States as second-class citizens.

Supreme Court Shifts Focus

Against this backdrop the Supreme Court began to take a closer look at the laws that discriminated on the basis of race.

From the end of the Civil War until 1937, the Supreme Court's primary concern was the protection of business from what it considered excessive regulation by the federal government. When these *laissez-faire* views jeopardized Roosevelt's New Deal programs, the president threatened in 1937 to "pack" the Court with additional justices who would construe the Constitution to support his economic policies.

The Court responded by relaxing its vigilant attitude toward economic regulation and shifting its focus to individual rights and liberties. A harbinger of this shift came in a 1938 footnote to an otherwise routine decision. In that note, Justice Harlan Fiske Stone implied that the Court might soon be required to decide whether

statutes directed at particular religious . . . or national . . . or racial minorities . . . [or] whether prejudice against discrete and insular minorities may be a special condition which tends seriously to curtail the operation of those political processes ordinarily to be relied upon to protect minorities, and which may call for a correspondingly more searching judicial inquiry.[10]

Slave or Free: The *Dred Scott* Case

Dred Scott, a slave seeking his freedom, brought about the first major individual rights ruling from the U.S. Supreme Court. Scott lost his case, and the Court's decision inflamed public opinion and contributed to the outbreak of the Civil War, which finally settled the question of slavery in the United States.

The case of *Dred Scott v. Sandford* was brought —with the financial support of Scott's owners—to test whether a slave who lived for a time on free soil would become free as a result. Scott had lived in Illinois and Wisconsin, where slavery was not permitted. He later returned to the slave state of Missouri, contending that he was free.

The Missouri Supreme Court held that under state law, Scott remained a slave. The case moved into the federal courts. The first federal court dismissed the case, finding that Scott, as a slave, was not a citizen of Missouri and so could not invoke the jurisdiction of the federal courts over suits between citizens of different states. By this time Scott had been sold outside of Missouri.

Scott appealed his case to the U.S. Supreme Court, which heard it argued twice in 1856. The nine justices voted 7-2 against him.

The majority would have resolved the case simply by declaring that Scott's status was a matter for Missouri, not federal officials, to decide. But the two dissenters, both fiercely antislavery, announced that their dissents would address broader issues: whether a slave could ever become a citizen, whether a stay on free soil made a slave free, and whether Congress had the power to ban slavery in the territories.

In response, each of the seven majority justices wrote his own opinion, setting out his views on these matters. The result was confusion. On March 6, 1857, the Court announced its decision. The opinion, by Chief Justice Roger B. Taney, is generally considered the official majority view.

Slaves May Not Be Citizens

Dred Scott could not be a citizen, declared Taney, nor could any slave or his descendant. Thus, the chief justice continued, blacks could "claim none of the rights and privileges which . . . [the Constitution] provides for and secures to citizens of the United States."[1]

When the Constitution used the word "citizens," it did not include slaves, Taney explained, reasoning from the fact that slaves "had for more than a century before [ratification of the Constitution] been regarded as being of an inferior order, and altogether unfit to associate with the white race, either in social or political relations; and so far inferior, that they had no rights which the white man was bound to respect."[2]

This last statement, taken out of its context as Taney's observation upon the historical view of slaves, was quoted time and again in the incendiary debates of the years before the war. Northern abolitionists were particularly incensed by it, viewing it as a statement of Taney's own belief in the inferiority of blacks.

Furthermore, wrote Taney, slaves were not included in the statement in the Declaration of Independence that "all men are created equal."[3]

Indeed, slaves were viewed as property, and the Constitution reflects this view. "The only two provisions which point to them and include them, treat them as property, and make it the duty of the government to protect it; no other power, in relation to this race, is to be found in the Constitution."[4]

Taney could have stopped there. He had given ample reason for dismissing Scott's case on the grounds that he was not a citizen. But Taney continued.

Congress lacked the power to declare certain territory "free" of slavery, he wrote, and so the "free territory" in which Scott had lived could not actually be so designated.

For Congress to do so, Taney reasoned, deprived slave-owning citizens of their property when they came into that territory—and thus denied slave owners due process of law, in violation of the Fifth Amendment.[5] Congress was officially declared powerless to stop the spread of slavery through the expanding nation.

Dred Scott Reversed

The Civil War rendered moot the question of congressional power over slavery. And in 1868 ratification of the Fourteenth Amendment reversed the Court's declaration that blacks were not and could not be citizens under the Constitution.

The first section of the amendment declares that all persons born or naturalized in the United States and subject to its jurisdiction are citizens of the United States and the state in which they live. That same section prohibits states from making any law abridging the privileges and immunities of citizens, depriving any person of life, liberty, or property without due process of law, or denying to anyone equal protection of the law.

It was this set of guarantees, indirectly the legacy of Dred Scott, a slave who sought to be free, that provide the basis for the modern revolution in civil rights.

1. *Dred Scott v. Sandford*, 19 How. 393 at 404 (1857).
2. Id. at 407.
3. Id. at 410.
4. Id. at 425.
5. Id. at 450.

That same year, the Court ruled that the separate but equal rule required a state to provide law schools for blacks if it provided them for whites, even though there might be only a single black law student. The Court also upheld the right of blacks to picket an employer to persuade him to hire more black workers.

In 1944, six years after Stone's footnote comment, the Court announced that it would give closer scrutiny to laws that treated one race differently from another, upholding such distinctions only if they were justified by a pressing governmental need. In that same year the Court held it unconstitutional for states to exclude black voters from primary elections and, in the first modern decision on job discrimination, the Court ruled in favor of black railroad workers.

In 1948 the Court took another look at restrictive covenants, ruling that although the Fourteenth Amendment did not prohibit them, it did prohibit states from enforcing them. With this decision, the Court began to expand its definition of state action covered by the Fourteenth Amendment to include private discrimination promoted in any way by official state action, even if the state action itself was not discriminatory.

But the decisions that portended the most for the future of black civil rights dealt with the question of whether separate facilities could be equal.

On June 5, 1950, the Court held first that Texas violated the equal protection clause because its black state law school was not the equivalent of the white school either in tangible aspects—such as the number of books in the library—or in intangible aspects such as the prestige of its faculty and alumni. In a second case decided the same day, the Court ruled that Oklahoma violated the equal protection guarantee when it separated a black from his white colleagues in classes, the library, and the cafeteria.

Four years later in the public school desegregation cases, familiarly known as *Brown v. Board of Education,* the unanimous Court declared that separation of the races in public schools was "inherently unequal." [11] After sixty years, the *Plessy* doctrine—and a way of life for an entire section of the nation—had been officially renounced.

The *Brown* decisions, wrote Professor G. Theodore Mitau,

> acknowledged judicially what many people had known or felt for a long time: Segregation was morally indefensible, socially irrational and politically undemocratic. It perpetuated a racial myth which imprisoned American values at home and weakened America's leadership abroad. Equally important to many, it defiled this country's claim to stand as a world model of freedom and human dignity in defense of which whites and Negroes fought side by side in all of this nation's major wars. [12]

In 1955 the Court issued guidelines directing school officials to desegregate schools with "all deliberate speed." Although many states complied with the Court order, many others embarked on programs of "massive resistance" in defiance of the Supreme Court order.

The governor of Arkansas in 1958 called out the state's national guard to prevent black students from entering a formerly all-white high school in Little Rock. In extraordinary session, the Supreme Court demanded unanimously that the state cease its resistance and that the students be admitted to the school.

For ten years after *Brown,* the Court left it to lower courts to implement school desegregation. The pace was slow: by 1964 less than 2 percent of black pupils in the former Confederate states were in desegregated schools. [13]

Civil Rights Revolution

During this same decade, however, the Court frequently cited *Brown* as precedent for rulings striking down other forms of segregation throughout the South, in parks and beaches, traffic courts and theaters, railroad cars and bus terminals.

These decisions spurred a revolution in civil rights. Blacks were no longer willing to let whites deny them their rights. Beginning in 1957 with a Montgomery, Alabama, bus boycott led by Dr. Martin Luther King, Jr., blacks organized to protest racial segregation and discrimination in jobs, housing, and public accommodations. The student sit ins and "freedom rides" of the early 1960s sensitized the rest of the nation to the black dilemma; the violence with which whites frequently countered black demonstrations drew the nation's sympathy.

The year that marked the 100th anniversary of the Emancipation Proclamation was particularly turbulent. In May 1963 police loosed dogs and turned high-pressure fire hoses on demonstrators in Birmingham, Alabama, provoking sympathy protests in several other cities. In August 200,000 blacks and whites marched peacefully in Washington, D.C., to present black demands for equal treatment to Congress, the president, and a closely watching country. One month later a bomb thrown into a black church in Birmingham killed four little girls. On November 22, an assassin shot and killed President John F. Kennedy, an unequivocal advocate of civil rights.

Hope, frustration, and outrage impelled Congress in 1964 to approve the most comprehensive civil rights act since Reconstruction. It barred discrimination in most public accommodations, prohibited job discrimination on the basis of race, and established a procedure for withholding federal funds from any program, including schools, that continued to discriminate against blacks.

That year also marked the end of the Court's silence on continuing questions of school desegregation. There has been "too much deliberation and not enough speed" in desegregating public schools, the Court declared in 1964, holding that a county could not close its schools to avoid desegregating them. Later in the year, the Court upheld that section of the 1964 Civil Rights Acts barring racial discrimination in most private accommodations. In 1966 the Court upheld Congress's 1965 Voting Rights Act.

In 1968 the Court reinterpreted an 1866 civil rights law as barring private individuals from refusing to sell their homes to persons of a different race. The Court also declared that state and school officials must do more than simply end segregation, that they had a duty to take affirmative action to ensure effective school desegregation. The Court also gave lower courts new guidelines for determining if desegregation efforts were sincere.

The Court's Remedies

Chief Justice Earl Warren's replacement in 1969 by Chief Justice Warren E. Burger coincided with a new phase in the civil rights movement and the Court's role in it. It was clear that racial discrimination was illegal; the Court's task was now to define the scope of remedies available to its victims.

The Burger Court approved a wide variety of measures to remedy school segregation, including busing, gerrymandered attendance zones, limited use of mathematical ratios, and compensatory education programs. The Court also extended the obligation to desegregate to nonsouthern school districts where existing segregation had not been imposed by law but rather through school-board policy.

At the same time, however, the Court insisted that these remedies be tailored to fit the extent of the proven discrimination. Thus a multidistrict busing plan was found too sweeping a remedy when deliberate discrimination had been found in only one of the affected districts. In another instance, a districtwide plan was held to be too broad because the proven discrimination had not been shown to infect the entire school district. The Court also held that once a school district was desegregated, school officials were not required to remedy its resegregation so long as it did not result from official state action.

After the Court reinterpreted the 1866 Civil Rights Act to bar housing discrimination by private individuals, it also read the act to prohibit private schools from refusing to admit black pupils and to invalidate neighborhood recreational association policies excluding black homeowners and renters from membership. In a major case in which federal and city housing officials admitted they had been guilty of intentional racial segregation, the Court backed a lower court's remedy that covered a metropolitan area. But in a second case, where a community was charged with exercising its zoning power to exclude blacks by omitting low-income housing, the Court held there was no constitutional violation because there was no evidence that the charges were true and that the zoning decision was motivated by racial considerations.

When charges of racial discrimination in employment have been brought under Title VII of the Civil Rights Act of 1964, the Court has placed the burden of proving nondiscrimination on the employer. Few employers have met this test. But when charges of job discrimination have been brought under the Fourteenth Amendment, the Court shifted the burden to the employees, requiring them to prove that the employer intended to discriminate; the discriminatory effect of an employment policy is not sufficient proof of intent. Few employees have met this test. Where job discrimination has been proved, however, the Court has sanctioned far-reaching remedies, including awards of back pay and retroactive seniority.

The success of the black civil rights movement encouraged other victims of discrimination, particularly women, to assert their right to equal treatment. It has also prompted some members of the majority to complain that they have suffered from "reverse discrimination," that is, that affirmative action programs to remedy past minority discrimination have in turn discriminated against whites.

The Court has held that the 1964 Civil Rights Act provides remedies to whites as well as blacks who have been discriminated against in employment because of their race and that it bars universities receiving federal funds from setting aside a specific number of seats in each class for minority applicants. But the Court has endorsed as within the bounds of the Constitution and the law the use of affirmative action, race-conscious remedies as a temporary means of remedying society's past discrimination.

EQUAL OPPORTUNITY FOR EDUCATION

When the Supreme Court in 1896 ruled that separate public facilities for blacks and whites did not violate the equal protection clause of the Fourteenth Amendment, it pointed to the nation's schools as "the most common instance" of segregation. "Establishment of separate schools for white and colored children has been held to be a valid exercise of the legislative power," the Court said in *Plessy v. Ferguson*, "even by courts of States where the political rights of the colored race have been longest and most earnestly enforced." [14]

Boston, 1849

The Court was referring to the fact that in an 1849 ruling a Massachusetts court first sanctioned separate schools for the two races. The city of Boston had maintained separate schools for blacks and whites since 1820. Sarah Roberts, a five-year-old black child, was forced, as a result of this segregation, to walk past five white primary schools on her way to the black school. When repeated attempts to place her in one of the closer white schools failed, Sarah's father hired Charles Sumner, the future senator and abolitionist, and went to court.

Appearing before Chief Justice Lemuel Shaw of Massachusetts in *Roberts v. City of Boston* (1849), Sumner made one of his most eloquent pleas, contending that the segregated schools violated state law which held all persons, "without distinction of age or sex, birth or color, origin or condition," to be equal before the law. Noting the general soundness of Sumner's contention, the state supreme court nonetheless rejected Roberts's challenge.

Shaw wrote that

> when this great principle [of equality before the law] comes to be applied to the actual and various conditions of persons in society, it will not warrant the assertion, that men and women are legally clothed with the same civil and political powers, and that children and adults are legally to have the same functions and be subject to the same treatment; but only that the rights of all, as they are settled and regulated by law, are equally entitled to the paternal consideration and protection of the law, for their maintenance and security. What those rights are, to which individuals, in the infinite variety of circumstances by which they are surrounded in society, are entitled, must depend on laws adapted to their respective relations and conditions. [15]

To Sumner's contention that segregation "brand[s] a whole race with the stigma of inferiority and degradation," Shaw responded:

> It is urged, that this maintenance of separate schools tends to deepen and perpetuate the odious distinction of caste, founded in a deep-rooted prejudice in public opinion. This prejudice, if it exists, is not created by law, and probably cannot be changed by laws. [16]

Massachusetts prohibited dual school systems six years after *Roberts*. In citing this case to support *Plessy*, the Court overlooked the fact that the state case was decided almost twenty years before ratification of the Fourteenth Amendment made blacks citizens and required the states to give all citizens equal protection of the laws.

Plessy and Schools

While the *Plessy* decision did not deal directly with school segregation, the Supreme Court in that opinion clearly condoned the practice. The Court confirmed this position in three subsequent cases challenging the "separate" half of the "separate but equal" doctrine as states applied it to schools. In all three instances the Court bowed to the right of the state to run its own schools, refusing to consider the constitutional question of whether state-required segregation denied black children equal protection of the laws.

The first of these cases was *Cumming v. Richmond (Ga.) County Board of Education*, decided in 1899, three years after *Plessy*. The school board had discontinued operating the black high school in order to use the building as an additional facility for black primary school pupils. The board continued to operate a high school for white girls and one for white boys. Blacks in the county sought an injunction to prevent taxes from being used to operate the white schools until a black high school was reestablished.

Refusing to grant the injunction, the Court said it would not address the issue of equal protection because it was not raised in the case. The Court then said:

> while all admit that the benefits and burdens of public taxation must be shared by citizens without discrimination against any class on account of their race, the education of the people in schools maintained by state taxation is a matter belonging to the respective States, and any interference on the part of the federal authority with the management of such schools cannot be justified except in the case of a clear and unmistakable disregard of rights secured by the supreme law of the land.[17]

Ironically, this opinion was written by Justice John Marshall Harlan, who had so vigorously dissented from *Plessy*. (Details, p. 248)

In 1908 Berea College, a private Christian school incorporated in Kentucky, challenged in the Supreme Court a state law requiring that any institution that taught both blacks and whites conduct separate classes for the two races.

The school said the state had illegally impaired the school's charter by denying it the right to teach students of both races together. The Court rejected the challenge, holding that since the college could still teach members of both races, the law had not significantly injured the school's charter.[18]

Twenty years later a girl of Chinese descent challenged her assignment to an all-black school in Mississippi as a denial of equal protection. In *Gong Lum v. Rice* (1927) the Court upheld her assignment to the black school, saying that the question raised "has been many times decided to be within the constitutional power of the state legislature to settle without intervention of the federal courts under the Federal Constitution."[19]

Separate and Unequal

In none of these early cases did the Court consider whether the segregated facilities were in fact equal. Nor was school segregation challenged on that specific basis. During the 1930s the NAACP determined that the separate-but-equal doctrine was most vulnerable on this point. Studies of dual school systems, particularly in the South, showed disproportionate amounts of money spent on white and black school facilities, materials, salaries, and transportation.

The NAACP decided first to attack the lack of equality in institutions of higher education. Inequality of facilities and instruction was even more apparent at the university level than at the primary and secondary school levels. Many states provided no school at all to blacks seeking certain advanced degrees. And NAACP officials reasoned that integration of a college or university by a few black students represented less of a threat to the segregated southern lifestyle than did wholesale integration of entire school districts.[20]

In 1938 the Supreme Court decided the first of these cases, *Missouri ex rel. Gaines v. Canada*. Because there were no black law schools in Missouri, Lloyd Gaines, a qualified black undergraduate, applied to the all-white University of Missouri Law School, which refused him admission solely because of his race. The school said it would pay Gaines's tuition at any law school in an adjacent state that would accept him. At the time, law schools in Kansas, Nebraska, Iowa, and Illinois accepted black out-of-state students. This solution was unacceptable to Gaines, who sued to compel the University of Missouri to admit him.

The Supreme Court ruled, 6-2, that Gaines had been denied equal protection and that he was entitled to be admitted to the state's all-white law school. Dismissing the state's contention that it intended to establish a black law school when it became practical, Chief Justice Charles Evans Hughes wrote:

> The question here is not of a duty of the State to supply legal training, or of the quality of the training which it does supply, but of its duty when it provides such training to furnish it to the residents of the State upon the basis of an equality of right. By the operation of the laws of Missouri, a privilege has been created for white law students which is denied to Negroes by reason of their race.[21]

The majority also rejected as inadequate the state's promise to pay tuition at an out-of-state school:

> We find it impossible to conclude that what otherwise would be an unconstitutional discrimination, with respect to the legal right to the enjoyment of opportunities within the State, can be justified by requiring resort to opportunities elsewhere. That resort may mitigate the inconvenience of the discrimination but cannot serve to validate it.[22]

Ten years later, the Court reaffirmed this ruling in *Sipuel v. Board of Regents of the University of Oklahoma* (1948) in which a black law school applicant had been refused admission to the University of Oklahoma because of her race. In a *per curiam* opinion, the Court said the state must provide Sipuel with legal training "in conformity with the equal protection clause."[23]

The next case, *Sweatt v. Painter* (1950), focused on

Famous Footnote: *Plessy* Refuted

One of the more controversial footnotes in Supreme Court history is footnote 11 in *Brown v. Board of Education* (1954). That footnote cited seven sociological and psychological studies of the effects of racial segregation, support for the Court's contention that segregation on the basis of race generated a feeling of inferiority among blacks that might never be erased. The text of the footnote follows:

> 11. K. B. Clark, Effect of Prejudice and Discrimination on Personality Development (Midcentury White House Conference on Children and Youth, 1950); Witner and Kotinsky, Personality in the Making (152), c. VI; Deutscher and Chein, The Psychological Effects of Enforced Segregation; A Survey of Social Science Opinion, 26 J. Psychol. 259 (1948); Chien, What are the Psychological Effects of Segregation Under Conditions of Equal Facilities?, 3 Int. J. Opinion and Attitude Res. 229 (1949); Brameld, Educational Costs, in Discrimination and National Welfare (MacIver, ed., 1949), 44-48; Frazier, The Negro in the United States (1949), 674- 681. And see generally Myrdal, An American Dilemma (1944).[1]

In his book *Simple Justice,* Richard Kluger quotes Chief Justice Earl Warren as saying of the footnote: "We included it because I thought the point it made was the antithesis of what was said in *Plessy.* They had said there that if there was any harm intended, it was solely in the mind of the Negro. I thought these things—these cited sources—were sufficient to note as being in contradistinction to that statement in *Plessy.*"[2]

Kluger's research indicates that at least two of the justices questioned inclusion of the footnote in the school desegregation opinion, but their objections were minor compared to those that came from critics of the decision. Mississippi senator James O. Eastland, (D, 1941, 1943-1979) in a May 27, 1954, speech in the Senate said:

> The Supreme Court could not find the authority for its decisions in the wording of the 14th Amendment, in the history of the amendment or in the decision of any court. Instead, the Court was forced to resort to the unprecedented authority of a group of recent partisan books on sociology and psychology. If this is the judicial calibre of the Court, what can the Nation expect from it in the future? What is to prevent the Court from citing as an authority in some future decision the works of Karl Marx?[3]

Even some who favored desegregation were displeased with the footnote. "It is one thing to use the current scientific findings, however ephemeral they may be, in order to ascertain whether the legislature has acted reasonably, in adopting some scheme of social or economic regulation.... It is quite another thing to have our fundamental rights rise, fall or change along with the latest fashions of psychological literature," wrote Professor Edmond Cahn.[4]

Another respected law professor, Alexander Bickel, concluded:

> It was a mistake to do it this way. If you're going to invoke sociology and psychology, do it right.... No matter how it had been done, no doubt, the enemies of the opinion were certain to seize upon it and proclaim the ruling unjudicial and illegal. The opinion therefore should have said straightforwardly that *Plessy* was based on a self-invented philosophy, no less psychologically oriented than the Court was being now in citing these sources that justify the holding that segregation inflicted damage. It was clear, though, that Warren wanted to present as small a target as possible, and that was wise. He did not want to go out to the country wearing a Hussar's uniform.[5]

1. *Brown v. Board of Education,* 347 U.S. 483 at 495 (1954).
2. Richard Kluger, *Simple Justice: The History of* Brown v. Board of Education *and Black America's Struggle for Equality* (New York: Alfred A. Knopf, 1976), 706.
3. U.S. Congress, Senate, *Congressional Record,* May 27, 1954, 100: 7252.
4. Edmond Cahn, *Jurisprudence* 30, New York University Law Review 150, 159 (1955).
5. Kluger, *Simple Justice,* 707.

the inequality of two state institutions at which legal training was provided. Refused admission to the all-white University of Texas law school, Sweatt sued in state court. The Court agreed that Sweatt had been denied equal protection but gave the state time to create a black law school. Sweatt refused to apply to the new school on the ground that its instruction would be inferior to that he would receive at the University of Texas. After state courts held the new school "equal" to the long-established university law school, Sweatt appealed to the Supreme Court.

Unanimously, the Court ordered that Sweatt be admitted to the University of Texas. The Court "cannot find substantial equality in the educational opportunities offered white and Negro law students by the state," wrote Chief Justice Fred M. Vinson. He elaborated:

> In terms of number of the faculty, variety of courses and opportunity for specialization, size of the student body, scope of the library, availability of law review and similar activities, the University of Texas Law

School is superior. What is more important, the University of Texas Law School possesses to a far greater degree those qualities which are incapable of objective measurement but which make for greatness in a law school. Such qualities, to name but a few, include reputation of the faculty, experience of the administration, position and influence of the alumni, standing in the community, traditions and prestige. It is difficult to believe that one who had a free choice between these law schools would consider the question close.[24]

For the first time, the Court had ordered a state to admit a black to an all-white school because the education provided by a black school was inferior. But Vinson said the Court saw no necessity to go on—as Sweatt's attorney, Thurgood Marshall, had asked it to do—to re-examine the separate but equal doctrine "in the light of contemporary knowledge respecting the purposes of the Fourteenth Amendment and the effects of racial segregation."[25]

A second case decided the same day, June 5, 1950, cast even more doubt upon the premise that separate could be equal. A black student admitted to the all-white University of Oklahoma as a candidate for a doctorate in education was assigned to a special seat in the classroom and to special tables in the library and cafeteria. The Supreme Court in *McLaurin v. Oklahoma State Regents for Higher Education* (1950) held that such state-imposed requirements produced inequities that could not be tolerated. The restrictions, the Court wrote, "impair and inhibit [McLaurin's] ability to study, to engage in discussion and exchange views with other students, and, in general, to learn his profession."[26]

Implicit in this decision was the fact that it was only McLaurin's segregation from the rest of the students that made his treatment unequal. He heard the same lectures, had access to the same books, and ate the same food.

Brown v. Board of Education

Even as the Court announced its decisions in *Sweatt* and *McLaurin*, the five cases in which the Court would make the implicit explicit were taking shape. In each of the five cases, parents of black school children asked lower courts to order school boards to stop enforcing laws requiring or permitting segregated schools.

The Cases

The challenge that gave the landmark school desegregation decision its name, *Brown v. Board of Education of Topeka,* was brought in 1951 by Oliver Brown in behalf of his daughter Linda.[27]

Under Kansas law permitting cities with populations over 15,000 to operate dual school systems, Topeka had opted to segregate its primary schools. As a result Linda Brown was forced to walk twenty blocks to an all-black grade school rather than attend an all-white school in her neighborhood. Several other black families joined the challenge.

In 1951 a federal district court found Topeka's segregation detrimental to black children but found no constitutional violation because the black and white primary schools were substantially equal with respect to buildings, curricula, transportation, and teachers.

The case of *Briggs v. Elliott* was actually the first to reach the Supreme Court. Federal proceedings began in 1950 when parents of black elementary and secondary school-aged children in Clarendon County, South Carolina, asked a federal district court to enjoin enforcement of state constitutional and statutory provisions requiring segregation in public schools. The court denied the request, but found the black schools inferior to the white and ordered the school board to equalize them immediately. The court refused, however, to order the school board to admit black children to the white school while the equalization took place. The children's parents then appealed to the Supreme Court, which in 1952 returned the case to the lower court to consider a report on the progress of the equalization program. The lower court found that the school board had either achieved substantial equality in all areas or soon would, and it again upheld the separate but equal doctrine. The case then returned to the Supreme Court.

Davis v. County School Board of Prince Edward County, Va. was almost identical to *Briggs.* Parents of black high school students sued to stop enforcement of the state's constitutional provisions requiring separate schools. While the district court found the black high school to be inferior and ordered its equalization, it upheld the validity of the segregation provisions. It also refused to admit the black students to white high schools while the black schools were being brought up to par with the white schools.

The fourth case, *Gebhart v. Belton,* involved the schools of New Castle County, Delaware. As in the other cases, parents of black children sued to stop enforcement of the constitutional provisions mandating a dual school system, but unlike the other cases, the state court granted the request. Finding the black schools inferior on a number of points, the court ordered white schools to admit black children. The state supreme court affirmed the decree, which the school board then appealed to the U.S. Supreme Court.

The fifth case, although argued with the other four, was decided separately.[28] *Bolling v. Sharpe* concerned public schools in the District of Columbia. Because the Fourteenth Amendment's guarantee of equal protection of the laws applies only to states, parents of black pupils based their challenge to school segregation in the District on the Fifth Amendment's guarantee of due process. A district court dismissed the suit, and the Supreme Court granted review of the dismissal. *(Box, p. 224)*

Together, the five cases brought to the Court grade school pupils and high school students, mandatory segregation laws and more permissive laws, the equal protection clause of the Fourteenth Amendment and the due process clause of the Fifth Amendment. Geographically, the five cases came from two southern states, one border state, a plains state, and the nation's capital. As one commentator noted, the "wide geographical range gave the anticipated decision a national flavor and would blunt any claim that the South was being made a whipping boy."[29]

In all five cases the lower courts found that education offered black students was substantially equal, or soon would be, to that given in the white schools. Thus the question presented to the Court was whether public school segregation per se was unconstitutional.

The Arguments

The school cases were argued in December 1952. In June 1953 the Court requested reargument, asking the attorneys to address themselves to three main questions.

● What historical evidence was there that the framers of the Fourteenth Amendment intended it to apply to segregation in public schools?

● If the answer to the first question was inconclusive, was it within the power of the Court to abolish segregation?

● If school segregation was found unconstitutional, what approach should the Court take to end it?

The cases were reargued in December 1953. Two months earlier former California governor Earl Warren had become chief justice, replacing Vinson, who had died in September. Because Congress had already adjourned when he was named, Warren presided over the Court by virtue of a recess appointment until his unanimous confirmation on March 1, 1954.

Although there were several lawyers on both sides, the two leading adversaries were Marshall, director of the NAACP Legal Defense and Educational Fund, which had been instrumental in guiding the challenge to school segregation through the courts, and John W. Davis, U.S. representative, D-W.Va. (1911-1913), solicitor general (1913-1918), and ambassador to Great Britain (1918-1921). In addition to being the 1924 Democratic presidential nominee, he had argued more cases before the Supreme Court than any other lawyer of his era.

Marshall, then forty-five, would become in 1967 the first black to sit *on* the Supreme Court. Davis, at age eighty, was making his final appearance before the Court, arguing in behalf of South Carolina in *Briggs* for the continuation of school segregation.

It is one of the ironies of these cases that in 1915 Davis as solicitor general had successfully persuaded the Court to strike down Oklahoma's "grandfather clause" that prohibited blacks from voting. In that case the fledgling NAACP supported Davis's position in its first friend-of-the-court brief.[30] *(Details, p. 109)*

Davis was first to present an answer to the Court's three questions. He contended that the framers of the Fourteenth Amendment never intended it to bar segregation in the nation's public schools. In addition to an intensive examination of the legislative history surrounding enactment of the amendment, Davis also recited the names of the states both north and south that instituted or continued to conduct segregated schools after the amendment was ratified; several of these same states had voted to ratify.

To the question whether the Court had the authority on its own to overturn the separate but equal doctrine, Davis reminded the Court that the doctrine had been upheld not only by the lower courts but by the Supreme Court, and had therefore become part of the law of the land. "[S]omewhere, sometime to every principle comes a moment of repose when it has been so often announced, so confidently relied upon, so long continued, that it passes the limits of judicial discretion and disturbance," he said.[31]

Making clear what he thought of earlier expert testimony concerning the detrimental effects of segregation on black children, Davis rhetorically asked what impact a desegregation order might have on a predominantly black school district such as Clarendon County:

If it is done on the mathematical basis, with 30 children as a maximum ... you would have 27 Negro children and three whites in one school room. Would that make the children any happier? Would they learn any more quickly? Would their lives be more serene?

Children of that age are not the most considerate animals in the world, as we all know. Would the terrible psychological disaster being wrought, according to some ... to the colored child be removed if he had three white children sitting somewhere in the same school room?

Would white children be prevented from getting a distorted idea of racial relations if they sat with 27 Negro children? I have posed that question because it is the very one that cannot be denied.[32]

Davis also said he did not believe the courts had the power to tell the states how to desegregate their schools. "Your Honors do not sit, and cannot sit as a glorified Board of Education for the State of South Carolina or any other state. Neither can the District Court," he declared. Davis then concluded:

Let me say this for the State of South Carolina.... It believes that its legislation is not offensive to the Constitution of the United States.

It is confident of its good faith and intention to produce equality for all of its children of whatever race or color. It is convinced that the happiness, the progress and the welfare of these children is best promoted in segregated schools, and it thinks it a thousand pities that by this controversy there should be urged the return to an experiment which gives no more promise of success today than when it was written into their Constitution during what I call the tragic era.

I am reminded—and I hope it won't be treated as a reflection on anybody—of Aesop's fable of the dog and the meat: The dog, with a fine piece of meat in his mouth, crossed a bridge and saw the shadow in the stream and plunged for it and lost both substance and shadow.

Here is equal education, not promised, not prophesied, but present. Shall it be thrown away on some fancied question of racial prestige?[33]

Marshall's response to Davis the following day illustrated the difference between the two men's styles and philosophies:

I got the feeling on hearing the discussion yesterday that when you put a white child in a school with a whole lot of colored children, the child would fall apart or something. Everybody knows that is not true.

Those same kids in Virginia and South Carolina— and I have seen them do it—they play in the streets together, they play on their farms together, they go down the road together, they separate to go to school, they come out of school and play ball together. They have to be separated in school.

There is some magic to it. You can have them voting together, you can have them not restricted because of law in the houses they live in. You can have them going to the same state university and the same college, but if they go to elementary and high school, the world will fall apart.... They can't take race out of this case. From the day this case was filed until this moment, nobody has in any form or fashion ... done anything to distinguish this [segregation] statute from the Black Codes, which they must admit, because nobody can dispute ... the Fourteenth Amendment was intended to deprive the states of power to enforce Black Codes or anything else like it.

De Facto Segregation: From Denver to Dayton

The Fourteenth Amendment prohibits state action denying anyone the equal protection of the law. It clearly applies to de jure segregation, which was imposed by law and which was declared unconstitutional in *Brown v. Board of Education.* De jure segregation existed in most southern and border states.

School segregation also existed in many northern and western urban communities, even though the states never required it or no longer practiced it. De facto segregation resulted from economic status, residential patterns, and other factors outside the usual scope of the equal protection clause.

Denver, 1973

In 1973, almost twenty years after *Brown,* the Court decided the first school segregation case from a state that had not imposed separation by law. In *Keyes v. School District #1, Denver,* the Court, 7-1, ruled that this type of school segregation might also be unconstitutional.

The case concerned two sets of schools in the Denver school system: some already found segregated by deliberate actions of the school board, and core city schools, which were segregated but not—a lower court had held—as a result of school board action. The Supreme Court directed the lower court to determine whether the school board's deliberate action in regard to the first set of schools so affected the other schools that it made the entire district a dual system. If not, the Court was to consider proof, which the school board must produce, that the core city schools were not intentionally segregated. If the proof was not persuasive, the Court should order desegregation.

With this decision the Court expanded the definition of de jure segregation to include that fostered by intentional school board policies, even in the absence of state law. Without a showing of intent to segregate, however, no constitutional wrong existed. "We emphasize that the differentiating factor between de jure segregation and so-called de facto segregation . . . is *purpose or intent to* segregate," Justice William J. Brennan, Jr., wrote.[1]

The majority indicated that the deliberate segregation of some of a system's schools could make the entire system a segregated one:

[C]ommon sense dictates the conclusion that racially inspired school board actions have an impact beyond the particular schools that are the subjects of those actions. . . . Plainly a finding of intentional segregation as to a portion of a school system is not devoid of probative value in assessing the school authorities' intent with respect to other parts of the same school system.[2]

Justice Lewis F. Powell, Jr., agreed with the decision, but not with retention of the de jure, de facto distinction. He contended that the Court should adopt instead the rule that

where segregated public schools exist within a school district to a substantial degree, there is a prima facie case that the duly constituted public authorities . . . are sufficiently responsible [for the segregation] to warrant imposing upon them a nationally applicable burden to demonstrate they nevertheless are operating a genuinely integrated school system.[3]

Disregarding Powell's suggestion, the Court in 1976 and 1977 continued to maintain the distinction between de jure and de facto segregation. In 1976 it told lower federal court judges to reconsider the school case of Austin, Texas, in light of that year's Supreme Court ruling in the job bias case of *Washington v. Davis* that discriminatory intent, as well as discriminatory effect, must be shown for a denial of equal protection to be proved.[4]

And in 1977 the Court in *Dayton Board of Education v. Brinkman* held that a lower court had erred in holding that the simple existence of racial imbalance in a city's schools constituted proof of deliberate segregation.[5]

Dayton, 1979

But when the Dayton case, along with a case from Columbus returned to the Court two years later, the Court abandoned its effort to distinguish between de jure and de facto segregation. The Court upheld massive court-ordered busing for both school systems, backing the finding of lower courts that both systems were unconstitutionally segregated.[6]

The majority stated that because the Dayton and Columbus systems had been largely segregated by race in 1954—at the time of *Brown*—the school boards in those cities had an affirmative constitutional responsibility to end that segregation. Because they had not, the busing orders were justified, declared the majority: the board's actions after 1954 "having foreseeable and anticipated disparate [racial] impact" were relevant evidence "to prove . . . forbidden purpose." [7]

1. *Keyes v. School District #1, Denver,* 413 U.S. 189 at 208 (1973); see also *Columbus (Ohio) Board of Education v. Penick,* 443 U.S. 449 (1979).
2. Id. at 203, 207 passim.
3. Id. at 224.
4. *Austin Independent School Board v. United States,* 429 U.S. 190 (1976); *Washington v. Davis,* 426 U.S. 229 (1976).
5. *Dayton (Ohio) Board of Education v. Brinkman,* 433 U.S. 406 (1977).
6. *Dayton Board of Education v. Brinkman, Columbus Board of Education v. Penick,* 443 U.S. 526 (1979).
7. Ibid.

. . . [T]he only way that this Court can decide this case in opposition to our position, is that there must be some reason which gives the state the right to make a classification that they can make in regard to nothing else in regard to Negroes, and we submit the only way to arrive at this decision is to find that for some reason Negroes are inferior to all other human beings. . . .

It can't be because of slavery in the past, because there are very few groups in this country that haven't had slavery some place back in the history of their groups. It can't be color because there are Negroes as white as the drifted snow, with blue eyes, and they are just as segregated as the colored man.

The only thing [it] can be is an inherent determination that the people who were formerly in slavery, regardless of anything else, shall be kept as near that stage as possible, and now is the time, we submit, that this Court should make it clear that that is not what our Constitution stands for.[34]

The Decision

All nine justices—including Robert H. Jackson, who had left a hospital bed—were present May 17, 1954, when Chief Justice Warren read the unanimous decision in *Brown v. Board of Education.* The opinion, described by many as the most socially and ideologically significant decision in the Court's history, was just thirteen paragraphs long.

Warren quickly disposed of the Court's first question—whether the framers of the Fourteenth Amendment intended it to bar school segregation. The evidence was inconclusive.

The Chief Justice then turned to the "separate but equal" doctrine. Unlike *Sweatt,* he said, children attending the segregated public schools in these cases were—or soon would be—receiving substantially equal treatment so far as "tangible" factors were concerned. Therefore, said Warren, the Court must look at the "effect of segregation itself on public education." [35]

That assessment could not be made by turning the clock back to 1868 when the amendment was adopted or to 1896 when the *Plessy* decision was written.

"We must consider public education in the light of its full development and its present place in American life throughout the Nation," wrote Warren. "Only in this way can it be determined if segregation in public schools deprives these plaintiffs of the equal protection of the laws." [36]

The Court found that education was "perhaps the most important function" of state and local government, as evidenced by their compulsory attendance laws and considerable expenditures. Education, wrote Warren, was the foundation of good citizenship and the basis for professional training and adjustment to society.

"In these days, it is doubtful that any child may reasonably be expected to succeed in life if he is denied the opportunity of an education," said Warren, adding that where the state had undertaken to make education available it must be available to all on equal terms.[37]

The question is then, said Warren, "Does segregation of children in public schools solely on the basis of race, even though the physical facilities and other 'tangible' factors may be equal, deprive the children of the minority group of equal educational opportunities?"

The Court's answer: "We believe that it does." [38]

Observing that intangible factors were considered in finding the treatment accorded Sweatt and McLaurin unequal, Warren said:

Such considerations apply with added force to children in grade and high schools. To separate them from others of similar age and qualifications solely because of their race generates a feeling of inferiority as to their status in the community that may affect their hearts and minds in a way unlikely ever to be undone.[39]

This belief "was amply supported by modern authority," Warren asserted, citing in a famous footnote, seven sociological studies on the detrimental effects of enforced racial segregation. *(Box, p. 223)*

Warren then stated:

We conclude that in the field of public education the doctrine of "separate but equal" has no place. Separate educational facilities are inherently unequal. Therefore, we hold that the plaintiffs and others similarly situated for whom the actions have been brought are, by reason of the segregation complained of, deprived of the equal protection of the laws guaranteed by the Fourteenth Amendment.[40]

In the District of Columbia case, considered separately from the other four because it involved a question of due process under the Fifth Amendment, Warren wrote:

Liberty under law extends to the full range of conduct which the individual is free to pursue, and it cannot be restricted except for a proper governmental objective. Segregation in public education is not reasonably related to any proper governmental objective, and thus it imposes on Negro children of the District of Columbia a burden that constitutes an arbitrary deprivation of their liberty in violation of the Due Process Clause.

In view of our decision that the Constitution prohibits the states from maintaining racially segregated public schools, it would be unthinkable that the same Constitution would impose a lesser duty on the Federal Government.[41]

In both the state cases and the District of Columbia suit, the Court postponed its decision on a remedy for the school segregation until after the parties presented their views on that question.

'All Deliberate Speed'

Among the issues the Court asked the parties to address in argument on appropriate remedies were:

● Should the Supreme Court formulate a detailed decree in each of the five cases, and if so, what specific issues should be addressed?

● Should the Court appoint a special master to take evidence and then make specific recommendations to the Court on the contents of the decrees?

● Should the Court remand the cases to the lower courts to fashion the decrees, and if so, what directions and procedural guidelines should the Supreme Court give the lower courts?

● Should black pupils be admitted to schools of their choice "forthwith" or might desegregation be brought about gradually?

In addition to hearing from the parties involved in the five cases, the Court invited the Eisenhower administration and all the states that required or permitted segregated public schools to submit their answers to these questions. The administration, Florida, North Carolina, Arkansas, Oklahoma, Maryland, and Texas accepted the invitation and participated in the oral argument in April 1955. Several other states declined the invitation.

On May 31, 1955, Chief Justice Warren announced the Court's final decision in an opinion commonly known as *Brown II,* to distinguish it from the 1954 decision. Warren first noted that the District of Columbia and the school districts in Kansas and Delaware had made substantial progress toward desegregation in the year since the first *Brown* decision was handed down but that Virginia and South Carolina were awaiting the Court's final decision before acting. He then moved to the heart of the matter:

Full implementation of these constitutional principles may require solution of varied local school problems. School authorities have the primary responsibility for elucidating, assessing, and solving these problems; courts will have to consider whether the action of school authorities constitutes good faith implementation of the governing constitutional principles. Because of their proximity to local conditions and the possible need for further hearings, the courts which originally heard these cases can best perform this judicial appraisal. Accordingly, we believe it appropriate to remand the cases to those courts.

In fashioning and effectuating the decrees, the courts will be guided by equitable principles.... At stake is the personal interest of the plaintiffs in admission to public schools as soon as practicable on a nondiscriminatory basis. To effectuate this interest may call for elimination of a variety of obstacles in making the transition to school systems operated in accordance with the constitutional principles set forth in our May 17, 1954, decision. Courts of equity may properly take into account the public interest in the elimination of such obstacles in a systematic and effective manner. But it should go without saying that the vitality of these constitutional principles cannot be allowed to yield simply because of disagreement with them.

While giving weight to these public and private considerations, the courts will require that the defendants make a prompt and reasonable start toward full compliance with our May 17, 1954, ruling. Once such a start has been made, the courts may find that additional time is necessary to carry out the ruling in an effective manner. The burden rests upon the defendants to establish that such time is necessary in the public interest and is consistent with good faith compliance at the earliest practicable date. To that end, the courts may consider problems related to administration, arising from the physical condition of the school plant, the school transportation system, personnel, revision of school districts and attendance areas into compact units to achieve a system of determining admission to the public schools on a nonracial basis, and revision of local laws and regulations which may be necessary in solving the foregoing problems. They will also consider the adequacy of any plans the defendants may propose to meet these problems and to effectuate a transition to a racially nondiscriminatory

school system. During this period of transition, the courts will retain jurisdiction of these cases.[42]

Desegregation of public schools, Warren concluded, was to proceed "with all deliberate speed."[43]

Reaction and Resistance

Reaction to the two *Brown* decisions was immediate.

At one extreme were those committed to segregation as a way of life. They castigated the Court, called the decisions a usurpation of state prerogatives, and urged defiance. The height of the rhetoric opposing the *Brown* decisions may have been the March 1956 "Declaration of Constitutional Principles," a tract signed by 101 of 128 members of Congress from eleven southern and border states. The signers called the *Brown* decisions "a clear abuse of judicial power," and commended those states that intended to "resist enforced integration by any means."[44]

At the other end of the spectrum were those who hailed the demise of the "separate but equal" doctrine as long overdue but felt that the Court seriously erred in *Brown II* by not ordering immediate desegregation. Many found themselves somewhere in the middle, unhappy with the command to desegregate but unwilling to defy it.

Massive resistance—a phrase coined by Virginia senator Harry F. Byrd, D (1933-1965)—did not begin in earnest until late 1955 and early 1956.

Relieved that the Court had not ordered immediate desegregation, many southern leaders opposed to desegregation apparently presumed that lower courts would ignore or otherwise delay implementation of the *Brown* decisions. By January 1956, however, nineteen lower courts had used the *Brown* precedents to invalidate school segregation and, as historian C. Vann Woodward characterized it, "[s]omething very much like panic seized many parts of the South . . . a panic bred of insecurity and fear."[45] White citizens councils, created to preserve segregation, spread throughout the South. The NAACP was barred from operating in some states. And many state and local officials sought ways to delay desegregation in the schools.

Official resistance took three main paths. Several states enacted "interposition" statutes declaring the *Brown* decisions of no effect. Mississippi and Louisiana also passed laws claiming that the decisions did not affect the states' execution of their police powers and then requiring school segregation in order to promote public health and morals and preserve the public peace.

Several states also adopted superficially neutral laws that resulted in separation of pupils by race. Among these types of statutes were laws that assigned pupils to specific schools and classes on the basis of their scholastic aptitude and achievement. Since black children had rarely received adequate educations, they were thus easily isolated.

Another tactic was to allow pupils to attend any public school (of the correct grade level) they chose. Few blacks had the courage to attend hostile white schools, and even fewer whites chose to attend black schools. Some states barred public funds to any school district that integrated; others permitted public schools to close rather than to accept black children.

In some instances, compulsory attendance laws were repealed and in still other cases states and localities allocated public funds to private segregated schools. Many states employed more than one of these methods to perpetuate segregation in the public schools.

Brown as Precedent

Adverse reaction to the desegregation decision did not deter the Court from applying it to other areas of life. In 1955 the Court ordered the University of Alabama to admit two blacks to its undergraduate program.[46] In March 1956 the Court in a *per curiam* opinion declared in *Florida ex rel. Hawkins v. Board of Control* that it would not permit institutes of higher education to delay desegregation.[47] Beginning with the 1954 case of *Muir v. Louisville Park Theatrical Assn.*, the Court, in brief orders that cited *Brown* as authority, struck down the separate but equal doctrine as it applied to state-imposed segregation of public places, such as parks, and vehicles of interstate transportation.[48] *(Public accommodations, p. 247)*

Resistance Rebuked

In 1958 the Court first addressed the problem of massive resistance. The occasion was the case of *Cooper v. Aaron,* in which Arkansas officials openly defied the Court's order to abandon segregation.

Less than a week after the Supreme Court struck down the separate but equal doctrine, the Little Rock school board announced its intention to develop a desegregation plan for the city schools. One year later—a week before the Court announced its decision in *Brown II*—the school board approved a plan that called for gradual desegregation beginning with Central High School in the fall of 1957. Meanwhile, the state adopted a constitutional amendment commanding the legislature to oppose the *Brown* decisions. In response, the state legislature enacted a law permitting children in racially mixed schools to ignore compulsory attendance laws.

On September 2, 1957, Governor Orval Faubus sent units of the Arkansas National Guard to Central High to prevent nine black students scheduled to attend the school from entering. Obeying a federal district court order, the school board proceeded with its integration plan and on September 4 the nine students tried to enter the school, only to find their way blocked by guardsmen standing shoulder to shoulder, along with a mob of hostile onlookers. This situation prevailed until September 20, when Faubus decided to obey a court order and withdraw the troops.

On September 23, the black students entered the high school but were quickly removed by police when a mob outside grew unruly. Two days later, President Dwight D. Eisenhower sent federal troops to protect the blacks as they entered and left the school. Federal troops remained there until November 27, when they were replaced by federalized national guardsmen who remained for the duration of the school year.

In the face of both official and public hostility to its desegregation plan, the school board in February 1958 asked the district court for permission to withdraw the black students from Central High and to postpone any further desegregation for two and a half years. Finding the situation at Central intolerable, the court agreed to the request. An appeals court reversed the decision, and the school board appealed to the Supreme Court.

A Special Term

The Court convened a special summer term August 28, 1958, in order to render its opinion before the school year

began. Arguments were heard September 11. The next day the Court issued an unsigned *per curiam* opinion affirming the appeals court's denial of the postponement. On September 29 the Court issued its formal opinion, which sharply rebuked Faubus and the Arkansas legislature for their obstructive actions.[49]

The Court indicated its sympathy for the Little Rock school board which, it said, had acted in good faith, but added that the "constitutional rights of [black] respondents are not to be sacrificed or yielded to the violence and disorder which have followed upon the actions of the Governor and Legislature."[50] The Court then reminded those officials that the Fourteenth Amendment prohibited state officials from denying anyone equal protection of the laws and said that it would not tolerate any state action perpetuating segregation in schools:

> State support of segregated schools through any arrangement, management, funds or property cannot be squared with the [Fourteenth] Amendment's command that no State shall deny to any person within its jurisdiction the equal protection of the laws.... The basic decision in *Brown* was unanimously reached by this Court only after the case had been briefed and twice argued and the issues had been given the most serious consideration.
>
> Since the first *Brown* opinion three new Justices have come to the Court. They are at one with the Justices still on the Court who participated in that basic decision as to its correctness, and that decision is now unanimously reaffirmed. The principles announced in that decision and the obedience of the States to them, according to the command of the Constitution, are indispensable for the protection of the freedoms guaranteed by our fundamental charter for all of us. Our constitutional ideal of equal justice under law is thus made a living truth.[51]

To emphasize the gravity with which they viewed the defiance of the Arkansas officials, each of the nine justices personally signed the opinion.

Governor Faubus and the Arkansas legislature chose to ignore this warning. With approval of the legislature, Faubus closed all four Little Rock high schools, which remained closed for the entire 1958-1959 school year. In June 1959 a federal district court declared the statute authorizing the closing a violation of due process and equal protection, and the Supreme Court affirmed that opinion.[52] Little Rock high schools opened to black and white students in the fall of 1959.

Other Decisions

Despite its protestation in the Arkansas case that it would not tolerate schemes to evade segregation, the Court in November 1958 affirmed without opinion an appeals court decision upholding Alabama's pupil placement law as constitutional on its face. (The lower court had made clear, however, that the law might be found unconstitutional if its application resulted in racial discrimination.)[53]

In two 1959 cases the Supreme Court refused to review lower court rulings requiring that all state remedies for segregation be exhausted before a case could move into federal court.[54]

Over the next three years, the Court affirmed lower court decisions striking down Louisiana laws clearly designed to continue school segregation.[55]

Then in June 1963 the Court began to express its impatience with dilatory school boards. In the first signed school case opinion since *Cooper v. Aaron*, the Court struck down a transfer scheme that worked to preserve segregated schools. Reversing the lower courts' approval of transfer plans in two Tennessee cities that allowed students assigned to schools where they were in the minority to transfer to schools where their race was in the majority, the unanimous Court in *Goss v. Board of Education of Knoxville* (1963) declared that because it was "readily apparent" that the plan would continue segregation, it was therefore unconstitutional.[56]

In a second case in 1963, *McNeese v. Board of Education*, the Court ruled that where federal rights were at stake, all state remedies need not be exhausted before relief was sought in federal court.[57]

Too Much Deliberation

The following year, a full ten years after *Brown I*, the Court announced that there had been too much deliberation and not enough speed in the effort to desegregate the nation's public schools.

The case of *Griffin v. County School Board of Prince Edward County* (1964) originated in the same Virginia county involved in *Brown*. Despite that decision, the county's schools remained segregated. In 1959 the county closed its schools rather than obey a lower court order to desegregate. The county then replaced the public schools for whites with private schools, partially financed by public funds.

The county offered to set up similar schools for blacks. The blacks refused the offer and pursued the legal battle for integrated public schools. Consequently, black children in Prince Edward County could not attend public school there from 1959 until 1963. Finally, federal, state, and local officials cooperated to open some desegregated public schools in the county.

In 1961 a federal district court ordered a halt in the flow of public funds to the all-white private schools. In 1962 it ordered the county to reopen the public schools, ruling that it could not constitutionally close the schools to avoid segregating them while all the other public schools in the state remained open. The county appealed the ruling to the Supreme Court.

"Whatever nonracial grounds might support a State's allowing a county to abandon public schools, the object must be a constitutional one, and grounds of race and opposition to desegregation do not qualify as constitutional," the Court said in 1964 affirming the lower court order.[58]

Dismissing the county's contention that the state courts should have been given an opportunity to determine whether the schools should be opened before the federal district court acted, the Court declared:

> [W]e hold that the issues here imperatively call for decision now. The case has been delayed since 1951 by resistance at the state and county level, by legislation, and by lawsuits. The original plaintiffs have doubtless all passed high school age. There has been entirely too much deliberation and not enough speed in enforcing the constitutional rights which we held in *Brown* ... had been denied Prince Edward County Negro children.[59]

The Court spoke even more sharply in a November 1965 ruling. "Delays in desegregating public school systems are no longer tolerable," the justices declared in a per curiam opinion in *Bradley v. School Board of City of Richmond*.[60] Three weeks later, in *Rogers v. Paul*, the Court in another per curiam opinion ordered an Arkansas school district to permit a black student "immediate transfer" to an all-white high school, adding that "those similarly situated" might transfer as well.[61] In December 1967 the Court affirmed without opinion lower court rulings requiring Alabama to desegregate its schools. It was the first time that a state was ordered to take such action; previously, desegregation orders had been directed only to local school systems.[62]

'Affirmative Duty'

In May 1968 the Supreme Court put its foot down. The unanimous Court ordered still-segregated school systems to devise desegregation plans that promised to be effective. In *Green v. County School Board of New Kent County, Va.*, the Court held that the county's freedom of choice plan did not accomplish the goals set out in *Brown I* and *Brown II*.

Freedom of choice plans allowed students to choose which school within the district they wanted to attend. Details varied from district to district, but in most instances custom and residential patterns served to keep the schools under such plans racially segregated.

Rural New Kent County, with a population divided almost evenly between whites and blacks, was originally segregated by Virginia law. In 1965 the school board adopted a freedom of choice plan but, as the Supreme Court noted, in three years of operation no white pupil chose to attend the black school and only 15 percent of the black children were enrolled in the formerly all-white school.

In an opinion written by Justice William J. Brennan, Jr., the Court said the school board's adoption of a freedom of choice plan did not fulfill its obligation to desegregate the county schools:

> In the context of the state-imposed segregated pattern of long standing, the fact that in 1965 the Board opened the doors of the former "white" school to Negro children and of the "Negro" school to white children merely begins, not ends, our inquiry whether the Board has taken steps adequate to abolish its dual, segregated system. *Brown II* was a call for the dismantling of well-entrenched dual systems tempered by an awareness that complex and multifaceted problems would arise which would require time and flexibility for a successful resolution. School boards such as the respondent then operating state-compelled dual systems were nevertheless clearly charged with the affirmative duty to take whatever steps might be necessary to convert to a unitary system in which racial discrimination would be eliminated root and branch.[63]

Observing that it had taken eleven years after *Brown I* for the district to begin desegregating, Brennan continued:

> This deliberate perpetuation of the unconstitutional dual system can only have compounded the harm of such a system.... Moreover, a plan that at this late date fails to provide meaningful assurance of prompt and effective disestablishment of a dual system is also intolerable.... The burden on a school board today is

to come forward with a plan that promises realistically to work, and promises realistically to work *now*.[64]

Effective Remedy

The Court refused to say that any one type of desegregation plan promised to be more effective than another, leaving it up to each individual school district to fashion a remedy best suited to its situation and needs. But it did give the district courts some guidance in assessing the effectiveness of desegregation plans. Brennan wrote:

It is incumbent upon the district court to weigh that claim [of plan effectiveness] in light of the facts at hand and . . . any alternatives which may be shown as feasible and more promising in their effectiveness. Where the court finds the board to be acting in good faith and the proposed plan to have real prospects for dismantling the state-imposed dual system "at the earliest practicable date," then the plan may be said to provide effective relief. Of course, the availability to the board of other, more promising courses of action may indicate a lack of good faith; and at the least it places a heavy burden upon the board to explain its preference for an apparently less effective method.[65]

Although it did not rule out freedom of choice plans entirely, the Court said experience indicated they were usually ineffective. Certainly, the Court said, New Kent County's plan was ineffective. There "the plan has operated simply to burden children and their parents with a responsibility which *Brown II* places squarely on the School Board." The Court ordered the board to formulate a new plan that promised to convert the county schools "to a system, without a 'white' school and a 'Negro' school, but just schools." [66]

In two other cases decided the same day, the Court applied *Green* to find a freedom of choice plan in an Arkansas school district and a free transfer plan in Jackson, Tennessee, unlikely to achieve desegregation.[67]

Green was the last major school desegregation case in which Chief Justice Warren participated; he retired in June 1969. In the first case heard by Chief Justice Burger, the Court reversed an appeals court order that allowed indefinite postponement of desegregation in thirty-three Mississippi school districts so long as they took "significant steps" in the forthcoming school year to dismantle their dual school systems.

The Court's brief decision in *Alexander v. Holmes Board of Education* (1969) took on added significance because the administration of President Richard M. Nixon had argued for allowing delay. In an unsigned opinion, the Court said that the standard of "all deliberate speed" was "no longer constitutionally permissible," and ordered the school districts to begin immediate operation of unitary school systems. The Court defined these as "systems within which no person is to be effectively excluded from any school because of race or color." [68]

The Scope of the Remedy

Chief Justice Burger's appointment to the Court coincided with a shift in the focus of school desegregation cases. With *Green* it became clear that schools could no longer avoid the duty to desegregate; the question now was what

Two Races, Two Districts?

One way some towns and cities avoided desegregation was to divide a school district so that most black children would attend the schools of one district and most white children the other. The Supreme Court did not view this ploy sympathetically. In two cases decided in 1972, it struck down such efforts.

Wright v. Emporia City Council concerned a Virginia city whose schools were part of the surrounding county school system. When the county was ordered to desegregate its schools, the city petitioned to operate its own school system. Although both city and county school systems would have had a majority of black students, the county schools would have been more black if the city school district were created than if the city's students were part of a countywide plan.

By a 5-4 vote the Court ruled the city's proposal impermissible because it would hinder desegregation. "Certainly desegregation is not achieved by splitting a single school system operating 'white schools' and 'Negro schools' into two new systems, each operating unitary schools within its borders, where one of the two new systems is, in fact, 'white' and the other is, in fact, 'Negro,' " the majority stated.[1]

The four dissenters denied that creation of the second school system would interfere with the desegregation process. A second system should not be rejected if its only effect was a slightly greater racial imbalance in both school systems, they said.

In the second case, the Court was unanimous in its opinion that the creation of a new school district was impermissible. The case of *United States v. Scotland Neck City Board of Education* involved the North Carolina legislature's creation of a school district for the city of Scotland Neck, which had been part of a county school system that was in the process of implementing a desegregation plan. The Court said there was no question that the statute was motivated by a desire to create a predominantly white school system in the city and so it must be struck down.[2]

1. *Wright v. Emporia City Council*, 407 U.S. 451 at 463 (1972).
2. *United States v. Scotland Neck Board of Education*, 407 U.S. 484 (1972).

methods could be used to accomplish that end? A major issue was whether schools were required to reflect the racial balance that existed in the community. Would neighborhood schools, whatever their racial balance, satisfy the desegregation requirement so long as they were open to students of all races? Or must pupils be transported beyond their normal geographic school zones to achieve some sort of racial balance?

The *Swann* Decision

School officials, the Court held in 1971, could choose from a broad range of desegregation tools those that would most effectively eliminate segregation in their district. In a unanimous decision the Court ruled in *Swann v. Charlotte-Mecklenburg County Board of Education* that busing, racial balance quotas, and gerrymandered school districts were all appropriate interim methods of eliminating the vestiges of school segregation.

The case arose from controversy over the desegregation of the Charlotte-Mecklenburg County, North Carolina, school system. That system in the 1969-1970 school year had 84,000 students, 71 percent white and 29 percent black. In that year almost 29,000 of those students were bused to school in an effort to desegregate the school system.

Of the 24,000 black students, 21,000 lived within the city of Charlotte. Because of the smaller number and dispersed residences of black pupils in the rural part of the county, there were no all-black schools in that part of the system. But in the city, most schools remained racially identifiable, and two of every three of the city's black students attended one of twenty-five schools which were 98 percent to 100 percent black. Three of every four of the area's white students attended schools that were primarily white.

In February 1970 a federal district judge ordered 13,000 additional students bused. More than 9,000 of these pupils were elementary school children. Under the order, no school remained all black, and the effort was made to reach a 71:29 white-black ratio in each school, reflecting the overall white-black ratio in the system.

The Fourth Circuit Court of Appeals first delayed, then reversed the elementary school part of the plan as imposing an unreasonable burden upon the school board. The NAACP Legal Defense Fund, representing the black parents concerned, appealed to the Supreme Court, arguing that the order should have been left intact. The school board also appealed, arguing that more of the order should have been modified.

Chief Justice Burger wrote the Court's opinion. He pointed out that federal courts became involved in the desegregation process only when local school authorities failed to fulfill their obligation to eliminate the dual school system. If school authorities did so default—as the lower federal court found that the Charlotte school board had in *Swann*—then the federal judge had wide discretion to select the means of desegregating the school system. Burger then discussed the four main issues *Swann* presented.

Racial Balance. The Court held that the federal district court had properly used mathematical ratios of whites and blacks as "a starting point in the process of shaping a remedy."

However, Burger wrote, a court could not require "as a matter of substantive constitutional right" any specific degree of racial mixing. "The constitutional command to desegregate schools does not mean that every school in every community must always reflect the racial composition of the school system as a whole." [69]

One-Race Schools. The Court acknowledged that residential patterns often result in schools that were attended only by children of one race. The presence of such schools did not necessarily indicate a system that was still segregated, but, wrote Burger, school authorities or the district court:

should make every effort to achieve the greatest possible degree of actual desegregation and will thus necessarily be concerned with the elimination of one-race schools. No *per se* rule can adequately embrace all the difficulties of reconciling the competing interests involved; but in a system with a history of segregation, the need for remedial criteria of sufficient specificity to assure a school authority's compliance with its constitutional duty warrants a presumption against schools that are substantially disproportionate in their racial composition. . . . [T]he burden upon the school authorities will be to satisfy the court that their racial composition is not the result of present or past discriminatory action on their part. [70]

The Court endorsed plans that allowed a child attending a school where his race was a majority to transfer to a school where his race was a minority. But to be successful, the justices added, such plans must assure the transferring pupil available space in the school and free transportation.

Attendance Zones. To overcome the effects of segregated residential patterns, the Court endorsed drastic gerrymandering of school districts and pairing, clustering, and grouping of schools that were not necessarily contiguous. "As an interim corrective measure, this cannot be said to be beyond the broad remedial powers of a court," the Chief Justice wrote. [71]

Busing. Bus transportation of students had been an "integral part of the public education system for years," Burger wrote, and was a permissible remedial technique to help achieve desegregation. The Court conceded that objections to busing might be valid "when the time or distance of travel is so great as to either risk the health of the children or significantly impinge on the educational process." The limits to busing would vary with many factors, "but probably with none more than the age" of the children, the Court said. [72]

The Court acknowledged that some of these remedies might be "administratively awkward, inconvenient and even bizarre in some situations and may impose burdens on some; but all awkwardness and inconvenience cannot be avoided in the interim period when the remedial adjustments are being made to eliminate the dual school systems." [73]

The Court was careful to say that its decision did not deal with de facto segregation, discrimination resulting from factors other than state law. Nor did it reach the question of what action might be taken against schools that were segregated as a result of "other types of state action, without any discriminatory action by the school authorities." [74]

In reference to the potential problem of resegregation, which might occur after achievement of a unitary school system, the Court concluded:

Neither school authorities nor district courts are constitutionally required to make year-by-year adjustments of the racial composition of student bodies once the affirmative duty to desegregate has been accomplished and racial discrimination through official action is eliminated from the system. This does not mean that federal courts are without power to deal with future problems; but in the absence of a showing that either the school authorities or some other agency of the state has deliberately attempted to fix or alter demographic patterns to affect the racial composition of the schools, further intervention by a district court should not be necessary.[75]

Related Rulings

The Court handed down three other related school desegregation decisions the same day—April 20, 1971. In *North Carolina State Board of Education v. Swann,* the Court struck down a state law that forbade school systems to bus or assign students to schools on the basis of race. The Court said the law was invalid because it prevented implementation of desegregation plans.

> [I]f a state-imposed limitation on a school authority's discretion operates to inhibit or obstruct the operation of a unitary school system or impede the disestablishing of a dual school system, it must fall; state policy must give way when it operates to hinder vindication of federal constitutional guarantees.... [T]he statute exploits an apparently neutral form to control school assignment plans by directing that they be "colorblind"; that requirement, against the background of segregation, would render illusory the promise of *Brown....* Just as the race of students must be considered in determining whether a constitutional violation has occurred, so also must race be considered in formulating a remedy. To forbid, at this stage, all assignments made on the basis of race would deprive school authorities of the one tool absolutely essential to fulfillment of their constitutional obligation to eliminate existing dual school systems.[76]

In *Davis v. Board of School Commissioners of Mobile County, Ala.,* the Court ordered an appeals court to reexamine its desegregation order for Mobile, Alabama, in light of the guidelines set down in *Swann.* The Court said the appeals court had not considered all the available techniques for desegregation. The plan included no busing for black children attending predominantly black high schools, and its insistence on geographically unified school zones tended to preserve single-race schools.[77]

In the third case, *McDaniel v. Barresi,* the Court upheld a Georgia county desegregation plan that assigned black pupils living in heavily black areas to schools in other attendance zones. The state supreme court had declared the plan invalid on the grounds that busing only black pupils denied equal protection of the laws. But the Supreme Court said the school board had acted properly in considering race as a factor in a desegregation plan.[78]

'Tailoring' the Remedy

In the early 1970s opposition to court-ordered desegregation focused on the school bus. The nearly universal antipathy to busing did not cause the Supreme Court to retract its opinion that busing was an appropriate remedy for segregation, but in 1974 the Court began to insist that the scope of the remedy not exceed the extent of the violation causing the segregation.

Richmond: Cross-District Busing

The first time the Court considered whether federal courts could require busing between school districts as part of a desegregation plan, it did not reach a conclusion.

The case of *Richmond School Board v. Virginia State Board of Education* (1973) came to the Court after a federal district judge ordered school officials to consolidate the predominantly black Richmond school district with the two neighboring mostly white county systems in order to desegregate the city schools.[79] The court of appeals overturned the order as too drastic.

The Supreme Court divided 4-4, automatically upholding the court of appeals. Justice Lewis F. Powell, Jr., did not participate in the case; he had formerly served on both the Richmond and Virginia school boards. There was no Court opinion and, because of the even vote, the case carried no weight as precedent.

Detroit: Multidistrict Busing

Little more than a year later, the Court, 5-4, struck down a district court plan to desegregate Detroit, Michigan, schools by busing students among fifty-four school districts in three counties. The majority held that a multidistrict remedy was not appropriate unless all of the districts were responsible for the segregation.

Milliken v. Bradley (1974) originated when a federal district judge concluded that both the Detroit school board and state officials had taken actions that fostered school segregation in the city. Because the city school system was predominantly black, the judge declared that a plan limited to its boundaries would fail to provide meaningful desegregation of the schools. He therefore ordered the multidistrict remedy. "[S]chool district lines are simply matters of political convenience and may not be used to deny constitutional rights," the judge ruled.[80] A court of appeals affirmed the order.

The Supreme Court majority overturned the order. Chief Justice Burger explained that both lower courts erred when they assumed that desegregation could not be achieved unless the Detroit schools reflected the racial balance of the surrounding metropolitan area. Although "boundary lines may be bridged where there has been a constitutional violation calling for interdistrict relief," wrote Burger, "... the notion that school district lines may be casually ignored or treated as a mere administrative convenience is contrary to the history of public education in our country."[81]

In any school desegregation case, said Burger, the scope of the remedy should not exceed the extent of the violation. He continued:

> Before the boundaries of separate and autonomous school districts may be set aside by consolidating the separate units for remedial purposes or by imposing a cross-district remedy, it must first be shown that there has been a constitutional violation within one district that produces a significant segregative effect in another district. Specifically, it must be shown that racially discriminatory acts of the state or local school districts, or of a single school district have been a substantial cause of interdistrict segregation. Thus an interdistrict remedy might be in order where the racially discriminatory acts of one or more school districts caused racial segregation in an adjacent district or where district lines have been deliberately drawn on the basis of race. In such circumstances, an interdistrict remedy would be appropriate to eliminate the interdistrict segregation directly.... Conversely, with-

Discrimination and Private Schools...

Private schools proliferated in most areas under pressure to desegregate public schools. Many of the private schools were created specifically as havens for whites fleeing desegregation.

As early as 1925, the Supreme Court acknowledged the right of parents to send their children to private schools. In *Pierce v. Society of Sisters* the Court ruled that an Oregon statute requiring all children to attend public schools "unreasonably interferes with the liberty of parents and guardians to direct the upbringing and education of children under their control." [1]

This holding, coupled with the Court's view that the Fourteenth Amendment did not prohibit acts of private discrimination, appeared to immunize private schools with racially discriminatory admissions policies from desegregation efforts. However, two Supreme Court rulings in the 1970s curtailed the forms of support that state and local governments could provide to racially discriminatory private schools. And in a third case the Court significantly narrowed the freedom of such schools to discriminate.

In *Norwood v. Harrison* (1973) a unanimous Court held that it was not permissible for Mississippi to lend textbooks to private schools that discriminated on the basis of race. Lending textbooks was direct state aid in violation of the Fourteenth Amendment, the Court said. (In other cases the Court has held that the First Amendment's clause prohibiting government establishment of religion bars states from lending textbooks to parochial schools but not from lending them to children who attend those schools.) *(Details, p. 95)*

Noting that it had affirmed lower court rulings barring state tuition grants to students attending racially discriminatory private schools, Chief Justice Warren E. Burger wrote:

> Free textbooks, like tuition grants directed to private school students, are a form of financial

assistance inuring to the benefit of the private schools themselves. An inescapable educational cost for students in both public and private schools is the expense of providing all necessary learning materials. When, as here, that necessary expense is borne by the State, the economic consequence is to give aid to the enterprise; if the school engages in discriminatory practices the State by tangible aid in the form of textbooks thereby supports such discrimination. Racial discrimination in state-operated schools is barred by the Constitution and "(i)t is also axiomatic that a State may not induce, encourage or promote private persons to accomplish what it is constitutionally forbidden to accomplish." [2]

The Court rejected Mississippi's contention that to deny such private schools state aid would deny them equal protection of the laws. "It is one thing to say that a State may not prohibit the maintenance of private schools and quite another to say that such schools must, as a matter of equal protection, receive state aid," declared the Court. [3]

Athletic Facilities

In 1974 the Court affirmed a lower court order forbidding Montgomery, Alabama, to permit racially discriminatory private schools to have exclusive use of its park and recreational facilities. Such permission "created, in effect, 'enclaves of segregation,'" which deprived black children and their families of equal access to the parks, the Court said in *Gilmore v. City of Montgomery.* [4]

Furthermore, the Court said, the city's action ran counter to the intent of a court order directing it to desegregate its public schools. Justice Harry A. Blackmun explained that the city, by permitting these schools to have exclusive use of public recreational facilities, enhanced the attractiveness of seg-

out an interdistrict violation and interdistrict effect, there is no constitutional wrong calling for an interdistrict remedy. [82]

Since none of the other fifty-three school districts had been shown to practice segregation or to have been affected by Detroit's segregation, the proposed remedy was "wholly impermissible," the majority concluded.

Nor did the fact that state officials contributed to the segregation empower the federal court to order the multidistrict remedy. "Disparate treatment of white and Negro students occurred within the Detroit school system, and not elsewhere, and on this record the remedy must be limited to that system," Burger wrote. [83]

Without an interdistrict remedy, wrote Justice Marshall, "Negro children in Detroit will receive the same

separate and inherently unequal education in the future as they have been unconstitutionally afforded in the past." [84] Marshall insisted that the segregative actions of state officials justified the multidistrict remedy:

> The essential foundation of interdistrict relief in this case was not to correct conditions within outlying districts.... Instead, interdistrict relief was seen as a necessary part of any meaningful effort by the State of Michigan to remedy the state-caused segregation within the city of Detroit. [85]

Detroit: A Broad-Based Remedy

The Supreme Court remanded *Milliken* to the district court to fashion a new remedy that affected only the De-

...State Aid and Admissions

regated private schools—formed in reaction to the desegregation order—by enabling them to offer athletic programs to their students at public expense.

Because the city provided the schools with stadiums and other recreational facilities, the schools were able to spend money they would have spent on athletic programs on other educational projects. At the same time, the schools realized revenue from the concessions operated at the stadiums and other facilities.

"We are persuaded," concluded Blackmun, "... that this assistance significantly tended to undermine the federal court order mandating the establishment and maintenance of a unitary school system in Montgomery." [5]

However, the Court was unable to decide whether it was unconstitutional for the state to allow the segregated private schools to use the facilities in common with other school children and private nonschool organizations.

Admissions Policies

Racially discriminatory admissions policies of private schools were directly challenged in the 1976 cases of *Runyon v. McCrary* and *Fairfax-Brewster School v. Gonzales.* Two private schools in northern Virginia, Bobbe's Private School and Fairfax-Brewster School, refused to admit Michael McCrary and Colin Gonzalez solely because they were black. Their parents filed suit on behalf of the boys, charging that discriminatory admissions policies violated the 1866 Civil Rights Act that gives "all persons within the jurisdiction of the United States the same right ... to make and enforce contracts ... as is enjoyed by white citizens." A federal district court and court of appeals agreed with the parents, and the Supreme Court affirmed the lower courts by a 7-2 vote. [6]

The majority, with Justice Potter Stewart as its spokesman, rejected the argument that the 1866 law did not reach private contracts. That claim was inconsistent with the Court's earlier rulings, said Stewart, in particular the 1968 decision in *Jones v. Alfred H. Mayer Co.* In that decision the Court held that a companion provision of the 1866 act forbade private racial discrimination in the sale or rental of property. [7] *(Details, p. 255)*

The Court also rejected the arguments that application of the 1866 law to admissions policies violated the constitutional right of parents to have their children associate only with certain persons and to send their children to schools that promote racial segregation. "[P]arents have a First Amendment right to send their children to educational institutions that promote the belief that racial segregation is desirable, and ... the children have an equal right to attend such institutions," Stewart wrote. "But it does not follow that the *practice* of excluding racial minorities from such institutions is also protected" by the right of association. [8]

Dissenting for himself and Justice William H. Rehnquist, Justice Byron R. White took issue with the extension of the contract provision of the 1866 law to private action. No person, black or white, has a right to enter into a contract with an unwilling party, White said. [9]

1. *Pierce v. Society of Sisters,* 268 U.S. 510 at 534-535 (1925).
2. *Norwood v. Harrison,* 413 U.S. 455 at 463-465 (1973); for state tuition grants cases, see *Brown v. South Carolina Board of Education,* 296 F. Supp. 199 (S.C. 1968), affirmed *per curiam* 393 U.S. 222 (1968); *Poindexter v. Louisiana Finance Commission,* 275 F. Supp. 833 (E D La. 1967), affirmed *per curiam* 389 U.S 571 (1968).
3. *Norwood v. Harrison,* 413 U.S. 455 at 462 (1973).
4. *Gilmore v. City of Montgomery,* 417 U.S. 556 at 566 (1974).
5. *Id.* at 569.
6. *Runyon v. McCrary, Fairfax-Brewster School v. Gonzales,* 427 U.S. 160 (1976).
7. *Jones v. Alfred H. Mayer Co.,* 392 U.S. 409 (1969).
8. *Runyon v. McCrary,* 427 U.S. 160 at 176 (1976).
9. *Id.* at 195.

troit city schools. In an opinion affirmed by the appeals court, the district court ordered the school board as part of the new remedy to institute comprehensive remedial education, testing, training, counseling, and guidance programs in the city schools. It also directed the state to pay half the costs of implementing these programs. These two parts of the remedy were appealed to the Supreme Court, which upheld them in 1977 by a 9-0 vote.

The Court found the comprehensive remedial programs appropriate to remedy the educational conditions caused by the segregation. "Pupil assignment alone does not automatically remedy the impact of previous unlawful educational isolation; the consequences linger and can be dealt with only by independent measures," the Court said. [86]

The justices also held that the order to the state to pay half the costs was not equivalent, as the state claimed, to an award for damages. In a nonschool-related case, the Court in 1974 had ruled that the Eleventh Amendment protected states against such payments of damages. [87] But the school payments were permissible, held the Court, because they amounted to prospective relief "designed to wipe out continuing conditions of inequality" caused by the state. [88]

Systemwide Remedies

In the 1974 *Milliken* decision the Court held that where segregation affected only one school district, a multidistrict remedy was excessive. Three years later the

Bilingual Education

A unanimous Supreme Court in *Lau v. Nichols* (414 U.S. 563, 1974) ruled that a public school system must make some effort to ensure that its non-English-speaking students are equipped with language skills necessary to profit from their required attendance at school. Non-English-speaking Chinese students in San Francisco charged that the city school board's failure to provide them with bilingual lessons or remedial English resulted in unequal educational opportunities and violated the Fourteenth Amendment.

The Court found it unnecessary to address the equal protection issue, ruling that the school board had violated the 1964 Civil Rights Act, which forbade discrimination based on national origin, race, or color in any program receiving federal aid, and a Department of Health, Education, and Welfare regulation requiring such school districts "to rectify ... language deficiency" to ensure that instruction was meaningful to non-English-speaking pupils.

Court held that where segregation did not affect an entire school district, a systemwide desegregation plan was excessive.

A federal district court found in *Dayton (Ohio) Board of Education v. Brinkman* that the city school board had discriminated against minority students in three specific instances. After a court of appeals rejected more limited remedies, the district court proposed a desegregation plan that involved the entire school district. The appeals court affirmed this plan, but the Supreme Court struck it down, 8-0.

In an opinion written by Justice William H. Rehnquist, the Court questioned the validity of the district court's finding of discrimination in two of the instances and observed that the discrimination in the third affected only high school students. Under these circumstances, the Court said, the appeals court overstepped its proper role when it ordered the district court to develop a systemwide plan without disputing the district court's findings of fact or legal opinion. Rehnquist wrote:

The duty of both the District Court and of the Court of Appeals in a case such as this, where mandatory segregation by law of the races in the schools has long since ceased, is to first determine whether there was any action in the conduct of the business of the school board which was intended to, and did in fact, discriminate against minority pupils, teachers or staff.... If such violations are found, the District Court in the first instance, subject to review by the Court of Appeals, must determine how much incremental segregative effect these violations had on the racial distribution of the Dayton school population as presently constituted, when that distribution is compared to

what it would have been in the absence of such constitutional violations. The remedy must be designed to redress that difference, and only if there has been a systemwide impact may there be a systemwide remedy.[89]

In 1979 the Court held that the board's discrimination had a systemwide impact and thus necessitated a systemwide remedy. *(See box, p. 236)*

A Continuing Balance

The Court in *Swann* said that once a school system was desegregated, school authorities would not be required to make annual adjustments in order to maintain a specific racial balance in each school. In the 1976 case of *Pasadena City Board of Education v. Spangler,* the Court elaborated on that point.

The Pasadena, California, school board adopted a desegregation plan stipulating that as of the 1970-1971 school year, no school in the district could have a majority of students of a minority race. In 1974 the school board asked the court to lift or modify the "no-majority" requirement. Observing that the board had complied with that requirement only in the initial year of the plan's implementation, the district court refused the request. It held that the requirement was applicable every year, even though residential patterns and other factors outside the school board's control resulted in a changing racial composition of the schools.

The Supreme Court, 6-2, reversed the district court, holding that its literal interpretation required the board to maintain a specific racial balance, something that the Court in *Swann* said it would disapprove. The majority wrote:

No one disputes that the initial implementation of the plan accomplished [its] objective. That being the case, the District Court was not entitled to require the [school district] to rearrange its attendance zones each year so as to ensure that the racial mix desired by the court was maintained in perpetuity. For having once implemented a racially neutral attendance pattern in order to remedy the perceived constitutional violations on the part of the defendants [the school board], the District Court has fully performed its function of providing the appropriate remedy for previous racially discriminatory attendance patterns.[90]

Joined in dissent by Justice Brennan, Justice Marshall noted that the desegregation plan fulfilled the no-majority requirement only for one year and that without its continued maintenance immediate resegregation of the school system was likely. Because a lasting unitary school system had therefore apparently not been achieved, Marshall said the majority's application of *Swann* was improper. *Swann,* wrote Marshall,

recognizes on the one hand that a fully desegregated school system may not be compelled to adjust its attendance zones to conform to changing demographic patterns. But on the other hand, it also appears to recognize that *until* such a unitary system is established, a district court may act with broad discretion—discretion which includes the adjustment of attendance zones—so that the goal of a wholly unitary system might be sooner achieved.[91]

TRAVEL AND PUBLIC ACCOMMODATIONS

During the first few years after the Civil War, blacks in many localities were treated substantially the same as whites. In the 1870s there was little state-imposed segregation of the races in transportation or public accommodations; in fact, three states—Massachusetts, New York, and Kansas—specifically prohibited separation of the races in public places. Whether to accept the patronage of blacks was left largely to individual choice, and the majority of operators of public transport systems, hotels, restaurants, theaters, and other amusements admitted blacks—if not always to first class accommodations, then at least to second class.[92]

Nonetheless, many proprietors, especially in the rural South, refused to serve blacks. Enactment of the 1866 Civil Rights Act granting blacks the same rights as whites to bring lawsuits encouraged blacks to challenge such exclusion. Although many of these suits were successful, some courts upheld the right of individual proprietors to deny service to whomever they chose.

In an attempt to reverse such rulings, the Republican Congress enacted the Civil Rights Act of 1875, declaring that "all persons within the jurisdiction of the United States shall be entitled to the full and equal enjoyment of the accommodations ... of inns, public conveyances on land or water, theaters, and other places of public amusement; subject only to the conditions and limitations established by law, and applicable alike to citizens of every race or color." Persons violating the act were subject to fine or imprisonment.

The *Civil Rights Cases*

This law became the basis for several dozen suits protesting denial of equal treatment to blacks. Federal courts in some states upheld the constitutionality of the act, while others found it invalid. Five of these cases—known collectively as the *Civil Rights Cases*—reached the Supreme Court. They involved theaters in New York and California that would not seat blacks, a hotel in Missouri and a restaurant in Kansas that would not serve blacks, and a train in Tennessee that prohibited a black woman from riding in the "ladies" car. *(United States v. Singleton, United States v. Ryan, United States v. Nichols, United States v. Stanley, Robinson & Wife v. Memphis and Charleston Railroad Company)*

Deciding these cases by an 8-1 vote, the Court in 1883 declared that Congress had exceeded its authority to enforce the Thirteenth and Fourteenth Amendments in passing the 1875 act, and so it was invalid. The Fourteenth Amendment applied only to discriminatory *state* actions, the Court reminded Congress. "Individual invasion of individual rights is not the subject-matter of the amendment," the Court asserted.[93]

Furthermore, said the majority, private discrimination against blacks did not violate the Thirteenth Amendment abolishing slavery:

such an act of refusal has nothing to do with slavery or involuntary servitude.... It would be running the slavery argument into the ground to make it apply to every act of discrimination which a person may see fit to make as to the guests he will entertain, or as to the people he will take into his coach or cab or car, or admit to his concert or theater.[94]

Although public opinion generally supported the Court's decision in these *Civil Rights Cases*, four states in 1884 barred discrimination in public places. By 1897, eleven more states, all in the North and West, had enacted similar laws. Those that were challenged were sustained as a proper exercise of state police power.[95]

Segregation and Commerce

The decision in the *Civil Rights Cases* left open the possibility that Congress, through its commerce power, might bar private discrimination against blacks on public carriers. The Constitution gave Congress authority to regulate interstate commerce. By the close of the Civil War, the Court had interpreted that authority to deny the states power to regulate anything other than local commerce with no significant impact on other states.

In 1878 a unanimous Supreme Court had declared unconstitutional a Louisiana law *forbidding* segregation on public carriers. So far as the state law required desegregation on carriers that traveled interstate, it was a burden on interstate commerce, the Court said in *Hall v. DeCuir*. Prohibition of segregation in interstate transportation was a matter on which there should be national uniformity, and thus only Congress·could adopt that policy. "If each state was at liberty to regulate the conduct of carriers while within its jurisdiction, the confusion likely to follow could not but be productive of great inconvenience and unnecessary hardship," the Court concluded.[96]

Hoping that the Court would apply this same reasoning to strike down state segregation laws, opponents of segregation in 1890 challenged a Mississippi law *requiring* segregation on public transportation. Their hopes went unfulfilled.

Distinguishing the 1890 case of *Louisville, New Orleans & Texas Railway v. Mississippi* from *DeCuir*, the Court ruled that the Mississippi law applied only to intrastate traffic and was therefore within a state's power to regulate local commerce.[97]

Plessy v. Ferguson

Six years later the Supreme Court gave its blessing to segregation in the case of *Plessy v. Ferguson*. The case was a deliberate test of the constitutionality of a Louisiana statute requiring separate but equal railroad accommodations for the races. Louisiana was one of six states that by 1896 had enacted such "Jim Crow" laws segregating blacks from whites on trains.

The suit was brought by Homer Plessy, a citizen of the United States and a Louisiana resident who was one-eighth black and appeared white. Plessy bought a first class ticket to travel from New Orleans to Covington, Louisiana, and took a seat in the coach reserved for whites. When he refused to move to the black coach, he was arrested. The state courts upheld the constitutionality of the state law. Plessy then appealed to the Supreme Court, which in 1896 affirmed the holdings of the state courts.

A Reasonable Rule

Writing for the majority, Justice Henry B. Brown said the state law did not infringe on congressional authority over commerce. "In the present case," said Brown, "no question of interference with interstate commerce can possibly arise, since the East Louisiana Railway appears to have been purely a local line, with both its termini within the State." [98]

Nor did the state statute violate the Thirteenth Amendment:

A statute which implies merely a legal distinction between the white and colored races—a distinction which is founded in the color of the two races, and which must always exist so long as white men are distinguished from the other race by color—has no tendency to destroy the legal equality of the two races, or reestablish a state of involuntary servitude. [99]

Plessy's challenge to the law as a violation of the Fourteenth Amendment also failed, the majority said, because that amendment guaranteed only political equality and did not encompass what the Court considered social distinctions:

The object of the [Fourteenth] Amendment was undoubtedly to enforce the absolute equality of the two races before the law, but in the nature of things it could not have been intended to abolish distinctions based upon color, or to enforce social, as distinguished from political equality, or a commingling of the two races upon terms unsatisfactory to either. Laws permitting, and even requiring, their separation in places where they are liable to be brought into contact do not necessarily imply the inferiority of either race to the other, and have been generally recognized as within the competency of the state legislatures in the exercise of their police powers. [100]

The question then, Brown continued, was whether the law was an unreasonable use of the state's police power. Noting that the Court thought it reasonable for a state to consider the traditions and customs of its people and to want to protect their comfort and peace, Brown wrote:

we cannot say that a law which authorizes or even requires the separation of the two races in public conveyances is unreasonable, or more obnoxious to the Fourteenth Amendment than the act of Congress requiring separate schools for colored children in the District of Columbia, the constitutionality of which does not seem to have been questioned, or the corresponding acts of state legislatures.

We consider the underlying fallacy of [Plessy's] argument to consist in the assumption that the enforced separation of the two races stamps the colored race with a badge of inferiority. If this be so, it is not by reason of anything found in the act, but solely because the colored race chooses to put this construction upon it. . . . Legislation is powerless to eradicate racial instincts or to abolish distinctions based upon physical differences, and the attempt to do so can only result in accentuating the difficulties of the present

situation. If the civil and political rights of both races be equal one cannot be inferior to the other civilly, or politically. If one race be inferior to the other socially, the Constitution of the United States cannot put them upon the same plane. [101]

A Colorblind Constitution

In lone dissent, as in the *Civil Rights Cases*, Justice Harlan predicted that the decision would prove "quite as pernicious" as had the 1857 *Dred Scott* decision. The Kentucky-born Harlan, himself a former slaveholder, acknowledged that whites were the dominant race in prestige, education, wealth, and power. "But in view of the Constitution," he declared, "in the eye of the law, there is in this country no superior, dominant, ruling class of citizens. There is no caste here. Our Constitution is colorblind and neither knows nor tolerates classes among citizens." [102] *(Dred Scott case, p. 229)*

Charging that the majority had glossed over the fact that the Louisiana law segregated blacks because whites considered them inferior, Harlan wrote:

The arbitrary separation of citizens, on the basis of race, while they are on a public highway, is a badge of servitude wholly inconsistent with the civil freedom and the equality before the law established by the Constitution. It cannot be justified upon any legal grounds. . . . We boast of the freedom enjoyed by our people above all other peoples. But it is difficult to reconcile that boast with a state of the law, which, practically, puts the brand of servitude and degradation upon a large class of our fellow-citizens, our equals before the law. The thin disguise of "equal" accommodations for passengers in railroad coaches will not mislead any one, nor atone for the wrong this day done. [103]

Equal Treatment

For sixty years the Court's stance in regard to segregation on public carriers was similar to that it maintained on school segregation cases. The Court upheld the right of the states to separate the races while requiring that their treatment be equal.

This insistence on equal treatment in transportation was first apparent in the 1914 case of *McCabe v. Atchison, Topeka & Santa Fe Railroad.* Oklahoma law required companies operating trains within the state to provide separate coaches for whites and blacks. McCabe sued the railroad because it provided sleeping cars for whites but none for blacks.

The railroad argued that there was not sufficient demand by blacks for sleeping car accommodations. The Court rejected this defense. In an opinion written by Justice Hughes, the Court said the railway's contention:

makes the constitutional right depend upon the number of persons who may be discriminated against, whereas the essence of the constitutional right is that it is a personal one. Whether or not particular facilities shall be provided may doubtless be conditioned upon there being a reasonable demand therefore, but, if facilities are provided, substantial equality of treatment of persons traveling under like conditions cannot be refused. It is the individual who is entitled to the equal protection of the laws, and if he is denied by a common carrier, acting in the matter under the authority of a state law, a facility or convenience in the course of his journey which under substantially the same circumstances is furnished to another traveler, he may properly complain that his constitutional privilege has been invaded.[104]

In 1941 the Court extended this principle to the case of an interstate traveler. A black member of the U.S. House of Representatives, Arthur W. Mitchell, D-Ill. (1935-1943), held a first class ticket for a trip from Chicago to Hot Springs, Arkansas. When the train reached the Arkansas border, Mitchell was required by state law to move to a car reserved for blacks where there were no first class accommodations.

Mitchell challenged the state law as a violation of the Interstate Commerce Act of 1887, which prohibited public carriers from subjecting "any person . . . to any undue or unreasonable prejudice or disadvantage in any respect whatsoever." The Interstate Commerce Commission (ICC) dismissed the complaint, but Mitchell appealed to the Supreme Court, which held he was entitled to first class accommodations just as any white would be. The Court, however, did not question Arkansas's right to require the segregated coaches.[105]

Five years later the Court took a significant step toward overturning segregation in public interstate transportation. The case of *Morgan v. Virginia* (1946) concerned a black woman traveling on a bus from Virginia to Maryland who defied a Virginia law when she refused to move to the back of the bus to make her seat available to whites.

Noting that ten states specifically required segregation in interstate bus travel and that eighteen specifically prohibited it, the Court said that a "burden [on interstate commerce] might arise from a state statute which requires interstate passengers to order their movements on the vehicle in accordance with local rather than national requirements."[106] The Court held that "seating arrangements for the different races in interstate motor travel require a single, uniform rule to promote and protect national travel."[107] The state law violated the commerce clause.

In 1948 the Court upheld a Michigan law prohibiting segregation in public transportation. The law did not interfere with Congress's power to regulate interstate and foreign commerce, it said. In 1950 the Court struck down segregated but unequal dining facilities on trains. In 1953 the Court applied two seldom-used laws to prohibit restaurants in the District of Columbia from discriminating against blacks.[108]

Plessy Overturned

Then, in 1954, the Supreme Court renounced the separate but equal doctrine as it applied to public schools.[109] Beginning with *Muir v. Louisville Park Theatrical Assn.* (1954), the Court summarily declared that state-imposed segregation in public accommodations and transportation was unconstitutional as well. Relying on *Brown*, the Court ordered an end to state-imposed segregation on public beaches, municipal golf courses, vehicles of interstate transportation, in public parks, municipal auditoriums and athletic contests, seating in traffic court, and in prisons and jails.[110]

Discriminatory Wills

In two sets of cases, the Supreme Court has held that the Fourteenth Amendment forbids a state agency, but not a private one, from acting as trustee for wills that discriminate against blacks.

In 1957 the Court considered *Pennsylvania v. Board of Directors of City Trusts of Philadelphia*, concerning a will that left money in trust for the establishment and maintenance of a school for poor white orphan boys. The trust was administered by a state agency. The case arose when the agency refused admittance to two black orphan boys.

In a per curiam opinion, the Court said the agency's refusal to admit the two boys amounted to state discrimination in violation of the Fourteenth Amendment. Administration of the school was then turned over to private trustees who continued to follow the discriminatory terms of the will. This policy was again challenged, but the Court in 1958 refused to review it.[1]

A decade later in 1966, the Court decided a case concerning a park in Macon, Georgia, which, under the terms of the will bequeathing the land, could only serve whites. In this case the Court held that even though the city, refusing to operate the park on a segregated basis, had turned over its management to private trustees, the park retained a public character that made it subject to the prohibitions of the Fourteenth Amendment.[2]

As a result, the park reverted to the original heirs and was closed. A group of blacks sued, claiming the closing violated their right to equal protection of the laws. But the Court in 1970 found no constitutional violation. Closing the park to the public did not treat one race differently from the other, but deprived both blacks and whites equally of the facility, the majority said.[3]

1. *Pennsylvania v. Board of Directors of City Trusts of Philadelphia*, 353 U.S. 230 (1957); 357 U.S. 570 (1958).
2. *Evans v. Newton*, 382 U.S. 296 (1966).
3. *Evans v. Abney*, 396 U.S. 435 (1970); see also *Palmer v. Thompson*, 403 U.S. 217 (1971).

Most of these decisions were issued without opinion. In 1963, however, the Court issued a full opinion in one case to emphasize its expectation that the states would proceed expeditiously to eliminate state-imposed segregation in public areas. The question in *Watson v. Memphis* (1963) was whether the Tennessee city should be granted more time to desegregate its public parks and other municipal facilities. Warning that it would not countenance indefinite delays, the Court said:

The rights here asserted are, like all such rights, *present* rights; they are not merely hopes to some *future* enjoyment of some formalistic constitutional promise. The basic guarantees of our Constitution are warrants for the here and now and, unless there is an overwhelmingly compelling reason, they are to be promptly fulfilled.[111]

In contrast to its continued insistence on school desegregation, a sharply divided Court held in 1971 that a city under a court order to desegregate its public facilities could close its public swimming pools rather than operate them on an integrated basis.

For the five-man majority in *Palmer v. Thompson*, Justice Hugo L. Black maintained that the Fourteenth Amendment did not impose an affirmative obligation on a local government to maintain public swimming pools. And, said Black, so long as the city government denied the same facility to both races, it was not denying either equal protection.

For the dissenters, Justice Byron R. White said that "a state may not have an official stance against desegregating public facilities in response to a desegregation order.... The fact is that closing the pools is an expression of public policy that Negroes are unfit to associate with whites." [112]

Semipublic Business

In a pair of cases, the Court in 1960 and 1961 prohibited racial discrimination by privately owned businesses operated on public property. *Boynton v. Virginia* (1960) concerned a privately owned restaurant in an interstate bus terminal. The restaurant refused to serve a black interstate traveler. The question presented to the Court was whether the refusal violated the Interstate Commerce Act. The Court decided it did:

> [I]f the bus carrier has volunteered to make terminal and restaurant facilities and service available to its interstate passengers as a regular part of their transportation, and the terminal and restaurant have acquiesced and cooperated in this undertaking, the terminal and restaurant must perform these services without discriminations prohibited by the Act. In performance of these services under such conditions, the terminal and the restaurant stand in the place of the bus company.[113]

The second case involved an intrastate situation and a constitutional question rather than a question of statutory law. The case of *Burton v. Wilmington Parking Authority* (1961) concerned the Eagle restaurant, which leased space in a city-owned parking building. The parking authority rented out the space in order to procure additional revenue to redeem its bonds. When the restaurant refused to serve a black, the question was whether the restaurant was so closely associated with the municipal parking authority as to make its discriminatory action state action in violation of the equal protection clause.

"Only by sifting facts and weighing circumstances can the nonobvious involvement of the State in private conduct be attributed its true significance," the Court said in answering the question.[114] It then pointed out that the land on which the parking garage and restaurant sat was publicly owned and that the restaurant was there for the purpose of maintaining the public garage as a self-sustaining entity. Thus, the Court concluded that:

> The State has so far insinuated itself into a position of interdependence with [the] Eagle [restaurant] that it must be recognized as a joint participant in the challenged activity, which, on that account, cannot be considered to have been so "purely private" as to fall without the scope of the Fourteenth Amendment.[115]

The Sit-In Cases

Boynton and *Burton* served as precedent for a series of cases decided in 1962 and commonly known as the "Sit-In Cases." Four of these concerned young blacks who had been convicted of criminal trespass after they had protested racially discriminatory policies of privately owned stores and restaurants by seeking service at "whites only" lunch counters and tables. The fifth involved two ministers convicted of aiding and abetting persons to commit criminal trespass by encouraging them to sit in.

The Supreme Court decided most such cases involving civil rights activists on First Amendment grounds. The sit-in cases were the only major cases decided on equal protection grounds. In each, a majority of the Court found sufficient state involvement with the private act of discrimination to warrant coverage by the Fourteenth Amendment's equal protection clause.

In the first case, *Peterson v. City of Greenville*, an eight-justice majority overturned the convictions of ten youthful protestors who attempted to desegregate a department store lunch counter in Greenville, South Carolina. A city ordinance required racial segregation of public eating places. By having the protestors arrested, the store's managers did what the ordinance required, and therefore, held the Court, the subsequent convictions amounted to state enforcement of the city ordinance denying equal protection. It was no defense that the store managers would have brought criminal trespass charges in the absence of the ordinance, the majority said.

> When a state agency passes a law compelling persons to discriminate against other persons because of race, and the State's criminal processes are employed in a way which enforces the discrimination mandated by that law, such a palpable violation of the Fourteenth Amendment cannot be saved by attempting to separate the mental urges of the discriminators.[116]

The *Peterson* case then became the rule for overturning similar criminal trespass convictions in *Gober v. City of Birmingham* and *Avent v. North Carolina*.[117] In both cases, city ordinances required separation of the races in eating places. Then, having overturned the trespass convictions in *Gober,* the Court overturned the aiding and abetting convictions of the two ministers who had urged participation in that sit in. "It is generally recognized that there can be no conviction for aiding and abetting someone to do an innocent act," the majority wrote in *Shuttlesworth v. Birmingham.*[118]

In the final case, *Lombard v. Louisiana,* there was no law requiring segregated eating places in New Orleans. Nonetheless, the Court found that public statements of the city mayor and police chief effectively "required" that public eating facilities be segregated. If it is constitutionally impermissible for a state to enact a law segregating the races, "the State cannot achieve the same result by an official command which has at least as much coercive effect as an ordinance," the justices said.[119]

Individual Discrimination

Still, most private owners of hotels, stores, restaurants, theaters, and other public accommodations remained "without the scope of the Fourteenth Amendment" until passage in 1964 of the most comprehensive civil rights act since 1875. The act barred discrimination in employment, provided new guarantees to ensure blacks the right to vote, and authorized the federal government to seek court orders for the desegregation of public schools.

Title II of the act was aimed at discrimination in public accommodations. It prohibited discrimination on grounds of race, color, religion, or national origin in public accommodations if the discrimination was supported by state law or other official action, if lodgings or other service were provided to interstate travelers, or if a substantial portion of the goods sold or entertainment provided moved in interstate commerce.

There was no question that the Fourteenth Amendment barred state officials from requiring or supporting segregation in public places. But the power of Congress to use the commerce clause as authority for barring private discrimination was uncertain. A case challenging that exercise of the commerce power reached the Supreme Court just six months after the 1964 law was enacted.

Heart of Atlanta Motel

The case of *Heart of Atlanta Motel v. United States* (1964) involved a motel in downtown Atlanta that refused to serve blacks in defiance of the new federal law. The motel owner charged that Congress had exceeded its authority under the commerce clause when it enacted Title II, and that the property owner's Fifth Amendment rights were denied when Congress deprived him of the freedom to choose his customers.

A unanimous Supreme Court upheld Title II. Writing for the Court, Justice Tom C. Clark first outlined the interstate aspect of the motel's business, noting that it was accessible to interstate travelers, that it sought out-of-state patrons by advertising in nationally circulated publications, and that 75 percent of its guests were interstate travelers. Clark then cited the testimony at the congressional hearings on the act that showed that blacks were frequently discouraged from traveling because of the difficulty encountered in obtaining accommodations. Congress had reasonably concluded that discrimination was an impediment to interstate travel, the Court said.

Clark next turned to the commerce power of Congress, finding that Congress had the authority not only to regulate interstate commerce but also to regulate intrastate matters that affected interstate commerce:

> [T]he power of Congress to promote interstate commerce includes the power to regulate the local incidents thereof, including local activities in both the States of origin and destination, which might have a substantial and harmful effect upon that commerce. One need only examine the evidence ... to see that Congress may—as it has—prohibit racial discrimination by motels serving travelers, however "local" their operations may appear.[120]

The Court also said that it made no difference that Congress had used its power under the commerce clause to achieve a moral goal. That fact, wrote Clark

---

Private Clubs

The freedom to associate with persons of one's own choosing is protected by the First Amendment, at least up to a point. Consequently, private clubs with racially discriminatory admissions policies are generally considered beyond the reach of the Fourteenth Amendment.

In 1972 the Supreme Court held, 6-3, that the issuance of a liquor license by the state to a private club that discriminated against blacks did not amount to discriminatory state action in violation of the Fourteenth Amendment. In *Moose Lodge 107 v. Irvis,* the majority said the Court had never forbidden a state to provide services to a private individual or group that practiced discrimination.[1] Such a ruling would mean that the state could not provide vital essentials such as fire and police protection, electricity, and water to private individuals who discriminate.

The degree of state involvement necessary to constitute state action varies from case to case, the majority continued. In this situation, the liquor regulations, with one exception, in no way promoted discrimination and therefore did not involve the state in the private discriminatory policy, they concluded. The exception was the liquor board's requirement that all club bylaws be obeyed. The majority found that in cases where the bylaws restricted membership by race, the state regulation amounted to enforcement of a discriminatory practice and the requirement should not be applied to the private club.

In a second case, the Court rejected the claim of a community recreation association that it was a private club exempt from the 1964 Civil Rights Act. The association limited membership in its swimming pool to white residents of the community and their white guests. In *Tillman v. Wheaton-Haven Recreation Association* (1973) the Court ruled that the association was not entitled to the exemption because it had no selection criteria for membership other than race and residence in the community.[2]

1. *Moose Lodge 107 v. Irvis,* 407 U.S. 163 (1972).
2. *Tillman v. Wheaton-Haven Recreational Association, Inc.,* 410 U.S. 431 (1973).

---

does not detract from the overwhelming evidence of the disruptive effect that racial discrimination has had on commercial intercourse. It was this burden which empowered Congress to enact appropriate legislation, and, given this basis for the exercise of its power, Congress was not restricted by the fact that the particular obstruction to interstate commerce with which it was dealing was also deemed a moral and social wrong.[121]

The Court also rejected the claim that Title II violated the motel owner's Fifth Amendment rights. Congress acted reasonably to prohibit racial discrimination, the Court said, noting that thirty-two states had similar civil rights laws in effect. Furthermore, the Court said, "in a long line of cases this Court has rejected the claim that the prohibition of racial discrimination in public accommodations interferes with personal liberty" [122]

The Court's decision upholding the constitutionality of the use of the commerce power to bar private discrimination seemed to conflict with the decision in the 1883 *Civil Rights Cases* that Congress lacked the power to enforce the Thirteenth and Fourteenth Amendments by barring private acts of discrimination in public accommodations. The Court said in its 1964 ruling that it found the 1883 decision "without precedential value" since Congress in 1875 had not limited prohibition of discrimination to those businesses that impinged on interstate commerce. Wrote Clark of that case:

> Since the commerce power was not relied on by the Government and was without support in the [trial] record it is understandable that the Court narrowed its inquiry and excluded the Commerce Clause as a possible source of power. In any event, it is clear that such a limitation renders the opinion devoid of authority for the proposition that the Commerce Clause gives no power to Congress to regulate discriminatory practices now found substantially to affect interstate commerce. [123]

Ollie's Barbecue

In the companion case of *Katzenbach v. McClung* (1964) the Court upheld the section of Title II barring discrimination by private proprietors who served to their clientele goods that moved in interstate commerce. Ollie's Barbecue, a Birmingham, Alabama, restaurant that discriminated against blacks, did not seek to serve customers from out of state, but 46 percent of the food it served was supplied through interstate commerce.

The restaurant claimed that the amount of food it purchased in interstate commerce was insignificant compared to the total amount of food in interstate commerce. The Court rejected this argument. The restaurant's purchase might be insignificant, the Court said, but added to all other purchases of food through interstate commerce by persons who discriminate against blacks, the impact on interstate commerce was far from insignificant. [124]

Commerce and Recreation

Five years later, in *Daniel v. Paul* (1969), the Court upheld Title II as applied to a small recreational area near Little Rock, Arkansas. The area admitted only whites, but claimed it did not fall under Title II because it did not seek interstate travelers and sold little food purchased through interstate commerce.

The Court disagreed, pointing out that the food sold was composed of ingredients produced in other states. Moreover, the facility advertised in Little Rock and at a military base, and it was unreasonable to think that the ads would not attract some interstate travelers. [125]

Justice Black objected to connecting the recreational area to interstate commerce, saying he would have supported a decision based on the Fourteenth Amendment.

THE RIGHT TO FAIR HOUSING

Even as the Supreme Court in the *Civil Rights Cases* of 1883 held that Congress lacked authority to protect blacks against persons who refused them public accommodations, it acknowledged the power of Congress to erase "the necessary incidents of slavery" and "to secure to all citizens of every race and color, without regard to previous servitude, those fundamental rights which are the essence of civil freedom." Among these, the Court said, was the right "to inherit, purchase, lease, sell and convey property." [126]

With this statement the Court by indirection upheld the Civil Rights Act of 1866, enacted by Congress to enforce the Thirteenth Amendment, which abolished slavery. The act gave blacks the same rights as whites to buy, lease, hold, and sell property. *(Box, p. 253)*

State Discrimination

As states and cities adopted more laws segregating whites from blacks, however, even these fundamental rights fell victim to "Jim Crow" laws. In 1917 the Supreme Court struck down one such housing law.

Buchanan v. Warley (1917) began in Louisville, Kentucky, where a city ordinance forbade members of one race to buy, reside on, or sell property on streets where a majority of the residents were of the other race. Buchanan, a white property owner, entered into a contract for the sale of his property to a black man named Warley. When Warley found the Louisville law prevented him from living on the property, he exercised a contract proviso allowing him to break his agreement to purchase. Buchanan then sued for performance of the contract and charged that the Louisville ordinance violated the Fourteenth Amendment. Defenders of the ordinance claimed that it was a valid exercise of the city's police power to prevent racial conflict, maintain racial purity, and prevent deterioration in property values.

The Supreme Court acknowledged a broad police power, but also recalled the Court's 1883 opinion that acquisition, use, and disposal of property were fundamental rights available to all citizens without regard to race or color. The Court then unanimously struck down the city ordinance. Justice William R. Day wrote for the Court.

> That there exists a serious and difficult problem arising from a feeling of race hostility which the law is powerless to control, and to which it must give a measure of consideration, may be freely admitted. But its solution cannot be promoted by depriving citizens of their constitutional rights and privileges. . . . The right which the ordinance annulled was the civil right of a white man to dispose of his property if he saw fit to do so to a person of color, and of a colored person to make such disposition to a white person. . . . We think this attempt to prevent the alienation of the property in question . . . was not a legitimate exercise of the police power of the state, and is in direct violation of the

fundamental law enacted in the Fourteenth Amendment of the Constitution preventing state interference with property rights except by due process of law.[127]

The Court subsequently upheld several lower court decisions invalidating similar laws by citing *Buchanan*.[128]

Restrictive Covenants

Officially imposed housing segregation was quickly replaced in many localities by private restrictive covenants. Under such covenants, the white residents of a particular block or neighborhood agreed to refuse to sell or lease their homes to blacks.

A challenge to the constitutional validity of such private covenants came before the Supreme Court in 1926. Adhering to its earlier rulings that Congress had no authority to protect individuals from private discrimination, the Court dismissed *Corrigan v. Buckley* (1926), effectively upholding as valid private restrictive convenants. The arguments that the covenant violated the Fifth, Thirteenth and Fourteenth Amendments, the Court said, were

> entirely lacking in substance or color of merit. The Fifth Amendment "is a limitation only upon the powers of the General Government," ... and is not directed against the action of individuals. The Thirteenth Amendment denouncing slavery ... does not in other matters protect the individual rights of persons of the Negro race.... And the prohibitions of the Fourteenth Amendment "have reference to state action exclusively, and not to any action of private individuals." [129]

No State Enforcement

Twenty-two years later, the Court effectively nullified restrictive covenants by forbidding the state to enforce them. *Shelley v. Kraemer* (1948) arose when a black couple bought property to which a restrictive covenant applied. A white couple who owned restricted property in the same neighborhood sued to stop the Shelleys from taking possession of the property. The trial court denied that request, holding that the covenant was not effective because it had not been signed by all the property owners in the affected area. The supreme court of Missouri reversed the decision, ruling the covenant effective and not a violation of the Shelleys' rights under the Fourteenth Amendment. The Shelleys appealed to the Supreme Court, where their case was combined with a similar one, *McGhee v. Sipes*.[130]

Writing for a unanimous Court (although three members did not participate), Chief Justice Vinson repeated the Court's earlier opinion that the Fourteenth Amendment does not reach "private conduct, however discriminatory or wrongful." Therefore, Vinson wrote, private restrictive covenants "effectuated by voluntary adherence to their terms" are not in violation of the amendment.[131]

However, the chief justice continued, official actions by state courts and judicial officers have never been considered to be outside the scope of the Fourteenth Amendment. In the two cases before the Court, Vinson said,

> the States have made available to [private] individuals the full coercive power of government to deny to petitioners, on the grounds of race or color, the enjoyment of property rights in premises which petitioners are

Civil Rights Act of 1866

Congress enacted the Civil Rights Act of 1866 to enforce the newly ratified Thirteenth Amendment prohibiting slavery. Following is the text of the portion of the Civil Rights Act that, the Supreme Court ruled in 1968, barred individuals from discriminating against racial minorities in the sale or rental of housing:

Section 1. Be it enacted by the Senate and House of Representatives of the United States of America in Congress assembled, That all persons in the United States and not subject to any foreign power, ... are hereby declared to be citizens of the United States; and such citizens, of every race and color, without regard to any previous condition of servitude ... shall have the same right, in every State and Territory in the United States, to make and enforce contracts, to sue, be parties, and give evidence, to inherit, purchase, lease, sell, hold, and convey real and personal property, and to full and equal benefit of all laws and proceedings for the security of person and property, as is enjoyed by white citizens, and shall be subject to like punishment, pains, and penalties, and to none other, any law, statute, ordinance, regulation, or custom, to the contrary notwithstanding.

Section 2. That any person who, under color of any law, statute, ordinance, regulation, or custom, shall subject, or cause to be subjected, any inhabitant of any State or Territory to the deprivation of any right secured or protected by this act, or to different punishment, pains, or penalties on account of such person having at any time been held in a condition of slavery or involuntary servitude, ... or by reason of his color or race, than is prescribed for the punishment of white persons, shall be deemed guilty of a misdemeanor, and, on conviction, shall be punished by fine not exceeding one thousand dollars, or imprisonment not exceeding one year, or both, in the discretion of the court.

willing and financially able to acquire and which the grantors are willing to sell. The difference between judicial enforcement and nonenforcement of the restrictive covenants is the difference to petitioners between being denied rights of property available to other members of the community and being accorded full enjoyment of these rights on an equal footing....

We hold that in granting judicial enforcement of the restrictive agreements in these cases, the States have denied petitioners the equal protection of the laws and that, therefore, the action of the state courts cannot stand.[132]

The Right to Challenge

Ordinarily, the Supreme Court does not allow a person to come before it to defend someone else's rights. However, the Court has sometimes bent this rule in housing discrimination cases.

Barrows v. Jackson (1953) concerned a woman who violated a restrictive covenant by selling her property to blacks. Other covenantors in the neighborhood sued her for damages, claiming that her action reduced their property values. The restrictive covenant did not affect the constitutional rights of the white seller who had breached its terms, but in defense of her action, she argued that the covenant infringed on the rights of racial minorities by forbidding them to buy homes in the neighborhood.

The Court allowed her to make this defense in behalf of minority group members. The reasons for ordinarily prohibiting such a third-party defense were "outweighed [in this case] by the need to protect the fundamental rights which would be denied by permitting the damages action to be maintained," the Court said.[1]

In 1972 the Court again took a broad view of the right to bring housing discrimination cases. Two white tenants in an apartment building claimed that their landlord's discriminatory policy against nonwhites harmed them by denying them social, business, and professional advantages gained from association with minorities. The tenants filed a complaint with the U.S. Department of Housing and Urban Development (HUD) under Section 810 of the 1968 Civil Rights Act.

When the complaint came to trial, a federal judge held that the tenants were not within the class of persons entitled to sue under the 1968 act. The Supreme Court reversed in *Trafficante v. Metropolitan Life Insurance Co.*

"We can give vitality to [section] 810 . . . ," wrote Justice William O. Douglas, "only by a generous construction which gives standing to sue to all in the same housing unit who are injured by racial discrimination in the management of those facilities within the coverage of the statute."[2]

But the Court has not consistently been so generous in construing standing to challenge alleged housing discrimination. In the 1975 case of *Warth v. Seldin*, a five-justice majority deflected an effort to attack a town's zoning ordinance that effectively excluded low- and moderate-income persons from living in the town.

The majority held that none of the groups seeking to bring the suit had the legal standing to do so because none could show that a decision in their favor invalidating the zoning ordinance would have a direct ameliorative effect on the injury they claimed to suffer as a result of its operation.[3]

1. *Barrows v. Jackson*, 346 U.S. 249 at 257 (1953).
2. *Trafficante v. Metropolitan Life Insurance Company*, 409 U.S. 205 at 212 (1972); see also *Gladstone Realtors v. Village of Bellwood*, 441 U.S. 91 (1979).
3. *Warth v. Seldin*, 422 U.S. 490 (1975).

Two companion cases, *Hurd v. Hodge* and *Urciola v. Hodge* (1948), challenged restrictive covenants in the District of Columbia. Because the Fourteenth Amendment applied only to states, the District covenants were alleged to violate the due process clause of the Fifth Amendment. But the Court found it unnecessary to address the constitutional issue, holding instead that the district courts were barred from enforcing the covenants by the Civil Rights Act of 1866.[133]

No Penalty

The Court expanded *Shelley v. Kraemer* five years later in *Barrows v. Jackson* (1953) when it ruled that state courts could not require a person who had violated a restrictive covenant to pay damages to other covenantors who claimed her action had reduced the value of their property.

Court enforcement of such a damage claim constitutes state action that violates the Fourteenth Amendment if it denies any class the equal protection of the laws, the Court said. "If a state court awards damages for breach of a restrictive covenant," the Court reasoned, "a prospective seller of restricted land will either refuse to sell to non-Caucasians or else will require non-Caucasians to pay a higher price to meet the damage which the seller may incur."[134] In either event, the Court concluded, non-Caucasians would be denied equal protection.

Housing Referenda

In the 1967 case of *Reitman v. Mulkey* the Court applied *Shelley v. Kraemer* to nullify a 1964 California constitutional amendment barring the state from interfering with the right of any person to sell or refuse to sell his property to anyone for any reason. The amendment effectively nullified several state fair housing laws.

When the Mulkeys sued Reitman on the grounds that he had declined to rent them an apartment solely because they were black, Reitman moved for dismissal of the complaint, citing the newly enacted constitutional amendment. The California Supreme Court, however, held that by the amendment the state had acted "to make private discriminations legally possible" and thus violated the equal protection clause.

By a 5-4 vote the Supreme Court affirmed that ruling.

For the majority, Justice White wrote that adoption of the amendment meant:

> The right to discriminate, including the right to discriminate on racial grounds, was now embodied in the State's basic charter, immune from legislative, executive or judicial regulation at any level of the state government. Those practicing racial discriminations need no longer rely solely on their personal choice. They could now invoke express constitutional authority, free from censure or interference of any kind from official sources.[135]

Justice Harlan, writing for the dissenters, said the amendment was neutral on its face and did not violate the equal protection clause. By maintaining that the amendment actually encourages private discrimination, Harlan said, the majority "is forging a slippery and unfortunate criterion by which to measure the constitutionality of a statute simply permissive in purpose and effect, and inoffensive on its face." [136]

Two years later the Court struck down a newly added provision of the Akron, Ohio, city charter that required a majority of voters to approve any ordinance dealing with racial, religious, or ancestral discrimination in housing.

Noting that the charter did not require similar referenda for other housing matters, such as rent control, public housing, and building codes, the majority in *Hunter v. Erickson* (1969) held that the charter singled out a special class of people for special treatment in violation of the equal protection clause. "[T]he State may no more disadvantage any particular group by making it more difficult to enact legislation in its behalf than it may dilute any person's vote or give any group a smaller representation than another of comparable size," the majority wrote.[137]

Justice Black dissented, protesting "against use of the Equal Protection Clause to bar States from repealing laws that the Court wants the States to retain." [138]

In the 1971 case of *James v. Valtierra,* however, the Court upheld a California constitutional amendment providing that no local government agency could construct low-income housing projects without first receiving the approval of a majority of those voting in a local referendum. Distinguishing this case from *Hunter,* the majority said the city charter at issue in *Hunter* created a classification based solely upon race, while the constitutional amendment involved in the *James* case "requires referendum approval for any low-rent public housing project, not only for projects which will be occupied by a racial minority." [139]

In dissent, Justice Marshall contended that the California amendment created a classification based on poverty that violated the equal protection clause just as much as classifications based on race. "It is far too late in the day to contend that the Fourteenth Amendment prohibits only racial discrimination," Marshall wrote, "and, to me, singling out the poor to bear a burden not placed on any other class of citizens tramples the values that the Fourteenth Amendment was designed to protect." [140] *(Poverty and equal protection, p. 287)*

Individual Discrimination

Despite the Court's rulings on state enforcement of restrictive covenants and housing referenda, blacks and other minorities still had little protection from housing discrimination by individual home and apartment owners.

Old Law, New Life

Then, in 1968, just weeks after Congress enacted the first federal fair housing law, the Supreme Court, 7-2, held that the 1866 Civil Rights Act barred individual as well as state-backed discrimination in the sale and rental of housing. The case was brought by Joseph Lee Jones, who contended that the Alfred H. Mayer Company violated the 1866 act by refusing to sell him a home in the Paddock Woods section of St. Louis County, Missouri, because he was black.

A federal district court dismissed the case; the court of appeals affirmed the dismissal on the grounds that the 1866 act (in modern form Section 1982 of Title 42 of the U.S. Code) applied only to state discrimination and not to the segregative actions of private individuals.

The Supreme Court reversed the court of appeals. Writing in *Jones v. Alfred H. Mayer Co.* (1968), Justice Potter Stewart said that the legislative history of the 1866 act persuaded the Court that Congress intended to ban private and state-backed discrimination:

> In light of the concerns that led Congress to adopt it and the contents of the debates that preceded its passage, it is clear that the Act was designed to do just what its terms suggest: to prohibit all racial discrimination, whether or not under color of law, with respect to the rights enumerated therein—including the right to purchase or lease property.[141]

The question was then: Did Congress have the power to enact the 1866 act? For the answer, Stewart looked to the Thirteenth Amendment rather than to the equal protection clause of the Fourteenth Amendment. The Thirteenth Amendment was adopted to remove the "badges of slavery" from the nation's blacks, Stewart observed, and gave Congress the power to enforce that removal.

> If Congress has power under the Thirteenth Amendment to eradicate conditions that prevent Negroes from buying and renting property because of their race or color, then no federal statute calculated to achieve that objective can be thought to exceed the constitutional power of Congress simply because it reaches beyond state action to regulate the conduct of private individuals.... Surely Congress has the power under the Thirteenth Amendment rationally to determine what are the badges and the incidents of slavery, and the authority to translate that determination into effective legislation. Nor can we say that the determination Congress has made is an irrational one.... [W]hen racial discrimination herds men into ghettoes and makes their ability to buy property turn on the color of their skin, then it too is a relic of slavery....
>
> At the very least, the freedom that Congress is empowered to secure under the Thirteenth Amendment includes the freedom to buy whatever a white man can buy, the right to live wherever a white man can live. If Congress cannot say that being a free man means at least this much, then the Thirteenth Amendment made a promise the Nation cannot keep.[142]

Justice Harlan, dissenting for himself and Justice White, said that the 1866 act was meant only to protect people from state-imposed discrimination.

The Zoning Power and Fair Housing

Since 1926, when it first upheld a comprehensive local zoning law, the Supreme Court has seldom interfered with state power over land use, even when those laws were challenged as violating the equal protection clause of the Fourteenth Amendment.

Such a challenge was raised in 1974 against a New York village's zoning ordinance that prohibited more than two unrelated persons from sharing a single-family home. The ordinance placed no limit on the number of family members that could share a house. Rejecting an equal protection challenge to the ordinance, the Court wrote that the zoning law was a reasonable means of attaining a permissible objective—the preservation of the family character of the village.[1]

Discriminatory Intent

In 1977 the Court again turned back an equal protection challenge to a local zoning decision. The case of *Village of Arlington Heights v. Metropolitan Housing Development Corporation* arose when a housing developer requested the predominantly white Chicago suburb of Arlington Heights to rezone certain land so that he could build housing for low- and moderate-income persons of both races there. When zoning officials refused the request, the developer went to court, charging the denial was motivated by a desire to keep black families from moving into the suburb.

By 5-3, the Supreme Court upheld the village's refusal to rezone, finding no evidence that it was racially motivated. Instead the evidence showed that the zoning decision was the result of the legitimate desire to protect property values.[2]

Without discriminatory intent, wrote Justice Lewis F. Powell, Jr., the fact that the refusal to rezone had a racially discriminatory effect was "without independent constitutional significance." The court referred to its 1976 job discrimination ruling in *Washington v. Davis*.[3]

There, said Powell, the Court made clear "that official action will not be held unconstitutional solely because it results in a racially disproportionate impact.... Proof of racially discriminatory intent or purpose is required to show a violation of the Equal Protection Clause."[4] *(Washington v. Davis, p. 259)*

Powell said that the factors that might be examined to determine whether a decision had been motivated by racial discrimination included its potential impact, the historical background, the specific sequence of events leading up to the decision, departures from normal procedures and the legislative or administrative history.

For example, Powell said, the Arlington Heights decision to refuse to rezone would appear in a different light if the village had not consistently applied its zoning policy, if unusual procedures had been followed in handling this particular request or if the zoning for the particular parcel had been recently changed from multifamily to single-family use.

Justice Byron R. White, author of the Court's opinion in *Washington v. Davis,* dissented, saying that the majority should not have applied that ruling to this case.

Discriminatory Effect

The Court sent the case back to the court of appeals to consider whether the zoning decision violated the Fair Housing Act of 1968. In July 1977 that court held that the village's refusal to rezone would violate the act if it had a discriminatory effect even though there was no intent to discriminate. "Conduct that has the necessary and foreseeable consequences of perpetuating segregation can be as deleterious as purposefully discriminating conduct in frustrating" the national goal of integrated housing, the appeals court wrote.[5]

1. *Village of Belle Terre v. Boraas,* 416 U.S. 1 (1974).
2. *Village of Arlington Heights v. Metropolitan Housing Development Corporation,* 429 U.S. 252 (1977).
3. *Washington v. Davis,* 426 U.S. 229 (1976).
4. *Village of Arlington Heights v. Metropolitan Housing Development Corporation,* 429 U.S. 252 at 264-265 (1977).
5. *Metropolitan Housing Development Corporation v. Village of Arlington Heights,* 558 F. 2d 1283 at 1289 (1977).

Community Clubs, Pools

In 1969 the Court held that the 1866 act also prohibited a community recreational club from refusing membership to a black man who received a club share as part of his lease of a home in the neighborhood.[143]

And in 1973 the Court ruled that a community recreation area violated the 1866 Civil Rights Act when it limited membership in its swimming pools to white residents of the community and their white guests.

In *Tillman v. Wheaton-Haven Recreation Associa-*tion, a unanimous Court wrote:

> When an organization links membership benefits to residence in a narrow geographical area, that decision infuses those benefits into the bundle of rights for which an individual pays when buying or leasing within the area. The mandate of [the 1866 Civil Rights Act] then operates to guarantee a nonwhite resident, who purchases, leases or holds this property, the same rights as are enjoyed by a white resident.[144]

Remedies for Discrimination

Although the Court has struck down several varieties of housing discrimination, it has had little occasion to consider remedies for that discrimination.

In the one case the Court has heard on the remedy issue, however, it unanimously upheld the power of a federal judge to order a metropolitan areawide remedy for segregated public housing in Chicago.

The question in *Hills v. Gautreaux* (1976) was whether the remedy for racial discrimination in public housing caused by state and federal officials must be confined to the city in which the discrimination occurred or could include the surrounding metropolitan area.[145] In holding that the remedy need not be restricted to the city alone, the Court made an important distinction between the facts in this case and those in 1974 case of *Milliken v. Bradley,* which overturned a metropolitan areawide plan of school desegregation.[146] (*Milliken decision, p. 243*)

In *Hills* the Chicago Housing Authority (CHA) was found guilty of discrimination in placing most of the city's public housing in black ghettoes, and the Department of Housing and Urban Development (HUD) was found guilty of sanctioning and aiding this discriminatory public housing program. A court of appeals ordered a metropolitan areawide plan to eliminate the segregated public housing system, but HUD asked the Supreme Court to reverse it, citing *Milliken v. Bradley.*

Distinguishing between the two cases, Justice Stewart said the Court struck down the school desegregation plan because "there was no finding of unconstitutional action on the part of the suburban school officials and no demonstration that the violations committed in the operation of the Detroit school system had any significant segregative effects in the suburbs." [147]

The situation in the Chicago housing case was different, Stewart's opinion said. HUD did not contest the finding that it had violated the Constitution and the 1964 Civil Rights Act, nor did it dispute the appropriateness of its being ordered to help develop public housing in desegregated neighborhoods:

The critical distinction between HUD and the suburban school districts in *Milliken* is that HUD has been found to have violated the Constitution. . . . Nothing in the Milliken decision suggests a *per se* rule that federal courts lack authority to order parties found to have violated the Constitution to undertake remedial efforts beyond the municipal boundaries of the city where the violation occurred.[148]

The Court's opinion continued:

[I]t is entirely appropriate and consistent with *Milliken* to order CHA and HUD to attempt to create housing alternatives for the respondents [the black plaintiffs] in the Chicago suburbs. Here the wrong committed by HUD confined the respondents to segregated public housing. The relevant geographic area for purposes of the respondents' housing option is the Chicago housing market, not the Chicago city limits. . . . To foreclose such relief solely because HUD's constitutional violation took place within the city limits of Chicago would transform *Milliken's* principled limitation on the exercise of federal judicial authority into an arbitrary . . . shield for those found to have engaged in unconstitutional conduct.[149]

A metropolitan remedy need not impermissibly interfere with local governments which had not been involved in the unconstitutional segregation, Stewart continued:

The remedial decree would neither force suburban governments to submit public housing proposals to HUD nor displace the rights and powers accorded local government entities under federal or state housing statutes or existing land-use laws. The order would have the same effect on the suburban governments as a discretionary decision by HUD to use its statutory powers to provide the respondents with alternatives to the racially segregated Chicago public housing system created by CHA and HUD.[150]

In 1977 the Court seemed to limit the potential impact of *Gautreaux.* In *Village of Arlington Heights v. Metropolitan Housing Development Corporation,* the Court said that, without a showing of discriminatory motive, the village's refusal to rezone property to permit building of a housing development for low- and moderate-income persons of both races did not violate the Fourteenth Amendment.[151] The Court's decision left open the possibility that the zoning decision might have violated the 1968 Fair Housing Act. (*Details, box, p. 256*)

EQUAL EMPLOYMENT OPPORTUNITY

Civil war and emancipation did little to free blacks from job discrimination. Most of the southern states enacted Black Codes restricting the kinds of jobs blacks could hold, thereby limiting competition with white workers and forcing blacks to continue as farm and plantation workers.

South Carolina enacted one of the harshest of these codes. It prohibited a black from working as an artisan or mechanic unless he obtained a license that cost ten dollars and from becoming a shopkeeper unless he had a license costing one hundred dollars. Licenses were issued by judges who decided whether the black applicants were skilled and morally fit for the work.

The only jobs that blacks could obtain without a license were as farm workers or servants, and in both cases they were required to sign labor contracts with their employers. In South Carolina, as in many other southern states, failure to fulfill the labor contract was a crime, and a black worker could avoid a jail term only by agreeing to work off the original contract, his fine for defaulting, and court costs. The Supreme Court struck down such peonage laws as unconstitutional in the early 1900s.[152]

Despite industrialization, blacks remained relegated to low-paying, unskilled jobs that promised little, if any, advancement. Even if a black qualified for a better job, he was often passed over in favor of a white employee. Until the enactment of state fair employment laws in the mid-1940s, few blacks who had been refused jobs because of their race had any legal recourse. The employer-employee relationship was considered private, outside the protection of the Fourteenth Amendment. Private employers and labor unions could discriminate against blacks with impunity and many of them did.[153]

Early Rulings

Because there were so few legal protections available, only a handful of employment discrimination cases reached the Court before 1964, the year that Congress prohibited such job bias. In almost all of these early cases, however, the Supreme Court interpreted available law to protect blacks.

The first of these cases came in 1938. Blacks organized a picket line outside a District of Columbia grocery to force the proprietor to hire blacks. A federal court ordered the picketing stopped; the blacks charged that the order violated the Norris-LaGuardia Act, which prohibited federal courts from issuing injunctions in legal labor disputes. The issue was whether picketing to force someone to hire blacks was a legal labor objective within the meaning of the law. By 7-2, the Court held that it was:

> Race discrimination by an employer may be reasonably deemed more unfair and less excusable than discrimination against workers on the ground of union affiliation. There is no justification . . . for limiting [the act's] definition of labor disputes and cases arising therefrom by excluding those which arise with respect to discrimination in terms and condition of employment based upon differences of race or color.[154]

The Court modified this position in 1950 when it held that picketing to demand that a store owner increase the number of blacks he employed constituted discrimination against already-hired white clerks.[155]

The first case involving union discrimination came in 1944 when the Court was asked to decide whether a union acting under federal law as the exclusive bargaining agent for a class of workers was obligated by that law to represent all workers without regard to race.

Steele v. Louisville and Nashville Railroad Co. involved the Brotherhood of Locomotive Firemen, the exclusive bargaining representative for train firemen of twenty-one railroad companies. The union, which excluded blacks from membership, agreed with the railroad companies to amend the work contract to end all employment of blacks as firemen. As a result, Steele, a black fireman, was reassigned to more difficult, less remunerative work and his job given to a white man with less seniority and no more qualifications.

In an opinion that carefully avoided any constitutional issues, the Court ruled that the Railway Labor Act of 1930 compelled the exclusive bargaining agent for an entire class of employees to represent all those employees fairly "without hostile discrimination" against any of them.[156]

The Court reached a similar conclusion in the 1952 case of *Brotherhood of Railroad Trainmen v. Howard.* A white brakemen's union threatened to strike unless the railroad company fired all its black "train porters," who performed the same functions as brakemen, and replaced them with white union members. Unlike the blacks in the *Steele* case, however, the black train porters had long been represented by their own union. Nonetheless, a majority of the Supreme Court saw no significant difference in the two cases. The black "train porters are threatened with loss of their jobs because they are not white and for no other reason, " wrote Justice Black. "The Federal [Railway Labor] Act . . . prohibits bargaining agents it authorizes from using their position and power to destroy colored workers' jobs in order to bestow them on white workers." [157]

State Antidiscrimination Laws

Black workers won another measure of job protection in 1945 when the Court upheld the validity of state fair employment laws. The New York Civil Rights Act contained a provision—one of the first of its kind ever enacted—prohibiting a union from denying membership on the basis of race, creed, or color. The Railway Mail Association, which represented postal clerks in New York and other states and which limited its membership to whites and Indians, appealed the state's judgment that this law applied to its policy of excluding blacks. The association claimed the state law violated the organization's right to due process and equal protection and encroached on Congress's power to regulate the mails. The Supreme Court denied all three claims:

> We see no constitutional basis for the contention that a state cannot protect workers from exclusion solely on the basis of race, color or creed by an organization functioning under the protection of the state, which holds itself out to represent the general business needs of employees.[158]

The question whether a state fair employment practices act placed an impermissible burden on interstate commerce came to the Court in *Colorado Anti-Discrimination Commission v. Continental Airlines* (1963).[159]

A black man named Marion Green applied for a job as a pilot with the interstate airline, which had its headquarters in Denver. He was rejected solely because of his race. The Colorado Anti-Discrimination Commission found the company had discriminated in violation of state law and ordered it to give Green the first opening in its next training course. A state court overruled the order, however, because the law unduly burdened interstate commerce.

The Supreme Court reversed the trial court and upheld the commission's order. The state antidiscrimination law did not conflict with or frustrate any federal law that might also regulate employment discrimination by airlines, said the Court. Nor did it deny the airlines any rights granted by Congress. Unlike several cases in which the Court has found that state-required racial separation of passengers in public transportation unduly burdened interstate commerce, the Court found hiring within a state, even for an interstate job, a "much more localized matter." Furthermore, the potential for diverse and conflicting hiring regulations among the states, which might hamper interstate commerce, was "virtually nonexistent," the Court said. *(Discrimination in interstate transportation, p. 248)*

The 1964 Civil Rights Act

The following year Congress enacted the first federal law prohibiting job discrimination. Title VII of the Civil Rights Act of 1964 prohibited employers of and unions representing more than twenty-five workers, union hiring halls, and employment agencies from discriminating on the grounds of race, color, religion, sex, or national origin in the hiring, classification, training, or promotion of anyone. The act also created the Equal Employment Opportunities Commission (EEOC) to hear complaints and seek compliance with the law.

The Question of Intent

Distinguishing between cases based on the Constitution's guarantee of equal protection and those based on civil rights laws, the Supreme Court has made clear that it is sometimes more difficult to prove some actions unconstitutional than to prove them illegal.

The seminal case was *Washington v. Davis*, decided in 1976. In order to prove an employer guilty of unconstitutional discrimination, his action must be shown to be discriminatory in effect and intent, the Court held.

Washington v. Davis arose when two blacks challenged as unconstitutionally discriminatory the District of Columbia police department's requirement that recruits pass a verbal ability test. The two men backed their challenge by arguing that the number of black police officers did not reflect the city's large black population, that more blacks than whites failed the test, and that the test was not significantly related to job performance.

Their challenge was based not on the Civil Rights Act of 1964, however, but on the due process clause of the Fifth Amendment, which implicitly includes the equal protection guarantee. *(Details, box, p. 224)*

A federal district court rejected the challenge because there was no evidence of intent to discriminate. The appeals court reversed, citing *Griggs v. Duke Power* (1971). *(Details, p. 258)*

The Supreme Court, however, reversed again, agreeing with the district court, 7-2, that there was no constitutional violation without proof of discriminatory intent.

Justice Byron R. White wrote that the Court had "not held that a law, neutral on its face and serving ends otherwise within the power of the government to pursue, is invalid under the Equal Protection Clause simply because it may affect a greater proportion of one race than another." [1]

The Court subsequently applied this principle—that a law or other official action must reflect some racially discriminatory intent to violate the equal protection guarantee—in other areas of discrimination, including schools and housing. [2] *(School case, p. 236, housing case, p. 256)*

In 1980 the Court extended this intent requirement to challenged voting practices, ruling 6-3, in *Mobile v. Bolden* that before it would strike down an at-large system for electing city officials as a violation of the equal protection guarantee or of the law barring racial discrimination in voting, the system must be found intentionally discriminatory—as well as discriminatory in effect. Congress quickly overrode this ruling with its 1982 amendments to the Voting Rights Act, which made plain that there was no need for this finding of intent to justify holding a voting practice impermissible under that law. [3]

Two years later the Court again applied the intent requirement in the job area, ruling 5-4 in *American Tobacco Co. v. Patterson*, that workers challenging a seniority system as discriminatory under the 1964 Act must prove both a discriminatory intent and effect. [4]

1. *Washington v. Davis*, 426 U.S. 229 at 242 (1976).
2. *Austin Independent School District v. United States*, 429 U.S. 990 (1976); *Village of Arlington Heights v. Metropolitan Housing Development Corporation*, 429 U.S. 252 (1977).
3. *City of Mobile, Ala. v. Bolden*, 446 U.S. 55 (1980); *Congress and the Nation*, vol. VI. (Washington, D.C.: Congressional Quarterly, 1985), 680.
4. *American Tobacco Co. v. Patterson*, 456 U.S. 63 (1982); see also *U.S. Postal Service Board of Governors v. Aikens*, 460 U.S. 711 (1983).

In 1972 Congress extended coverage to employers and unions with fifteen or more employees or members, state and local governments, and educational institutions. The only major group left uncovered were federal government employees. The 1972 act also authorized the EEOC to go into federal court to enforce the law. Federal courts were authorized to order employers to remedy proven discrimination by reinstating or hiring the employees concerned, with or without back pay, and by any other remedial measures the courts found appropriate.

Job Qualifications

The Supreme Court first fully discussed the scope of Title VII in its 1971 decision in *Griggs v. Duke Power Co.* Black employees charged that the North Carolina power company had unfairly discriminated when it required them to have a high school diploma or pass a generalized intelligence test as a condition for employment or promotion. The black workers claimed that neither requirement was related to successful job performance, that the requirements disqualified a substantially higher number of blacks than whites and that the jobs in question had been filled by whites under the company's former longstanding policy of giving whites first preference.

By 8-0 the Court ruled that under those circumstances the job qualification requirements were discriminatory. Chief Justice Burger set out the Court's interpretation of Title VII:

[T]he Act does not command that any person be hired simply because he was formerly the subject of discrimination, or because he is a member of a minority group. Discriminatory preference for any group, minority or majority, is precisely and only what Congress has proscribed. What is required by Congress is

Black *and* White

Title VII of the 1964 Civil Rights Act prohibits racial discrimination against whites as well as blacks in the workplace, the Court ruled in 1976.

In *McDonald v. Santa Fe Trail Transportation Co.*, a freight company fired two white men who had stolen sixty cans of antifreeze, but the firm did not dismiss a black man who had also participated in the theft.

The Court held this differential treatment a clear violation of Title VII. The law in its language and its legislative history makes plain that whites are to be protected as well as members of racial minorities, said Justice Thurgood Marshall. "While Santa Fe may decide that participation in a theft of cargo may render an employee unqualified for employment, this criterion must be 'applied alike to members of all races,' and Title VII is violated if . . . it was not." (427 U.S. 273 at 283, 1976)

The Court held, 7-2, that the two white men were also protected from such treatment by a provision of the 1866 Civil Rights Act, embodied in existing law as Section 1981 of Title 42 of the United States Code. The section declares that "all persons within the jurisdiction of the United States shall have the same right . . . to make and enforce contracts . . . as is enjoyed by white citizens. " *(Box, p. 253)*

the removal of artificial, arbitrary, and unnecessary barriers to employment when the barriers operate invidiously to discriminate on the basis of racial or other impermissible classification.[160]

Any test that operates to exclude blacks, even one that is neutral on its face, must be shown to have a significant relation to job performance, Burger continued. Neither the requirement for a high school diploma nor the intelligence test had this relation. The Court agreed that there was no evidence that the company had intended to discriminate against its black employees, but, wrote Burger, "Congress directed the thrust of the Act to the consequences of employment practices, not simply the motivation."[161]

The Supreme Court in 1975 reaffirmed its view that tests that excluded more blacks than whites and were not proven to be job-related were discriminatory.[162]

Illegal Protests

A unanimous Court held in 1973 that the 1964 Civil Rights Act did not require a company to rehire a black employee who had engaged in deliberate unlawful protests against it. But neither was the company permitted to use the protests as a pretext for refusing to rehire the employee just because of his race. The former employee should have an opportunity to prove that the employer was using the

illegal protest as an excuse to carry out a discriminatory hiring policy, the Court said in *McDonnell Douglas Corp. v. Green* (1973). If he could not show this, the refusal to rehire him could stand.[163]

Proof of Discrimination

In the 1978 case of *Furnco Construction Corp. v. Waters*, the Supreme Court held that an appeals court erred in ordering a construction company to adopt nondiscriminatory hiring practices before the company had been found guilty of job discrimination. The Court also said that an employer may point to the fact that he has hired a substantial number of black workers as part of his proof that he is not guilty of discrimination. But, wrote the Court, "a racially balanced work force cannot immunize an employer from liability for specific acts of discrimination." [164]

Remedies

The Supreme Court has upheld the broad authority of lower federal courts under Title VII to award back wages and retirement benefits to persons who have suffered illegal job discrimination.

Back Pay. The first such case was *Albemarle Paper Co. v. Moody* (1975). A federal district court found that the North Carolina paper mill had discriminated against blacks prior to enactment of Title VII and that the effects of that discrimination were apparent for several years afterward. But because the company no longer discriminated, the lower court decided against a backpay award. A court of appeals reversed that decision, and the paper mill appealed.

By 7-1 the Court ruled that back pay was a proper remedy for past job discrimination. Justice Stewart wrote:

> If employers faced only the prospect of an injunctive order, they would have little incentive to shun practices of dubious legality. It is the reasonably certain prospect of a backpay award that "provide[s] the spur or catalyst which causes employers and unions to self-examine and to self-evaluate their employment practices and to endeavor to eliminate, so far as possible, the last vestiges of an unfortunate and ignominious page in this country's history.". . . It is also the purpose of Title VII to make persons whole for the injuries suffered on account of unlawful employment discrimination.[165]

Back pay should be awarded in most cases where job discrimination in violation of Title VII has been proved, the majority held, even in cases such as this one, where the employer had acted in good faith to end discrimination. If back pay were awarded only for acts of bad faith, the majority said, "the remedy would become a punishment for moral turpitude, rather than a compensation for workers' injuries. . . . [A] worker's injury is no less real simply because his employer did not inflict it in "bad faith." [166]

In *Fitzpatrick v. Bitzer* (1976) the Court upheld the award of retroactive retirement benefits to male employees of the state of Connecticut who had been required to work longer than women employees before they could retire.[167] *(Details, p. 285)*

One of the first Supreme Court opinions by Justice Sandra Day O'Connor concerned back pay awards. In *Ford Motor Co. v. Equal Employment Opportunity Commis-*

sion, she explained the Court's view that an employer charged with job bias can terminate the period for which he may be held liable for back pay by unconditionally offering the person charging bias the job he had previously refused to offer. "The victims of job discrimination want jobs, not lawsuits," she wrote, expressing the hope that this ruling would encourage employers to make such offers.[168]

Seniority Rights. The Court also has upheld the authority of federal courts to award retroactive seniority rights to persons denied employment or promotion by biased policies.

In *Franks v. Bowman Transportation Co., Inc.* (1976) the Court, 5-3, approved seniority awards by lower courts dating back to rejection of the job application. Retroactive seniority was an appropriate remedy, and such awards should be made in most cases where a seniority system exists and discrimination is proved, the Court said.

Such awards fulfill the "make-whole" purposes of Title VII, held the Court. Without them, Justice Brennan wrote, the victim of job discrimination "will never obtain his rightful place in the hierarchy of seniority according to which these various employment benefits are distributed. He will perpetually remain subordinate to persons who, but for the illegal discrimination, would have been in respect to entitlement to these benefits his inferiors." [169]

The Court did not distinguish between benefit seniority, which determines such matters as length of vacation and pension benefits, and competitive seniority, which determines issues such as the order in which employees are laid off and rehired, promoted, and transferred.

In dissent Justice Powell opposed the award of retroactive competitive seniority because it did not affect the employer but rather "the rights and expectations of perfectly innocent employees. The economic benefits awarded discrimination victims would be derived not at the expense of the employer but at the expense of other workers." [170]

Retroactive Seniority Limited. Little more than a year later, the Court qualified its holding in *Franks* barring the award of retroactive seniority benefits dating back before July 2, 1965, the effective date of the 1964 Civil Rights Act.

In Title VII Congress specifically included language which immunized existing bona fide seniority systems from attack as discriminatory. By 7-2 the Court held that this immunity precluded any award of retroactive seniority benefits that would have been accumulated prior to July 2, 1965, absent racial discrimination.

This case—*Teamsters v. United States, T.I.M.E.-D.C. v. United States* (1977)—concerned a nationwide trucking firm and the truckers' union.[171] Lower courts found that the firm systematically denied intercity-line driver jobs to blacks and Spanish-surnamed employees and applicants. Seniority became an issue in determining the remedy for this discrimination.

Under the company's collective bargaining agreement with the Teamsters, competitive seniority for a line driver was counted from the time he took the post, not from the time he joined the company. Thus a black employee transferring to the line driver job would be required to give up any competitive seniority he had accumulated.

Citing *Franks,* the Court held unanimously that persons discriminated against after the effective date of the 1964 act were entitled to retroactive seniority as far back as that date. But with Justices Brennan and Marshall dissenting, the Court refused to order seniority awards stretching back further than July 2, 1965, for victims of discrimination.

Were it not for the specific immunity granted by the act to bona fide seniority systems, wrote Stewart for the majority, the seniority system challenged in this case would probably have been found invalid. But both the language of the immunization provision and the legislative history demonstrated that an

> otherwise neutral, legitimate seniority system does not become unlawful under Title VII simply because it may perpetuate pre-Act discrimination. Congress did not intend to make it illegal for employees with vested seniority rights to continue to exercise those rights, even at the expense of pre-Act discriminatees.[172]

Marshall and Brennan based their dissent on their view that a seniority system that perpetuated the effect of pre-1965 discrimination was not a bona fide system protected by Title VII.

In 1983 the Court, by a splintered majority, held that without proof of intent to discriminate, private persons suing their employer, a recipient of federal funds, for discrimination in violation of Title VI of the 1964 Civil Rights Act, may not win back pay or retroactive seniority, but only an injunction against the continuation of such conduct.[173]

AFFIRMATIVE ACTION

Affirmative action was the civil rights issue of the 1970s and 1980s. The focus on this matter, a question not of right, but of remedy, reflected the progress the nation had made into the second generation of the civil rights movement. From 1974—when the issue first came to the Supreme Court—until 1987, the Court considered ten affirmative action cases.

Over these years, the Court and the country pondered the questions of fairness and equal protection presented by a remedy designed to compensate for past discrimination. Was it proper to deny members of the majority fair treatment to make up for past unequal treatment of minorities? How did such a remedy fit within the equal protection guarantee?

The first time the issue came to the Court, in the 1974 case of *DeFunis v. Odegaard,* a five-justice majority sidestepped the issue. The Court avoided ruling on the reverse discrimination issue by finding the case moot, no longer presenting a live controversy.

The white plaintiff, who charged that he was denied admission to a state law school so that the school might accept a less-qualified minority student, had been admitted under court order. He was scheduled to graduate from law school in the spring of 1974, only months after the Court heard arguments in his case.

The majority held that the case was moot because their decision on the equal protection issue would have no effect on the plaintiff. The dissenting justices would have preferred to resolve the substantive question.[174]

By 1987 the record was mixed to the point of confusion. The Court had struck down as many affirmative action plans as it had upheld. Never with the agreement of more than six justices, the Court had approved some use of affirmative action in school admissions, job training, contract set-asides, admission to union membership, and promotions. It had forbidden the use of affirmative action in layoffs to preserve the jobs of blacks at the expense of more senior white employees.

Then in 1987 the Court came down firmly on the side of affirmative action, ruling that so long as it was carefully used, affirmative action was an appropriate remedy violating neither the Constitution nor any federal civil rights law.

The *Bakke* Case

When the Court in 1978 finally dealt with a live case of reverse discrimination, it handed down a split decision.

By 5-4, the Court ruled that state universities may not set aside a fixed quota of seats in each class for minority group members, denying white applicants the opportunity to compete for those places.

At the same time, a different five-justice majority held that it is constitutionally permissible for admissions officers to consider race as one of the complex of factors that determine which applicant is accepted and which rejected.

Background

Allan Bakke, a thirty-eight-year-old white engineer, was twice denied admission to the medical school at the University of California at Davis. To ensure minority representation in the student body, the university had set aside sixteen seats for minority applicants in each one hundred-member medical school class.

Challenging the set-aside as a violation of his constitutional right to equal protection of the laws, Bakke contended that he would have been admitted had it not been for this rigid preference system. In each year his application was rejected, the school had accepted some minority applicants with qualifications inferior to Bakke's.

Justice Powell's Votes

Justice Powell was the key to the Bakke decision. He was the only justice who agreed with both majorities in *University of California Regents v. Bakke*—in fact, it could be said that he created both majorities.

On the first point—the decision to strike down the Davis quota system—Powell voted with Chief Justice Burger and Justices Rehnquist, Potter Stewart, and John Paul Stevens, who saw *Bakke* as a controversy between litigants that could be settled by applying the 1964 Civil Rights Act without involving constitutional issues. Title VI of the act, they pointed out, barred any discrimination on the ground of race, color, or national origin in any program receiving federal financial assistance. When that ban was placed alongside the facts of the case, it was clear to them that the university had violated the statute. Stevens explained:

The University, through its special admissions policy, excluded Bakke from participation in its program of medical education because of his race. The University also acknowledges that it was, and still is, receiving federal financial assistance. . . . The meaning of the

Title VI ban on exclusion is crystal clear: Race cannot be the basis of excluding anyone from participation in a federally funded program.[175]

Powell's reasoning on this point differed. Where they found no constitutional involvement, he found the scope of the Title VI ban and the equal protection clause of the Fourteenth Amendment identical—what violated one therefore violated the other. And so he based his vote against the university's preference system on both the law and the Constitution.

The Davis special admissions program used an explicit racial classification, Powell noted. Such classifications were not always unconstitutional, he continued, "[b]ut when a state's distribution of benefits or imposition of burdens hinges on . . . the color of a person's skin or ancestry, that individual is entitled to a demonstration that the challenged classification is necessary to promote a substantial state interest." Powell could find no substantial interest that justified establishment of the university's specific quota system. Not even the desire to remedy past discrimination was a sufficient justification, he said; such a desire was based on "an amorphous concept of injury that may be ageless in its reach into the past."[176]

But Powell did not believe that all racial classifications were unconstitutional. He voted with Justices Brennan, Marshall, White, and Harry A. Blackmun to approve the use of some race-conscious affirmative action programs.

Powell's vote endorsing this position was cautious; he would limit the use of these programs to situations in which past discrimination had been proved. The other four contended that the university's wish to remedy past societal discrimination was sufficient justification. For the four, Brennan wrote:

Government may take race into account when it acts not to demean or insult any racial group, but to remedy disadvantages cast on minorities by past racial prejudice, at least when appropriate findings have been made by judicial, legislative, or administrative bodies with competence to act in this area.[177]

The four endorsed the broad remedial use of race-conscious programs, even in situations where no specific constitutional violation had been found.

The *Weber* Case

The Court's next affirmative action case, *United Steelworkers of America v. Weber,* decided in 1979, did not raise the constitutional issue of equal protection. It posed only the question whether the 1964 act barred an employer from voluntarily establishing an affirmative action training program that preferred blacks over whites.

By a 5-2 vote the Court held that Title VII did not bar such a program. Stewart, who had voted against racial quotas in the *Bakke* case, joined the four justices who had endorsed use of race-conscious programs in that case to form the majority in *Weber.* Burger and Rehnquist dissented; Powell and Stevens did not participate in the case.

Background

In 1974 Kaiser Aluminum and the United Steelworkers of America agreed upon an affirmative action plan that reserved 50 percent of all in-plant craft training slots for minorities. The agreement was a voluntary effort to increase the number of minority participants holding skilled jobs in the aluminum industry.

Brian Weber, a white, applied for a training program at the Kaiser plant where he worked in Gramercy, Louisiana. He was rejected. Weber, who had more seniority than the most junior black accepted for the program, charged that he had been a victim of "reverse discrimination." He won at both the federal district court and the court of appeals levels. The union, the company, and the Justice Department then asked the Supreme Court to review the appeals court decision.[178]

Permissible Plan

Reversing the lower courts, the majority said that in passing Title VII Congress could not have intended to prohibit private employers from voluntarily instituting affirmative action plans to open opportunities for blacks in job areas traditionally closed to them:

> It would be ironic indeed if a law triggered by a Nation's concern over centuries of racial injustice and intended to improve the lot of those who had "been excluded from the American dream for so long" ... constituted the first legislative prohibition of all voluntary, private, race-conscious efforts to abolish traditional patterns of racial segregation and hierarchy.[179]

The majority carefully distinguished between the language of Title VII prohibiting racial discrimination in employment and Title VI, the section of the act reviewed in *Bakke* and held to mean that programs receiving federal aid could not discriminate on the basis of race. In Title VI, Brennan said for the majority:

> Congress was legislating to assure federal funds would not be used in an improper manner. Title VII, by contrast was enacted pursuant to the Commerce power to regulate purely private decisionmaking and was not intended to incorporate and particularize the commands of the Fifth and Fourteenth Amendments

which guarantee equal protection of the laws against federal and state infringement.[180]

In separate dissents Chief Justice Burger and Justice Rehnquist objected to the majority's interpretation of Title VII and its legislative history. The Court's judgment, Burger wrote:

> is contrary to the explicit language of the statute and arrived at by means wholly incompatible with long-established principles of separation of powers. Under the guise of statutory "construction," the Court effectively rewrites Title VII to achieve what it regards as a desirable result. It "amends" the statute to do precisely what both its sponsors and its opponents agreed the statute was *not* intended to do.[181]

Rehnquist charged that the majority had contorted the language of Title VII. Its opinion, he said, is "reminiscent not of jurists such as Hale, Holmes and Hughes, but of escape artists such as Houdini." The Court, he continued, "eludes clear statutory language, 'uncontradicted' legislative history, and uniform precedent in concluding that employers are, after all, permitted to consider race in making employment decisions."[182]

The *Fullilove* Case

The following year the Court faced a constitutional challenge to the decision of Congress in the Public Works Employment Act of 1977 to set aside a certain percentage of federal funds for contracts with minority-owned businesses. The Court, 6-3, held the set-aside permissible.

This program, explained Chief Justice Burger, "was designed to ensure that, to the extent federal funds were granted under ... [this law], grantees who elect to participate would not employ procurement practices that Congress had decided might result in perpetuation of the effects of prior discrimination which had impaired or foreclosed access by minority businesses to public contracting opportunities."[183]

"In the continuing effort to achieve the goal of equality of economic opportunity," wrote Burger, "Congress has necessary latitude to try new techniques such as the limited use of racial and ethnic criteria to accomplish remedial objectives; this especially so in programs where voluntary cooperation with remedial measures is induced by placing conditions on federal expenditures."[184]

The justices in the majority were Burger, Brennan, Powell, Marshall, White, and Blackmun. Dissenting were Rehnquist, Stewart, and Stevens.

Layoffs: *Stotts* and *Wygant*

Affirmative action was anathema to Ronald Reagan's administration, which saw it as impermissible reverse discrimination, penalizing innocent whites—usually white men—for past discrimination by others against blacks and women.

The first two affirmative action cases heard by the Court during the Reagan years brought results the administration found quite congenial. Twice, the Court ruled that affirmative action was not appropriately used in layoff situations to protect the jobs of more recently hired blacks at the cost of the jobs of more senior white employees.

Background

In December 1983 the Court heard arguments in the first affirmative action case of the Reagan years, *Firefighters Local Union No. 1784 v. Stotts, Memphis Fire Department v. Stotts.*

After the Memphis fire department, operating under a consent decree settling charges of racial discrimination against the department, had hired a number of black firefighters, cutbacks in the city budget required some firemen to be laid off. The black fire captain, Carl Stotts, who had won the consent decree, persuaded a federal judge to order that whites with more seniority be laid off in order to preserve the jobs of more recently hired blacks.

With the backing of the Reagan administration, the city and the firefighters' union came to the Court seeking reversal of this order, arguing that layoffs should proceed along the general rule of "last hired, first fired," followed by the other parts of the city government.

The administration's friend-of-the-court argument contended that the firemen's seniority system was immunized by the 1964 Civil Rights Act against such judicial tampering—unless the system was shown to have been designed to discriminate against minority employees, a finding not made in the Memphis case.

Stotts Ruling

In June 1984 the Court agreed with the challenge, holding that the federal judge had overstepped his powers when he overrode the usual seniority rule to preserve the jobs of the junior black firemen. The administration hailed the decision as a victory, reading into it a broad disavowal of affirmative action.

In fact, Justice White tied the Court's opinion closely to the particular facts of this case, namely, the court order directing the city to ignore its usual rules for layoffs in order to preserve gains achieved under a consent decree.[185]

But White and the four other justices in the majority—Burger, Powell, Rehnquist, and Sandra Day O'Connor—did declare that Congress, in the 1964 Civil Rights Act, had intended to provide remedies of this affirmative sort only to persons who had themselves been the victims of illegal discrimination. Because there was no finding in this case that any of the newly hired black firefighters had suffered such personal rejection the judge's order was unwarranted, they said. Justice Stevens joined the majority, but not White's opinion. Justices Brennan, Blackmun, and Marshall dissented.

Wygant Decision

Two years later, the Court underscored its doubts about any use of affirmative action in layoff situations, ruling 5-4 that it was unconstitutional for a school board to lay off white teachers to preserve the jobs of blacks with less seniority. That, the Court held in *Wygant v. Jackson Board of Education,* denied the whites equal protection.[186]

The voluntary adoption of an agreement protecting black jobs in time of layoffs was not based on any showing of actual past discrimination by the board, nor was it narrowly tailored enough to be permitted, the majority held. It was one thing to use affirmative action in hiring, when "the burden to be borne by innocent individuals is diffused . . . generally," wrote Powell, but quite another to use it to deprive people of their existing jobs.[187]

No single opinion set out the Court's view in *Wygant.* And it was particularly notable, in light of the Reagan administration's position, that the Court went out of its way to point out that although the school board's use of affirmative action was not permissible, some affirmative action was appropriate.

"We have recognized . . . that in order to remedy the effects of prior discrimination, it may be necessary to take race into account," wrote Justice Powell. "As part of this nation's dedication to eradicating racial discrimination, innocent persons may be called upon to bear some burden of the remedy." [188]

Justice O'Connor also wrote to emphasize the Court's agreement on "core principles" concerning affirmative action. "The Court is in agreement," she wrote, that "remedying past or present racial discrimination by a state actor is a sufficiently weighty state interest to warrant the remedial use of a carefully constructed affirmative action program." [189]

O'Connor's opinion rejected the administration's position, which *Stotts* had seemed to endorse, that affirmative action was constitutional only when used to benefit specific identified victims of bias. Her opinion, her first substantive writing on the issue, moved her into the decisive "swing" position between the four justices who usually favored affirmative action—Brennan, Marshall, Blackmun, and Stevens—and the four who generally disapproved it—Burger, Rehnquist, White, and Powell.

Affirmative Action Upheld

Wygant marked a turning point. Six weeks later, on July 2, 1986, the Court ruled in two more affirmative action cases. In both the Court rebuffed the administration's argument against affirmative action. Only Chief Justice Burger and Justice Rehnquist accepted the administration's view.

Justice Brennan, the Court's most staunchly liberal member, spoke for the majority in both cases, holding that neither court-ordered minority quotas for union admission nor race-based job promotions violated the 1964 Civil Rights Act.

In *Local #28 of the Sheet Metal Workers' International v. Equal Employment Opportunity Commission,* the Court, 5-4, upheld an order requiring the union, which had persistently refused to admit blacks, to increase its nonwhite membership to 29.23 percent by August 1987.[190] In *Local #93, International Association of Firefighters v. City of Cleveland and Cleveland Vanguards,* the Court, 6-3, held that the Civil Rights Act did not prevent the city from resolving a bias complaint by agreeing to promote one black firefighter for every white promoted.[191]

In the the Cleveland case, O'Connor, who had dissented in the sheet metal workers case, criticizing racial quotas as impermissible, joined the majority, leaving Burger, Rehnquist, and White in dissent.

Paradise: Promotion Quota

For the third time in less than a year, the Supreme Court in February 1987 upheld a challenged affirmative action plan. Against a challenge that a one-black-for-one-white promotion quota denied white troopers the equal protection of the law, the Court, 5-4, in *United States v. Paradise,* upheld the plan imposed on Alabama's state troopers by a federal judge.[192]

Brennan spoke for the Court. "Strong measures were required in light of the . . . long and shameful record of delay and resistance," he wrote. The Alabama Department of Public Safety had hired no blacks before it was sued for discrimination in 1972. Eleven years later a federal judge found racial discrimination still pervasive and conspicuous in the department and therefore imposed the promotion quota. This quota "was amply justified and narrowly tailored to serve the legitimate and laudable purposes" of eradicating this history of discrimination, wrote Brennan.[193]

Powell, but not O'Connor, joined the majority in this case. Dissenting with O'Connor were Rehnquist, now the chief justice, White, and the Court's newest member, Antonin Scalia.

Johnson: A Boost for Women

Any remaining doubts about the Court's endorsement of the careful use of affirmative action were laid to rest in March 1987 with the Court's first decision concerning the use of affirmative action to benefit women.

The Court, 6-3—with the votes of O'Connor and Powell—upheld a voluntary affirmative action plan adopted by the Santa Clara County Transportation Department to move women into higher-ranking positions than they had held before. The plan resulted in the promotion of Diane Joyce to road dispatcher. Competing with Joyce for the job was Paul Johnson, who scored two points higher on a qualifying interview but, because of the affirmative action plan, lost out on the promotion.

It was appropriate, under the circumstances, to take Joyce's sex into account as a plus, wrote Justice Brennan in *Johnson v. Transportation Agency, Santa Clara County, Calif.* "The decision to do so was made pursuant to an affirmative action plan that represents a moderate, flexible, case-by-case approach to effecting a gradual improvement in the representation of minorities and women in the agency's work force.... Such a plan is fully consistent with Title VII [of the Civil Rights Act of 1964], for it embodies the contribution that voluntary employer action can make in eliminating the vestiges of discrimination in the workplace." [194]

Brennan looked back to the *Weber* ruling in writing this opinion, extending Weber's approval of voluntary affirmative action to include public as well as private employers. As in *Weber*, the plan in *Johnson* was permissible because it did not require white men to be fired and replaced by blacks or women nor impose an absolute bar to advancement by white males, and it was only a temporary remedy.

Dissenting were Rehnquist, White, and Scalia.

Notes

1. *Strauder v. West Virginia*, 100 U.S. 303 at 306-307 (1880).
2. John P. Frank, *Marble Palace: The Supreme Court in American Life* (New York: Alfred A. Knopf, 1961), 204. Other sources include John Hope Franklin, *From Slavery to Freedom: A History of Negro Americans*, 3d ed. (New York: Random House, Vintage Books, 1969); John A. Garraty, ed., *Quarrels That Have Shaped the Constitution* (New York: Harper & Row, 1964); United States Commission on Civil Rights, *Freedom to the Free: Century of Emancipation, 1863-1963* (Washington, D.C.: U.S. Government Printing Office, 1963); C. Vann Woodward, *The Strange Career of Jim Crow*, 2d rev. ed. (New York: Oxford University Press, 1966).
3. *Slaughterhouse Cases*, 16 Wall. 36 (1873).
4. *Civil Rights Cases*, 109 U.S. 3 (1883).
5. Carl B. Swisher, "Dred Scott One Hundred Years After," *Journal of Politics*, May 1957, 167-174, quoted in *Marble Palace*, 205.
6. Alan P. Westin, "The Case of the Prejudiced Doorkeeper," in *Quarrels That Have Shaped the Constitution*, 143.
7. *Plessy v. Ferguson*, 163 U.S. 537 (1896).
8. United States Commission on Civil Rights, *Freedom to the Free*, 71.
9. Franklin, *From Slavery to Freedom*, 480.
10. *United States v. Carolene Products Co.*, 304 U.S. 144 at 152-153, footnote 4 (1938).
11. *Brown v. Board of Education of Topeka*, 347 U.S. 483 (1954).
12. G. Theodore Mitau, *Decade of Decision: The Supreme Court and the Constitutional Revolution, 1954-1964* (New York: Charles Scribner's Sons, 1967), 62-63.
13. Franklin, *From Slavery to Freedom*, 644.
14. *Plessy v. Ferguson*, 163 U.S. 537 at 544 (1896).
15. *Roberts v. City of Boston*, 59 Mass. 198 at 206 (1849).
16. Id. at 209.
17. *Cumming v. Richmond County Board of Education*, 175 U.S. 528 at 545 (1899).
18. *Berea College v. Kentucky*, 211 U.S. 45 (1908).
19. *Gong Lum v. Rice*, 275 U.S. 78 at 86 (1927).
20. For general background, see Alfred H. Kelly and Winfred A. Harbison, *The American Constitution: Its Origins and Development*, 5th ed. (New York: W. W. Norton, 1976), 860; Richard Kluger, *Simple Justice* (New York: Alfred A. Knopf, 1976), 126-137.
21. *Missouri ex rel. Gaines v. Canada*, 305 U.S. 337 at 349 (1938).
22. Id. at 350.
23. *Sipuel v. Board of Regents of the University of Oklahoma*, 332 U.S. 631 at 633 (1948).
24. *Sweatt v. Painter*, 339 U.S. 629 at 633-634 (1950).
25. Id. at 636.
26. *McLaurin v. Oklahoma State Regents for Higher Education*, 339 U.S. 637 at 641 (1950).
27. *Brown v. Board of Education of Topeka, Briggs v. Elliott, Davis v. County School Board of Prince Edward County, Va., Gebhart v. Belton*, 347 U.S. 483 (1954).
28. *Bolling v. Sharpe*, 347 U.S. 497 (1954).
29. Loren Miller, *The Petitioners: The Story of the Supreme Court of the United States and the Negro* (New York: Random House, Pantheon Books, 1966), 345.
30. *Guinn v. United States*, 238 U.S. 347 (1915); see also Kluger, *Simple Justice*, 527.
31. Quoted in Leon Friedman, ed., *Argument: The Oral Argument Before the Supreme Court in Brown v. Board of Education of Topeka, 1952-55* (New York: Chelsea House Publishers, 1969), 215.
32. Ibid.
33. Ibid., 216.
34. Ibid, 239-240.
35. *Brown v. Board of Education of Topeka*, 347 U.S. 483 at 492 (1954).
36. Id. at 492-493.
37. Id. at 493.
38. Ibid.
39. Id. at 494.
40. Id. at 495.
41. *Bolling v. Sharp.*, 347 U.S. 497 at 499-500 (1954).
42. *Brown v. Board of Education of Topeka*, 349 U.S. 294 at 299-301 (1955).
43. Id. at 301.
44. U.S. Congress, Senate, "Declaration of Constitutional Principles," March 12, 1956, *Congressional Record*, 102:4460.
45. Woodward, *Strange Career of Jim Crow*, 154.
46. *Lucy v. Adams*, 350 U.S. 1 (1955).
47. *Florida. ex rel. Hawkins v. Board of Control*, 350 U.S. 413 (1956).
48. *Muir v. Louisville Park Theatrical Assn.*, 347 U.S. 971 (1954); see also: *Mayor and City Council of Baltimore v. Dawson*, 350 U.S. 877 (1955); *Holmes v. City of Atlanta*, 350 U.S. 879 (1955); *New Orleans City Park Improvement Assn. v. Detiege*, 358 U.S. 54 (1959); *Gayle v. Browder*, 352 U.S. 903 (1956); *Wright v. Georgia*, 373 U.S. 284 (1963).
49. *Cooper v. Aaron*, 358 U.S. 1 (1958).
50. Id. at 16.
51. Id. at 19-20.
52. *Faubus v. Aaron*, 361 U.S. 197 (1959).
53. *Shuttlesworth v. Birmingham Board of Education*, 162 F. Supp. 372, affirmed 358 U.S. 101 (1958).
54. *Holt v. Raleigh*, 265 F 2d 95, cert. denied, 361 U.S. 818 (1959); *Covington v. Edwards*, 264 F 2d 780, cert. denied, 361 U.S. 840 (1959).
55. *Bush v. Orleans Parish School Board*, 364 U.S. 500 (1960); *Orleans Parish School Board v. Bush*, 365 U.S. 569 (1961); *St Helena Parish School Board v. Hall*, 368 U.S. 515 (1962).
56. *Goss v. Board of Education of Knoxville*, 373 U.S. 683 (1963).
57. *McNeese v. Board of Education for Community School District 187, Cahokia, Ill.*, 373 U.S. 668 (1963).
58. *Griffin v. County School Board of Prince Edward County*, 377 U.S. 218 at 231 (1964).
59. Id. at 229.
60. *Bradley v. School Board, City of Richmond*, 382 U.S. 103 (1965).

61. *Rogers v. Paul*, 382 U.S. 198 (1965).
62. *Wallace v. United States, Bibb County Board of Education v. United States*, 386 U.S. 976 (1967).
63. *Green v. County School Board of New Kent County, Va.*, 391 U.S. 430 at 437-38 (1968).
64. Id. at 438-439.
65. Id. at 439.
66. Id. at 441, 442.
67. *Raney v. Board of Education of Gould School District*, 391 U.S. 443 (1968); *Monroe v. Board of Commissioners, City of Jackson*, 391 U.S. 450 (1968).
68. *Alexander v. Holmes Board of Education*, 396 U.S. 19 (1969); see also *Carter v. West Feliciana Parish School Board*, 396 U.S. 290 (1970); *Northcross v. Board of Education, City of Memphis*, 397 U.S. 232 (1970).
69. *Swann v. Charlotte-Mecklenburg County Board of Education*, 402 U.S. 1 at 25, 24 (1971).
70. Id. at 26.
71. Id. at 27.
72. Id. at 30-31.
73. Id. at 28.
74. Id. at 23.
75. Id. at 31-32.
76. *North Carolina State Board of Education v. Swann*, 402 U.S. 43 at 45-46 (1971).
77. *Dallas v. Board of School Commissioners of Mobile County Ala.*, 402 U.S. 33 (1971).
78. *McDonald v. Barresi*, 402 U.S. 39 (1971).
79. *Richmond School Board v. Virginia State Board of Education*, 412 U.S. 92 (1973).
80. Quoted by Chief Justice Warren E. Burger in *Milliken v. Bradley*, 418 U.S. 717 at 733 (1974).
81. Id. at 741.
82. Id. at 744-745.
83. Id. at 746.
84. Id. at 752.
85. Id. at 789.
86. *Milliken v. Bradley*, 433 U.S. 267 at 287-288 (1977).
87. *Edelman v. Jordan*, 415 U.S. 651 (1974).
88. *Milliken v. Bradley*, 433 U.S. 267 at 290 (1977).
89. *Dayton (Ohio) Board of Education v. Brinkman*, 433 U.S. 406 at 420 (1977); *Dayton Board of Education v. Brinkman* 443 U.S. 526 (1979).
90. *Pasadena City Board of Education v. Spangler*, 427 U.S. 424 at 437 (1976).
91. Id. at 443.
92. For general historical background in this area, see Commission on Civil Rights, *Freedom to the Free*, 60-71; Woodward, "The Case of the Louisiana Traveler," *Quarrels That Have Shaped the Constitution*, 145; Woodward, *Strange Career of Jim Crow*.
93. *Civil Rights Cases*, 109 U.S. 3 at 11 (1883).
94. Id. at 24.
95. Milton Konvitz and Theodore Leskes, *A Century of Civil Rights, with a Study of State Law Against Discrimination* (New York: Columbia University Press, 1961), 157. The states that passed antidiscrimination laws were: Connecticut, Iowa, New Jersey, and Ohio in 1884; Colorado, Illinois, Indiana, Michigan, Minnesota, Nebraska, and Rhode Island in 1885; Pennsylvania in 1887; Washington in 1890, Wisconsin in 1895, and California in 1897.
96. *Hall v. DeCuir*, 95 U.S. 485 at 489 (1878).
97. *Louisville, New Orleans and Texas Railway v. Mississippi*, 133 U.S. 587 (1890).
98. *Plessy v. Ferguson*, 163 U.S. 537 at 548 (1896).
99. Id. at 543.
100. Id. at 544.
101. Id. at 550-551.
102. Id. at 559.
103. Id. at 560-561.
104. *McCabe v. Atchison, Topeka and Santa Fe Railroad*, 235 U.S. 151 at 161-162 (1914).
105. *Mitchell v. United States*, 313 U.S. 80 (1941).
106. *Morgan v. Virginia*, 328 U.S. 373 at 380-381 (1946).
107. Id. at 386.
108. *Bob-Lo Excursion Co. v. Michigan*, 333 U.S. 28 (1948); *Henderson v. United States*, 339 U.S. 816 (1950); *District of Columbia v. Thompson Co.*, 346 U.S. 100 (1953).
109. *Brown v. Board of Education of Topeka*, 347 U.S. 483 (1954).
110. *Mayor and City Council of Baltimore v. Dawson*, 350 U.S. 877 (1955); *Holmes v. City of Atlanta*, 350 U.S. 879 (1955); *New Orleans City Park Improvement Assn. v. Detiege*, 358 U.S. 54 (1959); *Gayle v. Browder*, 352 U.S. 903 (1956); *Muir v. Louisville Park Theatrical Assn.*, 347 U.S. 971 (1954); *Wright v. Georgia*, 373 U.S. 284 (1963); *Schiro v. Bynum*, 375 U.S. 395 (1964); *State Athletic Commission v. Dorsey*, 359 U.S. 533 (1959); *Johnson v. Virginia*, 373 U.S. 61 (1963); *Lee v. Washington*, 390 U.S. 333 (1968).
111. *Watson v. City of Memphis*, 373 U.S. 526 at 533 (1963).
112. *Palmer v. Thompson*, 403 U.S. 217 (1971).
113. *Boynton v. Virginia*, 364 U.S. 454 at 460-461 (1960).
114. *Burton v. Wilmington Parking Authority*, 365 U.S. 715 at 722 (1961).
115. Id. at 725.
116. *Peterson v. City of Greenville*, 373 U.S. 244 at 248 (1963).
117. *Gober v. City of Birmingham*, 373 U.S. 374 (1963); *Avent v. North Carolina*, 373 U.S. 375 (1963).
118. *Shuttlesworth v. Birmingham*, 373 U.S. 262 at 265 (1963).
119. *Lombard v. Louisiana*, 373 U.S. 267 at 273 (1963).
120. *Heart of Atlanta Motel v. United States*, 379 U.S. 241 at 258 (1964).
121. Id. at 257.
122. Id. at 260.
123. Id. at 252.
124. *Katzenbach v. McClung*, 379 U.S. 294 (1964).
125. *Daniel v. Paul*, 395 U.S. 298 (1969).
126. *Civil Rights Cases*, 109 U.S. 3 at 22 (1883).
127. *Buchanan v. Warley*, 245 U.S. 60 at 80-82 (1917).
128. See, for example, *Harmon v. Tyler*, 273 U.S. 668 (1927); *City of Richmond v. Deans*, 281 U.S. 704 (1930).
129. *Corrigan v. Buckley*, 271 U.S. 323 at 330 (1926).
130. *Shelley v. Kraemer, McGhee v. Sipes*, 334 U.S. 1 (1948).
131. Id. at 13.
132. Id. at 19-20.
133. *Hurd v. Hodge, Urciola v. Hodge*, 334 U.S. 24 (1948).
134. *Barrows v. Jackson*, 346 U.S. 254 (1953).
135. *Reitman v. Mulkey*, 387 U.S. 369 at 377 (1967).
136. Id. at 393.
137. *Hunter v. Erickson*, 393 U.S. 385 at 393 (1969).
138. Id. at 396-397.
139. *James v. Valtierra*, 402 U.S. 137 at 141 (1971).
140. Id. at 145.
141. *Jones v. Alfred H. Mayer Co.*, 392 U.S. 409 at 436 (1968).
142. Id. at 438-443, passim.
143. *Sullivan v. Little Hunting Park, Inc.*, 396 U.S. 229 (1969).
144. *Tillman v. Wheaton-Haven Recreational Association*, 410 U.S. 431 at 437 (1973).
145. *Hills v. Gautreaux*, 425 U.S. 284 (1976).
146. *Milliken v. Bradley*, 418 U.S. 717 (1974).
147. *Hills v. Gautreaux* 425 U.S. 284 at 294 (1976).
148. Id. at 297.
149. Id. at 298-300.
150. Id. at 306.
151. *Village of Arlington Heights v. Metropolitan Housing Development Corporation*, 429 U.S. 252 (1977).
152. *Bailey v. Alabama*, 219 U.S. 219 (1911); *United States v. Reynolds*, 235 U.S. 133 (1914); see also *Taylor v. Georgia*, 315 U.S. 25 (1942); *Pollock v. Williams*, 322 U.S. 4 (1944).
153. For general historical accounts of job discrimination against blacks, see Miller, *The Petitioners;* Woodward, *Strange Career of Jim Crow.*
154. *New Negro Alliance v. Sanitary Grocery Co.*, 303 U.S. 552 at 561 (1938).
155. *Hughes v. Superior Court*, 339 U.S. 460 (1950).
156. *Steele v. Louisville and Nashville Railroad Company*, 323 U.S. 192 (1944); see also *Tunstall v. Brotherhood*, 323 U.S.

210 (1944); *Graham v. Brotherhood*, 338 U.S. 232 (1949); *Conley v. Gibson*, 355 U.S. 41 (1957).

157. *Brotherhood of Railroad Trainmen v. Howard*, 343 U.S. 768 at 774 (1951); see also *Syres v. Oil Workers International Union*, 350 U.S. 892 (1955).

158. *Railway Mail Association v. Corsi*, 326 U.S. 88 (1945).

159. *Colorado Anti-Discrimination Commission v. Continental Airlines*, 372 U.S. 714 (1963).

160. *Griggs v. Duke Power Co.*, 401 U.S. 424 at 430-431 (1971).

161. Id. at 432.

162. *Albemarle Paper Company v. Moody*, 422 U.S. 405 (1975).

163. *McDonnell Douglas Corporation v. Green*, 411 U.S. 807 (1973).

164. *Furnco Construction Corporation v. Waters*, 438 U.S. 567 at 579 (1978).

165. *Albemarle Paper Company v. Moody*, 422 U.S. 405 at 417-418 (1975).

166. Id. at 422.

167. *Fitzpatrick v. Bitzer*, 427 U.S. 445 (1976).

168. *Ford Motor Co. v. Equal Employment Opportunity Commission*, 458 U.S. 219 (1982).

169. *Franks v. Bowman Transportation Co., Inc.*, 424 U.S. 747 at 768 (1976).

170. Id. at 788-789.

171. *Teamsters v. United States, T.I.M. E.-D.C. v. United States*, 431 U.S. 324 (1977).

172. Id. at 354.

173. *Guardians Association v. Civil Service Commission of City of New York*, 463 U.S. 482 (1983).

174. *DeFunis v. Odegaard*, 416 U.S. 312 (1974).

175. *University of California Regents v. Bakke*, 438 U.S. 265 at 412, 418 (1978).

176. Id. at 320, 307.

177. Id. at 325.

178. *United Steelworkers of America v. Weber, Kaiser Aluminum & Chemical Corp. v. Weber, United States v. Weber*, 443 U.S. 193 (1979).

179. Id. at 204.

180. Id. at 206, footnote 6.

181. Id. at 216.

182. Id. at 222.

183. *Fullilove v. Klutznick*, 448 U.S. 448 at 473 (1980).

184. Id. at 490.

185. *Firefighters Local #1784 v. Stotts*, 467 U.S. 561 (1984).

186. *Wygant v. Jackson Board of Education*, 476 U.S. 267 (1986).

187. Id. at 282.

188. Id. at 280-281.

189. Id. at 286.

190. *Local #28 of the Sheet Metal Workers' International v. Equal Employment Opportunity Commission*, 478 U.S. 421 (1986).

191. *Local #93, International Association of Firefighters v. City of Cleveland and Cleveland Vanguards*, 478 U.S. 501 (1986).

192. *United States v. Paradise*, __ U.S. __ (1987).

193. Ibid.

194. *Johnson v. Transportation Agency of Santa Clara County*, __ U.S. __ (1987).

14

Aliens and Equal Protection

Congress has exclusive authority to determine who may enter the country, but once an alien is admitted to the United States, he or she is entitled to the equal protection of its laws. In 1886 the Court declared that the Fourteenth Amendment protected persons, not just citizens. The Supreme Court in *Yick Wo v. Hopkins* wrote that the Civil War amendment applied "to all *persons* within the territorial jurisdiction, without regard to any differences of race, of color, or of nationality; and the equal protection of the laws is a pledge of the protection of equal laws." [1]

It was eighty-five years before the Supreme Court in 1971 declared alienage, like race, a "suspect" category justifiable only by a compelling government interest. But beginning with *Yick Wo*, the Court, with one period of exception, required states to show more than a merely rational basis for a legal distinction between aliens and citizens. As a result, aliens initially fared better under the Court's application of the Fourteenth Amendment's equal protection clause than did the blacks who were expected by the authors of the clause to be its prime beneficiaries.

ALIENS AND PUBLIC PREJUDICE

Yick Wo involved a San Francisco ordinance, which, in order to minimize fire hazards, required operators of wooden laundries to obtain a license from the city. Although his laundry had been declared safe by city fire and health officials, Yick Wo was denied a renewal of his license. When he discovered that most Chinese owners of wooden laundries had been denied permits, while most white laundry owners were granted them, he sued, charging that he had been denied equal protection of the laws.

Sustaining the charge, a unanimous Supreme Court wrote:

Though the law itself be fair on its face and impartial in appearance, yet, if it is applied and administered by public authority with an evil eye and an unequal hand, so as practically to make unjust and illegal discriminations between persons in similar circumstances, material to their rights, the denial of equal justice is still within the prohibition of the Constitution. [2]

Because the city offered no explanation for its discrimination, "the conclusion cannot be resisted, that no reason for it exists except hostility to the race and nationality to which the petitioners belong, and which in the eye of the law is not justified," the Court wrote. [3]

Yick Wo's case involved his right to earn a living, a right the Court said was "essential to the enjoyment of life." The Court amplified this holding in the 1915 case of *Truax v. Raich*. Arizona law required that 80 percent of the workers in establishments with more than five employees be U.S. citizens. When a restaurant owner fired Mike Raich, an Austrian native, in order to comply with the statute, Raich charged that he had been denied equal protection. Agreeing, the Supreme Court declared the state law unconstitutional. Justice Charles Evans Hughes wrote the opinion:

It requires no argument to show that the right to work for a living in the common occupations of the community is of the very essence of the personal freedom and opportunity that it was the purpose of the [Fourteenth] Amendment to secure.... If this could be refused solely upon the ground of race or nationality, the prohibition of the denial to any person of the equal protection of the laws would be a barren form of words." [4]

Within twelve years *Raich* itself would prove rather barren. In 1915 the country was already growing suspicious of and antagonistic toward immigrants from certain countries. The prejudice, which would peak in the 1920s, is described by historians Alfred H. Kelly and Winfred A. Harbison:

The average middle class "old American" of the twenties believed firmly that both the Communist and anarchist menaces and the contemporary alarming increase in urban crime were due to the presence of undesirable aliens in the country. Much contemporary xenophobic sentiment also was laden with religious and racial prejudice. Conservative Protestants feared and resented the recent heavy influx of Catholic immigrants from Italy and Poland, while the swarthy newcomers from southern and eastern Europe as well as those from Japan and Asia were looked upon as "unassimilable" and a threat to American racial purity." [5]

In response, Congress passed laws requiring deportation for aliens convicted of crimes and subversive activity. Congress also established immigration quotas based on national origin; the quotas heavily favored the immigrants of northwest Europe. In 1924 Congress passed a second law that effectively barred most immigration from Asia.

ALIENS AND STATE GOVERNMENT

The Supreme Court was not immune to this public sentiment. Beginning in 1914, it condoned state laws excluding aliens from certain activities and jobs cloaked with a special public interest. In 1877 the Court had ruled in *McCready v. Virginia* that Virginia could prohibit residents of other states from planting oysters in its tidal streams. The right to use such streams was a property right, and the privilege and immunity clause did not invest "the citizens of one state ... with any interest in the common property of the citizens of another state." [6]

The Court extended this special public interest rule to aliens in 1914 when it upheld a Pennsylvania statute forbidding aliens to shoot wild game and, to that end, to possess shotguns and rifles. Wild game, like a tidal stream, was a natural resource that a state may preserve for its own citizens "if it pleases," the Court said in *Patsone v. Pennsylvania*. To that purpose, the state may make classifications, and if the class "discriminated against is or reasonably might be considered to define those from whom the evil mainly is to be feared," the classification is permissible, wrote Justice Oliver Wendell Holmes, Jr. [7] No evidence was presented to support a contention that aliens shot more game than any other class, but the majority would not say the state was wrong in identifying aliens "as the peculiar source of the evil that it desired to prevent." [8]

In 1915 the Court used the special public interest test to uphold the right of a state to confine hiring on state public works projects to U.S. citizens. [9]

In the early 1920s several western states seeking to discourage Japanese immigration passed laws barring aliens ineligible for citizenship from owning or leasing agricultural lands. The Court in 1922 interpreted the federal laws restricting citizenship as allowing only whites and blacks of African descent to become citizens. [10] As a result, the alien land laws applied primarily to Japanese aliens.

In 1923 the Court upheld these laws. Because the federal government recognized two classes of aliens—those who were eligible for citizenship and those who were not, the states were not required to justify similar state laws. "The rule established by Congress on this subject, in and of itself, furnishes a reasonable basis for classification in a state law," the Court said in *Terrace v. Thompson*. [11]

In 1927 the Court appeared to abandon its 1915 decision that states may not deny aliens opportunities to hold "the common occupations of the community" solely because they were aliens. At the same time the Court adopted a more relaxed standard of review for state classifications based on alienage.

Clarke v. Deckebach (1927) concerned a Cincinnati ordinance that barred aliens from operating pool and billiards halls. The city justified this classification by arguing that pool halls were evil places frequented by lawbreakers and were the scenes of many crimes. Because aliens were less familiar with the laws and customs of the country, their operation of these pool halls constituted a menace to the public, the city claimed.

Upholding the ordinance, the unanimous Court said that while the Fourteenth Amendment prohibits "plainly irrational discrimination against aliens ... it does not follow that alien race and allegiance may not bear in some instances such a relation to a legitimate object of legislation as to be made the basis of a permissible classification." [12]

Enunciating its new standard of scrutiny, the Court wrote:

> It is enough for present purposes that the ordinance, in the light of facts admitted or generally assumed, does not preclude the possibility of a rational basis for the legislative judgment and that we have no such knowledge of local conditions as would enable us to say that it is clearly wrong.
>
> It was competent for the city to make such a choice, not shown to be irrational, by excluding from the conduct of a dubious business an entire class rather than its objectionable members selected by more empirical means. [13]

The Fourteenth Amendment no longer protected aliens seeking to work at ordinary jobs. The Court now allowed a city or state to deny rights to all aliens on the presumption that some aliens would act in an unacceptable manner. It was left to the alien class to prove the presumption irrational. Fortunately for aliens, this standard was relatively shortlived.

A CLOSER SCRUTINY

The Court first indicated a changed attitude toward questions of alienage and national origin in two World War II cases that concerned U.S. citizens of Oriental descent. Both involved Japanese-Americans who had failed to comply with military orders first restricting the movements of Japanese-Americans living on the West Coast and then confining them to detention camps for eventual relocation away from the coast. In both the Court held that such extreme discrimination against these citizens was justified by the necessities of war and the need to protect the country from the possibility that some disloyal Japanese-Americans might collaborate with the Japanese enemy. But in both cases the Court said distinctions based on race and ancestry merited close scrutiny and could be justified only by such "pressing public necessity" as the war. [14]

In 1948 the Court effectively reversed its position on alien land laws. *Oyama v. California* involved a Japanese alien who had purchased some agricultural property as a gift to his minor son, a U.S. citizen by birth. Oyama was then appointed his son's guardian, which allowed him to work the land for the benefit of his son. The state charged Oyama with attempting to evade the alien land law, and Oyama in turn charged that both he and his son were denied equal protection of the laws by that law.

The Supreme Court ruled, 6-3, that the state law did deprive the citizen son of equal protection:

> There remains the question of whether discrimination between citizens on the basis of their racial descent, as revealed in this case, is justifiable. Here we start with the proposition that only the most exceptional circumstances can excuse discrimination on that basis in the face of the equal protection clause and a federal statute giving all citizens the right to own land.... The only justification urged upon us by the State is that the discrimination is necessary to prevent evasion of the Alien Land Law.... In the light most favorable to the State, this case presents a conflict between the State's right to formulate a policy of landholding within its bounds and the right of American citizens to own land anywhere in the United States. When these two rights clash, the rights of a citizen may not be subordinated merely because of his father's country of origin.[15]

The majority did not decide whether the alien father had been denied equal protection of the laws. But the decision stripped the law of much of its effectiveness.

Six months later, the Court, 7-2, rejected its reasoning in *Deckebach* and returned to its earlier position that the right to earn a living was a liberty that could not be denied an alien solely on the basis of race or national origin.

Takahashi v. Fish and Game Commission (1948) involved a 1943 California law that prohibited alien Japanese from fishing in the state's coastal waters. In 1945 the state amended the law to extend the ban to all aliens ineligible for citizenship, but a 1946 federal law making Filipinos and persons of races indigenous to India eligible for citizenship effectively restricted the disability imposed by the state law to Japanese aliens. Takahashi, a fisherman denied a license, charged that he had been denied equal protection of the law.

Sustaining the charge, the Supreme Court reversed its previous position that a state could make the same alienage classifications as the federal government. "It does not follow," wrote Justice Hugo L. Black for the majority, "that because the United States regulates immigration and naturalization in part on the basis of race and color classifications, a state can adopt one or more of the same classifications."[16]

The Constitution gave Congress complete authority over admission and naturalization of aliens. "State laws which impose discriminatory burdens upon the entrance or residence of aliens lawfully within the United States conflict with this constitutionally derived federal power to regulate immigration," he wrote.[17]

Furthermore, the majority rejected California's claim that the fish in its offshore waters were a natural resource that the state could reserve for its own citizens under the special public interest rule:

> To whatever extent the fish in the three-mile belt off

California may be "capable of ownership" by California, we think that the "ownership" is inadequate to justify California in excluding any or all aliens who are lawful residents of the State from making a living by fishing in the ocean off its shores while permitting all others to do so.[18]

THE MODERN STANDARD

Questions of discrimination against aliens did not come before the Court again until the 1970s. In its first important aliens case of this period, *Graham v. Richardson* (1971), a unanimous Court asserted that

> classifications based on alienage, like those based on nationality or race, are inherently suspect and subject to close judicial scrutiny. Aliens as a class are a prime example of a "discrete and insular" minority ... for whom such heightened judicial solicitude is appropriate.[19]

Graham concerned an Arizona statute that restricted certain welfare benefits to citizens and aliens who had resided in the United States for at least fifteen years. A second case, consolidated with *Graham,* tested a Pennsylvania statute that denied certain welfare benefits to all aliens. By its declaration that classification by alienage was inherently suspect, the Court required states to show a compelling governmental interest to justify making that distinction.

The claim that the special public interest rule allowed a state to "preserve limited welfare benefits for its own citizens is inadequate" to justify the classification, the Court said.[20]

Aliens as well as residents pay state and federal taxes. "There can be no 'special public interest' in tax revenues to which aliens have contributed on an equal basis with the residents of the State," the Court said.[21]

Over the next few years, the Court applied "close judicial scrutiny" and found no compelling interest in several state laws denying aliens certain benefits or the opportunity to work in certain professions. The Court struck down a Connecticut law that barred aliens from being licensed as lawyers, a Puerto Rico law that barred them from becoming engineers, a New York law that excluded aliens from the state's competitive civil service, and a Texas law barring resident aliens from the job of notary public. It also struck down a New York law that excluded resident aliens who did not intend to become citizens from eligibility for state financial aid for higher education.[22]

In *Sugarman v. Dougall,* the case concerning its competitive civil service, New York contended it should be allowed to exclude aliens from governmental policy-making positions because aliens might not be "free of competing obligations to another power."[23] The Court observed that not all members of the competitive civil service held policy-formulating positions. At the same time, the state allowed aliens to serve in other branches of the state civil service in both policy-making and nonpolicy-making jobs. Applying strict scrutiny, the Court held that the statute must fall because it "is neither narrowly confined nor precise in its application." [24]

But in *dicta* at the end of that unanimous opinion, the Court said states might require a person to be a citizen in order to exercise certain rights, such as voting, or to hold certain positions essential to the maintenance of representative government. Among these positions were "state elective or important nonelective executive, legislative, and judicial positions, for officers who participate directly in the formulation, execution, or review of broad public policy perform functions that go to the heart of representative government." [25] The Court further stated that its scrutiny would "not be so demanding where we deal with matters resting firmly within the State's constitutional prerogatives." [26]

In 1978 this statement provided the basis for a decision in which the Supreme Court, 6-3, upheld a New York statute requiring all its state police to be U.S. citizens. Writing for the majority, Chief Justice Warren E. Burger found police among the category of those who participated in making or carrying out governmental policy and whom, therefore, the state could require to be citizens. Burger explained: "The essence of our holdings to date is that although we extend to aliens the right to education and public welfare, along with the ability to earn a livelihood and engage in licensed professions, the right to govern is reserved to citizens." [27]

And because the right to govern fell within the state's constitutional prerogatives, the state needed only to prove that it had a rational basis for excluding aliens from police positions. Because police generally exercise a wide variety of discretionary powers that have a significant impact on citizens, the majority felt it was rational for the state to restrict such jobs to citizens. "Clearly the exercise of police authority calls for a very high degree of judgment and discretion, the abuse or misuse of which can have serious impact on individuals," Burger said. "In short, it would be as anomalous to conclude that citizens may be subjected to the broad discretionary powers of noncitizen police officers as it would be to say that judicial officers and jurors with power to judge citizens may be aliens." [28]

In 1979 the Court, 5-4, sustained a New York law prohibiting aliens who refuse to apply for U.S. citizenship the opportunity to work as public school teachers. Because teachers played a critical role in developing the attitudes of their students toward government, society, and the political process, they fell into the category of occupations "so bound up with the operation of the State as a governmental entity" as to permit the restriction of those jobs to citizens, the majority wrote. [29]

Subsequently, the Court, 5-4, upheld a California requirement that all peace officers be U.S. citizens. These officers, explained Justice Byron R. White in *Cabell v. Chavez-Salido*, exercise and symbolize the power of the political community and it is reasonable to require that they be citizens. [30]

But the Court did not see the education of public school age children the same way. Texas, home to a large number of illegal aliens who had crossed the border from Mexico, sought to curtail the costs those residents imposed on the state budget, by refusing to educate illegal alien children in the public schools. This policy was challenged, and in 1982 the Supreme Court, 5-4, rejected the state's choice.

Illegal aliens present in the United States are accorded the full protection of the equal protection clause, wrote Justice William J. Brennan, Jr., for the majority. Regardless of their illegal status, they are clearly persons and may not be denied the right to a free public education. There is no national policy nor state interest sufficient to justify denying them this right, held the Court. [31]

ALIENS AND THE FEDERAL GOVERNMENT

No matter what standard the Court finally settles on to determine whether the states have deprived aliens of equal protection of the laws, it appears unlikely that it will change its standard of review for judging federal laws that treat aliens and citizens differently.

Because the Constitution gives Congress absolute authority over admission and naturalization, the Supreme Court requires Congress only to present some rational basis for making a distinction between citizen and alien or between some aliens and other aliens.

In 1976 a unanimous Court in *Mathews v. Diaz* upheld a Medicare regulation denying aliens who were not permanent residents of the country for at least five years eligibility for supplementary medical benefits. The Court wrote:

> [T]he fact that Congress has provided some welfare benefits for citizens does not require it to provide like benefits for *all* aliens. Neither the overnight visitor, the unfriendly agent of a hostile foreign power, the resident diplomat, nor the illegal entrant, can advance even a colorable constitutional claim to a share in the bounty that a conscientious sovereign makes available to its own citizens and *some of* its guests. The decision to share that bounty with our guests may take into account the character of the relationship between the alien and this country: Congress may decide that as the alien's tie grows stronger, so does the strength of his claim to an equal share of the munificence....
>
> ... In short, it is unquestionably reasonable for Congress to make an alien's eligibility depend on both the character and the duration of his residence. Since neither requirement is wholly irrational, this case essentially involves nothing more than a claim that it would have been more reasonable for Congress to select somewhat different requirements of the same kind. [32]

And because the benefit issue raised was a question of degree rather than kind, the Court said it was "especially reluctant to question the exercise of congressional judgment." [33]

In a second case decided the same day, the Court, 5-4, ruled that the Civil Service Commission violated the Fifth Amendment due process guarantee by excluding all aliens from the federal competitive civil service and therefore denying them the opportunity for employment in a major sector of the economy. The denial affected an aspect of liberty protected by the Fifth Amendment, the majority said in *Hampton v. Mow Sun Wong*.

> Since these resident ... [aliens] were admitted as a result of decisions made by the Congress and the Pres-

ident ... due process requires that the decision to impose that deprivation of an important liberty be made either at a comparable level of government or, if it is permitted to be made by the Civil Service Commission, that it be justified by reasons which are properly the concern of that agency.[34]

The only reason offered that properly concerned the agency was administrative efficiency, the majority continued. And while it was reasonable for the agency to make a single rule applicable to all aliens, such an arbitrary rule did not outweigh "the public interest in avoiding the wholesale deprivation of employment opportunities caused" by the rule, which therefore must fall.[35]

Three months later, on September 2, 1976, President Gerald R. Ford issued an executive order authorizing the Civil Service Commission to continue to exclude noncitizens from the federal competitive civil service.

Notes

1. *Yick Wo v. Hopkins,* 118 U.S. 356 at 369 (1886).
2. Id. at 373-374.
3. Id. at 374.
4. *Truax v. Raich,* 239 U.S. 33 at 41 (1915).
5. Alfred H. Kelly and Winfred A. Harbison, *The American Constitution; Its Origins and Development,* 5th ed. (New York: W. W. Norton, 1976), 666.
6. *McCready v. Virginia,* 94 U.S. 391 at 395 (1877).
7. *Patsone v. Pennsylvania,* 232 U.S. 138 at 144 (1914).
8. Ibid.
9. *Heim v. McCall,* 239 U.S. 175 (1915); *Crane v. New York,* 239 U.S. 195 (1915).
10. *Ozawa v. United States,* 260 U.S. 178 (1922).
11. *Terrace v. Thompson,* 263 U.S. 197 at 220 (1923); see also *Porterfield v. Webb,* 263 U.S. 225 (1923); *Webb v. O'Brien,* 263 U.S. 313 (1923); *Frick v. Webb,* 263 U.S. 326 (1923); *Cockrill v. California* 268 U.S. 258 (1925).
12. *Clarke v. Deckebach,* 274 U.S. 392 at 396 (1927).
13. Id. at 397.
14. *Hirabayashi v. United States,* 320 U.S. 81 (1943); *Korematsu v. United States,* 323 U.S. 214 (1944).
15. *Oyama v. California,* 332 U.S. 633 at 646 (1948).
16. *Takahashi v. Fish and Game Commission,* 334 U.S. 410 at 418 (1948).
17. Id. at 419.
18. Id. at 421.
19. *Graham v. Richardson,* 403 U.S. 365 at 372.
20. Id. at 374.
21. Id. at 376.
22. *In re Griffiths,* 413 U.S. 717 (1973); *Examining Board of Engineers, Architects and Surveyors v. de Otero,* 426 U.S. 572 (1976); *Sugarman v. Dougall,* 413 U.S. 634 (1973); *Nyquist v. Mauclet,* 432 U.S. 1 (1977); *Bernal v. Fainter,* 467 U.S. 216 (1984).
23. *Sugarman v. Dougall,* 413 U.S. 634 at 641.
24. Id. at 643.
25. Id. at 647.
26. Id. at 648.
27. *Foley v. Connelie,* 435 U.S. 291 at 297 (1978).
28. Id. at 298-299.
29. *Ambach v. Norwick,* 441 U.S. 68 (1979).
30. *Cabell v. Chavez-Salido,* 454 U.S. 432 (1982).
31. *Plyler v. Doe, Texas v. Certain Named and Unnamed Undocumented Alien Children,* 457 U.S. 202 (1982).
32. *Mathews v. Diaz,* 426 U.S. 67 at 80-83, passim (1976).
33. Id. at 84.
34. *Hampton v. Mow Sun Wong,* 426 U.S. 88 at 1.
35. Id. at 115.

15

Sex Discrimination

It took the Supreme Court almost a century to extend the guarantee of equal protection to blacks, but it took even longer for it to extend the same guarantee to women.

Not until the 1970s did the Court begin to apply the equal protection guarantee to gender-based discrimination. But nearly twenty years later, this form of discrimination was still measured against a more relaxed standard than racial discrimination. The Court in that period had taken important steps toward placing men and women on an equal footing before the law, but at the same time it still upheld some laws—most notably that excluding women from the military draft—based on traditional beliefs about the respective roles of men and women.

'ROMANTIC' PATERNALISM

The Supreme Court's attitude toward women and their role in the political and economic life of the nation reflects prevailing societal attitudes. Early on, the Court adopted a protectionist philosophy, described as "romantic paternalism," to justify discrimination against women.

Relying on the view of woman as wife, mother, and homemaker, the Court in 1873 upheld a state's refusal to let a woman practice law. In *Bradwell v. Illinois* a Chicago woman appealed to the Supreme Court to overturn the state's refusal to license her to practice law.

In the Court's opinion, Justice Samuel F. Miller did not discuss the gender issue but simply held that the Fourteenth Amendment did not affect state authority to regulate admission of members to its bar. But in a concurring opinion, Justice Joseph P. Bradley gave judicial cognizance to the then-common belief that women were unfit by nature to hold certain occupations:

[T]he civil law, as well as nature herself, has always recognized a wide difference in the respective spheres and destinies of man and woman. Man is, or should be,

woman's protector and defender. The natural and proper timidity and delicacy which belongs to the female sex evidently unfits it for many of the occupations of civil life. The constitution of the family organization, which is founded in divine ordinance, as well as in the nature of things, indicates the domestic sphere as that which properly belongs to the domain and functions of womanhood.[1]

If the Fourteenth Amendment did not compel the states to admit women to the bar, neither did it compel them to allow women to vote or to serve on juries. In *Minor v. Happersett* (1875) the Court held that, although women were citizens, the right to vote was not a privilege or immunity of national citizenship before adoption of the Fourteenth Amendment, nor did the amendment add suffrage to the privileges and immunities of national citizenship. Therefore, the national government could not require states to permit women to vote.[2] In this respect, women fared worse than blacks, whose right to vote was specifically protected by the Fifteenth Amendment. Not until ratification in 1920 of the Nineteenth Amendment were women assured of the right to vote. *(Details of voting discrimination cases, p. 107)*

The Court in 1880 ruled that the Fourteenth Amendment did not prohibit the states from excluding women from jury duty. This position, reaffirmed as recently as 1961, was overturned by the Court's 1975 decision in *Taylor v. Louisiana*.[3] *(Details, box, p. 279)*

"Romantic paternalism" again came into play when the Court upheld laws intended to protect women's morals. In 1904 it affirmed the validity of a Denver ordinance prohibiting the sale of liquor to women and barring women from working in bars or stores where liquor was sold.[4] Four decades later—in the 1948 case of *Goesaert v. Cleary,* the Court sustained a Michigan law that forbade a woman to serve as a bartender unless she was the wife or daughter of the bar's owner. The majority thought it was reasonable for Michigan to believe "that the oversight assured through ownership of a bar by a barmaid's husband or father minimizes hardships that may confront a barmaid without such protecting oversight."[5]

But three justices disagreed, contending that the statute made an unjustifiable and therefore unconstitutional distinction between male and female bar owners. "A male bar owner, although he himself is always absent from his bar, may employ his wife and daughter as barmaids," they wrote, while a "female [bar] owner may neither work as a barmaid herself nor employ her daughter in that position." [6] The real purpose of the statute, implied the dissenters, was not to protect women's morals but men's jobs.

Paternalism was also evident in the Court's response to other cases involving working women. In the early 1900s the Court upheld state laws setting maximum hours and minimum wages for women while holding similar regulations for men a violation of the right to contract their labor. The typical justification of this distinction was provided by the Court's 1908 decision in *Muller v. Oregon,* backing a state law that set maximum hours for women laundry workers. The unanimous Court wrote:

> The two sexes differ in structure of body, in the functions to be performed by each, in the amount of physical strength, in the capacity for long-continued labor, particularly when done standing, the influence of vigorous health upon the future well-being of the race, the self-reliance which enables one to assert full rights, and in the capacity to maintain the struggle for subsistence. This difference justifies a difference in legislation and upholds that which is designed to compensate for some of the burdens which rest upon [women]. [7]

The civil rights movement of the 1950s and 1960s aroused a new national sensitivity to all forms of discrimination, including that based on sex. Even a cursory examination showed that the traditional protectionist view of women as wives and mothers had contributed substantially to the discrimination they suffered in a modern era where more and more women worked to support themselves and their families.

Because women had been expected to remain at home, they were generally less well educated than men. As a result, women seeking jobs outside the home usually qualified only for low-paying, low-skill jobs where opportunities for advancement were limited. Frequently women were paid less than men who performed the same job, often on the theory that women's earnings were less vital to the support of their families than men's. Certain legal rights and benefits accrued to women only through their presumed dependency on their husbands and not to them as individuals. As a lower court wrote in 1971: "The pedestal upon which women have been placed has, ... upon closer inspection, been revealed as a cage." [8]

Congress began to act to remedy some of the more obvious inequities in 1963 when it adopted the Equal Pay Act. Title VII of the 1964 Civil Rights Act prohibited employment discrimination on the basis of sex. In 1972 Congress barred gender-based discrimination in all education programs that received federal support. It also sent to the states for ratification the proposed Equal Rights Amendment, which would guarantee women and men equal rights under the law. In 1973 it approved a bill prohibiting lenders from denying credit on the basis of sex or marital status.

Challenges to sex discrimination began to reach the Court in the 1970s. While the Court consistently held that classifications based on sex were subject to judicial examination as possible violations of the equal protection guarantee, it was unable to agree on the standard to use in deciding whether such classifications were justified and constitutional.

THE SEARCH FOR A STANDARD

Rationality was the standard applied in the first case, *Reed v. Reed,* decided in 1971. The case arose after a minor child in Idaho died intestate (without a will). His adoptive parents, Sally and Cecil Reed, were separated; both filed competing petitions to serve as administrator of the child's estate. The Court awarded the appointment to the father because the Idaho statute designating those eligible to administer intestate estates gave preference to males. Sally Reed challenged the statute as a violation of the equal protection clause of the Fourteenth Amendment.

For the first time the Supreme Court held a state law invalid because it discriminated against women. In an opinion written by Chief Justice Warren E. Burger, a unanimous Supreme Court struck down the Idaho statute. Quoting from a 1920 decision, Burger said that to be constitutionally permissible, a gender-based classification "must be reasonable, not arbitrary, and must rest upon some ground of difference having a fair and substantial relation to the object of the legislation so that all persons similarly circumstanced shall be treated alike." [9]

Applying that standard to the Idaho statute, the Court could find no rational basis for giving men preference over women. The statute's purpose was to reduce the work of probate courts by eliminating one source of controversy in probate cases, the Court said. But "[t]o give a mandatory preference to members of either sex over members of the other, merely to accomplish the elimination of hearings on the merits, is to make the very kind of arbitrary legislative choice forbidden by the Equal Protection Clause," the Court concluded. [10]

Using the rationality standard, the Court in several cases upheld gender-based classifications, sustaining:

● A Florida property tax exemption for widows but not for widowers. The majority found the exemption "reasonably designed to further the state policy of cushioning the financial impact of spousal loss upon the sex for whom that loss imposes a disproportionately heavy burden." (*Kahn v. Shevin,* 1974) [11]

● A federal law that allows certain female naval officers to serve longer than male officers before mandatory discharge upon failure to win promotion. Observing that female officers could not compete with male officers to win promotion through combat or sea duty, the majority thought it reasonable for Congress to give them a longer period in which to earn advancement. (*Schlesinger v. Ballard,* 1975) [12]

● A Social Security regulation that denies survivors' benefits to widows married less than three months before their husband's death. The majority said such denials were a rational means of preventing sham marriages solely for the purpose of obtaining Social Security benefits. (*Weinberger v. Salfi,* 1975) [13]

● A Social Security regulation providing benefits to married women under age 62 with a minor dependent whose husbands were retired or disabled but not to divorced women in the same circumstances. (*Mathews v. deCastro,* 1976) [14]

In 1975 the Court used the rationality standard to

strike down a Utah law that required divorced fathers to support their sons to age twenty-one but their daughters only to age eighteen. The Court in *Stanton v. Stanton* rejected arguments that boys needed the longer period of parental support to obtain education and training, and that girls needed a shorter period of support because they tended to mature and marry earlier than males.

Present realities make education for girls as important as for boys, the majority said. "And if any weight remains in this day in the claim of earlier maturity of the female, with a concomitant inference of absence of need for support beyond 18, we fail to perceive its unquestioned truth or its significance," the Court added.[15]

Stricter Standard Advocated

As early as 1973, four members of the Court argued for adoption of a stricter standard for gender-based laws. *Frontiero v. Richardson* involved a female air force officer who sought increased benefits for her husband as a dependent. Her request was denied because the law stipulated that while wives of members of the uniformed services were assumed to be dependents eligible for additional benefits, husbands were not and must prove actual dependence in order to be eligible.

Because a federal law was involved, the officer could not challenge it under the Fourteenth Amendment's guarantee of equal protection of the laws against state action. Instead she challenged the law as a violation of the due process clause of the Fifth Amendment, which applies to federal action. Although the Fifth Amendment does not specifically guarantee equal protection, the Court has long held that some discriminations are so unjustifiable as to be violations of the amendment's promise of due process. *(Box, p. 224)*

The Supreme Court struck the law down 8-1. In a plurality opinion announcing the decision, Justice William J. Brennan, Jr., contended that gender-based classifications, like distinctions based on race and alienage, were inherently suspect. Brennan observed that a person's sex was a noncontrollable and immutable characteristic, and added:

> what differentiates sex from such nonsuspect statuses as intelligence or physical disability, and aligns it with the recognized suspect criteria, is that the sex characteristic frequently bears no relation to ability to perform or contribute to society. As a result, statutory distinctions between the sexes often have the effect of invidiously relegating the entire class of females to inferior legal status without regard to the actual capabilities of its individual members.[16]

Such inherently suspect classifications may be justified only by a compelling governmental interest, argued Brennan. But, he said, the government's only purpose for the gender-based distinction in this case appeared to be administrative convenience, and even under the less exacting standard of rationality, gender-based classifications made solely to suit administrative convenience were constitutionally impermissible.

Only three other justices agreed with Brennan's reasoning, and so his view that gender-based classifications were inherently suspect remained simply an opinion without the force of law.

Rights of Unwed Fathers

The fathers of illegitimate children have only recently been brought under the scope of the equal protection clause. In many states the law presumes that fathers have no fundamental interest in their illegitimate offspring.

In *Stanley v. Illinois* an unwed father of children whose mother had died challenged a state statute that made his children wards of the state without giving him an opportunity to prove his fitness as a parent. The law provided a fitness hearing in such circumstances for legitimate parents and unwed mothers.

The Court in 1972 ruled that due process entitled him to a hearing and that denial of the hearing would violate equal protection. Administrative convenience was insufficient reason to justify denying unwed fathers such hearings.[1]

The Court also has held that states need not grant unwed fathers a veto over the adoption of their children—unless they had been legitimated—nor need they notify unwed fathers of a child's adoption unless the father had established some legal relationship to his child.[2]

In 1979, however, the Court struck down a state law that gave the natural mother, but not the natural father, the right to veto an adoption.[3]

Questions concerning the relationship of a father to his illegitimate child recur. The Court has held that once a state grants children the right to support from their fathers, equal protection denies the state the power to make the exercise of that right any more difficult for illegitimate than for legitimate children.[4]

And the justices struck down a Tennessee law that required all paternity and support actions on behalf of illegitimate children to be filed by the time the child is two years old. No similar time limit was imposed on such actions by legitimate children.[5]

1. *Stanley v. Illinois*, 405 U.S. 645 (1972).
2. *Quilloin v. Walcott*, 434 U.S. 246 (1978), *Lehr v. Robertson*, 463 U.S. 248 (1983).
3. *Caban v. Mohammed*, 441 U.S. 380 (1979).
4. *Mills v. Habluetzel*, 456 U.S. 91 (1982).
5. *Pickett v. Brown*, 462 U.S. 1 (1983).

Justice Lewis F. Powell, Jr., joined by Chief Justice Burger and Justice Harry A. Blackmun, said he agreed that the classification under consideration violated the due process clause. He objected, however, to placing sex-based classifications among those considered inherently suspect and justifiable only by a compelling government interest. He maintained that application of the rationality standard to this case would have resulted in the same outcome.

Justice Potter Stewart concurred in the result without subscribing to either opinion.

Arbitrary Presumptions

In *Frontiero* the law fell because the legislators had made the unproven assumption that wives depended on their husbands for support while men did not so depend on their wives. Because this assumption did not take into account those situations where wives were financially independent of their husbands and where husbands were in fact dependent on their wives, the Court held that the law was too broad and therefore a violation of the equal protection guarantee.

In three subsequent cases, the Court found similar presumptions invalid.

In 1975 the Court struck down that portion of the Social Security Act that provided survivors' benefits to widows with small children but not to widowers with small children. Finding this distinction the same as the invalid classification in *Frontiero*, the Court ruled that it violated the due process clause by providing working women fewer benefits for their Social Security contributions than working men received.

The distinction challenged here was based on an "ar-

The Rights of Illegitimate Children

Until the 1970s illegitimate children were not under the scope of the equal protection clause. Many state and several federal laws denied illegitimate children the rights and benefits granted to legitimate children.

The Supreme Court requires more than a rational basis to justify different treatment of legitimate and illegitimate children. But it has not made illegitimacy a suspect classification justifiable only by a compelling government interest. In most instances the Court has rejected such a classification as unconstitutional when it irrationally punishes the child for something its parents did.

In 1972, as it struck down a state law that denied illegitimate children any share in workers' compensation survivors' benefits paid automatically to legitimate children, the Court said:

> The status of illegitimacy has expressed through the ages society's condemnation of irresponsible liaisons beyond the bonds of marriage. But visiting this condemnation on the head of an infant is illogical and unjust. Moreover, imposing disabilities on the illegitimate child is contrary to the basic concept of our system that legal burdens should bear some relationship to individual responsibility or wrongdoing. Obviously, no child is responsible for his birth and penalizing the illegitimate child is an ineffectual—as well as an unjust—way of deterring the parent.[1]

Using similar reasoning, the Court struck down state laws forbidding illegitimate children to recover damages in the wrongful death of their mother and, conversely, a mother from recovering damages for the wrongful death of her illegitimate child.[2] It also voided a state law giving legitimate, but not illegitimate, children an enforceable right to support from their natural fathers.[3]

Inheritance and Illegitimacy

The Court has been ambivalent about laws restricting the rights of illegitimate children to inherit from their fathers when their fathers die without a written will—in legal terms, intestate.

In 1971 the Court, 5-4, upheld a state law that prevented an acknowledged illegitimate child from inheriting property from her father, who died with no will. To strike down the law, said the majority, would be an unwarranted interference with an exercise of state power. The father could have written a will designating his illegitimate child as an heir or could have legitimated her, the majority pointed out.[4]

But six years later, the Court appeared to repudiate this decision when it struck down an Illinois statute that allowed illegitimate children to inherit intestate only from their mothers while legitimate children could inherit from both parents in the absence of a will.[5]

In 1978, however, the Court appeared to waver again on this point, upholding, 5-4, a New York law that forbade illegitimate children to inherit from their intestate fathers unless the father had acknowledged his paternity in a Court proceeding during his lifetime.[6]

Federal Laws and Benefits

The Court has evidenced similar indecision in its rulings on federal laws which distinguish between legitimate and illegitimate children, striking down a provision that denied disability insurance benefits to some illegitimate children[7] but upholding a provision requiring certain illegitimate children to prove actual dependence on their deceased parent in order to be eligible for surviving children's benefits. Such proof was not required for legitimate children.[8]

1. *Weber v. Aetna Casualty and Surety Co.*, 406 U.S. 164 at 175 (1972).
2. *Levy v. Louisiana*, 391 U.S. 68 (1968); *Glona v. American Guarantee and Liability Insurance Co.*, 391 U.S. 73 (1968); see also *Parham v. Hughes*, 441 U.S. 347 (1979).
3. *Gomez v. Perez*, 409 U.S. 535 (1973).
4. *Labine v. Vincent*, 401 U.S. 532 (1971).
5. *Trimble v. Gordon*, 430 U.S. 762 (1977).
6. *Lalli v. Lalli*, 439 U.S. 259 (1978).
7. *Jimenez v. Weinberger*, 417 U.S. 628 (1974).
8. *Mathews v. Lucas*, 427 U.S. 495 (1976).

chaic and overbroad" generalization, said the Court in *Weinberger v. Wiesenfeld.* The idea that men more frequently than women are the primary supporters of their families is "not without empirical support," Justice Brennan wrote. "But such a gender-based generalization cannot suffice to justify the denigration of the efforts of women who do work and whose earnings contribute significantly to their families' support." [17]

Pointing out that the intended purpose of the benefit was to allow a mother to stay home to care for her young children, Brennan said the distinction between surviving mothers and surviving fathers was "entirely irrational.... It is no less important for a child to be cared for by its sole surviving parent when that parent is male rather than female." [18] Two years later a five-justice majority invalidated a Social Security Act provision that provided survivors' benefits to widows regardless of their financial dependence on their husbands, but to widowers only if they proved they had received more than half their income from their wives. In *Califano v. Goldfarb* four members of the majority found that this impermissibly discriminated against female wage earners by diminishing the protection, relative to male wage earners, that they provided for their families. Justice Brennan wrote:

> The only conceivable justification for writing the presumption of wives' dependency into the statute is the assumption, not verified by the Government ... but based simply on "archaic and overbroad" generalizations ... that it would save the Government time, money and effort simply to pay benefits to all widows, rather than to require proof of dependency of both sexes. We held in *Frontiero,* and again in *Wiesenfeld,* and therefore hold again here, that such assumptions do not suffice to justify a gender-based discrimination in the distribution of employment-related benefits. [19]

The fifth member of the majority, Justice John Paul Stevens found that the provision impermissibly discriminated against the dependent widowers.

For the minority, Justice William H. Rehnquist argued that the classification was a rational one substantially related to the intended goal, which Rehnquist defined as a wish to aid "the characteristically [economically] depressed condition of aged widows." [20]

Again in 1980 the Court struck down such a law, this time a state law making widows automatically eligible for death benefits after the work-related death of their husband, but requiring widowers—in order to be eligible for such benefits—to prove that they were physically or mentally unable to earn a living or that they were dependent upon their wives' earnings. [21]

'Important Objectives'

Although he had been unable to convince a majority of the Court that gender-based discrimination was so invidious as to require a compelling government interest to justify it, Justice Brennan in 1976 won majority support for a standard that appeared midway between the standards of rationality and a compelling governmental interest.

Craig v. Boren (1976) involved a challenge to an Oklahoma law that permitted the sale of 3.2 beer to women at age eighteen but not to men until age twenty-one. Four

Women on Jury Duty

For nearly one hundred years, the Supreme Court held that, because a woman's place was in the home, she did not have to perform jury duty unless she expressed a wish to do so.

Exclusion of women from state court jury panels did not violate the Fourteenth Amendment, the Court ruled in the 1880 case of *Strauder v. West Virginia.* [1]

The Court stood by this view as recently as 1961. In the case of *Hoyt v. Taylor,* Hoyt sought to overturn her murder conviction on the ground that Florida's jury selection procedures were unconstitutional because only women who had registered for jury duty could be called. The effect was to exclude most women from service.

However, the Court majority found the statute valid. "[W]oman is still regarded as the center of home and family life," wrote Justice John Marshall Harlan. "We cannot say that it is constitutionally impermissible for a State ... to conclude that a woman should be relieved from the civic duty of jury service unless she herself determines that such service is consistent with her own special responsibilities." [2]

Fourteen years later the Court reversed itself. In *Taylor v. Louisiana* it ruled unconstitutional the automatic exemption of women from juries.

Billy Taylor, convicted of a crime by an all-male jury, challenged the Louisiana law that exempted women from jury service unless they specifically announced a willingness to serve. He said the law denied him his right to a fair trial. The Court agreed, reasoning that a jury comprised of a fair cross section of the community was fundamental to the right to jury trial guaranteed by the Sixth Amendment.

That guarantee was denied "if the jury pool is made up of only special segments of the populace or if large, distinctive groups are excluded from the pool," the majority said. Because 53 percent of the community was female—a large, distinctive group—the question then became whether women served "such a distinctive role" that their exclusion from jury service was justifiable.

The majority answered that it was "no longer tenable to hold that women as a class may be excluded or given automatic exemptions based solely on sex if the consequence is that criminal jury venires are almost totally male.... If it was ever the case that women were unqualified to sit on juries or were so situated that none of them could be required to perform jury service, that time has long since passed." [3]

1. *Strauder v. West Virginia,* 100 U.S. 303 (1880).
2. *Hoyt v. Florida,* 368 U.S. 57 at 62 (1961).
3. *Taylor v. Louisiana,* 419 U.S. 522 at 537 (1975).

justices agreed with Brennan that to "withstand constitutional challenge ... classifications by gender must serve important governmental objectives and must be substantially related to achievement of those objectives." [22] It was not enough that the classification was rational, Brennan said; the distinction must serve some "important governmental objective."

Applying this standard, the majority found that Oklahoma's desire to promote traffic safety was an important goal, but that the gender-based distinction prohibiting the

Personal Liberty and Privacy...

The effort of women to win equal rights in society and the workplace was affected immeasurably by a line of Supreme Court decisions beginning in the mid-1960s that recognize an individual's right to privacy in making decisions concerning marriage, procreation, and abortion. The Constitution does not mention privacy, but the Court recognizes personal privacy as a basic contitutional right with which government may not casually interfere.

Judicial recognition of this category of personal rights dates back to 1923 and *Meyer v. Nebraska*. Nebraska law forbade any school from teaching a modern foreign language other than English to children in the first eight grades. The Court held that the statute violated the Fourteenth Amendment's due process guarantee by depriving the teacher who had been convicted of violating it and the affected parents and children of a measure of personal liberty:

Without doubt, it [liberty] denotes not merely freedom from bodily restraint but also the right of the individual to contract, to engage in any of the common occupations of life, to acquire useful knowledge, to marry, establish a home and bring up children, to worship God according to the dictates of his own conscience, and generally to enjoy those privileges long recognized at common law as essential to the orderly pursuit of happiness by free men. [1]

Two years later the Court struck down an Oregon law that required all children to attend public schools. The Court in *Pierce v. Society of Sisters* declared that the statute "unreasonably interferes with the liberty of parents ... to direct the upbringing and education of [their] children." [2]

Marriage and Procreation

In a 1942 case the Court's development of protection for the right of personal privacy was reinforced by its evolving fundamental interest standard for equal protection cases.

Oklahoma law provided that certain convicted felons could be sterilized. The Supreme Court invalidated the law because it did not treat all persons convicted of similar crimes in a similar way.

Marriage and procreation were "fundamental to the very existence and survival of the race," the Court said. [3] Laws that affected such fundamental rights were subject to close scrutiny and could be justified only by a pressing governmental objective.

Twenty-five years later the Court affirmed this view in *Loving v. Virginia*, striking down a Virginia law that punished persons who entered into interracial marriages. This law, the Court held, violated the equal protection clause and denied those it affected due process:

The freedom to marry has long been recognized as one of the vital personal rights essential to the orderly pursuit of happiness by free men. ... To deny this fundamental freedom on so unsupportable a basis as the racial classification embodied in these statutes ... is surely to deprive all the State's citizens of liberty without due process of law. The Fourteenth Amendment requires that the freedom of choice to marry not be restricted by invidious racial discriminations. Under our Constitution, the freedom to marry or not marry a person of another race resides with the individual and cannot be infringed by the State. [4]

Contraceptives

Two years before *Loving,* the Court held that a state unconstitutionally interfered with personal privacy when it prohibited married couples from using contraceptives. The 7-2 decision in *Griswold v. Connecticut* rested on a variety of reasons for the individual votes.

Justice William O. Douglas, for the Court, held that the right of personal privacy was an independent right implicit in the First, Third, Fourth, Fifth, and Ninth Amendments. "[S]pecific guarantees in the Bill of Rights have penumbras, formed by emanations from those guarantees that help give them life and substance," he wrote. "Various guarantees create zones of privacy." [5]

Marriage was within a protected zone of privacy, Douglas continued, and the state impermissibly invaded that zone by prohibiting married couples from using contraceptives. "Would we allow the police to search the sacred precincts of marital bedrooms for telltale signs of the use of contraceptives? The very idea is repulsive to the notions of privacy surrounding the marriage relationship," he concluded. [6]

In an convincing opinion by Justice Arthur J. Goldberg, for himself, Chief Justice Earl Warren, and

sale, but not the possession, of a low-alcohol beverage to males under age twenty-one was not substantially related to the attainment of that objective. The classification was therefore invalid.

Five years later the Court upheld a sex-based distinc-

tion in criminal law, finding it justified as an appropriate means of accomplishing an important state end. California's statutory rape law permitted a man to be prosecuted for having sexual relations with a woman younger than eighteen to whom he is not married. The woman was ex-

... Constitutionally Protected Rights

Justice William J. Brennan, Jr., the right to personal privacy was declared to be one of those rights "retained by the people" under the Ninth Amendment, which states that the "enumeration in the Constitution of certain rights shall not be construed to deny or disparage others retained by the people." [7]

Justice John Marshall Harlan saw marriage as one of the basic values that the Court had found "implicit in the concept of ordered liberty" protected by the Fourteenth Amendment.[8] Justice Byron R. White held that because marriage was a fundamental interest, the Connecticut law deprived married couples of "liberty" without due process of law.[9]

Justices Potter Stewart and Hugo L. Black in dissent found no right of personal privacy either expressed or implied in the Constitution.

In 1972 the Court struck down a state law that permitted the distribution of contraceptives to single persons to prevent the spread of disease but not to prevent conception, finding it a violation of the equal protection guarantee.[10]

Abortion

The most controversial decision of the 1970s vastly enlarged a woman's right of privacy, striking down all state laws banning abortion. The Court's 1973 ruling in *Roe v. Wade* extended the right of personal privacy to embrace the right of a woman to have an abortion. Once again the Court reached a conclusion based on a constitutional right of privacy without agreeing on the precise location within the Constitution for that right.

"The Constitution does not explicitly mention any right of privacy," wrote Justice Harry A. Blackmun. "[H]owever, ... the Court has recognized that a right of personal privacy, or a guarantee of certain areas or zones of privacy does exist under the Constitution." [11]

Whatever its source, Blackmun declared, "[t]his right of privacy ... is broad enough to encompass a woman's decision whether or not to terminate her pregnancy." [12] But, Blackmun cautioned, the woman's right to have an abortion is a qualified one:

[A] state may properly assert important interests in safeguarding health, in maintaining medical standards, and in protecting potential life. At some point in pregnancy, these respective interests become sufficently compelling to sustain

regulation of the factors that govern the abortion decision.[13]

In the first trimester of pregnancy, the Court held that the state had no interest sufficiently compelling to warrant interfering with this decision. In the second trimester, when an abortion was more likely than continuation of the pregnancy to affect the health of the mother adversely, the Court held that the state had a compelling interest in protecting her and could therefore regulate the abortion procedure, by requiring, for example, that it be performed in a hospital.[14]

In the third trimester, when the fetus presumably could live on its own, the state's compelling interest lay in protecting that life. To that end the Court said a state could forbid abortions in the third trimester except when necessary to protect the life or health of the mother.[15]

Subsequently, the Court held that this right protects a mature woman's right to have an abortion, even in the face of strong family opposition. The Court held that states cannot require either the consent of the husband or, if the woman was an unmarried minor, the consent of her parents, as an essential condition for a first-trimester abortion.[16]

However, the Court has declined to require that public funds be used for abortions for poor women, upholding state and federal funding bans.[17]

1. *Meyer v. Nebraska*, 262 U.S. 390 at 399 (1923).
2. *Pierce v. Society of Sisters*, 268 U.S. 510 at 534-535.
3. *Skinner v. Oklahoma*, 316 U.S. 535 at 541 (1942).
4. *Loving v. Virginia*, 388 U.S. 1 at 12 (1967).
5. *Griswold v. Connecticut*, 381 U.S. 479 at 484 (1965).
6. Id. at 485-486.
7. Id. at 499.
8. Id. at 500, quoting from *Palko v. Connecticut*, 302 U.S. 319 at 325 (1937).
9. Id. at 502.
10. *Eisenstadt v. Baird*, 405 U.S. 438 (1972).
11. *Roe v. Wade*, 410 U.S. 113 at 152 (1973).
12. Id. at 153.
13. Id. at 154.
14. *Simopoulos v. Virginia*, 462 U.S. 506 (1983).
15. *Thornburgh v. American College of Obstetricians and Gynecologiss*, 476 U.S. 747 (1986).
16. *Planned Parenthood of Central Missouri v. Danforth*, 428 U.S. 52 (1976); *Bellotti v. Baird*, 443 U.S. 622 (1979); *H. L. v. Matheson*, 450 U.S. 398 (1981); *City of Akron v. Akron Center for Reproductive Health, Inc.*, 462 U.S. 416 (1983); *Planned Parenthood Asssociation of Kansas City, Mo. v. Ashcroft*, 462 U.S. 476 (1983).
17. *Harris v. McRae*, 448 U.S. 297 (1980); *Williams v. Zbaraz*, 448 U.S. 358 (1980).

empted from criminal liability. This was challenged as discriminating against the man, but was upheld by the Court, 5-4, as an appropriate means of preventing illegitimate teenage pregnancies.[23]

Also in 1981, the Court gave at least lip service to this standard when it decided, 6-3, that Congress was well within its authority when it decided to exclude women from the military draft. Writing for the majority in *Rostker v. Goldberg*, Justice Rehnquist declared this distinction justified because women were barred from combat and thus were not "similarly situated" with men for the purposes of maintaining a ready military force.[24]

DISCRIMINATION IN EMPLOYMENT

Women bear children and that often interrupts their employment outside the home. Employers have used potential pregnancy as a primary argument against hiring, training, and promoting women. Employers' restrictive policies on pregnancy have been a major target of women's rights advocates who see this issue as the heart of sex discrimination.

The Supreme Court has found it difficult to deal with cases involving pregnancy-related discrimination. For a time the Court declared that pregnancy classifications did not discriminate between men and women but rather between pregnant persons and nonpregnant persons. After Justice John Paul Stevens took issue with that view, lecturing his brethren in 1976 that "it is the capacity to become pregnant which primarily differentiates the female from the male," it was rarely invoked again.[25]

Maternity Leave

The Court's first major decisions on sex discrimination in the workplace came in 1974 and required employers to be more flexible in administering maternity leave. The Court, 7-2, held that it violated the due process guarantee to require all pregnant women to leave their jobs at the same point in pregnancy.

Cleveland Board of Education v. LeFleur and *Cohen v. Chesterfield County School Board*, decided together, involved school board policies that forced teachers to stop teaching midway through pregnancy.

"[F]reedom of personal choice in matters of marriage and family life is one of the liberties protected by the due process clause," the majority wrote. Due process requires that maternity leave regulations "not needlessly, arbitrarily, or capriciously impinge upon this vital area of a teacher's constitutional liberty."[26]

The Court rejected the school boards' arguments that mandatory leave policies ensured continuity of instruction by giving the school time to find qualified substitute teachers. Such an absolute requirement violated the test of rationality, the Court said, because in many instances it would interrupt continuity by requiring a teacher to leave her classroom in the middle of a term.

"As long as the teachers are required to give substantial advance notice of their condition, the choice of firm dates later in pregnancy would serve the boards' objectives just as well, while imposing a far lesser burden on the women's exercise of constitutionally protected freedom," the majority wrote.[27]

The Court also held that the regulations were too broad because they presumed that all women reaching the fifth or sixth month of pregnancy were physically incapable of continuing in their jobs. Such a presumption, which denies a pregnant woman the opportunity to prove she is fit to continue working, is contrary to the due process guarantees of the Fifth and Fourteenth Amendments.

"If legislative bodies are to be permitted to draw a general line anywhere short of the delivery room, I can find no judicial standard of measurement which says the lines drawn here are invalid," said Justice Rehnquist, dissenting for himself and Chief Justice Burger.[28]

Pregnancy and Disability

When the Court turned to look at an employer's obligation to provide disability payments to women unable to work because of pregnancy and childbirth, it was distinctly less sympathetic to the needs of working women. After the Court twice ruled against women workers in this context, Congress stepped in to correct the trend, by amending Title VII of the 1964 Civil Rights Act to prohibit discrimination against pregnant women in all areas of employment.

Six months after the maternity leave decision, the Court in *Geduldig v. Aiello* upheld a state disability insurance program excluding coverage of disabilities related to normal pregnancy and childbirth. The six-justice majority said the exclusion was based on physical condition, not sex:

> The California insurance program does not exclude anyone from benefit eligibility because of gender but merely removes one physical condition—pregnancy—from the list of compensable disabilities. While it is true that only women can become pregnant, it does not follow that every legislative classification concerning pregnancy is a sex-based classification.... Normal pregnancy is an objectively identifiable physical condition with unique characteristics. Absent a showing that distinctions involving pregnancy are mere pretexts designed to effect an invidious discrimination against the members of one sex or the other, lawmakers are constitutionally free to include or exclude pregnancy from the coverage of legislation such as this on any reasonable basis, just as with respect to any other physical condition.[29]

The question then became simply whether the exclusion was reasonable. Stewart observed that disability coverage for pregnancy would increase costs that would have to be offset by increased employee contributions, changes in other coverage, or lower benefit levels. He continued:

> The state has a legitimate interest in maintaining the self-supporting nature of its insurance program. Similarly, it has an interest in distributing the available resources in such a way as to keep benefit payments at an adequate level for disabilities that are covered, rather than to cover all disabilities inadequately. Finally, California has a legitimate concern in maintain-

ing the contribution rate at a level that will not unduly burden participating employees, particularly low-income employees who may be most in need of the disability insurance.

These policies provide an objective and wholly non-invidious basis for the State's decision not to create a more comprehensive insurance program than it has. There is no evidence in the record that the selection of the risks insured by the program worked to discriminate against any definable group or class in terms of the aggregate risk protection derived by that group or class from the program. There is no risk from which men are protected and women are not. Likewise, there is no risk from which women are protected and men are not.

The appellee simply contends ... she has suffered discrimination because she encountered a risk that was outside the program's protection.... [W]e hold that this contention is not a valid one under the Equal Protection Clause of the Fourteenth Amendment.[30]

In dissent Justice Brennan argued that the Court should regard gender-based classifications as inherently suspect, justifiable only to achieve a compelling government interest that could not otherwise be met. But the Court misapplied the standard it did use, he argued:

[T]he economic effects caused by pregnancy-related disabilities are functionally indistinguishable from the effects caused by any other disability: wages are lost due to a physical inability to work, and medical expenses are incurred for the delivery of the child and for post-partum care. In my view, by singling out for less favorable treatment a gender-linked disability peculiar to women, the State has created a double standard for disability compensation: a limitation is imposed upon the disabilities for which women workers may recover, while men receive full compensation for all disabilities suffered, including those that affect only or primarily their sex.... Such dissimilar treatment of men and women, on the basis of physical characteristics inextricably linked to one sex, inevitably constitutes sex discrimination.[31]

Two years later, the Court upheld a similar exclusion from a disability plan maintained by a private employer, General Electric. "[E]xclusion of pregnancy from a disability benefits plan providing general coverage is not a gender-based discrimination at all," wrote Rehnquist for the six-justice majority in *General Electric Co. v. Gilbert* (1976).[32]

The plan covered some risks, but not others; there was no risk from which men were protected, but not women, or vice versa. Rehnquist wrote:

[I]t is impossible to find any gender-based discriminatory effect in this scheme simply because women disabled as a result of pregnancy do not receive benefits; that is to say, gender-based discrimination does not result simply because an employer's disability benefits plan is less than all-inclusive.... To hold otherwise would endanger the commonsense notion that an employer who has no disability benefits program at all does not violate Title VII [of the 1964 Act].[33]

"Surely it offends common sense to suggest ... that a classification revolving around pregnancy is not, at the minimum, strongly 'sex related,'" wrote Justice Brennan in dissent. "Pregnancy exclusions ... both financially burden women workers and act to break down the continuity of the employment relationship, thereby exacerbating women's comparatively transient role in the labor force."[34]

Sick Pay and Seniority

Almost exactly one year after *General Electric* the Court ruled that employers can refuse sick pay to women employees absent from work due to pregnancy and childbirth, but they cannot divest those women of their accumulated seniority for taking maternity leave. All the justices concurred in the ruling in *Nashville Gas Co. v. Satty* (1977).

For the Court, Justice Rehnquist wrote that the divestiture of seniority clearly violated the 1964 Civil Rights Act's Title VII, which prohibited employment discrimination on the basis of sex. Although the policy appeared neutral—divesting of seniority all persons who took leaves of absence from work for any reason other than illness, a category from which childbirth-related absences were excluded—its effect was clearly discriminatory, depriving far more women than men of job opportunities and adversely affecting their status as employees.

The denial of sick pay was permissible, wrote Rehnquist, under the *General Electric* reasoning. Attempting to distinguish the seniority policy from the sick pay and disability benefits policies, Rehnquist emphasized that the gas company

has not merely refused to extend to women a benefit [sick pay, disability insurance] that men cannot and do not receive, but has imposed on women a substantial burden that men need not suffer. The distinction between benefits and burdens is more than one of semantics. We held in Gilbert that ... [Title VII] did not require that greater economic benefits be paid to one sex or the other "because of their differing roles in the scheme of human existence." ... But that holding does not allow us to read ... [Title VII] to permit an employer to burden female employees in such a way as to deprive them of employment opportunities because of their different role.[35]

Finding this distinction somewhat confusing, Justice Stevens said he saw the difference between the two policies as one of short-term versus long-term effect. Denial of sick pay did not affect the woman worker beyond the period of her leave; loss of seniority resulted in permanent disadvantage.

In a concurring opinion, Justices Brennan, Powell, and Thurgood Marshall suggested that the combination of the seniority and sick pay policies violated Title VII by resulting in less net compensation for women than for men employees.

Frustrated by the Court's position, women's rights activists turned to Congress for relief. Congress responded in 1978 by amending Title VII to prohibit discrimination against pregnant women in any area of employment, including hiring, promotion, seniority rights, and job security. The Pregnancy Discrimination Act of 1978 also required employers who offered health insurance and temporary disability plans to provide coverage to women for pregnancy, childbirth, and related medical conditions.[36]

That meant, the Court held later, that employers must provide health insurance pregnancy coverage for the wives of male employees that was as comprehensive as that provided for the female employees. On the other hand, the

Court held in 1987, the new law did not preclude states from requiring more benefits for workers disabled by pregnancy than for other temporarily disabled workers.[37]

The 1964 Civil Rights Act

The first Title VII sex discrimination case to come to the Supreme Court was *Phillips v. Martin Marietta Corp.* (1971). Martin Marietta refused to hire women with pre-school children, although it hired men regardless of the age of their children. The Court said that Title VII did not permit such a distinction unless it was "a bona fide occupational qualification reasonably necessary to the normal operation of that particular business or enterprise." [38]

Six years later, in *Dothard v. Rawlinson*, the Court struck down as discrimination on the basis of sex a state law that set minimum height and weight requirements for certain jobs, in this case that of a prison guard.

Dianne Rawlinson was rejected for a job as a prison guard in Alabama because she did not meet the requirement that guards be at least five feet, two inches tall and at least 120 pounds. She challenged the law on the grounds that it would disqualify more than 40 percent of the women in the country but less than 1 percent of the men.

The Court ruled this prima facie evidence of sex discrimination because the apparently neutral physical requirements "select applicants for hire in a significantly discriminatory pattern." The state was then required to show that the height and weight requirements had a "manifest relationship" to the job in question. This the state failed to do, the Court said.[39]

The Court did uphold, however, a provision of the Alabama statute that prohibited women from filling positions that brought them into close proximity with inmates. In this case, the majority said an employee's "very womanhood" would make her vulnerable to sexual and other attacks by inmates and thus "undermine her capacity to provide the security that is the essence of a correctional counselor's responsibility." [40]

Justices Brennan and Marshall dissented. The majority decision "perpetuates one of the most insidious of the old myths about women—that women, wittingly or not, are seductive sexual objects," wrote Marshall. The majority, he said, makes women "pay the price in lost job opportunities for the threat of depraved conduct by prison inmates.... The proper response to inevitable attacks on both female and male guards is ... to take swift and sure punitive actions against the inmate offenders." [41]

PENSION RIGHTS, SEXUAL HARASSMENT

Women, as a group, live longer than men as a group. Traditionally, that disparity has been reflected in differing treatment of men and women by life insurance plans. But the Supreme Court has made clear that the 1964 Civil Rights Act bars the use of this collective difference to discriminate, in premiums or annuities, against women by

---

Congress and Discrimination

Congress carefully exempted itself from the reach of the laws it enacted to bar job discrimination in the rest of the country, the Supreme Court in 1979 curtailed that exemption.

In *Davis v. Passman* the Court ruled that the Fifth Amendment, which guarantees individuals against loss of their lives, liberty, or property without due process of law, and which implicitly guarantees equal protection as well, provides grounds for suing federal officials—including members of Congress—who violate those guarantees. *(Federal equal protection, box, p. 224)*

Davis v. Passman for the first time gave individuals who felt that they had lost their jobs on Capitol Hill as a result of illegal discrimination a basis for suing those responsible. The immediate beneficiary was Shirley Davis, who had lost her job with Representative Otto E. Passman, D-La. (1947-1977), simply because he felt that her post was better filled by a man.

Davis sued Passman for damages, arguing that he had violated her constitutional rights to due process and equal protection. A lower court threw her case out, refusing to find such an "implied cause of action" in the Fifth Amendment.

But the Supreme Court, 5-4, reversed the lower court and upheld Davis's right to sue. The Court sent back to the lower court, for further consideration, Passman's claim that legislative immunity protected him from such suits.

Writing for the majority, Justice William J. Brennan, Jr., declared that the Fifth Amendment conferred on Davis a federal constitutional right to be free from sex discrimination unless such discrimination was necessary to serve important governmental objectives and was substantially related to those objectives.

Davis was the obvious person to come into federal court to seek protection for that right, Brennan continued. If such rights are to be effective, persons "who allege that their own constitutional rights have been violated and who at the same time have no effective means other than the judiciary to enforce these rights, must be able to invoke the existing jurisdiction of the courts for the protection of their justiciable constitutional rights." *(Davis v. Passman, 442 U.S. 228, 1979)*

charging them more than the generally shorter lived men.

In 1978 the Court, 5-3, ruled that a municipal employer could not require female employees to make higher contributions to a pension fund than male employees earning the same salary.

In *Los Angeles v. Manhart* the city contended that the differential contributions were not based on sex, but on longevity. Justice Stevens for the majority acknowledged that women generally lived longer than men and that without the differential, men would, in effect, subsidize the pension benefits eventually paid to women. However, such subsidies, Stevens said, are the essence of group insurance:

> Treating different classes of risk as though they were the same for purposes of group insurance is a common practice which has never been considered inherently unfair. To insure the flabby and the fit as though they were equivalent risks may be more common than treating men and women alike; but nothing more than habit makes one "subsidy" seem less fair than the other.[42]

It is the individual that the 1964 Civil Rights Act protects from discrimination: "Even a true generalization about the class is an insufficient reason for disqualifying an individual to whom the generalization does not apply."[43] Even though most women live longer than most men, many women workers who paid the larger contribution would not, in fact, live longer than some of their male colleagues, Stevens pointed out.

In dissent, Chief Justice Burger said if employers

> are to operate economically workable group pension programs, it is only rational to permit them to rely on statistically sound and proven disparities in longevity between men and women. Indeed, it seems to me irrational to assume Congress intended to outlaw use of the fact that, for whatever reasons or combination of reasons, women as a class outlive men....
>
> An effect upon pension plans so revolutionary and discriminatory—this time favorable to women at the expense of men—should not be read into the statute without either a clear statement of that intent in the statute, or some reliable indication in the legislative history that this was Congress' purpose.[44]

The majority may have been influenced by Burger's warning of the decision's revolutionary effect on pension plans. By a 7-1 vote, the Court reversed the lower court order awarding retroactive relief to the women contributors. In this instance the majority felt that retroactive relief was inappropriate because it "could be devastating for a pension fund."[45] Payment of the award from the pension fund would diminish the fund's assets; that might then prove inadequate to meet obligations, which in turn might decrease benefits to all employees or increase the contribution rates for current employees, the Court said.

In lone dissent on this point, Justice Marshall said the majority had been shown no proof of the predicted "devastating" effect. Repayment to women of their earlier excessive contributions was the only way to make them whole for the discrimination they had suffered, he said.

In an earlier case involving remedies for proven sex discrimination, the Court held that the Eleventh Amendment, which prohibits private suits in federal courts against unwilling states, did not protect a state from an order to pay retroactive benefits to employees who were discriminated against by the state.

In *Fitzpatrick v. Bitzer* (1976), the Court upheld a federal court order to Connecticut to pay retroactive benefits to men who had been forced by state law to work longer than women employees before they could retire.[46]

The Court said Congress had the power to enforce the guarantees of the Fourteenth Amendment by authorizing such orders requiring expenditures of states funds. States, by ratifying that amendment, surrendered some of their sovereign immunity to such federal orders, it said.

The proper allocation of retirement rights and costs is still a matter that closely divides the Court. In 1983 the Court divided twice, 5-4, in resolving a challenge to an employer's retirement plan under which women workers upon retirement received smaller monthly payments than men who had contributed the same amounts during their working years.

In *Arizona Governing Committee for Tax Deferred Annuity and Deferred Compensation Plans v. Norris*, the Court held—with reasoning similar to that set out by Stevens in *Manhart*—that the fact that women as a group outlive men as a group was not a permissible basis for paying them different monthly benefits.[47]

Voting together on that point were Justices Marshall, Brennan, Stevens, Sandra Day O'Connor, and Byron R. White.

But on a second point, of considerable practical importance to women who had already retired under this plan, the Court held that this decision would apply only to retirement benefits derived from contributions made after this ruling. O'Connor joined the dissenters from the other point—Burger, Blackmun, Powell, and Rehnquist to form this majority.

In June 1986—the week Rehnquist was promoted to chief justice—the Court unanimously applied Title VII to ban sexual harassment in the workplace as a form of sexual discrimination, and the usually conservative Rehnquist wrote the majority's opinion. Such harassment is illegal not only when it results in the loss of a job or promotion, but also when it creates an offensive or hostile working environment, Rehnquist wrote.

> The language of Title VII is not limited to "economic" or "tangible" discrimination. The phrase "terms, conditions, or privileges of employment" evinces a congressional intent "to strike at the entire spectrum of disparate treatment of men and women" in employment.[48]

Notes

1. *Bradwell v. Illinois,* 16 Wall. 130 at 141 (1873).
2. *Minor v. Happersett,* 21 Wall. 162 (1875).
3. *Strauder v. West Virginia,* 100 U.S. 303 (1880); *Hoyt v. Florida,* 368 U.S. 57 (1961), overruled by *Taylor v. Louisiana,* 419 U.S. 522 (1975).
4. *Cronin v. Adams,* 192 U.S. 108 (1904).
5. *Goesaert v. Cleary,* 335 U.S. 464 at 466 (1948).
6. Id. at 468.
7. *Muller v. Oregon,* 208 U.S. 412 at 422-423 (1908); see also *Riley v. Massachusetts,* 232 U.S. 671 (1914); *Miller v. Wilson,* 236 U.S. 373 (1915); *Bosley v. McLaughlin,* 236 U.S. 385 (1915); *West Coast Hotel v. Parrish,* 300 U.S. 379 (1937).
8. *Sail'er Inn, Inc. v. Kirby,* 5 Cal. 3d 1.20, 485 P 2d 529 (1971).
9. *Reed v. Reed,* 404 U.S. 71 at 76 (1971), quoting *Royster Guano Co. v. Virginia,* 253 U.S. 412 at 415 (1920).
10. *Reed v. Reed,* 404 U.S. 71 at 76 (1971).

11. *Kahn v. Shevin*, 416 U.S. 351 (1974).
12. *Schlesinger v. Ballard*, 419 U.S. 498 (1975).
13. *Weinberger v. Salfi*, 422 U.S. 749 (1975).
14. *Mathews v. deCastro*, 429 U.S. 181 (1976).
15. *Stanton v. Stanton*, 421 U.S. 7 at 15 (1975).
16. *Frontiero v. Richardson*, 411 U.S. 677 at 686-687 (1973).
17. *Weinberger v. Wiesenfeld*, 420 U.S. 636 at 645 (1975).
18. Id. at 651-652.
19. *Califano v. Goldfarb*, 430 U.S. 199 at 217 (1977).
20. Id. at 242.
21. *Wengler v. Druggists Mutual Insurance Co.*, 446 U.S. 142 (1980).
22. *Craig v. Boren*, 429 U.S. 190 at 197 (1976); see also *Orr v. Orr*, 440 U.S. 268 (1979).
23. *Michael M. v. Superior Court of Sonoma County*, 450 U.S. 464 (1981).
24. *Rostker v. Goldberg*, 453 U.S. 57 (1981).
25. *General Electric Co. v. Gilbert*, 429 U.S. 125 at 162 (1976).
26. *Cleveland Board of Education v. LaFleur, Cohen v. Chesterfield County School Board*, 414 U.S. 632 at 639-640 (1974).
27. Id. at 643.
28. Id. at 660.
29. *Geduldig v. Aiello*, 417 U.S. 484 at 496-497, footnote 20 (1974).
30. Id. at 496-497.
31. Id. at 500-501.
32. *General Electric Co. v. Gilbert*, 429 U.S. 125 at 136 (1976).
33. Id. at 138-139.
34. Id. at 149, 158.
35. *Nashville Gas Co. v. Satty*, 434 U.S. 136 at 142 (1977).
36. Congressional Quarterly, *Congress and the Nation*, vol. V (Washington, D.C.: Congressional Quarterly, 1981), 796.
37. *Newport News Shipbuilding & Dry Dock Co. v. Equal Employment Opportunity Commission*, 462 U.S. 669 (1983); *California Federal Savings & Loan v. Guerra*, ___ U.S. ___ (1987).
38. *Phillips v. Martin-Marietta Corp.*, 400 U.S. 542 (1971).
39. *Dothard v. Rawlinson*, 433 U.S. 321 at 329 (1977).
40. Id. at 336.
41. Id. at 345-346.
42. *Los Angeles v. Manhart*, 435 U.S. 702 at 710 (1978).
43. Id. at 708.
44. Id. at 726.
45. Id. at 722.
46. *Fitzpatrick v. Bitzer*, 427 U.S. 445 (1976).
47. *Arizona Governing Committee for Tax Deferred Annuity and Deferred Compensation Plans v. Norris*, 463 U.S. 1073 (1983).
48. *Meritor Savings Bank v. Vinson*, 477 U.S. 57 (1986).

16

Poverty and Equal Protection

Discrimination based on relative wealth has not been declared inherently unconstitutional by the Supreme Court, even though individual justices in recent years have endorsed that belief. The Court, however, has found classifications based upon wealth in violation of the equal protection guarantee when they work to deprive poor people of certain fundamental rights and interests and there is no compelling state interest to justify the discrimination.

On this basis, the Court has invalidated classifications by wealth that impede access to justice, the right to travel freely between states, and the right to vote and run for public office.

Efforts to persuade the Court to classify all distinctions based on wealth as inherently suspect and to raise vital interests, such as education, to the status of fundamental rights have been unsuccessful. Where the Court has found that a classification by wealth does not involve a fundamental interest, it has applied the traditional equal protection test in which the state must only show a rational basis to justify the distinction between rich and poor.

ACCESS TO JUSTICE

The first time the Supreme Court found that classification based on wealth violated the equal protection guarantee was in the 1956 case of *Griffin v. Illinois.* Judson Griffin and James Crenshaw were convicted of armed robbery. Because they were indigent, the two asked for a free transcript of their trial for use in preparing an appeal. After their request was refused, the two charged that the refusal denied them due process and equal protection. The Supreme Court agreed, 5-4.

However, only four justices subscribed to the opinion written by Justice Hugo L. Black, who said:

> Both equal protection and due process emphasize the central aim of our entire judicial system—all people

charged with crime must, so far as the law is concerned, "stand on an equality before the bar of justice in every American court." . . . Surely no one would contend that either a State or the Federal Government could constitutionally provide that defendants unable to pay court costs in advance should be denied the right to plead not guilty or to defend themselves in court. Such a law would make the constitutional promise of a fair trial a worthless thing. Notice, the right to be heard, and the right to counsel would under such circumstances be meaningless promises to the poor. In criminal trials a State can no more discriminate on account of poverty than on account of religion, race, or color. Plainly the ability to pay costs in advance bears no rational relationship to a defendant's guilt or innocence and could not be used as an excuse to deprive a defendant of a fair trial.[1]

A state is not required by the Constitution to provide an appeals procedure. But if it chooses to do so it may not limit access to it on the basis of wealth, Black continued. "There can be no equal justice where the kind of a trial a man gets depends on the amount of money he has."[2]

Justice Felix Frankfurter concurred in the judgment with a separate opinion.

The four dissenters held that so long as Illinois followed its established procedure for appellate review, due process had not been denied. And so long as the state opened its appeals procedure to all defendants convicted of the same crime, it did not violate equal protection even though

> some may not be able to avail themselves of the full appeal because of their poverty. . . . The Constitution requires the equal protection of the law, but it does not require the States to provide equal financial means for all defendants to avail themselves of such laws.[3]

An Equal Right to Appeal

By 1971, however, the entire Court agreed that poverty alone should not bar an indigent from appealing his conviction. In *Mayer v. Chicago* a unanimous Court expanded *Griffin* to hold that a state's refusal to provide a free transcript to a man so that he might appeal his misdemeanor conviction was a violation of equal protection. "The size of the defendant's pocketbook bears no more relationship to his guilt or innocence in a nonfelony than in a felony case," the Court declared.[4]

But in 1976 the Court limited the circumstances under which the federal government must provide transcripts at public expense. In *United States v. MacCollum* the Court declared that indigent convicts did not have an unlimited constitutional right to a free transcript of their trial. Congress did not violate the equal protection guarantee implicit in the Fifth Amendment when it made provision of such a transcript conditional upon a finding that the challenge to the conviction was not frivolous and that the transcript was necessary to resolve the issues presented.

These conditions, the five-justice majority conceded,

> place an indigent in somewhat less advantageous position than a person of means. But neither the Equal Protection Clause of the Fourteenth Amendment nor ... the Fifth Amendment ... guarantees "absolute equality or precisely equal advantages." ... In the context of a criminal proceeding, they require only an "adequate opportunity to present [one's] claims fairly." [5]

The Right to Legal Counsel

In 1963, on the same day that the Supreme Court held in *Gideon v. Wainwright* that a state violated due process when it refused to provide court-appointed attorneys to indigents charged with felonies, the Court also held that a state violated equal protection if it provided attorneys to indigents appealing convictions only when the appellate court decided legal counsel would be advantageous to the success of the appeal. For the majority in *Douglas v. California*, Justice William O. Douglas wrote:

> There is lacking that equality demanded by the Fourteenth Amendment where the rich man, who appeals as of right, enjoys the benefit of counsel's examination into the record, research of the law, and marshalling of arguments on his behalf, while the indigent, already burdened by a preliminary determination that his case is without merit, is forced to shift for himself.[6]

Justice John Marshall Harlan, who dissented in *Griffin* also dissented in *Douglas*, arguing that the Court should have relied on the due process clause rather than the equal protection guarantee to invalidate the state law:

> The States, of course, are prohibited by the Equal Protection Clause from discriminating between "rich" and "poor" *as such* in the formulation and application of their laws. But it is a far different thing to suggest that this provision prevents the State from adopting a law of general applicability that may affect the poor more harshly than it does the rich, or, on the other hand, from making some effort to redress economic imbalances while not eliminating them entirely.[7]

In subsequent cases the Court held that neither due process nor equal protection required a state to provide a convicted defendant with counsel so that he could seek discretionary review of his case in the state's higher courts or in the Supreme Court—rather than an appeal to which he had a right. Nor did a state deny equal protection when it required a convicted indigent who subsequently became capable of repayment to reimburse the state for the costs of his court-appointed attorney.[8]

Court Costs

Justice Harlan eventually persuaded a majority of the Court that due process was the proper constitutional basis for striking down state laws discriminating against the poor.

People who could not afford the sixty dollars in court costs associated with divorce proceedings were barred by Connecticut from filing for separation. Ruling against the state in *Boddie v. Connecticut*, Justice Harlan for the majority pointed out that the only way to obtain a divorce was in court. The state, by denying access to court to persons too poor to pay the fees amounted—in the absence of a "sufficient countervailing" justification from the state—to a denial of due process. Harlan acknowledged that the state had an interest in curbing frivolous suits and in using court fees to offset court costs. But these reasons were not sufficient, he said, "to override the interest of these [indigents] in having access to the only avenue open for dissolving their ... marriages." [9]

Justices Douglas and William J. Brennan, Jr., concurred in the result but argued that the case presented a classic denial of equal protection. "Affluence does not pass muster under the Equal Protection Clause for determining who must remain married and who shall be allowed to separate," wrote Douglas.[10]

Bankruptcy

By a 5-4 vote the Court sustained a federal law that required indigents to pay a fee to declare bankruptcy. "There is no constitutional right to obtain a discharge of one's debts in bankruptcy," the majority wrote in *United States v. Kras* (1973).[11]

Because the right to file for bankruptcy was not a fundamental one, the majority ruled that the federal government need only meet the rationality test. And since it was reasonable that the bankruptcy system be self-sufficient, the government met the test.

In dissent, Justice Potter Stewart said he could not agree with a decision that made "some of the poor too poor even to go bankrupt." [12]

Fines and Terms

In two unanimous decisions the Court has held that states may not substitute imprisonment for a fine that an indigent is unable to pay. In the 1970 case of *Williams v. Illinois*, the Court said that states could not hold poor people in prison beyond the length of the maximum sentence merely to work off a fine they were unable to pay. Forty-seven of the fifty states allowed such further imprisonment.

Writing for the Court, Chief Justice Warren E. Burger said:

> On its face the statute extends to all defendants an apparently equal opportunity for limiting confinement to the statutory maximum simply by satisfying a money judgment. In fact, this is an illusory choice for Williams or any indigent who . . . is without funds. . . . By making the maximum confinement contingent upon one's ability to pay, the State has visited different consequences on two categories of people.[13]

In 1971 the Court ruled that a "$30 or 30 days" sentence was also an unconstitutional denial of equal protection. That provision of the Fourteenth Amendment, held the Court, barred any state or municipality from limiting punishment for an offense to a fine for those who could pay, but expanding punishment for the same offense to imprisonment for those who could not.[14]

RIGHT TO TRAVEL, POLITICAL RIGHTS

Although the Supreme Court has not settled on which clause of the Constitution protects an individual's right to travel from state to state, since 1966 it has been established that this is a fundamental protected right.[15]

In 1969 the Court struck down two state laws and a District of Columbia statute setting residence requirements for welfare recipients. In *Shapiro v. Thompson* the Court ruled, 6-3, that the residency requirements infringed on the right of poor people to move from state to state and thereby denied them due process and equal protection of the laws. "[A]ny classification which serves to penalize the exercise of that right [to travel], unless shown to be necessary to promote a *compelling* governmental interest is unconstitutional," the majority said.[16] The majority recognized the state's valid interest in maintaining the fiscal integrity of its welfare plan, but found this interest not a compelling justification for making "invidious distinctions between classes of its citizens." [17]

The Court reiterated its *Shapiro* holding in 1974 when it ruled that Arizona violated the equal protection clause by requiring indigent persons to live in a county for a year before becoming eligible for free nonemergency medical care.[18]

The Court has ruled consistently that states may not place financial impediments in the way of a person's right to vote or otherwise participate in the political process. Rights associated with political participation are of fundamental interest to citizens, and classifications that prevent a group of people from participating may be justified only by a compelling governmental interest. *(Details, p. 225)*

The poll tax was the major financial barrier to voting for many people for years. Originally conceived of as an additional source of revenue, the poll tax became in the early 1900s a discriminatory tool to bar blacks from voting. In *Breedlove v. Suttles* (1937) the Court turned aside a charge that the poll tax denied equal protection of the laws, upholding it as a valid source of revenue.[19] In the 1966 case of *Harper v. Virginia State Board of Elections*, the Court overruled its 1937 decision on the ground that the poll tax denied equal protection to the poor by depriving them of the freedom to exercise their right to vote. "Wealth, like race, creed, or color, is not germane to one's ability to participate intelligently in the electoral process," the majority declared.[20] *(Details, p. 113)*

Twice the Court has held that states may not use filing fee requirements to keep poor candidates off the ballot. Such restrictions not only violate the guarantee of equal protection to candidates but also to voters by limiting the choice of candidates, the Court reasoned. *Bullock v. Carter* (1972) concerned a Texas statute that based the size of primary election filing fees on the costs of conducting those elections. The fees ran as high as $8,900 for some races.

The Court held that keeping spurious candidates off the ballot was a legitimate state objective, but that the method selected to achieve that objective was arbitrary since some serious candidates were unable to pay the high filing fees while some frivolous candidates could afford them. The test applied to the challenged law was not as demanding as the compelling interest test generally used for classifications affecting fundamental interests, but it was more rigorous than the traditional equal protection test that simply required the state to show that the challenged classification had a rational basis.[21]

Bullock was expanded in 1974 when the Court held that California could not deny an indigent candidate a ballot spot simply because he was too poor to pay the filing fee, no matter how reasonable that fee was. In *Lubin v. Panish* the Court said the state must provide alternative means for indigents to qualify for a ballot position.[22]

EDUCATION AND WEALTH

In 1973 the Court refused to make classifications by wealth inherently suspect or to give education the status of a "fundamental interest." This meant that the Court did not closely scrutinize a state's decision to continue financing public schools from local property taxes—even though that resulted in wide disparities in the amount spent per pupil in different districts.

Nor did the state have to prove that its financing system served a compelling state interest. As a result, the Court, 5-4, upheld this system of financing public education, challenged as a denial of equal protection of the laws.

In the early 1970s, school districts in every state but Hawaii operated primarily with money raised from taxing the real property within the district. Variations in districts—the amount of taxable property, the value of the property, and the tax rate—resulted in widely differing amounts that school districts in the same state could spend for the education of their children.

In Texas, where the case of *San Antonio School District v. Rodriguez* arose, the wealthiest district spent $594 for each schoolchild while the poorest spent only $356.

A bombshell shook the foundations of this traditional fees structure of public school financing on August 30, 1971, when the California Supreme Court declared this method unconstitutional because it resulted in less being

Family Matters

Because some matters of family and marital relations are of fundamental interest, classifications that restrict these relationships can be justified only by a compelling reason. However, in 1970 the Supreme Court ruled that a state statute that appeared to discriminate against large families was constitutional because it had a rational basis.

Dandridge v. Williams concerned a Maryland law that limited the maximum amount of welfare a family could receive. This meant that large families received less per child in benefits than families with fewer children. Large poor families consequently charged that the state had impermissibly denied them equal protection.

The Court held that the statute did not deliberately discriminate against large families but was simply a reasonable means for a state to use to allocate scarce welfare funds. (*Dandridge v. Williams*, 397 U.S. 471, 1970)

spent to educate a child in one school district than in another.[23]

Similar rulings followed from several other state and federal courts. In Texas the parents of Mexican-American pupils in San Antonio brought a similar suit, and in December 1971, a federal court found the Texas system unconstitutional. The state appealed to the Supreme Court.

Critical to the holding of the five-justice majority, for whom Justice Lewis F. Powell, Jr., wrote, were its findings that the Texas system did not disadvantage an identifiable group of poor persons and that the Constitution makes no mention of a right to education.

In previous cases classifications by wealth were found unconstitutionally discriminatory, wrote Powell, because the groups or individuals affected "were completely unable to pay for some desired benefit, and as a consequence, they sustained an absolute deprivation of a meaningful opportunity to enjoy that benefit."

But in *Rodriguez*, Powell continued, there was no showing that the financing system disadvantaged any definable indigent group or that the poorest people were concentrated in the poorest school districts. He explained:

The argument here is not that the children in districts having relatively low assessable property values are receiving no public education; rather, it is that they are receiving a poorer quality education than that available to children in districts having more assessable wealth. Apart from the unsettled and disputed question whether the quality of education may be determined by the amount of money expended for it, a sufficient answer ... is that at least where wealth is involved, the Equal Protection Clause does not require absolute equality or precisely equal advantages.[24]

"It is not the province of this Court to create substantive constitutional rights in the name of guaranteeing equal

protection of the laws," Powell said. " [T]he undisputed importance of education will not alone cause this Court to depart from the usual standard for reviewing a State's societal and economic legislation." [25]

The question remaining was whether it was reasonable for the state to use the property tax to finance public schools. The majority concluded that it was rational:

[T]o the extent that the Texas system of school finance results in unequal expenditures between children who happen to reside in different districts, we cannot say that such disparities are the product of a system that is so irrational as to be invidiously discriminatory.... The Texas plan is not the result of hurried, ill-conceived legislation. It certainly is not the product of purposeful discrimination against any group or class. On the contrary, it is rooted in decades of experience in Texas and elsewhere, and in major part is the product of responsible studies by qualified people.... One must also remember that the system here challenged is not peculiar to Texas.... In its essential characteristics, the Texas plan for financing public education reflects what many educators for a half century have thought was an enlightened approach to a problem for which there is no perfect solution. We are unwilling to assume for ourselves a level of wisdom superior to that of legislators, scholars, and educational authorities in 50 States, especially where the alternatives proposed are only recently conceived and nowhere yet tested. The constitutional standard under the Equal Protection Clause is whether the challenged state action rationally furthers a legitimate state purpose or interest.... We hold that the Texas plan abundantly satisfies this standard.[26]

The four dissenters wanted to overturn the Texas system. Justices Douglas and Thurgood Marshall contended that classification by wealth demanded strict scrutiny and that education was a fundamental interest. Children in property-poor districts were unconstitutionally discriminated against, wrote Marshall, and the Court should not judge the instrument of their discrimination against the "lenient standard of rationality which we have traditionally applied ... in the context of economic and commercial matters." [27]

Marshall rejected "the majority's labored efforts to demonstrate that fundamental interests ... encompass only established rights which we are somehow bound to recognize from the text of the Constitution itself." [28] The right to an education was fundamental, he said, because it was so intimately related to such rights as the right of expressing and receiving information and ideas as guaranteed by the First Amendment. Justices Douglas, Brennan, and Byron R. White said that the school financing system was not rational.

Notes

1. *Griffin v. Illinois,* 351 U.S. 12 at 12-13 (1956).
2. Id. at 19.
3. Id. at 28-29.
4. *Mayer v. Chicago,* 404 U.S. 189 at 196 (1971).
5. *United States v. MacCollum,* 426 U.S. 317 at 324 (1976).
6. *Douglas v. California,* 372 U.S. 353 at 357-358 (1963).
7. Id. at 361.

8. *Ross v. Moffitt*, 417 U.S. 600 (1974); *Fuller v. Oregon*, 417 U.S. 40 (1974).
9. *Boddie v. Connecticut*, 401 U.S. 371 at 381 (1971).
10. Id. at 386.
11. *United States v. Kras*, 409 U.S. 434 at 446 (1973).
12. Id. at 457.
13. *Williams v. Illinois*, 399 U.S. 235 (1970).
14. *Tate v. Short*, 401 U.S. 395 (1971).
15. *United States v. Guest*, 383 U.S. 745 (1966).
16. *Shapiro v. Thompson*, 394 U.S. 618 at 634 (1969).
17. Id. at 633.
18. *Memorial Hospital v. Maricopa County*, 415 U.S. 250 (1974).
19. *Breedlove v. Suttles*, 302 U.S. 277 (1937).
20. *Harper v. Virginia State Board of Elections*, 383 U.S. 663 at 668 (1966).
21. *Bullock v. Carter*, 405 U.S. 134 (1972).
22. *Lubin v. Panish*, 415 U.S. 709 (1974).
23. *Serrano v. Priest*, 96 Cal. Rptr. 601, 487 P. 2d 1241; 5 Cal. 3d 584 (1971).
24. *San Antonio Independent School District v. Rodriguez*, 411 U.S. 1 at 23-24 (1973).
25. Id. at 33, 35.
26. Id. at 54-55.
27. Id. at 98.
28. Id. at 99.

Appendix

Glossary of Legal Terms

Accessory. In criminal law, a person not present at the commission of an offense who commands, advises, instigates, or conceals the offense.

Acquittal. Discharge of a person from a charge of guilt. A person is acquitted when a jury returns a verdict of not guilty. A person may also be acquitted when a judge determines that there is insufficient evidence to convict him or that a violation of due process precludes a fair trial.

Adjudicate. To determine finally by the exercise of judicial authority to decide a case.

Affidavit. A voluntary written statement of facts or charges affirmed under oath.

A fortiori. With stronger force, with more reason.

Amicus curiae. A friend of the court, a person not a party to litigation, who volunteers or is invited by the court to give his views on a case.

Appeal. To take a case to a higher court for review. Generally, a party losing in a trial court may appeal once to an appellate court as a matter of right. If he loses in the appellate court, appeal to a higher court is within the discretion of the higher court. Most appeals to the U.S. Supreme Court are within the Court's discretion.

However, when the highest court in a state rules that a U.S. statute is unconstitutional or upholds a state statute against the claim that it is unconstitutional, appeal to the Supreme Court is a matter of right.

Appellant. The party that appeals a lower court decision to a higher court.

Appellee. One who has an interest in upholding the decision of a lower court and is compelled to respond when the case is appealed to a higher court by the appellant.

Arraignment. The formal process of charging a person with a crime, reading him the charge, asking whether he pleads guilty or not guilty, and entering his plea.

Attainder, Bill of. A legislative act pronouncing a particular individual guilty of a crime without trial or conviction and imposing a sentence upon him.

Bail. The security, usually money, given as assurance of a prisoner's due appearance at a designated time and place (as in court) in order to procure in the interim his release from jail.

Bailiff. A minor officer of a court usually serving as an usher or a messenger.

Brief. A document prepared by counsel to serve as the basis for an argument in court, setting out the facts of and the legal arguments in support of his case.

Burden of proof. The need or duty of affirmatively proving a fact or facts that are disputed.

Case Law. The law as defined by previously decided cases, distinct from statutes and other sources of law.

Cause. A case, suit, litigation or action, civil or criminal.

Certiorari, Writ of. A writ issued from the Supreme Court, at its discretion, to order a lower court to prepare the record of a case and send it to the Supreme Court for review.

Civil law. Body of law dealing with the private rights of individuals, as distinguished from criminal law.

Class action. A lawsuit brought by one person or group on behalf of all persons similarly situated.

Code. A collection of laws, arranged systematically.

Comity. Courtesy, respect; usually used in the legal sense to refer to the proper relationship between state and federal courts.

Common law. Collection of principles and rules of action, particularly from unwritten English law, which derive their authority from longstanding usage and custom or from courts recognizing and enforcing these customs. Sometimes used synonymously with case law.

Consent decree. A court-sanctioned agreement settling a legal dispute and entered into by the consent of the parties.

Contempt (civil and criminal). Civil contempt consists in the failure to do something that the party is ordered by the court to do for the benefit of another party. Criminal contempt occurs when a person willfully exhibits disrespect for the court or obstructs the administration of justice.

Conviction. Final judgment or sentence that the defendant is guilty as charged.

Criminal law. That branch of law which deals with the enforcement of laws and the punishment of persons who, by breaking laws, commit crimes.

Declaratory judgment. A court pronouncement declaring a legal right or interpretation but not ordering a specific action.

De facto. In fact, in reality.

Defendant. In a civil action, the party denying or defending itself against charges brought by a plaintiff. In a criminal action, the person indicted for commission of an offense.

De jure. As a result of law, as a result of official action.

Deposition. Oral testimony from a witness taken out of court in response to written or oral questions, committed to writing, and intended to be used in the preparation of a case.

Dicta. See Obiter dictum.

Dismissal. Order disposing of a case without a trial.

Docket. See Trial docket.

Due process. Fair and regular procedure. The Fifth and Fourteenth Amendments guarantee persons that they will not be deprived of life, liberty, or property by the government until fair and usual procedures have been followed.

Error, Writ of. A writ issued from an appeals court to a lower court requiring it to send to the appeals court the record of a case in which it has entered a final judgment and which the appeals court will now review for error.

Ex parte. Only from, or on, one side. Application to a court for some ruling or action on behalf of only one party.

Ex post facto. After the fact; an ex post facto law makes an action a crime after it has already been committed, or otherwise changes the legal consequences of some past action.

Ex rel. Upon information from; usually used to describe legal proceedings begun by an official in the name of the state, but at the instigation of, and with information from, a private individual interested in the matter.

Grand jury. Group of twelve to twenty-three persons impaneled to hear in private evidence presented by the state against persons accused of crime and to issue indictments when a majority of the jurors find probable cause to believe that the accused has committed a crime. Called a "grand" jury because it comprises a greater number of persons than a "petit" jury.

Grand jury report. A public report released by a grand jury after an investigation into activities of public officials that fall short of criminal actions. Grand jury reports are often called "presentments."

Guilty. A word used by a defendant in entering a plea or by a jury in returning a verdict, indicating that the defendant is legally responsible as charged for a crime or other wrongdoing.

Habeas corpus. Literally, "you have the body"; a writ issued to inquire whether a person is lawfully imprisoned or detained. The writ demands that the persons holding the prisoner justify his detention or release him.

Immunity. A grant of exemption from prosecution in return for evidence or testimony.

In camera. "In chambers." Refers to court hearings in private without spectators.

In forma pauperis. In the manner of a pauper, without liability for court costs.

In personam. Done or directed against a particular person.

In re. In the affair of, concerning. Frequent title of judicial proceedings in which there are no adversaries, but rather where the matter itself—as a bankrupt's estate—requires judicial action.

In rem. Done or directed against the thing, not the person.

Indictment. A formal written statement based on evidence presented by the prosecutor from a grand jury decided by a majority vote, charging one or more persons with specified offenses.

Information. A written set of accusations, similar to an indictment, but filed directly by a prosecutor.

Injunction. A court order prohibiting the person to whom it is directed from performing a particular act.

Interlocutory decree. A provisional decision of the court that temporarily settles an intervening matter before completion of a legal action.

Judgment. Official decision of a court based on the rights and claims of the parties to a case that was submitted for determination.

Jurisdiction. The power of a court to hear a case in question, which exists when the proper parties are present, and when the point to be decided is within the issues authorized to be handled by the particular court.

Juries. See grand jury and petit jury.

Magistrate. A judicial officer having jurisdiction to try minor criminal cases and conduct preliminary examinations of persons charged with serious crimes.

Mandamus. "We command." An order issued from a superior court directing a lower court or other authority to perform a particular act.

Moot. Unsettled, undecided. A moot question is also one that is no longer material; a moot case is one that has become hypothetical.

Motion. Written or oral application to a court or a judge to obtain a rule or an order.

Nolo contendere. "I will not contest it." A plea entered by a defendant at the discretion of the judge with the same legal effect as a plea of guilty, but it may not be cited in other proceedings as an admission of guilt.

Obiter dictum. Statement by a judge or justice expressing an opinion and included with, but not essential to, an opinion resolving a case before the court. Dicta are not necessarily binding in future cases.

Parole. A conditional release from imprisonment under conditions that if the prisoner abides by the law and other restrictions that may be placed upon him, he will not have to serve the remainder of his sentence. But if he does not abide by specified rules, he will be returned to prison.

Per curiam. "By the court." An unsigned opinion of the court or an opinion written by the whole court.

Petit jury. A trial jury, originally a panel of twelve persons who tried to reach a unanimous verdict on questions of fact in criminal and civil proceedings. Since 1970 the Supreme Court has upheld the legality of state juries with fewer than twelve persons. Because it comprises fewer persons than a "grand" jury, it is called a "petit" jury.

Petitioner. One who files a petition with a court seeking action or relief, including a plaintiff or an appellant. But a petitioner is also a person who files for other court action where charges are not necessarily made; for example, a party may petition the court for an order requiring another person or party to produce documents. The opposite party is called the respondent.

When a writ of certiorari is granted by the Supreme Court, the parties to the case are called petitioner and respondent in contrast to the appellant and appellee terms used in an appeal.

Plaintiff. A party who brings a civil action or sues to obtain a remedy for injury to his rights. The party against whom action is brought is termed the defendant.

Plea Bargaining. Negotiations between prosecutors

and the defendant aimed at exchanging a plea of guilty from the defendant for concessions by the prosecutors, such as reduction of charges or a request for leniency.

Pleas. See Guilty and Nolo contendere.

Presentment. See Grand jury report.

Prima facie. At first sight; referring to a fact or other evidence presumably sufficient to establish a defense or a claim unless otherwise contradicted.

Probation. Process under which a person convicted of an offense, usually a first offense, receives a suspended sentence and is given his freedom, usually under the guardianship of a probation officer.

Quash. To overthrow, annul, or vacate; as to quash a subpoena.

Recognizance. An obligation entered into before a court or magistrate requiring the performance of a specified act—usually to appear in court at a later date. It is an alternative to bail for pretrial release.

Remand. To send back. In the event of a decision being remanded, it is sent back by a higher court to the court from which it came for further action.

Respondent. One who is compelled to answer the claims or questions posed in court by a petitioner. A defendant and an appellee may be called respondents, but the term also includes those parties who answer in court during actions where charges are not necessarily brought or where the Supreme Court has granted a writ of certiorari.

Seriatim. Separately, individually, one by one.

Stare Decisis. "Let the decision stand." The principle of adherence to settled cases, the doctrine that principles of law established in earlier judicial decisions should be accepted as authoritative in similar subsequent cases.

Statute. A written law enacted by a legislature. A collection of statutes for a particular governmental division is called a code.

Stay. To halt or suspend further judicial proceedings.

Subpoena. An order to present one's self before a grand jury, court, or legislative hearing.

Subpoena duces tecum. An order to produce specified documents or papers.

Tort. An injury or wrong to the person or property of another.

Transactional immunity. Protects a witness from prosecution for any offense mentioned in or related to his testimony, regardless of independent evidence against him.

Trial docket. A calendar prepared by the clerks of the court listing the cases set to be tried.

Use immunity. Protects a witness against the use of his own testimony against him in prosecution.

Vacate. To make void, annul, or rescind.

Writ. A written court order commanding the designated recipient to perform or not perform acts specified in the order.

How to Read a Citation

The official version of Supreme Court decisions and opinions is contained in a series of volumes entitled *United States Reports*, published by the U.S. Government Printing Office.

Although there are several unofficial compilations of Court opinions— *United States Law Week*, published by the Bureau of National Affairs; *Supreme Court Reporter*, published by West Publishing Co.; and *United States Supreme Court Reports, Lawyers' Edition*, published by Lawyers Cooperative Publishing Co.—it is the official record that is generally cited. (An unofficial version or the official slip opinion might be cited if a decision has not yet been officially reported.) A citation to a case includes, in order, the name of the parties to the case, the volume of *United States Reports* in which the decision appears, the page in the volume that the opinion begins on, the page from which any quoted material is taken, and the year the decision was made.

For example, *Colegrove v. Green*, 328 U.S. 549 at 553 (1946) means that the Supreme Court decision and opinion in the case of Colegrove against Green may be found in volume 328 of *United States Reports* beginning on page 549. The specific quotation in question will be found on page 553. The case was decided in 1946.

Reporters of Decisions

Until 1875 the official reports of the Court were published under the names of the Court reporters and it is their names, or abbreviated versions, that appear in cites for those years. A citation such as *Marbury v. Madison*, 1 Cranch 137 (1803) means that the opinion in the case of Marbury against Madison is found in the first volume of reporter Cranch beginning on page 137. (Between 1875 and 1883 a Court reporter named William T. Otto compiled the decisions and opinions; his name appears on the volumes for those years as well as the *United States Reports* volume number, but Otto is seldom cited.)

The titles of the volumes to 1875, the full names of the reporters and the corresponding *United States Reports* volumes are:

1-4	Dall.	Dallas	1-4 U.S.
1-9	Cranch or Cr.	Cranch	5-13 U.S.
1-12	Wheat.	Wheaton	14-25 U.S.
1-16	Pet.	Peters	26-41 U.S.
1-24	How.	Howard	42-65 U.S.
1-2	Black	Black	66-67 U.S.
1-23	Wall.	Wallace	68-90 U.S.

Supreme Court Justices

Following are brief biographies of all the justices of the Supreme Court since 1789. The material is organized in the following order: name; relationship to other government officials; state; date of birth; date of death (if applicable); previous government service; name of nominating president and date of nomination; date of confirmation; date of swearing in (recess appointment noted, if applicable); date of resignation or retirement (in cases where the justice left the Court before death).

The major sources of information for this list were *Congressional Quarterly's Guide to the U.S. Supreme Court* and the United States Supreme Court.

Baldwin, Henry (Pa.) Jan. 14, 1780-April 21, 1844; House 1817-22; nominated by Jackson Jan. 4 1830; confirmed Jan. 6, 1830; sworn in Jan. 18, 1830; served until April 21, 1844.

Barbour, Philip Pendleton (Va.) May 25, 1783-Feb. 25, 1841; House 1814-25, 1827-30, Speaker 1821-23; nominated by Jackson Dec. 28, 1835; confirmed March 15, 1836; sworn in May 12, 1836; served until Feb. 25, 1841.

Black, Hugo Lafayette (Ala.) Feb. 27, 1886-Sept. 25, 1971; Senate 1927-37; nominated by Roosevelt Aug. 8, 1983; confirmed Aug. 17, 1937; sworn in Aug. 19, 1937; resigned Sept. 17, 1971.

Blackmun, Harry Andrew (Minn.) Nov. 12, 1908; nominated by Nixon April 14, 1970; confirmed May 12, 1970; sworn in June 9, 1970.

Blair, John Jr. (Va.) 1732-Aug. 31, 1800; nominated by Washington Sept. 24, 1789; confirmed Sept. 26, 1789; sworn in Feb. 2, 1790; resigned Jan. 27, 1796.

Blatchford, Samuel (N.Y.) March 9, 1820-July 7, 1893; nominated by Arthur March 13, 1882; confirmed March 27, 1882; sworn in April 3, 1882; served until July 7, 1893.

Bradley, Joseph P. (N.J.) March 14, 1813-Jan. 22, 1892; nominated by Grant Feb. 7, 1870; confirmed March 21, 1870; sworn in March 23, 1870; served until Jan. 22, 1892.

Brandeis, Louis Dembitz (Mass.) Nov. 13, 1856-Oct. 5, 1941; nominated by Wilson Jan. 28, 1916; con-firmed June 1, 1916; sworn in June 5, 1916; resigned Feb. 13, 1939.

Brennan, William Joseph Jr. (N.J.) April 25, 1906; nominated by Eisenhower Jan. 14, 1957; confirmed March 19, 1957; sworn in Oct. 16, 1956.

Brewer, David Josiah (nephew of Stephen Johnson Field, below) (Kan.) June 20, 1837-March 28, 1910; nominated by Harrison Dec. 4, 1889; confirmed Dec. 18, 1889; sworn in Jan. 6, 1890; served until March 28, 1910.

Brown, Henry Billings (Mich.) March 2, 1836-Sept. 4, 1913; nominated by Harrison Dec. 23, 1890; confirmed Dec. 29, 1890; sworn in Jan. 5, 1891; resigned May 28, 1906.

Burger, Warren Earl (Minn.) Sept. 17, 1907; nominated by Nixon May 21, 1969; confirmed as Chief Justice June 9, 1969; sworn in June 23, 1969; resigned Sept. 26, 1986.

Burton, Harold Hitz (Ohio) June 22, 1888-Oct. 28, 1964; Senate 1941-45; nominated by Truman Sept. 19, 1945; confirmed Sept. 19, 1945; sworn in Oct. 1, 1945; resigned Oct. 13, 1958.

Butler, Pierce (Minn.) March 17, 1866-Nov. 16, 1939; nominated by Harding, Nov. 23, 1922; confirmed Dec. 21, 1922; sworn in Jan. 2, 1923; served until Nov. 16, 1939.

Byrnes, James Francis (S.C.) May 2, 1879-April 9, 1972; House 1911-25, Senate 1931-41, Secy. of State 1945-47, Gov. 1951-55; nominated by Roosevelt June 12, 1941; confirmed June 12, 1941; sworn in July 8, 1941; resigned Oct. 3, 1942.

Campbell, John Archibald (Ala.) June 24, 1811-March 12, 1889; nominated by Pierce March 22, 1853; confirmed March 25, 1853; sworn in April 11, 1853; resigned April 30, 1861.

Cardozo, Benjamin Nathan (N.Y.) May 24, 1870-July 9, 1938; nominated by Hoover Feb. 15, 1932; confirmed Feb. 24, 1932; sworn in March 14, 1932; served until July 9, 1938.

Catron, John (Tenn.) 1786-May 30, 1865; nominated by Jackson March 3, 1837; confirmed March 8, 1837; sworn in May 1, 1837; served until May 30, 1865.

Chase, Salmon Portland (Ohio) Jan. 13, 1808-May 7, 1873; Senate 1849-55, 1861, Gov. 1856-60, Secy. of the Treasury 1861-64; nominated by Lincoln Dec. 6, 1864; confirmed as Chief Justice Dec. 6, 1864; sworn in Dec. 15, 1864; served until May 7, 1873.

Chase, Samuel (Md.) April 17, 1741-June 19, 1811; Cont. Cong. 1774-78, 1784-85; nominated by Washington Jan. 26, 1896; confirmed Jan. 27, 1796; sworn in Feb. 4, 1796; served until June 19, 1811.

Clark, Thomas Campbell (Texas) Sept. 23, 1899-June 13, 1977; Atty. Gen. 1945-49; nominated by Truman Aug. 2, 1949; confirmed Aug. 18, 1949; sworn in Aug. 24, 1949; resigned June 12, 1967.

Clarke, John Hessin (Ohio) Sept. 18, 1857-March 22, 1945; nominated by Wilson July 14, 1816; confirmed July 24, 1916; sworn in Oct. 9, 1916; resigned Sept. 18, 1922.

Clifford, Nathan (Maine) Aug. 18, 1803-July 25, 1881; House 1839-43, Atty. Gen. 1846-48; nominated by Buchanan Dec. 9, 1957; confirmed Jan. 12, 1858; sworn in Jan. 21, 1858; served until July 25, 1881.

Curtis, Benjamin Robbins (Mass.) Nov. 4, 1809-Sept. 15, 1874; nominated by Fillmore Dec. 11, 1851; confirmed Dec. 29, 1851; sworn in Oct. 10, 1851; resigned Sept. 30, 1857.

Cushing, William (Mass.) March 1, 1732-Sept. 13, 1810; nominated by Washington Sept. 24, 1789; confirmed Sept. 26, 1789; sworn in Feb. 2, 1790; served until Sept. 13, 1810.

Daniel, Peter Vivian (Va.) April 24, 1784-May 31, 1860; nominated by Van Buren Feb. 26, 1841; confirmed March 2, 1841; sworn in Jan. 10, 1842; served until May 31, 1860.

Davis, David (Ill.) March 9, 1815-June 26, 1886; Senate 1877-83, Pres. pro tempore 1881-83; nominated by Lincoln Dec. 1, 1862; confirmed Dec. 8, 1862; sworn in Dec. 10, 1862; resigned March 4, 1877.

Day, William Rufus (Ohio) April 17, 1849-July 9, 1923; Secy. of State 1898; nominated by Roosevelt Feb. 19, 1903; confirmed Feb. 23, 1903; sworn in March 2, 1903; resigned Nov. 13, 1922.

Douglas, William Orville (Conn.) Oct. 16, 1898-Jan. 19, 1980; nominated by Roosevelt March 20, 1939; confirmed April 4, 1939; sworn in April 17, 1939; resigned Nov. 12, 1975.

Duvall, Gabriel (Md.) Dec. 6, 1752-March 6, 1844; House 1794-96; nominated by Madison Nov. 15, 1811; confirmed Nov. 18, 1811; sworn in Nov. 23, 1811; resigned Jan. 14, 1835.

Ellsworth, Oliver (Conn.) April 29, 1745-Nov. 26, 1807; Cont. Cong. 1777-84, Senate 1789-96; nominated by Washington March 3, 1796; confirmed as Chief Justice March 4, 1796; sworn in March 8, 1796; resigned Dec. 15, 1800.

Field, Stephen Johnson (uncle of David Josiah Brewer, above) (Calif.) Nov. 4, 1816-April 9, 1899; nominated by Lincoln March 5, 1863; confirmed March 10, 1863; sworn in May 20, 1863; resigned Dec. 1, 1897.

Fortas, Abe (D.C.) June 19, 1910-April 5, 1982; nominated by Johnson July 28, 1965; confirmed Aug. 11, 1965; sworn in Oct. 4, 1965; resigned May 14, 1969.

Frankfurter, Felix (Mass.) Nov. 15, 1882-Feb. 22, 1965; nominated by Roosevelt Jan. 5, 1939; confirmed Jan. 17, 1939; sworn in Jan. 30, 1939; resigned Aug. 28, 1962.

Fuller, Melville Weston (Ill.) Feb. 11, 1833-July 4, 1910; nominated by Cleveland April 30, 1888; confirmed as Chief Justice July 20, 1888; sworn in Oct. 8, 1888; served until July 4, 1910.

Goldberg, Arthur Joseph (Ill.) Aug. 8, 1908; Secy. of Labor 1961-62; nominated by Kennedy Aug. 29, 1962; confirmed Sept. 25, 1962; sworn in Oct. 1, 1962; resigned July 25, 1965.

Gray, Horace (son-in-law of Stanley Matthews, below) (Mass.) March 24, 1828-Sept. 15, 1902; nominated by Arthur Dec. 19, 1881; confirmed Dec. 20, 1881; sworn in Jan. 9, 1882; resigned July 9, 1902.

Grier, Robert Cooper (Pa.) March 5, 1794-Sept. 25, 1870; nominated by Polk Aug. 3, 1846; confirmed Aug. 4, 1846; sworn in Aug. 10, 1846; resigned Jan. 31, 1870.

Harlan, John Marshall (grandfather of John Marshall Harlan, below) (Ky.) June 1, 1833-Oct. 14, 1911; nominated by Hayes Oct. 17, 1877; confirmed Nov. 29, 1877; sworn in Dec. 10, 1877; served until Oct. 14, 1911.

Harlan, John Marshall (grandson of John Marshall Harlan, above) (N.Y.) May 20, 1899-Dec. 29, 1971; nominated by Eisenhower Jan. 10, 1955; confirmed March 16, 1955; sworn in March 28, 1955; resigned Sept. 23, 1971.

Holmes, Oliver Wendell Jr. (Mass.) March 8, 1841-March 6, 1935; nominated by Roosevelt Dec. 2, 1902; confirmed Dec. 4, 1902; sworn in Dec. 8, 1902; resigned Jan. 12, 1932.

Hughes, Charles Evans (N.Y.) April 11, 1862-Aug. 27, 1948; Gov. 1907-10, Secy. of State 1921-25; nominated by Taft April 25, 1910; confirmed May 2, 1910; sworn in Oct. 10, 1910; resigned June 10, 1916; nominated by Hoover Feb. 3, 1930; confirmed as Chief Justice Feb. 13, 1930; sworn in Feb. 24, 1930; resigned July 1, 1941.

Hunt, Ward (N.Y.) June 14, 1810-March 24, 1886; nominated by Grant Dec. 3, 1872; confirmed Dec. 11, 1872; sworn in Jan. 9, 1873; resigned Jan. 27, 1882.

Iredell, James (N.C.) Oct. 5, 1751-Oct. 20, 1799; nominated by Washington Feb. 8, 1790; confirmed Feb. 10, 1790; sworn in May 12, 1790; served until Oct. 20, 1799.

Jackson, Howell Edmunds (Tenn.) April 8, 1832-Aug. 8, 1895; Senate 1881-86; nominated by Harrison Feb. 2, 1893; confirmed Feb. 18, 1893; sworn in March 4, 1893; served until Aug. 8, 1895.

Jackson, Robert Houghwout (N.Y.) Feb. 13, 1892-Oct. 9, 1954; Atty. Gen. 1940-41; nominated by Roosevelt June 12, 1941; confirmed July 7, 1941; sworn in July 11, 1941; served until Oct. 9, 1954.

Jay, John (brother-in-law of Henry Brockholst Livingston, below) (N.Y.) Dec. 12, 1745-May 17, 1829; Cont. Cong. 1774-75, 1777, 1778-79 (president), Secy. of Foreign Affairs 1784-89, Gov. 1795-1801; nominated by Washington Sept. 24, 1789; confirmed as Chief Justice Sept. 26, 1789; sworn in Oct. 19, 1789; resigned June 29, 1795.

Johnson, Thomas (Md.) Nov. 4, 1732-Oct. 26, 1819; Cont. Cong. 1774-77; nominated by Washington Nov. 1, 1791; confirmed Nov. 7, 1791; sworn in Aug. 6, 1792; resigned Feb. 1, 1793.

Johnson, William (S.C.) Dec. 27, 1771-Aug. 4, 1834; nominated by Jefferson March 22, 1804; confirmed March

24, 1804; sworn in May 7, 1804; served until Aug. 4, 1834.

Kennedy, Anthony (Calif.) July 23, 1936; nominated by Reagan Nov. 30, 1987; confirmed Feb. 3, 1988; sworn in Feb. 18, 1988.

Lamar, Joseph Rucker (cousin of Lucius Quintus Cincinnatus Lamar, below) (Miss.) Oct. 14, 1857-Jan. 2, 1916; nominated by Taft Dec. 12, 1910; confirmed Dec. 15, 1910; sworn in Jan. 3, 1911; served until Jan. 2, 1916.

Lamar, Lucius Quintus Cincinnatus (cousin of Joseph Rucker Lamar, above) (Miss.) Sept. 17, 1825-Jan. 23, 1893; House 1857-60, 1873-77, Senate 1877-85, Secy. of the Interior 1885-88; nominated by Cleveland Dec. 6, 1887; confirmed Jan. 16, 1888; sworn in Jan. 18, 1888; served until Jan. 23, 1893.

Livingston, Henry Brockholst (brother-in-law of John Jay, above, father-in-law of Smith Thompson, below) (N.Y.) Nov. 25, 1757-March 18, 1823; nominated by Jefferson Dec. 13, 1806; confirmed Dec. 17, 1806; sworn in Jan. 20, 1807; served until March 18, 1823.

Lurton, Horace Harmon (Tenn.) Feb. 26, 1844-July 12, 1914; nominated by Taft Dec. 13, 1909; confirmed Dec. 20, 1909; sworn in Jan. 3, 1910; served until July 12, 1914.

Marshall, John (Va.) Sept. 24, 1755-July 6, 1835; House 1799-1800, Secy. of State, 1800-01; nominated by Adams Jan. 20, 1801; confirmed as Chief Justice Jan. 27, 1801; sworn in Feb. 4, 1801; served until July 6, 1835.

Marshall, Thurgood (N.Y.) July 2, 1908; nominated by Johnson June 13, 1967; confirmed Aug. 30, 1967; sworn in Oct. 2, 1967.

Matthews, Stanley (father-in-law of Horace Gray, above) (Ohio) July 21, 1824-March 22, 1889; Senate 1877-79; nominated by Garfield March 14, 1881; confirmed May 12, 1881; sworn in May 17, 1881; served until March 22, 1889.

McKenna, Joseph (Calif.) Aug. 10, 1843-Nov. 21, 1926; House 1885-92, Atty. Gen. 1897-98; nominated by McKinley Dec. 16, 1897; confirmed Jan. 21, 1898; sworn in Jan. 26, 1898; resigned Jan. 5, 1925.

McKinley, John (Ala.) May 1, 1780-July 19, 1852; Senate 1826-31, 1837, House 1833-35; nominated by Van Buren Sept. 18, 1837; confirmed Sept. 25, 1837; sworn in Jan. 9, 1838; served until July 19, 1852.

McLean, John (Ohio) March 11, 1785-April 4, 1861; House 1813-16, Postmaster Gen. 1823-29; nominated by Jackson March 6, 1829; confirmed March 7, 1829; sworn in Jan. 11, 1830; served until April 4, 1861.

McReynolds, James Clark (Tenn.) Feb. 3, 1862-Aug. 24, 1946; Atty. Gen. 1913-14; nominated by Wilson Aug. 19, 1914; confirmed Aug. 29, 1914; sworn in Oct. 12, 1914; resigned Jan. 31, 1941.

Miller, Samuel Freeman (Iowa) April 5, 1816-Oct. 13, 1890; nominated by Lincoln July 16, 1862; confirmed July 16, 1862; sworn in July 21, 1862; served until Oct. 13, 1890.

Minton, Sherman (Ind.) Oct. 20, 1890-April 9, 1965; Senate 1935-41; nominated by Truman Sept. 15, 1949; confirmed Oct. 4, 1949; sworn in Oct. 12, 1949; resigned Oct. 15, 1956.

Moody, William Henry (Mass.) Dec. 23, 1853-July 2, 1917; House 1895-1902, Secy. of the Navy 1902-04, Atty. Gen. 1904-06; nominated by Roosevelt Dec. 3, 1906; con-

firmed Dec. 12, 1906; sworn in Dec. 17, 1906; resigned Nov. 20, 1910.

Moore, Alfred (N.C.) May 21, 1755-Oct. 15, 1810; nominated by Adams Dec. 6, 1799; confirmed Dec. 10, 1799; sworn in April 21, 1800; resigned Jan. 26, 1804.

Murphy, Francis William (Mich.) April 13, 1890-July 19, 1949; Gov. 1937-39, Atty. Gen. 1939; nominated by Roosevelt Jan. 4, 1940; confirmed Jan. 15, 1940; sworn in Feb. 5, 1940; served until July 19, 1949.

Nelson, Samuel (N.Y.) Nov. 10, 1792-Dec. 13, 1873; nominated by Tyler Feb. 4, 1845; confirmed Feb. 14, 1845; sworn in Feb. 27, 1845; resigned Nov. 28, 1872.

O'Connor, Sandra Day (Ariz.) March 26, 1930; nominated by Reagan Aug. 19, 1981; confirmed Sept. 21, 1981; sworn in Sept. 25, 1981.

Paterson, William (N.J.) Dec. 24, 1745-Sept. 9, 1806; Cont. Cong. 1780-81, 1787, Senate 1789-90, Gov. 1790-93; nominated by Washington March 4, 1793; confirmed March 4, 1793; sworn in March 11, 1793; served until Sept. 9, 1806.

Peckham, Rufus Wheeler (N.Y.) Nov. 8, 1838-Oct. 24, 1909; nominated by Cleveland Dec. 3, 1895; confirmed Dec. 9, 1895; sworn in Jan. 6, 1896; served until Oct. 24, 1909.

Pitney, Mahlon (N.J.) Feb. 5, 1858-Dec. 9, 1924; House 1895-99; nominated by Taft Feb. 19, 1912; confirmed March 13, 1912; sworn in March 18, 1912; resigned Dec. 31, 1922.

Powell, Lewis Franklin Jr. (Va.) Sept. 19, 1907; nominated by Nixon Oct. 21, 1971; confirmed Dec. 6, 1971; sworn in Jan. 7, 1972; resigned June 26, 1987.

Reed, Stanley Forman (Ky.) Dec. 31, 1884-April 2, 1980; nominated by Roosevelt Jan. 15, 1938; confirmed Jan. 25, 1938; sworn in Jan. 31, 1938; resigned Feb. 25, 1957.

Rehnquist, William Hubbs (Ariz.) Oct. 1, 1924; nominated by Nixon Oct. 21, 1971; confirmed Dec. 10, 1971; sworn in Jan. 7, 1972; nominated as Chief Justice by Reagan June 20, 1986; confirmed as Chief Justice Sept. 17, 1986; sworn in Sept. 26, 1986.

Roberts, Owen Josephus (Pa.) May 2, 1875-May 17, 1955; nominated by Hoover May 9, 1930; confirmed May 20, 1930; sworn in June 2, 1930; resigned July 31, 1945.

Rutledge, John (S.C.) June 1739-June 21, 1800; Cont. Cong. 1774-76, 1782-83; nominated by Washington Sept. 24, 1789; confirmed Sept. 26, 1789; sworn in May 12, 1790; resigned March 5, 1791; sworn in as Chief Justice Aug. 12, 1795 (recess appointment not confirmed, service terminated Dec. 15, 1795).

Rutledge, Wiley Blount (Iowa) July 20, 1894-Sept. 10, 1949; nominated by Roosevelt, Jan. 11, 1943; confirmed Feb. 8, 1943; sworn in Feb. 15, 1943; served until Sept. 10, 1949.

Sanford, Edward Terry (Tenn.) July 23, 1865-March 8, 1930; nominated by Harding Jan. 24, 1923; confirmed Jan. 29, 1923; sworn in Feb. 19, 1923; served until March 8, 1930.

Scalia, Antonin (D.C.) March 11, 1936; nominated by Reagan June 24, 1986; confirmed Sept. 17, 1986; sworn in Sept. 26, 1986.

Shiras, George Jr. (Pa.) January 26, 1832-Aug. 2, 1924; nominated by Harrison July 19, 1892; confirmed July 26, 1892; sworn in Oct. 10, 1892; resigned Feb. 23, 1903.

Stevens, John Paul (Ill.) April 20, 1920; nominated by Ford Nov. 28, 1975; confirmed Dec. 17, 1975; sworn in Dec. 19, 1975.

Stewart, Potter (Ohio) Jan. 23, 1915-Dec. 7, 1985; nominated by Eisenhower Jan. 17, 1959; confirmed May 5, 1959; sworn in Oct. 14, 1958 (recess appointment); resigned July 3, 1981.

Stone, Harlan Fiske (N.Y.) Oct. 11, 1872-April 22, 1946; Atty. Gen. 1924-25; nominated by Coolidge Jan. 5, 1925; confirmed Feb. 5, 1925; sworn in March 2, 1925; nominated as Chief Justice by Roosevelt July 2, 1941; confirmed as Chief Justice June 27, 1941; sworn in July 3, 1941; served until April 22, 1946.

Story, Joseph (Mass.) Sept. 18, 1779-Sept. 10, 1845; House 1808-09; nominated by Madison Nov. 15, 1811; confirmed Nov. 18, 1811; sworn in Feb. 3, 1812; served until Sept. 10, 1845.

Strong, William (Pa.) May 6, 1808-Aug. 19, 1895; House 1847-51; nominated by Grant Feb. 7, 1870; confirmed Feb. 18, 1870; sworn in March 14, 1870; resigned Dec. 14, 1880.

Sutherland, George (Utah) March 25, 1862-July 18, 1942; House 1901-03, Senate 1905-17; nominated by Harding Sept. 5, 1922; confirmed Sept. 5, 1922; sworn in Oct. 2, 1922; resigned Jan. 17, 1938.

Swayne, Noah Haynes (Ohio) Dec. 7, 1804-June 8, 1884; nominated by Lincoln Jan. 21, 1862; confirmed Jan. 24, 1862; sworn in Jan. 27, 1862; resigned Jan. 24, 1881.

Taft, William Howard (brother of Rep. Charles Phelps Taft, father of Sen. Robert Alphonso Taft, grandfather of Sen. Robert Taft, Jr.) (Ohio) Sept. 15, 1857-March 8, 1930; Gov. (prov.) 1901-04 (Philippines), Secy. of War 1904-08, President 1909-13; nominated by Harding June 30, 1921; confirmed as Chief Justice June 30, 1921; sworn in July 11, 1921; resigned Feb. 3, 1930.

Taney, Roger Brooke (Md.) March 17, 1777-Oct. 12, 1864; Atty. Gen. 1831-33, Acting Secy. of War 1831, Acting Secy. of the Treasury 1833-34; nominated by Jackson Dec. 28, 1835; confirmed as Chief Justice March 15, 1836; sworn in March 28, 1836; served until Oct. 12, 1864.

Thompson, Smith (son-in-law of Henry Brockholst Livingston, above) (N.Y.) Jan. 17, 1768-Dec. 18, 1843; Secy. of Navy, 1819-23; nominated by Monroe Dec. 8, 1923; confirmed Dec. 19, 1823; sworn in Sept. 1, 1823 (recess appointment); served until Dec. 18, 1843.

Todd, Thomas (Ky.) Jan. 23, 1765-Feb. 7, 1826; nominated by Jefferson Feb. 28, 1807; confirmed March 3, 1807; sworn in May 4, 1807; served until Feb. 7, 1826.

Trimble, Robert (Ky.) Nov. 17, 1776-Aug. 25, 1828; nominated by Adams April 11, 1826; confirmed May 9, 1826; sworn in June 16, 1826; served until Aug. 25, 1828.

Van Devanter, Willis (Wyo.) April 17, 1859-Feb. 8, 1941; Atty. Gen. 1897-1903; nominated by Taft Dec. 12, 1910; confirmed Dec. 15, 1910; sworn in Jan. 3, 1911; resigned June 2, 1937.

Vinson, Frederick Moore (Ky.) Jan. 22, 1890-Sept. 8, 1953; House 1924-29, 1931-38, Secy. of the Treasury 1945-46; nominated by Truman June 6, 1946; confirmed as Chief Justice June 20, 1946; sworn in June 24, 1946; served until Sept. 8, 1953.

Waite, Morrison Remick (Ohio) Nov. 29, 1816-March 23, 1888; nominated by Grant Jan. 19, 1874; confirmed as Chief Justice Jan. 21, 1874; sworn in March 4, 1874; served until March 23, 1888.

Warren, Earl (Calif.) March 19, 1891-July 9, 1974; Gov. 1943-53; nominated by Eisenhower Sept. 30, 1953; confirmed as Chief Justice March 1, 1954; sworn in Oct. 5, 1953 (recess appointment); resigned June 23, 1969.

Washington, Bushrod (nephew of George Washington) (Va.) June 5, 1762-Nov. 26, 1829; nominated by Adams Dec. 19, 1798; confirmed Dec. 20, 1798; sworn in Feb. 4, 1799; served until Nov. 26, 1829.

Wayne, James Moore (Ga.) 1790-July 5, 1867; House 1829-35; nominated by Jackson Jan. 7, 1835; confirmed Jan. 9, 1835; sworn in Jan. 14, 1835; served until July 5, 1867.

White, Byron Raymond (Colo.) June 8, 1917; nominated by Kennedy March 30, 1962; confirmed April 11, 1962; sworn in April 16, 1962.

White, Edward Douglass (La.) Nov. 3, 1845-May 19, 1921; Senate 1891-94; nominated by Cleveland Feb. 19, 1894; confirmed Feb. 19, 1894; sworn in March 12, 1894; nominated as Chief Justice by Taft Dec. 12, 1910; confirmed as Chief Justice Dec. 12, 1910, sworn in Dec. 19, 1910; served until May 19, 1921.

Whittaker, Charles Evans (Mo.) Feb. 22, 1901-Nov. 26, 1973; nominated by Eisenhower March 2, 1957; confirmed March 19, 1957; sworn in March 25, 1957; resigned March 31, 1962.

Wilson, James (Pa.) Sept. 14, 1742-Aug. 21, 1798; Cont. Cong. 1775-77, 1783, 1785-87; nominated by Washington Sept. 24, 1789; confirmed Sept. 26, 1789; sworn in Oct. 5, 1789; served until Aug. 21, 1798.

Woodbury, Levi (N.H.) Dec. 22, 1789-Sept. 4, 1851; Gov. 1823-24, Senate 1825-31, 1841-45; Secy. of the Navy 1831-34; Secy. of the Treasury 1834-41; nominated by Polk Dec. 23, 1845; confirmed Jan. 3, 1846; sworn in Sept. 23, 1845; served until Sept. 4, 1851.

Woods, William Burnham (Ga.) Aug. 3, 1824-May 14, 1887; nominated by Hayes Dec. 15, 1880; confirmed Dec. 21, 1880; sworn in Jan. 5, 1881; served until May 14, 1887.

Constitution of the United States

We the People of the United States, in Order to form a more perfect Union, establish Justice, insure domestic Tranquility, provide for the common defence, promote the general Welfare, and secure the Blessings of Liberty to ourselves and our Posterity, do ordain and establish this Constitution for the United States of America.

Article I

Section 1. All legislative Powers herein granted shall be vested in a Congress of the United States, which shall consist of a Senate and House of Representatives.

Section 2. The House of Representatives shall be composed of Members chosen every second Year by the People of the several States, and the Electors in each State shall have the Qualifications requisite for Electors of the most numerous Branch of the State Legislature.

No Person shall be a Representative who shall not have attained to the age of twenty five Years, and been seven Years a Citizen of the United States, and who shall not, when elected, be an Inhabitant of that State in which he shall be chosen.

[Representatives and direct Taxes shall be apportioned among the several States which may be included within this Union, according to their respective Numbers, which shall be determined by adding to the whole Number of free Persons, including those bound to Service for a Term of Years, and excluding Indians not taxed, three fifths of all other Persons.][1] The actual Enumeration shall be made within three Years after the first Meeting of the Congress of the United States, and within every subsequent Term of ten Years, in such Manner as they shall by Law direct. The Number of Representatives shall not exceed one for every thirty Thousand, but each State shall have at Least one Representative; and until such enumeration shall be made, the State of New Hampshire shall be entitled to chuse three, Massachusetts eight, Rhode-Island and Providence Plantations one, Connecticut five, New-York six, New Jersey four, Pennsylvania eight, Delaware one, Maryland six, Virginia ten, North Carolina five, South Carolina five, and Georgia three.

When vacancies happen in the Representation from any State, the Executive Authority thereof shall issue Writs of Election to fill such Vacancies.

The House of Representatives shall chuse their Speaker and other Officers; and shall have the sole Power of Impeachment.

Section 3. The Senate of the United States shall be composed of two Senators from each State, [chosen by the Legislature thereof,][2] for six Years; and each Senator shall have one Vote.

Immediately after they shall be assembled in Consequence of the first Election, they shall be divided as equally as may be into three Classes. The Seats of the Senators of the first Class shall be vacated at the Expiration of the second Year, of the second Class at the Expiration of the fourth Year, and of the third Class at the Expiration of the sixth Year, so that one third may be chosen every second Year; [and if Vacancies happen by Resignation, or otherwise, during the Recess of the Legislature of any State, the Executive thereof may make temporary Appointments until the next Meeting of the Legislature, which shall then fill such Vacancies.][3]

No Person shall be a Senator who shall not have attained to the Age of thirty Years, and been nine Years a Citizen of the United States, and who shall not, when elected, be an Inhabitant of that State for which he shall be chosen.

The Vice President of the United States shall be President of the Senate, but shall have no Vote, unless they be equally divided.

The Senate shall chuse their other Officers, and also a President pro tempore, in the Absence of the Vice President, or when he shall exercise the Office of President of the United States.

The Senate shall have the sole Power to try all Impeachments. When sitting for that Purpose, they shall be on Oath or Affirmation. When the President of the United States is tried the Chief Justice shall preside: And no Person shall be convicted without the Concurrence of two thirds of the Members present.

Judgment in Cases of Impeachment shall not extend further than to removal from Office, and disqualification to hold and enjoy any Office of honor, Trust or Profit under the United States: but the Party convicted shall nevertheless be liable and subject to Indictment, Trial, Judgment and Punishment, according to Law.

Section 4. The Times, Places and Manner of holding Elections for Senators and Representatives, shall be prescribed in each State by the Legislature thereof; but the Congress may at any time by Law make or alter such Regulations, except as to the Places of chusing Senators.

The Congress shall assemble at least once in every Year, and such Meeting shall [be on the first Monday in December],⁴ unless they shall by Law appoint a different Day.

Section 5. Each House shall be the Judge of the Elections, Returns and Qualifications of its own Members, and a Majority of each shall constitute a Quorum to do Business; but a smaller Number may adjourn from day to day, and may be authorized to compel the Attendance of absent Members, in such Manner, and under such Penalties as each House may provide.

Each House may determine the Rules of its Proceedings, punish its Members for disorderly Behaviour, and, with the Concurrence of two thirds, expel a Member.

Each House shall keep a Journal of its Proceedings, and from time to time publish the same, excepting such Parts as may in their Judgment require Secrecy; and the Yeas and Nays of the Members of either House on any question shall, at the Desire of one fifth of those Present, be entered on the Journal.

Neither House, during the Session of Congress, shall, without the Consent of the other, adjourn for more than three days, nor to any other Place than that in which the two Houses shall be sitting.

Section 6. The Senators and Representatives shall receive a Compensation for their Services, to be ascertained by Law, and paid out of the Treasury of the United States. They shall in all Cases, except Treason, Felony and Breach of the Peace, be privileged from Arrest during their Attendance at the Session of their respective Houses, and in going to and returning from the same; and for any Speech or Debate in either House, they shall not be questioned in any other Place.

No Senator or Representative shall, during the Time for which he was elected, be appointed to any civil Office under the Authority of the United States, which shall have been created, or the Emoluments whereof shall have been encreased during such time; and no Person holding any Office under the United States, shall be a Member of either House during his Continuance in Office.

Section 7. All Bills for raising Revenue shall originate in the House of Representatives; but the Senate may propose or concur with amendments as on other Bills.

Every Bill which shall have passed the House of Representatives and the Senate, shall, before it become a Law, be presented to the President of the United States; If he approve he shall sign it, but if not he shall return it, with his Objections to that House in which it shall have originated, who shall enter the Objections at large on their Journal, and proceed to reconsider it. If after such Reconsideration two thirds of that House shall agree to pass the Bill, it shall be sent, together with the Objections, to the other House, by which it shall likewise be reconsidered, and if approved by two thirds of that House, it shall become a Law. But in all such Cases the Votes of both Houses shall be determined by yeas and Nays, and the Names of the Persons voting for and against the Bill shall be entered on the Journal of each House respectively. If any Bill shall not be returned by the President within ten Days (Sundays excepted) after it shall have been presented to him, the Same shall be a Law, in like Manner as if he had signed it, unless the Congress by their Adjournment prevent its Return, in which Case it shall not be a Law.

Every Order, Resolution, or Vote to which the Concurrence of the Senate and House of Representatives may be necessary (except on a question of Adjournment) shall be presented to the President of the United States; and before the Same shall take Effect, shall be approved by him, or being disapproved by him, shall be repassed by two thirds of the Senate and House of Representatives, according to the Rules and Limitations prescribed in the Case of a Bill.

Section 8. The Congress shall have Power To lay and collect Taxes, Duties, Imposts and Excises, to pay the Debts and provide for the common Defence and general Welfare of the United States; but all Duties, Imposts and Excises shall be uniform throughout the United States;

To borrow Money on the credit of the United States;

To regulate Commerce with foreign Nations, and among the several States, and with the Indian Tribes;

To establish an uniform Rule of Naturalization, and uniform Laws on the subject of Bankruptcies throughout the United States;

To coin Money, regulate the Value thereof, and of foreign Coin, and fix the Standard of Weights and Measures;

To provide for the Punishment of counterfeiting the Securities and current Coin of the United States;

To establish Post Offices and post Roads;

To promote the Progress of Science and useful Arts, by securing for limited Times to Authors and Inventors the exclusive Right to their respective Writings and Discoveries;

To constitute Tribunals inferior to the supreme Court;

To define and punish Piracies and Felonies commited on the high Seas, and Offences against the Law of Nations;

To declare War, grant Letters of Marque and Reprisal,and make Rules concerning Captures on Land and Water;

To raise and support Armies, but no Appropriation of Money to that Use shall be for a longer Term than two Years;

To provide and maintain a Navy;

To make Rules for the Government and Regulation of the land and naval Forces;

To provide for calling forth the Militia to execute the Laws of the Union, suppress Insurrections and repel Invasions;

To provide for organizing, arming, and disciplining, the Militia, and for governing such Part of them as may be employed in the Service of the United States, reserving to the States respectively, the Appointment of the Officers, and the Authority of training the Militia according to the discipline prescribed by Congress;

To exercise exclusive Legislation in all Cases whatsoever, over such District (not exceeding ten Miles square) as may, by Cession of Particular States, and the Acceptance of Congress, become the Seat of the Government of the United States, and to exercise like Authority over all Places purchased by the Consent of the Legislature of the State in which the Same shall be, for the Erection of Forts, Magazines, Arsenals, dock-Yards, and other needful Buildings;—And

To make all Laws which shall be necessary and proper for carrying into Execution the foregoing Powers, and all other Powers vested by this Constitution in the Government of the United States, or in any Department or Officer thereof.

Section 9. The Migration or Importation of such Persons as any of the States now existing shall think proper to admit, shall not be prohibited by the Congress prior to the Year one thousand eight hundred and eight, but a Tax or duty may be imposed on such Importation, not exceeding ten dollars for each Person.

The Privilege of the Writ of Habeas Corpus shall not be suspended, unless when in Cases of Rebellion or Invasion the public Safety may require it.

No Bill of Attainder or ex post facto Law shall be passed.

No capitation, or other direct, Tax shall be laid, unless in Proportion to the Census of Enumeration herein before directed to be taken.[5]

No Tax or Duty shall be laid on Articles exported from any State.

No Preference shall be given by any Regulation of Commerce or Revenue to the Ports of one State over those of another; nor shall Vessels bound to, or from, one State, be obliged to enter, clear or pay Duties in another.

No Money shall be drawn from the Treasury, but in Consequence of Appropriations made by Law; and a regular Statement and Account of the Receipts and Expenditures of all public Money shall be published from time to time.

No Title of Nobility shall be granted by the United States: And no Person holding any Office of Profit or Trust under them, shall, without the Consent of the Congress, accept of any present, Emolument, Office, or Title, of any kind whatever, from any King, Prince or foreign State.

Section 10. No State shall enter into any Treaty, Alliance, or Confederation; grant Letters of Marque and Reprisal; coin Money; emit Bills of Credit; make any Thing but gold and silver Coin a Tender in Payment of Debts; pass any Bill of Attainder, ex post facto Law, or Law impairing the Obligation of Contracts, or grant any Title of Nobility.

No State shall, without the Consent of the Congress, lay any Imposts or Duties on Imports or Exports, except what may be absolutely necessary for executing it's inspection Laws: and the net Produce of all Duties and Imposts, laid by any State on Imports or Exports, shall be for the Use of the Treasury of the United States; and all such Laws shall be subject to the Revision and Controul of the Congress.

No State shall, without the Consent of Congress, lay any Duty of Tonnage, keep Troops, or Ships of War in time of Peace, enter into any Agreement or Compact with another State, or with a foreign Power, or engage in War, unless actually invaded, or in such imminent Danger as will not admit of delay.

Article II

Section 1. The executive Power shall be vested in a President of the United States of America. He shall hold his Office during the Term of four Years, and, together with the Vice President, chosen for the same Term, be elected, as follows.

Each State shall appoint, in such Manner as the Legislature thereof may direct, a Number of Electors, equal to the whole Number of Senators and Representatives to which the State may be entitled in the Congress: but no Senator or Representative, or Person holding an Office of Trust or Profit under the United States, shall be appointed an Elector.

[The Electors shall meet in their respective States, and vote by Ballot for two Persons, of whom one at least shall not be an Inhabitant of the same State with themselves. And they shall make a List of all the Persons voted for, and of the Number of Votes for each; which List they shall sign and certify, and transmit sealed to the Seat of the Government of the United States, directed to the President of the Senate. The President of the Senate shall, in the Presence of the Senate and House of Representatives, open all the Certificates, and the Votes shall then be counted. The Person having the greatest Number of Votes shall be the President, if such Number be a Majority of the whole Number of Electors appointed; and if there be more than one who have such Majority, and have an equal Number of Votes, then the House of Representatives shall immediately chuse by Ballot one of them for President; and if no Person have a Majority, then from the five highest on the list the said House shall in like Manner chuse the President. But in chusing the President, the Votes shall be taken by States, the Representation from each State having one Vote; a quorum for this Purpose shall consist of a Member or Members from two thirds of the States, and a Majority of all the States shall be necessary to a Choice. In every Case, after the Choice of the President, the Person having the greatest Number of Votes of the Electors shall be the Vice President. But if there should remain two or more who have equal Votes, the Senate shall chuse from them by Ballot the Vice President.][6]

The Congress may determine the Time of chusing the Electors, and the Day on which they shall give their Votes; which Day shall be the same throughout the United States.

No Person except a natural born Citizen, or a Citizen of the United States, at the time of the Adoption of this Constitution, shall be eligible to the Office of President; neither shall any Person be eligible to that Office who shall not have attained to the Age of thirty five Years, and been fourteen Years a Resident within the United States.

In Case of the Removal of the President from Office, or of his Death, Resignation, or Inability to discharge the Powers and Duties of the said Office,[7] the Same shall devolve on the Vice President, and the Congress may by Law provide for the Case of Removal, Death, Resignation or Inability, both of the President and Vice President, declaring what Officer shall then act as President, and such Officer shall act accordingly, until the Disability be removed, or a President shall be elected.

The President shall, at stated Times, receive for his Services, a Compensation, which shall neither be encreased nor diminished during the Period for which he shall have been elected, and he shall not receive within that Period any other Emolument from the United States, or any of them.

Before he enter on the Execution of his Office, he shall take the following Oath or Affirmation:—"I do solemnly swear (or affirm) that I will faithfully execute the Office of President of the United States, and will to the best of my

Ability, preserve, protect and defend the Constitution of the United States."

Section 2. The President shall be Commander in Chief of the Army and Navy of the United States, and of the Militia of the several States, when called into the actual Service of the United States; he may require the Opinion, in writing, of the principal Officer in each of the executive Departments, upon any Subject relating to the Duties of their respective Offices, and he shall have Power to grant Reprieves and Pardons for Offenses against the United States, except in Cases of Impeachment.

He shall have Power, by and with the Advice and Consent of the Senate, to make Treaties, provided two thirds of the Senators present concur; and he shall nominate, and by and with the Advice and Consent of the Senate, shall appoint Ambassadors, other public Ministers and Consuls, Judges of the supreme Court, and all other Officers of the United States, whose Appointments are not herein otherwise provided for, and which shall be established by Law: but the Congress may by Law vest the Appointment of such inferior Officers, as they think proper, in the President alone, in the Courts of Law, or in the Heads of Departments.

The President shall have Power to fill up all Vacancies that may happen during the Recess of the Senate, by granting Commissions which shall expire at the End of their next Session.

Section 3. He shall from time to time give to the Congress Information of the State of the Union, and recommend to their Consideration such Measures as he shall judge necessary and expedient; he may, on extraordinary Occasions, convene both Houses, or either of them, and in Case of Disagreement between them, with Respect to the Time of Adjournment, he may adjourn them to such Time as he shall think proper; he shall receive Ambassadors and other public Ministers; he shall take Care that the Laws be faithfully executed, and shall Commission all the Officers of the United States.

Section 4. The President, Vice President and all Civil Officers of the United States, shall be removed from office on Impeachment for, and Conviction of, Treason, Bribery, or other high Crimes and Misdemeanors.

Article III

Section 1. The judicial Power of the United States, shall be vested in one supreme Court, and in such inferior Courts as the Congress may from time to time ordain and establish. The Judges, both of the supreme and inferior Courts, shall hold their Offices during good Behaviour, and shall, at stated Times, receive for their Services, a Compensation, which shall not be diminished during their Continuance in Office.

Section 2. The judicial Power shall extend to all Cases, in Law and Equity, arising under this Constitution, the Laws of the United States, and Treaties made, or which shall be made, under their Authority;—to all Cases affecting Ambassadors, other public Ministers and Consuls;—to all Cases of admiralty and maritime Jurisdiction;—to Controversies to which the United States shall be a Party;—to Controversies between two or more States;—between a State and Citizens of another State;[8]—between Citizens of

different States;—between Citizens of the same State claiming Lands under Grants of different States, and between a State, or the Citizens thereof, and foreign States, Citizens or Subjects.[8]

In all Cases affecting Ambassadors, other public Ministers and Consuls, and those in which a State shall be Party, the supreme Court shall have original Jurisdiction. In all the other Cases before mentioned, the supreme Court shall have appellate Jurisdiction, both as to Law and Fact, with such Exceptions, and under such Regulations as the Congress shall make.

The Trial of all Crimes, except in cases of Impeachment, shall be by Jury; and such Trial shall be held in the State where the said Crimes shall have been committed; but when not committed within any State, the Trial shall be at such Place or Places as the Congress may by Law have directed.

Section 3. Treason against the United States, shall consist only in levying War against them, or in adhering to their Enemies, giving them Aid and Comfort. No Person shall be convicted of Treason unless on the Testimony of two Witnesses to the same overt Act, or on Confession in open Court.

The Congress shall have Power to declare the Punishment of Treason, but no Attainder of Treason shall work Corruption of Blood, or Forfeiture except during the Life of the Person attainted.

Article IV

Section 1. Full Faith and Credit shall be given in each State to the public Acts, Records, and judicial Proceedings of every other State. And the Congress may by general Laws prescribe the Manner in which such Acts, Records and Proceedings shall be proved, and the Effect thereof.

Section 2. The Citizens of each State shall be entitled to all Privileges and Immunities of Citizens in the several States.

A Person charged in any State with Treason, Felony, or other Crime, who shall flee from Justice, and be found in another State, shall on Demand of the executive Authority of the State from which he fled, be delivered up, to be removed to the State having Jurisdiction of the Crime.

[No Person held to Service or Labour in one State, under the Laws thereof, escaping into another, shall, in Consequence of any Law or Regulation therein, be discharged from such Service or Labour, but shall be delivered up on Claim of the Party to whom such Service or Labour may be due.][9]

Section 3. New States may be admitted by the Congress into this Union; but no new State shall be formed or erected within the Jurisdiction of any other State; nor any State be formed by the Junction of two or more States, or Parts of States, without the Consent of the Legislatures of the States concerned as well as of the Congress.

The Congress shall have Power to dispose of and make all needful Rules and Regulations respecting the Territory or other Property belonging to the United States; and nothing in this Constitution shall be so construed as to Prejudice any Claims of the United States, or of any particular State.

Section 4. The United States shall guarantee to every State in this Union a Republican Form of Government, and shall protect each of them against Invasion; and on Application of the Legislature, or of the Executive (when the Legislature cannot be convened) against domestic Violence.

Article V

The Congress, whenever two thirds of both Houses shall deem it necessary, shall propose Amendments to this Constitution, or, on the Application of the Legislatures of two thirds of the several States, shall call a Convention for proposing Amendments, which, in either Case, shall be valid to all Intents and Purposes, as Part of this Constitution, when ratified by the Legislatures of three fourths of the several States, or by Conventions in three fourths thereof, as the one or the other Mode of Ratification may be proposed by the Congress; Provided [that no Amendment which may be made prior to the Year One thousand eight hundred and eight shall in any Manner affect the first and fourth Clauses in the Ninth Section of the first Article; and][10] that no State, without its Consent, shall be deprived of its equal Suffrage in the Senate.

Article VI

All Debts contracted and Engagements entered into, before the Adoption of this Constitution, shall be as valid against the United States under this Constitution, as under the Confederation.

This Constitution, and the Laws of the United States which shall be made in Pursuance thereof; and all Treaties made, or which shall be made, under the Authority of the United States, shall be the supreme Law of the Land; and the Judges in every State shall be bound thereby, any Thing in the Constitution or Laws of any State to the Contrary notwithstanding.

The Senators and Representatives before mentioned, and the Members of the several State Legislatures, and all executive and judicial Officers, both of the United States and of the several States, shall be bound by Oath or Affirmation, to support this Constitution; but no religious Test shall ever be required as a Qualification to any Office or public Trust under the United States.

Article VII

The Ratification of the Conventions of nine States, shall be sufficient for the Establishment of this Constitution between the States so ratifying the Same. Done in Convention by the Unanimous Consent of the States present the Seventeenth Day of September in the Year of our Lord one thousand seven hundred and Eighty seven and of the Independence of the United States of America the Twelfth In witness whereof We have hereunto subscribed our Names, George Washington, President and deputy from Virginia.

New Hampshire: John Langdon,
             Nicholas Gilman.

Massachusetts: Nathaniel Gorham,
             Rufus King.

Connecticut: William Samuel Johnson,
             Roger Sherman.

New York: Alexander Hamilton

New Jersey: William Livingston,
             David Brearley,
             William Paterson,
             Jonathan Dayton.

Pennsylvania: Benjamin Franklin,
             Thomas Mifflin,
             Robert Morris,
             George Clymer,
             Thomas FitzSimons,
             Jared Ingersoll,
             James Wilson,
             Gouverneur Morris.

Delaware: George Read,
             Gunning Bedford Jr.,
             John Dickinson,
             Richard Bassett,
             Jacob Broom.

Maryland: James McHenry,
             Daniel of St. Thomas Jenifer,
             Daniel Carroll.

Virginia: John Blair,
             James Madison Jr.

North Carolina: William Blount,
             Richard Dobbs Spaight,
             Hugh Williamson.

South Carolina: John Rutledge,
             Charles Cotesworth Pinckney,
             Charles Pinckney,
             Pierce Butler.

Georgia: William Few,
             Abraham Baldwin.

[The language of the original Constitution, not including the Amendments, was adopted by a convention of the states on Sept. 17, 1787, and was subsequently ratified by the states on the following dates: Delaware, Dec. 7, 1787; Pennsylvania, Dec. 12, 1787; New Jersey, Dec. 18, 1787; Georgia, Jan. 2, 1788; Connecticut, Jan. 9, 1788; Massachusetts, Feb. 6, 1788; Maryland, April 28, 1788; South Carolina, May 23, 1788; New Hampshire, June 21, 1788.

Ratification was completed on June 21, 1788.

The Constitution subsequently was ratified by Virginia, June 25, 1788; New York, July 26, 1788; North Carolina, Nov. 21, 1789; Rhode Island, May 29, 1790; and Vermont, Jan. 10, 1791.]

Amendments

Amendment I

(First ten amendments ratified Dec. 15, 1791.)

Congress shall make no law respecting an establishment of religion, or prohibiting the free exercise thereof; or abridging the freedom of speech, or of the press; or the right of the people peaceably to assemble, and to petition the Government for a redress of grievances.

Amendment II

A well regulated Militia, being necessary to the security of a free State, the right of the people to keep and bear Arms, shall not be infringed.

Amendment III

No Soldier shall, in time of peace be quartered in any house, without the consent of the Owner, nor in time of war, but in a manner to be prescribed by law.

Amendment IV

The right of the people to be secure in their persons, houses, papers, and effects, against unreasonable searches and seizures, shall not be violated, and no Warrants shall issue, but upon probable cause, supported by Oath or affirmation, and particularly describing the place to be searched, and the persons or things to be seized.

Amendment V

No person shall be held to answer for a capital, or otherwise infamous crime, unless on a presentment or indictment of a Grand Jury, except in cases arising in the land or naval forces, or in the Militia, when in actual service in time of War or public danger; nor shall any person be subject for the same offence to be twice put in jeopardy of life or limb; nor shall be compelled in any criminal case to be a witness against himself, nor be deprived of life, liberty, or property, without due process of law; nor shall private property be taken for public use, without just compensation.

Amendment VI

In all criminal prosecutions, the accused shall enjoy the right to a speedy and public trial, by an impartial jury of the State and district wherein the crime shall have been committed, which district shall have been previously ascertained by law, and to be informed of the nature and cause of the accusation; to be confronted with the witnesses against him; to have compulsory process for obtaining witnesses in his favor, and to have the Assistance of Counsel for his defence.

Amendment VII

In Suits at common law, where the value in controversy shall exceed twenty dollars, the right of trial by jury shall be preserved, and no fact tried by a jury, shall be otherwise re-examined in any Court of the United States, than according to the rules of the common law.

Amendment VIII

Excessive bail shall not be required, nor excessive fines imposed, nor cruel and unusual punishments inflicted.

Amendment IX

The enumeration in the Constitution, of certain rights, shall not be construed to deny or disparage others retained by the people.

Amendment X

The powers not delegated to the United States by the Constitution, nor prohibited by it to the States, are reserved to the States respectively, or to the people.

Amendment XI *(Ratified Feb. 7, 1795)*

The Judicial power of the United States shall not be construed to extend to any suit in law or equity, commenced or prosecuted against one of the United States by Citizens of another State, or by Citizens or Subjects of any Foreign State.

Amendment XII *(Ratified June 15, 1804)*

The Electors shall meet in their respective states and vote by ballot for President and Vice-President, one of whom, at least, shall not be an inhabitant of the same state with themselves; they shall name in their ballots the person voted for as President, and in distinct ballots the person voted for as Vice-President, and they shall make distinct lists of all persons voted for as President, and of all persons voted for as Vice-President, and of the number of votes for each, which lists they shall sign and certify, and transmit sealed to the seat of the government of the United States, directed to the President of the Senate;—The President of the Senate shall, in the presence of the Senate and House of Representatives, open all the certificates and the votes shall then be counted;—The person having the greatest number of votes for President, shall be the President, if such number be a majority of the whole number of Electors appointed; and if no person have such majority, then from the persons having the highest numbers not exceeding three on the list of those voted for as President, the House of Representatives shall choose immediately, by ballot, the President. But in choosing the President, the votes shall be taken by states, the representation from each state having one vote; a quorum for this purpose shall consist of a member or members from two-thirds of the states, and a majority of all the states shall be necessary to a choice. [And if the House of Representatives shall not choose a President whenever the right of choice shall devolve upon them, before the fourth day of March next following, then the Vice-President shall act as President, as in the case of the death or other constitutional disability of the President —][11] The person having the greatest number of votes as Vice-President, shall be the Vice-President, if such number be a majority of the whole number of Electors appointed, and if no person have a majority, then from the two highest numbers on the list, the Senate shall choose the Vice-President; a quorum for the purpose shall consist of two-thirds of the whole number of Senators, and a majority of the whole number shall be necessary to a choice. But no person constitutionally ineligible to the office of President shall be eligible to that of Vice-President of the United States.

Amendment XIII *(Ratified Dec. 6, 1865)*

Section 1. Neither slavery nor involuntary servitude, except as a punishment for crime whereof the party shall have been duly convicted, shall exist within the United States, or any place subject to their jurisdiction.

Section 2. Congress shall have power to enforce this article by appropriate legislation.

Amendment XIV *(Ratified July 9, 1868)*

Section 1. All persons born or naturalized in the United States and subject to the jurisdiction thereof, are citizens of the United States and of the State wherein they reside. No State shall make or enforce any law which shall abridge the privileges or immunities of citizens of the United States; nor shall any State deprive any person of life, liberty, or property, without due process of law; nor deny to any person within its jurisdiction the equal protection of the laws.

Section 2. Representatives shall be apportioned among the several States according to their respective numbers, counting the whole number of persons in each State, excluding Indians not taxed. But when the right to vote at any election for the choice of electors for President and Vice President of the United States, Representatives in Congress, the Executive and Judicial officers of a State, or the members of the Legislature thereof, is denied to any of the male inhabitants of such State, being twenty-one years of age,[12] and citizens of the United States, or in any way abridged, except for participation in rebellion, or other crime, the basis of representation therein shall be reduced in the proportion which the number of such male citizens shall bear to the whole number of male citizens twenty-one years of age in such State.

Section 3. No person shall be a Senator or Representative in Congress, or elector of President and Vice President, or hold any office, civil or military, under the United States, or under any State, who, having previously taken an oath, as a member of Congress, or as an officer of the United States, or as a member of any State legislature, or as an executive or judicial officer of any State, to support the Constitution of the United States, shall have engaged in insurrection or rebellion against the same, or given aid or comfort to the enemies thereof. But Congress may by a vote of two-thirds of each House, remove such disability.

Section 4. The validity of the public debt of the United States, authorized by law, including debts incurred for payment of pensions and bounties for services in suppressing insurrection or rebellion, shall not be questioned. But neither the United States nor any State shall assume or pay any debt or obligation incurred in aid of insurrection or rebellion against the United States, or any claim for the loss or emancipation of any slave; but all such debts, obligations and claims shall be held illegal and void.

Section 5. The Congress shall have power to enforce, by appropriate legislation, the provisions of this article.

Amendment XV *(Ratified Feb. 3, 1870)*

Section 1. The right of citizens of the United States to vote shall not be denied or abridged by the United States or by any State on account of race, color, or previous condition of servitude.

Section 2. The Congress shall have power to enforce this article by appropriate legislation.

Amendment XVI *(Ratified Feb. 3, 1913)*

The Congress shall have power to lay and collect taxes on incomes, from whatever source derived, without apportionment among the several States, and without regard to any census or enumeration.

Amendment XVII *(Ratified Apr. 8, 1913)*

The Senate of the United States shall be composed of two Senators from each State, elected by the people thereof, for six years; and each Senator shall have one vote. The electors in each State shall have the qualifications requisite for electors of the most numerous branch of the State legislatures.

When vacancies happen in the representation of any State in the Senate, the executive authority of such State shall issue writs of election to fill such vacancies: *Provided,* That the legislature of any State may empower the executive thereof to make temporary appointments until the people fill the vacancies by election as the legislature may direct.

This amendment shall not be so construed as to affect the election or term of any Senator chosen before it becomes valid as part of the Constitution.

[Amendment XVIII *(Ratified Jan. 16, 1919)*

Section. 1. After one year from the ratification of this article the manufacture, sale, or transportation of intoxicating liquors within, the importation thereof into, or the exportation thereof from the United States and all territory subject to the jurisdiction thereof for beverage purposes is hereby prohibited.

Section 2. The Congress and the several States shall have concurrent power to enforce this article by appropriate legislation.

Section 3. This article shall be inoperative unless it shall have been ratified as an amendment to the Constitution by the legislatures of the several States, as provided in the Constitution, within seven years from the date of the submission hereof to the States by the Congress.][13]

Amendment XIX *(Ratified Aug. 18, 1920)*

The right of citizens of the United States to vote shall not be denied or abridged by the United States or by any State on account of sex.

Congress shall have power to enforce this article by appropriate legislation.

Amendment XX *(Ratified Jan. 23, 1933)*

Section 1. The terms of the President and Vice President shall end at noon on the 20th day of January, and the terms of Senators and Representatives at noon on the 3d day of January, of the years in which such terms would have ended if this article had not been ratified; and the terms of their successors shall then begin.

Section 2. The Congress shall assemble at least once in every year, and such meeting shall begin at noon on the 3d day of January, unless they shall by law appoint a different day.

Section 3.[14] If, at the time fixed for the beginning of the term of the President, the President elect shall have died, the Vice President elect shall become President. If a President shall not have been chosen before the time fixed for the beginning of his term, or if the President elect shall have failed to qualify, then the Vice President elect shall act as President until a President shall have qualified; and the Congress may by law provide for the case wherein neither a President elect nor a Vice President elect shall have qualified, declaring who shall then act as President, or the manner in which one who is to act shall be selected, and such person shall act accordingly until a President or Vice President shall have qualified.

Section 4. The Congress may by law provide for the case of the death of any of the persons from whom the House of Representatives may choose a President whenever the right of choice shall have devolved upon them, and for the case of the death of any of the persons from whom the Senate may choose a Vice President whenever the right of choice shall have devolved upon them.

Section 5. Sections 1 and 2 shall take effect on the 15th day of October following the ratification of this article.

Section 6. This article shall be inoperative unless it shall have been ratified as an amendment to the Constitution by the legislatures of three-fourths of the several States within seven years from the date of its submission.

Amendment XXI *(Ratified Dec. 5, 1933)*

Section 1. The eighteenth article of amendment to the Constitution of the United States is hereby repealed.

Section 2. The transportation or importation into any State, Territory or possession of the United States for delivery or use therein of intoxicating liquors, in violation of the laws thereof, is hereby prohibited.

Section 3. This article shall be inoperative unless it shall have been ratified as an amendment to the Constitution by conventions in the several States, as provided in the Constitution, within seven years from the date of the submission hereof to the States by the Congress.

Amendment XXII *(Ratified Feb. 27, 1951)*

Section 1. No person shall be elected to the office of the President more than twice, and no person who has held the office of President, or acted as President, for more than two years of a term to which some other person was elected President shall be elected to the office of the President more than once. But this Article shall not apply to any person holding the office of President when this Article was proposed by the Congress, and shall not prevent any person who may be holding the office of President, or acting as President, during the term within which this Article become operative from holding the office of President or acting as President during the remainder of such term.

Section 2. This Article shall be inoperative unless it shall have been ratified as an amendment to the Constitution by the legislatures of three-fourths of the several States within seven years from the date of its submission to the States by the Congress.

Amendment XXIII *(Ratified March 29, 1961)*

Section 1. The District constituting the seat of Government of the United States shall appoint in such manner as the Congress may direct:

A number of electors of President and Vice President equal to the whole number of Senators and Representatives in Congress to which the District would be entitled if it were a State, but in no event more than the least populous State; they shall be in addition to those appointed by the States, but they shall be considered, for the purposes of the election of President and Vice President, to be electors appointed by a State; and they shall meet in the District and perform such duties as provided by the twelfth article of amendment.

Section 2. The Congress shall have power to enforce this article by appropriate legislation.

Amendment XXIV *(Ratified Jan. 23, 1964)*

Section 1. The right of citizens of the United States to vote in any primary or other election for President or Vice President, for electors for President or Vice President, or for Senator or Representative in Congress, shall not be denied or abridged by the United States or any State by reason of failure to pay any poll tax or other tax.

Section 2. The Congress shall have power to enforce this article by appropriate legislation.

Amendment XXV *(Ratified Feb. 10, 1967)*

Section 1. In case of the removal of the President from office or of his death or resignation, the Vice President shall become President.

Section 2. Whenever there is a vacancy in the office of the Vice President, the President shall nominate a Vice President who shall take office upon confirmation by a majority vote of both Houses of Congress.

Section 3. Whenever the President transmits to the President pro tempore of the Senate and the Speaker of the House of Representatives his written declaration that he is unable to discharge the powers and duties of his office, and until he transmits to them a written declaration to the contrary, such powers and duties shall be discharged by the Vice President as Acting President.

Section 4. Whenever the Vice President and a majority of either the principal officers of the executive departments or of such other body as Congress may by law provide, transmit to the President pro tempore of the Senate and the Speaker of the House of Representatives their written declaration that the President is unable to discharge the powers and duties of his office, the Vice President shall immediately assume the powers and duties of the office as Acting President.

Thereafter, when the President transmits to the President pro tempore of the Senate and the Speaker of the House of Representatives his written declaration that no inability exists, he shall resume the powers and duties of his office unless the Vice President and a majority of either the principal officers of the executive department or of such other body as Congress may by law provide, transmit within four days to the President pro tempore of the Senate and the Speaker of the House of Representatives their written declaration that the President is unable to discharge the powers and duties of his office. Thereupon Congress shall decide the issue, assembling within forty-eight hours for that purpose if not in session. If the Congress, within twenty-one days after receipt of the latter written declaration, or, if Congress is not in session, within twenty-one days after Congress is required to assemble, determines by two-thirds vote of both houses that the President is unable to discharge the powers and duties of his office, the Vice President shall continue to discharge the same as Acting President; otherwise, the President shall resume the powers and duties of his office.

Amendment XXVI *(Ratified July 1, 1971)*

Section 1. The right of citizens of the United States, who are eighteen years of age or older, to vote shall not be denied or abridged by the United States or by any State on account of age.

Section 2. The Congress shall have power to enforce this article by appropriate legislation.

Notes

1. The part in brackets was changed by section 2 of the Fourteenth Amendment.
2. The part in brackets was changed by section 1 of the Seventeenth Amendment.
3. The part in brackets was changed by the second paragraph of the Seventeenth Amendment.
4. The part in brackets was changed by section 2 of the Twentieth Amendment.
5. The Sixteenth Amendment gave Congress the power to tax incomes.
6. The material in brackets has been superseded by the Twelfth Amendment.
7. This provision has been affected by the Twenty-fifth Amendment.
8. These clauses were affected by the Eleventh Amendment.
9. This paragraph has been superseded by the Thirteenth Amendment.
10. Obsolete.
11. The part in brackets has been superseded by section 3 of the Twentieth Amendment.
12. See the Twenty-sixth Amendment.
13. This Amendment was repealed by section 1 of the Twenty-first Amendment.
14. See the Twenty-fifth Amendment.

Source: U.S. Congress, House, Committee on the Judiciary, *The Constitution of the United States of America, As Amended Through July 1971,* H. Doc. 93-215, 93rd Cong., 2nd sess., 1974.

Selected Bibliography

Freedom of Expression

Barker, Lucius J., and Barker, Twiley W., Jr. *Civil Liberties and the Constitution: Cases and Commentaries*. 5th ed. Englewood Cliffs, N.J.: Prentice-Hall, 1986.

Berman, Harold J. "Religion and Law: The First Amendment in Historical Perspective." *Emory Law Journal* 35 (1986): 777-793.

Beth, Loren P. *The American Theory of Church and State*. Gainesville: University of Florida Press, 1958.

Bogen, David S. *Bulwark of Liberty: The Court and the First Amendment*. Port Washington, N.Y.: Associated Faculty Press, 1984.

Bollinger, Lee C. *The Tolerant Society: Freedom of Speech and Extremist Speech in America*. New York: Oxford University Press, 1986.

Branit, James R. "Reconciling Free Speech and Equality: What Justifies Censorship?" *Harvard Journal of Law and Public Policy* 9 (1986): 429-460.

Congressional Quarterly. *Congressional Quarterly's Guide to Congress*. 3d ed. Washington, D.C.: Congressional Quarterly Inc., 1982.

Cushman, Robert F. *Cases in Civil Liberties*. 4th ed. Englewood Cliffs, N.J.: Prentice-Hall, 1985.

Dowling, Noel T. *Cases on Constitutional Law*. 6th ed. Brooklyn, N.Y.: The Foundation Press, Inc., 1959.

Emerson, Thomas I. *The System of Freedom of Expression*. New York: Random House, Vintage Books, 1970.

Esbeck, Carl H. "1985 Survey of Trends and Developments on Religious Liberty in the Courts." *Journal of Law and Religion* 4 (1986): 211-240.

Forer, Lois G. *A Chilling Effect: The Mounting Threat of Libel and Invasion of Privacy Actions to the First Amendment*. New York: W. W. Norton, 1987.

Hemmer, Joseph J. *The Supreme Court and the First Amendment*. New York: Praeger, 1986.

Kalven, Harry, Jr. *The Negro and the First Amendment*. Chicago: University of Chicago Press, Phoenix Books, 1966.

Kelly, Alfred H., and Harbison, Winfred A. *The American Constitution: Its Origins and Development*. 6th ed. New York: W. W. Norton, 1982.

Konvitz, Milton R. *Fundamental Liberties of a Free People: Religion, Speech, Press, Assembly*. Ithaca, N.Y.: Cornell University Press, 1978. Reprint of 1957 ed.

Madison, James. *The Federalist Papers*. Ed Isaac Kramnick. New York: Penguin Books, 1987.

Marshall, William P. "Discrimination and the Right of Association." *Northwestern Law Review* 81 (1986): 68-105.

Mason, Alpheus T., and Beaney, William M. *The Supreme Court in a Free Society*. New York: W. W. Norton, 1968.

Miller, William, and Cureton, Charles. *Supreme Court Decisions on Church and State*. Charlottesville, Va.: Ibis Publications, 1986.

Miller, William Lee. *The First Liberty: Religion and the American Republic*. New York: Alfred A. Knopf, 1985.

Murphy, Paul L. *The Constitution in Crisis Times, 1918-1969*. New York: Harper & Row, Harper Torchbooks, 1972.

Pfeffer, Leo. *Church, State and Freedom*. 2 vols. Dobbs Ferry, N.Y.: Oceana Publishing, Inc., nd.

Redish, Martin H. *Freedom of Expression: A Critical Analysis*. Charlottesville, Va.: Michie Co., 1984.

Spitzer, Matthew Laurence. *Seven Dirty Words and Six Other Stories: Controlling the Content of Print and Broadcast*. New Haven, Conn.: Yale University Press, 1986.

Tedford, Thomas L. *Freedom of Speech in the United States*. New York: Random House, 1985.

Van Alstyne, William W. *Interpretations of the First Amendment*. Durham, N.C.: Duke University Press, 1984.

Political Participation

Atleson, James B. "The Aftermath of *Baker* v. *Carr:* An Adventure in Judicial Experimentation." *California Law Review* 51 (1963): 535-572.

Auerbach, Carl E. "The Reapportionment Cases: One Person, One Vote—One Vote, One Value." In *Supreme Court Review 1964*, ed. Philip B. Kurland. Chicago: University of Chicago Press, 1964.

Banzhaf, John F., III "Multi-Member Electoral Districts—Do They Violate the 'One Man, One Vote' Principle?" *Yale Law Journal* 75 (1966): 1309-1338.

Bickel, Alexander M. "The Voting Rights Cases." In *Supreme Court Review 1966*, ed. Philip B. Kurland. Chicago: University of Chicago Press, 1966.

Bontecou, Eleanor. *The Federal Loyalty-Security Program*. Westport, Conn.: Greenwood Press, 1974. Reprint of 1953 ed.

Brown, Ralph S., Jr. *Loyalty and Security: Employment Tests in the United States*. Jersey City, N.J.: Da Capo, 1972. Reprint of 1958 ed.

Cushman, Robert E. *Civil Liberties in the United States.* Ithaca, N.Y.: Cornell University Press, 1969. Reprint of 1956 ed.

DeGrazia, Alfred. *Essay on Apportionment and Representative Government.* Westport, Conn.: Greenwood Press, 1983. Reprint of 1963 ed.

Elliott, Ward E. Y. *The Rise of Guardian Democracy: The Supreme Court's Role in Voting Rights Disputes, 1845-1969.* Cambridge, Mass.: Harvard University Press, 1974.

Irwin, William P. "Representation and Election: The Reapportionment Cases in Retrospect." *Michigan Law Review* 67 (1969): 73-82.

Konvitz, Milton R. *Fundamental Liberties of a Free People.* Westport, Conn.: Greenwood Press, 1978. Reprint of the 1957 ed.

Lahava, Prina. *Press Law in Modern Democracies: A Comparative Study.* New York: Longman, 1985.

Latham, Earl. *The Communist Controversy in Washington.* Ann Arbor, Mich.: UMI, Books on Demand, 1966.

McKay, Robert. *Reapportionment: The Law and Politics of Equal Representation.* New York: Twentieth Century Fund, 1965.

Meiklejohn, Alexander. *Political Freedom: The Constitutional Powers of the People.* Westport, Conn.: Greenwood Press, 1979. Reprint of 1960 ed.

Mendelson, Wallace E. "Clear and Present Danger—From *Schenck* to *Dennis.*" *Columbia Law Review* 52 (1952): 313-333.

Murray, Robert K. *Red Scare: A Study in National Hysteria, 1919-1920.* Minneapolis: University of Minnesota Press, 1955.

Nathanson, Nathaniel L. "The Communist Trial and the Clear and Present Danger Test." *Harvard Law Review* 63 (1950): 1167-1175.

Polsby, Nelson W., ed. *Reapportionment in the 1970s.* Berkeley: University of California Press, 1971.

Pritchett, C. Herman. *Congress versus the Supreme Court, 1957-1960.* Minneapolis: University of Minnesota Press, 1961.

Thompson, Kenneth. *The Voting Rights Act and Black Electoral Participation.* Washington, D.C.: Joint Center for Political Studies, 1984.

Woodward, C. Vann. *Origins of the New South, 1877-1913.* Baton Rouge, La.: Louisiana State University Press, 1951.

——. *The Strange Career of Jim Crow.* 3d rev. ed. New York: Oxford University Press, 1974.

Due Process

Alexander, Frederick, and Amsden, John L. "Scope of the Fourth Amendment." *Georgetown Law Journal* 75 (1987): 713-727.

Allen, Francis A. "Federalism and the Fourth Amendment: A Requiem for Wolf." In *Supreme Court Review 1961,* ed. Philip B. Kurland. Chicago: University of Chicago Press, 1961.

Amsterdam, Anthony. "Perspectives on the Fourth Amendment." *Minnesota Law Review* 58 (1974): 349.

Angotti, Donna Louise, and Michael D. Warden. "Warrantless Searches and Seizures." *Georgetown Law Journal* 75 (1987): 742-790.

Barnett, Edward L., Jr. "Personal Rights, Property Rights and the Fourth Amendment." In *Supreme Court Review 1960,* ed. Philip B. Kurland. Chicago: University of Chicago Press, 1960.

Beaney, William M. "The Constitutional Right to Privacy in the Supreme Court." In *Supreme Court Review 1962,* ed. Philip B. Kurland. Chicago: University of Chicago Press, 1962.

——. *The Right to Counsel in American Courts.* Ann Arbor: University of Michigan Press, 1955.

Black, Charles L. *Capital Punishment: The Inevitability of Caprice and Mistake.* Rev. ed. New York: W. W. Norton, 1982.

Essaye, Anne. "Cruel and Unusual Punishment." *Georgetown Law Journal* 75 (1987): 1168-1195.

Fellman, David. *The Defendant's Rights Today.* Madison: University of Wisconsin Press, 1976.

Fingarette, Herbert. "Addiction and Criminal Responsibility." *Yale Law Journal* 84 (1975): 413.

Fisher, Louis. *Congress and the Fourth Amendment. Georgia Law Review* 21 (1986): 107-170.

Goldberger, Peter. "A Guide to Identifying Fourth Amendment Issues." *Search and Seizure Law Report* 13 (1986): 33-40.

Green, John Raeburn. "The Bill of Rights, the Fourteenth Amendment, and the Supreme Court" *Michigan Law Review* 46 (1948): 869.

Griswold, Erwin N. *Search and Seizure: A Dilemma of the Supreme Court.* Lincoln: University of Nebraska Press, 1976.

Hall, Livingston, Yale Kamisar, Wayne R. LaFave, and Jerrold H. Israel. *Modern Criminal Procedure.* 6th ed. St. Paul, Minn.: West Publishing Co., 1986.

Herman, Michele G. *Search and Seizure Checklists,* 4th ed. New York: Boardman Co., 1985.

Israel, Jerrold H. "*Gideon v. Wainwright:* The Art of Overruling." *Supreme Court Review 1963,* ed. Philip B. Kurland. Chicago: University of Chicago Press, 1963.

James, Joseph B. *The Ratification of the Fourteenth Amendment.* Macon, Ga.: Mercer University Press, 1984.

Kalven, Harry A., Jr., and Hans Zeisel. *The American Jury.* Chicago: University of Chicago Press, 1986.

Kroll, Robert. "Can the Fourth Amendment Go High Tech?" *American Bar Association* 73 (1987): 70-74.

LaFave, Wayne R. "'Case-by-Case Adjudication' versus 'Standardized Procedures'": The *Robinson* Dilemma," *Supreme Court Review 1974,* ed. Philip B. Kurland. Chicago: University of Chicago Press, 1974.

——. *Search and Seizure: A Treatise on the Fourth Amendment,* 2d ed. St. Paul, Minn.: West Publishing Co., 1986.

Landynski, Jacob W. *Searches and Seizures and the Supreme Court: A Study in Constitutional Interpretation.* Ann Arbor, Mich.: UMI, Books on Demand. Reprint of 1965 ed.

Levy, Leonard W. *Origins of the Fifth Amendment: The Right Against Self-Incrimination.* New York: Macmillan, 1986.

Lewis, Anthony. *Gideon's Trumpet.* New York: Random House, 1964.

Marshaw, Jerry L. *Due Process in the Administrative State.* New Haven, Conn.: Yale University Press, 1985.

Mason, Alpheus T., and William M. Beaney *American Constitutioal Law.* 6th ed. Englewood Cliffs, N.J.: Prentice-Hall, 1978.

Moore, Tim. "Constitutional Law: The Fourth Amendment and Drug Testing in the Workplace." *Harvard Journal of Law and Public Policy* 10 (1987): 762-768.

Oaks, Dallin. "Studying the Exclusionary Rule in Searches and Seizures." *University of Chicago Law Review* 37 (1970): 665.

Port, Joseph Clinton, Jr., and James D. Mathias. "Right to Counsel." *Georgetown Law Journal* 75 (1987): 1029-1052.

Rossum, Ralph A. "New Rights and Old Wrongs: The Supreme Court and the Problem of Retroactivity." *Emory Law Journal* 23 (1974): 381.

Sit, Po Yin. "Double Jeopardy, Due Process, and the Breach of Plea Agreements." *Columbia Law Review* 87 (1987): 142-160.

Strong, Frank R. *Substantive Due Process of Law: A Dichotomy of Sense and Nonsense.* Durham, N.C.: Carolina Academic Press, 1986.

White, James B. "The Fourth Amendment as a Way of Talking About People: A Study of *Robinson* and *Matlock.*" In *Supreme Court Review 1974,* ed. Philip B. Kurland. Chicago: University of Chicago Press, 1974.

White, Welsh S. *The Death Penalty in the Eighties: An Examination of the Modern System of Capital Punishment.* Ann Arbor, Mich.: University of Michigan Press, 1987.

Equal Rights

Abernathy, M. Glenn. *Civil Liberties Under the Constitution.* 4th ed. Columbia: University of South Carolina Press, 1985.

Berger, Morroe. *Equality by Statute: The Revolution in Civil Rights.* New York: Hippocrene Books, 1978. Reprint of 1967 ed.

Bickel, Alexander M. *Politics and the Warren Court.* Jersey City, N.J.: Da Capo, 1973. Reprint of 1955 ed.

Blaustein, Albert P., and Clarence Clyde Ferguson, Jr. *Desegregation and the Law: The Meaning and Effect of the School Segregation Cases.* Littleton, Colo.: Rothman, 1985. Reprint of 1957 ed.

"Developments in the Law: Equal Protection." *Harvard Law Review* 82 (March 1969): 1065.

Esdall, Thomas Byrne. *The New Politics of Inequality.* New York: W. W. Norton, 1984.

Franklin, John Hope. *From Slavery to Freedom: A History of Negro Americans.* 5th ed. New York: Alfred A. Knopf, 1980.

Garraty, John A., ed. *Quarrels That Have Shaped the Constitution.* Rev. ed. New York: Harper & Row, 1987.

Gunther, Gerald. "In Search of Evolving Doctrine on a Changing Court: A Model for a Newer Equal Protection." *Harvard Law Review* 86 (November 1972): 1.

Hartmann, Heidi I. *Comparable Worth: New Direction for Research.* Washington, D.C.: National Academy Press, 1985.

Hull, Elizabeth. *Without Justice for All: The Constitutional Rights of Aliens.* Westport, Conn.: Greenwood Press, 1985.

Karst, Kenneth L. "Equal Citizenship Under the Fourteenth Amendment." *Harvard Law Review* 91 (November 1977): 1.

Kelly, Alfred H., and Winfred A. Harbison. *The American Constitution: Its Origins and Development,* 6th ed. New York: W. W. Norton, 1982.

Kirp, David L., Mark G. Yudof, and Marlene Strong Franks. *Gender Justice.* Chicago: University of Chicago Press, 1985.

Kluger, Richard. *Simple Justice: The History of* Brown v. Board of Education *and Black America's Struggle for Equality.* New York: Alfred A. Knopf, 1976.

Konvitz, Milton R., and Theodore Leskes. *A Century of Civil Rights, with a Study of State Law Against Discrimination.* Ann Arbor, Mich.: UMI, Books on Demand, 1961.

Lawson, Steven F. *In Pursuit of Power: Southern Blacks and Electoral Politics, 1965-1982.* New York: Columbia University Press, 1985.

Levin-Epstein, Michael D., and Howard J. Anderson. *Primer of Equal Employment Opportunity,* 3d ed. Washington, D.C.: Bureau of National Affairs, 1984.

Morris, Frank C. *Judicial Wage Determination: A Volatile Spectre: Perspectives on Comparable Worth.* Washington, D.C.: National Legal Center for the Public Interest, 1984.

Phelps, Glenn A., and Robert A. Poirer. *Contemporary Debates on Civil Liberties: Enduring Constitutional Questions.* Lexington, Mass.: Lexington Books, 1985.

Remick, Helen. *Comparable Worth and Wage Discrimination: Technical Possibilities and Political Realities.* Philadelphia: Temple University Press, 1984.

Reskin, Barbara F., and Heidi I. Hartmann. *Women's Work, Men's Work: Sex Segregation on the Job.* Washington, D.C.: National Academy Press, 1985.

Schiller, Bradley R. *The Economics of Poverty and Discrimination.* 4th ed. Englewood Cliffs, N.J.: Prentice-Hall, 1984.

Schmid, Gunther, and Renata Weitzel. *Sex Discrimination and Equal Opportunity: The Labor Market and Employment Policy.* New York: St. Martin's Press, 1984.

Schuman, Howard, Charlotte Steeh, and Lawrence Bobo. *Racial Attitudes in America: Trends and Interpretations.* Cambridge, Mass.: Harvard University Press, 1985.

Tussman, Joseph, and Jacobus tenBroek. "The Equal Protection of the Laws." *California Law Review* 37: 341.

United States Commission on Civil Rights. *Comparable Worth: Issue for the 80's—A Consultation of the U.S. Commission on Civil Rights, June 6-7, 1984.* Washington, D.C.: Commission on Civil Rights, 1984.

Wechsler, Herbert. "Toward Neutral Principles of Constitutional Law." *Harvard Law Review* 73 (November 1959): 31.

Woodward, C. Vann. *The Strange Career of Jim Crow.* 3d rev. ed. New York: Oxford University Press, 1974.

Subject Index

Case Index

A Book Named "John Cleland's Memoirs of a Woman of Pleasure" v. Attorney General of Massachusetts, 383 U.S. 413 (1966), 59

Abbate v. United States, 359 U.S. 187 (1959), 213

Abel v. United States, 362 U.S. 217 (1960), 188

Ableman v. Booth, 21 How. 506 (1859), 5 (box)

Abrams v. Martin, 467 U.S. 253 (1984), 170 (box)

Abrams v. United States, 250 U.S. 616 (1919), 22, 25-26, 79

Adair v. United States, 208 U.S. 161 (1908), 158

Adams v. Williams, 407 U.S. 143 (1972), 175 (box), 188

Adamson v. California, 332 U.S. 46 (1947), 162, 193, 196

Adderly v. Florida, 385 U.S. 39 (1966), 22, 43

Adkins v. Children's Hospital, 261 U.S. 525 (1923), 158

Adler v. Board of Education of New York City, 342 U.S. 485 (1952), 148, 150

AFL v. Swing, 312 U.S. 321 (1941), 46

Agnello v. United States, 269 U.S. 20 (1925), 182

Aguilar v. Felton, 473 U.S. 402 (1985), 99

Aguilar v. Texas, 378 U.S. 108 (1964), 188

Ake v. Oklahoma, 470 U.S. 68 (1985), 208

Albemarle Paper Company v. Moody, 422 U.S. 405 (1975), 267

Alberts v. California, 354 U.S. 476 (1957), 59

Albertson v. Subversive Activities Control Board, 382 U.S. 70 (1965), 152, 191

Alderman v. United States, 394 U.S. 165 (1969), 187

Alexander v. Holmes Board of Education, 396 U.S. 19 (1969), 241

Allen v. Virginia Board of Elections, 393 U.S. 544 (1969), 118

Allgeyer v. Louisiana, 165 U.S. 578 (1897), 158

Almeida-Sanchez v. United States, 413 U.S. 266 (1973), 177 (box)

Amalgamated Food Employees Union, Local 590 v. Logan Valley Plaza, 391 U.S. 308 (1968), 44 (box), 51

Ambach v. Norwick, 441 U.S. 68 (1979), 273

American Communications Association v. Douds, 339 U.S. 382 (1950), 22, 138 (box), 144, 146

American Party of Texas v. White, 415 U.S. 767 (1974), 115 (box)

American Steel Foundries v. Tri-City Central Trades Council, 257 U.S. 184 (1921), 51

American Tobacco Co. v. Patterson, 456 U.S. 63 (1982), 259 (box)

Anastaplo, In re, 348 U.S. 946 (1955), 145 (box)

Anastaplo, In re, 366 U.S. 82 (1961), 145 (box)

Anderson v. Liberty Lobby, 477 U.S. 242 (1986), 79

Andresen v. Maryland, 427 U.S. 463 (1976), 180-181

Apodaca v. Oregon, 406 U.S. 404 (1972), 165-166

Aptheker v. Secretary of State, 378 U.S. 500 (1964), 13, 135 (box)

Argersinger v. Hamlin, 407 U.S. 25 (1972), 206, 208

Arizona v. Hicks, __ U.S. __ (1987), 188

Arizona v. Rumsey, 467 U.S. 203 (1984), 213

Arizona Governing Committee for Tax Deferred Annuity and Deferred Compensation Plans v. Norris, 463 U.S. 1073 (1983), 285

Arkansas Writers' Project v. Ragland, __ U.S. __ (1987), 79

Ashcraft v. Tennessee, 322 U.S. 143 (1944), 201

Ashton v. Kentucky, 384 U.S. 195 (1966), 64, 79

Associated Enterprises Inc. v. Toltec Watershed Improvement District, 410 U.S. 743 (1973), 123 (box)

Associated Press v. National Labor Relations Board, 301 U.S. 103 (1937), 55

Associated Press v. United States, 326 U.S. 1 (1945), 55

Associated Press v. Walker, 388 U.S. 130 (1967), 66, 68

Austin v. Tennessee, 179 U.S. 343 (1900), 158

Austin Independent School District v. United States, 429 U.S. 990 (1976), 259 (box)

Austin Independent School Board v. United States, 429 U.S. 190 (1976), 236 (box)

Avent v. North Carolina, 373 U.S. 375 (1963), 50, 250

Avery v. Georgia, 345 U.S. 559 (1952), 168

Avery v. Midland County, 390 U.S. 474 (1968), 123 (box)

Baggett v. Bullitt, 377 U.S. 360 (1964), 153

Bailey v. Alabama, 219 U.S. 219 (1911), 257

Bailey v. Richardson, 341 U.S. 918 (1951), 143

Baker v. Carr, 369 U.S. 186 (1962), 10, 121 (box), 122-123, 126

Bakery and Pastry Drivers v. Wohl, 315 U.S. 769 (1942), 46

Baldwin v. New York, 399 U.S. 66 (1970), 165

Ballard v. United States, 329 U.S. 187 (1946), 172

Ballew v. Georgia, 435 U.S. 223 (1978), 172

Barker v. Wingo, 407 U.S. 514 (1972), 170-171

Barron v. Baltimore, 7 Pet. 243 (1833), 3, 12, 18, 160, 161

DEC 2 0 1990

APR 2 0 1996